CCNA Voice Study Guide

Exam IIUC 640-460 Objectives

OBJECTIVE	CHAPTER
Describe the components of the Cisco Unified Communications Architecture	
Describe the function of the infrastructure in a UC environment	1
Describe the function of endpoints in a UC environment	1
Describe the function of the call processing agent in a UC environment	1
Describe the function of messaging in a UC environment	1
Describe the function of auto attendants and IVRs in a UC environment	2
Describe the function of Contact Center in a UC environment	3
Describe the applications available in the UC environment, including Mobility, Presence, and TelePresence	1
Describe how the Unified Communications components work together to create the Cisco Unified Communications Architecture	3, 10
Describe PSTN Components and Technologies	
Describe the services provided by the PSTN	2
Describe time division and statistical multiplexing	2
Describe supervisory, informational, and address signaling	2
Describe numbering plans	2
Describe analog circuits	2
Describe digital voice circuits	2
Describe PBX, trunk lines, key-systems, and tie lines	2

Sybex®
An Imprint of
WILEY

OBJECTIVE	CHAPTER
Describe the features available in Cisco Unity Express	8, 9
Configure Auto Attendant services using Cisco Unity Express	9
Configure basic voice mail features using Cisco Unity Express	9

Perform Basic Maintenance and Operations Tasks to Support the VoIP Solution

Describe basic troubleshooting methods for Cisco Unified Communications Manager Express	5, 6
Explain basic troubleshooting methods for Cisco Unity Express	9
Explain basic maintenance and troubleshooting methods for UC500	10

Exam objectives are subject to change at any time without prior notice and at Cisco's sole discretion. Please visit Cisco's website (www.cisco.com) for the most current listing of exam objectives.

Sybex®
An Imprint of
WILEY

Sybex®
An Imprint of
WILEY

OBJECTIVE	CHAPTER
Describe VoIP Components and Technologies	
Describe the process of voice packetization	2
Describe RTP and RTCP	3
Describe the function of and differences between codecs	3
Describe H.323, MGCP, SIP, and SCCP signaling protocols	3
Describe and Configure Gateways, Voice ports, and Dial Peers to Connect to the PSTN and Service Provider Networks	
Describe the function and application of a dial plan	7
Describe the function and application of voice gateways	3, 7
Describe the function and application of voice ports in a gateway	7
Describe the function and operation of call legs	3, 7
Describe and configure voice dial peers	3, 7
Describe the differences between PSTN and Internet Telephony Service provider circuits	1, 7
Describe and Configure a Cisco Network to Support VoIP	
Describe the purpose of VLANs in a VoIP environment	4
Describe the environmental considerations to support VoIP	4
Configure switched infrastructure to support voice and data VLANs	4
Describe the purpose and operation of PoE	4
Identify the factors that impact voice quality	4
Describe how QoS addresses voice quality issues	4
Identify where QoS is deployed in the UC infrastructure	4

Sybex®
An Imprint of
WILEY

CCNA® Voice
Study Guide

CCNA® Voice
Study Guide

Andrew Froehlich

WILEY

Wiley Publishing, Inc.

Acquisitions Editor: Jeff Kellum
Development Editor: Jim Compton
Technical Editor: Scott Morris
Production Editor: Dassi Zeidel
Copy Editor: Linda Recktenwald
Editorial Manager: Pete Gaughan
Production Manager: Tim Tate
Vice President and Executive Group Publisher: Richard Swadley
Vice President and Publisher: Neil Edde
Media Project Manager 1: Laura Moss-Hollister
Media Associate Producer: Shawn Patrick
Media Quality Assurance: Josh Frank
Book Designers: Judy Fung and Bill Gibson
Proofreader: Publication Services, Inc.
Indexer: Ted Laux
Project Coordinator, Cover: Lynsey Stanford
Cover Designer: Ryan Sneed

Library of Congress Cataloging-in-Publication Data

Froehlich, Andrew, 1977-

  CCNA voice study guide (640-460) / Andrew Froehlich. — 1st ed.

    p. cm.

  ISBN-13: 978-0-470-52766-5

  ISBN-10: 0-470-52766-8

  1. Internet telephony—Examinations—Study guides. I. Title.

  TK5105.8865.F76 2010

  004.69'5—dc22

                                              2009047259

10 9 8 7 6 5 4 3 2 1

Dear Reader,

Thank you for choosing *CCNA Voice Study Guide*. This book is part of a family of premium-quality Sybex books, all of which are written by outstanding authors who combine practical experience with a gift for teaching.

Sybex was founded in 1976. More than 30 years later, we're still committed to producing consistently exceptional books. With each of our titles, we're working hard to set a new standard for the industry. From the paper we print on, to the authors we work with, our goal is to bring you the best books available.

I hope you see all that reflected in these pages. I'd be very interested to hear your comments and get your feedback on how we're doing. Feel free to let me know what you think about this or any other Sybex book by sending me an email at nedde@wiley.com. If you think you've found a technical error in this book, please visit http://sybex.custhelp.com. Customer feedback is critical to our efforts at Sybex.

Best regards,

Neil Edde
Vice President and Publisher
Sybex, an Imprint of Wiley

Acknowledgments

I'd like to thank the entire team Sybex assembled for their hard work and dedication in putting this book together. I wish to acknowledge Jeff Kellum, my acquisitions editor, for giving me the opportunity to write my first book for Sybex. A big thanks to my development editor, Jim Compton. Jim's tireless effort helped to shape the book into a much more readable format. I'd also like to thank my technical editor, Scott Morris. Having a multi-CCIE like Scott edit the book gave me a big reassurance that it was accurately written. Also, thanks to Dassi Zeidel, my production editor, and copy editor Linda Recktenwald. As is common with many books, the copy editor's timeline is always shrinking because of slowdowns in authoring and other edits. Dassi and Linda were able to crank out the copy editing in record time so it could be placed into the readers' hands on schedule.

Finally, I'd like to thank my family and friends for all of their support and encouragement. The writing and editing of this book over the past year for me took place in multiple locations around the world including the United States, Colombia, and Thailand. In each of these countries, I had support of family and/or friends to keep me motivated and inspired. Starting with those in the United States, I'd specifically like to thank my mother and father, Ron and Elaine Froehlich, as well my Chicago friends, including Angie Barbini, Matt and Fabiana Liska, Kevin and Ruth Ann McQuire, and Sean and Heather Uhles. Also in Chicago, my friends and co-workers at the University of Chicago Medical Center. In Colombia, I want to thank my dear friend Adriana Castro. Finally, in Thailand, I want to thank Manta Jambanja and the School of Information Technology staff at Mae Fah Luang University.

About the Author

Andrew Froehlich, CCNA, CCDA, CCNA-Voice, CCNP, CCSP, CCDP, F5 systems engineer, is the president of West Gate Networks, a network and IT consulting firm based in Chicago. Andrew also holds the position of network architect at the University of Chicago Medical Center. In the past, Andrew has performed network design and support for large companies, including State Farm Insurance and United Airlines. In addition to having more than 12 years of network experience, he holds a degree in Management Information Systems from Northern Iowa University and a master of business administration degree from Northern Illinois University. He is also a freelance writer for IT publications, including *Network World* magazine. Andrew's most recent work is as a professor of Network Architecture at Mae Fah Luang University in Chiang Rai, Thailand.

Contents at a Glance

Contents

**Chapter   5   CUCM Express Installation and Basic
Configuration   173**

Introduction

Welcome to *CCNA Voice Study Guide*, a comprehensive guide that covers everything you need for Cisco's new exam 640-460. For readers who are new to Cisco certifications, there is a well-defined structure to the different levels that network administrators can achieve. Cisco's current certification structure has the following five levels of certification:

- Entry level
- Associate
- Professional
- Expert
- Architect

This book is written for the associate level of certification. Cisco considers this level to be the "apprentice or foundation level" for network administrators.

Cisco has recently broadened its associate-level certifications to include not only a certification for routing and switching (CCNA) and design (CCDA) but also more targeted associate-level certifications for security (CCNA Security), wireless (CCNA Wireless), and voice (CCNA Voice). These new certifications target specific areas of Cisco technology and are to be used as stepping-stones for the professional and expert levels of certification that Cisco offers.

Cisco's Voice Certifications

Cisco offers three distinct levels of voice certifications. The following diagram shows that the CCNA Voice certification is a building block to the professional- and expert-level voice certifications:

This book covers the CCNA Voice certification exam 640-460. As of the writing of this book, the exam costs $250 USD. The exam tests your knowledge a great deal in areas both theoretical and technically specific to Cisco hardware and software.

Once you achieve your CCNA Voice certification, you can choose to continue on the voice path and achieve higher certifications, such as the CCNP Voice or the ultimate CCIE Voice Expert. But even if you stop after achieving your CCNA Voice certification, you will have demonstrated to your current or prospective employers that you have a sound knowledge of the interoperations of voice and Cisco voice technologies. This assurance to employers will make it easier for you to land that dream job you've always wanted!

What Skills Do You Need to Become CCNA Voice Certified?

To meet the CCNA Voice certification skill level, you must possess the following skills:

- A thorough knowledge of analog and voice technologies, including but not limited to FXS, FXO, T1/E1, voice trunks, voice packetization, codecs, transcoding, PBX, key systems, and multiplexing

- The ability to install, configure, and operate Cisco Unified Communications Manager Express hardware and software. In addition, you must be able to install, configure, and manage Unity Express hardware and software to work in coordination with the CUCM Express.

How Do You Become CCNA Voice Certified?

There are two ways to become CCNA Voice certified. This book provides one method, which is to pass the 640-460 exam. This is considered the CCNA Voice Commercial track, which covers the CUCM Express hardware and software that are commonly found in small and medium-size organizations.

 The other way to obtain a CCNA Voice Certification is to study for and pass the 642-436 exam. This exam is known as the CCNA Voice Enterprise track, which covers the CUCM hardware and software used in large organizations. This exam is also a requirement for those pursuing their CCVP certification.

It is critical that you get some hands-on experience with a router installed with the CUCM Express software. It would be even more valuable to acquire an SBCS UC500 device that contains both CUCM Express functionality and Unity Express. In addition, you can practice working with the Cisco Configuration Assistant software to set up the UC500, which is a critical skill to have before attempting to pass the exam.

Finding UC500 hardware at a low cost can be very difficult. If you cannot afford to purchase a system, you'll be happy to know that I've worked hard to provide configuration examples and screenshots throughout this book to help test takers learn what they need to pass the 640-460 exam.

What Does This Book Cover?

This book covers everything you need to know in order to pass the CCNA 640-460 exam. In addition to this book, having the ability to study and practice with CUCM Express/ Unity Express hardware and software will provide you the confidence to complete the simulation questions found in the exam.

You will learn the following information in this book:

- **Chapter 1** introduces you to the Cisco hardware and software lineup for small to medium-size businesses as well as large enterprise organizations. In addition, you will learn about the different deployment options you can use to design your voice network.

- **Chapter 2** provides you with the background covering traditional telephony. Topics such as analog network signaling, analog interface types, the analog-to-digital conversion process, multiplexing, and numbering plans are detailed to give you a firm foundation in traditional voice terminology and processes.

- **Chapter 3** introduces you to Voice over Internet Protocol in a Cisco network environment. This chapter covers topics such as the Cisco Unified Communications Model, voice gateway purpose and components, dial peers and call legs, and voice gateway and endpoint communication protocols. You will also read about the protocol that is responsible for transporting voice over an IP network—RTP. Finally, you will be introduced to some of the more popular voice codecs used with Cisco voice equipment and shown how to calculate voice packet sizes.

- **Chapter 4** provides you with the core networking skills required to design, configure, and operate IPT equipment on a Cisco IP network. Cisco endpoint power options are covered so you can appropriately plan for powering your IP phones in office deployments. The chapter then goes on to discuss the importance of segmenting voice traffic from data using voice VLANs and trunks. The chapter then describes some QoS techniques that can be implemented on a Cisco IP network for more reliable delivery of time-sensitive traffic such as voice.

- **Chapter 5** exposes readers to CUCM Express licensing options required to operate a Cisco voice system. The chapter then moves on to describe how to install and set up CUCM Express software on compatible Cisco hardware. At the end of this chapter, readers will know how to configure ephones and ephone-DNs to the point where a phone call can be successfully made from one Cisco IP phone to another.

- **Chapter 6** dives into more complex CUCM Express techniques that show readers how to set up voice features such as ephone button options, user and network locales, and user directories. This chapter also covers configuration of voice-productivity features including call forwarding, call parking, hunt groups, and paging. Then you will learn about voice accessibility and accounting settings such as call blocking and call detail records. Lastly, you will learn how to configure Music on Hold settings for both unicast and multicast MoH.

- **Chapter 7** covers the design and configuration of voice gateways, including how to configure analog and digital interfaces as well as POTs and VoIP dial peers. In addition, the chapter covers how to develop a dial-plan strategy to provide a simple and expandable dial plan for current and future growth. Finally, the chapter covers the dial-peer decision-making process of a voice gateway and how to manipulate dial strings for proper call routing.

- **Chapter 8** introduces you to the various features found in the Unity Express voice mail system. Those features include users/groups, message waiting indicators, message notification, Auto Attendant (AA), and Interactive Voice Response (IVR). You will then learn how to install and configure the Unity Express software to work with the CUCM Express. Once Unity Express can interoperate with the CUCM Express, you will learn how to set up Unity Express using the Unity Express Initialization Wizard.

- **Chapter 9** covers how to configure Unity Express using the web GUI. Specifically, you will learn how to configure system settings such as NTP, time zone, and DNS. You will also learn how to create and modify user and group mailbox settings. You will also learn how to set up and modify the Auto Attendant feature as well as learn different tools used to create AA scripts. You will see how to configure message notification configuration to allow users to be remotely notified and listen to voice messages when the user is away from their desk. Finally, you will learn techniques an administrator can use to maintain and troubleshoot Unity Express.

- **Chapter 10** is an introduction to the Cisco Smart Business Communications System (SBCS) lineup, including the UC500 Series hardware, which is an ideal voice/data platform for small to medium-size businesses. This chapter also introduces the Cisco Configuration Assistant (CCA), which is an innovative GUI tool used to configure and maintain SBCS devices.

- **Chapter 11** goes into how to configure a SBCS UC500 device using the CCA. Specifically, the chapter shows readers how to configure telephony regions, network options, SIP trunking, voice features, voice mail features, Auto Attendant options, and dial plans.

- **Appendix A** provides a real-world scenario designing and implementing a small office with a Cisco SBCS UC500 using the Cisco Configuration Assistant Telephony Setup Wizard.

How to Use This Book

The *CCNA Voice Study Guide* is designed to prepare a reader to pass the 640-460 exam to achieve the associate-level certification in Cisco voice technologies. To get the most out of this book, I recommend you use the following study method:

1. Take the assessment test provided to you prior to Chapter 1 of this book. Try to answer each question without looking at the answers and explanations found in the back of the book. This should give you an indication of your skill level prior to reading the book. Once you have completed the assessment test and graded yourself, take time to carefully read over the explanations for any question you get wrong and note the chapters in which the material is covered. This information should help you identify sections of the book that you need to spend additional time on. Keep in mind, however, that the book was designed for you to read each chapter in order. Much of the material found in the chapters builds on knowledge learned from previous chapters.

2. Prior to reading each chapter, make sure to review the test objectives listed at the beginning. These objectives are what the exam taker must ultimately know in order to pass the CCNA Voice 640-460 exam.

3. Complete each written lab at the end of each chapter. These labs are created to make sure the reader fully understands key topics that are contained within that chapter. Using a written format instead of multiple-choice format forces the reader to know the answers off the top of their head instead of just eliminating options, as we often do with multiple-choice questions.

4. Work through and fully understand the commands found in the hands-on labs in the chapter. Not all chapters have hands-on labs, but the book focuses on the important tasks necessary for aspiring CCNA Voice–certified network engineers. See the accompanying sidebar for a recommended lab setup.

5. Answer all of the review questions related to each chapter. Once you have finished answering the questions, review the answers and explanations to not only understand the correct answers but also understand why the incorrect answers are actually incorrect! Keep in mind that these review questions will not be the exact questions you will find on the exam, but they will help you to understand the material that Cisco creates the actual exam questions from.

6. Take time to review the bonus exams that are included on the companion CD. Questions in these exams appear only on the CD.

7. Test yourself using all the flashcards on the included CD. These flashcards can be viewed on both PCs and mobile devices, so now you can take your study material with you wherever you go!

Recommended Home Lab Setup

As stated earlier, it is critical to get some hands-on experience with both CUCM Express and Unity Express hardware and software. Following is a list of equipment I recommend you try to acquire for your home lab studies. If you are concerned about the high cost of purchasing the equipment, keep in mind that Cisco hardware can be easily resold on used markets such as Craigslist or eBay. Combine that fact with adding an extremely hot certification to your resume, and it's an investment well worth the initial cost.

Qty	Item
1	Cisco SBCS UC520
1	Cisco 7940 IP phone
1	Cisco 7965 IP phone
1	Windows PC loaded with the Cisco IP Communicator and Cisco Configuration Assistant software
2	Analog telephones

Recommended Home Lab Setup *(continued)*

This equipment should give you the ability to practice configuring CUCM Express and Unity Express using the command line, web GUI, and CCA methods detailed in this book. The two different IP phones I recommend allow you to understand the differences between two- and six-line phones as well as the fact that different Cisco IP phones require different firmware files. A Windows PC will be needed to install both the Cisco IP Communicator softphone and the Cisco Configuration Assistant software used to configure SBCS devices such as the UC520. Finally, the analog phones in your lab are useful for testing FXS configurations.

What's on the CD?

The CD included with this book includes many supplemental tools that you can use to further your studies and achieve your goal of becoming a CCNA Voice–certified administrator. The following content is provided for you to use to further your study.

The Sybex Test Engine

The Sybex test engine software lets readers practice all of the review and assessment questions found in the book as well as two additional bonus exams that are found only on the CD. The exams let potential test takers practice in an electronic test-taking environment that is similar to the actual Cisco exam.

Electronic Flashcards for PCs and Handheld Devices

In addition to the Sybex test engine software, Sybex has included over 200 electronic flashcards for you to test yourself with on PCs and compatible handheld devices. These flashcards are designed to get the reader to quickly recognize and recall important CCNA Voice information that will be useful for them when taking the 640-460 exam.

CCNA Voice: Cisco Certified Network Associate Voice Study Guide in PDF

Finally, this book contains the entire *CCNA Voice Study Guide* in PDF format on the included CD so you can read the book on your PC or laptop or any handheld devices that reads PDF files such as a Blackberry or iPhone.

Tips for Taking Your CCNA Voice Exam

According to Cisco's website at https://learningnetwork.cisco.com/community/certifications/voice_ccna/iiuc?view=overview, the CCNA Voice exam contains anywhere from 60 to 70 questions and must be completed in 90 minutes or less. The languages this exam is offered in include English, Japanese, Chinese, Russian, Portuguese,

Korean, French, and Spanish. This information can change per exam. A passing score varies according to the types of questions found in the exam, but it is probably best to assume you need to get approximately 85 percent of the questions correct to pass the exam.

When taking the exam, thoroughly read each question to make sure you know what answer it is looking for. Cisco exam questions tend to have answers that look identical. You will find, however, that there are small differences in the answer that can determine a correct or incorrect answer.

Also, keep in mind that you should choose the answer that Cisco believes is the correct as opposed to what you or other vendors believe. This is a Cisco exam, after all, so the right answer is the one that Cisco recommends!

The format of the 640-460 exam questions might include any of the following:

- Multiple-choice single-answer
- Multiple-choice multiple-answer—Cisco will always tell you to choose two or three, depending on the proper number of multiple correct responses.
- Drag-and-drop
- Fill-in-the-blank
- CUCM Express and Unity Express simulations

Test-Day Tips for Certification Success

- Arrive at least 30 minutes early to the exam center. That way you can check in and mentally prepare for the exam without having to rush.

- Take the Cisco exam tutorial. This tutorial is offered prior to the official start of each exam before the test timer starts. In this tutorial you will be given an interactive lesson as to the format of the exam and how to navigate through the different question types, including multiple-choice, drag-and-drop, fill-in-the-blank, and simulation questions. Even if you have taken many Cisco exams, I highly recommend going through the tutorial in case there is something new to the exam format since the last time you took an exam.

- Read both the questions and answers very carefully. Cisco often will intentionally lead the hasty test taker, who simply glosses over a question, to quickly choose the incorrect answer. Patience and careful thinking pay off greatly when taking Cisco exams!

- Be aware that you cannot go back to change an answer once you have moved on to the next question. Make sure that the answer you choose is the one you want to stick with, because there is no way to change it later on.

Assessment Test

1. What two configuration steps are required for proper communication between the CUCM Express and Unity Express?

   A. A loopback interface needs to be configured.

   B. A default gateway needs to be configured on the service module pointing to the IP of the service engine (or integrated service engine).

   C. The service engine (or integrated service engine) must be on the same IP subnet as the service module.

   D. A default gateway needs to be configured on the service engine (or integrated service engine) pointing to the IP of the service module.

2. Which IP Telephony deployment model places independent call-processing and voice mail devices at each remote site?

   A. Multisite with distributed call processing

   B. Single site

   C. Multisite with centralized call processing

   D. Single site with SRST

   E. Clustering over the WAN

3. What type of license might you need if you want to add a new Cisco IP phone to your existing CUCM Express system? Choose all that apply.

   A. Cisco softphone license

   B. CCME Express feature license

   C. Cisco IOS license for voice capabilities

   D. Individual user license

4. When you order a T1 circuit from a PSTN, you request that only 12 channels be available. What term is used for this scenario?

   A. Timeslots

   B. Fractional

   C. LoopStart

   D. Ds0-group

5. What is the 3.5 mm port used for on the UC500 system?

   A. Wireless expandability

   B. ESW 500 series uplink

   C. Fax/modem connectivity

   D. External music source for MoH

6. What Windows application can be used to configure a UC500 system?

    A. CUCM Express GUI

    B. CCA

    C. SIP

    D. SRST

7. Which two are peer-to-peer signaling protocols?

    A. SCCP and H.323

    B. SIP and MGCP

    C. SIP and H.323

    D. SCCP and MGCP

    E. H.323 and MGCP

8. What queuing technique is considered the best option for voice traffic?

    A. FIFO

    B. LIFO

    C. LLQ

    D. PQ

    E. CQ

9. What CUCM Express config-telephony command modifies tone and cadence differences between geographic regions?

    A. `user-locale`

    B. `network-locale`

    C. `language-locale`

    D. `telephony-service-locale`

10. What type of hunt group algorithm rings the hunt group members in the order in which they were entered into the CUCM, always starting from the first number?

    A. Longest idle

    B. Peer

    C. Round robin

    D. Sequential

    E. FIFO

11. Using the Unity Express CLI, what show command lets you view the maximum number of configurable personal and GDM mailboxes?

    A. `router#show license`

    B. `router(config)#show license`

    C. `router#show software license`

    D. `router#show software mailbox`

12. When configuring voice features by using CCA, what tab would you use to exclude an IP address from the DHCP scope on a UC500?

    A. System

    B. SIP Trunk

    C. Voice Features

    D. Network

    E. User Extensions

13. When SCCP is used between two endpoints that call each other, how is RTP data transported when a connection is established?

    A. It must be proxied throughout the CUCM.

    B. It must be sent through a voice gateway.

    C. It is sent directly from one endpoint to another.

    D. Each RTP stream terminates at the CUCM.

14. When a telephone handset is in its cradle, what state is it in?

    A. Multiplex

    B. Dual-line

    C. Single-line

    D. Off-hook

    E. On-hook

15. What are the three different inter-VLAN routing methods that you can configure on your network?

    A. Layer 3 switching

    B. Layer 2 switching

    C. Individual router links

    D. Trunked router link

    E. Individual trunk link for each VLAN

16. By default, what type of signaling are FSX ports configured for?

   A. SIP

   B. GroundStart

   C. LoopStart

   D. SCCP

17. How are Unity Express backups run using the web GUI?

   A. Backups can be set to run automatically each day.

   B. Backups can be run only during evening hours or holidays.

   C. Backups can be run using the TUI interface as long as the user is an AvT administrator.

   D. Backups are run by navigating to Administration ➢ Backup/Restore ➢ Start Backup.

18. Which of the following is not a Trunk Priority dial-plan rule for outgoing calls?

   A. PSTN Only

   B. SIP Only

   C. FXO Only

   D. None

19. What does 2 represent in the command `button 1:2`?

   A. Extension #2 on the phone

   B. A dual-line ephone

   C. Ephone-DN #2

   D. Ephone #2

20. Which voice signaling protocol is proprietary?

   A. H.323

   B. SIP

   C. SCCP

   D. MGCP

   E. G.711

   F. G.729

21. What PBX service redirects a call to a different extension?

   A. Extension dialing

   B. Call forwarding

   C. Hunt group

   D. Paging group

   E. Call park

22. What step in the analog-to-digital conversion converts the data into binary?

   A. Encode

   B. Quantize

   C. Compress

   D. Sample

23. What percentage of dropped packets can be allowed on a network and still have quality voice calls according to Cisco?

   A. Less than 1 percent

   B. Less than 4 percent

   C. Less than 8 percent

   D. Less than 2 percent

24. Given the following `dir flash:` output, what command would you use to view Cisco IP phone firmware files?

```
Router#dir flash:
Directory of flash:/

    1  drw-            0    Apr 7 2009 18:17:56 +00:00  bacdprompts
   13  -rw-        22224    Apr 7 2009 18:25:56 +00:00  CME43-full-
readme-v.2.0.txt
   14  drw-            0    Apr 7 2009 18:18:06 +00:00  Desktops
   27  drw-            0    Apr 7 2009 18:18:14 +00:00  gui
   45  -rw-       496521    Apr 7 2009 18:26:22 +00:00  music-on-
hold.au
   46  drw-            0    Apr 7 2009 18:18:28 +00:00  phone
  127  drw-            0    Apr 7 2009 18:31:02 +00:00  ringtones
  161  -rw-     47576204    Apr 7 2009 18:37:22 +00:00  c3825-
ipvoicek9-mz.124-15.XZ2.bin
```

   A. dir flash:/Desktops

   B. dir tftp:/Desktops

   C. dir tftp:/phone

   D. dir flash:/phone

25. What are three situations where a voice gateway is required?

    A. Connecting a CUCM Express to the local IP network

    B. Connecting a CUCM Express to the PSTN

    C. Connecting a CUCM Express to an SIP phone

    D. Connecting a CUCM Express to a legacy PBX

    E. Connecting a CUCM Express to a second CUCM Express over an IP WAN

26. What is the absolute maximum number of devices supported by CCA within a single site?

    A. 20

    B. 15

    C. 25

    D. 50

27. When running through the Unity Express Initialization Wizard, when are changes actually made to the configuration?

    A. After pressing the Next button to move on to the next configuration screen.

    B. Changes are saved every 60 seconds.

    C. When the administrator selects the Save To Startup Configuration check box and clicks the Finish button.

    D. When the administrator presses the Finish button at the Initialization Wizard Commit page.

28. What are the two voice mail configuration tabs within the CCA?

    A. Network

    B. Pilot

    C. Mailboxes

    D. Setup

    E. Users

29. Out of the box, if a Cisco IP phone is plugged into an Ethernet interface on a UC500 system, what extension is automatically assigned to it?

    A. 2001

    B. 3001

    C. 201

    D. 301

    E. 101

30. What is the default call-transfer method on the CUCM Express for dual-line DN phones?

   A. `local-consult`

   B. `full-consult`

   C. `blind`

   D. `full-blind`

31. Which protocol is used to synchronize clocks on all voice and data network equipment?

   A. VTP

   B. NTP

   C. CDP

   D. Timezone

   E. DST

32. What portion of the E.164 International code is actually assigned by the ITU board?

   A. Country code

   B. National destination code

   C. Area code

   D. Station code

   E. Office code

33. Which Cisco Communications Manager runs on a router platform?

   A. CUCM

   B. CUCMBE

   C. CUCM Express

   D. All of the above

34. At what layer of the UC model is the Cisco Unity voice mail solution found?

   A. Infrastructure layer

   B. Data Link layer

   C. Call Control layer

   D. Applications layer

   E. Session layer

35. Which protocol is used to monitor and provide detailed information about the quality of an RTP stream?

A. cRTP

B. RTCP

C. UDP

D. TCP

E. H.323

36. When issuing a show ephone command on a CUCM Express system, you see that one of your ephones is in a DECEASED state. What does this mean?

A. The phone unregistered abnormally because of a keepalive timeout.

B. A hardware malfunction occurred at the phone endpoint.

C. The phone unregistered normally and is not currently active.

D. The phone unregistered abnormally because of a reverse proxy lookup.

E. The phone unregistered normally because of a keepalive timeout.

37. Which of the following is *not* a required configuration setting when setting up a T1 CAS?

A. Pri-group options

B. Framing type

C. Clock source

D. Ds0-group options

E. Linecode type

38. What methods are available to administrators when they want to run a trace on Unity Express?

A. Using the Unity Express command line

B. Using the Unity Express web GUI

C. Using the CUCM Express command line

D. Using the CUCM Express web GUI

39. What type of analog interface connects to standard analog telephones?

A. CO

B. DID

C. FXS

D. FXO

40. Given the following configuration output, what type of phone system does this represent?

```
Router(config)#ephone-dn  1
Router(config-dn)#number 5555558888
Router(config-dn)#ephone-dn  2
Router(config-dn)#number 5555559999
Router(config-dn)#exit
Router(config)#ephone  1
Router(config-ephone)#button  1:1 2:2
Router(config)#ephone  2
Router(config-ephone)#button  1:1 2:2
```

    A. PBX system

    B. Key system

    C. Hybrid system

    D. Publisher system

41. If you try to use the web GUI for Unity Express Configuration but you are unable to connect to the Unity Express web service, what must you do?

    A. You must enable HTTP server on the CUCM Express.

    B. You must enable SSH on the CUCM Express.

    C. You must enable HTTP server on Unity Express.

    D. You must enable SSH on Unity Express.

    E. You must configure a username/password on Unity Express.

42. What is a function of a voice gateway?

    A. Provides user authentication

    B. Provides call processing

    C. Translates between analog-to-digital and digital-to-analog connections

    D. Connects IP networks over a WAN

    E. Stores voice mail information

43. What limits the types of numbers that can be used by the message-notification feature?

    A. Extension blocking

    B. Message expiry

    C. Number profile

    D. Restriction tables

Answers to Assessment Test

1. B, C. The two interfaces must be located on the same IP subnet either by creating a brand-new subnet or by using a preexisting subnet and `ip unnumbered`. Also, the service module on the CUCM Express side of the network must point to the IP address of Unity Express. See Chapter 8 for more information.

2. A. The multisite with distributed call processing model places all voice functions out to the remote site edge. See Chapter 1 for more information.

3. B, D. You will need individual user licenses for each phone, and you might need to purchase additional feature licenses depending on how many feature licenses you have available. See Chapter 5 for more information.

4. B. When you order any capacity of lines on a T1 or E1 circuit that is less than the maximum, the term used to describe this circuit is "fractional." See Chapter 7 for more information.

5. D. The 3.5 mm jack is used to connect an external audio source for MoH. See Chapter 10 for more information.

6. B. The Cisco Configuration Assistant is a Windows application used for configuration of small-business hardware such as the UC500. See Chapter 1 for more information.

7. C. Both SIP and H.323 are considered peer-to-peer protocols. See Chapter 3 for more information.

8. C. Low Latency Queuing creates a priority queue for voice and sets aside a guaranteed rate for this traffic. See Chapter 4 for more information.

9. B. The `network-locale` command changes tone and tone cadences to match what users at a given geographic location are accustomed to. See Chapter 6 for more information.

10. D. The sequential algorithm always rings the first configured member first, then the second entered number, and so on. See Chapter 6 for more information.

11. C. The `show software license` command lets you view the maximum number of configurable personal and GDM mailboxes the license allows. See Chapter 8 for more information.

12. D. The Network tab includes DHCP configuration options. See Chapter 11 for more information.

13. C. SCCP information is passed from the endpoint to the CUCM, and RTP data is sent from one endpoint to another. See Chapter 3 for more information.

14. E. A phone is considered on-hook when the phone handset is in its cradle. See Chapter 2 for more information.

15. A, C, D. You can configure inter-VLAN routing using Layer 3 switches, individual links per VLAN, or a trunked link in router-on-a-stick mode. See Chapter 4 for more information.

16. C. The most common signaling for FXS ports is LoopStart, which is enabled by default. See Chapter 7 for more information.

17. D. Backing up Unity Express using the web GUI requires that the administrator navigate to Administration ➤ Backup/Restore ➤ Start Backup. See Chapter 9 for more information.

18. C. The Trunk Priority dial-plan rules can be set for PSTN Only, SIP Only, PSTN Then SIP, SIP Then PSTN, or None. See Chapter 11 for more information.

19. C. This command tells the CUCM Express system that button 1 is to be set with Ephone-DN 2. See Chapter 5 for more information.

20. C. The Skinny Call Control Protocol is proprietary to Cisco equipment. See Chapter 3 for more information.

21. B. Call forwarding allows a user to redirect calls from one extension to another automatically. See Chapter 2 for more information.

22. A. Encoding takes the quantized sample and converts it into binary code of 1s and 0s. See Chapter 2 for more information.

23. A. You can have approximately 1 percent or less of dropped IP packets on a network and still maintain a quality voice network. See Chapter 4 for more information.

24. D. This CUCME system used the `archive tar /xtract` command to uncompress files and place them into a directory structure. All of the phone firmware files will be located in the `flash:/phone` directory. See Chapter 5 for more information.

25. B, D, E. Voice gateways are required to connect to PSTNs, legacy PBX systems, or other voice gateways/call managers across an IP network. See Chapter 7 for more information.

26. C. CCA supports a maximum of 25 devices in a single site. See Chapter 10 for more information.

27. C. The Save To Startup Configuration check box must be checked on the Commit page for the changes to be saved on Unity Express. See Chapter 8 for more information.

28. C, D. The two CCA voice mail configuration tabs are Mailboxes and Setup. See Chapter 11 for more information.

29. C. Auto-registration of Cisco IP phones is used to set up the phone, and it is assigned a single extension beginning with 201. See Chapter 10 for more information.

30. B. `Full-consult` allows you to speak to the transfer number party prior to transferring the call. See Chapter 6 for more information.

31. B. The Network Time Protocol is used to synchronize network equipment to extremely accurate time sources on a network. See Chapter 4 for more information.

32. A. The ITU distributes the country code each country uses. See Chapter 2 for more information.

33. C. CUCM Express runs on Cisco router hardware. See Chapter 1 for more information.

34. D. CUCM Express runs on Cisco router hardware. See Chapter 3 for more information.

35. B. RTCP provides information regarding the quality of the RTP stream it is responsible for. See Chapter 3 for more information.

36. A. When a phone is in a DECEASED state, this means that the phone was on the network but failed to return keepalives. This is common when a phone loses power. See Chapter 5 for more information.

37. A. The `pri-group` command is used on T1 PRI interfaces and not on T1 CAS interfaces. See Chapter 7 for more information.

38. A. The only way to run a trace is to use the Unity Express command-line interface. See Chapter 9 for more information.

39. C. FXS interfaces connect analog devices to the PSTN. See Chapter 2 for more information.

40. B. Key systems typically share lines, and each ephone is identically configured. See Chapter 6 for more information.

41. A. Your CUCM Express must have HTTP server enabled by issuing the `ip http server` global configuration command. See Chapter 8 for more information.

42. C. A primary function of a voice gateway is to translate voice streams between analog and digital. See Chapter 3 for more information.

43. D. Restriction tables protect the organization from users employing message notification to forward calls to long-distance numbers. See Chapter 9 for more information.

Chapter

1

Cisco Unified Communication Solutions

THE FOLLOWING CCNA VOICE EXAM OBJECTIVES ARE COVERED IN THIS CHAPTER:

✓ **Describe the components of the Cisco Unified Communications Architecture.**

- Describe the function of the infrastructure in a UC environment.
- Describe the function of endpoints in a UC environment.
- Describe the function of the call processing agent in a UC environment.
- Describe the function of messaging in a UC environment.
- Describe the applications available in the UC environment, including Mobility, Presence, and TelePresence.

✓ **Describe and configure gateways, voice ports, and dial peers to connect to the PSTN and service provider networks.**

- Describe the differences between PSTN and Internet Telephony Service Provider circuits.

Cisco Systems seems to have the market cornered when it comes to product placement of telephones in television shows and movies. If you look closely at shows such as *The Office* and *24*, Cisco is cleverly placing their phones in the camera shots. While that placement is a good way to show off the sleekness of the phones, network engineers want to know what's powering the phones behind the scenes. This first chapter begins *CCNA: Voice Study Guide* with an overview of the Cisco Unified Communications (UC) hardware and software currently available. Knowing all the equipment that is in Cisco's IP telephony (IPT) arsenal will enable you not only to prepare for the CCNA Voice exam but ultimately to make intelligent engineering decisions for your company and clients.

Once the key hardware and software solutions are detailed, the discussion will turn toward the various best-practice design and deployment strategies for the Unified Communications system. This will help to clarify choices to be made regarding centralized versus distributed call-processing designs.

Why Should We Bother Integrating Voice and Data Services?

So, why are we here? What's the point of ripping out our old phone handsets and *PBX* hardware to replace everything with Cisco equipment that runs on our data network? Fortunately, there are many advantages that provide cost savings as well as increased capabilities that ultimately will change the way users communicate with each other. It's no secret that many businesses have already made the switch or are at least considering the increased benefits of IP telephony. An IPT system provides many business drivers. Let's break down the communications enhancements and monetary reasons to switch to an IP telephony–based solution such as one of the Cisco Unified Communications systems.

Communications Enhancements

IP telephony provides the following enhancements to communication:

Integration of voice and data networks   Combining communications methods such as voice, video, and data becomes much more feasible if all of them speak the same language. Applications can now seamlessly integrate features such as email and instant messaging into your voice functions to provide added functionality to users.

Unified messaging of voice, email, and fax messages   All of these once-separate communication methods can be combined into a single central repository. This allows users to have a single location where they store and retrieve messages and greatly reduces the need for communications in the workplace.

The ability to communicate while out of the office   If your voice system runs over IP, you can harness the power of the Internet to make remote connections back to your voice system while you are on the road. Cisco refers to this as *mobility*. The ability to function from a remote location as if you were sitting in your office allows for a great amount of workforce flexibility, which can increase overall productivity.

Cost Savings

IP telephony can save money in the following ways:

Reduced cabling costs   By integrating voice and data, businesses now maintain a single cabling structure. Previously, there was separate physical cabling for voice systems and data systems. Combining the two separate networks into a single integrated network can potentially cut cabling costs in half!

Reduction in telephone company charges   If you have remote site or branch offices that use telephones to communicate with one another, you can significantly reduce telephone charges. Instead of transporting your voice calls over public telephone lines that incur high monthly rates and long-distance charges, you can send them across your WAN links that are currently transporting only data services. The elimination of public telephone lines between branch sites can result in significant savings.

Preservation of investment in analog technology   Many businesses have a significant investment already in analog phones and other legacy phone technology. Cisco provides several methods where you can continue to use legacy hardware over an IP telephony network.

   Now that you're thoroughly convinced of the reasons to jump on board with an integrated voice and data network, let's look at the Cisco equipment offerings that meet virtually any business need.

Introducing the Cisco Unified Communications Manager Lineup

In Cisco's Unified Communications architecture, Unified Communications Managers are what makes IP telephony possible. These hardware/software devices are the brains that handle IP call processing. The call-processing portion of a Unified Communications system handles the sequence of operations from the time a user picks up a phone to make a call to the time the user ends the call by hanging up. All of the signaling, dial interpretation, ringing, and call connecting is performed by the call processor. From a phone user's standpoint, the call processor acts like a legacy-based analog or digital phone. All of the basic phone functions such as dialing, ring signals, and interactions are the same as they've always been. This is obviously by design; because users are so familiar with using phones, it would be very difficult to modify user behavior.

From an administrative standpoint, the call processor is where you configure dialing rules for end users. Things like how to reach an outside line, internal extension dialing, and other rules are configured and maintained in the call processor database. You can also administrate the individual phones from the call-processing unit. Additions, changes, and deletions of phone extensions, voice mail access, intercom, and other voice features are controlled centrally at the call-processing unit. The configurations are then pushed out to the individual phones on the network. All of these processes are transparent to the end users and require no manual interaction from them.

There are three distinct Unified Communications Manager systems:

- Cisco Unified Communications Manager (CUCM)

- Cisco Unified Communications Manager Business Edition (*CUCMBE*)

- Cisco Unified Communications Manager Express (*CUCM Express*)

Each of these voice solutions is feature rich and highly flexible. The major differences from an end user's point of view are the number of users that each solution can handle and which solutions provide high availability (HA) and redundancy. When you take a closer look at the hardware/software architecture, you will find that the CUCM and CUCMBE run on server-based hardware and a hardened Linux OS, while the CUCM Express runs on Cisco routers and utilizes the Cisco IOS to run on. Let's dive into the specifications of each of these IP telephony call-processing solutions.

Cisco Unified Communications Manager

The Unified Communications Manager is Cisco's IP telephony flagship system. Beginning with software version 5.0, it runs on a Linux-based operating system. The current CUCM version is 7.1. While Cisco supports a few select third-party hardware vendors to run the Unified Communications Manager, typical enterprise-class implementations are appliance-based, running on the Cisco 7800 Series Media Convergence Servers (MCS). Older versions of the CUCM ran on Windows 2000 Server operating systems. Cisco has moved away from the Windows-based systems and now provides only a version that runs on Linux.

Cisco packs in virtually every possible voice and video feature capability you can think of in the CUCM system. Each server appliance is capable of handling up to 7,500 endpoints and can be clustered to support up to 30,000 endpoints. Scalability is the name of the game here. If you have a large company or plan to grow quickly, the CUCM can grow right along with you. When clustering multiple CUCM servers together, one CUCM *Publisher* controls the read/write functions of the database. All other servers are called *subscriber* servers. Subscriber servers handle additional call processing or sit idle as standby servers in case an active subscriber were to fail. Subscriber servers are key components if your voice environment requires high availability in the event of a hardware or software failure. By providing a clustered call-processing environment, you can have a call processor go offline, whether because of failure or maintenance, and continue to process calls with the other subscriber servers that are still operational on the network.

It is important to keep in mind that the CUCM appliance offers only call-processing features. All voice mail functionality must be handled by a separate hardware/software solution. The voice mail could be a Cisco *Unity* or *Unity Express* system or another third-party voice mail solution. There is no integrated call-processing and voice mail solution because the CUCM is targeted toward very large enterprise-class environments with thousands of users and phones. In these environments, call-processing tasks require dedicated hardware to be able to handle the large call volumes that CUCM was intended for. Likewise, a large voice mail solution should also have its own dedicated hardware to handle the high number of users and the degree of functionality that is required in such large organizations.

When choosing a Cisco Unified Communications system for a particular environment, it is important to consider company growth in the equation. A communications system that meets the company's needs today may not meet future needs. Estimate the percentage of growth over a five- to seven-year period.

Cisco Unified Communications Manager Business Edition

The business edition of the full-blown CUCM is geared toward medium-size companies that require up to 500 endpoints. The CUCMBE is either a software- or appliance-based solution, much like its big brother. The call-processing features and functionality are identical to the CUCM. The only downside is that it does not provide redundancy and cannot be clustered with other CUCM or CUCMBE systems to add additional users. This lack of redundancy may or may not be an issue for your implementation, but it is important to keep it in mind. If redundancy is not an issue, CUCMBE might be a great solution for your medium-size environment because it offers many of the features of the larger CUCM system at a vastly reduced cost.

One major benefit of the CUCMBE is that it offers an integrated Unity voice mail system that runs on the same hardware as the call-processing system. This helps lower customer costs by allowing them to use only one piece of hardware for both purposes. The integrated *Unity Connection* is detailed later in this chapter.

Cisco Unified Communications Manager Express

The Unified Communications Manager Express solution is the call-processing system the CCNA Voice exam is mainly focused on. This software runs on Cisco routers such as the Integrated Service Router (ISR) line. *Integrated Service Router* is a term Cisco uses for routers that integrate multiple services into a single chassis. For example, an ISR can integrate full routing, switching, wireless, firewalling, and voice capabilities on a single unit. You can mix and match the services that you need because the add-on capabilities are hardware modules that are inserted into the router unit. This provides businesses with a very flexible platform that will scale well for many years to come.

A special version of Internetwork Operating System (IOS) software must be licensed for the router to run CUCM Express. The IOS is the software used by Cisco routers and switches that performs routing, switching and telecommunications functionalities. The Communications Manager Express software must also be installed in the router's flash memory. This software works alongside the router IOS and provides administrators with a single configuration file to help simplify and consolidate changes. Chapter 5 details instructions on how to install the CUCM Express software on compatible Cisco router hardware.

The ability to integrate voice, data, and security on a single Cisco platform appeals to many small-business owners. No separate servers or hardware are needed to handle the communications of a business up to 250 users. Here is a list of older IOS routers as well as the newer Cisco ISR router lineup that fully support CUCM Express:

Non-ISR routers supporting CUCM Express 7.1

- Unified Communications 500 Series (SBCS)
- Cisco IAD 2430
- Cisco 1751-V
- Cisco 1760 Series
- Cisco 2600XM Series
- Cisco 2691
- Cisco 3700 Series

ISR routers supporting CUCM Express 7.1 and above

- Cisco 1800 ISR Series
- Cisco 2800 ISR Series
- Cisco 3200 ISR Series
- Cisco 3800 ISR Series

Each router supports a different number of IP phones because of differences in hardware specifications. Following are the maximum specifications of CUCM Express:

- Integrated data, voice, and security on a single platform
- Up to 250 users on a 3845 ISR router running CUCM Express 7.1
- On-board Unity voice mail by installing either the NM-CUE module or AIM-CUE card in a compatible router

Comparing the Communications Manager Alternatives

As a summary, Table 1.1 compares the capabilities of the three CUCM systems.

TABLE 1.1   CUCM comparison

System	Platform	Max Endpoints	High Availability	Unity Options
CUCM	Server/Linux	7,500–30,000	Yes	Unity, Unity Express
CUCMBE	Server/Linux	500	No	Unity Connection
CUCM Express	Router/IOS	250	No	Unity, Unity Express

These three call-processing platforms, CUCM, CUCMBE, and CUCM Express, give businesses both small and large the opportunity to integrate voice with data and take advantage of Unified Communications features. Now that you have an understanding of the call-processing functionality that Cisco offers, we'll take a look at the Unity voice mail solutions that almost always accompany the CUCM.

Introducing the Cisco Unity Lineup

When a user cannot answer the phone because they are away from their desk or on another call, the calling party is directed to leave a voice message. Typically, every phone system offers its own voice mail box where users can log in and check personal messages. In the Cisco world, the voice mail product is called Unity. Much like Cisco's call-processing lineup, the Unity voice mail solutions can be broken down into three main categories:

- Cisco Unity
- Cisco Unity Connection
- Cisco Unity Express

The main differences are in the number of users supported and the platform the Unity software resides on. Let's take a closer look at each of these products. All of these products offer standard voice mail. What sets Unity systems apart from legacy voice mail systems is the fact that Unity can integrate with other communications mediums such as email, fax, and instant messaging to give users increased flexibility in the ways they conduct business on a daily basis.

Cisco Unity

The Unity product is Cisco's largest and most robust voice mail and unified messaging solution. The server-based appliance runs on the Microsoft Windows 2000 or 2003 operating system. A single server can support up to 15,000 mailboxes, and multiple servers can be clustered to provide additional mailboxes. The amount of voice mail storage depends on the size of the hard drives available on the server. The Unity product is the only solution that offers all the Unified Messaging (UM) functionality because it fully integrates with Microsoft Exchange. Unified Messaging includes a great number of value-added features for voice mail users. Essentially, it creates a single message-storage database for voice mail, fax, and email. All voice mail, email, and fax transmissions end up being stored on the Microsoft Exchange email server. This migrating of messages allows you to mesh voice with email to create some very helpful services. Here are some of the most popular Unified Messaging features available with the product:

- A single directory database for voice and email.

- Listening to and deleting voice mail on Microsoft Exchange–powered email. Deleting the voice mail on email also deletes the message from your message waiting box on the phone and turns off the message waiting indicator (MWI) lamp on the phone.

- Forwarding voice mail messages as email attachments.

- Email messages being read to users over the phone using Cisco's text to speech (TTS) conversion services.

- Reception of fax messages sent to the Unity system and the ability to view them as image files.

- Broadcasting of a voice mail message to multiple voice mail boxes.

The product can also be configured to be fully redundant. Unity servers are set up in a primary and standby configuration, where the primary server handles all messaging processes. In the event of a primary Unity server failure, the standby server automatically takes over the primary server duties. The primary server stays inactive until an administrator automatically brings it back online as the primary message-processing device.

Cisco Unity Connection

Unity Connection software runs on a Linux-based server platform. It often accompanies CUCMBE implementations and can even reside on the same hardware. It can be installed on separate hardware if desired. A Unity Connection server with full integrated messaging can handle up to 7,500 mailboxes. Much like the Unity system, the amount of voice mail storage available depends on the server the software resides on. Also similar to the Unity system, Unity Connection is designed to be fully redundant. The main difference between

Unity and Unity Connection from a functionality standpoint is that Unity Connection does not integrate as seamlessly with Microsoft Exchange. Instead of having a single message store between all voice mail, fax, and email messages, the Unity Connection server is responsible for handling voice mail and fax services, and the Microsoft Exchange server deals with email messages. The Unity Connection server does have the ability to send voice mail messages as attachments, so users can receive voice mails through their email. This process essentially makes a copy of the voice mail. Unfortunately, now you have two copies of the message. One message is in your email inbox, and the other is on Unity Connection. The deletion of one message does not delete all messages. These will have to be individually deleted by the user.

Cisco Unity Express

As with all Express products in Cisco's lineup, Unity Express runs on the same routers that CUCM Express supports. The Unity Express system can be thought of as a "bolted-on" solution. By this I mean the voice mail system resides on a piece of hardware that must be installed into a compatible Cisco router in order to function. It integrates with the router IOS to provide added services. This is where the Cisco marketing term *Integrated Services Router*, or ISR, came from. All of these added services, such as Unity Express voice mail, must integrate with the router hardware and software to function. Without this integration, they cannot function. Technically, however, the Unity Express system operates as a separate "server" within the router. It actually runs a hardened Linux OS for voice mail processing. You'll learn how to install and configure Unity Express properly in Chapters 8 and 9.

Unity Express offers the fewest messaging-integration features, but for such a small system, it packs quite a punch! Here are some of the voice messaging solutions available with Unity Express:

- Basic automated attendant (AA) functionality, in which the Unity Express system automatically answers calls using a computerized voice. The user is then presented with audible options from which to choose in order to direct their call to the proper recipient. It essentially eliminates the need to have a human receptionist transfer calls.

- Voice mail access through email. Unity Express can create a copy of the voice mail message and forward it to an email address. This is similar to the Unity Connection messaging process.

- Voice mail access by dialing into the system from an external phone. This allows users to receive messages when they cannot physically be at their desk.

- Voice mail access over a web-based interface. Users can download and listen to their voice mails using a web browser such as Internet Explorer.

Two hardware options are available for Unity Express:

NM-CUE   Unity Express NM-CUE is a network module card that slides into an open bay of the router. It contains a hard drive that stores the Unity Express software and provides additional storage for up to 250 mailboxes. Of the two Unity Express options currently available, this model offers the most storage for messages. The NM-CUE does come at a cost, however, because you are required to use up a network module slot on your router, which you may need for other services.

AIM-CUE   Unity Express AIM-CUE is an advanced integration module. It is a card that must be installed on the router motherboard. The module looks very similar to a RAM chip that you install in a PC or server. The benefit of this module over the NM-CUE is that you do not have to use up a module slot on your router. If you need to install other Integrated Service modules on your router, the AIM-CUE might be a good option to save precious NM slot space. The Unity Express software and mailbox storage space are housed on a compact flash (CF) card on the AIM card. The card comes with either 512 MB or 1 GB of storage. This is enough storage to handle up to 50 mailboxes. So here again we see a tradeoff between the AIM-CUE and the NM-CUE. While the AIM-CUE does not use up a network module slot, the amount of storage available for voice mail is very limited.

It is easy to remember which Unity product offers full Unified Messaging with Microsoft Exchange. Because Unity runs on the Microsoft Windows Server platform, it can integrate more completely than the other two Unity products, which run on Linux and IOS operating systems.

Table 1.2 compares the capabilities of the Unity systems.

TABLE 1.2   Unity comparison

System	Platform	Max Mailboxes
Unity	Windows Server 2000/2003	15,000+
Unity Connection	Integrated CUCMBE server/Linux	7,500
Unity Express NM-CUE	Router NM slot/IOS	250
Unity Express AIM	Router AIM slot/IOS	50

This should give you a good idea of the Unity voice mail systems that Cisco offers today. Later in the book you will learn more about the features offered with Unity Express and how to configure it to work with CUCM Express. Right now, we'll discuss what Cisco refers to as *VoIP endpoints*. These are IP phones and other voice/video solutions.

Introducing Cisco IP Phones and User Applications

IP phones include hardware- and software-based voice solutions. These IP phones allow the user to make phone calls on- and off-network just like any traditional telephone unit. Having an end-to-end Cisco voice solution provides many benefits in regard to increased functionality and ease of administration. Following are some examples of value-added functionality that Cisco IP phones possess and that third-party phone vendors may or may not provide:

The ability to power the phones using Power over Ethernet (PoE)   Using PoE-capable switches or powered patch panels, this allows the phones to be installed without the need to plug the handset directly into a power source.

A built-in data PC Ethernet port   Many phones allow you to use a single Ethernet connection to plug your phone into the access layer switch. The phone then has a second port that acts as a mini switch. You can plug your desktop PC into this port. This allows you to add phones to your network without the need to double your switch-port capacity.

Intelligent voice segmentation   Being able to differentiate between voice and data allows administrators to provide a higher quality of service (QoS). Being able to provide voice traffic with enough network bandwidth and throughput is essential for providing an acceptable voice stream end to end. The Cisco phone talks to the access switch using a proprietary communications protocol called Cisco Discovery Protocol (CDP) to tag traffic. You'll learn how this works in Chapter 4.

Fixed and programmable voice feature buttons   These buttons allow for value-added services to tailor fit a particular voice environment.

Software-based phones   These provide voice functionality using a standard PC with a microphone and sound card, giving users the ability to have a "virtual" phone anywhere they choose.

Integration with video services   This can be in the form of either an add-on webcam and software or a fully integrated video system housed within the phone unit itself.

Cisco has four main lines of IP hardware-based phones. The 7900 Series, 6900 Series, 3900 Series, and 500 Series phones offer different features and are designed for various IP telephony deployment scenarios. Cisco also has its version of a softphone, called the *IP Communicator*. This Microsoft Windows application emulates a full-featured 7900 Series phone without the need for a physical unit. Let's examine the capabilities of the various Cisco phone lineups.

Cisco 7900 Series IP Phones

The 7900 Series phones are Cisco's most popular line on the market today. Multiple models are available, from entry-level phones to high-end IP telephony solutions with built-in videoconferencing. There are also phones that are specifically designed to be used completely hands free in conference rooms and boardrooms. The 7900 Series also offers Wi-Fi–connected phones that operate using 802.11a and 802.11b/g radios. All 7900 Series phones support both the Session Initiation Protocol (SIP) and the Cisco proprietary Skinny Call Control Protocol (SCCP) for call signaling in an IP voice deployment. The other major distinction of the 7900 Series phones is its full support of advanced Extensible Markup Language (XML) functionality. XML is a programming language that can provide the phones with additional feature-rich services such as employee directories, company information, and other web content that can be made instantly visible to any phone in a CUCM cluster. Chapter 3 provides an in-depth discussion on how these protocols work. Table 1.3 lists some of the Cisco 7900 Series phones and their unique features. The list begins with the most basic phones and ends with the models with the most advanced features:

TABLE 1.3   7900 Series phone features

Phone Model	Display Type	Integrated PC Port	Number of Lines Available	Other Features
7906G	192 × 64 mono	None	1	Softkeys and basic XML support
7911G	192 × 64 mono	10/100	1	Softkeys and basic XML support
7931G	192 × 64 mono	10/100	24	Softkeys and basic XML support
7941GE	320 × 222 mono	10/100/1000	2	Full-duplex speakerphone and XML support
7945G	320 × 240 color	10/100/1000	2	Same features as 7941GE with 16-bit color display
7961GE	320 × 222 mono	10/100/1000	6	Full-duplex speakerphone and XML support
7945G	320 × 240 color	10/100/1000	6	Same features as 7961GE with 16-bit color display

Phone Model	Display Type	Integrated PC Port	Number of Lines Available	Other Features
7971G	320 × 240 color	10/100/1000	8	Large color touch screen display
7921G	176 × 220 color	None	1	802.11a/b/g wireless
7925G	176 × 220 color	None	1	802.11a/b/g wireless; rugged shell and Bluetooth support
7937G Conference Station	192 × 64 mono	None	1	Advanced speakerphone with 360-degree microphone coverage
7985G	Large multiresolution color	None	8	Built-in video camera for integrated videoconferencing

Cisco 7900 Expansion Modules

If you need additional phone line extension buttons in situations where a receptionist answers and transfers calls all day, you can use the 7900 Series expansion modules, which can plug into 796X and 797X Series phones. Table 1.4 lists the current Cisco 7900 expansion module devices and how many additional lines they support.

TABLE 1.4 7900 Series expansion modules

Model	Display Type	Number of Lines
7914	Mono LCD	14
7915	Mono LCD	24
7916	Color LCD	24

You can also connect as many as two of these expansion modules to a compatible Cisco 7900 Series phone to give you up to 48 additional lines.

Cisco 6900 Series IP Phones

Cisco's 6900 Series phones are midrange business phones for users who don't require all the advanced features found in the 7900 Series phones. The 6900 Series phones feature a straightforward design, which makes them very easy to use even for nontechnical users.

The phones feature fixed keys as opposed to softkeys used on the 7900 Series phones for features such as directory, call transfer, conference, hold, and voice mail. These fixed keys provide a clutter-free environment that is streamlined and easy to use. The 6900 Series phones boast the following features:

- Two, four, or twelve lines
- Full-duplex speakerphone
- 396 × 81 or 396 × 162 backlit, monochrome display
- Multilanguage support
- Integrated 10/100Mbps switch
- Power over Ethernet support

Cisco 3900 Series IP Phones

The 3900 Series phones are entry-level models that are targeted to areas where multiuse phones are needed, such as lobbies, hallways, and manufacturing floors. The phones could also be used as everyday cubicle phones, but some features are lacking, which may require an upgrade to the 6900 or 7900 Series IP phones. The major difference between the 3900 Series phones and the 7900 Series phones is that the 3900 Series phones communicate using the Session Initiation Protocol only and do not have the ability to run Cisco's proprietary SCCP signaling protocol. The 3900 Series phones also are not capable of running XML services and utilize fixed-feature buttons as opposed to the softkeys found on the higher-end 7900 Series phones. At the time of this writing, the only 3900 Series model available is the 3911. This phone has the following features:

- Single-line phone
- Half-duplex speakerphone
- 144 × 32 monochrome display
- Power over Ethernet support

Cisco IP Communicator

The Cisco IP Communicator is a software-based phone that delivers the capabilities of the 7900 Series phones through a PC running Microsoft Windows XP and Vista. This solution is perfect for travelers who require advanced telecommuting features. Using the IP Communicator gives users all the features of a 7970 IP hardware phone through a PC. In fact, the interface looks exactly like a 7970 hardware phone, so end users will immediately be familiar with how it works. All the features are available, including up to eight separate lines, direct access to voice mail, and XML services. Most third-party microphones and headsets are fully compatible with the IP Communicator. Figure 1.1 shows an image of the Cisco IP Communicator running on Windows XP.

FIGURE 1.1   The IP Communicator running on Windows XP

 **Real World Scenario**

The IP Communicator, a Telecommuter's Best Friend

Jennifer is an IT hardware reseller at a midsize company. A typical day for Jennifer would start off with a one-hour commute from her home to work. Many of Jennifer's customers contact her directly over the phone to place their orders.

This was no ordinary day, however. The temperatures outside were well below freezing, and her car wouldn't start. Fortunately for Jennifer, the company recently upgraded its phone system to a Cisco Unified Communications Manager. In addition, all of the salespeople were given IP Communicator software to use on the road and when getting into the office is impossible. So on this particular morning, instead of attempting to get her car started, Jennifer went back into her home and logged into the company network through her home Internet connection. She loaded up her Cisco IP Communicator from her laptop, and she was off and running.

All her calls to her office phone were forwarded to the softphone, and what started out to be a disastrous day turned into just another day at the (virtual) office.

Cisco 500 Series IP Phones

Cisco's 500 Series IP phones are cost-effective voice hardware devices that are specifically designed for the SBCS Unified Communication 500 Series hardware. In fact, the 500 Series phones will not function on any other Cisco IP telephony system. Unlike the 3900 Series phones, which use the SIP communications protocol, the 500 Series phones run Cisco's SCCP.

These are very low-cost phones geared toward small businesses. Just because they are low in cost doesn't mean they don't have any bells and whistles, however. The 500 Series phones can handle up to five lines per phone and have support for features such as conference calling, call parking, paging, and intercom. Table 1.5 lists the Cisco 500 Series phones and their unique features.

TABLE 1.5   500 Series phone features

Phone Model	Display Type	Integrated PC Port	Number of Lines Available	Other Features
521G	128 × 64 mono	None	1	Softkeys, backlit LCD
521SG	128 × 64 mono	10/100	1	Softkeys, backlit LCD
524G	128 × 64 mono	10/100	4	Softkeys, backlit LCD
524SG	128 × 64 mono	10/100/1000	4	Softkeys, backlit LCD
SPA525G	320 × 240 color	10/100/1000	5	Operates in wired or 802.11b/g wireless mode

Cisco Analog Telephony Adapter

The Cisco Analog Telephony Adapter (*ATA*) is a device that allows standard analog telephones and fax machines to operate on an Ethernet LAN. The *ATA* has one Ethernet port for network connectivity and two RJ-11 analog ports to connect up to two analog devices. This solution is good if the organization has analog telephony devices it wants to leverage throughout an IP telephony migration. Figure 1.2 shows how an ATA device connects an analog phone to the IP network.

Cisco VG224 and VG248 Series Voice Gateway

A second Cisco analog-to-IP conversion technology is the VG224. This device actually runs the Cisco IOS operating system that runs on a Cisco ISR router platform. Its sole purpose is the conversion of multiple analog lines into IP packets for transport over a data network.

FIGURE 1.2   An ATA device connecting an analog phone to an IP network

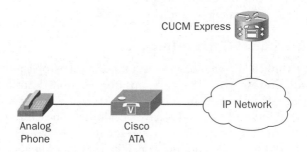

The VG224 can terminate up to 24 analog voice endpoints, while the VG248 can terminate up to 48 devices. They provide a cost-effective way to migrate your current analog voice system to IP. Following are some reasons to use the VG200 Series as a starting point into an IP telephony solution:

Investment protection   If you've invested a large amount of money into analog handsets and fax machines, this is a way to prolong their useful life while moving toward an integrated voice and data solution.

High voice quality   You experience the same quality calls as with a pure IP-based handset.

High availability   The VG224 and VG248 have the ability to detect WAN failures and route calls over backup PSTN lines.

Reduced cost of entry to IP telephony   You can lower the initial costs of an IP telephony implementation by using VG200 Series devices to provide a gateway for your existing analog phones. Eliminating the need to purchase new handsets can greatly reduce costs.

Additional Unified Communications Applications

In addition to the hard phones and softphones that Cisco offers, several user applications enhance the Unified Communications experience. In this section, I'm going to describe several of the Cisco applications available to you.

Cisco Video Advantage

The Cisco Video Advantage solution adds videoconferencing to your voice calls, a capability that seamlessly integrates with your Cisco Unified Communications system. Video Advantage comes with a USB web camera, called the Cisco VT Camera II. You can connect this camera to your desktop PC. You can then install the Video Advantage software onto your PC; this software integrates with your Cisco IP desk phone or IP Communicator. You can then make and receive not only standard audio voice calls but also videoconferencing calls with your Cisco phone. Video Advantage is an extremely scalable and cost-effective videoconferencing solution.

Cisco Unified Personal Communicator

You can think of the Unified Personal Communicator as a one-stop shop for all of your communication needs. Similar to the IP Communicator mentioned earlier, the Unified Personal Communicator is a piece of communications software that is installed on a computer and has the ability to make and receive standard phone calls. The Unified Personal Communicator takes things a step or two further, however, because the software is multiplatform and can be installed not only on Windows PCs but also on Apple computers running OS X. This product is marketed to larger companies with many remote employees who need to stay in constant contact with one another. Here are some of the integrated features that the Cisco Unified Personal Communicator offers:

- Softphone capabilities for standard phone calls and voice mail using any of the Cisco Unity products
- Instant messaging tool for real-time text-based communication
- Presence integration to notify other users of your whereabouts and to keep track of the availability of other Unified Personal Communicator users
- Integrated directory and contact services
- Videoconferencing using Cisco Video Advantage
- Web conferencing using Cisco Unified MeetingPlace software

Cisco Unified CallConnector

The Unified CallConnector is a Windows-based software application that installs on user PCs. This software is geared toward small and medium businesses. It fully integrates with the Cisco Unified Communications Express solution. Following are just some of the features available for use with the CallConnector applications:

- Integrates with Microsoft Outlook and Internet Explorer to provide a seamless integration of web, email, and voice functions
- Tracks user presence information to notify you when a user is available in real time
- Simple-to-use contact list that provides a single repository for your phone, email, and instant message contacts
- Lets users make and receive calls with the click of a mouse
- Allows users to be completely mobile

This should give you a good overview of the Cisco endpoints and endpoint applications that a Unified Messaging system can handle. In the next section, we'll discuss the hardware that allows our voice calls to be routed out to the public phone network.

Cisco TelePresence

TelePresence is an enterprise-class hardware and software video conferencing solution that uses large screen high-definition monitors to display remote video to simulate a virtual meeting room. The tool is designed to simulate face-to-face meetings over an IP network where members can be located all around the world. TelePresence hardware and software fully integrates into a CUCM system that is responsible for video conference call processing such as setups and tear-downs as well as scheduling.

Using Voice Gateways

The Cisco Unified Communications call-processing devices in the CUCM suite allow engineers to configure and deploy a voice system for on-network calling. On-network dialing means that the calls are contained within a private network fully controlled by a private organization. But what if you need to make a call to someone outside the local organization? This is where voice gateways come into play. Voice gateways are responsible for the setup of off-network calling. A voice gateway is simply an IOS router that is capable of translating legacy voice communication into IP packets for transport over data networks. It sits right on the border between your IP network and standard telephone networks. If you are familiar with configuring routers for Ethernet LANs and WANs, then you are already familiar with most of the configuration processes. What may be new to you are the voice interfaces that are needed to connect your IP network to the public telephone network. You'll learn more about these interfaces as well as other hardware that voice gateways utilize in a *VoIP* environment. For now, it is important to understand that voice gateways can connect your Cisco Unified Communications solution to the public switched telephone network (*PSTN*) either physically or virtually using a variety of methods. Let's briefly discuss the physical and virtual methods that can be used to connect to the PSTN.

Voice analog and digital interfaces are special PSTN connections configured on voice gateway routers to bridge the VoIP and PSTN networks so off-network calls can successfully be completed. Figure 1.3 shows how a voice gateway can be configured to connect directly to the PSTN.

FIGURE 1.3   A voice gateway connecting directly to the PSTN

A virtual method of connecting your voice gateway to the PSTN is to set up a VoIP trunk to an Internet Telephony Service Provider (*ITSP*). This VoIP trunk essentially creates a virtual tunnel from your local voice gateway to a service provider using your Internet connection. The calls are then switched out onto the PSTN at the ITSP site. The concept of using ITSPs for off-network calling is fairly new to the telephony world. This is because you need your voice system to be able to transport calls over IP using the Internet. But because you can leverage your existing Internet connection to provide transport for your off-network calls, many businesses find that they can eliminate expensive PSTN lines, which can cut operating costs significantly. Figure 1.4 shows how a voice gateway can be configured to connect virtually to the PSTN by tunneling voice traffic to an ITSP.

FIGURE 1.4   A voice gateway configured through an ITSP

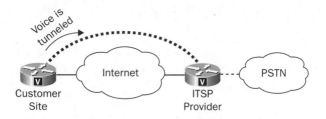

Voice gateways perform a great number of VoIP and PSTN services that will be covered in greater detail in subsequent chapters of this book. This section is provided simply to give you a 30,000-foot view of the way a voice gateway is responsible for the translation of voice between the IP network and legacy voice systems such as the PSTN.

Introducing the Cisco Unified Communications 500 Series

Cisco Unified Communications requires its own section because of the unique functionality that it brings to the table. The UC500 is part of Cisco's Smart Business Communication System (*SBCS*). Cisco has a unique suite of hardware that is geared toward small- to medium-size businesses. Table 1.6 lists the SBCS suite of hardware and shows what services each device performs.

TABLE 1.6   Cisco SBCS hardware platforms

Model	Functions
Unified Communications 500	Voice, data, security, and wireless
Catalyst Express 500	Layer 2 switching for desktops, servers, and IP phones
Wireless Express 500	Flexible controller-based 802.11b/g wireless solution
Unified 500 Series IP phones	Hardware-based IP phones
Cisco 500 Series secure router	Advanced firewalling, wireless, and dynamic routing protocol support for LANs and WANs

The CCNA Voice Exam focuses solely on the configuration of the UC520 hardware, which offers voice capabilities to small businesses. It is important to know, however, that other SBCS components are available that complement the UC520 in a network environment. The UC500 is an all-in-one solution that combines call processing, voice mail, voice gateway, standard IP data, optional Wi-Fi, and security into a single box. From a voice standpoint, the system runs the CUCM Express and Unity Express software with support for up to 48 IP phones. Because this is an all-in-one system, the UC500 has several voice gateway methods available for connecting your CUCM Express system for off-network calling using either physical or virtual methods. The SBCS Series is clearly targeted directly toward small businesses of 50 or fewer users who want a single, easy-to-manage system for all of their networking needs.

The SBCS UC500 can utilize any Cisco 7900 and 3900 Series IP phones. In addition, the SBCS system is also the only solution that is compatible with the Cisco 500 Series IP phones. These entry-level phones are ideal for small-office environments that are just making the transition from a legacy key system to an integrated voice/data system over IP.

Here is a list of features that the UC500 small business solution can provide:

- Support for 8 to 48 IP phones
- Integrated Unity Express voice mail
- Built-in eight-port Power over Ethernet (PoE) switch
- Integrated Auto Attendant (AA)
- Internal or external Music on Hold (MoH) sources
- Integrated analog voice ports to connect to the PSTN and to utilize analog phones and fax machines
- Static routing and Network Address Translation (NAT) support
- Virtual private network (VPN) support for up to 10 simultaneous remote access users

- Firewall configuration support using IOS firewall configuration commands
- Optional wireless 802.11a/b/g integration

One of the key features that the UC500 Series offers is a simple-to-use graphical configuration tool. The UC500 series can easily be managed using the Cisco Configuration Assistant (CCA). The CCA is a Windows-based application that allows administrators to connect to and configure the entire UC500 system using a graphical user interface (GUI). This tool greatly improves the ease of management and support for small businesses. In fact, the CCA can not only help you configure the UC500 device; it can also assist in the configuration of any of the SBCS 500 Series devices listed in Table 1.6. The ability to utilize the CCA for configuration and basic support sets the SBCS apart from Cisco's other offerings. Because everything can be run from a simple, graphics-driven interface on a PC, it appeals greatly to small businesses that may not have a full-time Cisco engineer on staff. Chapter 10 of this book is dedicated to the SBCS UC500 Series and its configuration using the CCA 2.0 software. In addition, Appendix A presents a case study of a detailed design and implementation of a UC500 system in a small-office environment.

Choosing an IP Telephony Deployment Option

Now that you understand the basic components of the Unified Communications system, let's talk about the four Cisco-supported deployment options that we can use to design an IP telephony solution. Each option has advantages and disadvantages that we will cover. Most deployments will fall nicely within one of the options depending on the end-user requirements. The four supported deployment options are as follows:

- Single site with centralized call processing
- Multisite with centralized call processing
- Clustering over the wide area network
- Multisite with distributed call processing

Single Site with Centralized Call Processing

The single-site deployment is a bit of a no-brainer. If all of your users are in the same geographic region and are interconnected with a high-speed network, then a centralized-call processing solution is the way to go. High availability can be achieved by clustering multiple Communications Managers on the same local network. Voice gateway redundancy can also be achieved by adding two or more voice gateway routers. The key factor to keep in mind is that even though the system needs multiple CUCM systems for redundancy, all users ultimately connect to a single system for their unified communication needs. Figure 1.5 shows a single-site design.

FIGURE 1.5   A single site with CUCM

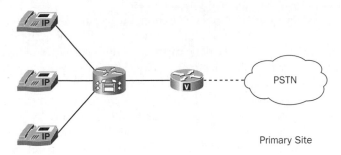

Primary Site

Most of your small-office environments will utilize the single-site deployment, and the CCNA Voice Exam does not go too far beyond this setup in the configuration knowledge it requires.

Multisite with Centralized Call Processing

The design options become more interesting when you need to provide unified communications to multiple sites that are interconnected across a wide area network (WAN). One option is to offer VoIP services to remote sites that communicate across the WAN to a CUCM system located at a central site. Figure 1.6 depicts a typical multisite design.

FIGURE 1.6   A typical multisite WAN with a central CUCM for VoIP

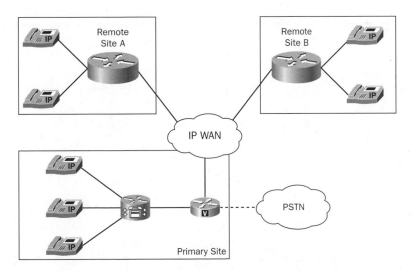

Phones located at Remote Site A and Remote Site B will communicate back to a single call-processing cluster located at the primary site. This solution is best when the vast majority of your users are located at a single site and you have a few remote sites. A reliable and high-speed WAN connection is obviously beneficial because all voice traffic will need to traverse the WAN to reach the primary site, where the call-processing, voice mail, and other Unified Communications applications are located.

If your remote sites have a single WAN connection, this creates a single point of failure. This may or may not be a concern to you. If it is critical that the remote sites maintain the ability to have at least basic PSTN calling capabilities during a WAN outage, you can implement the survivable remote site telephony service (*SRST*) to a voice-capable router at each remote site. SRST is a cost-effective method to provide high-availability voice features to remote sites that have a centralized call-processing design. Along with installing and configuring SRST on the router, you will need to purchase one or more local PSTN services to be used as a backup. When a WAN outage occurs, the remote site phones can no longer communicate with the call processor. An SRST-configured router will detect the WAN failure and begin routing calls out of the backup PSTN connections that are locally available. If you get the opportunity to configure a router for SRST redundancy, you'll be happy to find out that the configuration is very similar to a standard voice router with the CUCM Express software.

Clustering over the Wide Area Network

If your organization has two to six large and geographically dispersed locations that are interconnected by a high-speed and reliable WAN link, the clustering option may be the right choice for you. Basically, you provision a CUCM publisher server at one location and up to five subscriber servers at the remote site locations. The publisher and subscriber servers talk to one another and work as a single unit. This enables administrators to maintain a single system, but you must take care to ensure that the WAN is very stable and free of latency. On-network calls are made across the WAN, while off-network calls are made over the local PSTN connections. If the WAN were to fail, users would continue to connect to their local CUCM server, but all calls placed would go over the PSTN. Figure 1.7 shows a typical WAN clustering deployment model.

FIGURE 1.7   WAN clustering

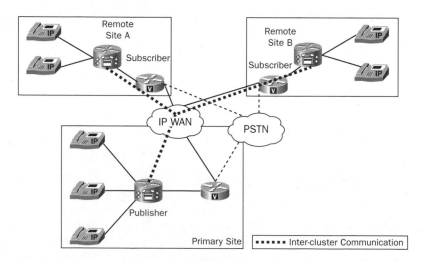

Because there is a limit to the number of active subscriber servers in a single CUCM deployment, this solution does not scale beyond six total sites. Because the clustered CUCM servers need to stay constantly updated and synchronized, the WAN links must provide quick response times for updates and keepalives.

Multisite with Distributed Call Processing

The distributed call-processing deployment is the best choice when you have many users who are geographically dispersed in multiple locations. The remote sites may also have low-speed WAN connections that are not highly reliable. If WAN conditions are not ideal for voice, then it might be best to distribute the call-processing and voice mail functionality out to the remote site itself. Figure 1.8 shows a typical multisite distributed call-processing deployment.

FIGURE 1.8   Distributed call processing

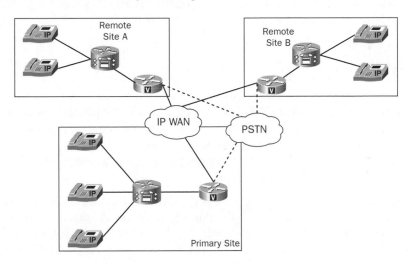

As you can see in the figure, each remote site has a Communications Manager and voice gateway to locally serve the remote-site phones, and each is completely independent of every other. The design can be configured for VoIP traffic to traverse WAN links to reach other internal destinations if possible. If the WAN is too congested, internal calls will be made over the PSTN.

Clearly this deployment offers the utmost in reliability but it comes at a high cost. Not only will the additional purchase of call-processing and voice mail services at each site be required, but you also need to keep in mind that support costs go up because you have to support multiple Unified Communications systems as opposed to one centralized system.

Summary

In this chapter, you learned the major components of a Cisco Unified Communications system, namely, the Unified Communications Manager, Unity voice mail, and the voice gateway. We discussed the features, architecture, and scaling capabilities of the three-tiered Communications Manager and Unity systems. You learned the difference between on- and off-network calling and therefore the need for a voice gateway to connect to the PSTN for external calls. In addition, you learned about the Cisco UC500 Series SBCS, which rolls up all three voice services along with security, wireless, and basic routing features into one little unit.

We also covered hardware- and software-based phones to give you an understanding of the various types of voice/video capabilities a Unified Communications system provides.

Finally, this chapter discussed the three recommended deployment methods of the Cisco Unified Communications system. You learned the pros and cons of each solution and when it would be best to implement a particular method. You also learned about how SRST can be used as a low-cost method to provide highly available voice service to remote sites that are configured in a centralized call-processing environment.

Exam Essentials

Understand the differences between the main components of a Unified Communications system.   The Communications Manager handles all call-processing and setup functions. The Unity system is responsible for the voice mail and unified or integrated messaging. The voice gateway handles off-network calls on the PSTN. Finally, the various hard and soft-phones are end units that users interact with.

Know the number of end devices that each Cisco Unified Communications Manager can handle.   When choosing a system, it is vital that you understand how it will scale. The CUCM supports a cluster environment of up to 30,000 end devices. The CUCMBE supports up to 500 end devices. Finally, the CUCM Express supports up to 250 end devices.

Understand the redundancy capabilities of each Communications Manager.   Full redundancy may or may not be an important issue for a particular implementation. Typically, users assume that when they pick up a phone, it will work. All three systems provide some form of redundant system to keep calls moving in the event of a failure. The CUCM uses clustered servers to provide call-processing redundancy. The CUCMBE and CUCM Express solutions provide PSTN redundancy by implementing SRST at the voice gateway.

Know the two Unity Express hardware options.   The NM-CUE takes up a module slot, and the AIM-CUE is a card inserted on the router system board.

Know the difference between the 7900, 6900, 3900, and 500 Series IP phones.   The 7900 supports both SCCP and SIP, the 6900 Series drops some of the advanced features of the 7900 but provides more features than the 3900 Series, the 3900 Series supports only SIP, and the 500 Series supports only SCCP and can be used only with the UC500 SBCS Series.

Understand what an IP Communicator is used for. The IP Communicator is Cisco's version of a softphone that is based on the 7970 hardware phone. It is excellent for people who are traveling or spend much of their time away from the office.

Understand the function of the ATA hardware endpoint. The ATA helps to connect analog phones and fax machines to an IP network.

Know when to design a single-site IP telephony deployment. Single-site deployments offer centralized calling to a group of users who are on the same high-speed network.

Know when to design a multisite centralized IP telephony deployment. When the majority of users are in a single location and you have a handful of remote sites, this design is ideal. It also requires less capital and has lower support costs because of the centralized nature of the voice equipment. WAN connections need to be fast and fairly reliable.

Know when to design an IP telephony cluster across an IP WAN. When you have two to six large remote sites that are interconnected by a high-speed IP WAN, you can cluster six CUCM servers together. This allows you to be able to administrate the cluster as one large system that is geographically dispersed. In the event of a WAN failure, remote users continue to use the local CUCM and send calls over the PSTN.

Understand when to use SRST. In multisite centralized deployments, SRST can be used at remote sites to give some voice functionality during a WAN outage.

Know when to design a multisite distributed IP telephony deployment. When users are distributed at multiple sites, you should take a distributed approach. Each site has local call processing, voice mail, and voice gateways. The downside is the increased cost and support of multiple systems.

Written Lab 1.1

Write the answers to the following questions:

1. What is the maximum number of endpoints a CUCMBE can handle?
2. Which Cisco Unified Communications Manager runs on an IOS router?
3. Which two Communications Managers and Unity systems can function within a single unit?
4. What is the name of Cisco's software-based phone?
5. What does ATA stand for?
6. What types and numbers of ports does an ATA 180 Series have?
7. What are the four IP telephony deployment types?
8. What does ITSP stand for?
9. Which Unity Express device uses up a router slot?
10. What is the maximum number of mailboxes Unity Express can support?

(The answers to Written Lab 1.1 can be found following the answers to the review questions for this chapter.)

Review Questions

1. Which Cisco IP phone series is not compatible with the CUCM Express system installed on ISR routers?

A. 7900 Series IP phones

B. 3900 Series IP phones

C. 500 Series IP phones

D. Cisco IP Communicator

E. Cisco ATA

2. Which Cisco voice mail system offers Unified Messaging?

A. Cisco Unity Express

B. Cisco Unity

C. Cisco Unity Connection

D. Cisco Unity and Cisco Unity Connection

3. Which of the following non-ISR routers is *not* compatible with CUCM Express?

A. Cisco 3725

B. Cisco 1761

C. Cisco UC520

D. Cisco 2621

4. What firmware is the Cisco IP Communicator based on?

A. Cisco 7965

B. Cisco 7970

C. Cisco 7940

D. Cisco 3925

E. Cisco 524

5. Which Unified Communications Manager runs on a Linux operating system? Select all that apply.

A. CUCM

B. CUCM Express

C. CUCMBE

D. None of the above

6. Which Unity solution uses compact flash (CF) for mailbox storage?

A. Unity Express NM-CUE

B. Unity Connection

C. Unity Express AIM-CUE

D. Unity

7. Which Communications Manager is best suited for large businesses that require high availability and uptime for thousands of phones?

   A. CUCMBE

   B. CUCM

   C. CUCM Express

   D. Unity

8. Which Cisco phone series can utilize SIP for voice signaling? Select all that apply.

   A. 7900 Series

   B. 3900 Series

   C. 500 Series

   D. 2800 ISR

9. What device allows you to connect analog devices to an IP network?

   A. IP Communicator

   B. SIP

   C. ATA

   D. SCCP

   E. UC500

10. What is responsible for handling off-network calls?

   A. ATA

   B. SCCP

   C. CUCM Publisher

   D. Voice gateway

11. What is the name of the call-processing device that handles the database read/write functions of the CUCM?

   A. Subscriber

   B. Publisher

   C. Unity Connection

   D. Unity

12. What is the maximum number of analog devices can you connect to a Cisco ATA?

   A. One

   B. Two

   C. Four

   D. Eight

13. What method can be used to connect a voice gateway to the PSTN for off-network calling? Select all that apply.

   A. Physical connection to the PSTN

   B. VoIP trunk to an ITSP

   C. VoIP trunk to a PSTN

   D. Virtual connection to the ITSP

14. Which phone cannot run SCCP?

   A. 7985

   B. 7921 wireless phone

   C. 524

   D. 3951

   E. IP Communicator

15. What GUI tool can be used to configure the UC500?

   A. Unity Express

   B. IP Communicator

   C. CCA

   D. SCCP

16. What platform does the CCA run on?

   A. Internet Explorer 6.0 and up

   B. MS Windows

   C. Mac OS X

   D. Terminal Emulator

17. What IP telephony deployment model would you use if you have 10 remote sites that require full availability of voice functions and applications in the event of a WAN outage? Select all that apply.

   A. Multisite with centralized call processing

   B. Single site

   C. Single site with distributed call processing

   D. Multisite with distributed call processing

18. What Cisco solution can be used at remote sites in a multisite with centralized call-processing design to allow basic voice functionality to remote-site users in the event of a WAN outage?

   A. SCCP

   B. SRST

   C. SIP

   D. CUCM Express

19. Which of the following is *not* an IP telephony deployment model Cisco recommends?

    A. Single site

    B. Multisite with centralized call processing

    C. Single site with distributed call processing

    D. Clustering over the WAN

    E. Multisite with distributed call processing

20. Which IP telephony deployment model is likely to cost the most?

    A. Single site

    B. Multisite with centralized call processing

    C. Multisite with distributed call processing

    D. Multisite with centralized call processing and SRST

Answers to Review Questions

1. C. The 500 Series IP phones are compatible only with the UC500 SBCS solution.

2. B. Only Unity offers Unified Messaging, which means it fully integrates with MS Exchange. The other two Unity systems offer Integrated Messaging with the use of IMAP.

3. D. The 2600 Series is not supported but the 2600XM Series is.

4. B. The IP Communicator is a softphone that is based on the 7970 phone firmware.

5. A, C. Both CUCM and CUCMBE run on a Linux OS. The CUCM Express runs on IOS.

6. C. The Unity Express AIM-CUE has a 512MB or 1GB CF for mailbox storage.

7. B. The CUCM allows for full clustering that offers complete HA for thousands of endpoints.

8. A, B. Both the 7900 and 3900 Series can run SIP for voice signaling.

9. C. The Analog Telephony Adapter (ATA) connects standard analog devices to an IP network.

10. D. The voice gateway handles off-network calling to the PSTN.

11. B. The publisher handles the read/write functions of the CUCM database.

12. B. The ATA 180 series has two RJ-11 interfaces to connect up to two analog phones.

13. A, D. You can connect to the PSTN by using a physical PSTN connection or by sending traffic across an IP network to an ITSP.

14. D. The 3900 Series phones run only SIP.

15. C. The Cisco Configuration Assistant (CCA) is a Windows application that uses a user-friendly GUI to help configure and support a number of Cisco products including the UC500.

16. B. The CCA is a Windows application.

17. D. The multisite with distributed call-processing model pushes the call-processing and other unified communications functions out to the remote site. In the event of a WAN outage, no voice services are affected.

18. B. Survivable remote site telephony (SRST) can be implemented on a voice-capable remote site router to set up basic voice calling using the PSTN in the event of a WAN outage.

19. C. It does not make sense to distribute call-processing functionality in a single site.

20. C. The distributed call-processing method forces you to purchase multiple CUCMs that are deployed throughout your environment. This is typically the most expensive deployment model.

Answers to Written Lab 1.1

1. 500 endpoints

2. CUCM Express

3. CUCMBE/Unity Connection and CUCM Express/Unity Express

4. IP Communicator

5. Analog telephony adapter

6. One Ethernet and two analog

7. Single site, multisite with centralized call processing, clustering over the WAN, and multisite with distributed call processing

8. Internet Telephony Service Provider

9. NM-CUE

10. 250

Chapter

2

Traditional Telephony

THE FOLLOWING CCNA VOICE EXAM OBJECTIVES ARE COVERED IN THIS CHAPTER:

✓ **Describe PSTN components and technologies.**

- Describe the services provided by the PSTN.

- Describe time division and statistical multiplexing.

- Describe supervisory, informational, and address signaling.

- Describe numbering plans.

- Describe analog circuits.

- Describe digital voice circuits.

- Describe PBX, trunk lines, key-systems, and tie lines.

✓ **Describe VoIP components and technologies.**

- Describe the process of voice packetization.

✓ **Describe the components of the Cisco Unified Communications Architecture.**

- Describe the function of auto attendants and IVRs in a UC environment.

The 1980s were an interesting time to grow up, in regard to technology. The personal computer was just being introduced, and a public Internet was many years away. Nearly all distance communication was done over the telephone. I was always fascinated with telephones and how they worked. To me, the "phone guy" was my version of the American cowboy—always out on the road and in the sun climbing phone poles to set up or restore service. The boom trucks and butt sets were the telco version of horses and six-shooters. Now that voice and data are converging, many aspects of the traditional telecommunications realm are changing while many others remain the same. This chapter will discuss traditional public switched telephone network (PSTN) components that are still being used today. This will give you the background you need to understand how they are integrated in IP telephony (IPT) networks.

We'll first discuss analog signaling and the different signaling functions each type performs. Then I'll describe analog and digital circuits and explain the differences between the two. I'll also describe multiplexing, to detail how multiple voice circuits can be transported over a single cable. Next we'll move on to PBX and key systems and how they connect to the PSTN. Finally, we'll end with a discussion of PSTN numbering plans and why they are so important from a planning and design point of view.

Understanding Analog Network Signaling

A standard analog telephone has such a simple interface that almost anyone can use it. All you have to do is pick up the handset, punch in the number of the person you are trying to reach, and all the wizards behind the curtain do the rest to connect your handset to another person, who may be located down the street or on the other side of the planet! We're going to pull back the curtain to see exactly what it takes for the magic of telephones to work. The most obvious place to start is with voice signaling.

Loop Start Signaling

When a telephone handset is sitting in the phone cradle, the telecommunications term for this state is *on-hook*. If someone wishes to make a phone call, the first thing they do is pick up the handset. This action sets off a series of signaling processes that notifies the phone switch that someone wishes to use the phone and places it in an off-hook state. In the analog world, this is called a *loop start* because it opens a circuit loop back to the PSTN. When the phone is on-hook, the loop is open. When you take the phone off-hook, it closes the loop, sending the voltage back to the CO so they can detect that you went off-hook.

You'll also receive audible feedback in the form of a dial tone when picking up a phone handset. This is to signal that the phone system is ready for you to begin dialing a number. You see, an analog line has two wires that plug into the back of your phone from the wall jack. One wire is called the tip or ground wire; it is your link back to the telephone company switch equipment. The second wire is called either the ring or the battery wire. This wire provides a constant flow of low-voltage power (−48 volts) to the phone. When the phone is on-hook, the connection between the ring and tip wires is severed. As soon as you pick up the handset and go off-hook, the connection between ring and tip on your phone connects power from the ring wire, and that power then flows over the tip wire to the phone company. Now that you have a fully powered loop, you can begin sending and receiving signaling information to and from the phone company equipment in order to make calls. Figure 2.1 displays the phone in an on-hook state where the loop is severed and also in an off-hook state where the circuit connects and the loop start occurs.

FIGURE 2.1   Loop start signaling

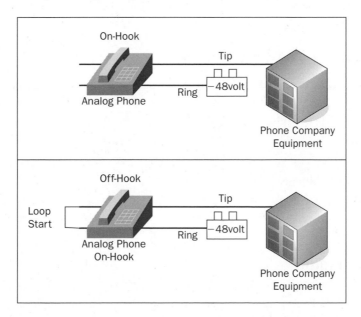

Glare is an interesting and somewhat common anomaly that occurs on analog lines that use loop start signaling. It occurs when both the local user and the telephone company attempt to access or seize the analog circuit simultaneously, that is, when someone is attempting to call your phone at the exact same time you want to use the line. When the local user picks up the phone, they are not given any warning (the phone didn't get the chance to ring) that someone is on the other end. This can lead to confusion because the local phone user is surprised to find a call is already in progress. Glare occurs in loop start signaling scenarios because the PSTN equipment does not check for a current on the wire prior to seizing the line. Glare typically isn't a problem in residential installations because call volume is typically low. In business settings, however, glare can become a real nuisance. To eliminate the glare problem, ground start signaling was developed.

Ground Start Signaling

A different approach to loop start in the analog world is *ground start*. From a pure signaling standpoint, ground start momentarily grounds one side of the circuit. This grounding is an indication to the PSTN equipment that the circuit is ready for use. This added signaling process avoids the glaring situation found in loop start signaling. A good example of ground start signaling is an analog pay phone. Pay phones require that the calling party first insert change prior to making a call; the physical insertion of coins into the phone activates ground start signaling. When a coin is inserted into a pay phone, it causes a lever within the phone to tip. This lever action is what grounds the circuit. Once the signal is grounded, the PSTN knows that money has been inserted, and a call can then be placed.

Analog Network Event Signaling

All analog phone calls need a way to signal events on the phone network in order to establish communication between end devices. There are three distinct types of network signaling in a voice network:

- Address signaling
- Informational signaling
- Supervisory signaling

Each type provides vital functions for call setup and end-user feedback to inform us that either a call is being processed properly or a problem has occurred. Let's look at each signaling type.

Address Signaling

Address signaling represents the transmission of digits to the remote party that the calling party wishes to dial. Two types of address signaling are in use. One method is *pulse dialing*, also called rotary dialing because the numbers are arranged on a round disk. The dial uses a mechanical method of quickly going on-hook and off-hook within a certain timeframe. Each digit 0 to 9 is represented by one of these on/off-hook transitions as it spins around. A different way to look at this is to think about what on-hook and off-hook sequences do. Basically we're momentarily turning on and off the power current to the phone switch. The phone switch then counts the number of starts and stops in the power flow and determines the intended digit to dial based on this calculation. It's very much like simple Morse code. For example, a user dials 5 by inserting their finger into the properly labeled slot and turning the dial clockwise until it stops. When the finger is removed, the dial rotates back to its original position. During this return motion, a series of five on/off-hook rapid transitions occurs. The phone recognizes these and collects the digits that the user wishes to dial.

The second and far more popular type of address signaling is dual-tone multi-frequency (*DTMF*). It is often called touch-tone dialing. This form of address signaling uses very specific audible tones that the phone network equipment recognizes. It combines two voice-band frequencies to represent twelve different numbers and symbols. The switch recognizes the tones and properly interprets the intended destination phone number. Figure 2.2 shows how the frequency combinations are used to represent the digits on a phone.

FIGURE 2.2   DTMF frequency creation

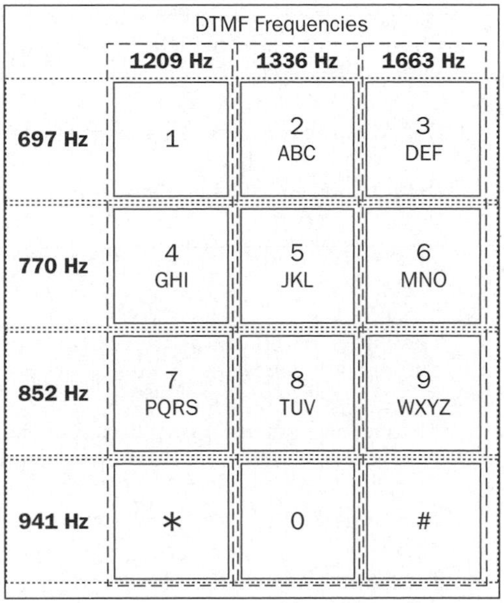

DTMF Frequencies		
1209 Hz	**1336 Hz**	**1663 Hz**
1	2 ABC	3 DEF
4 GHI	5 JKL	6 MNO
7 PQRS	8 TUV	9 WXYZ
*	0	#

(Row labels: 697 Hz, 770 Hz, 852 Hz, 941 Hz)

A Cisco voice gateway can be configured to recognize either DTMF or pulse address signaling. The default signaling is DTMF.

Timeout values are associated with the maximum and minimum speeds a user can dial numbers using DTMF. The quickest duration between dialed digits is 45 milliseconds, whereas the longest time allowed between dialed digits is 3 seconds.

Informational Signaling

Informational signaling is all about letting the calling party know what is going on with the phone system and the attempted call. As soon as you pick up the receiver of a phone, you hear a dial tone. This tone informs you that the phone is operational and talking to the phone switch. People commonly listen to make sure they hear the dial tone before dialing a number. Informational feedback is generated from the phone switch to the user in the form of audible tones and/or voice messages. Table 2.1 lists some of the most common informational signals and their meanings.

TABLE 2.1   Informational signals

Informational Signal Type	Signal Meaning
Dial tone	Phone is in an off-hook state and ready to accept user input with the keypad.
Busy	Called number phone is currently in use.
Number not in service	Called number is not available on the phone network.
Call waiting	An incoming call is being made to line 2 on the phone; line 1 is in use.
Ring-back	The phone company is attempting to establish the connection to the called party.
Reorder	All local circuits are busy; thus the call cannot be completed. This is also known as a "fast busy" signal.
Congestion	The long-distance company is unable to complete the call.
Handset off-hook	Someone has picked up the handset of a phone from the cradle.

Informational signaling may be different depending on what region you are in. A dial tone in the United States is different from a dial tone in Mexico, for instance.

Supervisory Signaling

Supervisory signaling deals with the behind-the-scenes part of call setup and teardown. There are many different types of supervisory signaling, depending on the types of circuits being used and the type of phone equipment making the signals. This signaling is done to ensure that the phone system properly interprets user input and that that user input is properly handled. For example, a phone seizure signal is a very common supervisory signal. When you pick up your phone, a seizure supervisory signal is first sent to the telephone switch to ensure that you have control over the analog circuit. As soon as the line is seized, you receive an informational signal in the form of a dial tone.

Supervisory signaling can occur in or out of band depending on the type of circuit being used. In-band signaling means that the signals are transported on the same wire as the voice traffic. Out-of-band signaling refers to signaling that utilizes a separate transport medium such as a separate pair of wires. Table 2.2 lists many common types of supervisory signaling.

TABLE 2.2 Supervisory signals

Supervisory Signal Type	Signal Meaning
Seizure	Signals the phone system to change the line/trunk state from idle to active.
Wink/hook flash	Indicates that the phone system is ready to receive address information in the form of DTMF or pulse digits.
Answer	Indicates when the remote-side phone is answered and two-way communication is established.
Disconnect	Indicates that either phone in the two-way communication goes on-hook. The call is torn down and the circuit returned to an idle state.
Robbed-bit	In-band bits are used to signal the start and end of address information.

Comparing Analog and Digital Circuits

The public switched telephone network established the framework for long-distance communication long before the Internet. The PSTN is a global network of telephony equipment that once was purely an analog system. Today the PSTN consists of mostly digital circuit-switched phone systems that are interconnected. It is important to understand both analog and digital circuits and why we're moving to a system that will eventually be 100 percent digital. Let's first look at analog circuits and how they transmit voice from one phone to another. Then we'll move on to digital circuits and how they convert analog into digital.

The Analog Signal

The goal of any voice circuit is to transmit sounds (typically the human voice) from one point to another. Using analog technology, the human voice is picked up from the transmitter portion of a telephone and is translated into an electrical signal that varies continuously with changes in the sound. Sounds such as the human voice are in analog form to begin with. The changes in pitch and tone as we pronounce various words create variations in the sound wave. A microphone and analog circuit are used to capture the analog sound waves and transmit them in an electrical form over copper wiring. Once the analog sound waves are in an electrical form, they can be transmitted across the PSTN to the other end of the phone connection. When the electrical signal reaches the intended destination, it is converted back into analog sound waves and sent through the receiver speaker. Figure 2.3 depicts a typical analog sound wave.

FIGURE 2.3 Analog sound wave

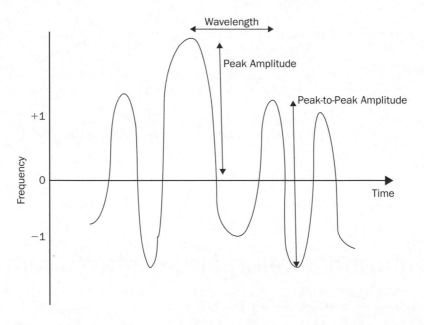

You'll notice that the figure shows the frequency of a sound over a period of time. A *wavelength* of a sound wave is the distance between each wave collected. The *frequency* of a wavelength is measured in cycles per second, or Hertz (Hz). You'll also note two different amplitudes listed. The *peak-to-peak amplitude* is the variation in the frequency over a one-wavelength period. The *peak amplitude* is the same frequency variation, but it is measured from the mean, which is 0 on the graph.

Analog circuits carry voice signals in a very pure form. A standard plain old telephone service (*POTS*) line from the phone company is typically delivered to a home or business on two wires. These two wires provide full-duplex voice conversation. The last hop on the PSTN before it goes to the customer premises is called the *central office* (CO). The central office bundles your circuit with other customers' circuits and switches them as needed to other COs on the PSTN. Your specific circuit coming into the central office is called a *local loop*. On the customer side of the analog circuit, Cisco has several types of analog interfaces to terminate various PSTN and analog endpoints on the voice gateway. Let's discuss each type.

Analog Voice Interfaces

Literally dozens of different analog interfaces can be used on Cisco hardware. The CCNA Voice exam focuses on the most popular types in use today. This next section covers FXS, FXO, and CAMA analog interfaces. Exam takers need to understand the situations where each interface type is used.

Foreign Exchange Station Interface

The *Foreign Exchange Station* (FXS) is an interface that connects directly to an analog endpoint such as an analog phone or fax machine. The connection handoff is a standard RJ-11 port. Figure 2.4 shows how you connect an analog line to an FXS port that connects to the PSTN.

FIGURE 2.4 An FXS interface

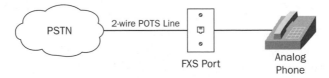

FXS ports are commonly found in residential homes that require very few analog lines. The interface provides voltage and signaling to analog devices. So in a residential home situation, we assume that all of the voltage and signaling will be provided to us from the PSTN switch equipment.

Analog devices don't really care what signaling you use, so FXS interfaces can use either loop start or ground start signaling from the source. Typically you will configure loop start signaling when connecting to analog devices like phones or fax machines. FXS ports can also be configured to use ground start. This is more common when you use an FXS port to connect to a legacy PBX.

Foreign Exchange Office Interface

Instead of plugging directly into an analog phone like the FXS port does, a *Foreign Exchange Office* (FXO) port connects to a PBX. The FXO interface assumes that all dial tones, ring indicators, and other call-progress signaling are provided locally by the equipment attached to it such as a key system or PBX. Contrast that with an FXS connection where the device that plugs into the port does not provide any form of signaling. Instead, it relies on the backend equipment to provide it. Typically, a business will provision a handful of FXO ports from the PSTN and then connect the phones to the PBX. If an analog phone or fax machine needs to make an off-network call, the PBX switches the connection to one of the free analog lines. This is beneficial to businesses because not every phone requires an off-network analog line at any given time. If you plan accordingly, you can get away with paying for a fraction of the number of analog lines than you have phones on your local network. Figure 2.5 shows a single analog line terminating at a PBX with an FXO interface.

FIGURE 2.5   An FXO interface

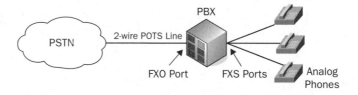

With this type of setup, there will be only one PSTN number per line. As with the FXS port, the connection handoff is RJ-11. The diagram also points out a simple way to remember the difference between FXS and FXO ports. FXS interfaces connect analog telephones, while FXO interfaces are used to connect to the PSTN. The first hop out to the PSTN cloud is called the central office. (A quick mnemonic: The central "o"ffice connects to your FX"O" interface.) In this scenario, either the single number would ring all phones on the PBX when dialed, or it would ring a single phone handled by a live operator, or the PBX would utilize an *auto attendant* (AA). An auto attendant is much like a live operator, but instead of a human, it is an automated system with voice prompts to assist the caller to be routed to the proper contact using internal extensions.

Analog Direct Inward Dial Service Interface

The analog *direct inward dial* (DID) service is very similar in functionality to the FXO circuit. The PSTN connection plugs into the PBX. The main difference between a standard FXO line and an analog DID is how the phone company handles the sending of digits. With an FXO connection, each physical analog line terminated at the PBX corresponds to a specific phone number. With an analog DID, the phone company can offer a service that bundles any number of analog lines and *trunks* them. *Trunking* means that a call can be sent to a specific number across any of the analog lines instead of specifically assigning them as in FXO connections. The phone company will then strip off all but the extension digits at the local PSTN central office. So in North America, when an off-network person calls your company's number, say 555-123-2221, the 555-123 digits are removed at the last hop on the PSTN and only the 2221 is sent to your PBX. Your PBX then takes that extension and switches it to the appropriate phone extension. Figure 2.6 shows this scenario.

FIGURE 2.6   Direct inward dial service interface

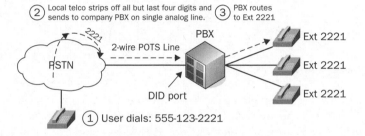

Centralized Automatic Message Accounting Service Interface

All of the previous analog interfaces that we discussed connected to the PSTN. An analog *Centralized Automatic Messaging Accounting* (CAMA) circuit is used exclusively for Emergency 911 (E911) service in North America. Some states require businesses over a certain size to connect directly to the E911 service. A CAMA link is one way to comply with this law.

The E911 service is largely built outside the PSTN, and calls are routed differently within the network. Typical PSTN phone calls are routed based on destination phone number. With the E911 service, phone calls are routed based on source phone number. The source number is used to route calls to an E911 because it can pinpoint the caller's location. When the location of the number has been determined, the call is then switched to the proper public service answering point (PSAP), where the 911 operator can assist. Figure 2.7 depicts what happens when a user dials 911.

FIGURE 2.7   CAMA service interface

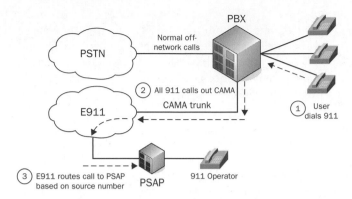

It is easy to understand why E911 calls rely so heavily on the source phone number. In an emergency, it is far more important for emergency services to be able to find you than for you to know where they are located!

 Real World Scenario

E911 to the Next Level

Voice engineers have just completed a major VoIP implementation at a major university campus. One of the tasks on the test plan was to test the 911 service to ensure that emergency services can correctly identify where users are calling from in any of the multiple buildings that cover several city blocks. When performing various testing with emergency services, they determined that no matter where users called from, it looked like the calls were being made from a single building. This was a big problem because some buildings were up to several miles away. Emergency services would not be able to properly identify the location of users within a reasonable distance.

The E911 service relies heavily on using the source number as the location of the person who requires emergency assistance. A major problem exists when you begin to build out an enterprise Unified Communication system that spans multiple buildings over a large geographical region. Depending on your design, you may have all of your PSTN lines terminated into a single location, like our university campus situation. If a phone user were to dial emergency services, that user could be several miles away from where the PSTN lines are physically located. So how can we better pinpoint where a person is on our network? Cisco to the rescue! Using what's known as the Cisco Emergency Responder, the server can dynamically track and update the location of Cisco IPT phones and place it into a database. This information is used to ensure that the emergency call is routed to the proper PSAP. It also better directs emergency personnel to the actual location of the caller instead of the location of the terminated phone line.

The Analog-to-Digital Conversion Process

The analog circuits just described seem to work well, so why do we need digital circuits? There are two main reasons. One deals with inefficiencies of analog, and the other deals with its distance limitations. In regards to efficiency, analog simply does not scale well. Based on what you've learned about analog signals, you know that for each voice call made with analog, we need two wires: one for the ring and the other for the tip. With digital signals, we have the capability to sample analog voice frequencies, turn the result into binary, compress it, and send it across an IP network using less bandwidth than just sending the analog waveform over the wire. Because of the smaller size, we can use other techniques to send multiple voice streams over fewer pairs of wires.

With analog signals there is also a distance limitation to contend with. Because analog signals are purely electrical on the wire, over longer distances these electrical signals become degraded. To address the analog degradation problem, electrical repeaters can be used to help extend the distance of analog. These repeaters sit on the wire at certain distance points. The repeater's job is to listen to the electrical signals coming in one end and reproduce the signals out the other. While this may work to extend analog distances a bit farther, they stop becoming productive at a certain point. This is because repeaters can interpret electrical pulses called noise on the wire and falsely assume they are part of the signal to be repeated. This noise gets retransmitted by the repeater. After the signal is repeated several times, a considerable amount of electrical noise is now accompanying our legitimate analog voice signal. When it finally reaches the other side, the electrical noise comes out as audible static on the receiving phone handset. You've probably played the "grapevine" game as a child, where one person whispers a message to the next, and then they whisper what they interpreted to the next child. By the time the message is repeated to the last kid on the grapevine, the message is almost always wrong! This game is very similar in concept to what happens with analog repeaters over time.

So now that you know we need digital circuits to overcome inefficiencies and distance limitations of analog circuits, let's look at how we can transform analog waves into a digital format. Digitizing voice solves our distance problem because instead of transporting electrical signals, we only have to worry about transporting numbers, as you will soon see. Then, after you've seen how to digitize analog waves, I'll explain how we can efficiently transport multiple voice streams over the same pair of wires using a technique called multiplexing.

Four steps are necessary to transform an analog signal into a compressed digital signal. The steps always occur in the following order:

1. Sample the analog voice signal.
2. Quantize the sample.
3. Encode the digital sample.
4. Compress the encoded sample.

Let's take a closer look at each of these steps so we can fully understand the digitizing process:

Step 1: Sample the Analog Voice Signal

A standard analog telephone can pick up sound waves from 0 to 4000 Hertz. Using this frequency range, the human voice is sampled 8,000 times per second. How did they come up with this sample rate? In 1924, a Bell Labs engineer by the name of Dr. Harry Nyquist found that by using a mathematical formula, he could find the optimal relationship between audio quality and acceptable bandwidth sample rates. Nyquist was doing theoretical research in the field of improving transmission speeds of data using analog lines. His research provided the base for digital transmissions that are currently being used. While performing this research, Nyquist discovered the bandwidth-saving benefits of continuously sampling analog signals and converting them to digital form. This theory is now referred to as the Nyquist formula:

max data rate(bits/sec) = 2 × B × log2 V

B = bandwidth and V = number of voltage levels

So what does all of this mean? Nyquist found that if you sample a sound wave at two times the highest frequency perceived, you can accurately reconstruct the signal digitally. Since 4000 Hz is approximately the highest frequency a human voice can achieve, sounds are sampled 8,000 times per second.

Even though the frequency range we use with the Nyquist formula is between 0 and 4000 Hz, the average human voice falls within the range of 200 to 2800 Hz. Filters are set up on the phone to collect any sound that falls within the range of 300 to 3300 Hz. Sound waves in the ranges 0–299 and 3301–4000 Hz are used for *out-of-band signaling*. Voice traffic is considered to be in-band.

Once the analog sounds are filtered, a technique called *Pulse Amplitude Modulation* (PAM) is performed on the waveform. PAM takes a slice of the wavelength at a constant number of 8,000 intervals per second. Using these *samples*, it is possible to reconstruct the entire wave on the other side of the connection without having to actually send the complete wave. Figure 2.8 shows a waveform sample being taken.

FIGURE 2.8 A digital sample

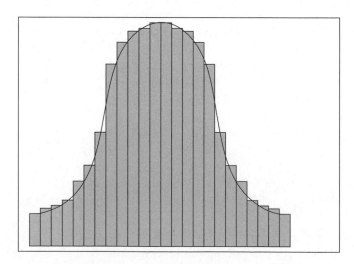

Step 2: Quantize the Sample

The process of digitizing voice is called *pulse code modulation* (PCM). PCM uses a method called *quantization* to encode the analog waveform into digital data for transport and then to decode the data to turn it back into analog form (the DC voltages that drive phone speakers). Quantization is the language used in this encoding process. Each analog sample is given a quantized number code that gets as close as possible to the amplitude of the signal. In the next step, these numbers will be used to encode the waveform for transport. Figure 2.9 shows the analog sample being quantized.

FIGURE 2.9   Quantization

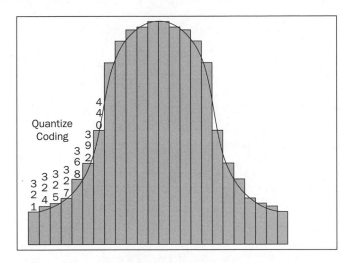

Step 3: Encode the Digital Sample

After quantization has been completed, step 3 of the PCM process is to put the data in a format that can be easily sent across the wire. We use the *binary* system to make this happen. Binary is the numbering system used in digital electronic systems. It consists of a series of 1s and 0s called *bits* to represent any numeric value.

No matter which PCM technique you use, the encoder uses the quantized numbers that represent analog waveforms and converts these numbers into binary. The 8,000 sample rate is converted into an 8-bit binary number. Therefore we need 64 Kbps of bandwidth to transport a single digital call. We arrive at the 64 Kbps (or 64,000 bits) using the following math:

8,000 samples × 8 bits per sample = 64,000 bits

There are multiple methods to *encode* the quantized signals. The intelligence or algorithm behind encoding and decoding is called a *codec* (short for compressor/decompressor). Depending on which codec is being used, the quality of the encoded waveforms as well as the size of the encoded data stream can differ. Either of two common types of PCM binary conversion techniques is used in most voice systems. The first PCM type is called u-law and is most commonly used in the United States, Canada, and Japan. The second PCM binary conversion type is a-law. It is used just about everywhere else on the planet. It is important to note that the two PCM techniques are not compatible with each other and need to be transcoded for interoperability. *Transcoding* is the process of translating one codec into another.

Now the signal is ready either to be sent across the wire immediately or to be optionally compressed prior to transport. Figure 2.10 shows the binary encoding process.

FIGURE 2.10   Binary encoding

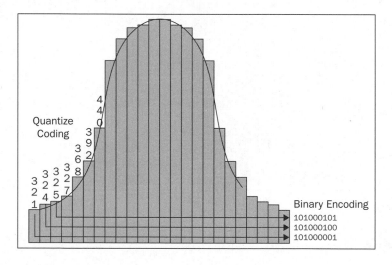

Step 4: Compress the Encoded Sample (Optional)

Compression is all about getting the biggest bang for the buck. As mentioned earlier, codecs are used for encoding and decoding digital voice data. Remember that even though we've been discussing traditional telephony circuits up to this point, compression is used only with newer voice technologies, which we'll discuss in the next chapter. These specifications also contain logic for compressing and decompressing this data so it can be more efficiently sent across the wire. When fewer bits are used per voice conversation, then more conversations can simultaneously exist on a finite amount of bandwidth. Compression attempts to eliminate redundancy in the data that is sent. It attempts to match your original encoded sample with something very similar to a known sample. It then uses this known sample, which can be identified with a much smaller binary stream, to send across the wire. The smaller the stream that is sent across the wire, the more individual streams can be sent across the same wire at the same time!

There is a tradeoff to compression, however. Because the actual encoded sample is not used, when the digital sample is decoded and turned back into analog, it is not an exact reproduction of the original sampled source. Typically what people notice is that the audio turns the human voice into a more robotic sound. And the more the sample is compressed, the more it loses any kind of uniqueness on the other end.

 Real World Scenario

Analog vs. Digital: You Can See the Difference!

Sometimes it's difficult to understand the value behind the movement toward abandoning analog for digital voice circuits. To better clarify why the change is good, let's look at a slightly different medium that might be easier to understand because we can literally see the difference in full high definition! Of course, I'm referring to the movement from analog to digital television transmission.

In the United States, a government regulation mandates that all over-the-air broadcasters must broadcast solely digital television transmissions. This began on June 12, 2009, and eliminated all analog forms of broadcasting.

It is interesting to compare the reception of digital and analog television transmissions over the air. If you've ever used an antenna to receive analog signals, if you didn't have optimal reception, you'd literally see the distortion in the form of snow. Even though there was distortion, however, you could still see the picture even though the clarity was degraded. This is the same distortion that you can encounter using an analog voice line. The signal might get through, but it may be full of distortion.

In contrast, when you pull in digital television signals over the air, it's all or nothing. Either you get a high-quality signal that is far superior to analog or you get a blank screen. There is no snowy, degraded signal as you might find with analog. Moving to digital is a bit of a tradeoff between quality and ability to receive the signal. If you have a weak digital signal, you won't see a picture, but if you have a strong signal, the picture is unrivaled compared to analog.

So why would the U.S. government enforce a law that forced television broadcasters to move to an all-digital transmission format? Just as we learned with digital voice, it is possible to digitize and compress video transmissions to use less radio frequency space when compared to analog television transmissions. Moving to all-digital transmissions freed up UHF frequencies that were at one time consumed by larger analog transmissions. These newly unused frequencies can then be redistributed for different purposes.

Digital Voice Interfaces

Analog circuits are fine if you require only a few PSTN lines into your business. If you need approximately 10 or more external lines, it is typically more cost effective to look into a digital trunk circuit such as a T1 or E1. From a physical point of view, T1 and E1 circuits are typically terminated at the customer site in the form of copper wiring, usually Category 5 cabling. This same cabling is used for Ethernet LAN connections. The circuits are terminated using a standard RJ-45 connector. Looking at the eight pinouts on the RJ-45, you can see that a T1 uses pins 1 and 2 for transmit and 4 and 5 for receive. Figure 2.11 shows T1/E1 pinouts to give you a better understanding of how the wiring is used.

FIGURE 2.11   T1 and E1 RJ-45 pinouts

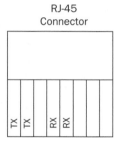

The digital circuit handed off to the customer is again called the local loop. Finally, most digital circuits bundle multiple voice lines on a single trunk line that is handed off to the customer. Let's look at some of the more popular digital circuits that PSTNs offer.

ISDN Basic Rate Interface

The ISDN *Basic Rate Interface* (BRI) circuit offers the ability to make two simultaneous calls on 64Kbps channels, called bearer channels, or B channels. The voice communication itself uses the entire amount of the 64Kbps channel. All call signaling is performed outside the voice channel. As you have already learned, this type of signaling is known as out-of-band signaling. On the ISDN BRI, signaling takes place on a third channel that has 16 Kbps of bandwidth. This signaling channel is referred to as the data, or D, channel. Thus, a single ISDN BRI circuit offers two B channels plus one D channel for signaling both bearer channels. The main type of BRI signaling used on the D channel is Q.931. This is the most popular signaling format used by PSTNs around the world.

It is important to note that there is a difference between the ISDN bit rate and the available bandwidth for making calls. The complete bit rate of an ISDN BRI circuit is 192 Kbps. This includes the 2 × 64Kbps B channels and 1 × 16Kbps D channel. The other

48 Kbps is used for framing and synchronization. So while the bit rate may be 192 Kbps for an ISDN BRI, the bandwidth is 144 Kbps.

T1 Channel Associated Signaling

The T1 channel associated signaling (CAS) has 24 channels associated with it. Each one of these channels can transport voice traffic. This means that 24 simultaneous voice calls can occur at the same time. Signaling for the traffic occurs in-band, meaning that bits that are typically used for voice are taken and reused to help with control and signaling of the circuit. This is often referred to *robbed-bit signaling* (RBS). 8 Kbps of each 64Kbps channel is used for signaling instead of utilizing an entire channel for shared out-of-band signaling. Let's break this down a bit further for your understanding.

Each T1 CAS has 24 channels that can transmit 8 bits per channel each. This gives us a total of 192 bits. The T1 has one additional bit for framing, bringing the total to 193 bits. Two types of line coding can be used on a T1 CAS. The first type of line coding is called Super Frame (SF). This is an older and less-efficient type of framing. Super Frame bundles 12 of these 193-bit frames together for transport. It then uses the even-numbered frames as signaling bits. The T1 CAS signaling then looks at every sixth frame for signaling information. This comes out to be 2 bits that are referred to as the A and B bits, which reside in frames 6 and 12. Figure 2.12 shows the robbed-bit framing process.

FIGURE 2.12   SF robbed-bit framing

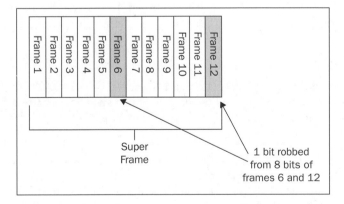

Frame 1
Frame 2
Frame 3
Frame 4
Frame 5
Frame 6
Frame 7
Frame 8
Frame 9
Frame 10
Frame 11
Frame 12

Super
Frame

1 bit robbed
from 8 bits of
frames 6 and 12

A newer CAS framing method is called Extended Super Frame (ESF). This method bundles 24 of the 193-bit frames together. Because ESF bundles larger groups of frames, this frees up additional bits. So now, with ESF we have 4 bits for signaling instead of the 2 that SF offered. The 4 bits are referred to as bits A, B, C, and D. They reside in frames 6, 12, 18, and 24. These extra framing bits allow for more intelligence and the ability to process error checking using the cyclical redundancy check (CRC) method. The better efficiency and error handling make ESF framing the far more optimal choice. Almost every modern telephone provider now uses ESF for their T1 circuits. Figure 2.13 shows the bits being robbed from the 4 frames using ESF.

FIGURE 2.13 ESF robbed-bit framing

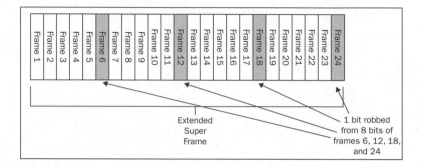

Three types of signaling methods are used on CAS circuits. These signaling methods use the four A, B, C, and D ESF framing bits for synchronization, control, and error handling of the circuit. When you provision a T1 CAS from the phone company, they need to tell you what type of signaling they will be using. You will have to configure the correct type of signaling on your T1 voice gateway interface. The three types of signaling methods are

- Loop start
- Ground start
- *E&M* (A supervisory signaling mode uses DC signals called the E and M leads. They were mostly found within the PSTN between phone switches. The technology is becoming obsolete in favor of PRI circuits.)

Did you ever wonder why a T1 is said to be 1.544 Mbps? Now that you understand framing, it is a bit easier to comprehend. We know that a T1 CAS has 24 channels at 8 bits per channel plus one framing bit. Because we sample voice 8,000 times every second using the Nyquist formula, we need to send 8,000 of these 193-bit frames across a T1 every second. 8,000 × 193 is 1,544,000 bps or 1.544 Mbps. Of course, this is the complete bit rate. To calculate the bandwidth rate, we must subtract the one bit that is used for framing and synchronization. So the true bandwidth for a T1 is 8,000 × 192, which is 1,536,000 bps or 1.536 Mbps.

For a T1 CAS this means that all 24 channels can be utilized. A downside to the CAS is that since signaling information is in-band, only 56 Kbps is available for voice calls. A more CPU-intensive encoding technique will be required to compress the voice from the standard 64 Kbps to 56 Kbps. Table 2.3 lists the components of the T1 CAS.

TABLE 2.3   T1 CAS components

Component	T1 CAS
Location used	North America
Total bit rate	1.544 Mbps
Total bandwidth	1.536 Mbps
Total number of channels	24
Number of usable voice channels	24
Voice bandwidth per channel	56 Kbps
Framing technique	SF or ESF
Signaling methods	Loop start, ground start, and E&M

E1 Channel Associated Signaling

The E1 CAS is a bit of an oddball. E1 circuits have a total of 32 channels, compared to 24 channels with a T1. Unlike the T1 CAS, which uses robbed-bit signaling for control and signaling of the circuit, the E1 uses out-of-band signaling on channels 1 and 17. Figure 2.14 breaks down the channel responsibilities of an E1 CAS.

FIGURE 2.14   E1 CAS channels

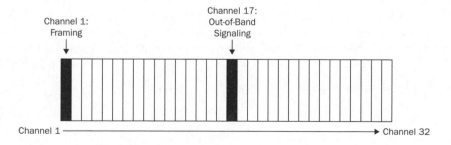

T1 and E1 Primary Rate Interface

The major difference between a *T1 PRI* and the previously mentioned CAS T1 is the way signaling is handled. Unlike the T1 CAS circuits that use in-band signaling, the T1 PRI circuits utilize out-of-band signaling. You might be surprised to learn that two very popular framing methods for the T1 PRI are Super Frame (SF) and Extended Super Frame (ESF). Although these are the way the circuit frames our voice for transport, the process stops there, because it doesn't have to bother with stealing a bit from every sixth frame for signaling. Instead, all signaling occurs on the separate out-of-band channel.

The T1 and E1 *Primary Rate Interface* (PRI) is the PSTN big brother of the ISDN BRI circuit. T1 circuits are most often found in North America and parts of Asia, while Europe and much of the rest of the world use the E1 PRI. This out-of-band signaling is called *common channel signaling* (CCS). Each individual voice connection has its own separate 64Kbps channel, and the signaling channel is also 64 Kbps. We'll first look at how the T1 circuit works and then highlight the differences between it and the E1 circuit.

T1 PRI   Twenty-four logically unique 64Kbps circuits make up a T1 PRI. Channel 24 is designated as the signaling channel for the circuit. The PRI is said to be a 23B + 1D, which means that there are 24 bearer channels for voice and 1 data channel for signaling. T1 circuits are most commonly offered by public telephone companies that operate in the United States, Canada, Japan, and South Korea. There is no real reason for this except that phone companies that operate within a country usually standardize on the type of PRI that is offered.

The T1 PRI uses Q.931 for signaling. As you can see, this is the same type of signaling used in ISDN BRI connections. Because we have a full 64Kbps DS0 channel for signaling, however, Q.931 can transmit all of the signaling information required for each of the 23 voice channels. In fact, enough bandwidth is available on the data channel that other signaling functions can be sent across the D channel. Many telecommunications vendors send proprietary signaling information across the D channel to add additional control and services.

E1 PRI   The E1 PRI bundles 32 logically unique 64Kbps channels. If we label the channels 1–32, channel 1 is responsible for framing and channel 17 is used as out-of-band signaling. This is exactly the same method as the E1 CAS described above. The difference is that the E1 PRI uses Q.931 signaling whereas the E1 CAS uses one of three other signaling formats. So if we subtract 2 channels from our E1, this leaves 30 channels with which to send voice traffic. Another way to put it is that the E1 PRI is a 30B + 2D circuit.

Table 2.4 lists the primary differences between a T1 and an E1 PRI circuit.

TABLE 2.4   T1/E1 PRI components

Component	T1 PRI	E1 PRI
Location used	North America	Europe
Total bit rate	1.544 Mbps	2.048 Mbps
Total bandwidth	1.536 Mbps	1.984 Mbps
Total number of channels	24	32
Number of usable voice channels	23	30
Voice bandwidth per channel	64 Kbps	64 Kbps
Channel used for out-of-band signaling	24	17
Common framing signaling	Q.931	Q.931

Comparing CAS and CCS Circuits

So, if given the opportunity, which T1 should you order, the T1 PRI that uses CCS or the T1 CAS that uses in-band RBS? Let's break down the positives and negatives of both:

T1 PRI Pros

- Full 64 Kbps for voice signals.
- Uses Q.931 signaling protocol, which is universally used around the world.
- Additional signaling bandwidth means more flexibility for vendors to communicate proprietary signaling information.
- Higher security because signaling is out-of-band.

T1 PRI Cons

- Only 23 usable signals to transport voice

T1 CAS Pros

- Can use all 24 channels for voice calls
- More efficient signaling mechanism
- Offers three different signaling methods

T1 CAS Cons

- Slightly degraded call quality
- Slightly increased router CPU utilization due to compression
- Signaling not as widely used

If I were given the choice, I would choose to use the T1 PRI circuit for my connection to the PSTN. Even though I do give up one full channel for signaling, it quite simply is the preferred standard and makes it much easier to understand how signaling works!

Multiplexing

In the previous section we discussed how digital circuits such as ISDN BRI/PRI and CAS T1s have multiple channels that divide the bandwidth into separate voice segments. For example, you can think of a T1 PRI as having 23 physical D channels for voice traffic and 1 D channel for signaling information. Figure 2.15 shows the logical representation of a T1 PRI.

FIGURE 2.15 PRI T1 circuit

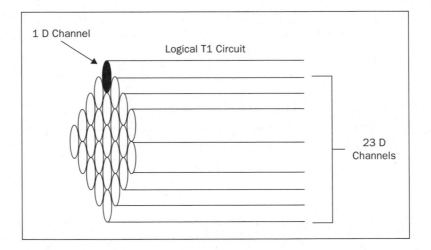

While it is useful to think of these channels as physically separate wires, that is not actually the case. Instead, all of the circuits are transmitted over the same pairs of copper or fiber-optic connections. In reality, the telecommunications equipment uses what is known as *multiplexing* to logically segment a single connection into multiple connections.

Multiplexing is the digital circuit's answer to the analog efficiency problem. With analog, every phone call requires a pair of wires to transmit the signal. If we digitize our voice calls, we can reduce the bandwidth requirements needed to transport the calls. And we can finally use multiplexing to transport multiple calls over the same pair of wires.

While there are many different types of multiplexing, the two main types you should become familiar with are Time-Division Multiplexing (TDM) and Statistical Time-Division Multiplexing (STDM). Both types handle multiplexing slightly differently and ultimately handle the circuit bandwidth in different ways. Now we'll take a closer look at these two methods.

Time-Division Multiplexing

Time-Division Multiplexing is often referred to as circuit mode multiplexing because of the fixed nature of the timeslots. Each timeslot reoccurs in a specific order. This means that a limited number of circuits can be transmitted on a single connection. This is the type of multiplexing typically found in current PSTN networks such as ISDN PRI circuits, where a fixed number of circuits or channels transmit voice in 64Kbps streams.

Let's look at an example of TDM. Figure 2.16 shows the timeslots of a T1 PRI circuit.

FIGURE 2.16 Time-Division Multiplexing

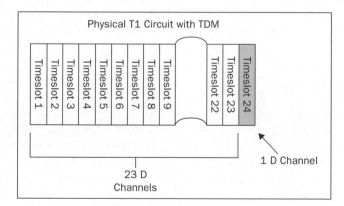

Each of the 24 T1 channels is actually a multiplexed timeslot on the same set of four wires. Each logical channel receives a timeslot at a specific interval. Once the voice segments come out the other side of the circuit, they are reassembled and put onto a single 64Kbps circuit that reaches the phone on the other end.

Statistical Time-Division Multiplexing

Statistical Time-Division Multiplexing is sometimes called packet-mode multiplexing. It is considered to be more advanced than standard TDM. While TDM reserves a timeslot for a channel regardless of any data requiring it, STDM reserves a timeslot on the wire only when the slot is required for sending or receiving data. Because of the bandwidth savings, it is actually possible to oversubscribe the circuit to connect more end devices than there is actual physical bandwidth for. The reasoning behind this is that it's unlikely that every phone would be in use at the exact same time, and therefore the circuit can be better utilized.

Private Phone Switching

Now that you are familiar with some of the most popular types of digital and analog circuits available from the PSTN, I'm going to move the focus back to the private portion of a phone network. Private switching allows a business to lower costs by eliminating a one-to-one ratio between PSTN extensions and telephone handsets. Using an intermediary switch that is privately managed, you can configure a many-to-few ratio scenario. A private phone switch also allows the administrator to configure advanced on-network functionality that enhances the communication experience. In a sense, you're becoming a mini-PSTN because you can now offer services such as dual lines, voice mail, intercom, and so on. All of these services are local to the key system or PBX. Let's look at the two types of private switching technologies found in most businesses: the key system and the private branch exchange (PBX).

The Key System

Small businesses typically deploy this type of internal phone-switching system. A typical *key system* has just a few analog or digital PSTN lines that are colocated in a single control unit. Most commonly, these are simple analog lines with FXO connections into the key system switch. Phones are then attached to the key system switch, which is also commonly referred to as the control unit. Each phone is set up identically and has every PSTN line available for use. This ensures that anyone in the office can answer an incoming call to any line. It also means that no single person has a unique phone number to call their own. Cisco calls this a shared-line scenario. Each PSTN extension is shared communally. When a user wants to make a call, they manually choose one of the unused extensions from which to place the call.

For users of key systems the vast majority of phone usage is for off-network calls. In small-business environments, you usually don't call from extension to extension using on-network dialing. Instead, you simply walk over to the person you want to talk to. An alternative method that is popular with key systems is the intercom feature. This feature is far more likely to be used than extension-to-extension dialing. The bottom line is that key systems are shared-line phone systems where the phones are identically set up and provide a small number of enhancement features.

Private Branch Exchange

Unlike a key system, where the end user manually selects an extension to use in order to make a phone call, the user on a private branch exchange (*PBX*) has a specific extension (or extensions) assigned to their phone. However, PBX resembles the key system in that all PSTN lines are colocated to a control switch, and all internal phones communicate with it to make on- and off-network calls. But unlike the key system, which most commonly uses analog PSTN circuits, the PBX typically works with digital circuits and interfaces such as the T1/E1 PRI. This is because PBX systems are usually in larger environments where more than a handful of outside PSTN lines are needed.

While key system end phones are typically identical in setup and functionality, phones connected to a PBX are often configured individually, depending on the voice functions required. An extension configured on the phone may be a DID number accessible directly from the PSTN, or it may be configured as internal only. In this type of setup, outside users call a main DID number and are either manually transferred to an internal number by an operator or transferred through the use of an auto attendant (AA).

PBX systems can also offer advanced services to their internal users. Table 2.5 briefly describes some of the most popular PBX services in use today.

TABLE 2.5   Common PBX services

Service Name	Function
Extension dialing	Truncated (typically 4–5 digits), used for on-network dialing
Call forwarding	Provides call redirection to a different extension that is either on or off network
Hunt groups	Provides one extension to a group of phones that ring on a rotating schedule
Conference bridge	Allows multiple extensions to participate in a single call
Call parking	Places a call on hold and resumes the call from a different phone
Paging	Provides notification of users/groups using phones
After hours support	Allows different dial rules depending on time of day/week

PSTN Numbering Plans

Public numbering plans are global and/or regional standard numbering formats created so that long-distance calls can be properly routed throughout the public network. Similar to networking, where public IP address spaces must not overlap, PSTN numbering plans help to ensure that each region has its own identification system so all calls can properly be routed. These numbering plans must be carefully maintained to insure that there is no overlap. Every phone number on the planet must be unique. Numbering plans help to group geographic blocks of users together to help assist with optimizing call routing on the PSTN. For the purpose of the CCNA Voice certification, you should be familiar with both the International Numbering Plan (ITU E.164) and the North American Numbering Plan (NANP).

The International Numbering Plan

The *International Numbering Plan* is commonly known as the International Telecommunications Union (ITU) E.164 standard. A globally recognized organization, the ITU is responsible for creating inter-border communications standards. The E.164 standard defines the format of PSTN numbers on a global scale. Table 2.6 details the ITU E.164 numbering system. As you can see, the structure consists of three distinct categories.

TABLE 2.6 ITU E.164 structure

Structure	Format	Description
Country code (CC)	1–3 digits	Defines the country of origin
National destination code (NDC)	0–15 digits	Optional country/region-specific code
Subscriber code (SC)	1–15 digits	Central office significant code

Within a given country code, the national destination and subscriber codes are primarily governed by the local country or region and can be in any format. The only caveat is that the ITU E.164 numbering plan stipulates that the maximum number of digits for an international call must be less than or equal to 15 and must use the assigned country code at the beginning of the dial string.

Table 2.7 lists a handful of country codes that the ITU has provisioned.

TABLE 2.7 ITU country code sampling

Country or Region	E.164 Country Code
North America	1
Mexico	52
United Kingdom	44
France	33
Germany	49
India	91
Hong Kong	852
Spain	34

This is just a sample list of the country codes available. You can get the most recent ITU-T E.164 country code assignments at this URL:

http://www.itu.int/publ/T-SP-E.164D-2009/

The North American Numbering Plan

The *North American Numbering Plan* (NANP) consists of a standard calling format for 24 countries and territories including the United States, Canada, and the Caribbean. The numbering structure consists of the three segments described in Table 2.8.

TABLE 2.8 NANP structure

Segment	Number Format	Description
Three-digit area code	[2-9][0-8][0-9]	Code dictated by geographic location
Three-digit office code	[2-9][0-9][0-9]	Code where circuit is terminated at the central office
Four-digit station code	[0-9][0-9][0-9][0-9]	Locally unique code at the central office

As you can see, neither the area code nor the office code can begin with a 1. Also, the area code can never have a 9 as the second digit. It is also important to keep in mind that the central office code's second and third digits cannot both be 1. This is because the X11 numbers are used for special purposes such as emergency services (911). Table 2.9 lists several X11 numbers along with other NANP numbers that are reserved for special use.

TABLE 2.9   NANP special numbers

Special Use Number	Description
0	Local operator
00	Long-distance operator
011	International access code
211	Community government information
311	City government information
411	Local/national directory assistance
511	Traffic and road conditions
611	Telephone repair service information
711	Hearing-disabled relay service
811	Underground pipe safety service
911	Emergency services

The rapid growth of additional PSTN numbers in the 1990s was due mainly to the deregulation of local phone services and the introduction of cellular phones. Because of this deregulation, multiple carriers received a portion of an area code's numbers. These numbers came in blocks of 10,000. Many cities quickly ran out of available numbers and required additional area codes to provide coverage for the same geographical region. These additional area codes are called overlay numbers. While overlay area codes fixed one problem, they introduced another. In order to call from one area code to another in an overlay region, you would have to make sure to dial the three-digit area code if the area codes of the called and calling party were not the same—even if the person you are trying to call is right next door! Ten- or 11-digit dialing may not seem like a big deal today, but it caused many problems when area code overlays were first introduced.

Combining the NANP with the International Numbering Plan

We know that there is an International Numbering Plan that all countries must abide by. We have also looked at the North American Numbering Plan to see how its components fit together. As an example, assume that we're in Spain and need to make an international phone call to a person In Chicago, Illinois. We have the NANP number of the person we wish to call in Chicago. It is 312-555-1234. If we simply dial this number when we are in Spain, we will not reach our intended destination. The most general piece of information we have is the 312 area code, which tells us the geographic location of our intended party while we are within the NANP calling area. But because our source phone is in Spain, we need to tell the Spanish PSTN that we need to make a call outside of their nation. If we don't notify the Spanish PSTN of this, it assumes that we want to make a call within their national boundaries. Since we are attempting to call a number in the United States, we can use the assigned country code that the ITU designated for the NANP, the number 1. So now we have all the pieces we need. Because we're dialing internationally, we need to dial the following number: 1-312-555-1234. Figure 2.17 breaks down the components of our combined International and NANP structure.

FIGURE 2.17   International and NANP example

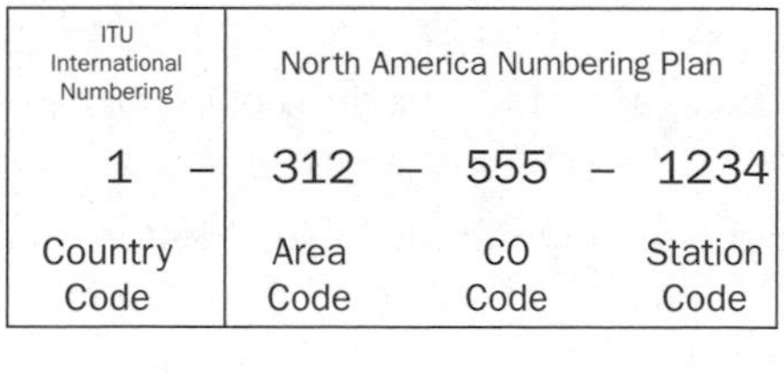

ITU International Numbering	North America Numbering Plan		
1 –	312 –	555 –	1234
Country Code	Area Code	CO Code	Station Code

Summary

In this chapter you learned about traditional IPT technology. The chapter covered the three types of PSTN network signaling and when they're used. In addition I explained the most common PSTN analog and digital circuits and how multiplexing is used to transport multiple channels over the same wire.

Next, you learned about the two types of private switching and when you'll typically see a key system setup versus a PBX. Finally, I covered both the ITU E.164 and NANP dial plans and explained why they are so important in order to create a uniform and scalable global PSTN system.

Hopefully I've uncovered much of the magic that the PSTN offers. While phone systems are moving from a circuit-based system to a network-friendly packet system, it is clear that the current PSTN system that fascinated me as a child is still alive and functioning today.

Exam Essentials

Understand the three types of phone network signaling.   Network signaling is broken into three distinct categories of address, supervisory, and informational. Each category is responsible for a part of each phone call made.

Know how to identify parts of an analog sound wave.   The key to understanding how voice travels across phone lines lies in understanding what analog sound waves look like and how they can be turned into an electrical form for transport.

Know the four most common types of analog voice interfaces.   Analog interfaces come in many types, but there are four interfaces to be familiar with. Understand the differences between FXS, FXO, DID, and CAMA interfaces and when each one is likely to be used.

Understand the proper steps and purpose for converting analog signals into a digital format.   Know why we would want to convert analog signals into digital and know the order of the four steps required to complete the process.

Know the four most common types of digital voice interfaces.   Make sure you know each digital interface type (ISDN BRI, T1 CAS, E1 CAS, and T1/E1 PRI), how they handle signaling, and how many voice calls can be made at one time. Also be sure to understand when you would utilize one digital circuit type over another.

Understand the purpose and types of multiplexing.   Multiplexing is a method to send multiple calls across the wire simultaneously. Understand that with TDM, a timeslot is reserved for each call regardless of any voice data being sent. STDM, on the other hand, requests a timeslot only if one is needed.

Know the difference between a PBX and a key system.   For the most part, there are two traditional private switches in use today. Understand the differences between a PBX and a key system, and know what types of office environments would be best suited for one system over the other.

Understand the International and NANP PSTN dial plans.   Know the purpose for having standards-based dial plans for PSTN networks, and understand the parts that make up the numbering plan. Also be aware of any requirements that each plan has designated.

Written Lab 2.1

Write the answers to the following questions:

1. What are the three types of voice network signaling?

2. What type of analog interface is typically used to connect to E911 services?

3. Name the type of PRI circuit typically used in Europe.

4. What type of multiplexing is considered to be circuit mode?

5. In what type of private phone system would the majority of calls made be off-network calls?

6. In what PBX service scenario will phone calls to a single extension rotate from phone to phone?

7. List the three categories of the ITU E.164 International Dial Plan.

8. What are the three NANP Dial Plan categories?

9. What term is used to describe the NANP designation when more than one area code is required for a single geographical region?

10. What NANP special code will connect a caller to local/national directory services?

(The answers to Written Lab 2.1 can be found following the answers to the review questions for this chapter.)

Review Questions

1. A dial tone is considered to be what type of network signaling?

   A. Address signaling

   B. Informational signaling

   C. Notification signaling

   D. Supervisory signaling

2. Which address signaling methods can be used to interpret phone numbers to place a call? Choose all that apply.

   A. DTMF

   B. Informational signaling

   C. Pulse dialing

   D. Supervisory signaling

3. Which multiplexing type is also referred to as packet-mode multiplexing?

   A. FIFO

   B. TDM

   C. STDM

   D. FHSS

   E. PTDM

4. What is the distance measured between each sound wave called?

   A. Analog signal

   B. Wavelength

   C. Peak-to-peak amplitude

   D. Peak amplitude

5. What is the variation in a sound wave amplitude over a one-wavelength period called?

   A. Peak-to-peak amplitude

   B. Peak amplitude

   C. Feedback

   D. POTS

   E. Hook flash

6. What is the name for an automated voice system that assists callers to their desired extension destination?

   A. DID

   B. FXO

   C. AA

   D. CO

   E. FXS

7. Which of the following is an analog interface that is typically found in small businesses with a few PSTN lines going into a PBX?

   A. E&M

   B. T1 PRI

   C. FXO

   D. FXS

   E. AA

8. Which of the following is an analog connection in which digits are stripped off at the PSTN switch prior to being sent to a private PBX?

   A. CAMA

   B. DID

   C. Amplitude

   D. FXS

9. Which analog interface routes calls based on the calling number?

   A. FXS

   B. FXO

   C. DID

   D. CAMA

   E. Trunk

10. What is the first step in the analog-to-digital conversion?

    A. Encode

    B. Quantize

    C. Compress

    D. Sample

11. Name the technique used to gather samples of an analog sound wave.

    A. POTS

    B. PAM

    C. Quantize

    D. Encode

    E. Compress

12. Which digital circuit consists of two B channels and one D channel?

    A. T1 PRI

    B. E1 PRI

    C. E&M

    D. FXO

    E. ISDN BRI

13. Which step in the analog-to-digital conversion process is optional?

   A. Compress

   B. Encode

   C. Quantize

   D. Codec

   E. Sample

14. How many voice calls can an E1 PRI handle at one time?

   A. 23

   B. 24

   C. 2

   D. 30

   E. 32

15. Which signaling method is used for T1 PRI circuits?

   A. Q.931

   B. HDB3

   C. ESF

   D. SF

   E. BRI

16. What type of T1 framing method is considered to be an older method?

   A. SF

   B. ESF

   C. Q.931

   D. HDB3

17. Which of the following digital circuits uses robbed-bit signaling?

   A. T1 PRI

   B. ISDN BRI

   C. T1 CAS

   D. E1 PRI

   E. ISDN CAS

18. Which type of multiplexing is considered to be more efficient?

   A. TDM

   B. DID

   C. T1 CAS

   D. STDM

   E. CAMA

19. What type of private switch typically has unique extension numbers configured on each phone?

    A. PBX

    B. CO

    C. Key system

    D. T1 CAS

20. What is the maximum number of digits that an international number can have and abide by the ITU E.164 numbering plan?

    A. 3

    B. 10

    C. 11

    D. 15

    E. 18

Answers to Review Questions

1. B. Informational signaling provides audible feedback to the called and/or calling party.

2. A, C. Address signaling can use either DTMF or pulse dialing to transmit phone numbers to the telecommunications switch.

3. C. Statistical Time-Division Multiplexing is also referred to as packet mode.

4. B. A wavelength of a sound wave is the distance between the two crests of each wave.

5. A. The peak-to-peak amplitude measures the entire variation of amplitude (highest and lowest points) over a one-wavelength period.

6. C. An auto attendant is similar to an operator but there is no human interaction.

7. C. FXO interfaces are individual lines that connect to a PBX.

8. B. With DID connections, the phone company strips off all address information digits except for the extension, which then are passed on to the private PBX.

9. D. CAMA interfaces are typically used for E911. These calls are routed to the PSAP based on the calling party's phone number.

10. D. The first step is to sample the analog signal.

11. B. Pulse Amplitude Modulation takes a slice of the analog sound wave at a constant interval over a period of time.

12. E. ISDN BRI circuits are composed of two bearer channels and one data channel.

13. A. Depending on the codec being used, compression may or may not occur.

14. D. The E1 PRI has 32 total channels; 30 are dedicated to voice calls while the other 2 are for framing and signaling.

15. A. Q.931 is used on both PRI and BRI digital circuits.

16. A. Super Frame is the older version for T1 CAS framing. Most T1 CAS circuits now use Extended Super Frame.

17. C. The T1 CAS uses RBS for in-band signaling so it can utilize all 24 channels for voice transport.

18. D. Statistical Time-Division Multiplexing is more efficient because it reserves a timeslot only when it is required.

19. A. A PBX is typically configured so that each phone has at least one unique extension assigned.

20. D. E.164 states that no phone number may exceed 15 digits including the country code.

Answers to Written Lab 2.1

1. Address signaling, informational signaling, supervisory signaling

2. CAMA

3. E1

4. Time-Division Multiplexing

5. Key system

6. Hunt group

7. Country code, national destination code, subscriber code

8. Area code, office code, station code

9. Overlay

10. 411

Chapter 3

Voice over IP (VoIP)

THE FOLLOWING CCNA VOICE EXAM OBJECTIVES ARE COVERED IN THIS CHAPTER:

✓ **Describe the components of the Cisco Unified Communications Architecture.**

  ▪ Describe how the Unified Communications components work together to create the Cisco Unified Communications Architecture.

  ▪ Describe the function of Contact Center in a UC environment.

✓ **Describe VoIP components and technologies.**

  ▪ Describe RTP and RTCP.

  ▪ Describe the function of and differences between codecs.

  ▪ Describe H.323, MGCP, SIP, and SCCP signaling protocols.

✓ **Describe gateways, and dial peers to connect to the PSTN and service provider networks.**

  ▪ Describe the function and application of voice gateways.

  ▪ Describe the function and operation of call legs.

  ▪ Describe voice dial peers.

Legacy voice and data networks consist of separate phone and data systems that occupy completely independent physical cabling and hardware and often have separate support staff. As data networks matured throughout the '90s and became more stable and efficient, it didn't take a genius to figure out that one could run both voice and data on the same infrastructure.

This chapter will focus on voice over IP (VoIP) technologies that allow phone calls to be reliably made over a packet-switched network. We're first going to discuss the four layers in the Unified Communications VoIP model. Next, we'll reexamine voice gateways in more detail to see exactly what services these devices can provide. We'll then look at the underlying voice transport protocols that provide a method for moving calls from one phone to another on the IP network. Following that, we'll look at different types of signaling protocols that assist with the setup and teardown of phone calls. Finally, the chapter will close with a look at various voice codecs, discussing what they do and when they should be used.

Understanding the Unified Communications Model

Cisco always has a knack for breaking up complex networking structures into simple, easy-to-understand hierarchical models. The Cisco Unified Communications Model is no exception. This model consists of four layers and their core components that build upon each other to provide a complete VoIP solution. Figure 3.1 displays the four layers and the core components within each layer.

Let's examine each of the Unified Communications Model layers to see how they build upon one another.

FIGURE 3.1   The Unified Communications Model

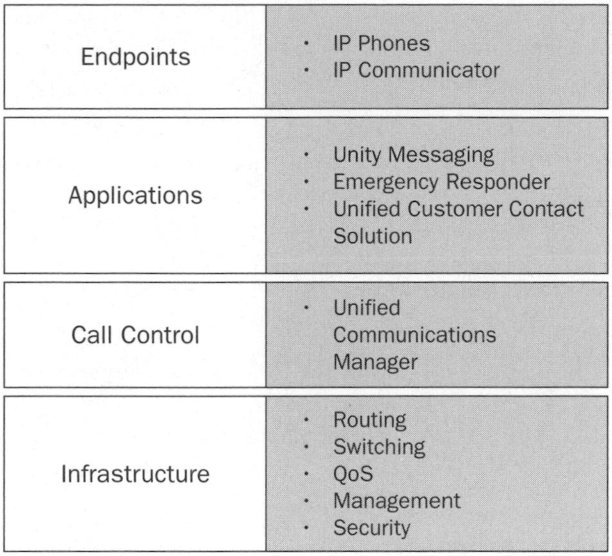

Endpoints	· IP Phones · IP Communicator
Applications	· Unity Messaging · Emergency Responder · Unified Customer Contact Solution
Call Control	· Unified Communications Manager
Infrastructure	· Routing · Switching · QoS · Management · Security

The Infrastructure Layer

The *Infrastructure layer* of the Unified Communications Model is where you will find your routers, switches, and voice gateways. The Infrastructure layer is responsible for moving IP packets from the source to the destination.

Because the Unified Communications Model is a converged network, multiple types of traffic are sent over the same infrastructure. Data, voice, and video traffic are all running over the same cabling and hardware in this layer. Because of the mixed traffic, there must be a way to distinguish voice and video from data and prioritize the types. Voice and video traffic are much more sensitive to delay on the network and ultimately must take priority over data. The Infrastructure layer typically incorporates quality of service (QoS) mechanisms to intelligently identify time-sensitive traffic and give it priority when there is congestion on the network.

Security also plays a key role in the Infrastructure layer. All access-control and IP restrictions are implemented at this layer. Typically, access control lists (ACLs) are created and implemented to limit the type of TCP/UDP traffic and source IP addresses that can access the Call Control layer, which is where the CUCM resides.

The Call Control Layer

Sitting on top of the Infrastructure layer is the *Call Control layer*. This is the heart of the Unified Communications system and is where the Call Manager is found. The CUCM is responsible for the following functions:

- Call processing
- Call signaling
- Endpoint control
- Dial plan control
- Media resource management
- User management

As you can see, the upper two layers of the Unified Communications Model fully rely on the Call Control layer to provide the underlying foundation from which the Application and Endpoint layers build. The majority of a UC phone system's intelligence is configured and maintained at this layer of the model.

The Applications Layer

The *Applications layer* builds on the Call Control layer to provide value-added functionality that makes a Unified Communications system feature rich. The Cisco Unity voice mail application is part of this layer. Not only does it provide full voice mail capabilities, but it can also integrate with email systems to provide integrated or unified messaging features.

The Cisco Emergency Responder is another application independent from the CUCM. This application is responsible for providing accurate information to emergency services in the event that an end user dials 911. While the Emergency Responder relies heavily on the Call Control layer, technically it is an independent application and sits one layer above the Call Control layer in the Unified Communications Model.

A third popular Unified Communications application found in large call centers is the Unified Customer Contact Center. Again, this separate application works in conjunction with the CUCM, found in the Call Control layer. It adds additional functionality to the call center in the form of collaboration and customer resource management tools to provide a more personal service. Specifically, the Contact Center application performs the following functions:

- Separates and delivers different customers to the proper call-handling representative based on intelligent routing decisions
- Monitors customer representative resource availability and idle times for proper staffing needs
- Utilizes detailed customer profiles using both dynamically and manually added customer information
- Integrates with Cisco Presence applications such as voice, video, email, instant messaging, and web collaboration

The Endpoints Layer

The *Endpoints layer* of the Unified Communications Model is probably the easiest to understand. This is where all voice/video communications begin and end for the user. In this layer you will find devices such as Cisco IP phones, IP Communicators, soft phones, Cisco Video Advantage devices, and Cisco ATA termination points. Essentially, any user device that utilizes the following endpoint signaling protocols is considered to be an endpoint in the Cisco Unified Communications Model:

- Skinny Call Control Protocol (SCCP)
- Session Initiation Protocol (SIP)

The users interact with these endpoints, and they require the support of the three layers below the Endpoints layer. Without the Applications layer, there would be no voice mail functions. Without the Call Control layer, there would be no intelligence to place a phone call. And without the Infrastructure layer, there would be no way to transport the traffic!

A Closer Look at Voice Gateways

Voice gateways are a vital part of VoIP communications and are often the most misunderstood. The purpose of voice gateways is to interconnect a VoIP packet-based network with a legacy phone network. A conversion process must take place for the two different systems to communicate with each other properly. Voice gateways can serve two primary functions on your network. They can be used to connect a CUCM to the PSTN or to connect a CUCM with a legacy PBX. Both of these services require a hardware component on the voice gateway, called a *digital signal processor (DSP)*. Let's first look at how DSP resources can be used to provide connectivity to the PSTN and legacy gateways. We'll look at both setups to see exactly how these two situations are used and the technology behind voice gateways. Then we'll move on to discuss voice gateway dial peers and call legs. Last, we'll cover the signaling protocols that facilitate the connection between the CUCM and the voice gateway.

Using DSP Resources on Voice Gateways to Connect a CUCM to the PSTN

The most common use for a voice gateway is to connect a CUCM to the PSTN. The voice gateway handles termination of any analog or digital trunks that you are leasing from the phone company. The magic of the voice gateway is how voice signals based on one voice technology are converted to a different technology. The voice gateway uses special hardware chips called digital signal processors (*DSPs*) to accomplish this goal.

DSPs perform several functions. Basically, they're specialized processor hardware that offloads voice processing services from the main router processor. After all, a router's main job is to route IP packets. We're asking the router, as a voice gateway, to provide additional services that go above and beyond its original intention. DSPs are installed to help support the additional services. Let's look at the two primary voice gateway functions: analog-to-digital conversion and digital transcoding. Then we'll look at echo cancellation and DTMF-relay, which are secondary voice gateway services.

Analog-to-Digital Conversion

Because DSPs are responsible for analog-to-digital conversion, they are required on voice gateways. Depending on the Cisco hardware used for a voice gateway, DSP modules can be found either attached to a network module (NM), WIC, or VWIC card or plugged directly into the motherboard of the router. It is important to note that a DSP resource is required for every legacy PSTN-circuit-to-IP-packet conversion that takes place on the voice gateway.

Your voice gateway router is also likely to include one or many different types of digital or analog voice interfaces, such as FXO, ISDN BRI, or T1 PRI circuit. The voice gateway sits between the legacy PSTN network and the VoIP network. The voice signals between the two networks do not speak the same language in terms of signaling, coding, and control. DSP resources are used to translate this information from one format to the other and thereby bridge the two networks.

Digital Transcoding

Even when two devices speak natively on an IP network, they still may need DSP resources to communicate properly. When two VoIP devices wish to talk to one another over the IP network, both need to be able to understand the codec that is being used. If one VoIP end unit uses a codec that the other end unit does not understand, a DSP can be used to *transcode* the stream into a codec that is supported. If you require hardware transcoding in your voice network, you can connect your CUCM to a DSP farm, which is normally found on a voice gateway. Essentially, you configure SCCP signaling between the CUCM and the voice gateway, which contains DSP resources. When the CUCM receives a voice stream that requires transcoding, the stream is directed to the voice gateway using SCCP. While it is important to understand the purpose of DSP farms, the actual configuration of a DSP farm is outside the scope of this book.

The types of codecs you need to transcode are a factor in how many DSP resources you need on your voice gateway. Usually, the more compressed the audio signal is, the more DSP resources are required for transcoding into another codec. Voice codecs are classified by complexity; they are considered to be either medium or high complexity.

🌐 Real World Scenario

Calculating DSP Requirements Online

Simon is a network consultant working on his first voice implementation for a client wanting to replace their current legacy PBX with a Cisco VoIP solution. During the course of the initial conversation meant to flesh out system requirements, Simon has determined that the site is best suited to utilize a 2800 series router with a T1 module, a four-port FXO card, and an eight-port FXS card. The four-port FXO card will be used for fax machine pass-through. Simon ended the meeting and compiled a bill of materials for a senior consultant to review. Upon looking at the information gathered, Max (the senior consultant) asked Simon if he knew how many DSP chips were required for this project. Simon had no idea what the senior consultant was talking about. Noticing the confused look on Simon's face, Max opened a web browser and navigated to

```
http://www.cisco.com/cgi-bin/Support/DSP/dsp-calc.pl
```

Max informed Simon that Cisco provides a DSP calculator to engineers to help them gauge which DSP chip will need to be ordered and in what quantity. The calculator asks for variables including router module, IOS version, and installed voice components. Simon entered all the information he gathered from the consulting session. The application then calculated the approximate number of DSP resources required and the DSP part numbers for easy ordering. Now that Simon has learned this little trick, he'll make sure to include this information in the bill of materials for future customers.

Let's use a couple of examples to make sure you understand when DSP resources may or may not be needed on your network. I'll discuss specific codec types later in the chapter, but to understand when they are required, it's sufficient to know that they are inoperable unless transcoding is performed. It is also important to note that all Cisco phones in use today support the G.729 and G.711 codecs.

Example 1: Cisco Phones Running G.711 and G.729

Suppose we have two Cisco phones, both 7960G desk phones. They are configured and running on a CUCM Express system. By default, the codec used for all VoIP on the CUCM Express is G.711. Let's say that we change the codec of one of the phones to G.729. Now we have a situation where one phone is using the G.711 codec and the other is using G.729. If one phone calls the other, we will need DSP resources to transcode one codec into another, right? Well, not necessarily! Because the Cisco IP phones understand both codecs, when the call setup occurs, the phones will actually negotiate which codec is used. If they can both talk natively using one codec, that's what they'll do. If they do not have a common codec, then DSP resources will be needed. In our example, the phones will negotiate and end up using the G.729 codec. Why did they choose G.729? If there is a choice between two or more codecs that both endpoints natively speak, they will choose the one that offers the most compression and therefore uses the least bandwidth.

Example 2: One Cisco Phone Running G.729 and a Third-Party Phone Running G.726

In this situation we have a Cisco phone that can understand G.729 and G.711. The third-party phone can use only the G.726 codec. In this situation, we'll need to tap into the DSP resources to perform transcoding between the two endpoints.

Echo Cancellation

Echo is the reflection of sound that arrives to the listener a period of time after the direct sound is heard. A certain amount of echo is experienced on most voice calls and up to a certain point is tolerated. When analog signals are converted to digital signals and then compressed using codecs, echo is often amplified to the point where it severely degrades the quality of the call. DSP resources are used to assist in the elimination of echo when converting from one voice signal into another. Echo cancellation is performed by default.

DTMF-Relay Services

VoIP devices do not support traditional DTMF digits by default. It may be necessary to allow your IP endpoints to use DTMF to communicate with non-VoIP-based services. DTMF-relay can be used to facilitate this conversion. There are several methods for configuring DTMF-relay. All of them require the use of DSPs to properly transport the DTMF tone uncompressed over an IP network. Just like DSP farms, the configuration of DTMF-relay is outside the scope of this book, but it is important to know the service exists.

Media Termination Points

When using H.323 or SIP endpoints or gateways, you can use DSP resources to assist with the process of functions such as call holds, parks, transfers, and conferences. These voice services are all very commonly used in most CUCM implementations. These supplementary services are referred to as *media termination points*. The DSPs are used to either help "park" calls while on hold or parking or provide audio multiplexing into a single audible stream for conference calls.

Using Voice Gateways to Connect a CUCM to a PBX

A second design methodology for using voice gateways is used when companies are making the migration to a Cisco Unified Communications solution. The process of migrating away from a traditional PBX typically involves interconnecting the CUCM and PBX for a period of time. Some users may have new Cisco phones, while others might still have the older phones that connect to the legacy PBX. End users on one system need to be able to communicate easily with users on the other. In this situation, a voice gateway can be used to provide a common channel-signaling method. A digital trunk interface on the voice gateway connects to a digital trunk interface on the legacy PBX. Figure 3.2 shows the physical setup of the design.

FIGURE 3.2 Connecting CUCM to a PBX

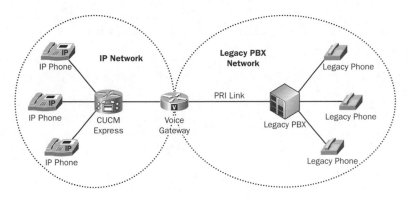

As you can see, the voice gateway represents the jumping-off point from the pure IP switched network and the legacy PBX network. In this particular setup, the two networks are interconnected by a PRI trunk. Depending on the type of PBX used, a different digital trunk might be used. The key point is that the PBX and voice gateway must use identical signaling on each side.

Voice Gateway Dial Peers

In order to route voice traffic properly from one point to another point using H.323 or SIP voice gateways, we need to configure *dial peers*. A dial peer is a device that can make or receive a call in a voice network. With VoIP networks, there are two types of dial peers:

- POTS dial peers
- VoIP dial peers

Let's review both of these to see how they function in IP and PSTN networks.

POTS Dial Peers

POTS dial peers are considered to be traditional telephony devices such as analog phones, cellular phones, and fax machines. From a voice gateway perspective, the POTS dial peer is a simple dial-string-to-port mapping. Figure 3.3 illustrates a POTS dial-peer scenario.

FIGURE 3.3 POTS dial peers

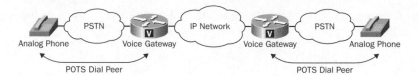

As you can see in this example, a single POTS dial peer runs from the analog phone located on the PSTN to our local voice gateway.

VoIP Dial Peers

These dial peers include any VoIP-capable endpoint, router, and gateway within the IP network. Just like POTS dial peers, *VoIP dial peers* use a dial string for mapping purposes. The difference is that instead of mapping the dial string to a physical interface, the VoIP dial peer maps the dial string to a remote IP network device. Figure 3.4 helps to explain VoIP dial peers.

FIGURE 3.4 VoIP dial peers

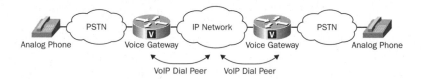

In this example, there is a VoIP dial peer for each side of the IP network. They are needed because each voice gateway requires a dial-peer configuration in order to identify the call source and destination endpoints.

Dial Peers and Call Legs

Call legs are logical connections between dial-peer origination and termination points on IP networks. They associate with dial peers on a one-to-one basis. A call leg is considered to be either a POTS or a VoIP leg, depending on which network the call leg represents. For example, Figure 3.5 shows a VoIP and POTS call communication scenario where phone A is making a call to phone B.

FIGURE 3.5 Call legs

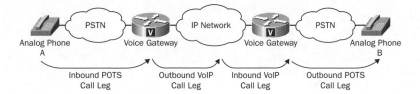

This example shows that every voice IP terminating device has a call leg associated with it. Any voice gateway will have two associated call legs/dial peers for each logical connection. By contrast, a POTS dial peer has only a single call leg/dial peer associated with it. This is because once the call is placed out on the PSTN, we don't really have any control over how it is switched. Therefore, we have control over only one dial peer and, ultimately, one call leg.

Comparing Voice Gateway Communication Protocols

As you have learned, voice gateways provide a bridge between the Cisco Unified Communications Manager and either the PSTN or a legacy PBX. There are two types of voice gateways in the CUCM Express system. The voice gateway might reside on the same router as your CUCM Express software; this is known as an *integrated voice gateway*. If the PSTN trunks reside on the same hardware as the CUCM Express software, calls can be directly switched from the PSTN lines to the IP phones with little configuration. Figure 3.6 shows the integrated gateway setup, which requires no voice gateway protocol:

FIGURE 3.6 Integrated voice gateway

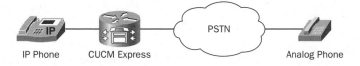

The *separated voice gateway* sits on a different router than the CUCM Express software. If the voice gateway is separate, you need a signaling protocol to transport the calls across the IP network between the CUCM and the voice gateway. Figure 3.7 depicts the separated voice gateway architecture and the link that requires a voice gateway signaling protocol.

FIGURE 3.7   Separated voice gateway

The Unified Communications system supports four methods of gateway communication. Let's briefly look at these four gateway protocols.

The H.323 Gateway Protocol

H.323 is an ITU standards-based peer-to-peer protocol. It is a bundle of multiple protocols signaling and controlling voice and video data. Table 3.1 lists the core protocols used within the H.323 suite and their functionality.

TABLE 3.1   H.323 core protocols

H.323 Subprotocol	Function
RAS	Messaging protocol used by the CUCM for gatekeeper discovery and registration. Also used to pass database lookup and CAC information.
H.245	Performs call control functions.
Voice Codecs (G.711, G.729, etc.)	Performs encoding/decoding of voice streams.
H.225	Performs call setup and codec negotiation over TCP 1720.

As you can see from the table, H.323 uses the various protocols within the suite to signal and control transport over IP. Transport and packetization are then performed using the Real-time Transport Protocol (RTP). RTP is an IETF standard for transport of time-sensitive packets such as voice. RTP will be described in detail later in this chapter. H.323 has been around since the mid-1990s and is considered to be the most mature of all voice gateway signaling protocols. The protocol suite is very versatile and can be utilized in multiple ways, including signaling for endpoints, gatekeepers, and voice gateways. For CUCM Express environments, which our book focuses on, you'll typically see H.323 used to communicate between CUCM Express and a voice gateway.

The H.323 architecture uses a peer-to-peer model. This means that the voice gateway is independent of the CUCM. Therefore, a more complex configuration is necessary on the voice gateway. This is because the gateway is responsible for maintaining the dial plans and route patterns.

You may run across a separate device in large legacy H.323 environments called an *H.323 gatekeeper.* This device is essentially a database that contains H.323 mappings (telephone numbers) to IP addresses. When a phone number is dialed, the gatekeeper is queried to determine what location (IP address) the remote phone is located in. For example, if a user dials 555-1212, the gatekeeper knows that this phone can be reached at the IP address of 10.10.4.220. Our Cisco voice gateway needs a way to communicate with the H.323 gatekeeper in order to facilitate this gatekeeper "lookup" functionality. It uses the RAS protocol to discover and communicate with the gatekeeper. Figure 3.8 shows the RAS communication between a voice gateway and an H.323 gatekeeper:

FIGURE 3.8 RAS between VG and H.323 gatekeeper

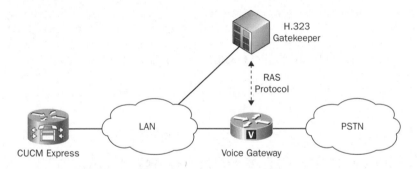

The gatekeeper is also responsible for any *call admission control (CAC)* that the administrator has configured. CAC is responsible for determining whether the caller has the right to ring the requested number. In addition, it can also determine whether there is enough bandwidth at the time of the call to make a successful connection.

The SIP Gateway Protocol

Session Initiation Protocol (*SIP*) is an IETF standard gateway communication method that uses a peer-to-peer architecture. It can run over TCP or UDP. By default, SIP uses UDP port 5060 when configured on a CUCM. Because it is a peer-to-peer system, the intelligence, such as dial plans and route patterns, resides on the voice gateway sides. It also means that the voice gateway configuration is more complex than with the client-server gateway protocols. SIP is considered the successor to H.323 and is in increasingly widespread use in new environments. But unlike H.323, SIP is merely responsible for call setup and control. Other protocols outside of SIP such as UDP/RTP/RTCP are ultimately responsible for the transport of the voice stream. We'll discuss these voice packet transport protocols in the next section.

The MGCP Gateway Protocol

The Media Gateway Control Protocol (*MGCP*) is a client-server architecture, which means all of the intelligence, such as dial peers and route plans, resides on the CUCM. This centralized call control model means the gateway simply facilitates the voice routing functions that the CUCM determines. It is an IETF standard protocol and is the newest of the standards-based voice gateway signaling protocols. It is also one of the simplest to configure on the voice gateway. Because of its client-server nature, the bulk of the configuration is performed on the CUCM and very little is required on the router itself. MGCP can run over either TCP or UDP. Signaling information between the CUCM and gateway runs over port UDP/2427 and TCP/2428 by default.

The SCCP Gateway Protocol

The Skinny Client Control Protocol (*SCCP*) is a Cisco proprietary gateway protocol. It uses a lightweight client-server architecture that allows the CUCM to maintain the dial plans and route patterns centrally and uses the gateway as a method of transport, similar to MGCP. Because SCCP is proprietary, your voice gateway must be a Cisco device. You may want to look into using SCCP as your voice gateway protocol, because it provides additional features that are not available with the standards-based protocols. The SCCP protocol runs over TCP port 2000.

We'll spend part of Chapter 7 configuring gateways and trunk communication between the CUCM Express and a separate voice gateway.

An Overview of Voice and Video Transport Protocols

Data payloads such as voice and video that our Cisco Unified Communications Systems facilitate require specific protocols to be handled properly. In regard to the CCNA Voice certification, you need to be aware of the protocols that the CUCM solutions use to transport voice endpoint packets from one endpoint to another. This section details the three protocols that are used in Cisco VoIP environments: Real-time Transport Protocol, Compressed Real-time Transport Protocol, and Real-time Control Transport Protocol.

The Real-Time Transport Protocol

The foundation of all voice and video communication over an IP network begins with the Real-time Transport Protocol (*RTP*). RTP is an IETF RFC 1889 and 3050 standard for the delivery of unicast and multicast voice/video streams. RTP almost always uses UDP for transport. UDP, unlike TCP, is an unreliable best-effort service. That may sound like a bad thing, but in reality it is the most efficient method for transport of streaming data. A best-effort service such as UDP does not attempt to retransmit or reorder packets as TCP does. If you think about it, once a voice packet is lost in transit, there is no reason to attempt to retransmit it, because once the packet reaches its destination, the sound wave contained in the packet would not make sense to the end user if it is delivered out of order. UDP also does not provide any flow control or error correction. This cuts down on the overhead of each datagram and therefore is much more efficient.

The RTP header does offer some important information about its payload in each encapsulated packet. Figure 3.9 lays out the RTP header information.

FIGURE 3.9 RTP header details

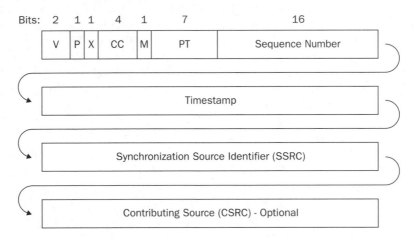

Let's briefly look at each segment of the RTP header:

Version (V): 2 bits   This field specifies the version of RTP that is being used.

Padding (P): 1 bit   If this bit is set, it indicates that this RTP packet has one or more octets at the end that are *not* part of the payload. Padding is often used for encrypting RTP payloads.

Extension (X): 1 bit   If this bit is set, it indicates that the fixed header is followed by a single header extension.

Marker (M): 1 bit   A field used to signify significant events to the application using the stream.

Payload Type (PT): 7 bits   This field identifies the type of RTP data that is inside the payload (either voice or video data).

Sequence Number: 16 bits   This field increments by one for each RTP packet in a particular stream. This may be used by upper-layer protocols to detect any packet loss or sequencing issues.

Timestamp: 32 bits   The timestamp marks each packet with an encapsulation time. It is most often used for jitter and synchronization calculations.

Synchronization Source Identifier (SSRC): 32 bits   This field marks each RTP stream differently so multiple RTP streams from the same source are kept separate.

Contributing Source (CSRC): 32 bits   An optional field that enumerates contributing sources to streams that come from multiple sources.

According to the RFC, RTP can utilize any UDP port as long as it is even numbered. It is up to the application to determine which port is used, although voice traffic is typically in the range of 16384 to 32767. The UDP port it uses for a practical RTP stream is chosen at random. That same port is used the entire duration of the stream. Once one of the IP phones hangs up, that RTP session is terminated and the port is released. RTCP, which we'll talk about in a moment, uses the next-incremented odd-numbered port, always creating a pair of ports representing a call leg.

Compressed RTP

You may have noticed that the entire RTP header is a hefty 12 bytes in length. Combined with a 20-byte IP header and a UDP header of 8 bytes, there is a whopping 40 bytes in header information alone. Because RTP data is very sensitive to any kind of delay, some way to compress this header information was needed. Compressed RTP (*cRTP*) was developed as a solution.

cRTP takes that massive 40-byte header compilation and cuts it down to anywhere between 2 and 5 bytes. Figure 3.10 shows the cRTP compression byte reduction rate.

FIGURE 3.10   RTP to cRTP

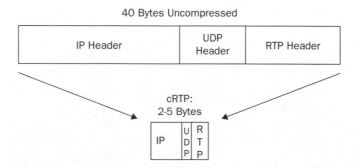

Because much of the information contained in the IP/UDP and RTP headers is static, cRTP essentially removes this information once it is known on both ends of the wire. By not sending this static data, it conserves precious bandwidth. In this sense, cRTP caches static information so it does not have to resend it across the same link. cRTP is most effective on WAN links that are T1 speed and below. Anything above this bandwidth renders the compression essentially useless.

If you implement cRTP in a production network, make sure you closely monitor the CPU utilization. Unless you have specialized compression hardware installed on your router, compression is performed in software and utilizes the main CPU. To see the utilization on a Cisco router, run a show processes cpu command while in privileged exec mode.

Real-Time Transport Control Protocol

RTP has a partner when it comes to the transport of real-time data. Real-time Transport Control Protocol (*RTCP*) works directly with RTP to provide out-of-band monitoring for the streaming of the RTP-encapsulated data. RTCP packets are sent to participants of a particular RTP stream. The main function of RTCP is to provide feedback about the quality of the RTP transmissions. The real-time application can use this information to adapt encoding settings if the protocol detects congestion. That means if congestion is discovered on the remote end of the stream, the receiver can inform the sender to use a lower-quality codec and therefore help with any bottlenecks. Following are some of the most common RTP data that RTCP tracks:

- Total packet count for the stream
- Packet loss of the stream
- Packet delay of the stream
- Amount of jitter on the stream

As mentioned, RTP uses even-numbered UDP ports for transport. RTCP uses the next-highest odd-numbered port for its transmission. For example, if RTP is running on UDP port 22864, then the corresponding RTCP packets run on UDP port 22865.

Keep in mind that an RTP/RTCP stream for voice traffic is one-way only. Thus for a single voice call, there are two RTP/RTCP streams. One instance is for transmission of voice to the called party; the other is for voice traffic being received.

Comparing VoIP Endpoint Signaling Protocols

You know that VoIP uses IP for routing decisions, UDP for packet delivery, and RTP/RTCP for real-time transport. You also need to understand how the CUCM solution handles the signaling responsibilities for voice endpoints. VoIP endpoint signaling protocols are responsible for locating endpoints, negotiation of various functions, and the setup and teardown of voice calls. You must be familiar with two endpoint signaling protocols: SCCP and SIP. Each protocol differs in architecture, call control, and other services. Let's look at each of them.

SCCP

The Skinny Call Control Protocol (SCCP) is a Cisco proprietary voice signaling protocol based on a client-server architecture. The clients can be any of the Cisco endpoint phones such as the Cisco 7971 or Cisco IP Communicator softphone. The server in the architecture is our Cisco Unified Communications Manager. All SCCP clients must communicate with the CUCM in order to place a call. In this regard, the phone is essentially a "dumb" device that fully relies on the CUCM to give it intelligence for call setup and teardown. So while the CUCM handles the call setup control, the phone is responsible only for the processing of RTP/RTCP packets. SCCP messages are transported over TCP port 2000. Because SCCP uses TCP for transport, messages can utilize TCP functionality such as error correction and guaranteed delivery of packets.

When an SCCP-enabled phone registers with it, the CUCM requests certain information from the phone: IP address, station ID, device types, and the codecs the phone can understand. The CUCM stores this information so it knows how to best handle the setup of calls to a particular endpoint. The CUCM uses SCCP messages for keepalives to the client phones. A *keepalive* is a message sent by one device to another at specific intervals to verify that communication between the two is functioning. If the CUCM does not receive a certain number of keepalive responses over a period of time, the stored endpoint information is cleared from the CUCM memory until it reconnects, at which time the phone will have to go through the information-gathering process again.

Once the phone capabilities are registered on the CUCM, SCCP is used again to send out all the necessary information that the phone requires, including its phone number, button templates, time/date synchronization, and any other configurable options and displays.

Messages are constantly sent between the client phone and the CUCM for everything that a user does on a phone. For example, when a user picks up the handset, an off-hook notification message is sent from the phone via SCCP to the CUCM. The CUCM then sends everything the phone should do in response to going off-hook. These include the message the LCD is to display, the softkeys that are to be displayed, and, of course, a dial-tone signal. So clearly, SCCP is very much a client-server technology, because control of the phone is strictly maintained by the Communications Manager. It is important to keep in mind that the client-server model between the endpoint and CUCM is only for signaling; the actual voice packets encapsulated in RTP and the RTCP control data are transported directly from one endpoint to the other. Figure 3.11 shows the traffic flow for SCCP and RTP/RTCP:

FIGURE 3.11   SCCP and RTP/RTCP flow

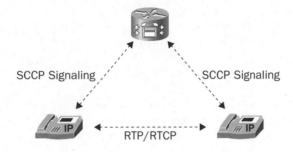

SIP

The Session Initiation Protocol (SIP) differs from SCCP in several ways. For one, it is an IETF RFC 3261 standard instead of the Cisco proprietary signaling protocol. This means that third-party phones and applications can be used on the CUCM system using SIP. The RFC for SIP states that the protocol was designed for the creation and management of multimedia sessions over the Internet. Its architecture is a peer-to-peer model in theory. Figure 3.12 shows how both SIP and RTP/RTCP communicate directly between endpoints.

FIGURE 3.12   SIP and RTP/RTCP flow

SIP phones working in a Cisco Unified Communications environment are set up in *SIP proxy* mode. The CUCM SIP proxy is used for making requests on behalf of endpoints. This helps to facilitate policy enforcement by the CUCM administrator. When the SIP phone is set up to work in a Cisco UC environment, the SIP proxy IP address is configured to be the IP address of the CUCM Express. Figure 3.13 shows how the CUCM is used as an SIP proxy.

FIGURE 3.13   CUCM SIP proxy

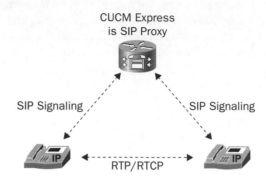

As soon as an SIP session is established between the two SIP endpoints, the actual voice stream flows between the users. The voice stream is managed by RTP and RTCP. The RTP/RTCP stream is identical whether you are using SIP or SCCP for signaling. This is because the voice streams use the signaling protocols only for setup and teardown. As soon as SIP sets up the call, RTC/RTCP proceeds independently from SIP.

Voice Signaling Protocols in Review

It is very important that you be able to successfully compare and contrast the different types of gateway and endpoint signaling protocols. Table 3.2 displays each protocol and its characteristics.

TABLE 3.2   Comparison of voice signaling protocols

Protocol	Standard	Architecture	Call Control	CUCM Uses
SCCP	Cisco proprietary	Client-server	Centralized	Voice gw/trunk and endpoint to CUCM
SIP	IETF	Peer-to-peer	Distributed	Voice gw/trunk and endpoint to CUCM
H.323	ITU	Peer-to-peer	Distributed	Voice gw/trunk
MGCP	IETF	Client-server	Centralized	Voice gw/trunk

Comparing the Common Voice Codecs

As you learned previously, voice codecs are responsible for the encoding and decoding of voice signals. They also can compress the digital signal so that more voice calls can be sent across a finite amount of bandwidth. In this section, we're going to compare the most common types of voice codecs used in a Unified Communications solution.

G.711

The *G.711* ITU standard codec is also known as pulse code modulation (PCM). This codec samples voice signals at a frequency of 8,000 samples per second. It provides the best quality among the most commonly used codecs, but that comes at a price. There are two common types of G.711 binary conversion techniques on most voice systems. The first G.711 type is called u-law and is most commonly used in the United States, Canada, and Japan. The second G.711 binary conversion type is called *a-law* and is used just about everywhere else on the planet. It is important to note that the two PCM techniques are not compatible with each other and need to be transcoded for interoperability.

Each phone call on the network requires 64 Kbps on the wire. Let's do some quick math to see how much compression is being used on the G.711 codec. Using Dr. Nyquist's formula, we will get 8,000 voice samples each second. Each of these samples is 8 bits in length. So if we multiply 8,000 × 8, we get 64,000 bps, or 64 Kbps. This means that G.711 uses no compression when it encodes the voice stream! If you have plenty of bandwidth, G.711 is the way to go. If you are running voice over a low-speed WAN link or are planning to use wireless IP phones, then you may want to consider a codec that compresses the call into a smaller data stream.

G.729

The *G.729* ITU standard codec samples the voice signal at the same rate as G.711 of 8,000 samples per second per the Nyquist rate theorem. Also like G.711, the bit rate is fixed at 8 per sample. The major difference between G.711 and the variations of G.729 has to do with compression. Using what's known as conjugative-structure algebraic-code-excited liner prediction (CS-ACELP), the G.729 codecs use alternate sampling methods and algebraic expressions as a codebook to predict the actual numeric representation. These smaller algebraic expressions are then sent to the remote side, where they are decoded and the audio is synthesized to mimic the original audio tones. This audio waveform prediction and synthesization degrades the quality of the voice signal by making the speaker's voice sound robotic. But the G.729's use of CS-ACELP allows the compressed voice signal to require only 8 Kbps per call as opposed to 64 Kbps required per stream of G.711. This means that eight voice calls using the G.729 codec can be made in the space of just one G.711 codec call. Not a bad tradeoff when you are attempting to run voice over low-speed WAN links!

G.729a

The *G.729a* ITU standard codec is very similar to G.729. They use the same 8Kbps bandwidth consumption per call. Where the two codecs differ is in the type of algorithm used to encode the voice signal. G.729 is considered a high-complexity codec and G.729 a medium-complexity codec. Table 3.3 displays the complexity level of several of the more popular codecs available today.

TABLE 3.3   Voice codec complexity

Medium Complexity	High Complexity
G.711	G.729
G.729a	G.728
G.726	iLBC

All codecs are classified as either medium or high complexity. These categories are important when dealing with DSPs, as we discussed earlier. We know that DSPs are required for translating digital signals to analog and for transcoding between different digital codecs. High-complexity codecs use more DSP processing power than medium-complexity codecs. Because DSP resources are finite, you may need to move from G.729 to G.729a to free up those DSP resources. The downside is that the voice quality of G.729a compared to G.729 is marginally worse.

iLBC

The Internet Low Bandwidth Codec is fairly new to the voice world and still waiting to fully catch on. The codec uses either 20ms or 30ms voice samples, and they end up consuming 15.2 Kbps or 13.3 Kbps, respectively. One other major benefit the iLBC touts is its ability to handle moderate amounts of packet loss. If some of your VoIP packets are lost in transit, iLBC's built-in techniques help the call continue with little notice to the user.

Where did this codec come from? Unlike all the other codecs we've discussed, it wasn't defined by the ITU. In 2000 a group of VoIP industry leaders collaborated and came up with the new codec. Hopefully, the cooperation between all the major players will finally get the industry to settle on a universal codec. iLBC is the first codec to attempt this. Fortunately, Cisco is now beginning to build their IP phones to be able to understand the iLBC codec. Other third-party vendors are also including iLBC support on their endpoints. So in addition to using the G.711 and G.729 codecs, the phones can utilize iLBC. As this book is being written, the following Cisco 7900 series phones understand the iLBC codec:

- 7906G
- 7911G
- 7921G
- 7925G
- 7942G
- 7945G
- 7962G
- 7965G
- 7975G

Which Codec Is Right for You?

In some instances there is a right or wrong choice in using one codec over another. But most of the time, it really depends on the business requirements. Here are some considerations to help you in making a codec decision:

What do my endpoints support?   As stated earlier, Cisco phones support G.711 and G.729. Newer phones also support the iLBC codec. So in Cisco environments you are going to use one of these three. Don't forget, however, that some codecs have variants, such as the G.729 and G.729a protocols.

How many DSP channels will I need?   DSP chips contain multiple channels with which to handle codec transcoding. If you find yourself having to constantly transcode one codec into another, you probably made a poor codec decision. DSP resources are not cheap. If you can limit transcoding, you should.

How much voice quality do I need?   Depending on your users and the environment they are used in, voice quality may or may not be a major factor in your decision-making process. A tried but true method of determining the quality of the audio of a voice codec is called the *Mean Opinion Score* (MOS). Developed by the ITU, this quality-measurement system rates the quality of voice streams for a particular codec. It is actually very nonscientific, because the MOS is an average "opinion" of a group of people who listen to the same sentence for each codec tested. These listeners then rank the voice quality on a scale of 1 to 5. A score of 1 is the worst quality, and a score of 5 is excellent quality. Table 3.4 lists the codecs we discussed and each one's MOS score.

TABLE 3.4 MOS scores of common VoIP codecs

Codec	MOS
G.711	4.1
iLBC	4.1
G.729	3.92
G.729a	3.7

How much bandwidth do I have to play with?   If you are going to run voice over low-bandwidth WAN links, then you should definitely look at codecs that use at least some compression.

Which codec works best for my environment?   If you have a high amount of packet loss on your network, you may want to look into the codecs that offer the best recoverability when VoIP packets are lost in transit.

Calculating IP Voice Packet Sizes

Continuing our topic of codec comparisons, let's focus on how different codecs affect the size of the IP packets that are sent across a network. Usually, choosing a codec depends on the type of environment the phones will operate in. You must be careful when you wish to use VoIP in low-bandwidth situations, such as running over low-speed WAN connections. If you need to run voice over the WAN, it's critical to know the size of the voice packets to determine how your network will scale. You should be able to calculate how much bandwidth a particular IP voice packet consumes so you can properly engineer you network for the approximate number of simultaneous calls you are anticipating. In calculating packet sizes, there are some packet components whose size is static and never changes. Other components are variable and can be manipulated depending on the codec used to change their size. The following sections present all of the static and variable services that change the size of the packets.

Voice Packet Payload

A voice packet payload consists of the following:

Sample times of audio streams: Typically, most codecs take sample sizes between 10ms and 30ms.

Codec bandwidth used: We already know how to calculate this using the Nyquist calculation.

One factor we always use to calculate the size of a single voice packet payload is the fact that we use an 8-bit sample. Therefore, to calculate how big our voice payload is in bytes, we use the calculations shown in the following example.

Let's say we're using the G.711 codec with a sample size of 20 ms. Using the Nyquist calculation, we already know that the codec bandwidth rate for G.711 is 64 Kbps. Therefore, to determine the number of bits per packet, it's a simple calculation of multiplying the codec bandwidth rate by our sample size:

Audio_payload_bits = 20 × 64

Audio_payload_bits = 1280

Now that we know what our payload is in bits, we divide by 8 to determine the bytes of audio contained in a single voice packet for the G.711 codec using a 20ms sample:

Audio_payload_bytes = 1280 / 8

Audio_payload_bytes = 160

Layer 2 Header Information

Layer 2 header information depends on the Layer 2 methods you are using on your network. Typically LANs use Ethernet as the Layer 2 transport. Two common WAN Layer 2 protocols are Frame Relay and PPP:

- Ethernet header: 20 bytes
- Frame Relay: 4–6 bytes
- Point-to-Point Protocol (PPP): 6 bytes

Layer 3 Header Information

Since we're dealing with VoIP, the Layer 3 numbers are static for our calculation. All VoIP must use IP, UDP, and RTP/RTCP. Therefore, we need header information, which uses up space! Here is the number of bytes each one uses:

- IP: 20 bytes
- UDP: 8 bytes
- RTP/RTCP: 12 bytes

Special Case Packet Additions

You may need to tunnel or encrypt voice traffic over your network. If this is the case, you must include the overhead for whatever protocol you are using. Here is a short breakdown of the bytes added by some of the more popular encryption techniques being used today:

- IPSec: 50–57 bytes
- GRE tunneling protocol: 4-20 bytes (Cisco uses 8 bytes)
- MPLS tagging: 4 bytes per tag (may be more than one tag present)

Now we can add everything together to determine how fat or skinny our VoIP packets are! This will give us the total packet size in bytes. This is great, but our LAN/WAN links are calculated in either Kbps or Mbps. We need to do two more calculations; first we must figure out our bandwidth requirements in bytes per second and ultimately how many bits per second.

Calculating Bytes per Second

In addition to the number of bytes your voice packet will consume, you'll need to go back and retrieve the sample size rate in ms that the codec uses. In our example, we are using 20ms samples. We're looking to calculate the number of bytes per second that a voice stream will generate. There are 1000 ms in 1 second. Therefore we can use this calculation to come up with the number of packets per second (packets_per_second):

packets_per_second = 1000 / sample_size

packets_per_second = 1000 / 20

packets_per_second = 50

With this information, we want to see how many bytes are consumed every second. Let's use the example voice packet size of 220 bytes (160 bytes in payload + 60 bytes for Ethernet and IP overhead) and our calculated 50 packets per second to come up with bytes per second. We can use the following equation to determine the number of bytes per second:

bytes_per_second = voice_packet_size 3 packets_per_second

bytes_per_second = 220 × 50

bytes_per_second = 11000

Calculating Bits per Second

Our last step is to convert our bytes per second into bits per second. This is just a matter of multiplying our bytes_per_second value by 8:

bits_per_second = bytes_per_second × 8

Using our 11,000 bytes_per_second number above, we can determine bits per second as follows:

bits_per_second = 11000 × 8

bits_per_second = 88000

This means that each RTP stream consumes 88,000 bps, or 88 Kbps, using the uncompressed G.711 codec over Ethernet.

You can use this information to help determine how many voice streams your network can support depending on the codec and L2/L3 technologies that you wish to utilize.

Size Calculation Examples

Let's practice our IP voice packet size calculations with the following two examples:

Example 1 information   The codec that we have chosen uses a sample time of 30 ms and a codec bandwidth of 8 Kbps. Our packet will be traversing only Ethernet networks. The packets will be tunneled using GRE.

Example 1 solution   First we need to calculate the voice packet payload size into bits:

>   audio_payload_bits = 30 × 8

>   audio_payload_bits = 240

Next we convert bits into bytes:

>   audio_payload_bytes = 240 / 8

>   audio_payload_bytes = 30

Then we need to add up our Layer 2 and Layer 3 header information:

>   Ethernet header: 20 bytes

>   IP: 20 bytes

>   UDP: 8 bytes

>   RTP/RTCP: 12 bytes

>   Total = 60 bytes

Because we're tunneling using GRE, this adds an additional 8 bytes to the packet size. Adding all three numbers together gives us our voice IP packet size:

>   Audio payload: 30 bytes

>   L2/L3 header: 60 bytes

>   GRE encapsulation: 8 bytes

>   Total voice packet: = 98 bytes

Now we can figure out the packets, bytes, and bits per second this stream uses:

Packets per second

>   packets_per_second = 1000 / sample_size

>   packets_per_second = 1000 / 30

>   packets_per_second = 33.33

Bytes per second

>   bytes_per_second = voice_packet_size 3 packets_per_second

>   bytes_per_second = 98 × 33.33

>   bytes_per_second = 3,266.34

Bits per second

bits_per_second = bytes_per_second 3 8

bits_per_second = 3,266.34 × 8

bits_per_second = 26,130.72

So this particular stream uses approximately 26,100 bps, or 26.1 Kbps, per stream.

Example 2 information   Our second example codec uses a sample time of 10 ms and a codec bandwidth of 32 Kbps. Our packet will be going across an MPLS WAN link. MPLS uses Ethernet for transport over the WAN, so it will use standard Ethernet headers in addition to the MPLS tags. The voice packets will be encrypted over the MPLS network using IPSec, which consumes 57 bytes for encapsulation.

Example 2 solution   First we need to calculate the voice packet payload size in bits:

audio_payload_bits = 10 × 32

audio_payload_bits = 320

Next we convert bits into bytes:

audio_payload_bytes = 320 / 8

audio_payload_bytes = 40

Then we need to add up our Layer 2 and Layer 3 header information:

Ethernet header: 20 bytes

MPLS header: 4 bytes

IP: 20 bytes

UDP: 8 bytes

RTP/RTCP: 12 bytes

Total = 64 bytes

We want to encrypt our sensitive voice traffic over the MPLS network using IPSec, which adds 57 bytes to the overall packet size. Adding all three numbers together gives us our voice IP packet size:

Audio payload: 40 bytes

L2/L3 header: 64 bytes

IPSec encryption: 57 bytes

Total voice packet = 161 bytes

Again, we can figure out the packets, bytes, and bits per second this stream uses:

Packets per second

packets_per_second = 1000 / sample_size

packets_per_second = 1000 / 10

packets_per_second = 100

Bytes per second

bytes_per_second = voice_packet_size 3 packets_per_second

bytes_per_second = 161 × 100

bytes_per_second = 161,000

Bits per second

bits_per_second = bytes_per_second × 8

bits_per_second = 161,000 × 8

bits_per_second = 128,800

So this particular stream uses 128,800 bps, or 128.8 Kbps, per stream.

Now you should have a good understanding of how to calculate the approximate size of a voice packet depending on the codec and additional services you require. You can then divide this number into the number of bytes available on your network links to see the maximum number of simultaneous calls your network could handle. Using Example 2, let's assume our MPLS network is 20 Mbps, or 20,000 Kbps, and 50 percent of the circuit is already being utilized with data traffic. This leaves us with 10,000 Kbps on average for voice. Given that each RTP stream consumes 128.8 Kbps, we can determine the number of simultaneous calls that can be made on the link:

simultaneous_calls = voice_in_Kbps / available_bw_in_Kbps

simultaneous_calls = 128.8 / 10,000

simultaneous_calls = 77.64

Reducing Voice Packet Sizes

You can reclaim some bytes from your voice streams in additional ways. One method that was already mentioned is the RTP header compression, or cRTP. As detailed earlier in this chapter, you can use cRTP to cache the 40-byte RTP/IP/UDP header information on one side of a link and send only the remainder of the header information to the other side of the link. This cuts the 40-byte header information down to 2–5 bytes.

Another great bandwidth-saving utility is called Voice Activity Detection (VAD). VAD monitors the voice conversation that is taking place, and when it detects silence on the RTP stream, it stops transmitting RTP packets across the wire. VAD is not enabled by default. When you make a phone call, you might be surprised to learn that anywhere from 35 to 40 percent of the conversation is complete silence! When VAD is disabled, the RTP stream will package up the silent voice slices and send them over as normal. VAD is more intelligent and will send only RTP data that actually contains voice. VAD must communicate with the other end on the connection so it will play a prerecorded "silence" VoIP packet instead of the actual packet from the source.

It is important to realize that the 35–40 percent is an average number based on several studies. If you have a Chatty Cathy on the other end, this number will obviously drop. Also, areas with a great deal of background noise—such as a data center with constantly buzzing fans—will not see much of an impact at all if VAD is enabled. When performing your bandwidth savings calculations, it's better to play it more conservatively and use a number between 10 and 20 percent.

Examples of When to Use Specific Codecs

At times it is highly recommended and sometimes required to use one type of codec over another. These are Cisco recommendations based on best-practice situations for common tasks. This section describes which codecs are recommended for voice and modem pass-through and when incorporating MoH over a low-speed WAN link.

ATA Fax and Fax Modem Pass-through

Using the Cisco ATA hardware, it is possible to connect analog phones and fax machines to an IP network. A problem arises when you attempt to use a fax machine without the correct codec. If you try to configure the port to use G.729 or G.729a, the compression methods used are not enough to correctly interpret the analog signals that the fax machine is transmitting. Therefore it is necessary to configure fax machines and fax modems to use the G.711 codec. Because that data is uncompressed, the analog signals that fax machines and modems use are more accurately digitized. When the digital signal is decoded on the other side, to the digital sample can successfully be rebuilt into an analog wave that is understood by the receiving fax machine or modem.

Music on Hold

The G.729 and G.729a codecs are designed to be optimized for human speech. This allows the data to be compressed down to a tiny 8Kbps stream. These compressed codecs are commonly used for transmission of voice over low-speed WAN links. But because the codecs are optimized solely for speech, they often do not provide adequate quality for Music on Hold (MoH) streams. If you determine that the MoH quality is unacceptable using the G.729 and G.729a codecs, there is a way to force MoH to use the higher-quality G.711 codec while voice communication still uses one of the lower-quality codecs using CUCM regions. This technique is outside the scope of this book.

Summary

Chapter 3 examined VoIP in Cisco networks beginning with an overview of the four layers of the Unified Communications Model—Infrastructure, Call Control, Applications, and Endpoints—and the components in each layer.

Voice gateways perform crucial infrastructure functions, and this chapter examined the four types of voice gateway protocols used in a Unified Communications environment. RTP and RTSP are the transport protocols for streaming media over IP networks, and we examined how they differ. The Cisco Unified Communications Manager uses two endpoint signaling protocols, SCCP and SIP, and this chapter showed how they differ.

The CUCM can use four common voice codecs: G.711, G.729, G.729a, and iLBC. The second half of the chapter described each one, how they differ, and the situations where each codec is most often used. As an administrator, your choice of which codec to use depends on calculating the voice packet size. The chapter concluded by discussing and illustrating those calculations.

This information should provide you with a thorough understanding of exactly how voice and data are transported on and between IP networks. Voice and data are two great services that can work together when VoIP is properly configured.

Exam Essentials

Know the Cisco Unified Communications Model.   The four layers of the communications model are the Infrastructure, Call Control, Applications, and Endpoints layers. Each layer plays a specific role in the Unified Communications system.

Understand how voice gateways connect to the PSTN and legacy PBX systems.   Voice gateways bridge an IP network to a non-IP legacy network, either of which may be public or private.

Understand the role DSPs play in the Unified Communications system.   DSPs provide analog-to-digital translation, codec transcoding, echo cancellation, DTMF relay services, and media termination points. DSP farms typically reside on voice gateway routers.

Understand the difference between POTS and VoIP dial peers.   POTS dial peers are traditional PSTN technology, while VoIP dial peers connect to endpoints using IP.

Know how dial peers and call legs are associated with each other and where they initiate and terminate on the voice network.   A call leg is always associated with a dial peer. It marks a logical point along the path of a phone call.

Understand the protocols that are responsible for signaling between the CUCM and a voice gateway.   The H.323, SIP, MGCP, and SCCP protocols can be used for voice gateway signaling. Each protocol has different setups that change the way the dial peers and route plans are located.

Know which protocol is responsible for the transport of the actual voice payloads.   RTP is used for the transport of voice packets on a Unified Communications system. RTCP is responsible for out-of-band monitoring of the RTP packets.

Know which protocol is used for compression of voice packets.   cRTP header compression can be used to shrink the IP, UDP, and RTP headers to decrease bandwidth consumption.

Understand the two Cisco Unified Communications endpoint signaling protocols.   SCCP is a Cisco proprietary protocol that uses client-server architecture. SIP is an IETF standards-based protocol that uses peer-to-peer architecture. SIP is used in a proxy server mode by the CUCM.

Be able to compare and contrast all voice signaling protocols.   Understand the differences in standards, architecture, call control, and CUCM uses for SCCP, SIP, H.323, and MGCP.

Understand the most common voice codecs and when to use them.   The three most common codecs are G.711, G.729, and G.729a. Each codec has advantages and disadvantages depending on the network speed it runs on.

Understand when specific codecs are either required or highly desirable.   It is important to know which codec is required in situations where fax machines and fax modems are used. Also, when using voice over low-speed WAN links, you need to understand why G.729 should be used for voice and G.711 for MoH.

Written Lab 3.1

Write the answers to the following questions:

1.   What are the four layers of the Unified Communications Model?

2.   What are the two signaling protocols used in the Endpoints layer?

3.   Name the layer where the Call Manager resides.

4.   What can you do at the Infrastructure layer of the UC Model to ensure that voice packets have priority over data packets?

5.   What is the term used when DSPs translate between two different codecs?

6.   List the two types of voice gateway dial peers.

7.   Name the two signaling protocols that can be used for both voice gateway and endpoint signaling.

8.   What is a possible side effect when using cRTP?

9.   What is the size of IP/UDP/RTP header information that is uncompressed?

10.   What is G.711 also known as?

(The answers to Written Lab 3.1 can be found following the answers to the Review Questions for this chapter.)

Review Questions

1. At which layer of the UC model can ACLs be implemented to limit which IPs and ports can access the CUCM?

   A. Infrastructure layer

   B. Data Link layer

   C. Call Control layer

   D. Applications layer

   E. Session layer

2. The CUCM is responsible for all of the following *except*:

   A. User management

   B. Call signaling

   C. Call processing

   D. QoS enforcement

   E. Media resource management

3. What can you use to help eliminate voice congestion on slow WAN links?

   A. RTCP

   B. RTP

   C. cRTP

   D. TCP/IP

4. What Unified Communications solution resides in the UC Model Applications layer and is responsible for handling endpoint location information for emergency services?

   A. Unity

   B. Cisco Unified Communications Manager

   C. E911

   D. Cisco Emergency Responder

   E. SRST

5. Which Cisco UC application provides integration with Cisco Presence applications such as voice, video, email, instant messaging, and web collaboration?

   A. Unity

   B. Customer Contact Solution

   C. Call Control

   D. Cisco Unified Communications Manager

   E. Real-time Transport

6. At which layer of the UC model are ATAs found?

    A. Infrastructure layer

    B. Endpoints layer

    C. Call Control layer

    D. Application layer

7. What is the centralized location for hardware that handles codec transcoding and voice translation services?

    A. Infrastructure layer

    B. Transcoding farm

    C. DSP farm

    D. Applications layer

    E. Unity

8. What is the term for the reflection of sound waves that arrive to the listener a short time after the direct sound is heard?

    A. Echo

    B. Refraction

    C. DTMF

    D. DSP

    E. Transcoding

9. Which method is *not* a valid hardware DSP option?

    A. Installed on a network module (NM)

    B. Installed on a compact flash (CF) card

    C. Installed on a WIC module

    D. Installed on a VWIC module

    E. Directly plugged into the router motherboard

10. When RTP payloads are encrypted, which RTP header bit is set?

    A. Extension

    B. Padding

    C. Payload Type

    D. SSRC

11. When a phone call is made between two IP endpoints, how many RTP and RTCP streams are established?

    A. Four RTP and four RTCP

    B. One RTP and one RTCP

    C. Two RTP and one RTCP

    D. One RTP and two RTCP

    E. Two RTP and two RTCP

12. What types of signaling protocols allow the endpoints to contain the intelligence to place their own calls?

    A. Client-server

    B. SCCP

    C. Peer-to-peer

    D. CDP

13. What is needed to convert G.729a to G.711?

    A. PSTN resources

    B. Analog voice gateway

    C. Transcoding resources

    D. H.323 signaling

    E. SCCP signaling

14. What function is commonly present in a VoIP network but never found in a purely traditional telephony network?

    A. Call processing

    B. Call supervision

    C. Dial plans

    D. Transcoding

15. When two voice gateways are separated by a VoIP network, what type of dial peer is required to complete calls between the two sites?

    A. VoIP dial peer

    B. POTS dial peer

    C. IP dial peer

    D. PSTN dial peer

16. What is in charge of translating an analog voice signal to digital?
    A. SCCP gateway
    B. H.323
    C. DSP
    D. Transcoder
    E. MGCP gateway

17. What are the names for logical hops along a voice network that are used to complete a call from one phone to another?
    A. Dial strings and dial plans
    B. SCCP and SIP
    C. VLAN and CDP
    D. FXS and FXO
    E. Dial peers and call legs

18. What situation would require a voice gateway?
    A. Connecting calls over an IP WAN
    B. Connecting calls over a LAN
    C. Connecting calls over a high-speed MAN
    D. Connecting calls to the PSTN
    E. Connecting calls between two Ethernet switches

19. What type of voice gateway signaling protocol would you implement if you wish to configure dial peers directly on the voice gateway router?
    A. SCCP
    B. H.323
    C. RTP
    D. cRTP

20. What protocol is responsible for the sequencing of voice packets?
    A. RTCP
    B. Jitter
    C. G.711
    D. UDP
    E. RTP

Answers to Review Questions

1. A. The Infrastructure layer is where all route/switch, QoS, and security are performed.

2. D. QoS enforcement is handled by network devices located in the Infrastructure layer of the Unified Communications Model.

3. C. cRTP compresses the IP/UDP/RTP headers to shrink the overall packet size of voice packets.

4. D. The Emergency Responder keeps a database listing the location of all endpoints on the system. This information is relayed to emergency services when needed.

5. B. The Customer Contact Solution integrates value-added communications features to improve customer relations.

6. B. ATAs are basically IP phones that have analog ports attached to them so analog signals can be converted to digital and packetized for transport.

7. C. A DSP farm is a router (commonly the voice gateway router) that contains one or more DSP hardware chips.

8. A. Echo is often experienced on voice calls and is amplified by codec compression. DSPs are used to help reduce excess echo.

9. B. DSPs are hardware modules. They are not installed on CF cards.

10. B. The Padding bit is set, which indicates that the RTP has one or more octets at the end of the encapsulated packet that are not part of the payload. This additional information is typically used for encryption purposes.

11. E. A single phone call requires one RTP and one RTCP stream for *each* phone. This means that two RTP/RTCP streams are established for every IPT call.

12. C. Peer-to-peer signaling protocols give call-making intelligence directly to the endpoint.

13. C. Transcoding is the process of translating between different digital voice codecs.

14. D. Transcoding is the process of translating between digital voice codecs.

15. A. VoIP dial peers interconnect two voice gateways running VoIP.

16. C. A digital signal processor converts analog voice into digital and digital into analog.

17. E. Dial peers and call legs are logical hops required to connect an end-to-end call.

18. D. You need a voice gateway to connect to the PSTN.

19. B. H.323 is a peer-to-peer protocol, so all dial-peer configuration is decentralized from the CUCM and is done on the voice gateway.

20. E. RTP includes a sequencing field in its header.

Answers to Written Lab 3.1

1. Infrastructure layer, Call Control layer, Applications layer, Endpoints layer

2. SCCP and SIP

3. Call Control layer

4. QoS

5. Transcode

6. POTS and voice network

7. SCCP and SIP

8. Increased CPU utilization

9. 40 bytes

10. Pulse code modulation (PCM)

Chapter

4

Configuring the Network Infrastructure for Voice

THE CCNA VOICE EXAM TOPICS COVERED IN THIS CHAPTER INCLUDE THE FOLLOWING:

✓ **Describe and configure a Cisco network to support VoIP.**

- Describe the purpose of VLANs in a VoIP environment.
- Describe the environmental considerations to support VoIP.
- Configure switched infrastructure to support voice and data VLANs.
- Describe the purpose and operation of PoE.
- Identify the factors that impact voice quality.
- Describe how QoS addresses voice quality issues.
- Identify where QoS is deployed in the UC infrastructure.

✓ **Implement Cisco Unified Communications Manager Express to support endpoints using CLI.**

- Describe the requirements and correct settings for DHCP and NTP.
- Configure DHCP and NTP.

Anyone who loves Chinese food knows that rice is the foundation of a typical Chinese meal, whether it's Mongolian beef, sweet and sour chicken, or mu shu pork. Even though these three dishes are quite different in taste, they all have one thing in common. They are always served with rice. You can think of the network infrastructure as your bed of rice. The "main dish" in our network may be data or it may be voice; both utilize the same network. In this chapter we'll discuss how to utilize the network infrastructure to support voice capabilities.

We'll also explore the options available for powering your Cisco IP phones. Then you'll see how we configure our network for voice by configuring VLANs, trunks, and inter-VLAN routing. Next we will explore the VLAN Trunking Protocol to see what it is used for and how to configure it. We'll cover some quality of service (QoS) basics, and you'll see how to configure auto-QoS for VoIP. We'll then discuss how to eliminate potential voice problems by configuring various link-efficiency techniques. Finally, we'll cover some network services that help support voice functionality, including DHCP and NTP services.

Power Options for IP Phones

So you've decided to take the plunge and order some Cisco IP phones. When you receive and unpack the phones, the first question you might ask yourself is, "How the heck do I power these things up?" There are three ways of providing power to your phones:

- Power brick
- Powered patch panel/power injector
- Power over Ethernet (PoE) switch

Let's review each power method in detail.

Power Brick

The *power brick* is an obvious choice. It connects to a power port on the back of the phone and plugs into a standard 110V AC outlet on your wall. You then connect a Category 5 or 6 Ethernet cable into a switch to provide network connectivity.

> Power bricks do not come standard on any Cisco IP phone! Cisco assumes that you will use some method of PoE. Many people forget about this and are very disappointed when they have to place a second order for power bricks.

The power brick option may be useful in situations when you will be using only a handful of phones. Otherwise, you may want to investigate a PoE option, because it can be more cost effective, and quite simply, it's nicer to combine power and Ethernet in one cable to eliminate the need for a second connection to the phone. Figure 4.1 shows a Cisco phone receiving power from the power brick with a separate connection to the LAN using Ethernet.

FIGURE 4.1 The power brick option

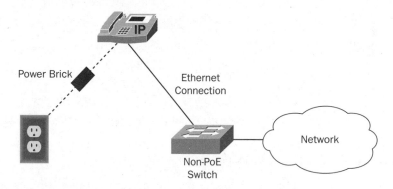

Powered Patch Panel/Power Injector

A second power option is to have a device that sits in between your IP phone and a non-PoE–capable switch. This is known as a midspan method because the power sits in the middle of the connection. A *powered patch panel* can terminate nonpowered Ethernet on one end and a powered Ethernet termination point on the other. These patch panels allow the power to be connected at the wiring closet, so no power brick is required, and the phone receives both power and Ethernet over a single Category 5 or 6 Ethernet cable. A standard Category 5/6 cable has a total of eight wires. 10BaseT and 100BaseT Ethernet utilize only RJ-45 pins 1, 2, 3, and 6. Pins 1 and 2 are for transmit and 3 and 6 are for receive. The other wires are essentially unused. Midspan switches will use the unused wires 4, 5, 7, and 8 to power the endpoints. The problem with this midspan setup is that 1000BaseT uses all four pairs of wires to transmit and receive. 1000BaseT must use pins 1, 2, 3, and 6 for power. Therefore, the midspan option is applicable only for 10/100BaseT.

Most patch panels typically come in either 24- or 48-port configurations. This may be the most cost-effective method if you have a significant investment in non-PoE–capable access switches. It also allows for a centralized location where you can provide uninterruptible power supply (UPS) power so the phones will remain functioning in the event of a power outage. Figure 4.2 shows how a powered patch panel can provide PoE functionality.

FIGURE 4.2   The powered patch panel option

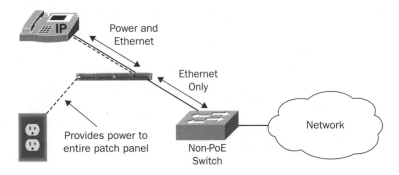

You can also purchase a *Cisco power injector*. These devices provide the same midspan "sit-in-the-middle" power function as the powered patch panel but only for a single phone.

Power over Ethernet Switch

The most streamlined and efficient method to provide power to phones (and other PoE-capable devices) is the *Power over Ethernet (PoE)* switch. The switch is responsible for detecting and outputting the required power on each switchport. By adding PoE functionality to the switch, fewer devices need UPS protection in the event of a power outage. Figure 4.3 shows how inline power switches provide power to endpoints.

FIGURE 4.3   The PoE switch option

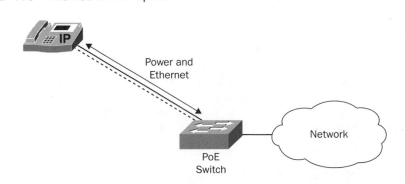

You need to be aware of a couple of "gotchas" when it comes to powering Cisco phones with any PoE option. The first deals with the type of inline power and quantity that the phone supports. The second thing to watch out for is ensuring your switch can properly handle the power load. Let's first look at the two inline power methods for Cisco switches, and then we'll look at switch power capacities.

Inline Power Method 1: Cisco Inline Power

Cisco began offering a proprietary Inline Power option to customers before a universal standard was available. In early 2000, Cisco began selling Catalyst switches with their proprietary *Inline Power (ILP)* functionality. Unlike the midspan switches, ILP uses the same RJ-45 pins 1, 2, 3, and 6 to provide power to the phones. Using the same wiring that Ethernet uses to transmit and receive is called *phantom power.* In a sense, ILP could have been used to power 1000Base-T Ethernet phones, but none were available at the time.

Cisco's proprietary Inline Power provides a fixed 6.3 watts of power to any device that supports the power method. ILP detects a capable device by sending a low-voltage AC signal across the transmit pairs and expects to receive the same signal coming back on the receive pairs. This is because the ILP capable phones have a low-pass filter that bridges the specific voltage signal from TX to RX. Once the switch receives the voltage back on the receive pair, it knows that the device requires power and initially sends 6.3 watts on that specific switchport. This provides enough power for the device to boot into low power mode. When the device has fully booted into low-power mode, CDP messages are exchanged between the switch and PoE device to negotiate the actual power required by the device up to 15.4 watts.

Inline Power Method 2: Cisco IEEE 802.3af

In mid-2003 the IETF came out with the *802.3af* PoE standard. This became the de facto standard for powering Ethernet over 10/100/1000BaseT. The standard states that power can be sent across the Cat5/6 cabling either on active transmit/receive pairs or over the inactive pairs for 10/100Base-T. Because 1000Base-T requires pins 1, 2, 3, and 6 for power, Cisco uses this standard on their 802.3af-supported PoE switches.

The 802.3af standard handles endpoint detection using a different method than ILP. It uses a low-powered DC signal sent across a copper pair. Just like ILP, the voltage is looped back to the switch by a slightly more advanced filter to signal that the end device is capable of receiving power. Unlike ILP, 802.3af has five specific classes of power that it can transmit. It knows the power level the end device requires by the voltage strength that it receives during the detection phase. Table 4.1 lists the 802.3af power classifications.

TABLE 4.1   IEEE 802.3af classifications

Class	Usage	Minimum Power Level at the Switch (in Watts)	Maximum Power Level at the Device (in Watts)
0	Default	15.4	0.44–12.95
1	Optional	4.0	0.44–3.84
2	Optional	7.0	3.84–6.49
3	Optional	15.4	6.49–12.95
4	Reserved for future	N/A	N/A

Class 0 is the default class and allocates a full 15.4 W of power to any device that falls into the category. This class is for devices whose vendor did not choose to implement a power classification. You'll commonly find this in inexpensive PoE products. Moving up, a device that declares itself as class 1 will have a maximum power requirement level between 0.44 and 3.84 W. The switch allocates 4.0 W of power for these devices. Class 2 allocates 7.0 W for devices requiring a maximum power level of 3.84 to 6.49 W. Class 3 is for any device that requires 6.49 to 12.95 W, and the switch allocates 15.4 W of power. Class 4 is not currently in use but was set aside so an additional power level can be added in the future.

Cisco Inline Power Switch Backward Compatibility

Because Cisco jumped the gun a few years early with their prestandard ILP, they now need to support the newer 802.3af as well as their proprietary ILP standard on their Catalyst line of PoE switches. The methods of power detection are somewhat different between ILP and 802.3af, and Cisco has come up with a method that allows its switches to detect the power requirements of Cisco phones. Here are the steps the PoE switch goes through for powering Cisco IP phones:

1. The switch uses continuous low-powered AC and DC signals to the PoE ports. If an AC signal is looped back to the switch, the device is ILP capable. If DC power is looped back to the switch, the device is 802.3af capable.

2. If the phone is only capable of using the ILP proprietary inline-power method, the phone boots into "low power mode" and negotiates the actual power required by the device using CDP. The phone then boots with the correct power requirements and the process ends.

3. If the phone is only capable of using 802.3af or supports both ILP and 802.3af, the switch and PoE device use additional low-voltage signaling to determine the power class. When the negotiation process is complete, the switch provides the necessary power to fully boot the IP phone.

Real World Scenario

The Right PoE for the Job

Tiana, a network engineer, was tasked with rolling out new Cisco 7971G IP desk phones with color displays to replace the older 7940 series phones already in place. Tiana thought this would be a simple project involving a few configuration changes on the CUCM and a matter of swapping out the old phones for new ones. However, this was not the case, because when Tiana attempted to swap the old phones with the new, she discovered that the new phones did not power up. Tiana was confused by this because the phones were using a PoE module in a 6500 series switch. The PoE module worked perfectly for the old phones, so why didn't it work for the new ones?

It turns out that the PoE module that was installed in the switch used the older Cisco ILP method. This worked fine for the 7940 phones because they supported both the ILP and 80.2.3af standard. The newer 7971G phones, however, are only capable of supporting the 802.3af standard.

This discovery caused a short delay in the rollout of the new phones. Tiana purchased a switch module offering 802.3af power, the 7965 phones powered up, and the project was finally complete.

Cisco PoE Intelligent Power Management

Depending on the types of endpoints you deploy and the type of switch and power supply used, you need to be aware that you can eventually exhaust the amount of power available to the switch. If you add too many PoE phones to a switchport, the switch may have already allocated all the available power, and therefore your device will not receive the necessary electricity to power the phone. Also, the 802.3af classification system can often set aside more power than is necessary, which can unnecessarily limit the number of PoE devices that can be powered. To better understand this situation, we need to briefly discuss how to determine how many watts a power supply can generate. While this will not give you an exact number, it should get you fairly close. It's really just a simple math equation:

watts = volts × amps

Let's use a Cisco Catalyst 4506-E with 2-48 port 10/100/1000 PoE modules and a Supervisor 4 module as our example. The standard AC power supply is 110 volts with a 15-amp circuit. Therefore

watts = 110 × 15

watts = 1650

Cisco plays its power limits conservatively, however, and it rates the 4500 Series 110V 15-amp power supplies at 1300 watts. This is to prevent any circuit trips when power reaches the limit of 1650 watts. The maximum amount of power to boot and run the switch supervisor module and line cards is approximately 600 watts. So let's subtract that from our total:

1300 − 600 = 700 watts

That's how much power we have to allocate to various PoE devices that we can run off the switch. Now let's say you want to add a number of Cisco 7965G IP phones to this switch. The 7965G is an 802.3af class 3 device. According to the 802.3af specification, each 7965G phone added to this switch consumes 15.4 watts of power. Therefore, how many phones can we put on this switch before the power is maxed out?

700/15.4 = 45.45

So even though we have 96 PoE ports on the switch, we can power only 45 of the 7965 phones. Technically, we do have two power supplies. By default they run in redundancy mode. This is basically an active/standby situation where you can utilize the power from only one power supply. You can configure them to utilize both power supplies by issuing the power redundancy-mode combined command.

I do not recommend you do this, however, unless you are really need the extra power. But you should at least know it's an option to have in your back pocket if needed.

Cisco switches also have the ability to throttle back allocated power resources so that unused watts can be put back into the power allocation pool. Using our 7965G phone example again, according to the 802.3af standard, 15.4 watts will be allocated to the phone. In reality, the phone will use a maximum of 12 watts. During the Cisco PoE switch-negotiation process using CDP, the switch will negotiate the power allocation down to the 12-watt limit. This is what Cisco refers to as *Intelligent Power Management (IPM)*. So now that we require only 12 watts of power per phone, let's recalculate how many phones we can fully power on our switch:

700/12 = 58.33

Using a Cisco PoE solution with IPM, we can power 58 phones instead of 45.

Cisco PoE Management Modes

The power inline IOS commands allow you to change PoE settings on a port-by-port basis. Let's look at the PoE interface commands available to us:

```
4506-switch(config-if)#power inline ?
  auto       Automatically detect and power inline devices
  never      Never apply inline power
  static     High priority inline power interface
```

This is the default setting. If the endpoint is a Cisco device such as a Cisco 7960 IP phone, the power settings will be negotiated automatically. To demonstrate this, let's look at a show power inline command output on the 4500 switch:

```
4506-switch#show power inline gigabitEthernet 3/2
Interface Admin  Oper         Power(Watts)      Device              Class
                              From PS    To Device
--------- ------ ----------   ---------- ---------- ------------------- -----

Gi3/2     auto   on           13.5       12.0       Cisco IP Phone 7965 3

Interface  AdminPowerMax
           (Watts)
---------- ---------------

Gi3/2      15.4
```

We can see that the Admin setting is set to auto. Using CDP, the switch detected the Cisco 7965 phone. The switch placed it into 802.3af power settings as a class 3 device and thus allocated 15.4 watts of power to it. However, the switch went one step further and dropped the power output to the device to 12.0 watts.

Now see what happens if we change port 3/2 so it will not send any power on the port regardless of what the device is on the other end:

```
4506-switch(config)#interface gi3/2
4506-switch(config-if)#power inline never
```

After running this command, you see that the port is no longer powering the phone. Note that both the Admin and Oper status are set to off:

```
4506-switch#show power inline gi3/2
Interface Admin  Oper         Power(Watts)      Device              Class
                              From PS    To Device
--------- ------ ----------   ---------- ---------- ------------------- -----

Gi3/2     off    off          0          0          n/a                 n/a

Interface  AdminPowerMax
           (Watts)
---------- ---------------

Gi3/2      15.4
```

Finally, let's see what the results are with our 7965 phone if we statically set the power first to 6 watts and then to 15.4 watts:

```
4506-switch(config)#interface gi3/2
4506-switch(config-if)#power inline static max 6000
4506-switch(config-if)#
1d22h: %ILPOWER-5-ILPOWER_POWER_DENY: Interface Gi3/2: inline power denied
```

When I set the max power to 6 watts, a log message is generated telling us "inline power denied." Because this is a class 3 device, we have to configure the minimum watts for the 802.3af standard. The show power inline instruction shows the Admin status as static but the Oper status as POWER_DENY. Also note that the switch does not identify the device as being a 7965, because that needs a minimum of 7 watts to exchange CDP information.

```
4506-switch#show power inline gi3/2
Interface Admin  Oper         Power(Watts)       Device              Class
                              From PS    To Device
--------- ------ ----------  ---------- ---------- ------------------- -----

Gi3/2     static power-deny 0          0          Ieee PD             3

Interface  AdminPowerMax
           (Watts)
---------- ---------------

Gi3/2     6.0
```

Let's bring the phone back online by configuring the static max to 15.4 watts:

```
4506-switch(config)#interface gi3/2
4506-switch(config-if)#power inline static max 15400
4506-switch(config-if)#
```

Now we see that the phone is recognized and boots. It is now utilizing more power (a full 15.4 watts) than when it is configured to auto-negotiate the power:

```
4506-switch#sh power inline gi3/2
Interface Admin  Oper         Power(Watts)       Device              Class
                              From PS    To Device
--------- ------ ----------  ---------- ---------- ------------------- -----

Gi3/2     static on          17.3       15.4       Cisco IP Phone 7965 3

Interface  AdminPowerMax
           (Watts)
```

```
---------  ---------------
```

```
Gi3/2      15.4
```

The `power inline static` command can be useful if you have non-Cisco phones that you know use only 8 watts, for example. Because non-Cisco devices cannot negotiate using CDP, each port will allocate the full 15.4 watts of power to the device. You can hard-code the power settings to 8 watts to save 7.4 watts per port!

Understanding and Configuring VLANs and Voice VLANs

I highly recommend that you logically separate voice and data devices on your network. To see why this step is necessary, you need to understand the concept of virtual LANs. We'll see how to configure VLAN trunk links to span logical VLANs across multiple physical Layer 2 switches. Then we'll look at how to configure Layer 3 inter-VLAN routing so that devices on separate VLANs can communicate with one another. I'll then introduce you to the VLAN Trunking Protocol (VTP), explaining what it is used for and how to configure it. Finally, we'll look at voice VLANs to see why they are needed and how to deploy them in your network. Let's get started:

An Overview of VLANs

A *virtual LAN (VLAN)* is a logical segmentation of the network that allows a group of devices to act as if they were on the same physical network. Devices that reside on the same VLAN share the same broadcast domain. Figure 4.4 shows how a single physical switch can be logically broken up into two separate "logical" switches.

FIGURE 4.4 Logical VLAN separation

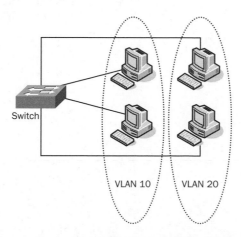

In this example we have four PCs connected to a Layer 2 switch. The switch is configured to have two PCs in VLAN 10 and the other two in VLAN 20. All devices within a VLAN are typically configured in the same IP subnet. So using our example, devices residing in VLAN 10 will be configured with an IP address within the 192.168.10.X/24 range, whereas devices in VLAN 20 are configured with an IP address within the 192.168.20.X/24 IP space.

Breaking up broadcast domains is critical on larger networks. Broadcast traffic in flat networks with hundreds or thousands of devices can lead to degraded performance. VLANs allow an administrator to break up a single broadcast domain into multiple domains to decrease broadcast traffic. Let's look at how we would configure VLANs on a Layer 2 Cisco switch.

Configuring VLANs

Using Figure 4.4 as our example, let's configure a Layer 2 switch for VLANs 10 and 20. We're going to say that VLAN 10 is our Sales department VLAN and VLAN 20 is our Marketing department. Before we configure anything, let's see what our switch is currently configured with by issuing a show vlan brief command:

Switch#**show vlan brief**

```
VLAN Name                             Status     Ports
---- -------------------------------- ---------  -------------------------------
1    default                          active     Fa0/1, Fa0/2, Fa0/3, Fa0/4
                                                 Fa0/5, Fa0/6, Fa0/7, Fa0/8
                                                 Fa0/9, Fa0/10, Fa0/11, Fa0/12
                                                 Fa0/13, Fa0/14, Fa0/15, Fa0/16
                                                 Fa0/17, Fa0/18, Fa0/19, Fa0/20
                                                 Fa0/21, Fa0/22, Fa0/23, Fa0/24
                                                 Fa0/25, Fa0/26, Fa0/27, Fa0/28
                                                 Fa0/29, Fa0/30, Fa0/31, Fa0/32
                                                 Fa0/33, Fa0/34, Fa0/35, Fa0/36
                                                 Fa0/37, Fa0/38, Fa0/39, Fa0/40
                                                 Fa0/41, Fa0/42, Fa0/43, Fa0/44
                                                 Fa0/45, Fa0/46, Fa0/47, Fa0/48
                                                 Gi0/1, Gi0/2
1002 fddi-default                     act/unsup
1003 token-ring-default               act/unsup
1004 fddinet-default                  act/unsup
1005 trnet-default                    act/unsup
```

The default setup for a Cisco switch is that all ports reside in VLAN 1. Now let's configure our two new VLANs and give them proper names:

```
Switch#configure terminal
Switch(config)# vlan 10
Switch(config-vlan)#name Sales
Switch(config)#vlan 20
Switch(config-vlan)#name Marketing
Switch(config-vlan)#end
Switch#show vlan brief
```

To verify that we properly created our two new VLANs, we'll run another show vlan brief command:

Switch#**show vlan brief**

```
VLAN Name                             Status    Ports
---- -------------------------------- --------- -------------------------------
1    default                          active    Fa0/1, Fa0/2, Fa0/3, Fa0/4
                                                Fa0/5, Fa0/6, Fa0/7, Fa0/8
                                                Fa0/9, Fa0/10, Fa0/11, Fa0/12
                                                Fa0/13, Fa0/14, Fa0/15, Fa0/16
                                                Fa0/17, Fa0/18, Fa0/19, Fa0/20
                                                Fa0/21, Fa0/22, Fa0/23, Fa0/24
                                                Fa0/25, Fa0/26, Fa0/27, Fa0/28
                                                Fa0/29, Fa0/30, Fa0/31, Fa0/32
                                                Fa0/33, Fa0/34, Fa0/35, Fa0/36
                                                Fa0/37, Fa0/38, Fa0/39, Fa0/40
                                                Fa0/41, Fa0/42, Fa0/43, Fa0/44
                                                Fa0/45, Fa0/46, Fa0/47, Fa0/48
                                                Gi0/1, Gi0/2
10   Sales                            active
20   Marketing                        active
1002 fddi-default                     act/unsup
1003 token-ring-default               act/unsup
1004 fddinet-default                  act/unsup
1005 trnet-default                    act/unsup
```

Our two new VLANs have successfully been configured, but all the ports still reside in VLAN 1. Let's move ports Fa0/1–24 into the Sales VLAN and Fa0/25–48 into the Marketing

VLAN by entering into config-if-range mode to configure multiple switchports and then issuing the switchport access vlan command to set the ports to reside in the proper VLAN:

```
Switch#configure terminal
Switch(config)#interface range fastEthernet 0/1 - 24
Switch(config-if-range)#switchport access vlan 10
Switch(config-if-range)#exit
Switch(config)#interface range fastEthernet 0/25 - 48
Switch(config-if-range)#switchport access vlan 20
Switch(config-if-range)#end
```

To verify that our ports are now in the correct VLANs, let's run the show vlan brief command one last time:

```
Switch#show vlan brief

VLAN Name                             Status    Ports
---- -------------------------------- --------- -------------------------------
1    default                          active    Gi0/1, Gi0/2
10   Sales                            active    Fa0/1, Fa0/2, Fa0/3, Fa0/4
                                                Fa0/5, Fa0/6, Fa0/7, Fa0/8
                                                Fa0/9, Fa0/10, Fa0/11, Fa0/12
                                                Fa0/13, Fa0/14, Fa0/15, Fa0/16
                                                Fa0/17, Fa0/18, Fa0/19, Fa0/20
                                                Fa0/21, Fa0/22, Fa0/23, Fa0/24
20   Marketing                        active    Fa0/25, Fa0/26, Fa0/27, Fa0/28
                                                Fa0/29, Fa0/30, Fa0/31, Fa0/32
                                                Fa0/33, Fa0/34, Fa0/35, Fa0/36
                                                Fa0/37, Fa0/38, Fa0/39, Fa0/40
                                                Fa0/41, Fa0/42, Fa0/43, Fa0/44
                                                Fa0/45, Fa0/46, Fa0/47, Fa0/48
1002 fddi-default                     act/unsup
1003 token-ring-default               act/unsup
1004 fddinet-default                  act/unsup
1005 trnet-default                    act/unsup
```

As you can see, ports Fa0/1–24 now reside in the Sales VLAN, and ports Fa0/25–48 are in the Marketing VLAN.

Configuring VLAN Trunks

The previous example showed how to configure VLANs on a single switchport. But what if you have a network that spans multiple floors and requires the interconnection of multiple switches? Taking this scenario one step further, what if you have Sales and Marketing employees connected to multiple switches, but you would like them to reside in the same logical VLAN? The solution to this problem is interconnecting switches with a *VLAN trunk* port. Figure 4.5 shows our new network topology with two switches that have VLANs 10 and 20 trunked between them.

FIGURE 4.5   A VLAN trunk

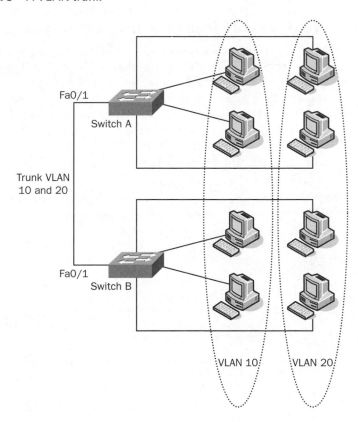

A VLAN trunk port is a link between two Layer 2 switches that can transport traffic from multiple VLANs. It keeps the traffic between the VLANs separate by tagging each frame. VLAN tagging essentially places a VLAN identifier on each frame. In our example, frames on VLAN 10 that need to go from one switch to the other are tagged as belonging to VLAN 10.

Detailed discussion of VLAN trunking is beyond the scope of this book, but it is an important part of preparing the network infrastructure for voice applications. I'll show you the most common method for configuring VLAN trunk links using the 802.1Q trunking protocol. 802.1Q is an IEEE standard that is supported by virtually every network vendor in the world.

Using Figure 4.5 as our example, let's configure a VLAN trunk link between Switches A and B using the 802.1Q trunking protocol on port Fa0/1. For simplicity's sake, let's assume that both Switch A and Switch B have been identically configured to switch VLAN 10 and 20. Configuring an 802.1Q trunk between the switches requires the following steps.

Step 1: Configure the VLAN Trunk Encapsulation Type

You can configure your VLAN trunk encapsulation for either the 802.1Q standard or Cisco's proprietary ISL trunking. I highly recommend that you configure your trunk using 802.1Q. I haven't seen anyone using ISL trunks for years. You can also configure one side of the trunk to negotiate the encapsulation method, but since we know we want to use 802.1Q, just keep it simple and specifically configure it as such. The command for configuring VLAN trunk encapsulation is `switchport trunk encapsulation`.

Step 2: Configure the VLAN Trunk Mode

There are several options for the VLAN trunk's operational mode, including dynamic desirable and dynamic auto. But since we know we want to configure the port as a trunk, we can simply hard-code the port using the `switchport mode trunk` command. Let's configure Switch A and Switch B for trunking on port Fa0/1.

Here's the Switch A configuration command:

```
Switch-A#configure terminal
Switch-A(config)#interface fa0/1
Switch-A(config-if)#switchport trunk encapsulation dot1q
Switch-A(config-if)#switchport mode trunk
Switch-A(config-if)#end
```

Here's the Switch B configuration command:

```
Switch-B#configure terminal
Switch-B(config)#interface fa0/1
Switch-B(config-if)#switchport trunk encapsulation dot1q
Switch-B(config-if)#switchport mode trunk
Switch-B(config-if)#end
```

Now let's issue a `show interfaces trunk` command on Switch A to see what our trunk looks like:

```
Switch-A#show interfaces trunk
```

```
Port        Mode            Encapsulation  Status       Native vlan
Fa0/1       on              802.1q         trunking     1

Port        Vlans allowed on trunk
Fa0/1       1-4094

Port        Vlans allowed and active in management domain
Fa0/1       1,10,20

Port        Vlans in spanning tree forwarding state and not pruned
Fa0/1       1,10,20
Switch-A#
```

At this point, our VLAN trunk is up and running and is successfully tagging frames on VLANs 10 and 20 between the two switches. There is one last cleanup step that is typically taken to keep the configuration clean. As you'll notice from the output of the show interfaces trunk command, the VLANs that are allowed to send traffic between the two switches are 1–4094. This basically means that any new VLANs created on the two switches can be trunked. Just as a precautionary measure, I typically limit which VLANs are allowed on the trunk by issuing a switchport trunk allowed command on both trunk interfaces to limit trunking to VLANs 10 and 20. Let's do this now.

Here's the Switch A configuration command:

```
Switch-A#configure terminal
Switch-A(config)#interface fa0/1
Switch-A(config-if)#switchport trunk allowed vlan 10,20
Switch-A(config-if)#end
```

Here's the Switch B configuration command:

```
Switch-B#configure terminal
Switch-B(config)#interface fa0/1
Switch-B(config-if)#switchport trunk allowed vlan 10,20
Switch-B(config-if)#end
```

Now when we run the show interfaces trunk command again, we see that only VLANs 10 and 20 are allowed to traverse the trunk:

Switch-A#**show interfaces trunk**

```
Port        Mode            Encapsulation  Status       Native vlan
Fa0/1       on              802.1Q         trunking     1
```

```
Port       Vlans allowed on trunk
Fa0/1      10,20

Port       Vlans allowed and active in management domain
Fa0/1      10,20

Port       Vlans in spanning tree forwarding state and not pruned
Fa0/1      10,20
Switch-A#
```

Now we have a two-switch network with two VLANs that are properly trunked together. A Sales department user on a PC on Switch A, VLAN 10, can communicate with another Sales department user attached to Switch B on VLAN 10. The same is true for the Marketing department users on VLAN 20. But what happens if a Sales department user PC needs to communicate with a Marketing department PC? Because VLANs break up switches into multiple logical switches, the PCs on different VLANs currently have no way of communicating with each other. To solve this dilemma, we need to configure inter-VLAN routing.

Implementing Inter-VLAN Routing

When you statically configure IP addressing on a PC, you are required to enter the following information:

- A unique IP address
- A subnet mask
- A default gateway

Every VLAN on your network is assigned its own IP subnet. For example, our Sales VLAN (VLAN 10) has been given the following IP space:

IP subnet: 192.168.10.X/24

Default gateway: 192.168.10.1

Because the IP space is a /24, the IP space has a subnet mask of 255.255.255.0. End devices such as PCs can be assigned to IP addresses between 192.168.10.2 and 192.168.10.254.

Our Marketing VLAN (VLAN 20) is in a separate IP space:

IP subnet: 192.168.20.X/24

Default gateway: 192.168.20.1

When a PC on VLAN 10 talks to another PC on the same VLAN, it uses broadcast messages to initially find the end device. Because broadcasts are contained within a specific VLAN, we need a different way for a PC on VLAN 10 to figure out how to reach a PC on VLAN 20. This is what the default gateway is for. The default gateway is configured on a Layer 3 device such as a router. It is the router's job to intercept requests from devices on one VLAN and send them to devices located on another VLAN. Thus the term *gateway*, because it is the only way to escape the confines of a VLAN. Router gateways keep track of other networks and store this information in a routing table. This is how *inter-VLAN routing* works.

There are essentially three methods for configuring inter-VLAN routing:

- Individual router links for each VLAN
- VLAN trunked router link (router-on-a-stick)
- Layer 3 switching

Let's look at each of these to see how they differ and how they are configured.

For simplicity's sake, we assume that in each of the three configuration scenarios we have the switch preconfigured with VLANs 10 and 20.

Individual Router Links

One way to set up inter-VLAN routing is to configure a separate router link for every VLAN on your network. In our two-VLAN environment, the design would be set up like Figure 4.6.

FIGURE 4.6 Individual router links

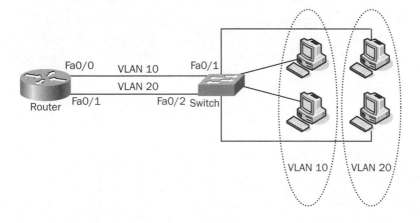

On the switch side, all that needs to be done is to ensure that the interface is configured as an access port in the correct VLAN. On the router side, we need to enable each router interface and configure it to be the default gateway. Let's look at how we go about configuring our router and switch to route VLANs 10 and 20 between themselves. Here is the switch configuration command:

```
Switch#configure terminal
Switch(config)#interface fa0/1
Switch(config-if)#switchport access vlan 10
Switch(config-if)#interface fa0/2
Switch(config-if)#switchport access vlan 20
Switch(config-if)#end
```

Here is the router configuration command:

```
Router#configure terminal
Router(config)#interface fastEthernet 0/0
Router(config-if)#ip address 192.168.10.1 255.255.255.0
Router(config-if)#exit
Router(config)#interface fastEthernet 0/1
Router(config-if)#ip address 192.168.20.1 255.255.255.0
```

You can verify that the routes for your two networks are configured by issuing a show ip route command on the router:

```
Router#show ip route
Codes: C - connected, S - static, I - IGRP, R - RIP, M - mobile, B - BGP
       D - EIGRP, EX - EIGRP external, O - OSPF, IA - OSPF inter area
       N1 - OSPF NSSA external type 1, N2 - OSPF NSSA external type 2
       E1 - OSPF external type 1, E2 - OSPF external type 2, E - EGP
       i - IS-IS, L1 - IS-IS level-1, L2 - IS-IS level-2, ia - IS-IS inter area
       * - candidate default, U - per-user static route, o - ODR
       P - periodic downloaded static route

Gateway of last resort is not set

C    192.168.10.0/24 is directly connected, FastEthernet0/0
C    192.168.20.0/24 is directly connected, FastEthernet0/1
```

Because both networks are directly connected, the router knows exactly how to reach the networks. When a PC on VLAN 10 communicates with a PC on VLAN 20, traffic goes out switchport Fa0/1 to router port Fa0/0. The router then looks up how to access the IP space that VLAN occupies. The router determines that VLAN 20 traffic should be sent out router interface Fa0/1, which sends it to switchport Fa0/2, where it ultimately reaches the PC.

If you have a very small number of VLANs on your network, the individual router link design may work for you. However, you can see that every new VLAN requires both a separate switchport and router port. Therefore, this type of inter-VLAN routing design does not scale well.

Next, let's look at how we can configure an 802.1Q trunk link between the router and switch so we can send multiple VLANs across the same link. Using this setup, we eliminate the need for separate ports per VLAN, and therefore this method scales much better.

VLAN Trunked Router Link

We've already discussed how to configure a VLAN trunk link between two Layer 2 switches. Configuring a trunked connection between a router and a switch is very similar. In fact, the switch configuration is identical. Figure 4.7 shows how a single VLAN trunk link can transport multiple VLANs from the switch to the router to provide inter-VLAN routing.

FIGURE 4.7 A VLAN trunked router link

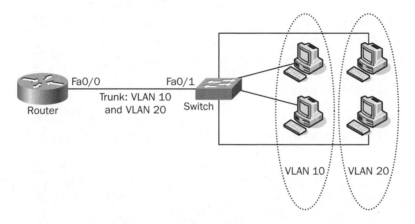

Looking at the figure, you can see how this design gets the nickname "router on a stick." A single link is responsible for handling inter-VLAN routing. Let's start configuring our VLAN trunked router link configuration by first setting up the 802.1Q trunk port on the switch:

Here's the switch configuration:

```
Switch#configure terminal
Switch-A(config)#interface fa0/2
Switch-A(config-if)#switchport trunk encapsulation dot1q
Switch-A(config-if)#switchport mode trunk
Switch(config-if)#switchport trunk allowed vlan 10,20
Switch(config-if)#end
```

Next, we'll configure VLAN trunking on the router Fa0/0 interface. To accomplish this, we need to ensure that the physical interface is enabled, by entering interface configuration mode and issuing a no shutdown command. Then we need to create subinterfaces on our Fa0/0 port. These subinterfaces handle traffic for a specific VLAN. You can think of them as virtual ports off a single physical port. On these subinterfaces, you configure the encapsulation as dot1Q (for 802.1Q trunking). This allows the router interface to understand 802.1Q tagging. Finally, you apply your gateway IP address to the subinterface.

Here's the router configuration:

```
Router#conf t
Enter configuration commands, one per line.  End with CNTL/Z.
Router(config)#int fa0/0
Router(config-if)#no shutdown
Router(config-if)#exit
Router(config)#int fa0/0.10
Router(config-subif)#encapsulation dot1Q 10
Router(config-subif)#ip address 192.168.10.1 255.255.255.0
Router(config-subif)#exit
Router(config)#interface fastEthernet 0/0.20
Router(config-subif)#encapsulation dot1Q 20
Router(config-subif)#ip address 192.168.20.1 255.255.255.0
Router(config-subif)#end
```

To verify that our VLAN trunk is properly configured, we'll go back to the switch we previously configured and issue a show interface trunk command:

```
Switch#show interface trunk

Port        Mode        Encapsulation  Status      Native vlan
Fa0/2       on          802.1Q         trunking    1

Port        Vlans allowed on trunk
Fa0/2       10,20

Port        Vlans allowed and active in management domain
Fa0/2       10,20

Port        Vlans in spanning tree forwarding state and not pruned
Fa0/2       10,20
Switch#
```

The VLAN trunk is properly configured on the switch and is ready to send both VLAN 10 and 20 traffic destined to the default gateway on switchport Fa0/2.

The limit to the number of subinterfaces configured on a physical router port varies from device to device, but this number is in the hundreds for newer Cisco routers. Keep in mind that all of these subinterfaces share the bandwidth of the single link, so it is important not to oversubscribe the link. For example, if we trunk VLAN 10 and 20 on a 100Mbps FastEthernet connection, they both have to share that 100 Mbps. The more VLANs you add, the more traffic is sent over the link, and ultimately the more congested the trunk links become.

To verify our routing, we'll connect to the router and issue the show ip route command:

```
Router#show ip route
Codes: C - connected, S - static, I - IGRP, R - RIP, M - mobile, B - BGP
       D - EIGRP, EX - EIGRP external, O - OSPF, IA - OSPF inter area
       N1 - OSPF NSSA external type 1, N2 - OSPF NSSA external type 2
       E1 - OSPF external type 1, E2 - OSPF external type 2, E - EGP
       i - IS-IS, L1 - IS-IS level-1, L2 - IS-IS level-2, ia - IS-IS inter area
       * - candidate default, U - per-user static route, o - ODR
       P - periodic downloaded static route

Gateway of last resort is not set

C    192.168.10.0/24 is directly connected, FastEthernet0/0.10
C    192.168.20.0/24 is directly connected, FastEthernet0/0.20
Router#
```

You'll notice that this routing table output looks very similar to the routing table for the individual router link. The main difference is that the router sees the IP networks as being on the same physical interface, Fa0/0, but it distinguishes the 192.168.10.0/24 subnet as belonging to subinterface Fa0/0.10 and the 192.168.20.0/24 network as belonging to Fa0/0.20. The router tags the packet with the proper destination 802.1Q VLAN identifier, and the switch is responsible for removing the tag and sending it to the correct destination switchport.

The VLAN trunked router link design is far more scalable than the individual router link design. You will find this setup in many small to medium-size businesses. If you have a fairly large Ethernet LAN and need the ability to add many VLANs on your network without being concerned about congestion on trunked router links, you can implement Layer 3 switching using special Cisco multilayer switches.

Layer 3 Switching

Layer 3 switching essentially takes the concept of a VLAN trunked router link between a Layer 2 switch and a router and combines the Layer 2 switch and router into a single device. A Layer 3 switch (also known as a *multilayer switch*) has the ability to create Layer 3 VLAN interfaces on the switch hardware. Now, instead of having to traverse a VLAN trunked link to reach a default gateway, which is rerouted directly back out the same link to the switch, this process is performed on the switch using dedicated hardware modules called Application-Specific Integrated Circuits (ASICs). The traffic is then switched on a Layer 3 backplane, which can typically handle several gigabits of bandwidth or more. This allows the administrator to create many more VLANs on a network without the worry of overutilizing a trunk link. It is also the preferred method for administrators because they need only support one Layer 3 switch instead of a Layer 2 switch and a router. Figure 4.8 shows how a Layer 3 switch is responsible for both the switching and routing functions.

FIGURE 4.8   A Layer 3 switch

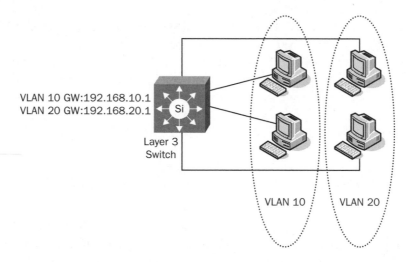

To configure Layer 3 switching, you need to ensure that your switch is capable of running in Layer 3 mode. By default, Layer 3 switching is disabled. To enable it, you must issue the ip routing configuration command. Next, you configure VLAN interfaces for each VLAN and assign the subnet gateway IP address to the virtual interface. Finally, you issue a no shutdown command to enable the virtual interface. Let's go ahead and start the configuration:

```
L3-Switch#configure terminal
L3-Switch(config)#ip routing
L3-Switch(config)#interface vlan 10
L3-Switch(config-if)#ip address 192.168.10.1 255.255.255.0
L3-Switch(config-if)#no shutdown
```

```
L3-Switch(config-if)#exit
L3-Switch(config)#interface vlan 20
L3-Switch(config-if)#ip address 192.168.20.1 255.255.255.0
L3-Switch(config-if)#no shutdown
L3-Switch(config-if)#end
```

Now that we've configured our VLAN interfaces, we can view them just as if they were physical Ethernet ports. Let's look at the VLAN 10 and VLAN 20 virtual interfaces by issuing a show interface vlan command:

```
L3-Switch#show interface vlan 10
Vlan10 is up, line protocol is up
  Hardware is EtherSVI, address is 000b.465e.5600 (bia 000b.465e.5600)
  Internet address is 192.168.10.1/24
  MTU 1500 bytes, BW 1000000 Kbit, DLY 10 usec,
     reliability 255/255, txload 1/255, rxload 1/255
  Encapsulation ARPA, loopback not set
  ARP type: ARPA, ARP Timeout 04:00:00
  Last input never, output never, output hang never
  Last clearing of "show interface" counters never
  Input queue: 0/75/0/0 (size/max/drops/flushes); Total output drops: 0
  Queueing strategy: fifo
  Output queue: 0/40 (size/max)
  5 minute input rate 0 bits/sec, 0 packets/sec
  5 minute output rate 0 bits/sec, 0 packets/sec
     0 packets input, 0 bytes, 0 no buffer
     Received 0 broadcasts (0 IP multicast)
     0 runts, 0 giants, 0 throttles
     0 input errors, 0 CRC, 0 frame, 0 overrun, 0 ignored
     0 packets output, 0 bytes, 0 underruns
     0 output errors, 0 interface resets
     0 output buffer failures, 0 output buffers swapped out

L3-Switch#show interface vlan 20
Vlan10 is up, line protocol is up
  Hardware is EtherSVI, address is 000b.465e.5800 (bia 000b.465e.5800)
  Internet address is 192.168.20.1/24
  MTU 1500 bytes, BW 1000000 Kbit, DLY 10 usec,
     reliability 255/255, txload 1/255, rxload 1/255
  Encapsulation ARPA, loopback not set
  ARP type: ARPA, ARP Timeout 04:00:00
```

```
Last input never, output never, output hang never
Last clearing of "show interface" counters never
Input queue: 0/75/0/0 (size/max/drops/flushes); Total output drops: 0
Queueing strategy: fifo
Output queue: 0/40 (size/max)
5 minute input rate 0 bits/sec, 0 packets/sec
5 minute output rate 0 bits/sec, 0 packets/sec
    0 packets input, 0 bytes, 0 no buffer
    Received 0 broadcasts (0 IP multicast)
    0 runts, 0 giants, 0 throttles
    0 input errors, 0 CRC, 0 frame, 0 overrun, 0 ignored
    0 packets output, 0 bytes, 0 underruns
    0 output errors, 0 interface resets
    0 output buffer failures, 0 output buffers swapped out
```

You can see that the VLAN 10 and 20 interfaces are up and the hardware states that it is EtherSVI. SVI stands for *switch virtual interface*. Essentially, it's a virtual interface created in software but switched in hardware using special ASICs.

Keep in mind that the VLAN interface will be in a "down" state until you have a device on that VLAN. If you are having problems configuring the VLAN and cannot get it to an "up" state, configure a switch access port to belong to that particular VLAN and attach a PC to the switchport. The VLAN will then move from being down to up. You may alternately have an enabled trunk port carrying that VLAN between switches to achieve the same up state.

You now have the skills to create VLANs and inter-VLAN routing. In larger networks with many switches and VLANs, configuration of VLANs can become an administrative nuisance. The next section will discuss VTP, a tool that you can use to help reduce the VLAN administration burden on your network.

Using the VLAN Trunking Protocol

Every switch on your network maintains a VLAN database for every VLAN it knows about. If your VLANs span multiple switches, it can become burdensome to configure the VLAN so that it is visible in every VLAN database switch. The *VLAN trunking protocol (VTP)* is a way to add, delete, and modify VLANs on a single switch and have that VLAN information propagate into the VLAN database on other switches within your network.

To completely delete previously configured VLANs that are in the VLAN database of a switch, you can issue the following global command:

`Switch#delete vlan.dat`

The `vlan.dat` file is where the VLAN database is stored on the switch. You can then reload the switch, and all the previously configured VLANs are no longer there.

You need to understand several concepts in VTP before using the protocol. In fact, you need to be very careful with VTP because it is possible to accidentally delete VLANs when adding new switches to the network if you aren't careful! I'll first tell you about the three VTP modes and when they should be used. Next I'll discuss VTP revision numbers and what they are used for. Then I'll review the most common VTP configuration options used in production networks.

Choosing a VTP Mode

You can configure a switch to be in one of three VTP modes: server, client, or transparent. Each mode serves a different purpose, and you should take care to configure each switch accordingly if you are planning to use VTP on your network. Here's a summary of the three VTP modes you can choose from.

VTP Server

The *VTP server* mode allows an administrator to add, delete, and modify VLANs on the network over trunked links. All changes are propagated to other switches within the VTP domain. VTP server is the default VTP mode on all Cisco switches.

VTP Client

VTP client mode listens to the VTP server and copies its VLAN settings to its own VLAN database. It also forwards the VTP update messages from the server to other switches within the same VTP domain on its trunked links. This mode does not allow you to add, delete, or modify VLANs.

VTP Transparent

VTP transparent mode basically disables VTP on the switch. You can add, delete, and modify VLAN information on the switch, but it never propagates this information to any other switch. Also, if the switch in this mode receives VTP update messages from other switches it is trunked with, it ignores the updates locally but will pass them on to connected neighbors.

Understanding VTP Revision Numbers

VTP uses the concept of revision numbers to help ensure that the most recent VLAN database changes are propagated to all other switches within the same VTP domain. The higher the revision number, the more trusted the information, and therefore that is the VLAN information that is updated to every other switch.

Each time a VLAN change is made on the switch (adding, deleting, or updating), the revision number increments. This revision number is then incremented on all switches within the VTP domain to ensure consistency.

You must be very careful when adding a switch to a network that is configured for VTP server mode and uses the same VTP domain and/ or password. If you have a switch that you've been tinkering around with in the lab setting up various test VLANs, each VLAN add/delete will increment the VLAN revision number. If the newly added switch's revision number ends up being higher than the revision number of the current production switches, VTP will assume that the new switch has more recent VLAN information and will overwrite all of your VLANs with the information contained on the new switch. To ensure that this does not happen, you should always reboot your switch before adding it to the network. Changing the VTP mode to transparent and then to either client or server will reset the revision number back to zero. One other tip is to use different VTP domain names and passwords on your lab equipment. Remember that the switches must be part of the same domain and share the same password in order to add, delete, modify, and forward VTP messages.

Configuring VTP on Your Network

As mentioned earlier, VTP is in server mode by default. If you plan to use VTP on your network, there is no need to have every switch on the network configured for server mode. Typically, your distribution block switches are set for server mode, and the access layer switches are set to run in client mode. In our example, we'll configure Switch A to be in VTP server mode, and it will send updates to Server B configured as a VTP client. Figure 4.9 depicts our network layout, which assumes that both switches have been preconfigured for 802.1Q trunking and have VLAN 10 and 20 already set up.

FIGURE 4.9   An example of VTP configuration

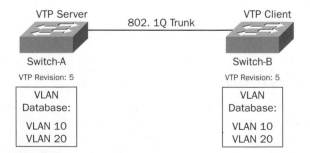

There are two versions of VTP. Both versions essentially perform the same functions on Ethernet networks, so it really doesn't matter which one you choose as long as everything in your network is running the same version. Typically, I recommend running VTP version 2 everywhere to ensure consistency.

The other vital configuration step is to configure the VTP domain. The VTP domain is the VTP group that a switch belongs to. Once a switch is in a specific domain, it listens only to updates within this group. All other VTP update messages are ignored. If the switch has never been configured, the VTP domain will be blank. Because the switch is in VTP server mode by default, it will join the first VTP domain from which it receives a VTP update message. The only way to change the VTP name once it is set is to change it manually while directly connected to the switch.

A third VTP configuration parameter that is optional but highly recommended is the VTP password. VTP passwords ensure that no unauthorized switches can be added to the network and no VLAN information is changed.

Now that you understand the VTP configuration options, let's configure our two switches with the following VTP setup:

- Switch A:
  - VTP Mode: Server
  - VTP Version: 2
  - VTP Domain: Sybex
  - VTP Password: CCNAVoice
- Switch B:
  - VTP Mode: Client
  - VTP Version: 2
  - VTP Domain: Sybex
  - VTP Password: CCNAVoice

Make sure you remember that both the VTP domain and VTP password you assign to the switches are case sensitive!

First let's issue the show vtp status command on Switch A so you can see how VTP is set up by default on all Cisco switches:

```
Switch-A#show vtp status
VTP Version                     : 2
Configuration Revision          : 5
Maximum VLANs supported locally : 1005
Number of existing VLANs        : 7
VTP Operating Mode              : Server
```

```
VTP Domain Name                 :
VTP Pruning Mode                : Disabled
VTP V2 Mode                     : Disabled
VTP Traps Generation            : Disabled
MD5 digest                      : 0xA7 0x2B 0x66 0xB2 0x7C 0x0A 0xC7 0x3C
```

Now we'll configure VTP on Switch A:

```
Switch-A(config)#vtp mode server
Switch-A(config)#vtp domain Sybex
Switch-A(config)#vtp version 2
Switch-A(config)#vtp password CCNAVoice
```

Another show vtp status command will verify that the changes were made correctly. We'll also run a show vtp password command to ensure that we have our VTP password set:

```
Switch-A#show vtp status
VTP Version                     : 2
Configuration Revision          : 5
Maximum VLANs supported locally : 1005
Number of existing VLANs        : 7
VTP Operating Mode              : Server
VTP Domain Name                 : Sybex
VTP Pruning Mode                : Disabled
VTP V2 Mode                     : Enabled
VTP Traps Generation            : Disabled
MD5 digest                      : 0x26 0x3A 0xA0 0x8C 0x66 0x01 0xA1 0xF
```

```
Switch-A#show vtp password
VTP Password: CCNAVoice
```

Now that we have our VTP server properly set up on our network, let's configure Switch B as our VTP client:

```
Switch-B(config)#vtp mode client
Switch-B(config)#vtp domain Sybex
Switch-B(config)#vtp version 2
Switch-B(config)#vtp password CCNAVoice
```

Running show VTP status and show vtp password shows us that the switch was set to VTP client and has all the proper configuration settings. Also notice that the Configuration

Revision number is 5, which is the same as the VTP server that it received VTP update messages from:

```
Switch-B#show vtp status
VTP Version                  : 2
Configuration Revision       : 5
Maximum VLANs supported locally : 1005
Number of existing VLANs     : 7
VTP Operating Mode           : Client
VTP Domain Name              : Sybex
VTP Pruning Mode             : Disabled
VTP V2 Mode                  : Enabled
VTP Traps Generation         : Disabled
MD5 digest                   : 0x26 0x3A 0xA0 0x8C 0x66 0x01 0xA1 0xF

Switch-B#show vtp password
VTP Password: CCNAVoice
```

Back on Switch A, we'll configure a new VLAN for our Management group. The new VLAN number is 30:

```
Switch-A#conf t
Switch-A(config)#vlan 30
Switch-A(config-vlan)#name Management
Switch-A(config-vlan)#end
```

This information should propagate over to Switch B. Figure 4.10 diagrams the process by which the VTP Server updates the VTP Client switch.

FIGURE 4.10   The VTP update process

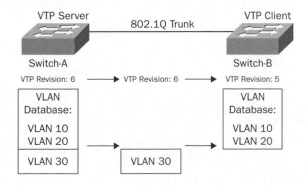

Let's take a look at the process by running the show vtp status and show vlan brief commands:

```
Switch-B#show vtp status
VTP Version                     : 2
Configuration Revision          : 6
Maximum VLANs supported locally : 1005
Number of existing VLANs        : 8
VTP Operating Mode              : Client
VTP Domain Name                 : Sybex
VTP Pruning Mode                : Disabled
VTP V2 Mode                     : Enabled
VTP Traps Generation            : Disabled
MD5 digest                      : 0xAA 0x10 0xFC 0x76 0xFD 0xD5 0xB3 0x4C
```

Notice that the Configuration Revision number has incremented, and now the number of existing VLANs is 8 instead of 7.

```
Switch-B#show vlan brief

VLAN Name                             Status    Ports
---- ------------------------------   --------- -------------------------------
1    default                          active    Gi0/1, Gi0/2
10   Sales                            active    Fa0/1, Fa0/2, Fa0/3, Fa0/4
                                                Fa0/5, Fa0/6, Fa0/7, Fa0/8
                                                Fa0/9, Fa0/10, Fa0/11, Fa0/12
                                                Fa0/13, Fa0/14, Fa0/15, Fa0/16
                                                Fa0/17, Fa0/18, Fa0/19, Fa0/20
                                                Fa0/21, Fa0/22, Fa0/23, Fa0/24
20   Marketing                        active    Fa0/25, Fa0/26, Fa0/27, Fa0/28
                                                Fa0/29, Fa0/30, Fa0/31, Fa0/32
                                                Fa0/33, Fa0/34, Fa0/35, Fa0/36
                                                Fa0/37, Fa0/38, Fa0/39, Fa0/40
                                                Fa0/41, Fa0/42, Fa0/43, Fa0/44
                                                Fa0/45, Fa0/46, Fa0/47, Fa0/48
30   Management                       active
1002 fddi-default                     act/unsup
1003 token-ring-default               act/unsup
1004 fddinet-default                  act/unsup
1005 trnet-default                    act/unsup
```

Sure enough, Switch B has the new VLAN 30 configured in its VLAN database!

Configuring and Verifying Voice VLANs

When it comes to configuring a separate VLAN for voice traffic, the process of configuration and VLAN creation is exactly the same whether traffic is going router-to-switch or switch-to-switch. The voice VLAN configuration differs when you want to use Cisco IP phones that incorporate a data port on the phone for PC connections. Many Cisco mid- and high-range phones such as the 7945G give users the ability to plug a PC into an Ethernet port on the phone to provide network connectivity. The phone essentially becomes a three-port switch at that point. One port connects the phone to the access-layer switch, the second (virtual) port is for voice traffic to the phone, and the third port is to connect to a PC for standard data transport. Figure 4.11 shows how a PC is plugged directly into the phone, which is essentially trunked with both a voice and data VLAN.

FIGURE 4.11 A Cisco IP phone switch

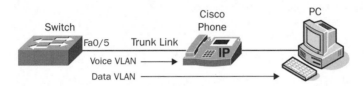

As you can see, the connection between the switch and the Cisco phone is an 802.1Q trunk link. It is necessary to have a VLAN trunk because we have our voice and data separated on two different VLANs. When configuring the VLAN trunk on the switchport that connects to the phone, we use a slightly different method. The Cisco IOS has a unique command to identify a VLAN as a *voice VLAN*. The command is switchport voice vlan. Even though the switchport command doesn't specifically reference 802.1a, in all actuality, this trunk link between our switch and the Cisco phone is not a full-fledged 802.1Q trunk like those we have practiced configuring between two switches and a switch and router. Instead, the Cisco switch and Cisco IP phone use CDP to implement this quasi-trunk. The VLAN that is configured as the voice VLAN is marked with an 802.1Q tag, while the data VLAN is considered to be the native VLAN and is left unmarked. This VLAN trunk is capable of handling only two VLANs—one tagged VLAN for voice and one untagged VLAN for data.

It used to be that the VLAN trunk link between the access switch and Cisco IPT phone was indeed a full-blown 802.1Q trunk. Unfortunately, it was easy to fool this setup, and PCs could easily join the voice VLAN and use sniffers to collect and re-create voice calls. Because the new quasi-trunk setup uses CDP to identify which devices can join the voice VLAN, the new method is much more secure.

With that understanding of the voice VLAN, let's add a new voice VLAN (VLAN 100) and configure port Fa0/5 to trunk the voice VLAN (using the `switchport voice vlan` command) and the Sales VLAN (data VLAN that is already configured on the switch) to the Cisco phone according to Figure 4.11. First we'll configure the voice VLAN:

```
Switch#configure terminal
Switch(config)#vlan 100
Switch(config-vlan)#name Voice
Switch(config-vlan)#end
```

Next let's configure the switchport to quasi-trunk VLAN 100 for voice and VLAN 10 for or data transport:

```
Switch#configure terminal
Switch(config)#interface fa0/5
Switch(config-if)#switchport voice vlan 100
Switch(config-if)#switchport access vlan 10
Switch(config-if)#end
```

Great! Now we'll run `show vlan brief` to verify that our port Fa0/5 is in both VLAN 10 and VLAN 100:

Switch#`sh vlan brief`

```
VLAN Name                             Status     Ports
---- -------------------------------- --------- -------------------------------
1    default                          active     Gi0/1, Gi0/2
10   Sales                            active     Fa0/1, Fa0/2, Fa0/3, Fa0/4
                                                 Fa0/5, Fa0/6, Fa0/7, Fa0/8
                                                 Fa0/9, Fa0/10, Fa0/11, Fa0/12
                                                 Fa0/13, Fa0/14, Fa0/15, Fa0/16
                                                 Fa0/17, Fa0/18, Fa0/19, Fa0/20
                                                 Fa0/21, Fa0/22, Fa0/23, Fa0/24
20   Marketing                        active     Fa0/25, Fa0/26, Fa0/27, Fa0/28
                                                 Fa0/29, Fa0/30, Fa0/31, Fa0/32
                                                 Fa0/33, Fa0/34, Fa0/35, Fa0/36
                                                 Fa0/37, Fa0/38, Fa0/39, Fa0/40
                                                 Fa0/41, Fa0/42, Fa0/43, Fa0/44
                                                 Fa0/45, Fa0/46, Fa0/47, Fa0/48
30   Management                       active
100  Voice                            active     Fa0/5
1002 fddi-default                     act/unsup
1003 trcrf-default                    act/unsup
```

```
1004 fddinet-default              act/unsup
1005 trbrf-default                act/unsup
Switch#
```

Sure enough, port Fa0/5 belongs to both the Sales (VLAN 10) and voice (VLAN 100) VLANs. Next we'll discuss how we can mark and prioritize the voice traffic using the most common QoS techniques.

Introduction to Quality of Service (QoS)

Quality of Service (QoS) is such an enormous topic in the world of networking that I could fill an entire book dedicated solely to it. In fact, the Cisco CCVP certification dedicates the 642-642 exam to QoS topics. Not only is there a great deal to discuss about QoS, many of the details of its mechanisms are very complex and difficult to grasp when you first start learning about them. The CCNA Voice track requires you to know the very basics of QoS in order to get some exposure to the topic. Fortunately for us, Cisco is making the actual implementation of QoS easier all the time with the concept of auto-QoS. We will start by discussing why we need QoS and the network requirements for voice packets. Then I'll explain the concept of QoS trust boundaries and where they should be located. Finally, I'll introduce you to auto-QoS and how it simplifies much of the complexity for proper implementation on a network.

Quality of Service (QoS) is the ability to identify time-sensitive traffic and give it priority over other forms of traffic. IP networks have restrictions on both the amount of bandwidth between two points and the *latency*, or time it takes for a packet to be moved between two points. From a pure bandwidth point of view, the goal is to eliminate or at least reduce bottlenecks on your network. *Bottlenecks* are network links interconnecting endpoints where the amount of data sent out an interface exceeds the physical capabilities of the interface. Figure 4.12 shows the network location where a bottleneck is most likely to occur.

FIGURE 4.12   A network bottleneck

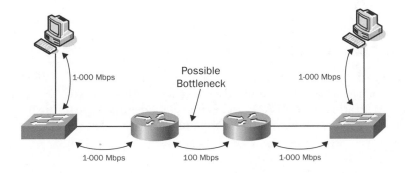

When we talk about network latency, we're mainly talking about network delay and network jitter. Some amount of network delay is always going to be present on even the fastest networks. This is called *fixed delay,* which means the time it takes to send an electrical or optical signal across a certain distance. This type of delay is very slight and does not affect time-sensitive traffic such as voice.

Variable delay, on the other hand, is what QoS attempts to eliminate or at least reduce. Variable delay refers to those bottleneck situations when your time-sensitive traffic has to sit in a queue and wait for other packets to be sent out of the interface before your voice packet can be sent. By incorporating QoS, we can give our voice packets priority over traffic that is not time-sensitive so that we won't be waiting in the queue and will thereby reduce variable delay.

Jitter refers to the variations in time of arrival for time-sensitive packets. If it takes 40 ms (milliseconds) for the first voice packet to arrive and 90 ms for the second packet to arrive, the jitter level is 50 ms.

One last network issue to watch out for with time-sensitive data is packet loss. If bottlenecks get to the point where the queues start filling up, packet loss occurs. If this happens, you can implement QoS to begin discarding less-critical data, which can be identified using QoS classification and marking methods.

Specific network requirements for QoS for voice and video have been established for you to use as guidelines. As long as you meet or beat the following criteria, your voice/video applications should not experience any problems.

- End-to-end delay: 150 ms or less
- Jitter: 30 ms or less
- Packet loss: 1 percent loss or less

So the goal for us is to implement QoS in order to provide a much more consistent and steady transport mechanism for our voice packets. While our best-effort design may work well for data, voice traffic requires a bit more care to function optimally. Now that we know what we're trying to accomplish with QoS, let's turn our attention to how it works.

The QoS function has three stages, which we'll look at in turn:

1. Traffic classification
2. Traffic marking
3. Traffic queuing

Traffic Classification

Traffic classification is the process of identifying time-sensitive packets. The identification process must be performed first because the equipment must be able to clearly identify certain traffic. Creating voice VLANS makes it easy to identify voice traffic because we can assume that any packets on the voice VLAN should be classified as such.

Traffic Marking

Traffic marking is the process of flagging critical packets so the rest of the network can properly identify them and give them priority over all other traffic. Cisco phones have the ability to mark voice packets with a Class of Service (CoS) value. The CoS is a field within the Layer 2 Ethernet frame header that marks traffic as being one of eight (0 to 7) classes. The higher the CoS value, the more priority is given. By default, voice traffic is marked with a classification of 5. If data is not marked with a CoS, it is given a value of 0. The CoS is used by Layer 2 switches for proper queuing.

The Cisco phone also marks the IP packet with a Type of Service (ToS) identifier. The ToS essentially does the same thing as the CoS but is intended to be used by Layer 3 devices such as routers and switches.

Traffic Queuing

Traffic queuing is the process of ordering certain types of traffic for transport over LAN/WAN interfaces. Many different queuing techniques are available, which can be overwhelming. Fortunately, one queuing technique is considered optimal for voice traffic, *Low Latency Queuing (LLQ)*. LLQ does the best job of eliminating variable delay, jitter, and packet loss on a network. LLQ on a switch creates a strict-priority queue for voice traffic. The auto-QoS configuration method utilizes LLQ as its default mechanism.

Now let's look at how and where we can classify and mark traffic using the high-level design concept of QoS trust boundaries.

Identifying QoS Trust Boundaries

We can classify, mark, and begin enforcing queuing strategies for IP traffic at several points along a network. But where should this process begin? The simplest answer is to push your *trust boundary* out as far to the endpoint as possible. But depending on the type of network, you may have to pull the boundary in a bit depending on how much you trust the end devices (that's why it's called a "trust" boundary!). If you have full control of endpoints, then you control the CoS and ToS markings that are generated, and you can push the trust boundary out to the phone and even PC level. If you do not have as much control over your network, it might be better to begin marking CoS/ToS values as soon as the traffic hits your switch. Also, you may run into a situation where your access-layer switches cannot be configured for QoS. Because of this, you have no choice but to configure the trust boundary at the distribution layer. Figure 4.13 displays where trust boundaries can be implemented within a typical network.

FIGURE 4.13   Trust boundaries

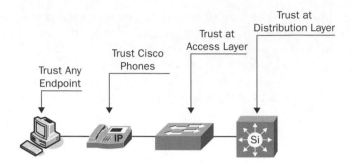

Most organizations will trust CoS/ToS markings from the Cisco phones but will not trust the markings from devices attached to the phone such as a PC. When network data from the PC reaches the Cisco phone, the switch will ignore the CoS/ToS markings and consider all data packets to have a value of 0.

Now that you understand the basics of QoS and trust boundaries, let's see how we can easily implement them on our network using auto-QoS.

Auto-QoS Implementation Options

There are only three options for configuring *auto-QoS* on an interface using the `auto qos voip` command. Once you understand these three options, configuring QoS on your network will be a snap! Here is the output of the switch when configuring auto-QoS:

```
Switch(config-if)#auto qos voip ?
  cisco-phone       Trust the QoS marking of Cisco IP Phone
  cisco-softphone   Trust the QoS marking of Cisco IP SoftPhone
  trust             Trust the DSCP/CoS marking
```

Let's look at the options to understand when each one should be used.

cisco-phone   You should use this option when you want to trust the QoS markings from your Cisco phone. Note that I said "Cisco" phone and not "IP" phone. Cisco uses CDP between the switch and phone to ensure that the device is indeed a phone and not some other device attempting to get a better classification for its traffic. Because CDP is Cisco proprietary, it works only when Cisco phones are connected or when other companies license CDP technology (such as Mitel IP Phones).

cisco-softphone   This option is very similar to the `cisco-phone` option except it trusts the CoS/ToS markings on PCs that are running the Cisco IP Communicator software. The IP Communicator software runs CDP once again to ensure that the device is properly identified as a Cisco phone.

trust   The trust option basically means that the switch will trust any CoS/ToS value received and treat the traffic accordingly. Be cautious when configuring this on access ports, because people "in-the-know" can manipulate the classification markings of data traffic on their PCs and have their data sent as priority traffic when it should be treated as normal traffic. But where the trust option should absolutely be used is between all of the switch and router interfaces that interconnect your network equipment. As soon as you set a location for your trust boundary, all other devices within that boundary can safely trust the CoS/ToS markings they receive.

That's all there is to auto-QoS. Let's use Figure 4.14 as our network example for configuring QoS on a production network. Assume that the Sales, Marketing, Management, and Voice VLANs are preconfigured on the network. Switchport Fa0/5 is configured to use VLAN 10 for data and VLAN 100 for voice traffic. Also assume that 802.1Q trunking is configured between the switch and the CME router.

FIGURE 4.14   An example of QoS

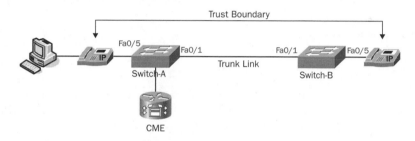

First, we need to set our trust boundary. Let's assume that we'll trust the Cisco phones but not trust ordinary PCs. Therefore, our trust boundary is set at the phone, using the auto qos voip cicso-phone command:

```
Switch-A#confure terminal
Switch-A(config)#interface fastEthernet 0/5
Switch-A(config-if)#auto qos voip cisco-phone
Switch-A(config-if)#end
```

Let's see exactly what auto-QoS is configured on our port, using the show run interface command:

```
Switch-A#sh run int fa0/5
Building configuration...
```

```
Current configuration : 487 bytes
!
interface FastEthernet0/5
 switchport access vlan 10
 switchport mode dynamic desirable
 switchport voice vlan 100
 mls qos trust device cisco-phone
 mls qos trust cos
 auto qos voip cisco-phone
 wrr-queue bandwidth 10 20 70 1
 wrr-queue min-reserve 1 5
 wrr-queue min-reserve 2 6
 wrr-queue min-reserve 3 7
 wrr-queue min-reserve 4 8
 wrr-queue cos-map 1 0 1
 wrr-queue cos-map 2 2 4
 wrr-queue cos-map 3 3 6 7
 wrr-queue cos-map 4 5
 priority-queue out
 spanning-tree portfast
```

We can see that the auto qos voip command actually configured all kinds of things on the interface! The important thing we need to identify is that we're trusting the Cisco phone with the auto qos voip cisco-phone entry.

Once the trust boundary is set, we know that the interfaces connecting our Layer 2 switch to the CME router should be configured using the auto qos voip trust command. Here's the switch trunk port configuration for Fa0/1:

```
Switch-A#confure terminal
Switch-A(config)#interface fastEthernet 0/1
Switch-A(config-if)#auto qos voip trust
Switch-A(config-if)#end
```

Let's look at our running configuration for our switch uplink to see the differences between the auto qos voip trust configurations and the auto qos voip cisco-phone output:

```
Switch-A#show run interface fa0/1
Building configuration...

Current configuration : 436 bytes
!
interface FastEthernet0/1
```

```
switchport trunk encapsulation dot1q
switchport trunk allowed vlan 10,20,100
switchport mode trunk
mls qos trust cos
auto qos voip trust
wrr-queue bandwidth 10 20 70 1
wrr-queue min-reserve 1 5
wrr-queue min-reserve 2 6
wrr-queue min-reserve 3 7
wrr-queue min-reserve 4 8
wrr-queue cos-map 1 0 1
wrr-queue cos-map 2 2 4
wrr-queue cos-map 3 3 6 7
wrr-queue cos-map 4 5
priority-queue out
```

Notice that from a QoS configuration standpoint, the only difference between the `trust` and `cisco-phone` configuration is the `auto qos voip trust` command.

The configuration of the opposite-end switch is identical. Once you've completed configuring all the interfaces, congratulations; you've successfully implemented QoS for voice on your network!

Configuring Other Link Efficiency Techniques

In addition to configuring QoS on your network for voice support, you can use two other link efficiency techniques to help with the consistent transport of VoIP. These techniques are compression and link fragmentation and interleaving (LFI).

Compression Techniques

Compression can come in many forms. I've already touched on how to use different voice codecs to compress the audio payload. I will cover how to implement various codecs on your CME in the next chapter. I've also mentioned the concept of using RTP compression (cRTP) across WAN links to help ease any congestion issues as the result of the WAN link being a bottleneck. Here is how to configure cRTP on a T1 PPP serial interface, which is a common place to implement this type of compression. Figure 4.15 shows the network layout for our example.

FIGURE 4.15 An example of compression

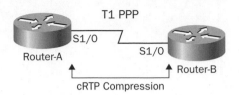

Configuration Steps

Configuring basic cRTP requires only one step, defining the `ip rtp header-compression ietf-format` command on the link. Of course, the link also needs a common serial link encapsulation type and IP addressing scheme for IP transport to work properly. Here are the basic steps for configuring your serial links for cRTP.

The Router-A configuration looks like this:

```
Router-A(config)# interface serial 1/0
Router-A(config-if)# encapsulation ppp
Router-A(config-if)#ip add 10.1.1.1 255.255.255.252
Router-A(config-if)# ip rtp header-compression ietf-format
Router-A(config-if)# end
```

The Router-B configuration looks like this:

```
Router-B(config)# interface serial 1/0
Router-B(config-if)# encapsulation ppp
Router-B(config-if)#ip add 10.1.1.1 255.255.255.252
Router-B(config-if)# ip rtp header-compression ietf-format
Router-B(config-if)# end
```

We can now verify that cRTP is enabled and compressing RTP headers by issuing the `sho ip rtp header-compression` command. Here's the output of this command on Router-A:

```
Router-A#show ip rtp header-compression

RTP/UDP/IP header compression statistics:
  Interface Serial1/0 (compression on, IETF)
    Rcvd:    1473 total, 1452 compressed, 0 errors, 0 status msgs
             0 dropped, 0 buffer copies, 0 buffer failures
    Sent:    1234 total, 1216 compressed, 0 status msgs, 379 not predicted
             41995 bytes saved, 24755 bytes sent
             2.69 efficiency improvement factor
```

```
Connect: 16 rx slots, 16 tx slots,
         6 misses, 0 collisions, 0 negative cache hits, 13 free contexts
         99% hit ratio, five minute miss rate 0 misses/sec, 0 max
```

Link Fragmentation Interleaving (LFI)

A second link-efficiency technique that is commonly used on PPP multilink circuits is called *link fragmentation interleaving (LFI)*. This process takes much larger data packets and fragments them into smaller, more manageable sizes. It then is able to send voice packets in between the newly fragmented data packets. This process ensures that voice packets have a more consistent variable delay and significantly cuts down on voice jitter. You configure LFI over a PPP multilink by using the ppp multilink command to enable multilink PPP and then the ppp multilink interleave command to enable LFI.

Network Infrastructure Services for VoIP support

The network infrastructure equipment can also provide supplementary services to assist in the support of a Cisco Unified Communications solution. Routers or Layer 3 switches can provide *Dynamic Host Control Protocol (DHCP)* services to your phones to dynamically assign IP addresses and other network information to the phones. The infrastructure can also serve as a centralized point for synchronizing your UC equipment clocks by being the *Network Time Protocol* point of reference. Let's look at how we configure both of these network services for our VoIP solution.

Configuring DHCP for Voice Functionality

DHCP allows an endpoint device (such as a Cisco IP phone) to boot up on the network and request network information, which it dynamically receives from a DHCP server. This section shows how to configure DHCP on your CME router for your end devices.

DHCP server functionality is considered a service on your IOS router. It is disabled by default. To enable the DHCP service you use the following configuration command:

Router(config)# service dhcp

The next step in your DHCP server-configuration process is to ensure that specific IP addresses on your network are never handed out to endpoints. You must specifically exclude IPs such as default gateways and other static interfaces that are already in use. If you skip this step, you run the risk of having an endpoint assigned an IP address that is already in use, which causes an IP conflict. IP conflicts are a very bad thing because they disrupt proper IP transport on your network for the devices with the conflict. You can configure a range of IP addresses to exclude with a single command. Typically, I configure all of my network interface and other critical IP address assignments on lower IP space. Therefore, if I'm creating a DHCP pool using a 255.255.255.0 subnet mask, I will exclude the first 20 IP addresses within that range. For example, suppose I want to configure a DHCP pool for the 192.168.100.0/24 range. My excluded command would then look like this:

```
Router(config)# ip dhcp excluded-address 192.168.100.1 192.168.100.20
```

Next, you want to create the DHCP pool for your network space. The first part in creating the pool is to name it. Because we want to create a pool for our IP phones, we'll name the pool voip-pool. Here is the command to complete this step:

```
Router(config)# ip dhcp pool voip-pool
```

As soon you name your DHCP pool, you are placed into dhcp-config mode. This is where you actually create your IP scope with the network command and any additional DHCP information you want to give to the endpoints. Following are the common parameters for endpoints.

Default-router   This parameter is mandatory for any endpoints. It tells the endpoint what IP address to use for its default-gateway.

Domain-name   This parameter specifies the domain name you want your endpoints to use.

DNS-server   This parameter informs the endpoints about the IP addresses of their DNS servers for name resolution. You can specify up to eight DNS servers with a single command.

Lease   This command allows you to specify how long an endpoint is to maintain the dynamically assigned IP address. You can specify the number of days, hours, or minutes or even tell it to maintain the address infinitely.

Another critical parameter that you will want to configure when setting up DHCP for your Cisco IP phones is the IP address of the TFTP server where the Cisco phone configuration files are located. All Cisco phones (SIP and SCCP) must download a configuration file when they first boot. This configuration file contains important information for the phone to properly function with the CUCM. The IP phones must know the location of the TFTP server so they can request the configuration file. The DHCP option 150 parameter is used to provide the IP address of the server.

For example, to implement the following information

- Network: 192.168.100.0/24
- Default router: 192.168.100.1
- Domain name: ccnavoice1.com
- DNS server: 192.168.10.5
- TFTP server: 192.168.100.10
- Lease time: 6 hours

we would use these DHCP configuration parameters:

```
Router(dhcp-config)#network 192.168.100.0 255.255.255.0
Router(dhcp-config)#default-router 192.168.100.1
Router(dhcp-config)#domain-name ccnavoice1.com
Router(dhcp-config)#dns-server 192.168.10.5
Router(dhcp-config)#option 150 ip 192.168.100.10
Router(dhcp-config)#lease 0 6 0
Router(dhcp-config)#end
```

Once those configuration steps are complete, when your IP phones are on the voice VLAN, they will dynamically receive.

Monitoring and Troubleshooting the DHCP Service

You can monitor your DHCP service with the following useful show commands:

show ip dhcp binding   Use this command to display the dynamic IP to MAC address mappings. It also lets you know when a specific lease will expire. The following example shows the binding for the DHCP leased IP address 192.168.100.101:

```
Router# show ip dhcp binding 192.168.100.101
```

IP address	Hardware address	Lease expiration	Type
192.168.100.101	00a0.9802.32de	Mar 01 2009 12:00 AM	Automatic

show ip dhcp conflict   This command lists any IP address conflicts and the time the detection occurred. It also indicates the method of conflict detection. The example shows a conflict for the IP address 192.168.100.101:

```
Router# show ip dhcp conflict
```

IP address	Detection Method	Detection time
192.168.100.101	Ping	Mar 01 2009 12:28 PM

Configuring the Network Time Protocol

The Network Time Protocol (NTP) should be configured on every single piece of network equipment in a production network. It is very important to have synchronized times for all of your logging information. It is also important in the voice world to have your phones properly synchronized for time. Issues can arise when clocks are mismatched. For instance, your Unity voice mail needs to know the proper time so it can correctly inform a user when a person called and left a message.

Usually, I will specify two devices on a network that have access to a public time source from the National Institute of Standards and Technology (NIST). Keep in mind that NTP runs over UDP port 123, so make sure you have this port open on your firewall ruleset to allow access. Configuring a time source on a Cisco IOS device is quite simple. First, you specify the time zone that your equipment resides in, using the clock timezone command. Next, you issue the command ntp server and specify an IP address of one of the public time servers. Then you can configure all of your other network devices to peer with the device receiving an external clock. Let's configure a router for an external NTP server. This example will use the external time source IP address of 192.5.41.41.

```
Router#configure terminal
Router(config)#clock timezone CHICAGO -6
Router(config)#ntp server 192.5.41.41
Router(config)#end
```

 You may live in a location that adheres to daylight savings time. If that is the case, you will need to let the Cisco device know by using a clock summer-time command option. We can issue a show ntp status command to verify that Router-A is synchronized. Keep in mind that it may take several minutes for the synchronization process to complete.

```
Router#show ntp associations
address          ref clock     st  when  poll reach  delay  offset    disp
*~192.5.41.41     .USNO.        1   285   512  377    33.9   1.23      1.0
 * master (synced), # master (unsynced), + selected, - candidate, ~ configured
```

Our NTP server is listed and synchronized. We know it is properly synchronized because of the asterisk (*) to the left of the IP address.

Summary

In this chapter we began with the three options available for powering your Cisco IP phones. You then learned about network configuration basics such as VLAN configuration and how to route properly between VLANs. We also spent some time examining the proper way to implement VTP on the network for ease of managing VLANs. We then went over quality of service basics and how to configure auto-QoS for VoIP. We discussed additional link-efficiency techniques to help you to eliminate any bottlenecks on the network. Lastly, we covered how to configure network services that help support voice functionality.

As you can see, you need to configure some modifications on your network infrastructure route/switch gear to ready it for voice traffic. But at its heart, the infrastructure is basically the same in terms of moving your packets from point A to point B. Just like with Chinese food, you may have different main dishes (voice and data traffic), but they're always served with a foundation of rice (network infrastructure).

Exam Essentials

Know the three different power options for IP phones.   The power brick is attached to the phone and plugs directly into the wall outlet. A power patch panel or power injector sits between an IP phone and a standard non-PoE switch; power is sent to the phone over the same cable that voice traffic resides on. Finally, the PoE switch offers power directly from the switch to the phone over an Ethernet cable.

Understand the different PoE proprietary and IETF standards of IP phones and PoE switches.   As long as the power source can meet the requirements of the IP phone, the Cisco PoE switch uses CDP to negotiate the best power option.

Know how to calculate and manipulate power requirements for your IP phone deployment for PoE switches.   It is important to determine your power requirements for any PoE devices on the network. You should also understand how to change the PoE management modes on a per-switch and per-switchport basis.

Understand the purpose of VLANs.   VLANs segment broadcast domains. A logical VLAN acts as a physically separate network.

Know what VLAN trunks are used for.   VLAN trunks transport multiple VLANs across the same physical link while keeping the traffic separate using VLAN tags.

Understand the need of inter-VLAN routing.   When you have two separate VLANs, you need a way for the two VLANs to communicate with each other. Inter-VLAN routing is a Layer 3 feature that routes Layer 2 traffic for inter-VLAN communication.

Understand the VLAN Trunking Protocol (VTP).   VTP is a service to help assist with the adds/changes/deletions of VLANs on a network. The three VTP modes are server, client, and transparent. VTP uses revision numbers to keep track of the latest updates on the network.

Understand the difference between data and voice VLANs.   Cisco switches use CDP to identify Cisco IP phones on the network. Voice VLANs are configured differently at the switchport level. Finally, voice VLANs are tagged on the switchport, while any PC that is connected to a switch or Cisco IP phone is untagged.

Know the network requirements for voice.   End-to-end delay should be 150 ms or less. Jitter should be 30 ms or less. Packet loss should be at 1 percent or less.

Know the three QoS classification steps.   QoS requires the traffic to be first classified, then marked, and finally queued.

Understand QoS traffic trust boundaries.   The closer to the source your boundary is, the better the QoS will ultimately be.

Know how to implement auto-QoS on a network.   Auto-QoS is designed to simplify the QoS implementation for voice traffic. You should be familiar with a few auto-QoS commands to properly configure your infrastructure for QoS of voice.

Understand basic link-efficiency techniques.   Techniques such as compression and LFI can help transport your voice traffic as efficiently as possible across the infrastructure.

Know how to configure network services for VoIP support.   Cisco IP phones rely heavily on DHCP servers for information such as IP address, default-router, DNS, and the location of IP phone configuration files by defining the option 150 parameter for a TFTP server.

Understand the purpose of NTP and how to configure it.   NTP is used to synchronize time for all of your phone equipment on the network. Synchronization of time helps to ensure proper operation and support of your VoIP network.

Written Lab 4.1

Write the answers to the following questions:

1. What is the command to display the power settings on a PoE switchport?

2. What is the command to see what VLAN all of your switchports belong to?

3. What two commands are used to configure a new VLAN 100 with the name of Voice?

4. What interface command assigns a switchport to a voice VLAN of 55?

5. What interface command assigns a switchport to a VLAN of 105?

6. What two interface commands configure the port to be a VLAN trunk that uses 802.1Q tagging?

7. What interface command sets the VLAN trunk to allow only VLANs 10, 20, and 30 to be transported over the link?

8. What command lets you view the VTP information currently configured on a switch?

9. What command lets you view the VTP password configured on the switch?

10. What command enables DHCP on the router?

(The answers to Written Lab 4.1 can be found following the answers to the review questions for this chapter.)

Hands-on Labs

Here is a list of the labs in this chapter:

Lab 4.1: Setting Power Options on PoE Ethernet Interfaces

Lab 4.2: Configuring Voice and Data VLANs and Switchport Assignment

Lab 4.3: Setting up VTP

Lab 4.4: Configuring Auto-QoS

Lab 4.5: Setting up a DHCP Server

To complete these labs, you need the following equipment:

Lab 4.1: one Cisco PoE switch

Lab 4.2: one Cisco switch

Lab 4.3: one Cisco switch

Lab 4.4: one Cisco switch

Lab 4.5: one Cisco router

Hands-on Lab 4.1: Setting Power Options on PoE Ethernet Interfaces

1. Log into your PoE switch and go into privileged exec mode by typing **enable**.

2. View the current power settings by typing **show power inline fa0/1**. You should see that the switchport is set for an Admin state of auto. This is the default PoE configuration.

3. Enter into interface configuration mode for PoE port Fa0/1 by typing **configuration terminal** and **interface fa0/1.**

4. View your power options by typing **power inline ?**. You should see the following options:

```
PoE-switch(config-if)#power inline ?
  auto      Automatically detect and power inline devices
  never     Never apply inline power
  static    High priority inline power interface
```

5. Configure the switchport so that it never supplies power to end devices by typing **power inline never**. Exit configuration mode by typing **end.**

6. Verify your configuration changes by again viewing the power settings by typing **show power inline fa0/1**. You should now see that the Admin state is off and no power is allocated to the switchport.

Hands-on Lab 4.2: Configuring Voice and Data VLANs and Switchport Assignment

1. Log into your switch and go into privileged exec mode by typing **enable**.

2. Enter configuration mode by typing **configuration terminal**.

3. Configure two new VLANs on the switch. VLAN 10 is named Data and VLAN 20 is named Voice. To accomplish this, type **vlan 10**, and you will enter VLAN configuration mode. Type **name Data**. Then configure VLAN 20 by typing **vlan 20**. Once in VLAN 20 configuration mode you can label the VLAN by typing **name Voice**.

4. Exit configuration mode by typing **end**.

5. Verify your configuration changes by typing **show vlan brief**. You should see something similar to the following:

```
PoE-switch#show vlan brief


VLAN Name                             Status    Ports
---- -------------------------------- --------- -------------------------------
1    default                          active    Fa0/1, Fa0/2, Fa0/3, Fa0/4
                                                Fa0/5, Fa0/6, Fa0/7, Fa0/8
                                                Fa0/9, Fa0/10, Fa0/11, Fa0/12
                                                Fa0/13, Fa0/14, Fa0/15, Fa0/16
                                                Fa0/17, Fa0/18, Fa0/19, Fa0/20
                                                Fa0/21, Fa0/22, Fa0/23, Fa0/24
                                                Fa0/25, Fa0/26, Fa0/27, Fa0/28
                                                Fa0/29, Fa0/30, Fa0/31, Fa0/32
                                                Fa0/33, Fa0/34, Fa0/35, Fa0/36
                                                Fa0/37, Fa0/38, Fa0/39, Fa0/40
                                                Fa0/41, Fa0/42, Fa0/43, Fa0/44
                                                Fa0/45, Fa0/46, Fa0/47, Fa0/48
                                                Gi0/1, Gi0/2
10   Data                             active
20   Voice                            active
1002 fddi-default                     act/unsup
```

```
1003 token-ring-default            act/unsup
1004 fddinet-default               act/unsup
1005 trnet-default                 act/unsup
```

6. Next, we want to configure port Fa0/1 to belong to VLAN 10 if the end device is a PC and VLAN 20 if the end device is a Cisco IP phone. To set this up, we must enter interface configuration mode by typing **configuration terminal** and **interface fa0/1**.

7. Assign VLAN 10 to the port by typing **switchport access vlan 10**. Then configure the voice VLAN to 20 by typing **switchport voice vlan 20**.

8. Exit configuration mode by typing **end**.

9. Verify your configuration changes by typing **show vlan brief**. You should now see that port Fa0/1 belongs to both VLAN 10 and 20:

```
PoE-switch#show vlan brief

VLAN Name                         Status    Ports
---- ----------------------------- --------- -------------------------------
1    default                       active    Fa0/2, Fa0/3, Fa0/4, Fa0/5
                                             Fa0/6, Fa0/7, Fa0/8, Fa0/9
                                             Fa0/10, Fa0/11, Fa0/12, Fa0/13
                                             Fa0/14, Fa0/15, Fa0/16, Fa0/17
                                             Fa0/18, Fa0/19, Fa0/20, Fa0/21
                                             Fa0/22, Fa0/23, Fa0/24, Fa0/25
                                             Fa0/26, Fa0/27, Fa0/28, Fa0/29
                                             Fa0/30, Fa0/31, Fa0/32, Fa0/33
                                             Fa0/34, Fa0/35, Fa0/36, Fa0/37
                                             Fa0/38, Fa0/39, Fa0/40, Fa0/41
                                             Fa0/42, Fa0/43, Fa0/44, Fa0/45
                                             Fa0/46, Fa0/47, Fa0/48, Gi0/1
                                             Gi0/2
10   Data                          active    Fa0/1
20   Voice                         active    Fa0/1
1002 fddi-default                  act/unsup
1003 token-ring-default            act/unsup
1004 fddinet-default               act/unsup
1005 trnet-default                 act/unsup
```

Hands-on Lab 4.3: Setting Up VTP

1. Log into your switch and go into privileged exec mode by typing **enable**.

2. View the VTP settings by typing **show vtp status**. You should see that the default VTP mode is server.

3. Enter configuration mode by typing **configuration terminal**.

4. We want this switch to be able to receive and forward VTP messages but not make any additions, changes, or deletions. Therefore, we type **vtp mode client**.

5. We want the switch to belong to the VTP domain called lab-domain. Type **vtp domain lab-domain**.

6. Our VTP domain uses VTP version 2. We then need to type **vtp version 2**.

7. Finally, all of our switches within the VTP domain lab-domain use a password of mypassword. To configure this, type **vtp password mypassword**.

8. Exit configuration mode by typing **end**.

9. Verify your configuration changes by typing **show vtp status** and **show vtp password**. You should see the following configuration:

```
PoE-switch#show vtp status
VTP Version                    : 2
Configuration Revision         : 5
Maximum VLANs supported locally : 1005
Number of existing VLANs       : 8
VTP Operating Mode             : Client
VTP Domain Name                : lab-domain
VTP Pruning Mode               : Disabled
VTP V2 Mode                    : Enabled
VTP Traps Generation           : Disabled
MD5 digest                     : 0x26 0x3A 0xA0 0x8C 0x66 0x01 0xA1 0xF

Switch-A#show vtp password
VTP Password: mypassword
```

Hands-on Lab 4.4: Configuring Auto-QoS

1. Log into your switch and go into privileged exec mode by typing **enable**.

2. Enter interface configuration mode for port Fa0/1 by typing **configuration terminal** and **interface fa0/1**.

3. Check your Auto-QoS options by typing **auto qos voip ?**. You should see the following output:

    ```
    PoE-switch(config-if)#auto qos voip ?
      cisco-phone       Trust the QoS marking of Cisco IP Phone
      cisco-softphone   Trust the QoS marking of Cisco IP SoftPhone
      trust             Trust the DSCP/CoS marking
    ```

4. Configure the switchport to trust the QoS marking of a Cisco IP phone. Type **auto qos voip cisco-phone**.

5. Exit interface configuration mode by typing **end**.

Hands-on Lab 4.5: Setting Up a DHCP Server

1. Log into your router and go into privileged exec mode by typing **enable**.

2. Enter configuration mode by typing **configuration terminal**.

3. Enable the DHCP service by typing **service dhcp**.

4. We'll use the 172.16.1.0/24 network as our DHCP pool. We also want to exclude the first five IP addresses from being handed out. To do this, type **ip dhcp excluded address 172.16.1.1 172.16.1.5**.

5. Enter DHCP configuration mode and name the pool lab-pool by typing **ip dhcp pool lab-pool**.

6. Now that we're in DHCP configuration mode, configure the IP pool space by typing **network 172.16.1.0 255.255.255.0**.

7. Set the default-gateway for the DHCP devices to 172.16.1.1 by typing **default-router 172.16.1.1**.

8. Set the domain name for the DHCP devices to lab-domain.com by typing **domain-name lab-domain.com**.

9. Set the DNS server for the DHCP devices to 4.2.2.2 by typing **dns-server 4.2.2.2**.

10. Set the TFTP server for the DHCP devices to 192.168.100.100 by typing **option 150 ip 192.168.100.100**.

11. Exit DHCP configuration mode by typing **end**.

Review Questions

1. What Cisco IP phone power options power the phones using the Ethernet connection? To accomplish this, they sit between the IP phone and non-PoE switch. Choose all that apply.

   A. Power brick

   B. 802.3af switch

   C. ILP switch

   D. Powered patch panel

   E. Power injector

2. An ILP PoE switch can power devices of up to how many watts?

   A. 6.0 W

   B. 15.4 W

   C. 6.3 W

   D. 7.0 W

3. What protocol does a Cisco IP phone use to tell the PoE switch how much power it requires for the phone?

   A. PoE protocol

   B. iLBC

   C. VTP

   D. STP

   E. CDP

4. What Cisco power saving method helps to negotiate the exact power requirements of a Cisco IP phone?

   A. IPM

   B. 802.3af

   C. ILP

   D. CDP

5. What protocol is used to notify the Cisco IP phone of its voice VLAN number?

   A. PoE

   B. Spanning Tree Protocol

   C. Cisco Discovery Protocol

   D. VLAN Trunking Protocol

6. What command syntax properly configures a Cisco switchport for a Cisco IP phone on VLAN 50 while in interface configuration mode?

   A. `switchport mode access 50`

   B. `switchport access vlan 50`

   C. `switchport voice vlan 50`

   D. `switchport access voice 50`

   E. `switchport access voice vlan 50`

7. Devices that reside in the same VLAN share what?

   A. The same collision domain

   B. The same VTP domain

   C. The same voice VLAN domain

   D. The same broadcast domain

8. What IOS command lets you view which interfaces are configured as VLAN trunk links?

   A. `show trunk`

   B. `show interfaces trunk`

   C. `show switchport trunk`

   D. `show trunk interfaces`

9. What do you need to configure to allow devices on one VLAN to communicate with devices on a different VLAN?

   A. Inter-VTP routing

   B. Inter-VLAN routing

   C. Broadcast bridging

   D. VLAN bridging

   E. Spanning Tree Protocol

10. Which VTP mode allows administrators to add, delete, and modify VLAN information on the switch without propagating that information to any other switch?

    A. VTP server

    B. VTP client

    C. VTP cluster

    D. VTP transparent

    E. VTP access

11. How are the voice and native data VLANs treated differently on the link between the Cisco switch and the Cisco IP phone?

    A. The voice VLAN is tagged using 802.1Q and the data VLAN is not tagged.

    B. The voice VLAN is tagged using ISL and the data VLAN is tagged using 802.1Q.

    C. The voice VLAN is not tagged and the data VLAN is tagged using ISL.

    D. The voice VLAN is not tagged and the data VLAN is tagged using 802.1Q.

12. What is the cause of jitter, a form of variable delay on a network?

   A. CODEC processing

   B. Compression techniques

   C. Transcoding delay

   D. Queuing delay

13. What is the maximum end-to-end delay for voice packets on a network according to Cisco?

   A. 200 ms

   B. 100 ms

   C. 150 ms

   D. 80 ms

   E. 250 ms

14. What is the first step in the QoS process?

   A. Traffic marking

   B. Traffic classification

   C. Traffic queuing

   D. Traffic forwarding

15. Ideally, where should the QoS trust boundary be located?

   A. At the distribution layer

   B. At the core layer

   C. As close to the endpoint as possible

   D. As far away from the endpoint as possible

   E. At the L3 gateway

16. When you configure auto-QoS on your Cisco switches using the `auto qos voip` command, what queuing technique is used?

   A. PQ

   B. LLQ

   C. Fast Queuing

   D. Custom Queuing

17. Which of the following can be used to eliminate delay and jitter of time-sensitive traffic such as voice? Choose all that apply.

   A. Interface buffering

   B. LFI

   C. VTP

   D. Increasing the bandwidth

   E. QoS

18. Why is it important to configure DHCP option 150 for Cisco voice networks?

    A. It defines the default gateway for the phone.

    B. It defines the IP address of the TFTP server.

    C. It defines the IP address of the communications manager.

    D. It defines the IP address for CDP.

19. What IOS configuration mode syntax can be used to remove the first 10 IP addresses from DHCP scope using the 192.168.1.1/24 subnet?

    A. `ip excluded-address 192.168.1.1 192.168.1.10`

    B. `ip excluded-address dhcp 192.168.1.1 192.168.1.10`

    C. `dhcp excluded-address 192.168.1.1 192.168.1.10`

    D. `ip dhcp excluded-address 192.168.1.1 192.168.1.10`

20. A Cisco 7985 IP phone is an 802.3af class 3 device that requires 15.4 W of power to operate. You plug the phone into a Cisco PoE switch and the phone does not properly power up. What could be the problem? Choose all that apply.

    A. The PoE switch supports both ILP and 802.3af but only up to class 2 devices.

    B. The PoE switch supports only ILP.

    C. The PoE switch is overutilized and cannot power any additional devices.

    D. The PoE switch supports 802.3af devices up to class 3.

Answers to Review Questions

1. D, E. Both the powered patch panel and the power injector sit between the IP phone and switch and power the phone on the Ethernet cable.

2. B. An ILP PoE switch provides up to 15.4 watts of power to capable devices.

3. E. The Cisco Discovery Protocol (CDP) is used to discover IP phones and negotiate power options.

4. A. Cisco Intelligent Power Management (IPM) works between Cisco PoE switches and Cisco IP phones to negotiate and allocate the exact amount of power needed by the phone.

5. C. CDP is used between a Cisco switch and Cisco IP phone to inform the phone of its voice VLAN number.

6. C. The `switchport voice vlan 50` command is the correct syntax.

7. D. Devices within the same VLAN share a broadcast domain.

8. Answer: B. The `show interfaces trunk` command is the proper syntax to see which interfaces are configured as VLAN trunk links.

9. B. You must configure some type of inter-VLAN routing for devices located on separate VLANs to communicate with each other.

10. D. VTP transparent mode does not propagate any changes to any other connected switches.

11. A. Voice VLANs are tagged with 802.1Q and the native data VLAN is left untagged.

12. D. Variable delay occurs in bottleneck situations where voice traffic has to sit in a queue and wait for other packets to be sent out of the interface before a voice packet can be sent. This delay is the cause of jitter.

13. C. A maximum of 150 ms end-to-end can be handled and still maintain high-quality voice calls.

14. B. Traffic is always classified first in the QoS process.

15. C. QoS performs best when the trust boundaries are as close to the endpoints as possible.

16. Answer: B. Low Latency Queuing (LLQ) is the queuing mechanism used when you configure auto-QoS.

17. B, D, E. You can implement LFI and QoS techniques and/or increase bandwidth to help eliminate bottlenecks on the wire that can cause delay and jitter.

18. B. Option 150 defines the IP address of the TFTP server, where the phone can download configuration files.

19. D. The ip dhcp excluded-address syntax is the proper way to exclude IP addresses from the DHCP scope.

20. B, C. Some older Cisco PoE switches support only the Cisco proprietary ILP option, which can power devices requiring up to 6.3 W. A second possibility is that the switch is powering many other PoE devices and has simply run out of power to allocate to the newly added phone.

Answers to Written Lab 4.1

1. `show power inline`

2. `show vlan brief`

3. `vlan 100, name Voice`

4. `switchport voice vlan 55`

5. `switchport access vlan 105`

6. `switchport mode trunk` and `switchport trunk encapsulation dot1q`

7. `switchport trunk allowed vlan 10,20,30`

8. `show vtp status`

9. `show vtp password`

10. `service dhcp`

Chapter

5

CUCM Express Installation and Basic Configuration

THE CCNA VOICE EXAM TOPICS COVERED IN THIS CHAPTER INCLUDE THE FOLLOWING:

✓ **Implement Cisco Unified Communications Manager Express to support endpoints using CLI.**

  ▪ Describe the appropriate software components needed to support endpoints.

  ▪ Describe the requirements and correct settings for TFTP.

  ▪ Configure TFTP.

  ▪ Describe the differences between key-system and PBX modes.

  ▪ Describe the differences between the different types of ephones and ephone-DNs.

  ▪ Configure Cisco Unified Communications Manager Express endpoints.

✓ **Perform basic maintenance and operations tasks to support the VoIP solution.**

  ▪ Describe basic troubleshooting methods for Cisco Unified Communications Manager Express.

In Chapter 5 we're going to start configuring the CUCM Express. Up until now, you've been reading all the theory and rhetoric behind PSTN and VoIP technology as well as how to design and build your network to support VoIP. Now you're finally going to be able to dig in and install software to support voice.

This chapter starts off discussing the CUCM licensing options available to you. Then we'll move on to installing the Cisco IOS that supports voice as well as show how to download and install the CUCM Express software, which interacts with the Cisco IOS software to function. Then you will learn the essential command-line configuration steps required on a CUCM Express system for call processing to function, and you will configure phones and extensions to the point where you can make phone calls. Once you can properly configure basic phone capabilities using the command line, you will learn how to enable and use the CUCM Express graphical web interface to configure and manage your voice environment. Lastly, we'll go over a troubleshooting methodology that helps you quickly identify and resolve common CUCM Express problems. I will also detail some handy show and debug commands to assist you with the troubleshooting process.

Understanding CUCM Express Licensing

One of the more complex tasks required when ordering Cisco voice gear is the way Cisco handles licensing structures. You need three Cisco licenses to run your CUCM Express system and Cisco phones on your network:

- Cisco IOS license for voice capabilities
- CCME Express feature license
- Individual user licenses for the total number of Cisco phones

In this section we'll review each of these so you can properly license and run a CUCM Express system and Cisco IP phones.

IOS Licenses for Voice

The first license allows you to download and operate a version of Cisco IOS that has CUCM Express functionality. When you purchase a router, it comes with an *IOS feature set* with which you can run the router. The license also allows you to download and install new versions of this IOS feature set when they become available.

CUCM Express Feature Licenses

Just because you own the license to run the voice-capable IOS image doesn't mean you can start adding Cisco IP phones. The second license you need is the *CUCM Express feature license*. This license determines how many phones you can run on the CUCM. They are sold in bundles; the smallest bundle is 25 Cisco IP phones. Table 5.1 shows the current CUCM Express feature license bundles available.

TABLE 5.1   CUCM Express 7965 feature license bundles

License	Description
FL-CCME-250	CUCM Express support for up to 250 IP phones
FL-CCME-175	CUCM Express support for up to 175 IP phones
FL-CCME-100	CUCM Express support for up to 100 IP phones
FL-CCME-50	CUCM Express support for up to 50 IP phones
FL-CCME-35	CUCM Express support for up to 35 IP phones
FL-CCME-25	CUCM Express support for up to 25 IP phones

Let's say you have an environment that on day one requires 150 IP phones. For this number, you should purchase the FL-CCME-175 license. Then, as the business grows, the next installment of phones on this network is 30, bringing the total number to 180. Instead of purchasing all new licenses, you can simply add to your 175-license total by purchasing the FL-CCME-25 license. Now you have CUCM Express license support for up to 200 phones.

Cisco Phone User Licenses

Finally, you need the *Cisco phone user license*. When you place an order for Cisco phones, you are given three different license options for each Cisco phone. For example, Table 5.2 lists the part numbers and descriptions for the 7965G phone:

TABLE 5.2 Cisco IP phone part numbers

Part Number	Description
CP-7965G=	Spare phone w/o license
CP-7965G-CH1	Phone w/ CUCM user license
CP-7965G-CCME	Phone w/ CUCM Express user license

As you can see, you are given several ordering choices for a single phone! The CP-7965G= is simply a spare phone. It does not come with a license. These are most commonly purchased to serve as "cold spares" at businesses. If a licensed phone on the network were to break, it could be replaced with the unlicensed spare as a one-to-one trade. These unlicensed phones are less expensive but they can be used only as replacements.

The other two license options are for either the CUCM/CUCMBE or the CUCM Express call-processing systems. The pricing is slightly different for these two parts. The CH1 licenses are more expensive than the CCME licenses, but the CH1 licenses can legitimately be used by the larger CUCM system. By contrast, the CCME licenses cannot be used for the CUCM/CUCMBE systems. So if you think you may upgrade from a CUCM Express system to one of the bigger CUCM systems, you may want to go ahead and purchase the CH1 licenses so you won't have to purchase phone user licenses twice.

Cisco CUCM Express License Bundles

Cisco is attempting to make licensing for voice capabilities easier on the purchaser by bundling Cisco ISR hardware with both the IOS and CUCM Express feature licenses. These *CUCM Express license bundles* are basically ready to go. All you need to do after buying one is to choose which Cisco phones you want to install and make sure each phone purchased comes with either the CH1 or CCME license. Table 5.3 shows a few examples of the types of ISR voice bundles that Cisco currently offers.

TABLE 5.3 ISR bundle examples

Bundle Part Number	Description	CUCM Express Licenses
CISCO3825-CCME/K9	Cisco 3825 ISR with IOS SP and voice services	Up to 168 Cisco phones
CISCO2851-CCME/K9	Cisco 2851 ISR with IOS SP and voice services	Up to 48 Cisco phones
CISCO2801-CCME/K9	Cisco 2801 ISR with IOS SP and voice services	Up to 8 Cisco phones

Cisco Voice IOS and CUCM Express Software Installation

The CUCM Express upgrade/installation process requires the installation of two separate but dependent pieces of software. One is the Cisco IOS with voice services, and the other is the CUCM Express software. The versions of these two software items must be compatible with each other to avoid any operability issues. Cisco has a handy website that gives you a very clear *IOS compatibility matrix* for the version of IOS/CUCM Express software you wish to run. This matrix is frequently updated and can be found at http://www.cisco .com/en/US/docs/voice_ip_comm/cucme/requirements/guide/33matrix.htm

Once you've decided on the IOS and CUCM Express software you wish to run on your supported router hardware, you can download the software from the http://www.cisco .com/go/software website. Downloading the IOS software from the Cisco website is quite simple. The IOS is a single file with a .bin extension. Once it is downloaded, you can put the software on a TFTP server and transfer it over to the router.

In order to download software from Cisco, you must register at www.cisco.com and have a valid service contract for the software you wish to acquire.

The process of uploading an IOS image to your router is fairly simple. For example, suppose you've just downloaded the c3825-ipvoicek9-mz.124-15.XZ2.bin IOS image and have it sitting on your TFTP server at 192.168.1.11. On your Cisco router, you issue the copy tftp: flash: command to upload the image to the router compact flash (CF) drive. The router then asks you for additional information such as the IP address of your TFTP server and the filename of the image you wish to TFTP. You can also rename the file if you want it to be named something different on the router. Here is the TFTP upload process in action:

```
Router#copy tftp: flash:
Address or name of remote host [192.168.1.11]?
Source filename [c3825-ipvoicek9-mz.124-15.XZ2.bin]?
Destination filename []? c3825-ipvoicek9-mz.124-15.XZ2.bin
Accessing tftp://192.168.1.11/c3825-ipvoicek9-mz.124-15.XZ2.bin...
Erase flash: before copying? [confirm]n
Loading c3825-ipvoicek9-mz.124-15.XZ2.bin from 192.168.1.11
(via GigabitEthernet0/0): !!!!!!!!!!!!!!!!!!!!!!!!!!!!!!!!!!!!!!!!!!
!!!!!!!!!!!!!!!!!!!!!!!!!!!!!!!!!!!!!!!!!!!!!!!!!!!!!!!!!!!!!!!!!!!!!!
!!!!!!!!!!!!!!!!!!!!!!!!!!!!!!!!!!!!!!!!!!!!!!!!!!!!!!!!!!!!!!!!!!!!!
```

```
[OK - 47576204 bytes]

Verifying checksum... CCCCCCCCCCCCCCCCCCCCCCCCCCCCCCCCCCCCCCCCCCCCCCCCCCC
CCCCCCCCCCCCCCCCCCCCCCCCCCCCCCCCCCCCCCCCCCCCC OK (0xB420)
47576204 bytes copied in 859.716 secs (55339 bytes/sec)
Router#
```

 Make sure you have sufficient storage space on your router prior to uploading any files. To verify the amount of space on the flash drive of a router, issue a show flash privileged exec command to see the total number of bytes free. If you don't have enough space, you'll have to delete other files/images using the delete flash:<*file name*> command.

Using a USB Thumb Drive as an Alternate Method for Uploading Software

If you have a router with USB ports such as any of the newer Cisco ISRs, you might find that uploading IOS and CUCM Express software just got a little easier and faster! You could go through the typical process of setting up a TFTP server and transferring the files across the network. This can take a great deal of time and effort to accomplish. If you happen to have physical access to the router, you can simply load the image files onto your trusty USB thumb drive and insert it into the router. The router will mount your USB thumb drive as usbflash1 (or usbflash2 if you have two USB ports), and you can run copy usbflash1: flash: to move your images to the router CF. For example:

```
TechRepublic-Router# copy usbflash1:/c3825-ipvoicek9-mz.124-15.XZ2.bin flash:
 Destination filename [c3825-ipvoicek9-mz.124-15.XZ2.bin]?
 Copy in progress...CCCCCCCCCCCCCCCCCCCCCCCCCCCCCCCCCCCCCCCCCCCCCCCCCCCCCCCC
CCCCCCCCCCCCCCCCCCCCCCCCCCCCCCCCCCCCCCCCCCCCCCCCCCCCCCCCCCCCCCCCCCCCCCCCCCCC
CCCCCCCCCCCCCCCCCCCCCCCCCCCCCCCCCCCCCCCCCCCCCCCCCCCCCCCCCCCCCCCCCCCCCCCCCCCC
CCCCCCCCCCCCCCCCCCCCCCCCCCCCCCCCCCCCCCCCCCCCCCCCCCCCCCCCCCCCCCCCCCCCCCCCCCCC
CCCCCCCCCCCCCCCC
 [output omitted]
 Verifying checksum... CCCCCCCCCCCCCCCCCCCCCCCCCCCCCCCCCCCCCCCCCCCCCCCCCCCC
CCCCCCCCCCCCCCCCCCCCCCCCCCCCCCCCCCCCCCCC OK (0xB420)
47576204 bytes copied in 68.756 secs (1193025 bytes/sec)
```

This method also works for uploading the CME software using the archive tar /xtract command, which you will learn how to use next. Not only does this save time setting up a TFTP server, but copying from a USB flash drive is much faster than TFTP!

Installing CUCM Express software on your IOS router can either be a pain or a real snap depending on the method you choose. The CUCM Express software consists of over 100 separate files that can be downloaded individually or as a Zip file from the cisco.com/software website. If you download the Zip package, you must unzip the files prior to uploading them to the router. That leaves you with quite a task, because you need to TFTP every file to the router flash drive.

An alternative method is to download and archive a prepackaged CUCM Express system that comes as a single .tar file. The .tar packages will be labeled cme-full.X.X.X.tar or cme-basic.X.X.X.tar, where X.X.X is the CUCM Express version number. The *cme-basic package* contains the more common Cisco phone load files, whereas the *cme-full package* includes all the load files. In addition, the cme-basic package includes the necessary web GUI files. The cme-full version includes all of the same web GUI files as well but also contains additional ring tone files, desktop backgrounds, and basic automatic call distribution (B-ACD) files.

Once you've selected the .tar package that is compatible with the IOS image you've already uploaded, you can upload the CUCM Express software via TFTP, using the archive tar /xtract command. This command automatically extracts the individual files and places them in an orderly directory structure for your convenience.

If you download and install a .tar package, you can always download and install additional software functionality that you need but was not included in the package. To do so, find the software files you require and TFTP them onto the router flash drive where the prepackaged software has been extracted.

The next example shows us again using 192.168.1.11 as our TFTP server, and we are uploading and extracting files from the single cme-full-4.3.0.0.tar file:

```
Router#archive tar /xtract tftp://192.168.1.11/cme-full-4.3.0.0.tar flash:
Loading cme-full-4.3.0.0.tar from 192.168.1.11 (via GigabitEthernet0/0): !
extracting bacdprompts/app-b-acd-2.1.2.2-ReadMe.txt (18836 bytes)
extracting bacdprompts/app-b-acd-2.1.2.2.tcl (24985 bytes)
extracting bacdprompts/app-b-acd-aa-2.1.2.2.tcl (35485 bytes)
extracting bacdprompts/en_bacd_allagentsbusy.au (75650 bytes)
extracting bacdprompts/en_bacd_disconnect.au (83291 bytes)
extracting bacdprompts/en_bacd_enter_dest.au (63055 bytes)!
extracting bacdprompts/en_bacd_invalidoption.au (37952 bytes)
extracting bacdprompts/en_bacd_music_on_hold.au (496521 bytes)!!
extracting bacdprompts/en_bacd_options_menu.au (123446 bytes)!
extracting bacdprompts/en_bacd_welcome.au (42978 bytes)
extracting bacdprompts/en_bacd_xferto_operator.au (34794 bytes)!
```

```
extracting CME43-full-readme-v.2.0.txt (22224 bytes)
extracting Desktops/320x212x12/CampusNight.png (131470 bytes)
extracting Desktops/320x212x12/CiscoFountain.png (80565 bytes)!
extracting Desktops/320x212x12/List.xml (628 bytes)
extracting Desktops/320x212x12/MorroRock.png (109076 bytes)
extracting Desktops/320x212x12/NantucketFlowers.png (108087 bytes)
extracting Desktops/320x212x12/TN-CampusNight.png (10820 bytes)
extracting Desktops/320x212x12/TN-CiscoFountain.png (9657 bytes)
extracting Desktops/320x212x12/TN-Fountain.png (7953 bytes)
extracting Desktops/320x212x12/TN-MorroRock.png (7274 bytes)!
extracting Desktops/320x212x12/TN-NantucketFlowers.png (9933 bytes)
extracting Desktops/320x212x12/Fountain.png (138278 bytes)
extracting gui/Delete.gif (953 bytes)
extracting gui/admin_user.html (3845 bytes)
extracting gui/admin_user.js (647358 bytes)!!!
extracting gui/CiscoLogo.gif (1029 bytes)!
[output cut]
```

This process takes a few minutes. Once it's complete, we can issue a dir flash: command to see the contents and structure of our CUCM Express system on the compact flash drive:

```
Router#dir flash:
Directory of flash:/

    1   drw-           0   Apr 7 2009 18:17:56 +00:00  bacdprompts
   13   -rw-       22224   Apr 7 2009 18:25:56 +00:00  CME43-full-readme-v.2.0.t
xt
   14   drw-           0   Apr 7 2009 18:18:06 +00:00  Desktops
   27   drw-           0   Apr 7 2009 18:18:14 +00:00  gui
   45   -rw-      496521   Apr 7 2009 18:26:22 +00:00  music-on-hold.au
   46   drw-           0   Apr 7 2009 18:18:28 +00:00  phone
  127   drw-           0   Apr 7 2009 18:31:02 +00:00  ringtones
  161   -rw-    47576204   Apr 7 2009 18:37:22 +00:00  c3825-ipvoicek9-mz.124-15
.XZ2.bin

511664128 bytes total (395001856 bytes free)
```

From the output of the dir flash:command, you can see that our IOS image is on the CF along with several CUCM Express software directories. You can look into the various directories as well. For instance, if you want to view the contents of the gui directory, you would do the following:

Router#**dir flash:/gui**
Directory of flash:/gui/

```
28   -rw-       953    Apr 7 2009 18:26:06 +00:00   Delete.gif
29   -rw-      3845    Apr 7 2009 18:26:06 +00:00   admin_user.html
30   -rw-    647358    Apr 7 2009 18:26:10 +00:00   admin_user.js
31   -rw-      1029    Apr 7 2009 18:26:12 +00:00   CiscoLogo.gif
32   -rw-       174    Apr 7 2009 18:26:12 +00:00   Tab.gif
33   -rw-     16344    Apr 7 2009 18:26:12 +00:00   dom.js
34   -rw-       864    Apr 7 2009 18:26:12 +00:00   downarrow.gif
35   -rw-      6328    Apr 7 2009 18:26:14 +00:00   ephone_admin.html
36   -rw-      4558    Apr 7 2009 18:26:14 +00:00   logohome.gif
37   -rw-      3724    Apr 7 2009 18:26:14 +00:00   normal_user.html
38   -rw-     76699    Apr 7 2009 18:26:16 +00:00   normal_user.js
39   -rw-       843    Apr 7 2009 18:26:16 +00:00   sxiconad.gif
40   -rw-      1347    Apr 7 2009 18:26:16 +00:00   Plus.gif
41   -rw-      2399    Apr 7 2009 18:26:18 +00:00   telephony_service.html
42   -rw-       870    Apr 7 2009 18:26:18 +00:00   uparrow.gif
43   -rw-      9968    Apr 7 2009 18:26:18 +00:00   xml-test.html
44   -rw-      3412    Apr 7 2009 18:26:20 +00:00   xml.template

511664128 bytes total (395001856 bytes free)
```

The gui directory lists all of the files needed for utilizing the CUCM Express web graphical user interface (GUI). Another important directory is the phone directory. It contains the files requested by any Cisco phones on the CUCM Express. Let's drill into the phone directory and its subdirectory, labeled 7945-7965:

Router#**dir flash:phone/7945-7965**
Directory of flash:phone/7945-7965/

```
48   -rw-    2496963    Apr 7 2009 18:26:30 +00:00   apps45.8-3-2-27.sbn
49   -rw-     585536    Apr 7 2009 18:26:34 +00:00   cnu45.8-3-2-27.sbn
50   -rw-    2453202    Apr 7 2009 18:26:44 +00:00   cvm45sccp.8-3-2-27.sbn
51   -rw-     326315    Apr 7 2009 18:26:46 +00:00   dsp45.8-3-2-27.sbn
52   -rw-     555406    Apr 7 2009 18:26:48 +00:00   jar45sccp.8-3-2-27.sbn
53   -rw-        638    Apr 7 2009 18:26:50 +00:00   SCCP45.8-3-3S.loads
```

```
54  -rw-        642    Apr 7 2009 18:26:50 +00:00  term45.default.loads
55  -rw-        642    Apr 7 2009 18:26:52 +00:00  term65.default.loads
```

511664128 bytes total (395001856 bytes free)

This directory stores all of the files that a Cisco 7945 through 7965 series IP phone will require. These files are requested by the Cisco phones and are downloaded using TFTP. We'll configure CUCM Express telephony services later in this chapter.

Initial CUCM Express Configuration

Cisco IP phones using the SCCP signaling protocol rely on servers to receive information such as the firmware and configuration files. This section details the files that the phones require and shows how to configure them on the CUCM Express router. First, you'll see how to turn the CUCM Express into a TFTP server to offer up specific Cisco phone firmware files. Then we'll move on to the four mandatory CUCM Express system configurations needed to support IP phones. Finally, I'll show you how to configure and generate individual phone configuration files to allow each Cisco phone to have unique functionality within the voice system. After all these steps are completed, your Cisco phone will be able to connect successfully to its host CUCM Express and use the information gathered to function as a VoIP phone!

Configuring CUCM Express as a TFTP Server

When a Cisco IP phone successfully powers up, it will use CDP to determine the voice VLAN it should belong to and then request and receive, at a minimum, an IP address/ subnet mask and gateway IP address via DHCP. It also must have the all-important option 150 IP address, which is the location of the TFTP server. As you've already learned, for voice the TFTP server is responsible for delivering Cisco phone firmware and configuration files to the phones when requested. The TFTP server can be located anywhere on your network, but in smaller environments, the CUCM Express router is configured for TFTP. This is the first server the IP phone gets its information from. One group of files that our Cisco IP phone will request is its firmware, which is specifically tailored to the type of Cisco phone hardware. If you are using your CUCM Express router to handle TFTP server functionality, you must configure the IOS to serve up the firmware that your phones will request. Because we've downloaded and extracted the .tar CUCM Express software, the extraction process neatly placed all the necessary firmware files needed by most phones into an easy-to-understand directory structure. All you need to do is figure out which Cisco phones you will want to allow on your network and then configure the router to serve the appropriate files. You can see all of the firmware file directories by issuing the `dir flash:/phone` command:

```
Directory of flash:/phone/

   47   drw-            0    Apr 7 2009 18:18:28 +00:00   7945-7965
   56   drw-            0    Apr 7 2009 18:18:56 +00:00   7937
   58   drw-            0    Apr 7 2009 18:19:24 +00:00   7914
   60   drw-            0    Apr 7 2009 18:19:26 +00:00   7906-7911
   69   drw-            0    Apr 7 2009 18:19:52 +00:00   7920
   71   drw-            0    Apr 7 2009 18:19:58 +00:00   7931
   79   drw-            0    Apr 7 2009 18:20:24 +00:00   7942-7962
   88   drw-            0    Apr 7 2009 18:28:46 +00:00   7921
   96   drw-            0    Apr 7 2009 18:29:30 +00:00   7940-7960
  101   drw-            0    Apr 7 2009 18:29:38 +00:00   7970-7971
  110   drw-            0    Apr 7 2009 18:30:06 +00:00   7975
  118   drw-            0    Apr 7 2009 18:30:34 +00:00   7941-7961
511664128 bytes total (395001856 bytes free)
```

Let's assume that we are going to be configuring Cisco 7945, 7965, and 7970 phones in our environment. Therefore, we need to configure our TFTP server to offer all of the files within the `flash:/phone/7945-7965` and `flash:/phone/7970-7971` directories. Note that some of the firmware files work for multiple phones. For example, the firmware files required by the Cisco 7945 are the same as those required by the 7965. This is because the phones are essentially identical except for the number of extension buttons they have. The 7945 has four extension buttons, whereas the 7965 has six.

Configuring the Cisco CUCM Express router to serve as a TFTP server for the firmware files is quite simple. Each firmware file needs to have its own `tftp-server flash:/phone/<firmware_file>` command. Also note that because our CUCM Express files are organized with a directory structure, we must provide a *directory alias* for the Cisco phones. Remember that Cisco phones are unintelligent devices for the most part. They know only the name of the firmware files and not where they are located. Because we've organized our CUCM Express software into directories, we must create aliases so that when the Cisco phone asks for a file, it knows which subdirectory the file is located in. Let's use the 7945-7965 phone firmware files as an example. We'll first run the `dir flash:/phone/7945-7965` command to see what firmware files those specific phones will require:

```
Router#dir flash:phone/7945-7965
Directory of flash:phone/7945-7965/

   48   -rw-      2496963    Apr 7 2009 18:26:30 +00:00   apps45.8-3-2-27.sbn
   49   -rw-       585536    Apr 7 2009 18:26:34 +00:00   cnu45.8-3-2-27.sbn
```

```
50  -rw-   2453202   Apr 7 2009 18:26:44 +00:00   cvm45sccp.8-3-2-27.sbn
51  -rw-    326315   Apr 7 2009 18:26:46 +00:00   dsp45.8-3-2-27.sbn
52  -rw-    555406   Apr 7 2009 18:26:48 +00:00   jar45sccp.8-3-2-27.sbn
53  -rw-       638   Apr 7 2009 18:26:50 +00:00   SCCP45.8-3-3S.loads
54  -rw-       642   Apr 7 2009 18:26:50 +00:00   term45.default.loads
55  -rw-       642   Apr 7 2009 18:26:52 +00:00   term65.default.loads
```

These phones will need all eight files to fully function properly. To offer up these files for downloading to the phones, we need to configure the following:

```
Router#configure terminal
Enter configuration commands, one per line.  End with CNTL/Z.
Router(config)#tftp-server flash:/phone/7945-7965/apps45.8-3-2-27.sbn alias
apps45.8-3-2-27.sbn
Router(config)#tftp-server flash:/phone/7945-7965/cnu45.8-3-2-27.sbn alias
cnu45.8-3-2-27.sbn
Router(config)#tftp-server flash:/phone/7945-7965/cvm45sccp.8-3-2-27.sbn alias
cvm45sccp.8-3-2-27.sbn
Router(config)#tftp-server flash:/phone/7945-7965/dsp45.8-3-2-27.sbn alias
dsp45.8-3-2-27.sbn
Router(config)#tftp-server flash:/phone/7945-7965/jar45sccp.8-3-2-27.sbn alias
jar45sccp.8-3-2-27.sbn
Router(config)#tftp-server flash:/phone/7945-7965/SCCP45.8-3-3S.loads alias
SCCP45.8-3-3S.loads
Router(config)#tftp-server flash:/phone/7945-7965/term45.default.loads alias
term45.default.loads
Router(config)#tftp-server flash:/phone/7945-7965/term65.default.loads alias
term65.default.loads
Router(config)#
```

We've now successfully configured our CUCM Express router to serve up firmware files for the Cisco 7945 and 7965 phones using TFTP. Let's go ahead and finish off this example by configuring the router to serve up firmware files for the Cisco 7971 phones. First we look in the phone directory for the 7970 and 7971 phones:

```
Router#dir flash:/phone/7970-7971
Directory of flash:/phone/7970-7971/

102  -rw-   2494499   Apr 7 2009 18:29:46 +00:00   apps70.8-3-2-27.sbn
103  -rw-    547706   Apr 7 2009 18:29:48 +00:00   cnu70.8-3-2-27.sbn
104  -rw-   2456051   Apr 7 2009 18:29:58 +00:00   cvm70sccp.8-3-2-27.sbn
105  -rw-    530601   Apr 7 2009 18:30:00 +00:00   dsp70.8-3-2-27.sbn
106  -rw-    538527   Apr 7 2009 18:30:04 +00:00   jar70sccp.8-3-2-27.sbn
107  -rw-       638   Apr 7 2009 18:30:06 +00:00   SCCP70.8-3-3S.loads
```

```
108  -rw-      642   Apr 7 2009 18:30:06 +00:00  term70.default.loads
109  -rw-      642   Apr 7 2009 18:30:06 +00:00  term71.default.loads
```

```
511664128 bytes total (395001856 bytes free)
```

Now we configure IOS to begin serving up these files using TFTP:

```
Router#configure terminal
Enter configuration commands, one per line.  End with CNTL/Z.
Router(config)#tftp-server flash:/phone/7970-7971/apps70.8-3-2-27.sbn alias
apps70.8-3-2-27.sbn
Router(config)#tftp-server flash:/phone/7970-7971/cnu70.8-3-2-27.sbn alias
cnu70.8-3-2-27.sbn
Router(config)#tftp-server flash:/phone/7970-7971/cvm70sccp.8-3-2-27.sbn alias
cvm70sccp.8-3-2-27.sbn
Router(config)#tftp-server flash:/phone/7970-7971/dsp70.8-3-2-27.sbn alias
dsp70.8-3-2-27.sbn Router(config)#tftp-server flash:/phone/7970-7971/
jar70sccp.8-3-2-27.sbn alias jar70sccp.8-3-2-27.sbn
Router(config)#tftp-server flash:/phone/7970-7971/SCCP70.8-3-3S.loads alias
SCCP70.8-3-3S.loads
Router(config)#tftp-server flash:/phone/7970-7971/term70.default.loads alias
term70.default.loads
Router(config)#tftp-server flash:/phone/7970-7971/term71.default.loads alias
term71.default.loads
Router(config)#
```

That's all there is to it! At this point, if you were to add one of these phones to your network, it would receive all the necessary IP information and download the phone firmware files from the TFTP server. The phone will *not* register to the CUCM Express, however. It is still missing vital configurations that must be set up on the CUCM Express for the registration process to occur. The next section of this chapter shows how to configure the CUCM Express to allow Cisco phones to work with the call processor and how to identify and serve up default configuration files to your Cisco IP phones.

Configuring the Mandatory CUCM Express System Settings

The majority of CUCM Express configuration tuning happens while in config-telephony mode. You must accomplish four configuration steps to get the system to properly register phones for call processing. These steps are:

1. Configure the source IP address for the CUCM Express.
2. Configure the maximum number of ephones and ephone-DNs (directory numbers) allowed on the CUCM Express.

3. Identify and set the firmware load files that Cisco IP phones should request based on the Cisco phone model.

4. Generate and serve up default phone configuration files via TFTP to the Cisco IP phones.

The next four sections detail each of these steps.

Step 1: Configure the Source CUCM Express IP Address

The *source IP address* defines the location of the CUCM Express call-processing unit. All of the Cisco IP phones on the network will use this address for all communications with the CUCM Express hardware. After a Cisco phone downloads the correct firmware used via TFTP, it requests and receives generic information about the CUCM Express. One item is the source IP address where the CUCM Express can be found. In the example shown in Figure 5.1, we'll assume that all of our IP phones reside on the voice VLAN of 192.168.10.0/24.

FIGURE 5.1   A sample CUCM Express network

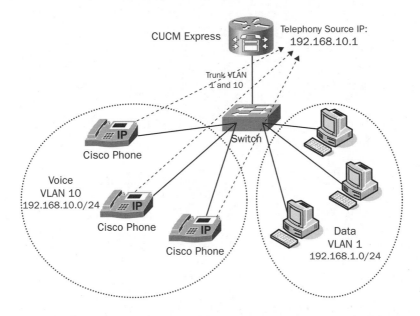

We're going to use the 192.168.10.1 IP address as our source IP for the Call Manager. The configuration of the CUCM Express source IP address is as follows:

```
Router#configure terminal
Router(config)#telephony-service
Router(config-telephony)#ip source-address 192.168.10.1
Router(config-telephony)#end
Router#
```

You'll see later how this information is eventually packaged within a default configuration file and sent to all Cisco IP phones on the network.

Step 2: Configure Max Ephones and DNs

Step 2 of our CUCM Express system configuration involves setting the maximum number of ephones and ephone-DNs. *Ephones* represent physical phones. They are how you identify a particular device within the IOS. *Ephone-DNs*, on the other hand, are the number extensions configured on each phone. Figure 5.2 shows a Cisco phone with buttons for multiple ephone-DNs. This particular Cisco phone has buttons to handle up to six ephone-DNs.

FIGURE 5.2   Cisco IP phone extension buttons

By default, the maximum number of both ephones and ephone-DNs is 0. You might ask, what's the point of Cisco setting the defaults to 0 if I have to set them to 1 or more to get a single phone to work? The answer has to do with memory allocation. When a maximum ephone and ephone-DN are set, the router sets aside memory for each one. For example, if you set max ephones to 10 and max-dn to 50, the router allocates memory for each of the 10 ephones and all 50 ephone-DNs regardless of whether you actually use them or not! You should keep in mind to not set the maximums too high, because you could overtax your router. In our example, we're going to set our max ephones to 8 and our max-dn to 20:

```
Router#configure terminal
Router(config)#telephony-service
Router(config-telephony)#max-ephones 8
Router(config-telephony)#max-dn 20
```

The maximum number of ephones and ephone-DNs that can be configured depends on the hardware, because different devices have different amounts of memory installed in them. Also, let's say that our max-ephones is 8 and we attempt to add a ninth phone to the CUCM Express. When this occurs, the phone will not be allowed to register and we will see a "Registration Rejected" message on the phone display, as shown in Figure 5.3.

FIGURE 5.3   "Registration Rejected" message

Also, if you exceed the max-dn number, you will receive an error when you attempt to configure the maximum +1 ephone-DN. The following example has max-dn set to 20, so on the 21st ephone-DN configuration, we'll see this log message on the CUCM Express console:

```
Router(config)#ephone-dn 21
dn 21 exceeds max-dn 20
Router(config)#
```

Step 3: Identify and Set Firmware Load Files

Step 3 of the CUCM Express system configuration process deals with how we handle the distribution of firmware for our Cisco phones. As I've already shown you, we've identified the files that our Cisco phones need and have configured our router to serve them using TFTP. The CUCM Express telephony processes must also be configured to set the firmware files we choose to define for each phone hardware type. As mentioned earlier, when the phones first communicate, they have very little information and must be told virtually everything. One piece of information a phone does possess is its hardware type (Cisco phone model). The CUCM Express uses this information to determine which *firmware load file* the phone should request. The firmware load file basically tells the CUCM Express what firmware to instruct the Cisco phone to download. It can be a bit difficult to figure out which firmware load file you need to configure for each phone. The best way to find out which load files you need is to do a search on the cisco.com website. Search for "CME X.X firmware," where X.X is the version of the CUCM Express software you are running. For example, Figure 5.4 shows a search for CME 4.3 firmware on Cisco's website.

FIGURE 5.4   Searching for Cisco phone firmware

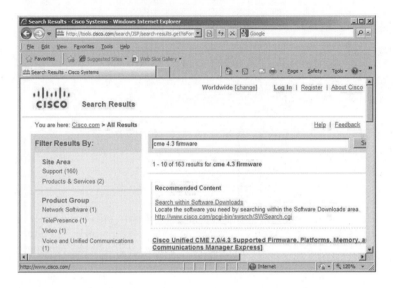

Now that we have a listing for the firmware files each phone requires, we can determine the single load file for each phone that needs to be configured within config-telephony mode. In Figure 5.5, we see that we need to configure SCCP45.8-3-3S.loads as our load file.

FIGURE 5.5   Cisco phone load file table

Cisco Unified IP Phone Support			
Device Type	SCCP Firmware Filename	SIP Firmware Filename	Comments
Cisco Unified IP Phone 7945G and 7965G	SCCP45.8-3-3S.loads* term45.default.loads term65.default.loads apps45.8-3-2-27.sbn cnu45.8-3-2-27.sbn cvm45sccp.8-3-2-27.sbn dsp45.8-3-2-27.sbn jar45sccp.8-3-2-27.sbn	SIP45.8-3-3S.loads* term45.default.loads term65.default.loads apps45.8-3-2-27.sbn cnu45.8-3-2-27.sbn cvm45sip.8-3-2-27.sbn dsp45.8-3-2-27.sbn jar45sip.8-3-2-27.sbn	

We know that we need to use SCCP45.8-3-3S.loads as our key load file because

1. We are using SCCP as our signaling protocol.

2. The file marked with an asterisk (*) is the load file.

Let's configure our Call Manager to tell our Cisco 7945, 7965, and 7970 phones which firmware load files they should request:

```
Router#configure terminal
Router(config)#telephony-service
Router(config-telephony)#load 7945 SCCP45.8-3-3S.loads
Updating CNF files
CNF files update complete for phonetype(7945)

Router(config-telephony)#load 7965 SCCP45.8-3-3S.loads
Updating CNF files
CNF files update complete for phonetype(7965)

Router(config-telephony)#load 7970 SCCP70.8-3-3S.loads
Updating CNF files
CNF files update complete for phonetype(7970)
```

If you are using CUCM Express software that is earlier than version 4.3, do not include the .sbin or .loads extension at the end of the load command. For versions 4.3 and above, use the complete filename including the .sbin or .loads suffix.

Step 4: Generate and Serve Default Phone Configuration Files

The *default phone configuration* is the file that informs a Cisco phone of all the general information it needs to communicate with the CUCM Express system. Included in this default phone configuration is the source IP address and port with which the phones can communicate to the Call Manager. It also includes the load configuration filenames we just finished setting up.

At this point, I'm referring to the phone configuration files as "default" because there is nothing unique about the configurations yet. Once we begin configuring phone extensions and other settings unique to the phones, this information will be compiled and stored as a single phone configuration file. But since none of that information is configured at this time, the configuration files have only the default information that all Cisco phones share.

The phone configuration file is automatically updated every time a change is made that affects the configuration. For example, if you need to add additional load files for a Cisco phone, as soon as an addition occurs in the telephony-service configuration prompt, the configuration file updates itself. You can also manually update the phone configuration file by issuing the create cnf-files config-telephony command. Here is an example of this command:

```
Router(config-telephony)#create ?
  cnf-files  create XML cnf for ethernet phone

Router(config-telephony)#create cnf-files
Creating CNF files
```

Once these four steps have been completed, we can back out of config-telephony mode and finish our basic configuration by configuring ephones and ephone-DNs.

 Real World Scenario

Troubleshooting IP Registration Problems

A brand-new Cisco IPT deployment was taking place at a manufacturing facility. After configuring the CUCM Express for proper deployment, Matt, the engineer responsible for implementation of the project, began installing 7945, 7965, and 7971 phones on desks within the office. While powering up the phones, Matt discovered that not all of the IP phones were properly registering. The 7945 and 7965 phones registered properly, but the 7971 phones did not. To determine the source of the problem, Matt went through the following troubleshooting steps:

1. Matt's first thought was that the maximum number of ephones and ephone-DNs had been reached. This was not possible, however, because the phones were implemented at random, so some of the 7945 and 7965 phones registered properly after a 7971 phone failed. Also, there were no "Registration Rejected" messages on the phone display.

2. Another possibility was that there might be an incorrect configuration with the DHCP server. Matt verified that the 7971 phones were indeed receiving an IP address and that the option 150 IP address was correct. Also, all of the Cisco phones were on the same voice VLAN and received the same DHCP pool information, so if there was a problem with DHCP, it would affect all phones and not just the 7971s.

3. Matt then verified that the firmware load files were properly set up on the CUCM Express. Indeed, the configuration showed the proper load commands within the telephony-service section.

4. Finally, it dawned on Matt that even though the option 150 was properly configured within the DHCP settings, he may have forgotten to actually configure the TFTP server to hand out the 7971 firmware files. Checking this within the CUCM Express, Matt found that he had correctly configured the TFTP service to serve up 7945 and 7965 load files but not those for the 7971 phones.

To remedy this, Matt used the `tftp-server flash:` command to serve up all the necessary `.loads` files. Once this was completed, Matt rebooted the 7971 phones, and they were then able to register with the CUCM Express properly.

Configuring Ephone and Ephone-DNs

Up until now, all of the configuration information that the Cisco IP phones receive from the CUCM Express has been generic information that all of the phones share. Ephone and ephone-DN configurations are the way the administrator can control the unique features that belong to each phone. We'll first look at what an ephone-DN is and how to configure the most basic type. Then we'll learn about ephones and how to apply an ephone-DN to an ephone.

Configuring an Ephone-Directory Number

An ephone-DN is what you would think of as a telephone number. This is the extension that a user dials when they wish to ring your phone. On the CUCM Express, we can use many different ephone-DN configuration settings to add functionality, but for now, all we want to do is add a single ephone-DN to a phone. We'll get fancier with the configurations in the next chapter. From a directory number standpoint, you need to first create an ephone-DN logical tag. Then, once you are in config-ephonedn configuration mode, you give the ephone-DN an extension number. Let's configure our first ephone-DN with an extension of 4001 and a second ephone-DN with the extension 4002:

```
Router#configure terminal
Router(config)#ephone-dn 1
Router(config-ephone-dn)#number 4001
Router(config-ephone-dn)#exit
Router(config)#ephone-dn 2
Router(config-ephone-dn)#number 4002
Router(config-ephone-dn)#end
Router#
```

Now that we have two directory numbers configured, let's apply them to two Cisco phones using the ephone configuration command.

Configuring an Ephone

An ephone configuration is the logical representation of a physical IP phone. This is where you apply all the unique ephone-DNs and other settings that are ultimately pushed down to the phone hardware. Every phone on the CUCM Express has a unique ephone tag in which all of the phone configurations are applied. The CUCM Express maps the ephone configuration to the unique MAC address of the phone. By using the MAC address, the phone can physically move around the network and continue to maintain the same configuration settings wherever it goes. The MAC address of each Cisco phone can be found in four locations, for your convenience:

- On the box the Cisco phone ships in. The MAC address is also stored on a *UPC bar code* located below the MAC address on the box. You can use a bar code scanner to scan the MAC address into a spreadsheet and then export this spreadsheet to your CUCM, which can be a great convenience if you are adding hundreds of phones or more.

- On the back of the Cisco phone. A UPC bar code is also located here.
- Within the Settings menu of a powered-up Cisco phone.
- On the console connection or VTY interface by issuing a `show cdp neighbors detail` command when a phone is connected to a Cisco switch.

Since we're using the most basic phone configuration, the only information we'll need to configure ephones is the MAC address of each phone and the ephone-DN tag we wish to apply. Let's configure two Cisco phones with our ephone-DN extension numbers. Ephone 1 will be configured to use extension 4001 and ephone 2 will be configured with extension 4002:

```
Router#configure terminal
Router(config)#ephone 1
Router(config-ephone)#mac-address 0014.1c4d.2589
Router(config-ephone)#button 1:1
Router(config-ephone)#exit
Router(config)#ephone 2
Router(config-ephone)#mac-address 0014.4c7f.a49b
Router(config-ephone)#button 1:2
Router(config-ephone)#end
Router#
```

The CUCM can automatically assign extensions to brand-new phones that do not have a specific ephone-to-MAC-address mapping configured. Using the auto assign command in config-telephony mode, you can specify the hardware types eligible for auto-assign as well as the ephone-DNs to be assigned. As soon as you power up an eligible phone and it registers to the CUCM Express, auto-assign kicks in and builds an ephone configuration. It pulls in the MAC address of the phone and configures the lowest unused tagged ephone-DN from the range specified. This option is perfect for new environments where it doesn't matter who receives a particular extension number or for fast deployments where editing can come later.

The `mac-address` configuration is self-explanatory, but the `button` config-ephone mode configuration needs some explanation. The first number of the `button` command indicates the Cisco IP phone button that is being configured. For example, on a Cisco 7960, six extension buttons are available, so this number could be 1–6. On the other hand, a 7940 series has only two buttons, so this number could only be 1 or 2. The colon (:) indicates that you want a standard ring for this extension. We'll sort out the many different types of audible and silent rings later on, but for now we just want a standard ring for our phone. The last number in the configuration specifies the ephone-DN to apply to the physical phone. Since we specified that ephone 1 uses ephone-DN 1, the extension on button 1 of ephone 1 will be 4001. And therefore ephone 2 will be configured to use ephone-DN 2 or extension 4002.

Making Your First Call Powered by CUCM Express

This is the moment you've all been waiting for—the opportunity to actually pick up a phone handset, hear a dial tone, and dial the second extension to hear it ring! If you haven't done so already, you can connect your phones to the network and power them up so they properly register. Alternatively, if the phones have been connected throughout the configuration processes, chances are that they have registered to your CUCM Express but did not get an updated configuration file that includes the phone extension. If the phone is registered and communicating with the CUCM Express, you can either restart or reset the phones via the command line. As you'll see next, these two methods are slightly different.

Restart

A *restart* is a quick reset of the phone. The phones connect to the TFTP server and update any changes to the configuration file. The restart command will update the following information:

- Directory numbers (DNs)
- Phone buttons
- Speed dial

    You have the ability to restart either all of the connected phones at once or one at a time. If you wish to restart all of the phones, you must be in config-telephony mode and issue a restart all command. Here is an example of the output of this command:

```
Router(config)#telephony-service
Router(config-telephony)#restart all
Reset 2 phones: at 5 second interval        - this could take several minutes
per phone
Starting with 7960 phones


Router(config-telephony)#
Reset/Restart-all looking for phones registered as type 30008 7902
Reset/Restart-all looking for phones registered as type 20000 7905
[output omitted]
Reset/Restart-all looking for phones registered as type 436 7965
Reset-All: Requesting Restart for phone SEP0021A086D04D at 192.168.10.12
deviceType 436  Idle [count=1]
May  2 07:28:51.878: %IPPHONE-6-UNREGISTER_NORMAL: ephone-1:SEP0021A086D04D
IP:192.168.10.12 Socket:1 DeviceType:Phone has unregistered normally.
Reset/Restart-all looking for phones registered as type 30006 7970
[output omitted]
Reset/Restart-all looking for phones registered as type 30016 CIPC
Reset-All: Requesting Restart for phone SEP001E68E1AFE9 at 192.168.1.15
```

```
deviceType 30016  Idle [count=2]
May  2 07:29:04.858: %IPPHONE-6-UNREGISTER_NORMAL: ephone-2:SEP001E68E1AFE9
IP:192.168.1.15 Socket:3 DeviceType:Phone has unregistered normally.
May  2 07:29:05.250: %IPPHONE-6-REG_ALARM: 23: Name=SEP001E68E1AFE9 Load=
7.0.1.0 Last=Reset-Restart
May  2 07:29:06.122: %IPPHONE-6-REGISTER: ephone-2:SEP001E68E1AFE9
IP:192.168.1.15 Socket:3 DeviceType:Phone has registered.
Reset/Restart-all looking for phones registered as type 39999 none
[output omitted]
Reset/Restart-all looking for phones registered as type -1 Unknown Ephone type
Restart-All issued for 2 phones
```

To restart a single phone, you navigate into config-ephone configuration mode of the specific phone you wish to restart and issue a restart command. Here's an example:

```
Router(config)#ephone 1
Router(config-ephone)#restart
restarting 0021.A086.D04D
Router(config-ephone)#
May  2 07:55:12.377: %IPPHONE-6-UNREGISTER_NORMAL: ephone-1:SEP0021A086D04D
IP:192.168.10.12 Socket:1 DeviceType:Phone has unregistered normally.
```

Reset

The *reset* command performs a full boot of the phone. This process requires the phone to go through both the TFTP download and DHCP renewal processes, so it takes more time for the phone to become fully operational within the CUCM Express system. In addition to handling the same three configuration updates that the restart command can perform, the reset command updates the phone if any of the following were added, deleted, or modified:

- Date/time
- Phone firmware
- CUCME source IP address
- TFTP download path
- Voice mail access number

Just like the restart command, reset can be performed on all phones or a single phone. To reset all phones, you must be in config-telephony mode and issue a reset all command. For a single ephone, navigate to the ephone you desire and enter a reset command. Here is the command-line output when we reset all the phones on the system:

```
Router(config)#telephony-service
Router(config-telephony)#reset all
```

```
ITS configuration has been changed, selecting sequence-all reset
Reset 2 phones: sequentially with 240 second per-phone timeout to guarantee
TFTP access
        - this could take several minutes per phone
you may abort this process using 'reset cancel'

Starting reset sequence with 7960 phones

Router(config-telephony)#
Reset/Restart-all looking for phones registered as type 30008 7902
Reset/Restart-all looking for phones registered as type 20000 7905
[output omitted]
Reset/Restart-all looking for phones registered as type 436 7965
Reset-All: Requesting Reset for phone SEP0021A086D04D at 192.168.10.12
deviceType 436 7965 Idle [count=1]
Reset-All received Unregister from ephone-1 SEP0021A086D04D
May  2 07:56:31.941: %IPPHONE-6-UNREGISTER_NORMAL: ephone-1:SEP0021A086D04D
IP:192.168.10.12 Socket:6 DeviceType:Phone has unregistered normally.
May  2 07:57:08.905: %MGCP-3-INTERNAL_ERROR:  mgcp_cfg_commands: nvgen lawful-
intercept: should not happen
May  2 07:57:33.149: %IPPHONE-6-REG_ALARM: 25: Name=SEP0021A086D04D Load=
SCCP45.8-3-2S Last=Initialized
May  2 07:57:33.165: %IPPHONE-6-REGISTER: ephone-1:SEP0021A086D04D
IP:192.168.10.12 Socket:1 DeviceType:Phone has registered.
Reset sequence-all, Ready to reset next phone (last 61 sec)
Reset sequence-all, Ready to reset next phone (last 61 sec)
Reset/Restart-all looking for phones registered as type 30006 7970
[output omitted]
Reset/Restart-all looking for phones registered as type 30016 CIPC
Reset-All: Requesting Reset for phone SEP001E68E1AFE9 at 192.168.1.15
deviceType 30016 CIPC Idle [count=2]
Reset-All received Unregister from ephone-2 SEP001E68E1AFE9
May  2 07:57:41.885: %IPPHONE-6-UNREGISTER_NORMAL: ephone-2:SEP001E68E1AFE9
IP:192.168.1.15 Socket:3 DeviceType:Phone has unregistered normally.
May  2 07:57:48.545: %IPPHONE-6-REG_ALARM: 22: Name=SEP001E68E1AFE9 Load=
7.0.1.0 Last=Reset-Reset
May  2 07:57:50.269: %IPPHONE-6-REGISTER: ephone-2:SEP001E68E1AFE9
IP:192.168.1.15 Socket:3 DeviceType:Phone has registered.
Reset sequence-all, Ready to reset next phone (last 8 sec)
[output omitted]
```

Reset/Restart-all looking for phones registered as type -1 Unknown Ephone type
Reset-All issued for 2 phones

And here's an example of resetting the single ephone 1:

```
Router(config)#ephone 1
Router(config-ephone)#reset
reseting 0021.A086.D04D
Router(config-ephone)#
May  2 07:53:49.937: %IPPHONE-6-UNREGISTER_NORMAL: ephone-1:SEP0021A086D04D
IP:192.168.10.12
```

You can also reset a Cisco phone using the handset unit by pressing the Settings button followed by **#** on the keypad.

Once your phones restart or reset, they will receive the updated configuration file containing their individual extension configured for button 1. Figure 5.6 shows what ephone 2 looks like with its configured extension:

FIGURE 5.6 Configured Cisco phone extension

Go ahead and use a phone to dial the other phone extension. Congratulations, you've officially configured basic call processing on a Cisco CUCM Express!

Basic Configuration Using the Telephony Service Setup Script

One configuration method that is often brought up is the telephony-service setup script command. The *telephony service setup script* is a command-line script that walks an administrator through a series of DHCP and voice questions to automatically configure ephones and ephone-DN settings. The CUCM Express is then set up for auto-assign so that it hands out extension numbers automatically when you begin adding phones to your network. At the same time, it grabs the phone's MAC address and puts it into the ephone configuration so it will continue to receive the same extension from that point on. To demonstrate this functionality, we'll configure two phones with single lines that begin with extension 8001. We'll first be asked if we want to configure DHCP. The single subnet that our two phones will be on is 192.168.10.0/24. The CUCM Express, gateway, and TFTP server IP address will be 192.168.10.1. To use the script, we enter configuration mode and type the following:

```
Router#configure terminal
Router(config)#telephony-service ?
  setup  Start setup for Cisco Unified Communications Manager Express. Please
         refer to
         http://www.cisco.com/en/US/products/sw/voicesw/ps4625/tsd_products_
support_
series_home.html
         for full documentation.
  <cr>
Router(config)#telephony-service setup

 --- Cisco IOS Telephony Services Setup ---

Do you want to setup DHCP service for your IP Phones? [yes/no]: yes
Configuring DHCP Pool for Cisco IOS Telephony Services :

  IP network for telephony-service DHCP Pool:192.168.10.0
  Subnet mask for DHCP network :255.255.255.0
  TFTP Server IP address (Option 150) :192.168.10.1
  Default Router for DHCP Pool :192.168.10.1

Do you want to start telephony-service setup? [yes/no]: yes
Configuring Cisco IOS Telephony Services :

  Enter the IP source address for Cisco IOS Telephony Services :192.168.10.1
```

```
Enter the Skinny Port for Cisco IOS Telephony Services :   [2000]:
How many IP phones do you want to configure :   [0]: 2
Do you want dual-line extensions assigned to phones? [yes/no]: no
What Language do you want on IP phones :
      0  English
      1  French
      2  German
      3  Russian
      4  Spanish
      5  Italian
      6  Dutch
      7  Norwegian
      8  Portuguese
      9  Danish
      10 Swedish
      11 Japanese
 [0]: 0
Which Call Progress tone set do you want on IP phones :
      0  United States
      1  France
      2  Germany
      3  Russia
      4  Spain
      5  Italy
      6  Netherlands
      7  Norway
      8  Portugal
      9  UK
      10  Denmark
      11  Switzerland
      12  Sweden
      13  Austria
      14  Canada
      15  Japan
 [0]: 0
  What is the first extension number you want to configure (maximum 32 digits):
8001

Do you have Direct-Inward-Dial service for all your phones? [yes/no]: no

Do you want to forward calls to a voice message service? [yes/no]: no
```

Do you wish to change any of the above information? [yes/no]: **no**

```
 ---- Setup completed config ---
```

```
Router(config)#
*May 19 18:45:32.007: %LINK-3-UPDOWN: Interface ephone_dsp DN 1.1, changed
state to up
*May 19 18:45:32.007: %LINK-3-UPDOWN: Interface ephone_dsp DN 2.1, changed
state to up
```

That's all there is to the script; now we can issue a show telephony-service command to see what this script has configured on our CUCM Express:

```
Router#show telephony-service
CONFIG (Version=7.0(0))
=====================
Version 7.0(0)
Cisco Unified Communications Manager Express
For on-line documentation please see:
http://www.cisco.com/en/US/products/sw/voicesw/ps4625/tsd_products_support_
series_home.html

ip source-address 192.168.10.1 port 2000
max-ephones 2
max-dn 2
max-conferences 12 gain -6
dspfarm units 0
dspfarm transcode sessions 0
conference software
privacy
no privacy-on-hold
hunt-group report delay 1 hours
hunt-group logout DND
max-redirect 5
cnf-file location: system:
cnf-file option: PER-PHONE-TYPE
network-locale[0] US   (This is the default network locale for this box)
network-locale[1] US
network-locale[2] US
network-locale[3] US
network-locale[4] US
user-locale[0] US    (This is the default user locale for this box)
```

```
user-locale[1] US
user-locale[2] US
user-locale[3] US
user-locale[4] US
srst mode auto-provision is OFF
srst ephone template is 0
srst dn template is 0
srst dn line-mode single
time-format 12
date-format mm-dd-yy
timezone 0 Greenwich Standard Time
no transfer-pattern is configured, transfer is restricted to local SCCP phones
only.
keepalive 30 auxiliary 30
timeout interdigit 10
timeout busy 10
timeout ringing 180
timeout transfer-recall 0
timeout ringin-callerid 8
timeout night-service-bell 12
caller-id name-only: enable
edit DN through Web:  disabled.
edit TIME through web:  disabled.
Log (table parameters):
    max-size: 150
    retain-timer: 15
create cnf-files version-stamp 7960 May 19 2009 14:08:11
transfer-system full-consult
transfer-digit-collect new-call
auto assign 1 to 2
local directory service: enabled.
Extension-assigner tag-type ephone-tag.
Router#
```

You can now boot two phones on the network. Once they have fully booted and received the phone numbers 8001 and 8002, you can run show telephony-service ephone and show telephony-service ephone-dn to verify their configurations:

```
Router#show telephony-service ephone
Number of Configured ephones 2 (Registered 1)
ephone 1
Device Security Mode: Non-Secure
```

```
mac-address 001E.68E1.AFE9
type CIPC
button  1:1
keepalive 30 auxiliary 0
max-calls-per-button 8
busy-trigger-per-button 0
Always send media packets to this router: No
Preferred codec: g729r8 pre-ietf
conference drop-mode never
conference add-mode all
conference admin: No
privacy: Yes
privacy button: No
user-locale US
network-locale US
!
ephone 2
Device Security Mode: Non-Secure
mac-address 0021.A086.D04D
type 7965
button  1:2
keepalive 30 auxiliary 0
max-calls-per-button 8
busy-trigger-per-button 0
Always send media packets to this router: No
Preferred codec: g729r8 pre-ietf
conference drop-mode never
conference add-mode all
conference admin: No
privacy: Yes
privacy button: No
user-locale US
network-locale US
!

Router#show telephony-service ephone-dn

ephone-dn 1
number 8001
preference 0 secondary 9
huntstop
call-waiting beep
```

```
ephone-dn 2
number 8002
preference 0 secondary 9
huntstop
call-waiting beep
```

This script gives you a basic phone setup, but many engineers new to the CUCM Express system find it provides a good way to get started using the command line to set up phone lines. As you become more comfortable setting up phones manually, you'll find that to be the better option simply because the setup script is very limited in what it can configure.

Basic Configuration Using the GUI

The Cisco Communications Manager Express has two configuration methods. You've just seen the first—using the command line. This method is what engineers need to be most familiar with, because it allows you to configure 100 percent of the voice features and is much faster to use over time. If you are transitioning support of the CUCM Express to a less technically skilled administrator, they may find that the *graphical user interface* (GUI) is more user friendly and intuitive for basic tasks such as setting up new phones and extensions. The web GUI allows an administrator to use a web browser to connect to the CUCM Express to configure many of the telephony features available on the system. This section will cover enabling the GUI interface and show you some of the basics of navigating the interface.

Enabling the GUI Interface

By default, the CUCM Express GUI interface is disabled. You must work through four steps using the command-line interface to enable the web GUI. You first must enable either the HTTP or the HTTPS server on the router. You also need to tell the router the location of the root web directory. Third, you need to allow for HTTP authentication from locally configured usernames and passwords. Lastly, you must configure a telephony service web administrator username and password. Following is an example of how to accomplish all of these tasks on the IOS router.

Enabling the HTTP(S) Server Process

Cisco routers have the ability to run web server processes for basic router IOS monitoring and configuration. Because our IOS router is also a CUCM Express router, you must enable the web processes to use the Call Manager web GUI as well. You can enable HTTP,

HTTPS, or both forms of access. The following commands configure both HTTP and HTTPS server processes on the router:

```
Router#configure terminal
Router(config)#ip http server
Router(config)#ip http secure-server
% Generating 1024 bit RSA keys, keys will be non-exportable...[OK]
Router(config)#exit
Router#
```

Setting the Root Web Directory

Even though you've enabled web services on your router, the CUCM GUI still will not work until you tell the router where it can find the web pages that are stored somewhere on the router. Typically, the web page files are found in just two locations. If you extracted all the CUCM Express files directly onto the router flash drive without a directory structure, you can simply issue the following command:

```
Router#configure terminal
Router(config)#ip http path flash:/
Router(config)#end
Router#
```

If your CUCM Express files are organized in a directory structure, you will need to let the CUCM Express router know where your web page files are in a subdirectory referred to as a *root web directory*. If you have your files in a directory structure, the web files are in the flash:/gui directory. Here is the output of the show dir flash:/gui command:

```
Directory of flash:/gui/

    28  -rw-       953   Apr 7 2009 18:26:06 +00:00  Delete.gif
    29  -rw-      3845   Apr 7 2009 18:26:06 +00:00  admin_user.html
    30  -rw-    647358   Apr 7 2009 18:26:10 +00:00  admin_user.js
    31  -rw-      1029   Apr 7 2009 18:26:12 +00:00  CiscoLogo.gif
    32  -rw-       174   Apr 7 2009 18:26:12 +00:00  Tab.gif
    33  -rw-     16344   Apr 7 2009 18:26:12 +00:00  dom.js
    34  -rw-       864   Apr 7 2009 18:26:12 +00:00  downarrow.gif
    35  -rw-      6328   Apr 7 2009 18:26:14 +00:00  ephone_admin.html
    36  -rw-      4558   Apr 7 2009 18:26:14 +00:00  logohome.gif
    37  -rw-      3724   Apr 7 2009 18:26:14 +00:00  normal_user.html
    38  -rw-     76699   Apr 7 2009 18:26:16 +00:00  normal_user.js
    39  -rw-       843   Apr 7 2009 18:26:16 +00:00  sxiconad.gif
    40  -rw-      1347   Apr 7 2009 18:26:16 +00:00  Plus.gif
    41  -rw-      2399   Apr 7 2009 18:26:18 +00:00  telephony_service.html
```

```
42  -rw-        870    Apr 7 2009 18:26:18 +00:00  uparrow.gif
43  -rw-       9968    Apr 7 2009 18:26:18 +00:00  xml-test.html
44  -rw-       3412    Apr 7 2009 18:26:20 +00:00  xml.template
```

To inform your CUCM Express router that it should look inside the `flash:/gui` directory for the web files, run the following command:

```
Router#configure terminal
Router(config)#ip http path flash:/gui
Router(config)#end
Router#
```

Now the CUCM Express will look in the `gui` subdirectory for all web files.

Enabling Local Web Authentication

Next on the task list is to set your CUCM Express router so that it allows for authentication from locally configured usernames and passwords. To do this, use the `ip http authentication local` command. Here's the configuration output that accomplishes this task:

```
Router#configure terminal
Router(config)#ip http authentication local
Router(config-telephony)#end
Router#
```

Creating a CUCM Express Administrator Account

The CUCM Express administrator account is separate from any user accounts that are made on the router side of the configuration. These special administrators have access only to the CUCM Express configuration capabilities, so you can create a separation of duties between route/switch administrators and voice administrators. There are several methods for creating these users, but the most basic is to create a system administrator using a local username and password. The following example shows how I created an administrator named WebAdmin with a secret password of cisco. The `secret 0` portion of the command specifies that we will be entering our password in plaintext form (0) and that we want the secret password to be encrypted when the command is applied to the running configuration.

```
Router#configure terminal
Router(config)#telephony-service
Router(config-telephony)#web admin system name WebAdmin secret 0 cisco
Router(config-telephony)#end
Router#
```

At this point, you can connect to the CUCM Express web GUI by pointing your web browser at `https://<CUCM Express source IP address>/ccme.html`

Figure 5.7 shows the SSL warning message that our web browser displays.

FIGURE 5.7   SSL warning message

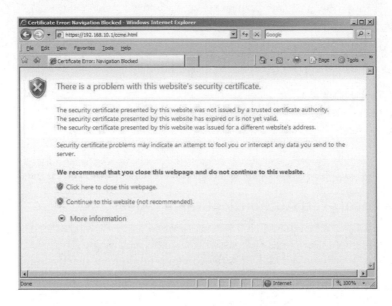

We're receiving this message because the SSL certificate that the router created when we enabled HTTPS was self-signed. In a production environment, you may want to purchase a certificate from a trusted certificate authority such as VeriSign to avoid receiving this warning message from your browser. Setting up a trusted certificate is beyond the scope of this book. For now, just click to continue on to the website.

The next screen we are presented with is an access popup asking us for a username and password. These are the CUCM Express administrator username and password that we just created. Figure 5.8 shows the access window with our credentials being entered.

FIGURE 5.8   CUCM Express GUI login

Now that we're logged in, we can see the CUCM Express GUI for the first time, as indicated in Figure 5.9.

FIGURE 5.9   CUCM Express GUI main page

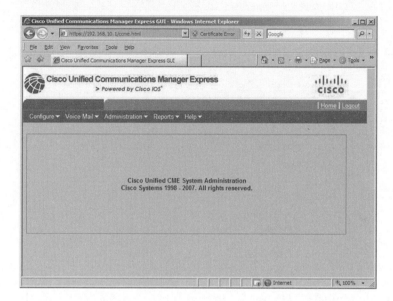

Along the top of the screen are drop-down menus for Configure, Voice Mail, Administration, Reports, and Help. Next, we'll take a quick look at some of the most frequently used web GUI options.

CUCM Express Web GUI Basics

The CUCM Express Web GUI is divided into five tabs. The Voice Mail tab is strictly for the configuration of a Unity system. Because we haven't yet covered Unity Express, we'll save that section for later on in the book. The Help tab is a basic help tool to assist new users with the "where and why" of the configuration tool. This section will focus on the other three tabs, and you'll see where to look to configure and verify the most important options the system has available to it.

Using the Configure Menu

The Configure tab is where administrators will spend most of their time. Here, you can add, change, and delete phones and phone extensions. Figure 5.10 shows the phones currently configured on the system.

FIGURE 5.10   Configured phones

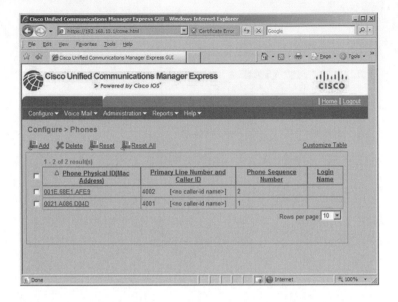

To configure a new phone, you click the Add button to set up the new phones.

To add a new extension, you click the Extensions option within the Configure tab. This lists all currently configured extensions. To configure a new extension, you click the Add button here. If you do that now, however, you will receive a pop-up message indicating that this configuration option is disabled on your system, as shown in Figure 5.11.

FIGURE 5.11   Add Extension Number alert pop-up message

This is one of the few web GUI features that are disabled by default on the CUCM Express system. To enable the web administrator to add or change extensions, you must issue the dn-webedit config-telephony command using the command line:

```
Router#configure terminal
Router(config)#telephony-service
Router(config-telephony)#dn-webedit
Router(config-telephony)#end
Router#
```

Now when you click the Add button to add an extension on your system, instead of receiving the disabled message, you will see the display shown in Figure 5.12.

FIGURE 5.12   The Add An Extension Number display

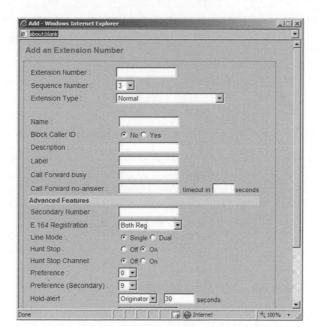

A third important Configure menu option is labeled System Parameters. This is where you configure all of the global voice parameters, including dial plans, hunt groups, and system messages. Figure 5.13 shows this section's GUI interface.

FIGURE 5.13   Configuring system parameters

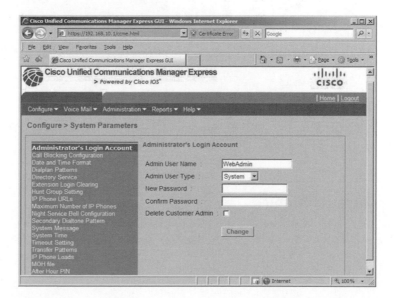

Using the Administration Menu

When you make any changes to the voice system, the modifications are automatically made. Some changes require you to either restart or reset the phone, but the changes themselves are automatically put into the IOS running configuration. As you've learned from your CCNA studies, however, if the router were to reboot, the changes that are in the running configuration are erased and the router loads the last-saved startup configuration. To ensure that our changes are maintained after a router reboot, we need to move to the Administration menu and choose the Save Router Config option. This essentially performs a *write memory* on the router to save the running configuration into the startup configuration.

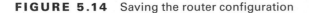

 If your router administrator is not also the CUCM Express web GUI administrator, you need to coordinate this action because it will save not only the CUCM Express configuration changes but also any changes the router administrator has made using the command line.

Figure 5.14 shows this process being performed on the web GUI.

FIGURE 5.14   Saving the router configuration

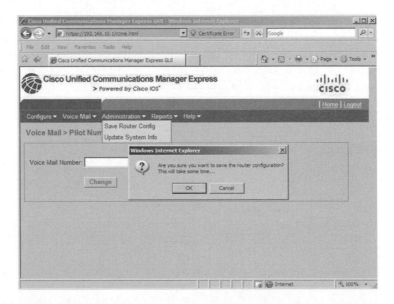

Using the Reports Menu

The Reports menu within the web GUI maintains data and displays it in the form of basic reports. The most widely used report is *Call History*, which shows call origin and destination along with start and end dates/times. This report can be useful for troubleshooting or other administrative tasks that management may need to perform. Figure 5.15 shows the output of a Call History report on the web GUI.

FIGURE 5.15 A Call History report

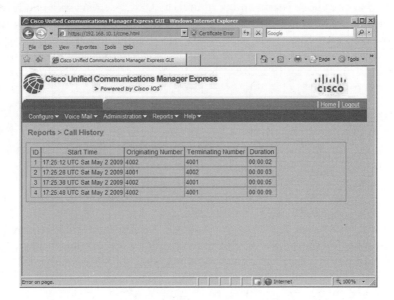

Using CUCM Express Verification and Troubleshooting Commands

When setting up a CUCM Express for the first time, you may need some basic troubleshooting skills. This section goes through some of the more common troubleshooting steps, including how to figure out why a Cisco phone won't register and how to determine the state of an ephone on your network.

Troubleshooting Cisco Phone Registrations

There will come a time when you add a new Cisco phone to your CUCM Express environment and it will not register. Because we understand the boot process, we have a methodical way of troubleshooting the problem. Here is the order in which troubleshooting should be performed:

1. Troubleshoot DHCP issues.

2. Troubleshoot TFTP issues.

3. Troubleshoot ephone registration issues.

Troubleshooting these three issues in order will help you to find and fix the vast majority of phone registration problems you'll encounter.

Troubleshooting DHCP Issues

When the phone boots up, one of the first things it displays is a "Configuring IP" message. This tells you that the phone is attempting to find the DHCP servers so it can receive the IP address and TFTP information needed to download the firmware and configuration files. You can verify that your phone is receiving DHCP information by using the debug ip dhcp server events command. Here's an example of the output you will receive when a device successfully receives an IP address from the DHCP server that is configured on your CUCM Express router:

```
Router#debug ip dhcp server events
DHCP server event debugging is on.
May 17 18:18:54.303: DHCPD: Sending notification of ASSIGNMENT:
May 17 18:18:54.303:  DHCPD: address 192.168.10.2 mask 255.255.255.0
May 17 18:18:54.303:   DHCPD: htype 1 chaddr 0021.a086.d04d
May 17 18:18:54.303:   DHCPD: lease time remaining (secs) = 86400
```

On a Cisco IP phone, you can verify that your phone received DHCP information by pressing the Settings button and navigating to the Network Configuration area. If your phone is not receiving an IP address, you should begin troubleshooting this as a DHCP problem and not a VoIP firmware or configuration problem.

If your Cisco IP phone is not receiving an IP address, it might be because the DHCP broadcast message is not reaching the DHCP server. If your DHCP server is set up on a subnet other than the subnet where the IP phone resides, then the DHCP broadcast message will never reach the server because, as you learned in chapter 4, broadcasts are contained within a single VLAN. You can either set up a DHCP server on every single VLAN on your network or use the ip helper-address X.X.X.X command on your router or VLAN Layer 3 interfaces. X.X.X.X is the IP address of your DHCP server. Maintaining multiple DHCP servers can be a cumbersome task, so you are much better off using the helper-address command to forward the DHCP requests on to your DHCP server that is located on a different subnet. What does this command do when configured? When the Layer 3 gateway interface hears a broadcast message from a DHCP client, the broadcast request is turned into a unicast message and forwarded to the IP address of the DHCP server. The DHCP server can then receive the request and hand out the appropriate IP address based on the source IP address, which will be the gateway IP of the Layer 3 interface.

Troubleshooting TFTP Issues

If your phone is receiving DHCP information, the next thing it attempts to do is download the firmware and configuration files required to operate. If your phone is stuck with the "Registering" notification on the screen, you can try to run the debug tftp events command to see if your phone is requesting files that are not on your TFTP server. Keep in mind that this command is useful only if your router is acting as the TFTP server. Here is an example of the output of this command for a phone that successfully receives some but not all of the requested firmware and configuration files:

```
Router#debug tftp events
TFTP Event debugging is on
Router#
May 17 18:51:36.855: TFTP: Looking for CTLSEP001E68E1AFE9.tlv
May 17 18:51:37.887: TFTP: Looking for SEP001E68E1AFE9.cnf.xml
May 17 18:51:37.887: TFTP: Opened system:/its/XMLDefaultCIPC.cnf.xml, fd 9,
size 1056 for process 248
May 17 18:51:37.891: TFTP: Finished system:/its/XMLDefaultCIPC.cnf.xml, time
00:00:00 for process 248
May 17 18:51:42.315: TFTP: Looking for Communicator/LdapDirectories.xml
May 17 18:51:43.423: TFTP: Looking for Communicator/LdapDialingRules.xml
May 17 18:51:49.823: TFTP: Looking for SEP001E68E1AFE9.cnf.xml
May 17 18:51:49.823: TFTP: Opened system:/its/XMLDefaultCIPC.cnf.xml, fd 9,
size 1056 for process 248
May 17 18:51:49.827: TFTP: Finished system:/its/XMLDefaultCIPC.cnf.xml, time
00:00:00 for process 248
May 17 18:51:50.035: TFTP: Looking for CTLSEP001E68E1AFE9.tlv
May 17 18:51:50.043: TFTP: Looking for English_United_States/ipc-sccp.jar
May 17 18:51:50.059: TFTP: Looking for CTLSEP001E68E1AFE9.tlv
May 17 18:51:50.063: TFTP: Looking for United_States/g3-tones.xml
May 17 18:51:50.315: %IPPHONE-6-REG_ALARM: 25: Name=SEP001E68E1AFE9 Load=
7.0.1.0 Last=Initialized
May 17 18:51:51.791: %IPPHONE-6-REGISTER: ephone-1:SEP001E68E1AFE9 IP:
192.168.10.4 Socket:1 DeviceType:Phone has registered.
Router#
```

Any line that begins with Looking means that the Cisco phone is requesting the file. If the TFTP server knows where a file is located, it will process the file, giving you the Opening statement. Finally, once the file is transferred you will receive a Finished message.

 As you can see in the sample output, this phone registered to the CUCM Express even though it did not receive all of the files it requested. Some of the files, such as LdapDirectories.xml, are supplementary services that do not affect phone registration. The TFTP server did manage to serve up the required files for the phone to register on the system.

If your phones are not receiving the necessary firmware or configuration files, you should make sure that your TFTP server is configured to serve up the files your phone is requesting. To do so, you can issue a show telephony-service tftp-bindings command. Here's a sample of typical output from this command:

```
Router#show telephony-service tftp-bindings
tftp-server system:/its/united_states/7960-tones.xml alias United_States/7960-
tones.xml
tftp-server system:/its/united_states/7960-font.xml alias English_United_States
/7960-font.xml
tftp-server system:/its/united_states/7960-font.xml alias English_United_States
/7920-font.xml
tftp-server system:/its/united_states/7960-dictionary.xml alias English_United_
States/7960-dictionary.xml
tftp-server system:/its/united_states/7960-kate.xml alias English_United_States
/7960-kate.xml
tftp-server system:/its/united_states/7960-kate.xml alias English_United_States
/7920-kate.xml
tftp-server system:/its/united_states/SCCP-dictionary.xml alias English_United_
States/SCCP-dictionary.xml
tftp-server system:/its/SEPDEFAULT.cnf alias SEPDefault.cnf
tftp-server system:/its/XMLDefault.cnf.xml alias XMLDefault.cnf.xml
tftp-server system:/its/ATADefault.cnf.xml alias ATADefault.cnf.xml
tftp-server system:/its/XMLDefaultCIPC.cnf.xml alias SEP001E68E1AFE9.cnf.xml
tftp-server system:/its/XMLDefault7965.cnf.xml alias SEP0021A086D04D.cnf.xml
```

If there are any files that are being requested and not listed by this command, you should locate them on your flash drive and serve them up using the tftp-server configuration command.

Troubleshooting Ephone Registration Issues

If you believe your TFTP server is serving up all the necessary files to your phone, the final step is to look at the *ephone registration* process itself. To do so, you can issue the debug ephone register command. Following is an example of a successful registration of a 7965 phone. There's a great deal of information here, but as you sift through the output, you can see how the phone at IP 192.168.10.3 initiates the registration process. The unique phone configuration file of this phone, SEP0021A086D04D, is then used to configure all of the necessary information into the phone, including the following steps:

- Sets IP address of the CUCM Express system
- Sets the date/time format
- Sets softkeys
- Verifies voice codec capabilities
- Configures extensions

```
Router#debug ephone register
EPHONE registration debugging is enabled
Router#
May 17 19:23:48.243: New Skinny socket accepted [1] (1 active)
May 17 19:23:48.243: sin_family 2, sin_port 51244, in_addr 192.168.10.3
May 17 19:23:48.243: skinny_add_socket 1 192.168.10.3 51244
May 17 19:23:48.307: %IPPHONE-6-REG_ALARM: 25: Name=SEP0021A086D04D Load=
SCCP45.8-3-2S Last=Initialized
May 17 19:23:48.307:
Skinny StationAlarmMessage on socket [2] 192.168.10.3 SEP0021A086D04D
May 17 19:23:48.307: severityInformational p1=0 [0x0] p2=0 [0x0]
May 17 19:23:48.307: 25: Name=SEP0021A086D04D Load= SCCP45.8-3-2S Last=
Initialized
May 17 19:23:48.335: ephone-(2)[2] StationRegisterMessage (1/2/21) from
192.168.10.3
May 17 19:23:48.335: ephone-(2)[2] Register StationIdentifier DeviceName
SEP0021A086D04D
May 17 19:23:48.335: ephone-(2)[2] StationIdentifier Instance 0    deviceType
436
May 17 19:23:48.335: ephone-2[1/-1]:stationIpAddr 192.168.10.3
May 17 19:23:48.335: ephone-2[1/-1][SEP0021A086D04D]:maxStreams 5
May 17 19:23:48.335: ephone-2[1/-1][SEP0021A086D04D]:From Phone raw protocol
Ver 0x8570000C
May 17 19:23:48.335: ephone-2[1/-1][SEP0021A086D04D]:protocol Ver 0x8570000C
May 17 19:23:48.335: ephone-2[1/-1][SEP0021A086D04D]:phone-size 13200 dn-size
784
May 17 19:23:48.335: ephone-(2) Allow any Skinny Server IP address 192.168.10.1
May 17 19:23:48.335: ephone-2[1/-1][SEP0021A086D04D]:Found entry 1 for
0021A086D04D
May 17 19:23:48.335: %IPPHONE-6-REGISTER: ephone-2:SEP0021A086D04D IP:
192.168.10.3 Socket:2 DeviceType:Phone has registered.
May 17 19:23:48.335: Phone 1 socket 2
May 17 19:23:48.335: Skinny Local IP address = 192.168.10.1 on port 2000

May 17 19:23:48.335: Skinny Phone IP address = 192.168.10.3 51244
May 17 19:23:48.339: ephone-2[1/2][SEP0021A086D04D]:Signal protocol
ver 9 to phone with ver 12
May 17 19:23:48.339: ephone-2[1/2][SEP0021A086D04D]:Date Format M/D/Y
May 17 19:23:48.339: ephone-2[1/2]:RegisterAck sent to sockettype ephone
socket 2: keepalive period 30 use sccp-version 9
May 17 19:23:48.339: ephone-2[1/2]:CapabilitiesReq sent
```

```
May 17 19:23:48.355: ephone-2[1/2][SEP0021A086D04D]:Skinny IP port 3500
set for socket [2]
May 17 19:23:48.355: ephone-2[1/2]:ButtonTemplateReqMessage
May 17 19:23:48.355: ephone-2[1/2]:ButtonTemplateReqMessage waiting for
Caps
May 17 19:23:48.355: ephone-2[1/2]:StationSoftKeyTemplateReqMessage
May 17 19:23:48.355: ephone-2[1/2]:StationSoftKeyTemplateResMessage
May 17 19:23:48.355: ephone-2[1/2]:StationSoftKeySetReqMessage
May 17 19:23:48.355: ephone-2[1/2]:StationSoftKeySetResMessage
May 17 19:23:48.359: ephone-2[1/2]:StationConfigStatReqMessage
May 17 19:23:48.359: ephone-2[1/2][SEP0021A086D04D]:
StationConfigStatMessage sent for device SEP0021A086D04D (40/280)
May 17 19:23:48.363: ephone-2[1/2]:CapabilitiesRes received
May 17 19:23:48.363: ephone-2[1/2][SEP0021A086D04D]:Caps list 9
WideBand_256K  40 ms, is_mtp 0
G711Ulaw64k  40 ms, is_mtp 0
G711Alaw64k  40 ms, is_mtp 0
ILBC  60 ms, is_mtp 0
G729AnnexB  60 ms, is_mtp 0
G729AnnexAwAnnexB  60 ms, is_mtp 0
G729  60 ms, is_mtp 0
G729AnnexA  60 ms, is_mtp 0
Unrecognized Media Type 257  1 ms, is_mtp 0

May 17 19:23:48.363: ephone-2[1/2]:Process pending button template
May 17 19:23:48.363: ephone-2[1/2]:ButtonTemplateReqMessage
May 17 19:23:48.363: ephone-2[1/2][SEP0021A086D04D]:
StationButtonTemplateReqMessage set max presentation to 6
May 17 19:23:48.363: ephone-2[1/2]:CheckAutoReg
May 17 19:23:48.363: ephone-2[1/2]:AutoReg is disabled
May 17 19:23:48.363: ephone-2[1/2][SEP0021A086D04D]:Setting 6 lines 0
speed-dials on phone (max_line 6)
May 17 19:23:48.363: ephone-2[1/2][SEP0021A086D04D]:First Speed Dial
Button location is 0 (0)
May 17 19:23:48.363: ephone-2[1/2]:ButtonTemplate lines=6 speed=0
buttons=6 offset=0
May 17 19:23:48.363: ephone-2[1/2][SEP0021A086D04D]:ButtonTemplate
buttonCount=6 totalButtonCount=6 buttonOffset=0
May 17 19:23:48.363: ephone-2[1/2][SEP0021A086D04D]:Configured 0 speed
dial buttons
May 17 19:23:48.423: ephone-2[1/2][SEP0021A086D04D]:StationLineStatReqMessage
from ephone line 1
```

```
May 17 19:23:48.423: ephone-2[1/2]:StationLineStatReqMessage ephone line 1
DN 2 = 8002 desc = 8002 label =
May 17 19:23:48.423: ephone-2[1/2][SEP0021A086D04D]:
StationLineStatResMessage sent to ephone (1 of 6)
May 17 19:23:48.435: ephone-2[1/2][SEP0021A086D04D]:
StationForwardStatReqMessage line 1 from ephone
May 17 19:23:48.435: Skinny StationForwardStatMessage line 1 sent on ephone
socket [2] for ephone-2
May 17 19:23:48.435: activeForward 0 AllActive 0 BusyActive 0
NoAnswerActive 0
May 17 19:23:48.435: ephone-2[1/2][SEP0021A086D04D]:
StationLineStatReqMessage from ephone line 2
May 17 19:23:48.435: ephone-2[1/2][SEP0021A086D04D]:
StationLineStatReqMessage from ephone line 2 Invalid DN -1
May 17 19:23:48.435: ephone-2[1/2][SEP0021A086D04D]:
StationLineStatResMessage sent to ephone (2 of 6)
May 17 19:23:48.435: ephone-2[1/2][SEP0021A086D04D]:
StationForwardStatReqMessage line 2 from ephone
May 17 19:23:48.435: Skinny StationForwardStatMessage line 2 sent
on ephone socket [2] for ephone-2
May 17 19:23:48.435: activeForward 0 AllActive 0 BusyActive 0
NoAnswerActive 0
May 17 19:23:48.435: ephone-2[1/2][SEP0021A086D04D]:
StationLineStatReqMessage from ephone line 3
May 17 19:23:48.435: ephone-2[1/2][SEP0021A086D04D]:
StationLineStatReqMessage from ephone line 3 Invalid DN -1
May 17 19:23:48.435: ephone-2[1/2][SEP0021A086D04D]:
StationLineStatResMessage sent to ephone (3 of 6)
May 17 19:23:48.435: ephone-2[1/2][SEP0021A086D04D]:
StationForwardStatReqMessage line 3 from ephone
May 17 19:23:48.435: Skinny StationForwardStatMessage line 3 sent on
ephone socket [2] for ephone-2
May 17 19:23:48.435: activeForward 0 AllActive 0 BusyActive 0 NoAnswerActive 0
May 17 19:23:48.435: ephone-2[1/2][SEP0021A086D04D]:
StationLineStatReqMessage from ephone line 4
May 17 19:23:48.435: ephone-2[1/2][SEP0021A086D04D]:
StationLineStatReqMessage from ephone line 4 Invalid DN -1
May 17 19:23:48.435: ephone-2[1/2][SEP0021A086D04D]:
StationLineStatResMessage sent to ephone (4 of 6)
May 17 19:23:48.435: ephone-2[1/2][SEP0021A086D04D]:
StationForwardStatReqMessage line 4 from ephone
May 17 19:23:48.435: Skinny StationForwardStatMessage line 4 sent on
```

```
ephone socket [2] for ephone-2
May 17 19:23:48.435: activeForward 0 AllActive 0 BusyActive 0 NoAnswerActive 0
May 17 19:23:48.435: ephone-2[1/2][SEP0021A086D04D]:StationLineStatReqMessage
from ephone line 5
May 17 19:23:48.435: ephone-2[1/2][SEP0021A086D04D]:StationLineStatReqMessage
from ephone line 5 Invalid DN -1
May 17 19:23:48.435: ephone-2[1/2][SEP0021A086D04D]:StationLineStatResMessage
sent to ephone (5 of 6)
May 17 19:23:48.435: ephone-2[1/2][SEP0021A086D04D]:StationForwardStatReqMessage
line 5 from ephone
May 17 19:23:48.435: Skinny StationForwardStatMessage line 5 sent on ephone
socket [2] for ephone-2
May 17 19:23:48.435: activeForward 0 AllActive 0 BusyActive 0 NoAnswerActive 0
May 17 19:23:48.435: ephone-2[1/2][SEP0021A086D04D]:StationLineStatReqMessage
from ephone line 6
May 17 19:23:48.435: ephone-2[1/2][SEP0021A086D04D]:StationLineStatReqMessage
from ephone line 6 Invalid DN -1
May 17 19:23:48.435: ephone-2[1/2][SEP0021A086D04D]:StationLineStatResMessage
sent to ephone (6 of 6)
May 17 19:23:48.435: ephone-2[1/2]:SkinnyCompleteRegistration
May 17 19:23:48.435: ephone-2[1/2][SEP0021A086D04D]:StationForwardStatReqMessage
line 6 from ephone
May 17 19:23:48.435: Skinny StationForwardStatMessage line 6 sent on ephone
socket [2] for ephone-2
May 17 19:23:48.435: activeForward 0 AllActive 0 BusyActive 0 NoAnswerActive 0
May 17 19:23:48.667: ephone-2[1/2]:MediaPathEventMessage
May 17 19:23:48.667: ephone-2[1/2]:MediaPathEventMessage
May 17 19:23:48.739: ephone-2[1/2][SEP0021A086D04D]:Skinny Available Lines
6 set for socket [2]
May 17 19:23:48.739: ephone-2[1/2]:Already done SkinnyCompleteRegistration
```

In the above debug output, there are several Invalid messages that state the following:

```
StationLineStatReqMessage from ephone line 2 Invalid
```

This same log message is repeated for lines 2–6 on a 7965 phone. This is because the 7965 phone can have up to six line buttons, but only button 1 is configured for an extension. The Invalid log essentially states that line buttons 2–6 are not usable.

Determining the State of an Ephone

Once your phones are configured and registered on your CUCM Express system, you'll want to familiarize yourself with the show ephone command, because it provides a wealth of information that can prove very useful when troubleshooting. We'll be going back to this show command throughout the book, but this is a good time to show how you can determine the state of an Ephone registration process and the state of a configured extension. First, let's look at the different registration states you will see.

Ephone Registration States

An Ephone can be in three different states. Table 5.4 lists the states and what each state means.

TABLE 5.4   Ephone registration states

State	Meaning
REGISTERED	Indicates the phone is registered to the CUCM Express and is active.
UNREGISTERED	Indicates the phone unregistered normally form the CUCM Express and is not active.
DECEASED	Indicates the phone unregistered abnormally because of a keepalive timeout.

Let's look at all three of these states by issuing the show ephone command:

```
Router#show ephone

ephone-1[0] Mac:0021.A086.D04D TCP socket:[-1] activeLine:0 DECEASED
mediaActive:0 offhook:0 ringing:0 ringRate: 0 reset:0 reset_sent:0 paging 0
debug:0 caps:9
IP:192.168.10.12 51055 7965  keepalive 8 max_line 6
button 1: dn 1  number 4001 CH1   DOWN
Preferred Codec: g711ulaw


ephone-2[1] Mac:0021.A02E.7D9A TCP socket:[5] activeLine:0 REGISTERED in SCCP
ver 12/9
mediaActive:0 offhook:0 ringing:0 ringRate: 0 reset:0 reset_sent:0 paging 0
debug:0 caps:9
IP:192.168.10.13 50271 7965  keepalive 6 max_line 6
button 1: dn 2  number 4002 CH1   IDLE
Preferred Codec: g711ulaw

ephone-3[2] Mac:001E.68E1.AFE9 TCP socket:[1] activeLine:0 UNREGISTERED
mediaActive:0 offhook:0 ringing:0 ringRate: 0 reset:0 reset_sent:0 paging 0
```

```
debug:1 caps:8
IP:192.168.10.14 1556 CIPC  keepalive 127 max_line 8
button 1: dn 1  number 4003 CH1   DOWN
Preferred Codec: g711ulaw
```

Three ephones are configured on this CUCM Express. Ephone-1 is in a DECEASED state, which means that the CUCM Express has lost contact with the switch. The CUCM Express uses keepalives to monitor the state of the phones. After six missed keepalive messages, the phone is placed into a DECEASED state. This typically happens when a phone loses power. Ephone-2 is in a REGISTERED state. This means that this phone is operational on the network and is ready to make and receive calls. Lastly, ephone-3 is in an UNREGISTERED state. This state means that the phone gracefully unregistered from the CUCM Express. We can see what type of phone this is on line 3 where it says the phone hardware is CIPC. Given that ephone-2 is a Cisco IP Communicator, the phone likely unregistered when the user exited the application.

Ephone Extension States

A second piece of information that we can gain from the show ephone command is the state of a phone extension. An ephone extension can have six *ephone extension states*. Table 5.5 provides a description of each of these states.

TABLE 5.5   Ephone extension states

State	On- or Off-hook	Ephone Registration State	Description
DOWN	N/A	UNREGISTRED / DECEASED	Ephone registration is not registered to the CUCM Express.
IDLE	On-hook	REGISTERED	Ephone is ready to make and receive calls.
SEIZE	Off-hook	REGISTERED	Ephone handset has been picked up, but no call has been made.
RINGING	Off-hook	REGISTERED	Ephone is calling another extension.
ALERTING	On-hook	REGISTERED	Ephone is receiving a call from another extension.
CONNECTED	Off-hook	REGISTERED	An active call is in progress between two or more extensions.

Let's look at the show ephone command to see what each of the ephone extension states looks like while we go through the process of ephone registration and call processing.

Ephone Extension DOWN State

The two following examples of ephone extensions show that the ephone registration process is in either a DECEASED or an UNREGISTRED state for the extensions to be in a DOWN state:

```
ephone-1[0] Mac:0021.A086.D04D TCP socket:[-1] activeLine:0 DECEASED
mediaActive:0 offhook:0 ringing:0 ringRate: 0 reset:0 reset_sent:0 paging 0
debug:0 caps:9
IP:192.168.10.12 51055 7965  keepalive 8 max_line 6
button 1: dn 1  number 4001 CH1   DOWN
Preferred Codec: g711ulaw


ephone-3[2] Mac:001E.68E1.AFE9 TCP socket:[1] activeLine:0 UNREGISTERED
mediaActive:0 offhook:0 ringing:0 ringRate: 0 reset:0 reset_sent:0 paging 0
debug:1 caps:8
IP:192.168.10.14 1556 CIPC  keepalive 127 max_line 8
button 1: dn 1  number 4003 CH1   DOWN
Preferred Codec: g711ulaw
```

Ephone Extension IDLE State

A phone is ready to either make or receive calls when the extension is in an IDLE state. In order for this to happen, the ephone must be properly REGISTERED to the CUCM Express, as shown here:

```
ephone-1[0] Mac:0021.A086.D04D TCP socket:[1] activeLine:0 REGISTERED in SCCP
ver 12/9
mediaActive:0 offhook:0 ringing:0 ringRate: 0 reset:0 reset_sent:0 paging 0
debug:0 caps:9
IP:192.168.10.12 52084 7965  keepalive 0 max_line 6
button 1: dn 1  number 4001 CH1   IDLE
Preferred Codec: g711ulaw
```

Ephone Extension SEIZE State

When an end user on ephone-2 wishes to make a call, they pick up the handset of the phone. As we know, this action changes the phone from an on-hook state to an off-hook state. This is called a *line seizure*. When this happens, the show ephone command has the ephone extension in an IDLE state, as shown here:

```
ephone-2[1] Mac:0021.A02E.7D9A TCP socket:[5] activeLine:1 REGISTERED in SCCP
ver 12/9
```

```
mediaActive:0 offhook:1 ringing:0 ringRate: 0 reset:0 reset_sent:0 paging 0
debug:0 caps:9
IP:192.168.10.13 50271 7965   keepalive 16 max_line 6
button 1: dn 2   number 4002 CH1    SEIZE
Preferred Codec: g711ulaw
Active Call on DN 2 chan 1 :4002 0.0.0.0 0 to 0.0.0.0 0 via 0.0.0.0
G711Ulaw64k   160 bytes no vad
Tx Pkts 0 bytes 0 Rx Pkts 0 bytes 0 Lost 0
Jitter 0 Latency 0 callingDn -1 calledDn -1
```

Ephone Extension RINGING and ALERTING States

Let's say that a user picks up a phone and dials an extension. Once that process reaches the CUCM, the phone where the user called from is put into a RINGING state. At this point the CUCM sends back the audible ringing tone through the phone handset to indicate that the call is being processed, and the user is waiting for the handset of the called phone to be picked up to complete the call. At the same time, the called phone goes into an ALERTING state. In this state the called phone is on-hook but ringing to alert the end user that someone is attempting to speak with them. The show ephone output looks like this:

```
ephone-1[0] Mac:0021.A086.D04D TCP socket:[1] activeLine:0 REGISTERED in SCCP
ver 12/9
mediaActive:0 offhook:0 ringing:1 ringRate: 0 reset:0 reset_sent:0 paging 0
debug:0 caps:9
IP:192.168.10.12 52084 7965   keepalive 1 max_line 6
button 1: dn 1   number 4001 CH1    RINGING
Preferred Codec: g711ulaw
call ringing on line 1


ephone-2[1] Mac:0021.A02E.7D9A TCP socket:[5] activeLine:1 REGISTERED in SCCP
ver 12/9
mediaActive:0 offhook:1 ringing:0 ringRate: 0 reset:0 reset_sent:0 paging 0
debug:0 caps:9
IP:192.168.10.13 50271 7965   keepalive 17 max_line 6
button 1: dn 2   number 4002 CH1    ALERTING
Preferred Codec: g711ulaw
Active Call on DN 2 chan 1 :4002 0.0.0.0 0 to 0.0.0.0 0 via 0.0.0.0
G711Ulaw64k   160 bytes no vad
Tx Pkts 0 bytes 0 Rx Pkts 0 bytes 0 Lost 0
Jitter 0 Latency 0 callingDn -1 calledDn 1
```

Ephone Extension CONNECTED State

The remote phone rings and the end user picks up the phone to answer it. At this point, the CUCM places both phones into a CONNECTED state. You can also see in the show ephone command that it lists the source and destination IP addresses.

```
ephone-1[0] Mac:0021.A086.D04D TCP socket:[1] activeLine:1 REGISTERED in SCCP
ver 12/9
mediaActive:1 offhook:1 ringing:0 ringRate: 0 reset:0 reset_sent:0 paging 0
debug:0 caps:9
IP:192.168.10.12 52084 7965  keepalive 2 max_line 6
button 1: dn 1  number 4001 CH1   CONNECTED
Preferred Codec: g711ulaw
Active Call on DN 1 chan 1 :4001 192.168.10.12 25848 to 192.168.10.13 23436 via
192.168.10.12
G711Ulaw64k  160 bytes no vad
Tx Pkts 219 bytes 37668 Rx Pkts 219 bytes 37668 Lost 0
Jitter 0 Latency 0 callingDn 2 calledDn -1


ephone-2[1] Mac:0021.A02E.7D9A TCP socket:[5] activeLine:1 REGISTERED in SCCP
ver 12/9
mediaActive:1 offhook:1 ringing:0 ringRate: 0 reset:0 reset_sent:0 paging 0
debug:0 caps:9
IP:192.168.10.13 50271 7965  keepalive 18 max_line 6
button 1: dn 2  number 4002 CH1   CONNECTED
Preferred Codec: g711ulaw
Active Call on DN 2 chan 1 :4002 192.168.10.13 23436 to 192.168.10.12 25848 via
192.168.10.13
G711Ulaw64k  160 bytes no vad
Tx Pkts 470 bytes 80840 Rx Pkts 468 bytes 80496 Lost 0
Jitter 0 Latency 0 callingDn -1 calledDn 1
```

Summary

Chapter 5 got us to the nuts and bolts of configuring the CUCM Express, which is a key goal in the process of learning how to configure CUCM Express hardware and ultimately passing the 640-460 exam. We began with Cisco's licensing options to ensure that you properly license your hardware and software. I then showed you how to download and install both the Cisco IOS and CUCM Express software onto a Cisco voice-capable router.

Once the software was up and running, we moved into the configuration phase of the chapter. Here I gave you the four mandatory configuration steps required for the CUCM Express to operate: configure the source IP address, configure the maximum number of ephones and ephone-DNs allowed, identify and set the firmware load files that Cisco IP phones should request, and generate and serve up default phone configuration files via TFPT. From there, we set up basic ephones and ephone-DNs to the point where a call could be made between two Cisco IP phones. You then saw how to set up and use the GUI interface for administration of the voice system. Although the GUI is less efficient than working from the command line, it allows you to delegate some tasks to less-experienced administrators. Finally, you learned some troubleshooting steps and techniques to help you resolve any CUCM configuration or registration issues you may see in your studies and in day-to-day work.

Exam Essentials

Understand the three CUCM Express licenses.   Cisco has three different licenses for CUCM environments. One license is for the voice-capable IOS. The second is the CCME Express feature license. The third is the individual user license.

Know how to download and install the voice-capable IOS and CUCM Express software.   On Cisco-capable router hardware, you must know how to download and properly install the software. To do so, you must download compatible software from cisco.com and either TFTP or use an external flash drive to transfer the software to the router's internal flash drive.

Know how to find CUCM Express software files on the router flash drive.   When you install the CUCM Express software using the archive tar /xtract command, the software is set up in a directory structure. It is important to know how to find phone firmware and other files by using the dir flash: commands.

Know how to configure your CUCM Express router as a TFTP server.   TFTP is required in a Cisco voice environment because Cisco phones request firmware and configuration files from TFTP servers. You should know how to configure your CUCM Express router to serve up the necessary files that are stored in flash.

Know how to configure the four mandatory CUCM Express system configuration settings using the command line.   The four mandatory configuration settings to get a CUCM Express router ready for operation are source IP address, max ephones and ephone-DN, firmware load files, and default configuration files.

Understand what the auto-assign configuration command does.   Auto-assign allows you to set up a pool of ephone-DNs. When Cisco IP phones connect to the CUCM Express for the first time, the auto-assign function registers the ephone. It maps an ephone-DN taken from the pool to the MAC address of the phone. This functionality is a great way to partially automate a phone rollout.

Understand the difference between the telephony-service restart **and reset commands.** Restart is a quick reset of the phone. It is good to use when you make changes to the configuration file, including changes to DNs, phone buttons, and speed dial. Reset is a full boot of the phone. This command causes the phone to go through a DHCP renewal process. It is also required when you change global parameters such as date/time, CUCME source IP, and TFTP download path.

Understand how to configure basic CUCM Express parameters using the telephony-service startup script. This script helps you to configure basic parameters by asking a series of questions regarding the needs of the phone system. Once you have answered the questions, the script automatically configures the telephony-service parameters.

Know how to navigate and administrate the CUCM Express system using the GUI interface. The CUCM Express has a GUI interface that can be enabled to allow administrators to manage and monitor the voice system.

Know how to troubleshoot CUCM Express registration and extension states. Understand how to best troubleshoot registration and extension problems using command line debug and show commands.

Written Lab 5.1

Write the answers to the following questions:

1. What privileged exec command do you use when you want to copy a file from TFTP to the router's internal flash drive?

2. What privileged exec command do you use when you want to copy and extract CUCM Express software that is compressed as a .tar file?

3. What configuration command tells the CUCM Express to serve up the flash:/ phone/7945-7965/SCCP45.8-3-2-27.sbn file via TFTP?

4. What config-telephony command sets the source IP address for the CUCM Express system to 172.16.55.100?

5. What config-telephony command sets the maximum number of ephones to 30?

6. What config-telephony command sets the maximum number of ephone-DNs to 50?

7. What config-telephony command tells the CUCM Express that when a 7945 phone requests a firmware load file, the file offered is SCCP45.8-3-3S.loads?

8. What configuration command begins the setup script process for the CUCM Express?

9. What configuration command enables the HTTPS server?

10. What debug command can you use to troubleshoot TFTP server issues?

(The answers to Written Lab 5.1 can be found following the answers to the review questions for this chapter.)

Hands-on Labs

To complete the labs in this section, you need a CUCM Express router and two Cisco IP phones. The phones used in this example are 7940s, but you can use any phone or IP Communicator you wish. The labs will follow the logical network design shown in Figure 5.16.

FIGURE 5.16　CUCM Express lab diagram

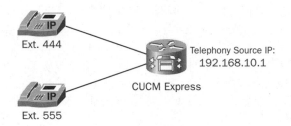

Ext. 444

Telephony Source IP:
192.168.10.1

CUCM Express

Ext. 555

These labs build on each other, so it is best to perform them in the order listed:

Lab 5.1: Configuring the CUCM Express as a TFTP Server

Lab 5.2: Configuring the CUCM Express for Basic Phone Operation

Lab 5.3: Enabling HTTP/HTTPS GUI Administration on the CUCM Express

Hands-on Lab 5.1: Configuring the CUCM Express as a TFTP Server

In this lab, we are going to add 7940 phones to our voice network. In order for them to work properly, we need to configure the CUCM Express router as a TFTP server to serve up the firmware files that the 7940 phones require.

1. Log into your CUCM Express router and go into privileged exec mode by typing **enable**.

2. Check to see which firmware files the 7940 phones need by viewing the files on the flash drive. To do this, type **dir flash:/phone/7940-7960**. You should see something similar to the following output:

```
Directory of flash:/phone/7940-7960/

    97  -rw-     129824    Apr 7 2009 18:29:32 +00:00  P00308000500.bin
    98  -rw-        458    Apr 7 2009 18:29:32 +00:00  P00308000500.loads
    99  -rw-     705536    Apr 7 2009 18:29:36 +00:00  P00308000500.sb2
   100  -rw-     130228    Apr 7 2009 18:29:36 +00:00  P00308000500.sbn
```

3. Enter into configuration mode by typing **configuration terminal**.

4. Configure the CUCM Express router to serve up the 7940 firmware files. Note that because the files are organized in a directory structure, you need to include the **alias** command:

```
tftp-server flash:/phone/7940-7960/P00308000500.bin alias P00308000500.bin
tftp-server flash:/phone/7940-7960/P00308000500.loads alias P00308000500.bin
tftp-server flash:/phone/7940-7960/P00308000500.sb2 alias P00308000500.bin
tftp-server flash:/phone/7940-7960/P00308000500.sbn alias P00308000500.bin
```

5. Exit configuration mode by typing **end**.

Hands-on Lab 5.2: Configuring the CUCM Express for Basic Phone Operation

1. Log into your CUCM Express router and go into privileged exec mode by typing **enable**.

2. Enter into config-telephony mode by typing **configuration terminal** and then **telephony-service**.

3. Configure the IP source address to the address given in the diagram by typing **ip source-address 192.168.10.1**.

4. Configure the maximum ephones to 5 and maximum ephone-DNs to 10 by typing **max-ephones 5** and then **max-dn 10**.

5. Set the firmware load files for the 7940 phones by typing **load 7960-7940 PPPPPPPP .loads**.

6. Exit config-telephony mode by typing **exit**.

7. Configure ephone-DN 1 to have the number 444 by typing **ephone-dn 1** and then **number 444**.

8. Configure ephone-DN 2 to have the number 555 by typing **ephone-dn 2** and then **number 555**.

9. Configure the MAC address of ephone 1 by typing **ephone 1** and then **mac-address XXXX.XXXX.XXXX.** Your MAC address will be unique.

10. Configure the MAC address of ephone 2 by typing **ephone 2** and then **mac-address XXXX.XXXX.XXXX.** Your MAC address will be unique.

11. Configure button 1 of ephone 1 to use ephone-DN 1 by typing **ephone 1** and then **button 1:1**.

12. Configure button 1 of ephone 2 to use ephone-DN 2 by typing **ephone 2** and then **button 1:2**.

13. Exit config-ephone mode by typing **end**.

Hands-on Lab 5.3: Enabling HTTP/HTTPS GUI Administration on the CUCM Express

1. Log into your CUCM Express router and go into privileged exec mode by typing **enable**.

2. Enter into configuration mode by typing **configuration terminal**.

3. Enable both HTTP and HTTPS services by typing **ip http server** and **ip http secure-server**.

4. Verify that your web files are in a directory structure by typing **dir flash:/gui**. The output will look like this:

```
Directory of flash:/gui/

    28  -rw-        953   Apr 7 2009 18:26:06 +00:00  Delete.gif
    29  -rw-       3845   Apr 7 2009 18:26:06 +00:00  admin_user.html
    30  -rw-     647358   Apr 7 2009 18:26:10 +00:00  admin_user.js
    31  -rw-       1029   Apr 7 2009 18:26:12 +00:00  CiscoLogo.gif
    32  -rw-        174   Apr 7 2009 18:26:12 +00:00  Tab.gif
    33  -rw-      16344   Apr 7 2009 18:26:12 +00:00  dom.js
    34  -rw-        864   Apr 7 2009 18:26:12 +00:00  downarrow.gif
    35  -rw-       6328   Apr 7 2009 18:26:14 +00:00  ephone_admin.html
    36  -rw-       4558   Apr 7 2009 18:26:14 +00:00  logohome.gif
    37  -rw-       3724   Apr 7 2009 18:26:14 +00:00  normal_user.html
    38  -rw-      76699   Apr 7 2009 18:26:16 +00:00  normal_user.js
    39  -rw-        843   Apr 7 2009 18:26:16 +00:00  sxiconad.gif
    40  -rw-       1347   Apr 7 2009 18:26:16 +00:00  Plus.gif
    41  -rw-       2399   Apr 7 2009 18:26:18 +00:00  telephony_service.html
    42  -rw-        870   Apr 7 2009 18:26:18 +00:00  uparrow.gif
    43  -rw-       9968   Apr 7 2009 18:26:18 +00:00  xml-test.html
    44  -rw-       3412   Apr 7 2009 18:26:20 +00:00  xml.template
```

5. Set the CUCM Express router to look for web files inside the flash:gui/ directory by typing **ip http path flash:/gui**. Or if your web files are not in a subdirectory, type **ip http path flash:/**.

6. Allow for local HTTP authentication by typing **ip http authentication local**.

7. Enter into config-telephony mode by typing **telephony-service**.

8. Create an admin account with the username of Adam and a secret password of cisco123 by typing **web admin system name Adam secret 0 cisco123**.

9. Exit config-telephony mode by typing **end**.

Review Questions

1. Which of the following is *not* a CUCM Express license?

    A. Cisco SCCP license

    B. Cisco IOS license for voice capabilities

    C. CCME Express feature licenses

    D. Individual user license

2. When ordering new Cisco 7985 IP phones, which part number should you order if you want the phones to be properly licensed for both CUCM Express and the bigger CUCM solutions?

    A. CP-7985-CH1

    B. CP-7985-SCCP

    C. CP-7985=

    D. CP-7985-CCME

3. What is the correct Cisco IOS command-line syntax to TFTP a file to a Cisco voice router's internal flash?

    A. `put tftp: flash:`

    B. `copy flash: tftp`

    C. `put flash: tftp:`

    D. `copy tftp: flash`

4. Which IOS command is used when you want to uncompress CUCM Express software that is stored as a `.tar` file?

    A. `uncompress tar /xtract`

    B. `unzip tar /xtract`

    C. `archive tar /xtract`

    D. `uncompress file /xtract`

5. What is the `tftp-server` IOS command used for?

    A. To identify the IP address of the TFTP server

    B. To set option 150 for DHCP clients

    C. To identify files the router serves via TFTP

    D. To enable Secure FTP

6. Which of the following is *not* a mandatory CUCM Express setting?

   A. Configure source IP address.

   B. Configure auto-assign.

   C. Configure max ephones and ephone-DNs.

   D. Set the firmware load files for the phones.

   E. Generate and serve default phone configuration files.

7. What command is used to manually update the phone configuration load files on a CUCM Express?

   A. `create firmware`

   B. `create cnf-files`

   C. `load cnf-files`

   D. `load firmware`

8. Which of the following places can the Cisco IP phone MAC address be found? Choose all that apply.

   A. On the box the Cisco phone shipped in

   B. In the Settings menu of the Cisco IP phone

   C. On the back of the phone

   D. On the phone handset

9. Which command-line operation does a quick reset of all phones currently registered on a CUCM Express system using a single command?

   A. `Router(config-telephony)#restart reset`

   B. `Router(config-ephone)#restart all`

   C. `Router(config-telephony)#restart all`

   D. `Router(config-ephone)#restart reset`

   E. `Router(config-ephone)#reset all`

   F. `Router(config-telephony)#reset`

10. Besides power cycling a Cisco IP phone, how can you reset it using the keypad buttons?

   A. Press **#**.

   B. Press the Help button and then **#**.

   C. Press the Directory button and then **#**.

   D. Press the Settings button and then **#**.

11. Why would you not want to set `max-ephones` and `max-DN` to the highest allowable number for your hardware unless necessary?

   A. The router CPU has to run additional processes, which can slow down the voice system.

   B. The router allocates memory for each ephone and ephone-DN allocated. The router's memory can quickly fill up and cause performance problems.

   C. The router allocates flash storage for each ephone and ephone-DN allocated. This space can fill up and cause performance problems.

   D. The router will log error messages until all ephones and ephone-DN allocations are used.

12. Which four configuration steps are required using the IOS command line to enable the web GUI interface?

   A. Configure the enable password.

   B. Configure the enable secret password.

   C. Enable the HTTP/HTTPS server.

   D. Configure http local authentication.

   E. Configure the web administrator username and password.

   F. Configure TACACS+ authentication.

   G. Set the web root directory.

13. In which GUI configuration menu would you add an ephone-DN?

   A. Administration

   B. Configure

   C. Reports

   D. Voice Mail

14. In what tab can you perform the GUI equivalent to a "write memory" in the command line?

   A. Administration

   B. Configure

   C. Reports

   D. Reset

15. When troubleshooting a Cisco phone that powers up and connects to the network but will not register, what is the first logical thing to check?

   A. Ensure that the proper firmware and configuration files are accessible to the phone.

   B. Ensure that the ephone is properly configured in the CUCM Express configuration.

   C. Make sure that the phone is receiving the correct IP address and other network parameters through DHCP.

   D. Check to see if the clock is properly synchronized with NTP.

16. On a Cisco phone, where can you verify that you received all the proper network parameters through DHCP?

    A. Press the * button; then select Network Configuration.

    B. Press the Help button; then select Network Configuration.

    C. Press the Directory button; then select Network Configuration.

    D. Press the Settings button; then select Network Configuration.

17. What two commands are best used to troubleshoot when you believe your Cisco IP phone is not getting the proper firmware file?

    A. debug ephone register

    B. debug tftp events

    C. debug ip packet

    D. show telephony-service tftp-bindings

    E. debug tftp-bindings

18. When viewing show ephone output like the following, what does SEIZE mean on the extension?

    ```
    ephone-2[1] Mac:0021.A02E.7D9A TCP socket:[5] activeLine:1 REGISTERED in SCCP
    ver 12/9
    mediaActive:0 offhook:1 ringing:0 ringRate: 0 reset:0 reset_sent:0 paging 0
    debug:0 caps:9
    IP:192.168.10.13 50271 7965  keepalive 16 max_line 6
    button 1: dn 2  number 4002 CH1    SIEZE
    Preferred Codec: g711ulaw
    Active Call on DN 2 chan 1 :4002 0.0.0.0 0 to 0.0.0.0 0 via 0.0.0.0
    G711Ulaw64k  160 bytes no vad
    Tx Pkts 0 bytes 0 Rx Pkts 0 bytes 0 Lost 0
    Jitter 0 Latency 0 callingDn -1 calledDn -1
    ```

    A. The phone is currently in a call.

    B. The phone is on-hook.

    C. The phone is off-hook and unregistered.

    D. The phone is off-hook.

    E. The phone is receiving a call.

19. When viewing `show ephone` output like the following, what does ALERTING mean on the extension?

```
ephone-2[1] Mac:0021.A02E.7D9A TCP socket:[5] activeLine:1 REGISTERED in SCCP
ver 12/9
mediaActive:0 offhook:1 ringing:0 ringRate: 0 reset:0 reset_sent:0 paging 0
debug:0 caps:9
IP:192.168.10.13 50271 7965  keepalive 17 max_line 6
button 1: dn 2  number 4002 CH1   ALERTING
Preferred Codec: g711ulaw
Active Call on DN 2 chan 1 :4002 0.0.0.0 0 to 0.0.0.0 0 via 0.0.0.0
G711Ulaw64k  160 bytes no vad
Tx Pkts 0 bytes 0 Rx Pkts 0 bytes 0 Lost 0
Jitter 0 Latency 0 callingDn -1 calledDn 1
```

A. The phone is currently in a call.

B. The phone is on-hook.

C. The phone is calling another extension.

D. The phone is receiving a call.

20. If your CUCM Express is configured with `max-ephone` 10, what happens when the 11th phone is added to the network?

A. The new phone will register but will only be able to receive calls.

B. The new phone will register, but the oldest registered phone will be forced to unregister.

C. The new phone will not be able to register.

D. The new phone will register and a log message will be generated notifying the administrator that the `max-ephone` limit has been exceeded.

Answers to Review Questions

1.   A. You need a license for the voice IOS, the CUCME software for a specific number of endpoints, and the individual user licenses for endpoints.

2.   A. If you want to be properly licensed for both the CUCM Express and the bigger CUCM voice solutions, you should order the CH1 part. This is a great idea if you think you might upgrade from an Express solution to one of the bigger Cisco Communications Managers in the future.

3.   D. The correct syntax to TFTP a file from a TFTP server to a voice router flash is `copy tftp: flash`.

4.   C. The correct syntax to TFTP a file from a TFTP server to a voice router flash is `archive tar /xtract`.

5.   C. The command is used to specify files that the router can serve to clients using TFTP.

6.   B. The auto-assign configuration is not necessary for the operation of a CUCM Express system.

7.   B. You manually update configuration load files using the `create cnf-files` command.

8.   A, B, C. The MAC address can be found on the box, on the back of the phone, and within the Settings menu of a powered-up phone.

9.   C. The `restart all` command within config-telephony mode performs a quick reset of all registered phones.

10.   D. To reset a phone locally, press the Settings button and then **#**.

11.   B. The CUCM Express allocates a specified amount of memory for each ephone and ephone-DN. This memory is essentially wasted if it is not needed. It could possibly cause performance problems if your router requires that memory for other uses.

12.   C, D, E, G. You must enable the HTTP server, HTTPS server, or both and then set the root directory. Also, you need to create a web administrator and password. This is the username/password used to authenticate to the GUI interface. Lastly, you must allow users to log in using locally configured usernames and passwords.

13.   B. You add, delete, and change ephone-DN configurations in the Configure menu tab.

14.   A. You can save configuration changes on the GUI under the Administration menu by selecting Save Router Config.

15.   C. When a phone powers up and connects to the network, its first task is to receive network parameters such as an IP address, gateway, subnet mask, and the option 150 parameter. If your phone is not receiving one or more of these, it will fail to properly register.

16.   D. You can find the Network Settings information by pressing the Settings button on a Cisco IP phone.

17. B, D. You can use debug tftp events to see which files a Cisco phone is asking for. With this information, you can then view which files are configured to be served via TFTP by issuing a show telephony-service tftp-bindings command.

18. D. When a user picks up the phone handset, the phone goes into an off-hook state. This is referred to as an extension seizure.

19. D. Alerting means that someone is trying to call that ephone-DN but the user has not yet picked up the handset.

20. C. The phone will not register until another phone unregisters or max-ephone is changed to 11.

Answers to Written Lab 1

1. `copy tftp: flash`

2. `archive tar /xtract`

3. `tftp-server flash:/phone/7945-7965/SCCP45.8-3-2-27.sbn alias SCCP45.8-3-2-27.sbn`

4. `ip source-ip 172.16.55.100`

5. `max-ephones 30`

6. `max-dn 50`

7. `load 7945 SCCP45.8-3-3S.loads`

8. `telephony-service setup`

9. `ip http secure-server`

10. `debug tftp events`

Chapter

6

CUCM Express Advanced Configuration

THE CCNA VOICE EXAM TOPICS COVERED IN THIS CHAPTER INCLUDE THE FOLLOWING:

✓ **Implement Cisco Unified Communications Manager Express to support endpoints using CLI.**

- Configure call-transfer per design specifications.

- Configure voice productivity features including hunt groups, call park, call pickup, paging groups, and paging/intercom.

- Configure Music on Hold.

✓ **Perform basic maintenance and operations tasks to support the VoIP solution.**

- Describe basic troubleshooting methods for Cisco Unified Communications Manager Express.

Whenever I go to buy a new car, the first things I look at are the basics. How reliable is the car? How much legroom is there? Does it get decent gas mileage? Does the value hold up for resale? Answering these questions will give me the basic functionality that I desire in my next automobile. This is similar to what we've done up to this point in configuring our CUCM Express. We have the basics nailed down, so we can make and receive calls. Once that's done, we need to start thinking about the bells and whistles. Call parking, hunt groups, intercom, Music on Hold—all these phone features are similar to added features of a car such as a six-disc CD changer, satellite radio, and built-in Bluetooth. While they may not be absolutely necessary, they're great to have! In Chapter 6 we cover many of the most popular configuration features on the CUCM Express.

Chapter 6 will begin by showing the difference in ephone-DN and ephone configuration between key-system and PBX models. We'll also cover the various phone button separator options. Next, you'll learn how to configure telephony service features that assist in tailoring the phone system to meet the geographical and business environment where the system and its users reside. Then you'll learn how to configure advanced voice productivity features that provide additional functionality to your users. After that, we'll look at how to configure some of the access and accounting features available on the CUCM Express. Finally, you'll learn how to configure Music on Hold in both unicast and multicast environments.

Configuring Key System and PBX DNs and Ephones

A key system is commonly used in small businesses where the vast majority of calls come from the PSTN. The key-system model is based on one extension being shared among many phones. Alternatively, a PBX system uses a model of one extension per phone. This section will show typical DN and ephone configurations for each setup so you can not only configure these models yourself but also identify the configuration differences between the two.

Configuring Key Systems

In a key-system environment, you historically see the entire PSTN extension configured on the line instead of a truncated four- or five-digit extension. Furthermore, all phones must be capable of answering any call. This means that all the ephone-DNs will be configured as buttons on every phone. This is known as a *shared line*. One way of creating this shared-line setup is to configure a single ephone-DN and apply it on multiple ephones.

The following key system example configuration shows two phone DNs that represent two separate external PSTN phone numbers. The DNs are assigned to both phones, and both will ring when the number is dialed. The first phone to answer gets the call.

```
Router#configure terminal
Router(config)#ephone-dn  1
Router(config-dn)#number 5555552121
Router(config-dn)#ephone-dn  2
Router(config-dn)#number 5555559191
Router(config-dn)#exit
Router(config)#ephone  1
Router(config-ephone)#button  1:1 2:2
Router(config)#ephone  2
Router(config-ephone)#button  1:1 2:2
Router(config-ephone)#end
Router#
```

Figure 6.1 shows what ephone 1 looks like after these configurations are made and the phone is reset.

FIGURE 6.1   One DN, multiple ephones

Let's say that a phone call is placed to 555-555-2121. Both ephone 1 and ephone 2 would ring. If ephone 2 answers the call first, line 1 of ephone 1 shows this line as in use by lighting the extension button red and showing the double-handset icon next to the line number. Figure 6.2 shows line 1 of ephone 1 in use.

FIGURE 6.2   DN 1 in use

Because line 1 is in use, if ephone 1 needs to make a call, it must use line 2, which is currently not in use.

An alternative shared-line method is to configure multiple ephone DNs with the same extension number. You can then configure the ephones to use the separate ephone-DN configurations. You set a *preference* on the ephone-DN configuration so one particular phone will always ring first. If the preferred ephone is busy, then the ephone with the next preference will ring instead. In the CUCM, preferences range from 0 to 9, with the lowest number being the first preference. We can accomplish this configuration, multiple ephone-DNs with a shared line, using the `preference` configuration command. The following configuration example shows how to configure two ephone-DNs with a single phone number. You can see that ephone-DN 1 has a preference of 0, which means that when a call is made to this extension, it will choose to ring the phone that is configured to use ephone-DN 1 first:

```
Router#configure terminal
Router(config)#ephone-dn 1
Router(config-ephone-dn)#number 5555557777
Router(config-ephone-dn)#preference 0
Router(config-ephone-dn)#ephone-dn 2
Router(config-ephone-dn)#number 5555557777
Router(config-ephone-dn)#preference 1
Router(config-ephone-dn)#exit
```

```
Router(config)#ephone 1
Router(config-ephone)#button 1:1
Router(config-ephone)#ephone 2
Router(config-ephone)#button 1:2
Router(config-ephone)#end
Router#
```

 If you did not configure a preference on the ephone-DNs or you set them to be the same, the CUCM would round-robin the calls between the two ephones. The preference command gives you control of where the CUCM Express routes calls.

If ephone 1 is in use, any new call will also be sent to ephone 1 because it is the lowest preferred DN regardless of whether the phone is busy or not. So a second call placed to our extension would receive a busy signal, and ephone 2 would never receive any calls. To get around this problem, we configure ephone-DN 1 with the no huntstop command. The no huntstop command tells the CUCM Express that it should look for the next preferred ephone-DN if the most preferred phone is busy. Now when ephone 1 is busy, a second call placed on the shared extension will roll over and ring ephone 2:

```
Router#configure terminal
Router(config)#ephone-dn 1
Router(config-ephone-dn)#number 5555557777
Router(config-ephone-dn)#preference 0
Router(config-ephone-dn)#no huntstop
Router(config-ephone-dn)#ephone-dn 2
Router(config-ephone-dn)#number 5555557777
Router(config-ephone-dn)#preference 1
Router(config-ephone-dn)#exit
Router(config)#ephone 1
Router(config-ephone)#button 1:1
Router(config-ephone)#ephone 2
Router(config-ephone)#button 1:2
Router(config-ephone)#end
Router#
```

Another shared-line key system configuration we need to look at is when the phone extensions are configured as dual-line and octo-line DNs. So far, we've configured only single-line phones. A single-line phone can make or receive only one call at a time. So if the line is already in use, you cannot place the call on hold to make a second call. Likewise, if line 1 is in use, a second phone call to the extension will receive a busy signal.

Dual-line phones, on the other hand, allow the phone to place calls on hold or receive a second call when in use. And *octo-line* phones are capable of handling up to eight simultaneous calls on a single phone button extension. Dual- and octo-line phones are configured within the ephone-DN as shown here:

```
Router(config)#ephone-dn 1 ?
  dual-line  dual-line DN (2 calls per line/button)
  octo-line  octo-line DN (8 calls per line/button)
```

Configuring ephone-DNs with dual lines is extremely beneficial because it allows additional functionality when your phone is in use. For now, let's assume that our small business has a single PSTN line that is to be shared between two phones configured with dual-line ephone-DNs. Just as in the previous configuration example, we want to ensure that the first call made to the extension is received on ephone 1 and that a second call rolls over to ephone 2 if ephone 1 is already in a call. Let's say we configure the following:

```
Router#configure terminal
Router(config)#ephone-dn 1 dual-line
Router(config-ephone-dn)#number 5555557777
Router(config-ephone-dn)#preference 0
Router(config-ephone-dn)#no huntstop
Router(config-ephone-dn)#ephone-dn 2 dual-line
Router(config-ephone-dn)#number 5555557777
Router(config-ephone-dn)#preference 1
Router(config-ephone-dn)#exit
Router(config)#ephone 1
Router(config-ephone)#button 1:1
Router(config-ephone)#ephone 2
Router(config-ephone)#button 1:2
Router(config-ephone)#end
Router#
```

In this situation, the first call will always go to ephone 1. But because the ephone-DN is configured as a dual line, a second call will also go to ephone 1. Only a third simultaneous call will make it to ephone 2. To get around this dual-line problem, we can use the huntstop channel command on ephone-DN 1. The huntstop command prevents calls from hunting for the second channel of the ephone-DN. So if we combine the no huntstop command with the huntstop channel command, the first call always goes to ephone 1, and if channel 1 of ephone 1 is busy, the second call is sent to ephone 2. Here is the full configuration example to accomplish our goal:

```
Router#configure terminal
Router(config)#ephone-dn 1 dual-line
Router(config-ephone-dn)#number 5555557777
Router(config-ephone-dn)#preference 0
Router(config-ephone-dn)#no huntstop
Router(config-ephone-dn)#huntstop channel
```

```
Router(config-ephone-dn)#ephone-dn 2 dual-line
Router(config-ephone-dn)#number 5555557777
Router(config-ephone-dn)#preference 1
Router(config-ephone-dn)#exit
Router(config)#ephone 1
Router(config-ephone)#button 1:1
Router(config-ephone)#ephone 2
Router(config-ephone)#button 1:2
Router(config-ephone)#end
Router#
```

Additional phone button options also expand the shared-line experience of key systems. In particular, you'll learn about overlay buttons in the "Configuring Ephone Button Options" section of this chapter.

Configuring PBX Systems

PBX systems are more commonly found in larger office environments and assign a unique phone extension to every phone. This allows a caller to reach a specific person within an organization directly. Also, because of the size of the environment, a large percentage of phone calls are within the network. To help make life easier for the phone users, phone extensions are used instead of the full phone number. Typical extensions are four or five digits in length. These digits may correspond to the last digits of the full PSTN direct inward dial (DID) if that is how their PSTN circuits are configured. Also, you will find that the phones almost always are configured as dual-line ephone-DNs. This is because you need a second line to enable the additional functionality the PBX system offers. In the last section, you learned how to configure the most common key-system methods of sharing a single phone number with multiple phones. Here is a very basic and common method of configuring two PBX system phones with separate extension numbers:

```
Router#configure terminal
Router(config)#ephone-dn 1 dual-line
Router(config-ephone-dn)#number 8001
Router(config-ephone-dn)#ephone-dn 2 dual-line
Router(config-ephone-dn)#number 8002
Router(config-ephone-dn)#exit
Router(config)#ephone 1
Router(config-ephone)#button 1:1
Router(config-ephone)#ephone 2
Router(config-ephone)#button 1:2
Router(config-ephone)#end
Router#
```

Now you have two phones with separate extensions. You can then configure the CUCM Express system for additional features to tailor your system to your environment. The remainder of this chapter details how to configure the most common advanced voice features and options you'll find in use today.

Configuring Ephone Button Options

When it's time to assign ephone-DNs to specific ephones, we use the button ephone-config command. The separator between the line button you wish to configure and the ephone-DN identifier is an *ephone button separator*. Many button separator options are available. Let's look at all the options:

```
Router(config-ephone)#button ?
  LINE  button-index:dn-index pairs example 1:2 2:5
Configuration line:button with separator feature options:
: normal phone lines
        example    button 1:2 2:5
s silent ring, ringer muted, call waiting beep muted
        example    button 1s2 2s5
b silent ring, ringer muted, call waiting beep not muted
        example    button 1b2 2b5
f feature ring
        example    button 1f2 2f5
        see also 'no dnd feature-ring'
m monitor line, silent ring, call waiting display suppressed
        example    button 1m2 2m5
        see also 'transfer-system full-consult dss'
w watch line (BLF), watch the phone offhook status via the phone's primary
ephone-dn
        example    button 1w2 2w5
o overlay lines, combine multiple lines per physical button
        example    button 1o2,3,4,5
c overlay call-waiting, combine multiple lines per physical button
        example    button 1c2,3,4,5
        see also 'huntstop channel' for ephone-dn dual-line
x expansion/overflow, define additional expansion lines that are
        used when the primary line for an overlay button is
        occupied by an active call
        Expansion works with 'button o' and not with 'button c'
        example    button 4o21,22,23,24,25
                   button 5x4
                   button 6x4
Different separator options may be use for each button
        example    button 1:2 2s5 3b7 4f9 5m22 6w10
```

Table 6.1 details the function of each button separator.

TABLE 6.1 Button separator options

Separator	Option Name	Function
:	Normal ring	Phone rings normally with default ring tone. Also uses flashing lights on line button and headset lamp to indicate ring.
s	Silent ring	No audible ring when calls come into the phone. Uses flashing lights on line button and headset lamp to indicate ring. No audible call-waiting beep.
b	Silent with beep	No audible ring when calls come into the phone. Uses flashing lights on line button and headset lamp to indicate ring. Call-waiting beep is audible.
f	Feature ring	Phone rings using an alternate ring tone from the default.
m	Monitor line	Used to monitor status (on- or off-hook) of a line. Commonly used on receptionist phones to see if an employee is currently using the phone. No audible ring when calls come into the phone, and the line cannot be used to make or take calls.
w	Watch phone	Similar to the monitor mode except that it allows the user to monitor all ephone-DNs on a phone instead of a single ephone-DN. This mode presents a more accurate picture of user availability than using the m separator.
o	Overlay line	Associates multiple ephone-DNs with a single line button. No call-waiting functionality.
c	Overlay with call waiting	Same as the overlay line but with call-waiting functionality added.
x	Expansion line	Another overlay line option. The difference is that if the line button extension is in use, new calls are allowed to overflow to additional line buttons to help prevent a busy signal.

The ring phone button options (:, s, b, and s) are fairly straightforward and need no more explanation. We'll focus on when you would want to use the monitor and overlay button options.

Monitor Line

Let's say you have an administrative assistant who is tasked with taking your calls and transferring them to your phone when you are not busy with other calls. The *monitor line* (m) button separator option allows the assistant's phone to monitor your ephone-DN and see if you are currently on a call using that ephone-DN. If you are already busy on the line, the assistant can take a message for you. The line configured in monitor mode cannot make or receive any calls. Instead, it is a visual aid to see if another line is being used. In this example, my phone is assigned the number 4040. My administrative assistant has their own number, 4041, assigned to button 1. Also configured is button 2 to monitor my ephone-DN.

```
Router(config)#ephone-dn 1
Router(config-ephone-dn)#number 4040
Router(config-ephone-dn)#ephone-dn 2
Router(config-ephone-dn)#number 4041
Router(config-ephone-dn)#exit
Router(config)#ephone 1
Router(config-ephone)#button 1:1
Router(config-ephone)#ephone 2
Router(config-ephone)#button 1:2 2m1
Router(config-ephone)#end
Router#
```

Now when I pick up my phone to make a call, my administrative assistant can see that I'm busy on that ephone-DN. Figure 6.3 shows the administrative assistant's phone when the 4040 line is in use.

FIGURE 6.3   A phone configured to monitor extension 4040

One of the drawbacks to this setup would become apparent if my phone were to be configured with multiple ephone-DNs. I would then need to create multiple monitor button operators for each extension. A way around the monitor line limitation is to use the watch phone button separator.

Watch Phone

The *watch phone* (w) button option does exactly the same thing as the monitor line option with the exception that it monitors all of the ephone-DNs of an ephone instead of just one. You configure the button to watch the primary line of a phone, and it monitors all lines on the phone. This is far more useful than the monitor line option because you can see if any of the lines on a phone are in use instead of just a single ephone-DN. As with the monitor line option, a line configured with the watch phone option cannot make or receive any calls. We'll use the boss-and-assistant scenario again for this example. The boss has two extensions (5111 and 5112) configured on lines 1 and 2. The administrative assistant's phone is configured to use extension 5113 on button 1. Button 2 is then configured to watch the primary ephone-DN 1, as shown here:

```
Router(config)#ephone-dn 1
Router(config-ephone-dn)#number 5111
Router(config-ephone-dn)#ephone-dn 2
Router(config-ephone-dn)#number 5112
Router(config-ephone-dn)#ephone-dn 3
Router(config-ephone-dn)#number 5113
Router(config-ephone-dn)#exit
Router(config)#ephone 1
Router(config-ephone)#button 1:1 2:2
Router(config-ephone)#ephone 2
Router(config-ephone)#button 1:3 2w1
Router(config-ephone)#end
Router#
```

With this command, when the boss uses either ephone-DN 1 or 2, the administrative assistant's button 2 will show the line as in use. The watching phone's display button shows the phone in use when the following conditions occur on the watched phone:

- Off-hook and/or in use

- Unregistered or deceased phone

- In DnD (do not disturb) mode

Overlay Line

Overlay (o) lines allow you to configure multiple ephone-DNs to a single phone button on a Cisco phone. Cisco phones have a finite number of phone buttons. You can use the overlay button option to assign multiple ephone-DNs to a single physical phone button.

Ephone-DNs that are configured on a particular ephone with the overlay option must all be single-line or dual/octo-line phones. There cannot be a mix of single- and multiline phones.

An overlay line is commonly used when a main line is answered by anyone in a specific department. This overlay shared-line configuration is best paired with the preference and no huntstop commands. In the next example, we have a department with two employees. Each employee has a unique extension for their phone. There is also a shared-line number (5454) that is configured as an overlay line on button 1. When we configure the ephone-DN, we make sure to configure the unique extension first. The first ephone configured is the number that is displayed on the phone display LCD panel. The overlay line is configured, but that number is never seen on the phone button display. The shared line is configured on ephone-DN 3 and ephone-DN 4. Ephone-DN 3 has the lower preference and will handle the first call. It also is configured to use the no huntstop command to look for the next-preferred ephone-DN with the same extension if the most-preferred phone is busy.

```
Router#configure terminal
Router(config)#ephone-dn 1
Router(config-ephone-dn)#number 6001
Router(config-ephone-dn)#ephone-dn 2
Router(config-ephone-dn)#number 6002
Router(config-ephone-dn)#ephone-dn 3
Router(config-ephone-dn)#number 5454
Router(config-ephone-dn)#preference 0
Router(config-ephone-dn)#no huntstop
Router(config-ephone-dn)#ephone-dn 4
Router(config-ephone-dn)#number 5454
Router(config-ephone-dn)#preference 1
Router(config-ephone-dn)#exit
Router(config)#ephone 1
Router(config-ephone)#button 1o1,3,4
Router(config-ephone)#ephone 2
Router(config-ephone)#button 1o2,3,4
Router(config-ephone)#end
Router#
```

Each phone's button 1 is configured with its unique number as well as the shared-line number for the department. Calls placed to 6001 go only to ephone 1. Calls placed to 6002 go only to ephone 2. But calls placed to 5454 are sent to both phones. The configuration uses only one phone button on each phone. Now other buttons are available to be configured for additional lines or speed-dial capabilities if desired. Following is the output of show ephone for our two configured ephones. As you can see, the first number assigned in the overlay configuration is bound to the phone and idle. The shared number is visible but not the primary number.

Router#**sh ephone**

```
ephone-1 Mac:0021.A084.4F0C TCP socket:[3] activeLine:0 REGISTERED in SCCP ver
12/8
mediaActive:0 offhook:0 ringing:0 reset:0 reset_sent:0 paging 0 debug:0 caps:9
IP:192.168.10.2 49242 7965   keepalive 11 max_line 6
button 1: dn 1  number 6001 CH1   IDLE         overlay
overlay 1: 1(6001) 3(5454) 4(5454)


ephone-2 Mac:0021.A02E.7D9A TCP socket:[4] activeLine:0 REGISTERED in SCCP ver
12/8
mediaActive:0 offhook:0 ringing:0 reset:0 reset_sent:0 paging 0 debug:0 caps:9
IP:192.168.10.3 49219 7965   keepalive 11 max_line 6
button 1: dn 2  number 6002 CH1   IDLE         overlay
overlay 1: 2(6002) 3(5454) 4(5454)
```

Let's say a call is placed to extension 5454, and ephone 2 answers the call. Now a show ephone looks like this:

Router#**sh ephone**

```
ephone-1 Mac:0021.A084.4F0C TCP socket:[3] activeLine:0 REGISTERED in SCCP ver
12/8
mediaActive:0 offhook:0 ringing:0 reset:0 reset_sent:0 paging 0 debug:0 caps:9
IP:192.168.10.2 49242 7965   keepalive 14 max_line 6
button 1: dn 1  number 6001 CH1   IDLE         overlay
overlay 1: 1(6001) 3(5454) 4(5454)

ephone-2 Mac:0021.A02E.7D9A TCP socket:[4] activeLine:1 REGISTERED in SCCP ver
12/8
mediaActive:1 offhook:1 ringing:0 reset:0 reset_sent:0 paging 0 debug:0 caps:9
IP:192.168.10.3 49219 7965   keepalive 14 max_line 6
button 1: dn 3  number 5454 CH1   CONNECTED    overlay shared
overlay 1: 2(6002) 3(5454) 4(5454)
Active Call on DN 3 chan 1 :5454 192.168.10.3 27418 to 192.168.1.100 24646 via
192.168.10.3
G711Ulaw64k   160 bytes no vad
Tx Pkts 196 bytes 33712 Rx Pkts 192 bytes 33024 Lost 0
Jitter 7 Latency 0 callingDn 5 calledDn -1
```

At this point, ephone-DN 3, which is number 5454, is owned and controlled by ephone 2. A second call is made to 5454; this time, ephone-DN 3 is in use, so the call rolls over to the next ephone-DN, which is 4. Because ephone 2 is configured with an overlay with both ephone-DNs 3 and 4, the phone rings on ephone 2. A show ephone with both ephone-DNs 3 and 4 in use looks like this:

```
ephone-1 Mac:0021.A084.4F0C TCP socket:[3] activeLine:1 REGISTERED in SCCP ver
12/8
mediaActive:1 offhook:1 ringing:0 reset:0 reset_sent:0 paging 0 debug:0 caps:9
IP:192.168.10.2 49242 7965    keepalive 19 max_line 6
button 1: dn 4  number 5454 CH1   CONNECTED     overlay shared
overlay 1: 1(6001) 3(5454) 4(5454)
Active Call on DN 4 chan 1 :5454 192.168.10.2 27274 to 192.168.1.101 24648 via
192.168.10.2
G711Ulaw64k  160 bytes no vad
Tx Pkts 0 bytes 0 Rx Pkts 0 bytes 0 Lost 0
Jitter 0 Latency 0 callingDn 5 calledDn -1

ephone-2 Mac:0021.A02E.7D9A TCP socket:[4] activeLine:1 REGISTERED in SCCP ver
12/8
mediaActive:1 offhook:1 ringing:0 reset:0 reset_sent:0 paging 0 debug:0 caps:9
IP:192.168.10.3 49219 7965    keepalive 19 max_line 6
button 1: dn 3  number 5454 CH1   CONNECTED     overlay shared
overlay 1: 2(6002) 3(5454) 4(5454)
Active Call on DN 3 chan 1 :5454 192.168.10.3 26148 to 192.168.1.100 24640 via
192.168.10.3
G711Ulaw64k  160 bytes no vad
Tx Pkts 738 bytes 126936 Rx Pkts 736 bytes 126592 Lost 0
Jitter 2 Latency 0 callingDn 6 calledDn -1
```

As you can see, this shared-line overlay configuration is a very good option in many office environments. It also highlights a combination of PBX and key-system capabilities on the CUCM Express. Installations that combine both PBX and key-system functionality are commonly called *hybrid systems*.

Overlay with Call Waiting

This button separator option, c, is the same as the overlay, except that it adds call-waiting functionality. *Call waiting* is the ability for a phone to receive two or more simultaneous calls at the same time. The user can place a currently engaged call on hold to answer the second call. To see this difference, we will configure our CUCM Express router with the same configuration as the overlay example except we will use the call-waiting button separator option. We'll also have to configure ephone-DN 3 as a dual-line phone so it can utilize call waiting:

```
Router#configure terminal
Router(config)#ephone-dn 1
Router(config-ephone-dn)#number 6001
Router(config-ephone-dn)#ephone-dn 2
Router(config-ephone-dn)#number 6002
Router(config-ephone-dn)#ephone-dn 3 dual-line
Router(config-ephone-dn)#number 5454
Router(config-ephone-dn)#preference 0
Router(config-ephone-dn)#no huntstop
Router(config-ephone-dn)#ephone-dn 4
Router(config-ephone-dn)#number 5454
Router(config-ephone-dn)#preference 1
Router(config-ephone-dn)#exit
Router(config)#ephone 1
Router(config-ephone)#button 1c1,3
Router(config-ephone)#ephone 2
Router(config-ephone)#button 1c2,3
Router(config-ephone)#end
Router#
```

So what are the results of this configuration? The first call to extension 5454 is handled by ephone-DN 3 because of its lower preference. A second call rolls over to ephone-DN 4, because the no huntstop option was set. Ephone-DN 4 rings ephone 1, but it also sends the call-waiting beep to ephone 2, which is currently in a call. This way, the user on ephone 2 is notified of a second call. He or she can place the first call on hold and answer the second.

Expansion Line

The *expansion* button separator, x, is used to expand line coverage for an overlay button (o). It does not work when the overlay separator button is configured for call waiting (c). When the extensions configured as overlay lines are in use, the expansion lines begin taking calls. In this example, we have ephone 1 configured to overlay ephone-DNs 1 and 2, which are both 7001. Ephone-DN 1 is also a dual-line phone. We also have button 2 configured as an overlay for line 1 on the phone:

```
Router#configure terminal
Router(config)#ephone-dn 1 dual-line
Router(config-ephone-dn)#number 7001
Router(config)#ephone-dn 2
Router(config-ephone-dn)#number 7001
Router(config-ephone-dn)#exit
```

```
Router(config)#ephone 1
Router(config-ephone)#button 1o1,2 2x1
Router(config-ephone)#end
Router#
```

In this example, the first call to 7001 goes to button 1. The second call also goes to button 1, because it is a dual line and channel 2 is free. The third call will overflow to button 2 because both lines are busy on button 1. Always remember that overflow lines will be used only when all other lines are occupied.

Configuring Telephony Service Features

You'll configure most telephony service features while in config-telephony mode. These features provide multiple ways to tailor your voice environment to better fit the needs of your end users. This section will show you how to configure several of the most important telephony service features. We'll look at how to change the language and ring tone settings to match the location where your endpoints will reside. I'll also show you how to modify the date and time formats and modify the phone handset system message to personalize your voice system. Lastly, you'll learn how to create a local directory to assist users in looking up phone extensions.

How to Configure User Locale and Network Locale

By default, the Cisco CUCM Express is set for the English (US) language for its location. What happens if you need to deploy this system in say, Colombia, where Spanish is the native language? To modify the language used on the Cisco phone handsets, including softkeys, help, and other buttons, we can use the *user-locale* command. Let's see what language options are currently available:

```
Router(config-telephony)#user-locale ?
<0-4>  user locale index 0 to 4 (0 is default)
  DE      Germany
  DK      Denmark
  ES      Spain
  FR      France
  IT      Italy
  JP      Japan
  NL      Netherlands
  NO      Norway
  PT      Portugal
  RU      Russian Federation
```

SE	Sweden
US	United States

Using our Colombian deployment example, we'll choose ES for our locale, so Spanish will be displayed on our handsets:

```
Router#configure terminal
Router(config)#telephony-service
Router(config-telephony)#user-locale ES
Updating CNF files
CNF files update complete
Please issue 'create cnf' command after the locale change
Router(config-telephony)#create cnf-files
CNF file creation is already On
Updating CNF files
CNF files update complete
```

Whenever we make changes to the configuration of a telephone, we will need to reset the phone in order to obtain all of the updated configuration and settings as manipulated.

Figure 6.4 shows a screenshot of the settings menu now that we've changed the language and reset our phones.

FIGURE 6.4   Spanish phone settings

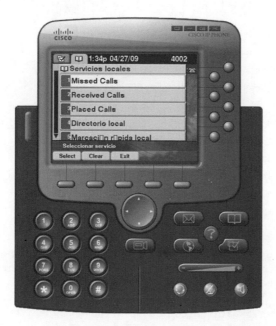

The *network-locale* command modifies tones and cadence differences between geographic regions. Unlike the user-locale, which changes language functions of the phones, the network-locale settings are based on regional telephone standards in terms of telephone signaling. Using our Colombia deployment example, we can use ES for the user-locale because Colombians speak the same language as Spaniards. The network-locale settings differ, however, because each region has different tones within its geographic regions:

```
Router(config-telephony)#network-locale ?
<0-4>  network locale index 0 to 4 (0 is default)
   AT     Austria
   CA     Canada
   CH     Switzerland
   CO     Colombia
   DE     Germany
   DK     Denmark
   ES     Spain
   FR     France
   GB     United Kingdom
   IT     Italy
   JP     Japan
   NL     Netherlands
   NO     Norway
   PT     Portugal
   RU     Russian Federation
   SE     Sweden
   US     United States
Router(config-telephony)#network-locale CO
Updating CNF files
CNF files update complete
Please issue 'create cnf' command after the locale change
Router(config-telephony)#create cnf-files
CNF file creation is already On
Updating CNF files
CNF files update complete
```

If you need to configure a user-locale and network-locale that are not currently in your CUCM Express software, you can download the individual user-locale .tar files here:

http://www.cisco.com/cgi-bin/tablebuild.pl/CME-Locale

Real World Scenario

Can You Translate This for Me?

Jeff was an IT consultant who recently began installing CUCM Express solutions in businesses. All of his implementations up to this point had been for local businesses in the United States, where English is the dominant language. A recent client, however, called for a Canadian deployment. Some employees had English as their primary language and others had French. In addition, the company regularly had visits from consultants from Spain, which required a third language. Since Jeff was new to the language-localization features of the CUCM Express, he had to do a bit of research to figure out the best configuration method to provide the three different language options to users. He learned that if the CUCM Express is going to be in a mixed-language environment, his best option was to configure user-locale and network-locale ephone templates. This is an example of how the ephone templates were used to remedy this situation:

```
Router#configure terminal
Router(config)#telephony-service
Router(config-telephony)# user-locale 1 ES
Router(config-telephony)# user-locale 2 FR
Router(config-telephony)# network-locale 1 ES
Router(config-telephony)# network-locale 2 FR
Router(config-telephony)#ephone-template 1
Router(config-ephone-template)# user-locale 1
Router(config-ephone-template)# network-locale 1
Router(config-ephone-template)#ephone-template 2
Router(config-ephone-template)# user-locale 2
Router(config-ephone-template)# network-locale 2
Router(config-ephone-template)#ephone 1
Router(config-ephone)# button 1:1
Router(config-ephone)#ephone 2
Router(config-ephone)# button 1:2
Router(config-ephone)# ephone-template 1
Router(config-ephone)#ephone 3
Router(config-ephone)# button 1:3
Router(config-ephone)# ephone-template 2
Router(config-ephone)#exit
```

```
Router(config)#telephony-service
Router(config-telephony)#create cnf-files
CNF file creation is already On
Updating CNF files
CNF files update complete
Router(config-telephony)#restart all
```

This method sets up a very simple and streamlined way to configure ephones that fits the needs of the local user. Note that by default, the English (US) locale is configured if you do not specify a template. So, for example, ephone 1 is for English-speaking users because there is no ephone template 1 or 2 specified.

Configuring the Date and Time Format

Similar to user-locale is the date and time format. Different countries display the date and time differently. In the United States, the date is displayed as mm/dd/yy. In other regions, such as Europe, the date is displayed as dd/mm/yy. The default format is mm/dd/yy. If you wish to change the format on your Cisco IP phones, you use the date-format command. You can specify the following formats:

```
Router(config-telephony)#date-format ?
  dd-mm-yy  Set date to dd-mm-yy format
  mm-dd-yy  Set date to mm-dd-yy format
  yy-dd-mm  Set date to yy-dd-mm format
  yy-mm-dd  Set date to yy-mm-dd format
```

Let's change the date format to the European dd/mm/yy:

```
Router#configure terminal
Router(config)#telephony-service
Router(config-telephony)#date-format dd-mm-yy
Router(config-telephony)#end
Router#
```

Now when we reset our phones, we get the date to display with the day first. See Figure 6.5.

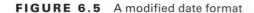

FIGURE 6.5   A modified date format

Configuring the System Message

The CUCM Express system message is a custom-display text message that appears on certain Cisco IP phones with large displays, such as the 7940 and 7960 grayscale displays or the 7945 and 7965 color displays. The system message defaults to "Cisco Unified CME" by default.

We can modify the default message with the `system message` config-telephony command. The next example shows how to change the message to "ACME Incorporated":

```
Router#configure terminal
Router(config)#telephony-service
Router(config-telephony)#system message ACME Incorporated
Router(config-telephony)#end
Router#
```

The system message does not need a reset or restart of the phones because this is updated every time the phone receives a keepalive message from the CUCM Express. Figure 6.6 shows the modified message on our phone.

FIGURE 6.6 A customized system message

 The maximum length of a system message on a CUCM Express is 34 characters.

Configuring a Local Directory

The CUCM Express *local directory* is like a built-in phone book. The directory can be used to search for and locate extensions based on caller-ID information that is configured on the system. Configuration of the local directory takes place in config-ephone-DN and config-telephony modes. Let's look at our configuration options to see how all the pieces fit together to make a custom-tailored directory to meet all your needs.

Configuring Caller-ID Ephone-DN Entries

When you configure an ephone, the name configuration command configures caller ID for this extension. For example, let's configure ephone-DN 1 with the extension 4001 and the caller ID John Smith:

```
Router#configure terminal
Router(config)#ephone-dn 1 dual-line
Router(config-ephone-dn)#number 4001
Router(config-ephone-dn)#name John Smith
Router(config-ephone)#end
Router#
```

When we assign this ephone-DN to an ephone and make a call from that ephone using the 4001 extension, we see that the caller-ID information comes through on the called phone, as shown in Figure 6.7.

FIGURE 6.7 A caller-ID display

The name config-ephone-DN mode command also automatically enters this name into the local directory. You can access the local directory using the Directory button located on the Cisco phone to see the display shown in Figure 6.8.

FIGURE 6.8 The local directory in default first-name-first order

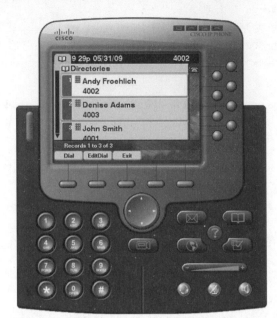

As you can see, by default, the directory displays names with first name showing first. This may not be the way you want to have your directory listed. You can change this by going into config-telephony mode and using the `directory last-name-first` command to switch the listings around. Now all of your directory names will be listed alphabetically by last name, as shown in Figure 6.9.

Configuring Manual Local Directory Entries and System-Level Speed Dial

You can also add directory listings directly using the `directory entry` config-telephony mode command. For example, let's add a directory entry for Branch Chicago using this method:

```
Router#configure terminal
Router(config)#telephony-service
Router(config-telephony)#directory entry 1 3125552777 name Branch Chicago
Router(config-telephony)#end
Router#
```

FIGURE 6.9 The local directory in last-name-first order

You can configure up to 100 manual directory entries (numbered 1–100). Directory entries listed within the 34–99 range are eligible to be configured as systemwide speed-dial entries if desired.

Configuring Voice Productivity Features

Voice productivity features are phone features that enhance the user's calling experience. In this section, you will learn how to configure the following productivity features:

- Call forward
- Call transfer
- Call pickup
- Call parking
- Hunt groups
- Intercom
- Paging

Call Forwarding

If you want to be able to answer your phone extension but are located somewhere else, you can use the *call forward* voice productivity feature to direct all of your calls to a different phone. There are two different types of call forwarding on the CUCM Express. One method is to forward all calls on the Cisco phone handset itself. We'll refer to this as dynamic call forwarding. The second method is to configure forwarding within the Cisco IOS. This is referred to as static call forwarding. Let's look at how to set up both methods.

Setting Up Dynamic Call Forwarding

To forward all incoming calls using the handset, you can press the CFwdAll softkey on the phone, enter the phone number you want to forward calls to, and then press either the End softkey or the # button. Figure 6.10 shows that extension 204 has been forwarded to the phone with the extension 201.

FIGURE 6.10   Call forwarding implemented on an IP phone

You can see that the icon in the upper-right corner next to the extension has changed to indicate that this phone has been forwarded. To stop the phone from forwarding calls, press the CFwdAll softkey again.

Setting Up Static Call Forwarding

Unlike dynamic call forwarding, static call forwarding allows for more options than to simply forward all incoming calls. It is important to note that static forwarding can be overridden using the CFwdAll softkey on Cisco phones. There are five ways to configure static call forwarding on an ephone-DN. Table 6.2 lists each configuration option and its function.

TABLE 6.2   Static call-forwarding options

Option	Description
All	Forward all incoming calls
Busy	Forward calls only when phone is busy
night-service	Forward calls only when CUCM Express is in night-service active time mode
Noan	Forward calls after a specified amount of time when the phone has not been answered

As an example, suppose we want our extension at 204 to be forwarded to extension 201 when we do not answer it after five rings. In the United States, a ring consists of a 4-second audible tone followed by 4 seconds of silence. Using this as our guide, we can configure our extension to forward calls after 30 seconds without answer:

```
Router#configure terminal
Router(config)#ephone-dn 4
call-forward noan 201 timeout ?
  <3-60000>  Ringing no answer timeout duration in seconds

Router(config-ephone-dn)#call-forward noan 201 timeout 30
Router(config-ephone-dn)#end
Router#
```

The call-forward all and call-forward busy options are fairly self-explanatory. The call-forward night-service option is useful only when the after-hours night service functionality is configured on your CUCM Express. Night-service is a way of having calls routed directly to voice mail during specified periods of time. It is typically used in key-system configurations. Once it is properly configured, you can configure call forwarding to take advantage of the night-service configuration.

 One additional static call-forwarding configuration needs to be addressed. The call-forward max-length option sets a maximum number of digits that end users can enter for forwarding. This option helps to prevent employees from forwarding calls to numbers that would ultimately incur long-distance charges.

Call Transfer

Call transfer is the process of moving an active phone conversation from one phone number to another. On Cisco phones, you perform this process by pressing the Trnsfer softkey and dialing the number where you wish to forward the call. Figure 6.11 shows a phone call in progress with the Trnsfer key option available for use.

FIGURE 6.11   The result of pressing the Transfer (call transfer) softkey

There are three ways to configure transfer on the CUCM Express within config-telephony mode. Table 6.3 lists the three call transfer options available.

TABLE 6.3   Call transfer options

Option	Description
full-blind	Transfers the call immediately after entering a forward number. Available on single-line ephone-DNs.
full-consult	Allows you to speak to the transfer number party prior to forwarding the phone conversation. This setup requires dual-line ephone-DNs.
local-consult	Similar in functionality to the full-consult option, but the handling of voice traffic flow is inefficient. This is a Cisco proprietary method and should be used only for backward compatibility with older Cisco phones.

Most of your implementations will be configured for either full-blind or full-consult. For single-line ephone-DNs, the only option is full-blind because consult transfers require the use of a second line. On all dual- and octo-line ephone-DNs, the default transfer method is full-consult. If the phone that is transferring is configured as a dual-line ephone-DN but the second line is not available, the transfer method falls back to full-blind.

You can also configure either a blind or consult transfer on each individual ephone-DN. This example shows ephone-DN 1 being configured for blind transfers:

```
Router#configure terminal
Router(config)#ephone-dn 1
Router(config-ephone-dn)#transfer-mode ?
  blind    Perform blind call transfers (without consultation) using single
           phone line
  consult  Perform call transfers with consultation using second phone line if
           available
Router(config-ephone-dn)#transfer-mode blind
Router(config-ephone-dn)#end
Router#
```

The CUCM Express has a built-in toll-fraud protection that is enabled by default. Unless otherwise configured, calls can be transferred only to local on-network numbers on the system. If you want to allow users to transfer calls off network, you must use the config-telephone transfer-pattern command to specify which dial strings are acceptable. The permitted numbers can be specific configurations that must exactly match. For example, let's configure a transfer pattern for the CEO to be able to transfer calls to his home number at 555-332-3112:

```
Router#configure terminal
Router(config)#telephony-service
Router(config-telephony)#transfer-pattern 5553323112
Router(config-telephony)#end
Router#
```

This number is now the only off-network number allowed to be forwarded.

You can also configure off-network numbers using standard CUCM wildcard characters. *Wildcards* let you configure multiple allowable off-network numbers without having to specify every allowable number. These wildcards are used in multiple different configuration options so it is very important that you properly identify each option. Table 6.4 lists the wildcard options and their use.

TABLE 6.4 Telephone number wildcard options

Option	Description
.	Matches any number 0–9 or the * key.
[ ]	A range of single number digits within the brackets. For example, [1-3] means the number can be 1, 2, or 3. Commas can also be used to indicate nonconsecutive numbers. For example, [1,3] means the number can either be 1 or 3. Finally, the carat (^) is used to indicate that the digit is *not* a number listed in the brackets. For example, [^1-3] means the number is anything other than 1, 2, or 3.
( )	Indicates a pattern. This can be used in conjunction with the ?, %, or + wildcard option.
?	The preceding digit occurs 0 or 1 time.
%	The preceding digit occurs either 0 or more times.
+	The preceding digit occurs either 1 or more times.
T	An inter-digit timeout. This essentially tells the router to pause to allow time to collect additional digits. By default, the system will wait 10 seconds or until the # key is pressed.

Table 6.5 lists telephone number wildcard examples to demonstrate how each option is used.

TABLE 6.5 Telephone number wildcard examples

Number Pattern	Description
555.......	Matches a number that must begin with 555. The last 7 digits can be any number.
555[3-5]......	Matches a number that must begin with 555. The next digit can be 3, 4, or 5. The final 6 digits can be any number.
312(555)?....	Matches a number that must begin with 312. The 555 may be used either 0 or 1 time. The final 4 digits can be any number.
011T	Matches a number that must begin with 011. The router than waits for up to 32 digits to be entered before moving on. If the user stops dialing, a timer (10 seconds by default) must complete before the router processes the digits.

Getting back to our transfer pattern example, let's assume that we want our users to be able to transfer calls to any number within the North American Numbering Plan. Here is the best way to set up the transfer pattern using wildcards:

```
Router#configure terminal
Router(config)#telephony-service
Router(config-telephony)#transfer-pattern [2-9][0-8].[2-9]......
Router(config-telephony)#end
Router#
```

As you learned in Chapter 2, the NANP has a three-digit area code. Every area code must start with a digit between 2 and 9. The second digit can be within 0 and 8. The last digit of the area code can be any number. The first digit of the office code can be any number between 2 and 9, while all the rest of the office codes and station codes can be any number.

 Real World Scenario

No More Missed Calls

Steve is the data center manager for a midsize ISP. He spends the vast majority of his time inside the data center monitoring equipment to ensure stability. Steve often spends time on the phone there talking to server and network engineers. One of his biggest complaints about the phone is that he often cannot hear the call-waiting beep on the line over the noise of the constantly running fans that keep network and server gear cool.

By default, call waiting is enabled on SCCP phones that are configured as dual/octo-line phones or with multiple ephone-DNs configured. When the user is on the phone and a second call comes through, the user will hear a subtle beep through the handset speaker indicating the second call. Users nearly always want this setup, so no configuration changes are required.

In a data center or other noisy environment, a call-waiting beep may not be loud enough to be heard. In this case, you may want to alter the call-waiting tone so it will actually ring like a second call coming in. To accomplish this, you can configure specific ephones to alert using an external ring rather than a beep through the handset. Here is an example of how to configure ephone-DN 10 to use a call-waiting ring:

```
Router#configure terminal
Router(config)#ephone-dn 10
Router(config-ephone-dn)# call-waiting ring
Router(config-ephone-dn)#end
Router#
```

After this configuration change, when a second call comes into Steve's phone in the data center, the phone will ring, which is much more likely to be heard.

Call Pickup

Call pickup is the process of answering a remote extension on your local phone. For example, suppose ephone 10 is configured with extension 210 and it begins to ring. You happen to be sitting at ephone 9, which is configured for extension 209. Using the PickUp softkey button, you can answer extension 210 on ephone 9. You simply press the PickUp key on your Cisco phone and enter the extension you want to answer (210 in our example). The call would be rerouted to ephone 9 and use the 209 extension line. All of this functionality is enabled by default on the CUCM Express. If you choose to disable this feature, you can issue a no service directed-pickup command within config-telephony mode.

You can also get fancy with call pickup by creating pickup groups to enhance the user experience for users who commonly answer each other's phones. To do so, we use the pickup-group command in config-ephone-DN mode. This example shows how to configure two different pickup groups with the IDs of 5110 and 5111:

```
Router#configure terminal
Router(config-ephone-dn)#ephone-dn 10
Router(config-ephone-dn)#pickup-group 5110
Router(config-ephone-dn)#ephone-dn 11
Router(config-ephone-dn)#pickup-group 5110
Router(config-ephone-dn)#ephone-dn 12
Router(config-ephone-dn)#pickup-group 5111
Router(config-ephone-dn)#ephone-dn 13
Router(config-ephone-dn)#pickup-group 5111
Router(config-ephone-dn)#end
Router#
```

Now, instead of using the PickUp softkey, you can use the GPickUp group softkey. After pressing the softkey, you enter the pickup-group identification number.

Call Parking

Call parking lets you place a phone call in "parked" state using an unassigned ephone-DN and then resume the call from any Cisco phone on the CUCM Express. Call park is essentially is the same functionality as hold except that with hold, the call can be resumed only from the local phone. Parking the call gives you more flexibility as to where the call is resumed from.

As stated previously, an unused ephone-DN must be configured and specifically designated as a call parking space. In this example, we configure ephone-DNs 30 and 31 as call parking spaces:

```
Router#configure terminal
Router(config)#ephone-dn 30
Router(config-ephone-dn)#number 3030
```

```
Router(config-ephone-dn)#name Parking 1
Router(config-ephone-dn)#park-slot
Router(config-ephone-dn)#ephone-dn 31
Router(config-ephone-dn)#number 3031
Router(config-ephone-dn)#name Parking 2
Router(config-ephone-dn)#park-slot
Router(config-ephone-dn)#end
Router#
```

Figure 6.12 shows a Cisco phone that placed a call into parking slot with the extension of 3030. Now that the call has been placed into call park, the recipient can resume the call from any CUCM Express phone by pressing the PickUp softkey and then entering the 3030 extension number.

FIGURE 6.12   Call-parked IP phone

There are several other park-slot options that we should look at. Here are the options available to us:

```
Router(config-ephone-dn)#park-slot ?
  reserved-for  Reserve this park slot for the exclusive use of the phone with
                the extension indicated by the transfer target extension number
  timeout       Set call park timeout
  <cr>
```

Use the `reserved-for` option if you want to have a parking space reserved for a specific extension. No other extensions will be able to use this parking slot.

The `timeout` option allows you to configure parking slot timer values and notification options when timers expire. These options are to help prevent people from parking calls and then forgetting about them. That's not the best way to treat your callers!

Hunt Groups

Hunt groups refer to the setup of a single phone number (the pilot number) that is answered by one of several extensions that take turns ringing first. The extension that receives the next call to the pilot number depends on the hunt group selection algorithm that is configured. Let's first look at the components of a hunt group, and then we'll learn how to configure them on the CUCM Express. Table 6.6 describes the hunt group components.

TABLE 6.6   Hunt group components

Component	Description
Hunt group tag	The tag to differentiate multiple hunt groups on the CUCM Express.
Pilot number	The ephone-DN that is dialed to reach a hunt group. A secondary DN can also be configured using the secondary keyword.
Algorithm type	The algorithm method used to select which phone in the hunt group should ring next. The options are `longest-idle`, `peer`, and `sequential`.
Member list	The ephone-DNs that belong to the hunt group.
Hops	The number of extensions that the algorithm will try to ring before going to the final number. This is a valid command for longest idle and peer algorithms.
Timeout	The number of seconds an extension in the hunt group will ring before moving to the next extension in the group.
Final number	The number that is tried last after the number of hops has been exceeded.

Hunt groups are configured by using the `ephone-hunt` configuration command. In addition to the key command, you also specify the hunt group tag and algorithm type. The tag can be any number between 1 and 100. The three different algorithm types are described in Table 6.7.

TABLE 6.7 Hunt group algorithms

Algorithm	Descriptions
Longest idle	Rings the phone in the hunt group that has been idle the longest.
Sequential	Rings the extensions in the exact order they were configured. Once it gets to the end of the list, it dials the configured final number.
Peer	A circular algorithm where the first number tried is configured directly to the right of the last number attempted.

As an example, we'll configure hunt group 10 for pilot number 5001. This pilot has four members with the extensions 201, 202, 203, and 204. We want to use the circular peer method of choosing extensions to ring. An extension should ring for 20 seconds before the call moves to the next extension in the list. Finally, we want to try up to three group members before contacting the manager at extension 205:

```
Router#configure terminal
Router(config)#ephone-hunt 10 peer
Router(config-ephone-hunt)#pilot 5001
Router(config-ephone-hunt)#list 201 202 203 204
Router(config-ephone-hunt)#hops 3
Router(config-ephone-hunt)#timeout 20
Router(config-ephone-hunt)#final 205
Router(config-ephone-hunt)#end
Router#
```

Using this example, we'll pretend that a call is placed into 5001, and it happens that the first number to ring is 203. That extension will ring for 20 seconds, and then the call will try extension 204. That phone will ring for 20 seconds, and then the call will wrap around the list and ring 201. Finally, if 201 does not answer the call, the maximum number of hops is reached and the call will be forwarded one last time to extension 205. This extension will continue to ring until someone answers it.

Intercom

Intercoms are mostly found in key-system CUCM Express systems, but they can also be used in key-system/PBX hybrid setups. The *intercom* feature is essentially a speed dial with automatic answer on the speakerphone. The speakerphone auto-answer on the called party is in a mute state. The user must unmute the phone to be heard on the other end.

Intercoms must have at least two phones configured for the service to work. Two new ephone-DNs need to be configured. To ensure that these extensions are not accidentally dialed by other phones, it is highly recommended that the number use a digit that cannot be dialed using a phone handset. The letters *a*, *b*, *c*, and *d* can be used here. These letters are DTMF priority and override tones that come in handy when you don't want anyone accidentally dialing this extension.

Once the ephone-DNs are configured using the `intercom` command and have extension numbers, they need to be assigned to buttons on the ephones you want to have intercom capability. In our example, we'll configure ephone-DNs 15 and 16. One ephone-DN will have the extension A900 and the other will be for A901. The intercom feature will be configured on each ephone-DN to be able to use the intercom between the two extensions. We'll then assign the intercom extensions to button 2 of ephones 1 and 2:

```
Router#configure terminal
Router(config)#ephone-dn 15
Router(config-ephone-dn)#number A900
Router(config-ephone-dn)#intercom A901
Router(config-ephone-dn)#ephone-dn 16
Router(config-ephone-dn)#number A901
Router(config-ephone-dn)#intercom A900
Router(config-ephone-dn)#exit
Router(config)#ephone 1
Router(config-ephone)#button 2:15
Router(config-ephone)#ephone 2
Router(config-ephone)#button 2:15
Router(config-ephone)#end
Router#
```

We need to discuss a few key intercom configuration options because they might be useful depending on how your users want to use the intercom voice-productivity feature. Let's look at the options:

```
Router(config-ephone-dn)#intercom A900 ?
  barge-in        Allow intercom calls received on this DN to force other calls
                  into the call HOLD state to allow the incoming intercom call
                  to immediately connect without waiting
  label           Define a text label for the intercom
  no-auto-answer  Disable intercom auto-answer
  no-mute         Disable intercom mute-on-answer
  <cr>
```

- The `barge-in` option is useful when the intercom extension on the remote end is already in progress. When you use this command, the current call will be placed on hold and the new intercom call will connect.

- The `label` option allows you to configure a name for the intercom to identify the calling party.

- The `no-auto-answer` option forces the called user to answer the intercom call manually.

- As stated earlier, the default behavior for intercom calls is to auto-answer the call on the remote end and put it into mute state. The `no-mute` option performs the auto-answer without putting the call into the muted state.

Paging

Paging is a one-way intercom. The best way to think about its use is at the grocery store. When you accidentally drop a jar of spaghetti sauce, your action will quickly be followed by an audible page from a store employee: "Cleanup on aisle 3." Whereas the intercom is typically to one phone, the page is a broadcast to multiple or possibly all phones. You can configure paging groups to determine which ephone-DNs will receive a specific page.

 A phone can be assigned to only one paging ephone-DN. However, you can assign paging groups to include multiple ephone-DNs.

Paging can be configured as either unicast or multicast. Unicast configurations are limited to a maximum of 10 receiving devices because of the inefficiencies and high overhead of transmitting 10 separate streams containing the same information. A better method is to configure multicast paging, which is much more efficient and scales well beyond 10 receiving devices. You must also configure a UDP port number for your multicast stream. The default UDP port for paging is 2000.

 Multicast addressing IP space is designated in the range of 224.0.0.0 to 239.255.255.255. However, all CUCM Express capabilities including multicast paging and Music on Hold exclude the 224.x.x.x range from use. You must also ensure that your network is properly configured for multicast routing prior to implementing any CUCM Express multicast features. Configuration of multicast routing is outside the scope of this book.

Our first paging example will configure a single ephone-DN to be used as our paging extension of 5555. Pages will be multicast on 239.1.1.100 to ephones 1, 2, and 3:

```
Router#confure terminal
Router(config)#ephone-dn 1
Router(config-ephone-dn)#number 5555
Router(config-ephone-dn)#paging ip 239.1.1.100 port 2000
Router(config-ephone-dn)#exit
```

```
Router(config)#ephone 1
Router(config-ephone)#paging-dn 1 multicast
Router(config-ephone)#ephone 2
Router(config-ephone)#paging-dn 1 multicast
Router(config-ephone)#ephone 3
Router(config-ephone)#paging-dn 1 multicast
Router(config-ephone)#end
Router#
```

Now that our paging group is configured, a user simply picks up the phone and dials extension 5555 to automatically have a connection to ephones 1, 2, and 3 over their speakerphones!

With our second paging configuration example, we'll configure three different paging ephone-DNs, labeled 1, 2, and 3. The numbers will be 5555, 5556, and 5557. We'll use different multicast IPs to ensure there is no overlap. Ephones 1 and 2 will be part of paging group DN 1. Ephones 3 and 4 will be part of paging group DN 2. Finally, all four ephones will be part of paging group DN 3: Here's how we configure this setup:

```
Router#confure terminal
Router(config)#ephone-dn 1
Router(config-ephone-dn)#number 5555
Router(config-ephone-dn)#paging ip 239.1.1.100 port 2000
Router(config)#ephone-dn 2
Router(config-ephone-dn)#number 5556
Router(config-ephone-dn)#paging ip 239.1.1.101 port 2000
Router(config)#ephone-dn 3
Router(config-ephone-dn)#number 5557
Router(config-ephone-dn)#paging group 1 2
Router(config-ephone-dn)#exit
Router(config)#ephone 1
Router(config-ephone)#paging-dn 1 multicast
Router(config-ephone)#ephone 2
Router(config-ephone)#paging-dn 1 multicast
Router(config-ephone)#ephone 3
Router(config-ephone)#paging-dn 2 multicast
Router(config-ephone)#ephone 4
Router(config-ephone)#paging-dn 2 multicast
Router(config-ephone)#end
Router#
```

Make note of the way we use the paging group ephone-DN configuration command to add DNs 1 and 2 to DN 3 so that all four ephones will be paged. This allows us to get around the limitation that an ephone can be configured with only a single paging-dn tag.

Configuring Voice Access and Accounting Features on the CUCM Express

This section will cover how to configure voice access and accounting features on the CUCM Express. First you'll see how to define the voice access that specific phones will have to specific phone numbers. Different environments require different levels of voice access restrictions. You'll learn how to use different configuration techniques to limit access to virtually any phone number based on time, date, and dial string.

The accounting portion of this section will show how you can log calls directly on the CUCM Express and how to offload this information to a server for long-term storage. It is very important to learn how to keep historical records of calls coming to and from your phone system. This section shows you how to accomplish this task.

Call Blocking

There's no doubt that certain phones should be configured to block specific destination phone numbers. Not everyone should be allowed to dial long-distance and international numbers. And it is likely that you'll want to restrict all phones from being able to connect to 900 and 976 numbers. On the Cisco CUCM Express, we can use the `after-hours` config-telephony mode commands for call blocking based on time and dialing number. There are also methods to exempt phones and users from call-blocking rules that are in place. This way, you can have a great deal of flexibility in your calling plan to restrict calls that should not be made in the first place from office phones. Let's first look at the different call-blocking options available, and then we'll discuss various ways to exempt phones and users from these call-block rules.

Blocking Calls by Date and Time (Toll Bar)

A *toll bar* allows you to block calls from being made on specific dates and/or during certain hours of the day. To accomplish this, you must first set the dates and times when the toll bar is in place. Second, you need to configure dial-string patterns of the numbers you choose to disallow. If a user dials a number that matches both the date/time and the dial-string pattern, the call is not processed. Instead, the user hears a fast busy tone for 10 seconds and then the phone will go on-hook.

The syntax required to configure call blocking is to use the `after-hours` config-telephony mode commands. To give you an idea of how call blocking works, here is an example of how we can block all long-distance and international calls on the weekend beginning Friday at 6:00 pm. and on Christmas day:

```
Router#confure terminal
Router(config)#telephony-service
```

```
Router(config-telephony)# after-hours day Fri 18:00 23:59
Router(config-telephony)# after-hours day Sat 00:00 23:59
Router(config-telephony)# after-hours day Sun 00:00 23:59
Router(config-telephony)# after-hours date Dec 25 00:00 23:59
Router(config-telephony)# after-hours block pattern 1 91..........
Router(config-telephony)# after-hours block pattern 2 9011T
Router(config-telephony)#end
Router#
```

As you can see, you can set the date/time by using either the after-hours day or after-hours date command. The time 00:00 23:59 is considered to be one entire day. Even though 23:59 is listed, the seconds are automatically included, so it's read by the router as 0:00:00 to 23:59:59. The after-hours block pattern command has a tag associated with it. The tag is a numerical number to differentiate the different block patterns. These tags can be between 1 and 100. When you create the block patterns, you can use wildcards to help cover larger blocks of numbers with the fewest commands. These are the same telephone number wildcards shown in Table 6.5 earlier in this chapter.

Configuring a Global Override Code

If you want certain people to be able to override any call-blocking functions from any phone on the network, you can configure an *override code* using the after-hours override-code config-telephony mode command. Here's an example of the command where a user can use softkeys to enter a PIN of 1234 to override the call blocks configured previously:

```
Router#confure terminal
Router(config)#telephony-service
Router(config-telephony)#after-hours override-code 1234
Router(config-telephony)#end
Router#
```

Now a user who knows the override code can use any phone to dial either long-distance or international destinations and use the Override softkey to first enter the 1234 PIN (personal identification number) that allows the override to occur. Once successfully logged in using the override code, the user can make calls that would previously be blocked.

Configuring Override PIN per Ephone

Override PINs can also be created on an individual ephone. To do so, you use the pin *string* config-ephone command. This example shows that the PIN of 4321 is used to override the after-hours configurations we created earlier:

```
Router#confure terminal
Router(config)#ephone 1
```

```
Router(config-ephone)# pin 4321
Router(config-telephony)#end
Router#
```

Now, any user who knows the PIN to this ephone can override the after-hours call blocking by first pressing the Login soft key and then entering the PIN. The user can then dial any number that would previously have been blocked.

Configuring Auto Exempt Ephone

A third method is to completely *exempt* an ephone from the call-blocking setups. Now users who have access to an ephone do not have to enter any sort of PIN to be able to make long-distance and international calls. To accomplish this, we use the config-ephone mode after-hours **exempt** command. Here's how to configure this on ephone 1:

```
Router#confure terminal
Router(config)#ephone 1
Router(config-ephone)# after-hour exempt
Router(config-ephone)#end
Router#
```

Configuring Global Call Block

You will want to be able to block some numbers 24/7 to everyone, including phones with override and exempt status. For these cases we can use the 7-24 option when configuring the after-hours block command. In this example, we're going to block absolutely everyone from ever dialing 900 and 976 numbers on the phone system.

```
Router#confure terminal
Router(config)#telephony-service
Router(config-telephony)#after-hours block pattern 3 91900 7-24
Router(config-telephony)#after-hours block pattern 4 91976 7-24
Router(config-telephony)#after-hours block pattern 5 91...976 7-24
Router(config-telephony)#end
Router#
```

Call Detail Records

One accounting feature that most businesses wish to implement is the *call detail record (CDR)*. This feature keeps track of all calls made on the CUCM Express system. That way, a business can keep track of who is calling whom, not only for budgeting but also to track fraud and for emergency reasons. The CDR logs phone source and destination numbers for both on- and off-network calls. This information can be stored in the router's internal logging buffer memory or on an external logging server. It can also be configured to be sent to both. At a minimum, you should have this information sent to a syslog server. This is because the log buffer on the router is not a permanent solution. Eventually it will run out of memory, and the oldest log data will be overwritten. Also, if the voice router loses power, all logs in the buffer are lost. The next two examples will show how to configure the CDR to use the router's internal buffer memory and then an external syslog server.

Configuring CDR to the Internal Buffer Memory

If we want to enable logging of call history to the buffer, we first must enable the buffer. Logging to memory is disabled by default. To enable this feature, we use the `logging buffered` command to turn on logging, using a portion of the router's memory. You can allocate various amounts of memory depending on how many logs you wish to keep. By default, logs can use 4 KB of memory. You likely will want to set this to something higher. The following example shows how to enable logging to the buffer and allocates 32 KB of memory to this task.

```
Router#configure terminal
Router(config)#logging buffered 32768
Router(config)#end
Router#
```

At this point, the log buffer is set. The only problem is that the default number of call records and the time that the records are stored in the buffer are very low. To change these settings, you use the `dial-control-mib` command. The `mib` portion of the command stands for Management Information Base. An MIB is an International Standards Organization (ISO) standard format for databases used to manage communications devices. Because our CUCM Express is a communications device, Cisco decided to use this standards-based format for logging to the buffer. Here are the size and timer options as shown on the CUCM Express system:

```
Router#configure terminal
Router(config)#dial-control-mib ?
  max-size      Specify the maximum size of the dial control history table
  retain-timer  Specify timer for entries in dial control history table

Router(config)#dial-control-mib max-size ?
  <0-500>  Number of entries in the dial control history table

Router(config)#dial-control-mib retain-timer ?
  <0-35791>  Time (in minutes) for removing an entry
```

Because the CDR is a database, we must set a `max-size` that the database can be. The maximum number of dial control history entries that can be saved depends on hardware. By default, it is only 50 entries. The `retain-timer` option sets the maximum amount of time the database will be kept on the router's memory. This time is specified in minutes and again is hardware dependent because it depends on the amount of memory the router has.

By default, the timer is set for only 15 minutes. In our example, we will change the defaults to more reasonable numbers. We'll set the maximum number of entries to 400 and store the database for three days (4320 minutes).

```
Router#confure terminal
Router(config)#dial-control-mib max-size 400
Router(config)#dial-control-mib retain-timer 4320
Router(config)#end
Router#
```

Finally, you must configure the call detail records to be logged. To accomplish this, you use the gw-accounting syslog command. After you enter this command, go ahead and place a call from one IP phone to another. Once you hang up the phone, issue a show logging command on the CUCM Express where you are logging CDR information to the internal buffer memory. Here's an example of the output you will see:

```
Router#show logging
Syslog logging: enabled (1 messages dropped, 0 messages rate-limited,
                0 flushes, 0 overruns, xml disabled, filtering disabled)

[output cut]

    Console logging: disabled
    Monitor logging: level debugging, 0 messages logged, xml disabled,
                     filtering disabled
    Buffer logging:  level debugging, 5 messages logged, xml disabled,
                     filtering disabled
    Logging Exception size (4096 bytes)
    Count and timestamp logging messages: disabled
    Persistent logging: disabled

[output cut]

Log Buffer (32768 bytes):

*May 26 02:58:04.307: %SYS-5-CONFIG_I: Configured from console by console
*May 26 02:58:21.819: %VOIPAAA-5-VOIP_CALL_HISTORY: CallLegType 1,
ConnectionId E3E3F81B48D711DE82A887E7220CC055, SetupTime
*02:58:14.629 UTC Tue May 26 2009, PeerAddress 5002, PeerSubAddress ,
DisconnectCause 10  , DisconnectText normal call clearing (16), ConnectTime
*02:58:19.139 UTC Tue May 26 2009, DisconnectTime *02:58:21.819 UTC
Tue May 26 2009, CallOrigin 2, ChargedUnits 0, InfoType 2, TransmitPackets
0, TransmitBytes 0, ReceivePackets 0, ReceiveBytes 0
```

```
*May 26 02:58:21.819: %VOIPAAA-5-VOIP_FEAT_HISTORY: FEAT_VSA=fn:TWC,ft:05/26/2009
02:58:14.623,cgn:5002,cdn:,frs:0,fid:250,fcid:E3E3F81B48D711DE82A887E7220CC055
,legID:F6,bguid:E3E3F81B48D711DE82A887E7220CC055
*May 26 02:58:21.819: %VOIPAAA-5-VOIP_CALL_HISTORY: CallLegType 1, ConnectionId
E3E3F81B48D711DE82A887E7220CC055, SetupTime *02:58:17.239 UTC
Tue May 26 2009, PeerAddress 5001, PeerSubAddress , DisconnectCause 10  ,
DisconnectText normal call clearing (16), ConnectTime *02:58:19.139 UTC
Tue May 26 2009, DisconnectTime *02:58:21.819 UTC Tue May 26 2009, CallOrigin
1, ChargedUnits 0, InfoType 2, TransmitPackets 0, TransmitBytes 0,
ReceivePackets 0, ReceiveBytes 0
*May 26 02:58:21.819: %VOIPAAA-5-VOIP_FEAT_HISTORY: FEAT_VSA=fn:TWC,
ft:05/26/2009 02:58:17.239,cgn:5002,cdn:5001,frs:0,fid:251,fcid:E3E3
F81B48D711DE82A887E7220CC055,legID:F7,bguid:E3E3F81B48D711DE82A887E7220CC055
```

It may seem cryptic, but all the information is there. You can obtain valuable information from the CDR, as detailed in Table 6.8.

TABLE 6.8 CDR information

Label	Description
PeerAddress	Phone number
DisconnectText	Method of disconnect
ConnectTime	Start call time/date
DisconnectTime	End call time/date

Look through the log entries shown previously to see if you can pick out each of these details for yourself.

Configuring CDR to an External Syslog Server

As you've learned, logging this information to the router's memory is not a permanent solution. *Syslog servers* are used to offload and store computer and network hardware log information for long periods of time. This is a great way to keep CDR information for historical purposes. Syslog servers are easy to set up and maintain. Dozens of different types of syslog servers are available today. Once you set up a server to store log information, you simply point the CUCM Express router at the syslog server. To do this, you use the logging *ip-address* command, where *ip-address* is the address of your syslog server. Here is an example of how we can configure logging to a syslog server at 172.16.8.5:

```
Router#confure terminal
Router(config)#logging 172.168.8.5
Router(config)#end
Router#
```

That's all there is to it. As stated earlier, it is possible and advisable to log CDR information to both a syslog server and the local router buffer. That way, if you need to look up recent CDR information, you can log in to the CUCM Express and check the logs. And if you need to check historical CDR information, you can go to your syslog server, which stores historical logs for a much longer time.

Configuring Music on Hold (MoH)

"Can you hold please?" Everyone hates to wait on hold. This is partly why *Music-on-Hold (MoH)* was invented. So now, at least you can listen to music while you wait. Besides making the wait less bothersome, it also helps the end user to know that they have not been disconnected from the call. This section will detail how to use audio files stored on the router flash for MoH.

On the CUCM Express system, a phone that uses either the g.711 or g.729 codec can utilize MoH. The music file is presented in a g.711 format by default, so keep in mind that any g.729 phones will require transcoding resources to use MoH. The sound quality will also suffer because of the downgrade in fidelity from g.711 to g.729. You can store audio files directly on the flash of the CUCM Express. The audio files that are compatible for use on a CUCM Express system must have the following requirements:

- File format of `.au` or `.wav`
- G.711 codec format
- 8-bit rate at 8 kHz

Cisco includes a copyright-free MoH file when you download the CUCM Express software. There also are audio-editing applications that can convert your MP3 files to the proper format for use on the CUCM Express system. Just make sure you are fully aware of any laws that prohibit the use of copyrighted music on your phone system.

There are two methods of providing audio file MoH on the CME. You can provide MoH as a unicast stream or as a multicast stream. You configure unicast MoH streams by using the `moh` command followed by the filename of the audio file. This command is performed within config-telephony mode. Here is an example of how to configure `mymusic.wav` as a unicast stream for our CUCM Express:

```
Router#confure terminal
Router(config)#telephony-service
Router(config-telephony)#moh mymusic.wav
Router(config-telephony)#end
Router#
```

Keep in mind that this specific MoH configuration setup requires a separate audio stream to be sent over the network for each phone that requests it. Every phone that is on hold is another RTP stream on the network. Clearly this does not scale well, because it adds more bandwidth overhead and increases the CPU usage on the CUCM Express. On the other hand, if your Cisco IPT implementation spans multiple subnets, and these subnets are not enabled for multicast routing, the unicast MoH method is your only choice.

An alternative method to the unicast MoH streams is to configure multicast MoH. If your network is enabled for multicast routing, then you should utilize the multicast functionality in the CUCM Express. Think of multicast as a radio station. If users tune into that radio station, they all listen to the same stream. This is exactly how multicast MoH works. You configure your "radio station" channel in the form of a multicast IP address. When a user places someone on hold, they tap into that audio stream on the network for the audio file. Additional users who are placed on hold also tap into this same audio stream. This way, there is a single MoH RTP stream on the network, and it is broadcast to any users who require it. To configure multicast MoH, you need to first identify the audio file just like in the unicast MoH configuration. In addition, you need to configure the multicast IP address and port. Multicast addresses fall into the range of 224.0.0.0 to 239.255.255.255. However, multicast for MoH will not function within the 224.x.x.x range. The phones specifically do not support multicast in this range. A good multicast IP range to configure multicast MoH with is the 239.x.x.x range. This IP block is specifically set aside for private use within an organization.

By default, the MoH stream uses UDP port 2000. You can optionally change this port if necessary, but it is not recommended, because the phones and CUCM are already set to listen for RTP media transmissions on port 2000. Following is an example that enables multicast MoH and specifies a multicast address for the audio stream. Just as in multicast paging, the phones are set to listen to multicast MoH on UDP port 2000.

```
Router#confure terminal
Router(config)#telephony-service
Router(config-telephony)#moh mymusic.wav
Router(config-telephony)# multicast moh 239.23.4.10 port 2000
Router(config-telephony)#end
Router#
```

Using the Multicast MoH Route Command

One last optional multicast MoH command we need to address is the route command, which allows you to configure up to four IP addresses to use as the source IP of the multicast stream. The IP addresses must be either physical router IP addresses on the CUCM Express or a loopback address. If the route command is not used, multicast MoH will be sourced from the IP address assigned as the ip source-address command within config-telephony mode. Let's look at an example code snippet of a CUCM Express router:

```
Router#confure terminal
Router(config)#telephony-service
Router(config-telephony)#ip source-address 10.1.1.1
Router(config-telephony)#moh mymusic.wav
Router(config-telephony)#multicast moh 239.10.16.16 port 2000
Router(config-telephony)#end
Router#
```

Here you can see that we are multicasting our MoH music on the IP of 239.10.16.16. The IP address that will be used as the source of the multicast stream is 10.1.1.1. Let's say we want to change that source IP address to 192.168.10.100, which is a loopback address on the CUCM Express. It is always the best practice to source services using loopback interfaces because they never go down. To do so we configure the following:

```
Router#confure terminal
Router(config)#telephony-service
Router(config-telephony)#multicast moh 239.10.16.16 port 2000 route
192.168.10.100
Router(config-telephony)#end
Router#
```

Disabling Multicast MoH on a Per-Ephone Basis

If part of your network is configured for multicast and another part is not, you can disable multicast MoH on a per-ephone basis. If multicast MoH is disabled on an ephone, it will use unicast for the stream instead. That way, you utilize multicast when you can and fall back to unicasting the streams where needed. Multicast MoH is enabled by default on all ephones. To disable it, you can use the no `multicast-moh` command within config-ephone mode. Here's an example of disabling multicast MoH on ephone 12:

```
Router#confure terminal
Router(config)#ephone 12
Router(config-ephone)# no multicast-moh
Router(config-ephone)#end
Router#
```

Summary

Chapter 6 began with the configuration differences between key systems and PBX systems. Then you learned how to configure telephony service features such as `user-locale` and `network-locale` to tailor your CUCM Express to any business and/or geographical region. You also learned advanced productivity configurations such as hunt groups and paging that give users added functionality. Access and accounting configuration options were also covered so you can limit user access and log calls on the system properly. Lastly, you learned how to set up Music on Hold within a CUCM Express environment.

Even though having a great car stereo or Xenon headlights might not be absolutely necessary, the add-on features of a car can be very nice to have. The same goes with the added features of a CUCM Express system. The added features we configured here help to add value to a business by streamlining and simplifying the way we handle calls. Without these added features, we still have a phone system—but it's not nearly as interesting or useful without the bells and whistles!

The next chapter looks at configuring voice gateways.

Exam Essentials

Know how to configure key systems and PBX system DNs.   The CUCM can be configured to act as a key system or a PBX depending on the needs of the environment. Key-system phones are typically configured identically and share DNs. PBX systems are configured with unique DNs on each phone and are individually tailored to meet the needs of the user.

Understand the different types of ephone button options.   Using the button separator when configuring extensions lets you set various ring options, phone monitoring, and overlay features.

Know how to configure your CUCM Express to meet the needs of your users. Depending on where you set up your CUCM Express, you may need to modify user options to match the native language. In addition, the network options can be modified to match the PSTN tone and cadence that are familiar to the area, and the CUCM Express can be modified to display the date and time in a familiar format. The system message display can be changed to customize the system for your environment.

Know how to configure local directory services.   The local directory contains the phone extension to name mapping on the CUCM Express. You can create these entries when configuring the ephone-DN. In addition, you can manually enter listings that are not directly configured as ephone-DNs on the system.

Understand the concept of static and dynamic call forwarding.   Dynamic call forwarding is performed by the user at the phone level. Static call forwarding is configured on the CUCM Express.

Know the three call transfer option types and when to use them.   Understand the difference between full-blind, full-consult, and local-consult and the circumstances of when you would want to use each of them.

Know how to configure call pickup groups.   These groups allow a user to answer another extension remotely. This functionality is important in call centers where people call into a main number around the clock.

Understand the purpose of and how to configure call parking lines.   Call parking spaces allow a user to "park" a call in a designated ephone-DN and resume the call from any other phone on the CUCM Express.

Understand the purpose of and how to configure hunt groups.   Hunt groups allow multiple phones to alternatively answer a shared ephone-DN. Different algorithms determine which phone receives the next call.

Know how to configure the CUCM Express for intercom functionality.   The intercom is a great way for quick, two-way communication between predefined ephones.

Understand the concept of paging and how to configure It.   Paging is one-way communication to multiple predefined phones. The paging communication can be configured either as multiple unicast streams or as a single multicast stream.

Know how to configure call blocking.   Call blocking can be performed by date, time, or the 7-24 option. There are also techniques to exempt a specific phone or user from the call-blocking rules.

Know how to configure call detail records to log to the router buffer and to an external syslog server.   CDR information keeps track of phone calls on the CUCM Express. This information can be useful for billing and fraud purposes.

Know how to configure Music on Hold.   Much like paging, Music on Hold can be configured to be sent as either a unicast stream to each phone on hold or as a multicast stream. Understand the various options for each method.

Written Lab 6.1

Write the answers to the following questions:

1. What is the config-ephone command to configure DN 1 on button 2 and DN 2 on button 1?
2. What is the config-ephone-DN command to make DN 10 have dual lines?
3. What is the config-ephone command to assign button 2 to DN 8 and have it use an alternate ring?
4. What is the config-ephone-DN command to set a DN to be more preferred than a DN that has its preference set to 2?
5. What show command lists all ephones, buttons, overlay lines, status, and call source and destinations?
6. What config-telephony command changes the date layout to show yy-mm-dd?
7. How would you configure a manual directory entry 1 for John Smith at extension 1001 while in config-telephony mode?

8. While in config-telephony mode, how would you configure users to be able to transfer calls to any off-network 10-digit number that begins with 555-777?

9. How would you configure call blocking on Saturdays after 6:00 p.m. while in config-telephony mode?

10. What is the config-telephony command to configure multicast MoH using 239.100.100.240 and port 2001?

(The answers to Written Lab 6.1 can be found following the answers to the review questions for this chapter.)

Hands-on Labs

To complete the labs in this section, you need a CUCM Express router and two Cisco IP phones. The CUCM Express should be properly set up and ready for configuring IP phones. Each lab in this section builds on the last and will follow the logical CUCM Express PBX model design shown in Figure 6.13.

FIGURE 6.13 CUCM Express lab diagram

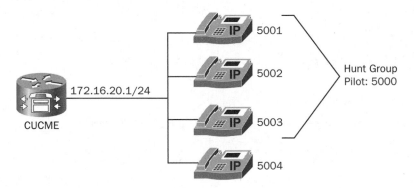

Here is a list of the labs in this chapter:

> Lab 6.1: Configuring a Hunt Group
>
> Lab 6.2: Configuring a Call Parking Slot
>
> Lab 6.3: Configuring Multicast Paging
>
> Lab 6.4: Configuring Multicast MoH

Hands-on Lab 6.1: Configuring a Hunt Group

In this lab, we're going to configure a PBX-modeled CUCM Express with four phones. Each phone will be configured with its individual extension on phone button 1. In addition, three of the phones should be configured for a hunt group. Table 6.9 provides additional phone information.

TABLE 6.9   Lab 6 phone setup details

Phone	MAC Address	Primary Number
Ephone 1	XXXX.XXXX.XXXX	DN 1: 5001: dual-line
Ephone 2	XXXX.XXXX.XXXX	DN 2: 5002: dual-line
Ephone 3	XXXX.XXXX.XXXX	DN 3: 5003: dual-line
Ephone 4	XXXX.XXXX.XXXX	DN 4: 5004

The following information will help you configure the hunt group:

- Hunt group tag: 1
- Pilot number: 5000
- Member extensions: 5001, 5002, 5003
- Number of rings before moving to next member: 5
- Algorithm: sequential
- Final number: 5004

1. Log into your CUCM Express router and go into configuration mode by typing **enable** and then **configuration terminal**.

2. Configure ephone-DN 1 to have the number 5001 by typing **ephone-dn 1 dual-line** and then **number 5001**.

3. Configure ephone-DN 2 to have the number 5002 by typing **ephone-dn 2 dual-line** and then **number 5002**.

4. Configure ephone-DN 3 to have the number 5003 by typing **ephone-dn 3 dual-line** and then **number 5003**.

5. Configure ephone-DN 4 to have the number 5004 by typing **ephone-dn 4** and then **number 5004**.

6. Configure the MAC address of ephone 1 by typing **ephone 1** and then **mac-address XXXX.XXXX.XXXX**. Your MAC address will be unique.

7. Configure button 1 of ephone 1 to use ephone-DN 1 by typing **button 1:1**.

8. Configure the MAC address of ephone 2 by typing **ephone 2** and then **mac-address XXXX.XXXX.XXXX**. Your MAC address will be unique.

9. Configure button 1 of ephone 2 to use ephone-DN 2 by typing **button 1:2**.

10. Configure the MAC address of ephone 3 by typing **ephone 3** and then **mac-address XXXX.XXXX.XXXX**. Your MAC address will be unique.

11. Configure button 1 of ephone 3 to use ephone-DN 3 by typing **button 1:3**.

12. Configure the MAC address of ephone 4 by typing **ephone 4** and then **mac-address XXXX.XXXX.XXXX**. Your MAC address will be unique.

13. Configure button 1 of ephone 4 to use ephone-DN 4 by typing **button 1:4**.

14. Exit config-ephone mode by typing **exit**.

15. Enter into config-ephone-hunt mode by typing **ephone-hunt 1 sequential**.

16. Enter the pilot number by typing **pilot 5000**.

17. Configure the members by typing **list 5001 5002 5003**.

18. Configure the number of rings allowed before moving to the next phone by typing **timeout 20**.

19. Enter the final number by typing **final 5004**.

20. Exit config-ephone-hunt mode by typing **end**.

Hands-on Lab 6.2: Configuring a Call Parking Slot

1. Log into your CUCM Express router and go into configuration mode by typing **enable** and then **configuration terminal**.

2. We want to create a single parking slot. For our lab parking slot, we'll use ephone-DN 10. To do this type **ephone-dn 10**.

3. Assign the extension 3000 to the ephone-DN by typing **number 3000**.

4. Configure the ephone-DN to be a call park extension by typing **park-slot**.

5. Name the ephone-DN Parking 1 by issuing **name Parking 1**.

6. Exit config-ephone-DN mode by typing **end**.

Hands-on Lab 6.3: Configuring Multicast Paging

1. Log into your CUCM Express router and go into configuration mode by typing **enable** and then **configuration terminal**.

2. We want to create a single paging ephone-DN. For our paging extension, we'll use ephone-DN 11. To do this, type **ephone-dn 11**.

3. Assign the extension 7777 to the ephone-DN by typing **number 7777**.

4. Configure multicast paging on address 239.254.254.254 by typing **paging ip 239.254.254.254 port 2000**.

5. Assign ephones 1, 2, and 3 to be alerted when someone dials 7777. To do this, type the following:

```
ephone 1
paging-dn 11 multicast
ephone 2
paging-dn 11 multicast
ephone 3
paging-dn 11 multicast
```

6. Exit config-ephone mode by typing **end**.

Hands-on Lab 6.4: Configuring Multicast MoH

1. Log into your CUCM Express router and go into configuration mode by typing **enable** and then **configuration terminal**.

2. Enter into config-telephony mode by typing **telephony service**.

3. We will use music-on-hold.au as our music file to play. To configure this, type **moh music-on-hold.au**.

4. Configure MoH for multicast at 239.1.1.250 by typing **multicast moh 239.1.1.250**.

5. Exit config-telephony mode by typing **end**.

Review Questions

1. With multiple ephone-DNs sharing a single number, what command can you use to prioritize which ephone-DN will always receive the incoming call if it is not in use?

   A. `priority`

   B. `preference`

   C. `state`

   D. `no huntstop`

2. With multiple ephone-DNs sharing a single number, when the phone preference for each ephone-DN is the same, how is call routing handled for incoming calls?

   A. Calls will be received on the ephone-DN with the lowest tag.

   B. This configuration will not work. The ephone-DNs must be configured with different priorities.

   C. Calls will be received on the ephone with the lowest tag.

   D. Calls will be handled round-robin style.

3. What config-ephone-DN command prevents calls from hunting to the second channel on dual-line ephone-DNs?

   A. `huntstop channel`

   B. `no huntstop`

   C. `no huntstop channel`

   D. `huntstop`

4. What ephone overlay button separator would you use if you want calls to come in on this extension only when all other lines are busy?

   A. `o`

   B. `c`

   C. `w`

   D. `x`

   E. `m`

5. What is the term used to describe the configuration of multiple ephone-DNs on a single physical phone button?

   A. Ephone

   B. Ephone-DN

   C. Dual-line

   D. Call waiting

   E. Overlay line

6. What configuration option can you change so that Cisco phones will display information on the screen in a different language?

   A. `network-locale`

   B. `language-locale`

   C. `user-locale`

   D. `telephony-service-locale`

7. What configuration mode do you need to be in to configure the CUCM Express system message that displays on Cisco IP phones?

   A. config t

   B. config-ephone

   C. config-telephony

   D. config-ephone-DN

   E. config-voiceport

8. How are directory names and numbers entered into the local directory on a CUCM Express? Choose all that apply.

   A. By configuring a name and number on an ephone-DN and assigning it to an ephone

   B. By entering the name and number into the system using the config-telephony mode's `directory entry` command

   C. By uploading a spreadsheet onto the CUCM Express router that has an `.xls` extension

   D. By manually entering the name and number using the Cisco IP phone handset.

9. What is the proper syntax to statically configure call forwarding to extension 2020 on a phone when the phone is currently in use?

   A. `Router(config-ephone)#call-forward noan 2020`

   B. `Router(config-ephone)#call-forward busy 2020`

   C. `Router(config-ephone-DN)#call-forward busy 2020`

   D. `Router(config-ephone-DN)#call-forward noan 2020`

10. What are the three call-transfer configuration methods?

   A. Blind

   B. Full-blind

   C. Partial-consult

   D. Full-consult

   E. Full-local

   F. Local-consult

11. By default, the CUCM Express allows calls to be transferred only to extensions that are on-network. If you want users to be able to transfer calls off-network to any number within the 555-555-XXXX range, how do you configure this?

    A. Router(config-telephony)#transfer-pattern 555555....

    B. Router(config-telephony)#transfer-pattern 555555????

    C. Router(config-telephony)#transfer-pattern 555555T

    D. Router(config-telephony)#transfer-pattern 5555554%

12. What Cisco telephony feature allows a user to answer, on their local phone, an extension that is configured on a different phone?

    A. Call transfer

    B. Call waiting

    C. Hunt group

    D. Call pickup

13. What is the main difference between call hold and call park?

    A. Call hold allows the user to resume the call from any phone on the CUCM Express system.

    B. Call hold disconnects the call after 120 seconds.

    C. Call park allows the user to resume the call from any phone on the CUCM Express system.

    D. Call park disconnects the call after 120 seconds.

14. When referring to hunt groups, what is the name of the ephone-DN that is used to call a hunt group?

    A. Hunt group tag

    B. Member list

    C. Pilot number

    D. Final number

15. On a CUCM Express, how would you configure extension 4001 as the last number that a hunt group should attempt?

    A. Router(config-ephone-hunt)#list 4001

    B. Router(config-ephone-hunt)#final 4001

    C. Router(config-ephone-hunt)#last 4001

    D. Router(config-ephone-hunt)#timeout 4001

16. When configuring multicast broadcasting for features such as paging and Music on Hold, what multicast IP range is not usable on the CUCM Express?

    A. 239.0.0.0 to 239.255.255.255

    B. 224.0.0.0 to 228.255.255.255

    C. 224.0.0.0 to 224.255.255.255

    D. 223.0.0.0 to 224.255.255.255

17. Given the following configuration, which ephones will be paged when you dial the 6003 paging extension?

```
Router(config)#ephone-dn 1
Router(config-ephone-dn)#number 6001
Router(config-ephone-dn)#paging ip 239.1.80.100 port 2000
Router(config)#ephone-dn 2
Router(config-ephone-dn)#number 6002
Router(config-ephone-dn)#paging ip 239.1.80.101 port 2000
Router(config)#ephone-dn 3
Router(config-ephone-dn)#number 6003
Router(config-ephone-dn)#paging group 1 2
Router(config-ephone-dn)#exit
Router(config)#ephone 1
Router(config-ephone)#paging-dn 1 multicast
Router(config-ephone)#ephone 2
Router(config-ephone)#paging-dn 1 multicast
Router(config-ephone)#ephone 3
Router(config-ephone)#paging-dn 2 multicast
Router(config-ephone)#ephone 4
Router(config-ephone)#paging-dn 2 multicast
Router(config-ephone)#end
```

    A. Ephones 1 and 2

    B. Ephone 1

    C. Ephones 1, 2, 3, and 4

    D. Ephones 3 and 4

18. Changes were made to add call-pickup groups to phones on your CUCM Express. The problem is, the call-pickup group function is not available on the phones. What is likely the problem?

    A. Call pickup is only available on high-end phones such as the 7975.

    B. The CUCM Express configuration has not been written to memory.

    C. The Cisco IP phones need to be restarted.

    D. You must configure multicast on your network for call-pickup groups to function.

19. What is the proper syntax to block all users from being able to dial 900 numbers out the PSTN on the CUCM Express? Assume that you must dial 9 to access the PSTN.

    A. `Router(config-telephony)#after-hours block pattern 91900 7-24`

    B. `Router(config-telephony)#after-hours block pattern 91900 Mo-Su`

    C. `Router(config-telephony)#after-hours block pattern 91900 exempt`

    D. `Router(config-telephony)#after-hours block pattern 91900 all`

20. Why is it recommended that you configure CDR to log to a syslog server and not just the internal router memory? Choose all that apply.

    A. The router has a limited amount of space, and the oldest logs will be overwritten over time.

    B. The syslog server will provide additional call details that the buffer logs will not have.

    C. The router will lose all logs if it is restarted or loses power.

    D. The syslog server will lose all logs if it is restarted or loses power.

Answers to Review Questions

1. B. The preference command allows you to set which ephone-DN will receive all calls when not in use. The lower number is the more preferred ephone-DN.

2. D. If preferences are the same, then calls will be handled in a round-robin manner.

3. A. The huntstop channel command informs the CUCM Express that it should not route the call to the second channel of a dual-line phone. Instead, the call will be routed to the ephone-DN that is next in line according to the algorithm being used.

4. D. The expansion (x) line button separator helps prevent a caller from receiving a busy signal. The calls will go to this line only when all other lines are busy.

5. E. An overlay line is a phone button separator configuration option that allows you to configure multiple ephone-DNs on a single phone button.

6. C. The user-locale option allows you to change the language displayed on the LCD screens of Cisco IP phones.

7. C. The system message displays any message you wish on all Cisco IP phones that are registered on the CUCM Express. The command can be configured while in config-telephony mode.

8. A, B. You can add names and numbers by adding a name and number to the ephone-DN and assigning it to an ephone or by manually entering a number using the directory config-telephony command.

9. C. The correct syntax is call-forward busy 2020. This command is run while in config-ephone-DN mode.

10. B, D, F. The three call transfer configuration methods on a CUCM Express are full-blind, full-consult, and local-consult.

11. A. Answer A is the correct wildcard sequence to allow calls to be transferred to any number in the 555-555-XXXX range. Answer C would also work, but the phone will have to wait 10 seconds to time out before it processes the digits. It is incorrect, however, because a user could dial other numbers outside the 555-555-XXXX range.

12. D. Call pickup is the process of answering a remote extension on a local phone. To do so, you can use the PickUp or GPickUp softkey depending on how your call pickup is configured.

13. C. With call park, you configure a separate ephone-DN where you place calls that are waiting. You can then answer the parked calls from any phone on the CUCM Express system as long as you know the ephone-DN where the call is parked.

14. C. The pilot number is the main DN that is used to call into a hunt group.

15. B. The final command is a config-ephone-hunt configuration that lists the last number that should be attempted after all members in the hunt group have not answered.

16. C. The entire 224.X.X.X multicast IP range cannot be used.

17. C. The ephone-DN 6003 is configured with paging group 1 and 2. Ephones 1–4 are configured with paging-DN 1 or 2. This means that when 6003 is dialed, it pages all four phones simultaneously.

18. C. Don't forget that many of the phone features require the phones to be restarted after configuring them on the CUCM Express.

19. A. The 7–24 option restricts the pattern at all times with no exemptions.

20. A, C. The router has a limited amount of memory. Also, if the router is rebooted or loses power, all logging is erased. The syslog server stores the logs to a storage drive, so it is better for maintaining historical logs over time.

Answers to Written Lab 6.1

1. `button 1:2 2:1`

2. `ephone-dn 10 dual-line`

3. `button 2f8`

4. `preference 1` (or `preference 0`, which is the default)

5. `show ephone`

6. `date-format yy-mm-dd`

7. `directory entry 1 1001 name John Smith`

8. `transfer-pattern 5557777....` (or `5557777T`)

9. `after-hours day Sat 18:00 23:59`

10. `multicast moh 239.100.100.240 port 2001`

Chapter
7

Configuring Voice Gateways for POTS and VoIP

THE CCNA VOICE EXAM TOPICS COVERED IN THIS CHAPTER INCLUDE THE FOLLOWING:

✓ **Configure gateways, voice ports and dial peers to connect to the PSTN and service provider networks.**

- Describe the function and application of a dial plan.

- Describe the function and application of voice gateways.

- Describe the function and application of voice ports in a gateway.

- Describe the function and operation of call legs.

- Configure voice dial peers.

- Describe the differences between PSTN and Internet Telephony Service provider circuits.

When I think of voice gateways, I like to use the Star Trek teleporter as a visual analogy. The teleporter on the starship *Enterprise* is responsible for taking a human (or Vulcan), dematerializing them into energy, and then rematerializing that person to a different location. A voice gateway does something similar; it takes a voice stream that works on one network and repackages it so the stream can be understood and sent over a different type of network. Ultimately the voice stream reaches its intended target destination on the other end of the connection. This chapter will discuss how we configure our voice gateways to properly package and direct voice streams to nonnative (alien) networks.

In Chapter 7, you'll first learn how to configure FXS and FXO voice ports. Then you'll see how to direct calls over these analog voice ports using POTS dial peers. We'll move on to how to configure the physical characteristics of digital T1 CAS and PRI interfaces and how to use POTS dial peers for call routing. Next we'll use VoIP dial peers to route off-network calls over the IP WAN connections. Once the analog and digital and basic IP WAN configurations are covered, we'll discuss the importance and process of coming up with a dial-plan strategy. We'll also go over the dial-peer decision-making process to learn how the CUCM Express makes decisions when routing calls. Next, we'll cover how to manipulate phone numbers so that calls can be properly routed both on and off network. Finally, we'll go over how to configure trunks between voice gateways using both H.323 and SIP.

Configuring Analog FXS and FXO Ports with Basic Dial Peers

When you insert an analog voice card into a Cisco router installed with a supported version of IOS voice software, the router will automatically detect and add the new voice interfaces to the configuration. You can view the configuration status of these interfaces by performing a show run. Here is an example of show run output from a CUCM Express router with a four-port FXS and a four-port FXO installed:

```
Router#sh run | begin voice-port
voice-port 0/0/0
!
voice-port 0/0/1
!
```

```
voice-port 0/0/2
!
voice-port 0/0/3
!
voice-port 0/1/0
!
voice-port 0/1/1
!
voice-port 0/1/2
!
voice-port 0/1/3
```

Another command that's useful for viewing the voice ports your voice gateway has installed is show voice port summary. Here is the output of this command. Notice how you can easily distinguish an FXS from an FXO port with this command as well as determine the signaling type (-ls for loopStart, -gs for groundStart) that is currently set:

```
Router#show voice port summary

                                      IN        OUT
PORT             CH   SIG-TYPE   ADMIN OPER STATUS    STATUS     EC
=============== ==   ============ ===== ==== ======== ======== ==
0/0/0            --   fxs-ls      up    dorm on-hook  idle      y
0/0/1            --   fxs-ls      up    dorm on-hook  idle      y
0/0/2            --   fxs-ls      up    dorm on-hook  idle      y
0/0/3            --   fxs-ls      up    dorm on-hook  idle      y
0/1/0            --   fxo-ls      up    dorm idle     on-hook   y
0/1/1            --   fxo-ls      up    dorm idle     on-hook   y
0/1/2            --   fxo-ls      up    dorm idle     on-hook   y
0/1/3            --   fxo-ls      up    dorm idle     on-hook   y

Router#
```

I will begin by showing you how to configure FXS ports for attached analog telephones. You will see how a phone number dial peer is properly applied to the FXS port, so anytime a phone calls that number, the CUCM Express knows that the desired party is physically attached to a specific analog interface.

We'll then move on to see how FXO ports are configured to connect to the PSTN. You'll see that the configuration of FXS and FXO ports is similar except for the dial-peer options. With FXS ports, they are connected to a physical end device such as an analog phone or fax machine, which implies a simple dial-peer mapping to an extension. In the case of FXO port connectivity to the PSTN, we need to set up our dial peers to be able to handle any off-network phone numbers that we want to be able to reach. Because of this, dial peers for FXO ports can become much more complex. You'll learn how to accomplish this setup more easily by using wildcards in your dial-peer statements.

Configuring FXS Ports

As you learned back in Chapter 2, FXS ports are responsible for connecting analog endpoints such as analog phones, fax machines, and modems. Figure 7.1 shows two phones connected to FXS ports on the CUCM Express.

FIGURE 7.1   Two phones connected via FXS ports as dial peers

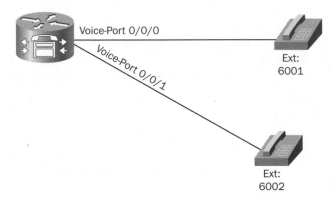

You can see in the diagram that extension 6001 should be configured for the analog phone on FXS voice-port 0/0/0, and the phone connected to voice-port 0/0/1 should be configured with extension 6002. The following example shows how we can use the `station-id number` command to set our caller ID number to the port. The first task is to enable caller ID on the FXS port because it is disabled by default. The `caller-id enable` command enables caller ID on a per-port basis.

Because analog devices are not intelligent, the phone has no idea what number is assigned to it. This way, you can swap analog phones at any time and not have to worry about any firmware/configuration file issues that you may run into when swapping out IP phones. A second command demonstrated here is `station-id name`. This configures the caller ID information to the analog FXS port. Here is the output for configuring a name and number to two FXS ports, as detailed in Figure 7.1:

```
Router#configure terminal
Router#voice-port 0/0/0
Router(config-voiceport)#caller-id enable
Router(config-voiceport)#station-id ?
  name    A string describing station name
  number  A full E.164 telephone number
```

```
Router(config-voiceport)#station-id number 6001
Router(config-voiceport)#station-id name Adriana Castro
Router(config-voiceport)#exit
Router#voice-port 0/0/1
Router(config-voiceport)#caller-id enable
Router(config-voiceport)#station-id number 6002
Router(config-voiceport)#station-id name Brett Cowan
Router(config-voiceport)#end
Router#
```

In addition to extension numbers, we need to specify the type of signaling we wish to use. The choices are ground start and loop start signaling, which we discussed in Chapter 2. Table 7.1 details the configuration differences between the two signaling options.

TABLE 7.1 FXS ground and loop start configuration choices

Signaling Type	Description	Default on FXS	Common Uses
Loop start	Closes loop immediately after off-hook is detected.	Default setting	When connecting analog end devices. Not recommended for high-volume analog trunks because of glare.
Ground start	Requires ground detection prior to the loop closing.	Not the default setting	When connecting to the PSTN or another PBX.

You have already seen how you can configure the CUCM Express router to match either the user or network locale for Cisco IP phones. Along those same lines, we can configure our FXS analog port to match the location standards for analog phones. To accomplish this, we can use the cptone config-voiceport command. Let's look at the cptone location options available to us:

```
Router#configure terminal
Router(config)#voice-port 0/0/0
Router(config-voiceport)#cptone ?
  locale   2 letter ISO-3166 country code

AR Argentina        IN India           PE Peru
AU Australia        ID Indonesia       PH Philippines
AT Austria          IE Ireland         PL Poland
BE Belgium          IL Israel          PT Portugal
BR Brazil           IT Italy           RU Russian Federation
```

CA Canada	JP Japan	SA Saudi Arabia
CN China	JO Jordan	SG Singapore
CO Colombia	KE Kenya	SK Slovakia
C1 Custom1	KR Korea Republic	SI Slovenia
C2 Custom2	KW Kuwait	ZA South Africa
CY Cyprus	LB Lebanon	ES Spain
CZ Czech Republic	LU Luxembourg	SE Sweden
DK Denmark	MY Malaysia	CH Switzerland
EG Egypt	MX Mexico	TW Taiwan
FI Finland	NP Nepal	TH Thailand
FR France	NL Netherlands	TR Turkey
DE Germany	NZ New Zealand	AE United Arab Emirates
GH Ghana	NG Nigeria	GB United Kingdom
GR Greece	NO Norway	US United States
HK Hong Kong	OM Oman	VE Venezuela
HU Hungary	PK Pakistan	ZW Zimbabwe
IS Iceland	PA Panama	

```
Router(config-voiceport)#cptone
```

The cptone command stands for *call progress tone*. By default, cptone is configured for the US locale. Let's change the default in our example to match the tones found in Thailand for both of the analog phones in our example:

```
Router#configure terminal
Router(config)#voice-port 0/0/0
Router(config-voiceport)#cptone TH
Router(config-voiceport)# voice-port 0/0/1
Router(config-voiceport)#cptone TH
Router(config-voiceport)#end
Router#
```

One final configuration option that you should be familiar with is the ring frequency command. Like the cptone command, ring frequency may need to be modified depending on the location of the deployment. Telephone endpoints such as analog phones may be country dependent. Depending on the phone in question, the *ring frequency* may need to be adjusted for it to ring properly. This command sets the AC power output over the wires to make the phone ring. The frequencies are measured in Hertz, and only a handful of options are available, as shown here:

```
Router#configure terminal
Router(config)#voice-port 0/0/0
Router(config-voiceport)#ring frequency ?
```

```
20   ring frequency 20 Hertz
25   ring frequency 25 Hertz
30   ring frequency 30 Hertz
50   ring frequency 50 Hertz
```

```
Router(config-voiceport)#ring frequency
```

If you're in a situation where you are setting up an analog phone and it just won't ring for some reason, you may need to adjust the frequency to match the standards of the country's PSTN. By default, Cisco sets the ring frequency to 25 Hz, which is the standard for North America. In some European countries such as France, the maximum ring frequency is 50 Hz. Here's how to modify the frequency to match Europe's default power limit for analog phones:

```
Router#configure terminal
Router(config)#voice-port 0/0/0
Router(config-voiceport)#ring frequency 50
Router(config-voiceport)#exit
Router(config)#voice-port 0/0/1
Router(config-voiceport)#ring frequency 50
Router(config-voiceport)#end
Router#
```

Reviewing FXS Port Configuration and Status

A great way to review your FXS port configuration and line status is to use the show voice port privileged exec command. Here we can check the configuration parameters and port status of our voice ports. Following is an example of the information this command displays about FXS port 0/0/0, which happens to be in use (off-hook):

```
Router#show voice port 0/0/0

Foreign Exchange Station 0/0/0 Slot is 0, Sub-unit is 0, Port is 0
 Type of VoicePort is FXS  VIC3-4FXS/DID
 Operation State is UP
 Administrative State is UP
 No Interface Down Failure
 Description is not set
 Noise Regeneration is enabled
 Non Linear Processing is enabled
 Non Linear Mute is disabled
 Non Linear Threshold is -21 dB
 Music On Hold Threshold is Set to -38 dBm
 In Gain is Set to 0 dB
```

```
Out Attenuation is Set to 3 dB
Echo Cancellation is enabled
Echo Cancellation NLP mute is disabled
Echo Cancellation NLP threshold is -21 dB
Echo Cancel Coverage is set to 64 ms
Echo Cancel worst case ERL is set to 6 dB
Playout-delay Mode is set to adaptive
Playout-delay Nominal is set to 60 ms
Playout-delay Maximum is set to 1000 ms
Playout-delay Minimum mode is set to default, value 40 ms
Playout-delay Fax is set to 300 ms
Connection Mode is normal
Connection Number is not set
Initial Time Out is set to 10 s
Interdigit Time Out is set to 10 s
Call Disconnect Time Out is set to 60 s
Supervisory Disconnect Time Out is set to 750 ms
Ringing Time Out is set to 180 s
Wait Release Time Out is set to 30 s
Companding Type is u-law
Region Tone is set for TH

Analog Info Follows:
Currently processing Voice
Maintenance Mode Set to None (not in mtc mode)
Number of signaling protocol errors are 0
Impedance is set to 600r Ohm
Station name Adriana Castro, Station number 6001
Translation profile (Incoming):
Translation profile (Outgoing):

Voice card specific Info Follows:
Signal Type is loopStart
Ring Frequency is 25 Hz
Hook Status is Off Hook
Ring Active Status is inactive
Ring Ground Status is inactive
Tip Ground Status is inactive
Digit Duration Timing is set to 100 ms
InterDigit Duration Timing is set to 100 ms
Hookflash-in Timing is set to max=1000 ms, min=150 ms
```

```
Hookflash-out Timing is set to 400 ms
No disconnect acknowledge
Ring Cadence is defined by CPTone Selection
Ring Cadence are [10 40] * 100 msec
Ringer Equivalence Number is set to 1
```

As you can see, we can learn a ton of information by issuing this command. We know that the port is physically working because the Administrative State is UP; the Operation State is also UP, which means the phone is off-hook. You can also see the configuration options set, including Station name, Station number, and Region Tone. Now let's look at FXS port 0/0/1:

Router#**sh voice port 0/0/1**

```
Foreign Exchange Station 0/0/1 Slot is 0, Sub-unit is 0, Port is 1
 Type of VoicePort is FXS  VIC3-4FXS/DID
 Operation State is DORMANT
 Administrative State is UP
 No Interface Down Failure
 Description is not set
 Noise Regeneration is enabled
 Non Linear Processing is enabled
 Non Linear Mute is disabled
 Non Linear Threshold is -21 dB
 Music On Hold Threshold is Set to -38 dBm
 In Gain is Set to 0 dB
 Out Attenuation is Set to 3 dB
 Echo Cancellation is enabled
 Echo Cancellation NLP mute is disabled
 Echo Cancellation NLP threshold is -21 dB
 Echo Cancel Coverage is set to 64 ms
 Echo Cancel worst case ERL is set to 6 dB
 Playout-delay Mode is set to adaptive
 Playout-delay Nominal is set to 60 ms
 Playout-delay Maximum is set to 1000 ms
 Playout-delay Minimum mode is set to default, value 40 ms
 Playout-delay Fax is set to 300 ms
 Connection Mode is normal
 Connection Number is not set
 Initial Time Out is set to 10 s
 Interdigit Time Out is set to 10 s
 Call Disconnect Time Out is set to 60 s
 Supervisory Disconnect Time Out is set to 750 ms
```

```
Ringing Time Out is set to 180 s
Wait Release Time Out is set to 30 s
Companding Type is u-law
Region Tone is set for TH

Analog Info Follows:
Currently processing none
Maintenance Mode Set to None (not in mtc mode)
Number of signaling protocol errors are 0
Impedance is set to 600r Ohm
Station name Brett Cowan, Station number 6002
Translation profile (Incoming):
Translation profile (Outgoing):

Voice card specific Info Follows:
Signal Type is loopStart
Ring Frequency is 25 Hz
Hook Status is On Hook
Ring Active Status is inactive
Ring Ground Status is inactive
Tip Ground Status is active
Digit Duration Timing is set to 100 ms
InterDigit Duration Timing is set to 100 ms
Hookflash-in Timing is set to max=1000 ms, min=150 ms
Hookflash-out Timing is set to 400 ms
No disconnect acknowledge
Ring Cadence is defined by CPTone Selection
Ring Cadence are [10 40] * 100 msec
Ringer Equivalence Number is set to 1
Router#
```

This port looks very similar except for the difference in Station name and Station number. Also note that the Operation State is DORMANT, which means that the phone attached to FXS port 0/0/1 is on-hook. Next up, you'll learn how to set POTS dial peers to point to our FXS ports.

Configuring POTS Dial Peers for the FXS Ports

Now that the physical FXS port is configured and ready to go, we need to create a POTS dial peer to hard-code a phone number to that port. Because both of our ports are analog endpoints, the destination-pattern is limited to creating a destination pattern number and assigning that to our analog FXS port. In this example, we assign the numbers 6001 and 6002 to our previously configured FXS ports.

```
Router#configure terminal
Router(config)#dial-peer voice ?
  <1-2147483647>  Voice dial-peer tag

Router(config)#dial-peer voice 6001 pots
Router(config-dial-peer)#destination-pattern 6001
Router(config-dial-peer)#port 0/0/0
Router(config-dial-peer)#dial-peer voice 6002 pots
Router(config-dial-peer)#destination-pattern 6002
Router(config-dial-peer)#port 0/0/1
Router(config-dial-peer)#end
Router#
```

At this stage, any analog phone can be attached to these ports. The attached analog phones can then be reached by dialing the destination pattern. Keep in mind that the extension number is statically assigned to the FXS port and not the analog phone. The `dial-peer voice` tag number does not need to be equivalent to the extension number, but this is often done for ease of remembering the configuration.

FXS PLAR Configuration

A special analog FXS configuration type that you'll likely run across is the *private line automatic ringdown (PLAR)* port. This specialized port will automatically ring any number that is configured on the port as soon as the phone goes off-hook. A good way to think about this type of port is as a "hotline" phone for emergency or informational purposes such as an emergency phone inside an elevator. PLAR is also often used on phones in public places outside locked doors. When someone wishes to gain access through the locked doors, they pick up the phone, which automatically rings the security desk. Let's use the security desk PLAR as our example. Figure 7.2 shows our PLAR-configured phone that resides outside the locked doorway.

FIGURE 7.2 An FXS PLAR secure door scenario

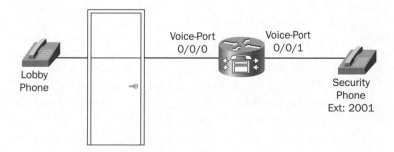

To accomplish this goal using the minimum number of steps, we first must configure voice-port 0/0/0 to function as a PLAR port. We can use the `connection plar` command in config-voiceport mode to do this. Here are the configuration steps to configure voice-port 0/0/0 as a PLAR to ring extension 2001 automatically when the receiver is picked up.

```
Router#configure terminal
Router(config)#voice-port 0/0/0
Router(config-voiceport)#connection plar 2001
Router(config-voiceport)#end
Router#
```

Next, we'll configure a POTS dial peer for extension 2001 and apply it to voice-port 0/0/1.

```
Router#configure terminal
Router(config)#dial-peer voice 2001 pots
Router(config-dial-peer)#destination-pattern 2001
Router(config-dial-peer)#port 0/0/0
Router(config-dial-peer)#end
Router#
```

 In this example, both phones are analog and use FXS ports. In reality, for an analog PLAR connection only the phone configured as the PLAR line needs to be analog. The destination extension can be analog, IP based, or somewhere off network if desired. PLAR can also be enabled on IP phones running either SIP or SCCP, but their configuration setup is different and outside the scope of this book.

Now when you take the PLAR phone off hook, it will immediately ring the security phone at extension 2001.

Configuring FXO Ports

Configuring FXO ports is similar to configuring FXS ports at the interface level. Just like the FXS interfaces, FXO interfaces can use the same `station-id`, `cptone`, and `ring frequency` config-voiceport commands. The main difference in configuration setup between the two is that we'll want to use either the `signal groundStart` or `signal cama` config-voiceport command for signaling to the PSTN or to the PSAP (Public Switch Answering Point). Remember that in some circumstances in North America, you need to route your emergency service calls out using a CAMA-configured port. I'll show you how to configure your port for CAMA operation later in this section. For now, we'll configure our FXO port for ground-start signaling. We'll use Figure 7.3 as our FXO interface and dial-peer configuration example.

FIGURE 7.3 Configuring an FXO port with POTS dial peer

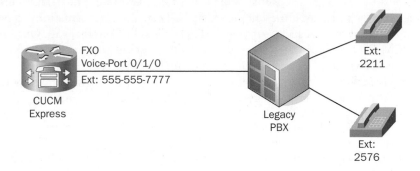

In our example, we're going to keep most of our defaults and simply configure ground-start signaling and provide caller-ID information on the port:

```
Router#configure terminal
Router(config)#voice-port 0/1/0
Router(config-voiceport)#station-id name Acme Inc
Router(config-voiceport)#station-id number 5555557777
Router(config-voiceport)#signal groundStart
Router(config-voiceport)#end
Router#
```

Two additional commands are used only with FXO hardware configurations. The first configuration option is the `dial-type` config-voiceport command, which allows you to set the address signaling used on this FXO port for outgoing calls. We know that we have two options for address signaling. DTMF is the default and is used virtually everywhere these days. You can also set the address signaling to pulse dialing if you find yourself in a part of the world that still uses it. Here are the command options as they appear on the CUCM Express:

```
Router(config-voiceport)#dial-type ?
  dtmf   touch-tone dialer
  pulse  pulse dialer

Router(config-voiceport)#
```

A second FXO-only configuration option when configuring voice ports is the `ring number` command. The *ring number* command signifies the maximum number of rings detected by the router before answering the call. Remember that on FXO interfaces, the line actually terminates at the router and not at a phone endpoint, as was discussed in Chapter 3.

In our example, the number 555-555-7777 belongs to the FXO port itself. The `ring number` command specifies how many rings it should wait before answering. The default number is 1, which means it will answer the call immediately. There are some situations where you might want to set this higher, such as if your PSTN line is split from the wall. One line goes to your CUCM Express and another to a standard analog phone. Let's say that you would like to be able to answer all incoming calls on your analog phone on the first one to three rings. If nobody is there to answer the calls, then the FXO should answer and handle the call accordingly. To accomplish this, configure the following on your FXO port:

```
Router#configure terminal
Router(config)#voice-port 0/1/0
Router(config-voiceport)#ring number ?
  <1-10>  The number of rings detected before closing loop

Router(config-voiceport)#ring number 3
Router(config-voiceport)#end
Router#
```

Now you have the ability to catch the call on your other analog phone before it is handled automatically by the CUCM Express FXO port.

Reviewing FXO Port Configuration and Status

Just as with the FXS ports, we can view configuration and status information of our FXO ports by using the `show voice port` privileged exec command. Here's what our FXO port 0/1/0 looks like:

```
Router#sh voice port 0/1/0

Foreign Exchange Office 0/1/0 Slot is 0, Sub-unit is 1, Port is 0
 Type of VoicePort is FXO
 Operation State is DORMANT
 Administrative State is UP
 No Interface Down Failure
 Description is not set
 Noise Regeneration is enabled
 Non Linear Processing is enabled
 Non Linear Mute is disabled
 Non Linear Threshold is -21 dB
 Music On Hold Threshold is Set to -38 dBm
 In Gain is Set to 0 dB
 Out Attenuation is Set to 3 dB
```

Echo Cancellation is enabled
Echo Cancellation NLP mute is disabled
Echo Cancellation NLP threshold is -21 dB
Echo Cancel Coverage is set to 64 ms
Echo Cancel worst case ERL is set to 6 dB
Playout-delay Mode is set to adaptive
Playout-delay Nominal is set to 60 ms
Playout-delay Maximum is set to 1000 ms
Playout-delay Minimum mode is set to default, value 40 ms
Playout-delay Fax is set to 300 ms
Connection Mode is normal
Connection Number is not set
Initial Time Out is set to 10 s
Interdigit Time Out is set to 10 s
Call Disconnect Time Out is set to 60 s
Ringing Time Out is set to 180 s
Wait Release Time Out is set to 30 s
Companding Type is u-law
Region Tone is set for US

Analog Info Follows:
Currently processing none
Maintenance Mode Set to None (not in mtc mode)
Number of signaling protocol errors are 0
Impedance is set to 600r Ohm
Station name Acme Inc, Station number 5555557777
Translation profile (Incoming):
Translation profile (Outgoing):

Voice card specific Info Follows:
Signal Type is groundStart
Battery-Reversal is enabled
Number Of Rings is set to 3
Supervisory Disconnect is signal
Answer Supervision is inactive
Hook Status is On Hook
Ring Detect Status is inactive
Ring Ground Status is inactive
Tip Ground Status is inactive
Dial Out Type is dtmf

```
Digit Duration Timing is set to 100 ms
InterDigit Duration Timing is set to 100 ms
Pulse Rate Timing is set to 10 pulses/second
InterDigit Pulse Duration Timing is set to 750 ms
Percent Break of Pulse is 60 percent
GuardOut timer is 2000 ms
Minimum ring duration timer is 125 ms
Hookflash-in Timing is set to 600 ms
Hookflash-out Timing is set to 400 ms
Supervisory Disconnect Timing (loopStart only) is set to 350 ms
OPX Ring Wait Timing is set to 6000 ms
Router#
```

We can see that our FXO port is UP and in a DORMANT state. We can also see our configuration settings, including station name, station number, and number of rings. Next, you'll learn how to configure a dial peer for our FXO interface.

Configuring POTS Dial Peers for the FXO Ports

Now that we have our physical FXO analog port set up, we need to configure our POTS dial peer to define whom we can reach on this interface. This task gets a bit more complex because FXO ports typically connect to the PSTN or a legacy PBX. That being said, we can use a POTS dial peer to control the calls that are allowed on this interface. We can use dial-peer wildcards to help accomplish our goal. Table 7.2 lists the available dial-peer wildcards on a CUCM Express system.

TABLE 7.2   Dial-peer wildcards

Wildcard	Description	Common Example
.	A single digit 0–9 or *.	5... matches 5 plus three additional numbers or *.
[ ]	A range of single-numbered digits. Incorporates – for consecutive range or , for nonconsecutive ranges.	[4–7] matches any number 4, 5, 6, or 7. [5,8] Matches either 5 or 8.
( )	Indicates a pattern. It is used in conjunction with the ?, %, and/or + symbols.	N/A
?	The last digit or ( ) pattern occurs zero or one time.	543 matches 54 or 543. 6(54)? matches 6 or 654.

TABLE 7.2 Dial-peer wildcards (*continued*)

Wildcard	Description	Common Example
%	The last digit or ( ) pattern occurs 0 or more times.	765% matches 76 or 765 or up to any number of 5s to a total of 32 digits. 3(21)% matches 3 or 321 or up to any number of 21s to a total of 32 digits.
+	The last digit or ( ) occurs 1 or more times.	987+ matches 987 or 9877 or up to an infinite number of 7s. 6(54)+ matches 654 or 65454 or up to any of 54s to a total of 32 digits.
T	The CUCM pauses to collect any number of digits entered 0–9 or *.	9T matches 9 plus up to 31 additional digits 0–9 and *.

You'll notice that the dial-peer wildcards are virtually identical to other telephone-digit wildcards used on the system. Once you learn them, you can use them in multiple scenarios and not just with dial peers.

In our example, we connect to a legacy PBX system with an FXO port. The PBX has two phones attached to it. Using a simple destination-pattern dial peer, we can use a wildcard to cover all of the phones that the legacy PBX has with a single command:

```
Router#configure terminal
Router(config)#dial-peer voice 2000 pots
Router(config-dial-peer)#destination-pattern 2...
Router(config-dial-peer)#no digit-strip
Router(config-dial-peer)#port 0/1/0
Router(config-dial-peer)#end
Router
```

Now the router is set up so that when any CUCM Express–configured phones dial 2XXX, those calls are routed over to the legacy PBX on FXO port 0/1/0.

We had to include the command no digit-strip in this FXO POTS dial-peer configuration. This command is explained in the "Dial-Peer Digit Manipulation" section of this chapter. For now, all you need to know is that the command is needed to forward all four digits to the PBX, which is the next hop along the call leg.

FXO PLAR Configuration

FXO interfaces cannot utilize direct inward dials (DIDs). Instead, they have only a single PSTN number assigned to the interface. They also cannot use *Dialed Number Identification Service (DNIS)*. DNIS is a service the public phone company offers on digital circuits that lets the CUCM Express determine which telephone number was dialed by a customer. It is useful for inbound calls because it allows you to switch the calls internally based on the DNIS number.

Because our FXO interfaces cannot use DIDs or DNIS, and because the PSTN numbers terminate the phone number directly on the voice-port interface, it is very common to use PLAR to forward the call transparently to either a receptionist or an automated attendant system for all inbound calls from the PSTN or a legacy PBX. If PLAR is not set up on the FXO port, when a call from a user on the PSTN hits the FXO interface, that caller receives a second dial tone. If the user knows the internal extension they want to call, they can enter it then. That might work for people who know the exact internal extension they want to call, but it can be confusing to others. A better way is to use PLAR to forward the calls to a receptionist or automated attendant. That way, the receptionist can receive the inbound calls and forward them to the proper internal extension. The same situation holds true for an auto attendant. The inbound calls can be forwarded to the AA, and then the caller can use automated prompts to be connected to the internal extension they choose. Figure 7.4 illustrates our configuration example.

FIGURE 7.4   An example of PLAR set up on an FXO port

Here we have a single FXO port connected to the PSTN. The port is configured with a 555-555-1212 number. We want all calls going to this number to be automatically switched to our receptionist IP phone at extension 1000, which is already configured on the CUCM Express. So all we need to do is configure our FXO port for proper signaling and set up the PLAR to point to extension 1000:

```
Router#configure-terminal
Router(config)#voice-port 0/1/0
Router(config)#signal groundStart
Router(config-voiceport)#connection plar 1000
Router(config-voiceport)#end
Router#
```

In our previous example, the PLAR number we used is an IP-based phone. If the phone were an analog phone attached to an FXS port, we would want to use the following config-voiceport command when setting up our PLAR:

Router(config-voiceport)#connection plar opx 1000

The opx option stands for *off-premise exchange*. When an outside call comes into voice-port 0/1/0, typically the voice gateway completes the call immediately and then forwards it to the PLAR number. This works for both IPT and analog (FXS) numbers. The problem arises when nobody is able to answer the phone. If this occurs, the voice gateway cannot roll the call over to voice mail, because the call has already been terminated. If we include the opx option, the FXO port waits until the FXS port goes off-hook before connecting the call. We can then set up an option to roll the incoming call to voice mail if the analog phone is not answered after a specified number of seconds.

FXO CAMA Configuration

In Chapter 2 you learned that CAMA interfaces connect to the PSAP for E911 calling. They connect to the PSAP so the call can be directed to the proper E911 dispatch center based on the calling party's phone number. This helps to ensure that emergency service calls are routed to the proper dispatch station. In this section you will learn how to configure FXS ports for CAMA connections to the PSAP. Figure 7.5 shows our previously configured FXO port 0/1/0 going to the PSTN.

FIGURE 7.5   An example of FXO with CAMA

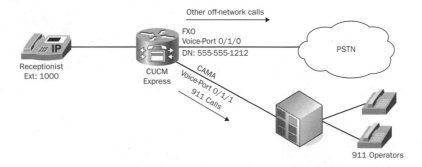

As you can see from the diagram, we want to configure 0/1/1 to go to the E911 PSAP as a CAMA port. The diagram depicts 911 calls being routed out the CAMA interface on voice-port 0/1/1 and all other calls going out to the PSTN on voice-port 0/1/0.

Configuration elements that are unique to the CAMA FXO interface involve signaling. Instead of using loopStart or groundStart, we use the signal cama config-voiceport command. In addition, we can choose from several options for the CAMA signaling. Here are the options listed on the router:

```
Router#configure terminal
Router(config)#voice-port 0/1/0
Router(config-voiceport)#signal cama ?
  KP-0-NPA-NXX-XXXX-ST                          Type 2 CAMA Signaling
  KP-0-NXX-XXXX-ST                              Type 1 CAMA Signaling
  KP-2-ST                                       Type 3 CAMA Signaling
  KP-II-NPA-NXX-XXXX-ST-KP-NPA-NXX-XXXX-ST  Type 5 CAMA Signaling
  KP-NPD-NXX-XXXX-ST                            Type 4 CAMA Signaling
  <cr>

Router(config-voiceport)#signal cama
```

The type of signaling required will be specified by the emergency services technicians in your area. Let's assume that we want to configure KP-0-NXX-XXXX-ST as our CAMA signaling type. Here's how the configuration of the voice port looks:

```
Router(config-voiceport)#signal cama KP-0-NPA-NXX-XXXX-ST
Note: need to shut/no shut to complete the CAMA signal type configuration.

Router(config-voiceport)#
```

Notice that after we changed signaling to CAMA, the router gave us a console message stating that we must perform a shut and no shut on the FXO port to put the interface into CAMA mode. Once the FXO port is configured, we can create the dial peer to send 911 and 9911 calls out the CAMA interface. Here's how to accomplish this task:

```
Router#configure terminal
Router(config)#dial-peer voice 911 pots
Router(config-dial-peer)#destination-pattern 911
Router(config-dial-peer)#no digit-strip
Router(config-dial-peer)#port 0/1/0
Router(config-dial-peer)#exit
Router(config)#dial-peer voice 911 pots
Router(config-dial-peer)#destination-pattern 9911
Router(config-dial-peer)#forward-digits 3
Router(config-dial-peer)#port 0/1/0
Router(config-dial-peer)#end
Router#
```

We introduce a new command called forward-digits here. This command is explained in more detail in the "Dial-Peer Digit Manipulation" section of this chapter. For now, you just need to understand that the command tells the voice gateway to send the last three digits of the matched destination pattern. Therefore, when a user dials 9911, only 911 is sent out the CAMA port 0/1/0.

Now anytime a user dials either 911 or 9911, the call is routed out the CAMA port. Notice that we have both 911 and 9911 set to route calls out the CAMA port. This is common if users are accustomed to dialing 9 for an outside line. Because the dial peer for our CAMA port matches a specific number, it takes precedence over any other 9XXX numbers. You'll learn more about how the CUCM Express selects the best destination routes later in this chapter. For now, just know that the more specific dial peer is best.

Configuring Digital T1 Ports

T1 ports are more commonly found in larger environments because they can carry multiple phone lines over a single trunk link. This section will show you how to configure a T1 CAS, which uses all 24 channels for voice. We'll then move on to configure the T1 PRI circuit, which uses 23 channels for voice and the 24th channel for out-of-band signaling. Along with the physical configuration of the digital circuits, you'll learn how to set up basic dial peers to be able to call inbound and outbound on the T1s.

Configuring T1 CAS Ports

A T1 CAS circuit comes into your voice gateway on a single copper connection. It has the ability to handle up to 24 concurrent calls. This first section will show you the various configuration steps and options available. Depending on your service provider, the options you choose may be different. You'll have to work closely with your PSTN provider to make sure you have the correct settings to have the T1 function properly. This book will use the most common configuration used in North America for framing and linecoding, which is ESF and B8ZS.

Framing and linecoding are outside the scope of this book. Just keep in mind that Cisco supports a few types, but you will most likely see B8ZS/ESF circuits.

Once we have the physical interface set up, we'll configure a basic POTS dial peer so calls can be properly routed out our interface.

A T1 that carries multiple calls on a single connection is referred to as a trunk line. The T1 hardware that is installed on your router will be seen as "controller" interfaces in the IOS configuration. To configure the T1 CAS card, you need to enter into config-controller mode and choose the slot/port where your T1 card is located on the router. Once in config-controller mode, you must configure the following four settings:

- Framing type
- Linecode type
- Clock source
- Ds0-group options

Let's briefly discuss each of these options to understand what they are used for.

Framing Type

The framing type sets the framing that your PSTN provider has configured on their end. You can see the options listed here while in config-controller mode:

```
Router#config t
Router(config)#controller t1 0/1/0
Router(config-controller)#framing ?
  esf  Extended Superframe
  sf   Superframe

Router(config-controller)#framing esf
Router(config-controller)#
```

Super Frame (SF) is the older of the two framing types available, and most telco providers now use Extended Super Frame (ESF).

Linecode Type

The linecode type you choose again depends on your PSTN provider. You have to set your linecode to match whatever coding they provide to you on the circuit. Here are the options available to you on the T1 card:

```
Router(config-controller)#linecode ?
  ami   AMI encoding
  b8zs  B8ZS encoding

Router(config-controller)#linecode b8zs
Router(config-controller)#
```

The most common option in much of the world is B8ZS.

Clock Source

The *clock source* option allows you to determine where the T1 circuit synchronizes its timing clock. We know that the digital T1 circuits use Time-Division Multiplexing

(TDM) to send multiple voice channels over a single circuit. A clock mechanism ensures that both sides of the T1 remain in sync so TDM can function properly. Here are the options available for setting the clock source:

```
Router(config-controller)#clock source ?
  internal      Internal Clock
  line          Recovered Clock


Router(config-controller)#clock source line
Router(config-controller)#
```

The line option specifies that the T1 uses the clock from the T1 line itself. This means that it synchronizes using the clock configured from the PSTN. The internal option tells us that the T1 uses its own internal interface clock. You should use this option if you are connecting to an internal PBX and want the router to handle the clock.

Ds0-group Options

The ds0-group options are where you can configure multiple or individual channels of the 24-line T1 CAS. Each T1 CAS channel is called a timeslot. Listed here are the different timeslot signaling types you can choose from:

```
Router(config-controller)#ds0-group 0 timeslots 1-24 type ?
  e&m-delay-dial       E & M Delay Dial
  e&m-fgd              E & M Type II FGD
  e&m-immediate-start  E & M Immediate Start
  e&m-wink-start       E & M Wink Start
  ext-sig              External Signaling
  fgd-eana             FGD-EANA BOC side
  fgd-os               FGD-OS BOC side
  fxo-ground-start     FXO Ground Start
  fxo-loop-start       FXO Loop Start
  fxs-ground-start     FXS Ground Start
  fxs-loop-start       FXS Loop Start
  none                 Null Signalling for External Call Control
  <cr>


Router(config-controller)#ds0-group 0 timeslots 1-24
```

You can configure signaling for each timeslot to be identical to or different from one another, depending on what you want to accomplish, by using the timeslots *X-X* option where *X-X* lists the timeslot range. When you want to use a group of timeslots for the same task, you should put them into the same ds0-group. If another set of timeslots is for a different task, you should put them into a second ds0-group. To show what I'm talking about, let's configure a ds0-group using the first 12 channels on ds0-group 0 and the second 12 channels for ds0-group 1. The first group will use fxo-loop-start signaling, and the second group will be set up using e&m-immediate-start:

```
Router#configure terminal
Router(config)#controller t1 0/1/0
Router(config-controller)#ds0-group 0 timeslots 1-12 type fxo-loop-start
Router(config-controller)#ds0-group 1 timeslots 13-24 type e&m-immediate-start
Router(config-controller)#
```

This example shows how you can split up the 24 channels into different ds0-groups for different purposes. In the next section, you'll see how to configure POTS dial peers to route off-network calls to the PSTN.

So far, we've been discussing T1 circuits that have a full 24 channels for use. If your environment does not need this many channels, most PSTN providers offer *fractional T1* circuits, in which they provide a T1 circuit but limit the number of usable channels. For example, if you need 12 POTS lines, the PSTN will give you a full T1 but only timeslots 1–12 will be usable. If you were to define all 24 timeslots, but only 12 were usable, you may reach a point where calls cannot go through. In this situation you would need to configure your ds0-group timeslots for only 1–12, as shown in this example:
```
Router(config-controller)#ds0-group 0 timeslots 1-12 type
fxo-loop-start
```

Configuring POTS Dial Peers for T1 CAS Ports

One thing to keep in mind about digital circuits such as T1s is that they're still considered POTS lines because they do not use IP for transport. In that regard, configuring POTS dial peers for T1 CAS interfaces is very similar to configuring POTS dial peers for FXO interfaces. The difference is that the T1 CAS circuits have multiple timeslots. In the next configuration example, we will assume that the CAS T1 is set up to use all 24 channels for the same signaling type. The following command output shows how to route off-network calls out the T1 CAS located at port 0/1/0:

```
Router(config-dial-peer)#dial-peer voice 91 pots
Router(config-dial-peer)#destination-pattern 91.........
Router(config-dial-peer)#port 0/1/0:D
Router(config-dial-peer)#end
Router#
```

This configuration looks very similar to a standard FXO line except for the fact that this dial peer allows 24 calls to be placed at a single time.

Configuring T1 PRI Ports

Configuration of a T1 PRI circuit is very similar to that of a T1 CAS circuit. I must mention a few differences, however. Because T1 PRIs use Q.931 ISDN signaling, we must configure the *ISDN switch type* that our PSTN provider uses. Also keep in mind that T1 PRIs use common channel signaling (CCS), which is out of band. That means that channel 24 (timeslot 23) is set aside for signaling, so only timeslots 0–22 are available for voice calls. Nothing from a configuration standpoint needs to be addressed. As soon as you set the T1 to use Q.931 signaling, timeslot 23 is automatically reserved for signaling. Here are the different ISDN switch type options. Note that this is a global router configuration option. It can be overridden on a per-interface basis if needed:

```
Router#configure terminal
Router(config)#isdn switch-type ?
  primary-4ess     Lucent 4ESS switch type for the U.S.
  primary-5ess     Lucent 5ESS switch type for the U.S.
  primary-dms100   Northern Telecom DMS-100 switch type for the U.S.
  primary-dpnss    DPNSS switch type for Europe
  primary-net5     NET5 switch type for UK, Europe, Asia and Australia
  primary-ni       National ISDN Switch type for the U.S.
  primary-ntt      NTT switch type for Japan
  primary-qsig     QSIG switch type
  primary-ts014    TS014 switch type for Australia (obsolete)

Router(config)#isdn switch-type primary-ni
Router(config)#
```

In the United States, you will typically choose `primary-5ess` or `primary-ni` for your switch type.

Just like the T1 CAS circuit, the T1 PRI is configured within config-controller mode. Here are the four options you need to be aware of for configuring the T1 PRI:

- Framing type
- Linecode type
- Clock source
- Pri-group options

The framing type, linecode type, and clock source options are identical to those for the T1 CAS configuration detailed earlier in this chapter. Notice, however, that instead of ds0-group options, the T1 PRI uses pri-group options. Let's take a closer look at this command.

Pri-group Options

The `pri-group` option simply sets the timeslots you wish to use. Here is how to configure a pri-group for a full PRI:

```
Router#configure terminal
Router(config)#controller t1 0/1/0
Router(config-controller)#pri-group timeslots 1-24
```

Did you notice that the pri-group is just a single global group that cannot be broken up into subgroups? This is one of the benefits that the T1 CAS has over the T1 PRI. The more granular control over timeslot signaling provided by using multiple ds0-groups is not an option with the `pri-group` commands.

T1 PRIs that utilize the Q.931 ISDN signaling can allow for the phone endpoint's full DID number to be used as the identity for off-network calls. This functionality is not available on the T1 CAS. This feature is nice when you want to use the PSTN call accounting records to keep track of your outbound calls.

Just like T1 CAS circuits, T1 PRIs can be ordered as fractional T1s. Keep in mind, though, that the signaling is always performed on channel 24, which is timeslot 23. When you configure a T1 pri-group command, you'll find that the D channel has automatically been created for you in the form of an interface serial and voice-port format. Here's the output showing what these two configurations look like:

```
Router# show run | section 0/1/0:23
Building configuration...
interface Serial0/1/0:23
 no ip address
 encapsulation hdlc
 isdn switch-type primary-ni
 isdn incoming-voice voice
 isdn bind-l3 ccm-manager
 no cdp enable
!
voice-port 0/1/0:23
```

We can also verify the operational status of each of the 23 voice channels on our T1 by issuing the `show voice port summary` privileged exec command, as shown here:

```
Router1#show voice port summary
```

PORT	CH	SIG-TYPE	ADMIN	OPER	IN STATUS	OUT STATUS	EC
0/1/0:23	01	xcc-voice	up	dorm	none	none	y
0/1/0:23	02	xcc-voice	up	dorm	none	none	y

```
0/1/0:23        03   xcc-voice   up    dorm none    none    y
0/1/0:23        04   xcc-voice   up    dorm none    none    y
0/1/0:23        05   xcc-voice   up    dorm none    none    y
0/1/0:23        06   xcc-voice   up    dorm none    none    y
0/1/0:23        07   xcc-voice   up    dorm none    none    y
0/1/0:23        08   xcc-voice   up    dorm none    none    y
0/1/0:23        09   xcc-voice   up    dorm none    none    y
0/1/0:23        10   xcc-voice   up    dorm none    none    y
0/1/0:23        11   xcc-voice   up    dorm none    none    y
0/1/0:23        12   xcc-voice   up    dorm none    none    y
0/1/0:23        13   xcc-voice   up    dorm none    none    y
0/1/0:23        14   xcc-voice   up    dorm none    none    y
0/1/0:23        15   xcc-voice   up    dorm none    none    y
0/1/0:23        16   xcc-voice   up    dorm none    none    y
0/1/0:23        17   xcc-voice   up    dorm none    none    y
0/1/0:23        18   xcc-voice   up    dorm none    none    y
0/1/0:23        19   xcc-voice   up    dorm none    none    y
0/1/0:23        20   xcc-voice   up    dorm none    none    y
0/1/0:23        21   xcc-voice   up    dorm none    none    y
0/1/0:23        22   xcc-voice   up    dorm none    none    y
0/1/0:23        23   xcc-voice   up    dorm none    none    y


PWR FAILOVER PORT          PSTN FAILOVER PORT
=================          ==================

Router#
```

Notice that all the ports are labeled as port 0/1/0:23, indicating that timeslot 23 is the out-of-band signaling channel. Keep this in mind as we configure the dial peers in the next section.

Configuring POTS Dial Peers for T1 PRI Ports

In this section, we're going to configure the pri-group for a full T1 and then configure a POTS dial peer for off-network calling using a very basic destination pattern. There is very little difference between configuring a T1 PRI POTS dial peer and any other POTS dial peer, as you will see here:

```
Router(config-dial-peer)#dial-peer voice 91 pots
Router(config-dial-peer)#destination-pattern 91..........
Router(config-dial-peer)#port 0/1/0:23
Router(config-dial-peer)#end
Router#
```

The one difference in the PRI setup is the :23 that specifies the D timeslot of the PRI circuit. This is because all of the channels within the PRI are labeled as port 0/1/0:23, as we saw previously in the show voice port summary command.

Now that we have the POTS dial-peer configurations taken care of, let's move on to configuring VoIP dial peers.

Configuring VoIP Dial Peers over WAN Connections

Now that we've covered how to configure physical analog and digital ports and pair them with POTS dial peers, we're going to move on to how to utilize an IP WAN circuit and VoIP dial peers for transporting voice from one voice gateway to another. Because this book focuses mainly on voice-configuration topics, I'm going to assume you know how to configure IP WAN interfaces. From a voice standpoint, it really doesn't matter what physical medium your WAN link uses. It could be point-to-point data T1s, SONET, Opt-E-MAN, MPLS, or any other IP technology, as long as it runs IP; the only thing you have to consider is bandwidth and delay requirements for voice. That being said, we're going to mostly focus on configuring VoIP dial peers across the WAN links using various options available to us.

We're going to create a point-to-point scenario in which we have a two-site WAN environment. The WAN is set up with a P2P link between two CUCM Express routers. See Figure 7.6 for a visual representation of our scenario:

FIGURE 7.6   An example of a VoIP WAN dial-peer gateway

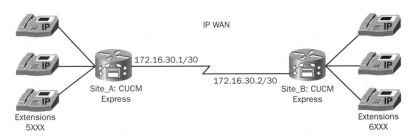

We can send calls across the IP WAN connection by configuring VoIP dial peers. Figure 7.6 shows that all extensions at Site_A are within the 5XXX range and extensions configured at Site_B are in the 6XXX range. We first must configure a VoIP dial peer and use a unique tag to identify it. Let's assume we are on the CUCM Express router at Site_A. We will configure a VoIP dial peer with the 6000 tag, as follows:

```
Site_A#configure terminal
Site_A(config)#dial-peer voice 6000 voip
Site_A(config-dial-peer)#
```

At this point, we need to configure our VoIP dial-peer options. You should be familiar with three important configuration steps:

- Destination pattern
- Session target
- Codec type

The destination pattern of a VoIP dial peer is identical to the POTS dial peer. This is the command used to identify a number or range of numbers that are to be directed over the WAN link. In our example, we will use the wildcard of 6..., which means that all four-digit extensions beginning with 6 are sent over the IP WAN to Site_B. Also remember that you must add the no digit-strip command so all digits are sent over to the remote CUCM Express:

```
Site_A(config-dial-peer)#destination-pattern 6...
Site_B(config-dial-peer)#no digit-strip
```

The *session target* command is similar to the POTS port dial peer command. It tells the dial peer that calls matching the defined destination pattern should be sent to the IP address listed in the session target. Using our example, we'll configure Site_A to forward calls to the IP address of the WAN interface configured on the CUCM Express of Site_B, which is 172.16.30.2:

```
Site_A(config-dial-peer)#session target ipv4:172.16.30.2
```

> The session target command lets you configure session targets using the IP address or DNS name. To configure using a DNS name, the syntax is as follows:
> Router(config-dial-peer)#session target dns:<dns-name>
> If you want to use DNS names for targets, you must ensure that your CUCM Express or voice gateway has a name server configured on it so it can perform DNS lookups. To configure a DNS server, you use the ip name-server <ip address> command.

The final VoIP configuration option that needs mentioning is the codec type. This is where you can set the codec you wish to use over the IP WAN link. The following output shows all of the different codec options available:

```
Router(config-dial-peer)#codec ?
  clear-channel  Clear Channel 64000 bps (No voice capabilities: data transport
                 only)
  g711alaw       G.711 A Law 64000 bps
```

```
g711ulaw        G.711 u Law 64000 bps
g722-48         G722-48K 64000 bps - Only supported for H.320<->H.323 calls
g722-56         G722-56K 64000 bps - Only supported for H.320<->H.323 calls
g722-64         G722-64K 64000 bps
g723ar53        G.723.1 ANNEX-A 5300 bps (contains built-in vad that cannot be
                disabled)
g723ar63        G.723.1 ANNEX-A 6300 bps (contains built-in vad that cannot be
                disabled)
g723r53         G.723.1 5300 bps
g723r63         G.723.1 6300 bps
g726r16         G.726 16000 bps
g726r24         G.726 24000 bps
g726r32         G.726 32000 bps
g728            G.728 16000 bps
g729br8         G.729 ANNEX-B 8000 bps (contains built-in vad that cannot be
                disabled)
g729r8          G.729 8000 bps
ilbc            iLBC 13330 or 15200 bps
```

```
Router(config-dial-peer)#codec
```

Depending on the amount of bandwidth on your WAN, you may want to use a codec that is optimal for low-bandwidth links (codec choices were discussed in Chapter 3). For our example, we'll set the codec to g729br8:

```
Site_A(config-dial-peer)#codec g729br8
```

That's all we need to do to configure the VoIP dial peer on Site_A. Let's move over to the CUCM Express on Site_B and configure a dial peer so users at Site_B will send calls destined to extensions 5XXX over the WAN to Site_A:

```
Site_B#configure terminal
Site_B(config)#dial-peer voice 6000 voip
Site_B(config-dial-peer)#destination-pattern 5...
Site_B(config-dial-peer)#no digit-strip
Site_B(config-dial-peer)#session target ipv4:172.16.30.1
Site_B(config-dial-peer)#codec g729br8
Site_B(config-dial-peer)#end
Site_B#
```

Now we have a fully operational VoIP dial peer that routes internal extension calls between the two sites over an IP WAN. Next we're going to look at how we should plan our dialing strategy to meet current and future needs in a way to ensure that our dial-peer destination patterns remain fairly simple.

Dial-Plan Strategy

You've already learned that phone routing decisions are made using either POTS or VoIP dial peers. More specifically, the routing decision is made in the destination patterns within the dial peers. Once the telephone number decision is made at the destination-pattern level, the dial peer is assigned a port (for POTS dial peers) or a session target address (for VoIP dial peers) where the calls are directed to.

When you begin to roll out a new voice system, you should take care to ensure that you have a solid plan in place for the assignment of internal and external DID numbers. If you begin to randomly assign numbers to users without a plan, you may find that you need to create very elaborate dial-plan destination patterns to route calls properly. Obviously you should avoid doing this. If you plan your dial-peer strategy for not only today's needs but future needs, you should be able to have a fairly simple dial-peer structure that doesn't require fancy wildcard setups or intensive digit manipulation. Let's look at a fictitious company voice network as depicted in Figure 7.7.

FIGURE 7.7   The voice network where we'll implement a dial-plan strategy

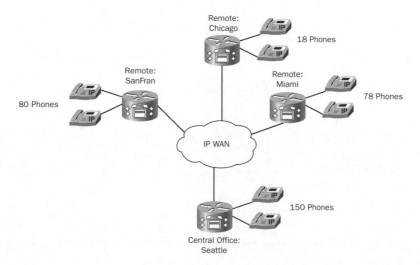

Here we have a central office with three remote sites. All of the sites have WAN connections back to the central office located in Seattle. They're using a distributed call-processing design, so each office has its own call manager. The Seattle central office currently has 150 phones and isn't expected to grow much over the next five years. The San Francisco office has 80 phones, and expected growth over five years is 5 percent. The Miami office has 12 phones and expects a 10 percent growth in five years. The Chicago office currently has 18 phones and is not expected to grow any further. Finally, an additional four remote offices are expected to pop up throughout the United States, bringing the total number of offices to nine. These new offices will have approximately 5 phones each. Our job is to take the current and expected growth states into account and plan our internal dialing structure. One additional requirement given is that the company desires to use three-digit extensions.

The idea behind a dial-plan strategy is to be able to efficiently route calls between the remote sites with the fewest number of `destination-pattern` commands. Given our restriction of three-digit extensions, we have approximately 800 numbers to play with and break up as we choose. Table 7.3 shows how the 800 number limit was derived.

TABLE 7.3 Three-digit dialing scope

Extension Range	Availability
0XX	Not available: used for operator
1XX	Available
2XX	Available
3XX	Available
4XX	Available
5XX	Available
6XX	Available
7XX	Available
8XX	Available
9XX	Not available: used for off-network and 911

Generally, it's best practice to exclude all internal extension numbers beginning with 0 and 9 so they can be used for operator and off-network/911 service dialing.

Because we want our dial-plan strategy to be usable in the future, we need to do some simple math to determine the approximate state of our voice endpoints across the multiple sites five years down the road, as shown in Table 7.4.

TABLE 7.4 Extension requirements (five-year plan)

Site Name	IP Endpoints
Seattle	150
SanFran	84
Miami	13
Chicago	18
New Site 1	5
New Site 2	5
New Site 3	5
New Site 4	5

This gives us a total of 285 endpoints. With 800 extension numbers available, this should be no problem, right? Your first thought might be to assign the one of the first digits to each location and call it a day. The Seattle office would receive 1XX numbers, SanFran would receive 2XX, and so on. The problem with this is that there are only 100 usable extensions per block. Because the Seattle office requires 150 extensions, they'll need to have two of these blocks. A second problem is that we need to plan for growth for up to nine remote sites. Unfortunately, we have only eight usable blocks of 100 numbers. One obvious option would be to dump the three-digit extension requirement and go with four- or even five-digit extensions. But to prove that we can fairly easily create destination patterns in this scenario using three-digit extensions, we're going to stick with this rule. What we can do is plan for blocks of 100 extensions for some locations and blocks of 10 numbers for others. This way, we can properly segment the dial plan to meet our needs. Table 7.5 lists a suggested breakdown of a dial-plan strategy that meets the needs of our example company.

TABLE 7.5 A dial-plan strategy

Site Name	IP Endpoints	Extension Blocks
Seattle	150	1XX, 2XX
SanFran	84	3XX
Miami	13	40X, 41X
Chicago	18	42X, 43X

TABLE 7.5   A dial-plan strategy (*continued*)

Site Name	IP Endpoints	Extension Blocks
New Site 1	5	44X
New Site 2	5	45X
New Site 3	5	46X
New Site 4	5	47X

Using this *dial-plan strategy*, we've successfully fit our 285 endpoints into a three-digit extension plan with room for growth. Now that you understand the importance of a dial-plan strategy, we can explore the details of how voice routers make call-routing decisions.

If you purchase blocks of DIDs from the PSTN, you may or may not be able to get contiguous blocks, as shown in our example. This example is a simplified scenario intended to give you an understanding of why it is important to have a dial-plan strategy.

Understanding the Dial-Peer Decision-Making Process

The process of routing voice calls boils down to understanding the decisions made for handling both outbound and inbound dial peers. At each call leg, an inbound and outbound match must be made prior to forwarding the call to the next call leg. *Inbound dial peers* come into the voice gateway, and *outbound dial peers* leave the voice gateway. This section will discuss the dial-peer attributes and call-setup elements that voice gateways use to make matches.

The Selection Process for Outbound Dial Peers

The outbound dial-peer decision-making process is the easiest to understand. To match outbound dial peers, the router uses the destination pattern to match the phone number. Once a match is made, it then uses either the port number or the IP session target to forward the call to the next destination. You should understand the two rules the router follows in determining the best destination pattern to use:

1. The router will always choose the most specific destination pattern.

2. Once a match is found, the router will immediately route the call.

To better understand these two rules, let's look at an example. On our CUCM Express, we have four configured dial peers with the following destination patterns:

Dial-peer 1: 555[4-7] . . .

Dial-peer 2: 5554 . . .

Dial-peer 3: 5555 . . .

Dial-peer 4: 5555

Now let's say that a call is made on the CUCM Express to 555-6712. Looking at our dial-peer options, the number matches only dial-peer 1, and the call is forwarded to the port or session target configured for that dial peer.

A second call is made to 555-4213. Now dial-peer 1 and dial-peer 2 are in the decision-making process because the number fits into both wildcard scenarios. Because of rule 1 stated previously, the router will choose dial-peer 2 as its best option. This is because dialpeer 2 matches 1000 different numbers within its wildcard setup, whereas dial-peer 1 matches 4000 different numbers. The most specific pattern wins, so in this case it's dial-peer 2.

Finally, a third call is made to 555-5111. This time the number matches dial-peers 1, 3, and 4. Even though seven digits were dialed, the first four digits were an exact match on dial-peer 4. According to rule 2, once a match is found, the router immediately routes the call. Therefore, the final three digits play no role in determining the best destination pattern to use and may not be sent.

Selection Process for Inbound Dial Peers

A voice gateway can utilize information found in call setup messages when a call arrives at a voice gateway and matches this information against one of four dial-peer attributes you can configure. First we'll look at the types of call setup information we can gain from inbound setup messages; then you'll see how to match this information against the dial-peer attributes.

Inbound Dial-Peer Call-Setup Information

Depending on the type of connection your inbound dial peers are being received on, the following call setup information can be used to route calls correctly based on inbound dial peers:

Dialed Number Identification Service The DNIS is a number or extension that represents the destination number the calling party wants to reach. DNIS is found only within Q.931 (ISDN BRI and PRI) and CAS signaling. Analog ports do not carry DNIS information.

Automatic Number Identification The *Automatic Number Identification (ANI)* is a number or extension that represents the originating phone number. It is also referred to as caller ID.

Inbound Port This is the port number that a POTS call comes in on.

Inbound Dial-Peer Configuration Attributes

We can gather the call setup information to help match our inbound call leg. Once we have this information, we can match it against one of the four following dial-peer configuration attributes. They are listed in the order in which the voice gateway checks them. As soon as a match is made, the call is checked against the next outbound dial peer:

1. `incoming called-number`   The number configured in this command is matched against the DNIS if one is provided in the setup message.

2. `answer-address`   The number configured in this command is matched against the ANI if one is provided in the setup message.

3. `destination-pattern`   The number configured in this command is matched against the ANI if one is provided in the setup message.

4. `port`   The port configured in this command is matched against the port that the inbound call is made on if the call comes from a POTS line.

An inbound dial peer must have at least one match before it can move on to the next call leg. If none of the four dial-peer configuration attributes match, there is a fifth "default" dial peer, known as dial-peer 0. It is explained in detail in the next section.

When All Else Fails: Dial-Peer 0

Dial-peer 0 (or pid 0) is the last-resort method that POTS and/or VoIP inbound dial peers are matched with if the first four methods do not provide a match. It is needed because the inbound dial peer must match something if the call is to move on to the next call leg. Unfortunately, if no match is found using the first four attributes, you have to play by the dial-peer 0 default rules, which cannot be modified. Following are the dial-peer 0 rules, which, as you will see, likely won't be the optimal choice for your voice calls:

- Uses any voice codec that the router can understand for VoIP dial peers.

- No Resource Reservation Protocol (RSVP) support for VoIP dial peers. This feature can reserve bandwidth along the call path to ensure that there is sufficient bandwidth.

- Uses fax-rate voice settings. This limits the amount of bandwidth available to fax calls to the absolute minimum.

- Does not use DTMF relay or any other nondefault voice-network capabilities that can offer a more stable network infrastructure and thus ensure higher-quality calls. This is true for both POTS and VoIP dial peers. The only difference is that VAD on VoIP dial peers is enabled by default using dial-peer 0.

- No DID support. You cannot use DIDs to forward off-network calls to on-network phones.

- No Interactive Voice Response (IVR) support for POTS dial peers.

Because most of these default settings are probably not ideal for your voice calls, you should make sure that you attempt to match one of the four dial-peer configurations listed previously.

Dial-Peer Digit Manipulation

The process of *digit manipulation* converts a dialed number into a different number to reach the intended destination. There are many reasons to manipulate digits on your voice system. You can manipulate dialed numbers by addition, subtraction, or substitution. Listed here are some more common reasons:

- To translate a full PSTN number (such as a 10-digit E.164 number) to a shorter extension so both internal and external calls can be made to a single extension.
- To have users dial an access code for PSTN calls. This access code must then be stripped prior to actually placing the call on the PSTN.
- To block calls to specific numbers.
- To redirect calls to specific numbers.

The CUCM Express has several methods for manipulating numbers the way the administrator wants them. This next section will cover digit-manipulation commands including the following:

- `digit-strip`
- `prefix`
- `forward-digits`
- `num-exp`
- `translation-profile`

Let's look at each of these and use them in some situations that you will encounter in the real world.

POTS Digit Manipulation Using Stripped Digits

When you configure a dial peer using wildcards, the leftmost digits in the destination pattern that are explicitly defined are stripped off. This is because dial-peer statements have digit stripping enabled by default. Here is an example POTS dial-peer configuration:

```
Router_A#configure terminal
Router_A(config)#dial-peer voice 10 pots
Router_A(config-dial-peer)#destination-pattern 555....
```

```
Router_A(config-dial-peer)#port 1/0:1
Router_A(config-dial-peer)#end
Router_A#
```

This is a simple POTS dial peer that matches any dialed number beginning with 555. When a call comes in that is destined for 555-1212, it matches the destination pattern and is forwarded out port 1/0:1. Before the call is sent out the port along the call leg, the leftmost explicitly defined digits are stripped, because *digit stripping* is enabled. This means that only 1212 will be sent out port 1/0:1. For some situations, this may be desired. But in other circumstances, you may want to send the 555 on the outbound call leg. To accomplish this, we can add a `no digit-strip` command within the dial-peer statement. Here is what the full configuration should look like if you want to send all seven digits out the call leg:

```
Router_A#configure terminal
Router_A(config)#dial-peer voice 10 pots
Router_A(config-dial-peer)#destination-pattern 555...
Router_A(config-dial-peer)#no digit-strip
Router_A(config-dial-peer)#port 1/0:1
Router_A(config-dial-peer)#end
Router_A#
```

POTS Digit Manipulation Using Prefixes

Digit prefix is the process of adding additional digits and/or pauses to the beginning of the dialed number prior to passing it on. This can be useful in situations where you need to add in specific digits that may have been stripped off when digit stripping is active in a dial peer. Let's look at an example where a DID number comes into the CUCM Express as 1-312-555-4773. The internal extension structure is configured for five-digit dialing. Therefore we need to end up with 54773 as the number we wish to pass on. Here's the POTS dial peer that we have configured:

```
Router_B#configure terminal
Router_B(config)#dial-peer voice 50 pots
Router_B(config-dial-peer)#destination-pattern 131255.....
Router_B(config-dial-peer)#port 1/0:1
Router_B(config-dial-peer)#end
Router_B#
```

Because digit stripping is enabled, the CUCM Express will pass on only the last four digits instead of the required five digits. To remedy this, we can use the `prefix <number-string>` command to add our needed digit back in. Following is the full configuration with the included `prefix` command:

```
Router_B#configure terminal
Router_B(config)#dial-peer voice 50 pots
Router_B(config-dial-peer)#destination-pattern 131255.....
Router_B(config-dial-peer)#prefix 5
Router_B(config-dial-peer)#port 1/0:1
Router_B(config-dial-peer)#end
Router_B#
```

Now our router can successfully pass on the required five digits for proper internal extension dialing.

A second popular use for the `prefix` command is to add the number 9 to the beginning of a dialed number so the router can use an outside line for off-network dialing. Let's look at this example:

```
Router_B#configure terminal
Router_B(config)#dial-peer voice 1 pots
Router_B(config-dial-peer)#destination-pattern 131255.....
Router_B(config-dial-peer)#no digit-strip
Router_B(config-dial-peer)#prefix 9,
Router_B(config-dial-peer)#port 1/1:1
Router_B(config-dial-peer)#end
Router_B#
```

Here you can see that we're going to match 1312555 and then the 4 wildcard digits after that. As you can see, we do not have digit stripping configured, so all the digits will be sent to the PSTN. In addition, we have a prefix configured to add 9, to the beginning of the string. The 9 allows for off-network calling for PSTN calls. The comma (,) is called a pause and informs the router to wait for one second before continuing to dial digits. In this situation, the voice gateway will dial 9 and pause for one second. This allows time for the PSTN to interpret the 9 as a signal to provide a second dial tone for off-network dialing. After the voice gateway pauses, it continues to dial the remaining 11 digits.

POTS Digit Manipulation Using Forward-Digits

You have already learned that you can disable the default digit stripping of leftmost explicit digits in a POTS dial-peer destination pattern. But what if you want only a certain number of leftmost digits to remain? A handy command for this is the `forward-digits number` command. With the *forward digits* command, you can inform the voice gateway to forward either all digits received or a specific number of rightmost digits. Let's say that you have the following POTS dial peer configured:

```
Router_C#configure terminal
Router_C(config)#dial-peer voice 5 pots
Router_C(config-dial-peer)#destination-pattern 91312.......
```

```
Router_C(config-dial-peer)#port 1/0:1
Router_C(config-dial-peer)#end
Router_C#
```

By default, the voice gateway will strip off 91312 and forward only the 7 remaining digits. We want to be able to forward the 312 to the PSTN. Therefore, we can use the forward-digits POTS dial-peer command to let the voice gateway know that we want the last 10 dialed digits to be sent out the port. Here is the full POTS dial-peer configuration to accomplish this goal:

```
Router_C#configure terminal
Router_C(config)#dial-peer voice 5 pots
Router_C(config-dial-peer)#destination-pattern 91312.......
Router_C(config-dial-peer)#forward-digits 10
Router_C(config-dial-peer)#port 1/0:1
Router_C(config-dial-peer)#end
Router_C#
```

POTS and VoIP Digit Manipulation Using Number Expansion

The num-exp command is a global configuration command that you can use to match either POTS or VoIP strings and change the number to anything you want. One good example of *number expansion* is translating from extension numbers to full E.164 DIDs. In most PBX environments configured today, internal dialing between phones that are both on network can be accomplished by dialing a shortened extension as opposed to the full DID number. Typically the internal extension is 3 to 5 digits in length. Let's say that our ephone-DNs are configured with the full E.164 10-digit number, as shown with these two example ephone-DN configurations:

```
Router_D#configure terminal
Router_D(config)#ephone-dn 1
Router_D(config-ephone-dn)#number 7735553784
Router_D(config-ephone-dn)#ephone-dn 2
Router_D(config-ephone-dn)#number 7735553991
Router_D(config-ephone-dn)#exi
Router_D(config)#ephone 1
Router_D(config-ephone)#button 1:1
Router_D(config-ephone)#ephone 2
Router_D(config-ephone)#button 1:2
Router_D(config-ephone)#end
Router_D#
```

Now when ephone 1 wants to call ephone 2, the user must dial the full 10-digit E.164 number to reach the destination. One way to get around this problem and allow users to dial the preferred 4-digit extensions is to use the num-exp command. Because the first 7 digits (7735553) match both of our ephone-DNs, we can use the 7th digit for matching and prepend the additional 6-dial string to match the full 10-digit ephone-DN. Here is how to configure num-exp on a voice gateway to solve our example problem:

```
Router_D#configure terminal
Router_D(config)#num-exp 3... 7735553...
Router_D(config)#exit
```

Now the user at ephone 1 can dial 3991 and have the 6 additional digits added, which will match ephone-DN 2 and ultimately ring ephone 2.

You can also completely change a number with the num-exp command. Let's say we have the following POTS dial peer configured:

```
Router_E#configure terminal
Router_E(config)#dial-peer voice 5 pots
Router_E(config-dial-peer)#destination-pattern 5040
Router_E(config-dial-peer)#port 1/0:1
Router_E(config-dial-peer)#end
Router_E#
```

The user at this extension wants to forward to 7447, which a POTS dial peer configured on the voice gateway. We can do the following to forward all calls that match 5040 to 7447:

```
Router_E#configure terminal
Router_E(config)#num-exp 5040 7447
Router_E(config)#exit
```

To verify that your num-exp configurations are correct, you can use the show dialplan number <number-string> command to verify that your phone number properly maps to a dial peer, as follows:

```
Router_E#show dialplan number 5040
Macro Exp.: 7447

VoiceOverIpPeer7447
        peer type = voice, system default peer = FALSE, information type = voice,
        description = `',
        tag = 7447, destination-pattern = `7447',
[output cut]
```

> The show dialplan number <number-string> command can be used in verifying more than just show num-exp manipulations. This command is useful anytime you want to verify which outgoing dial peer is reached when a particular number is dialed.

You can also run a show num-exp to see all of the extension numbers you have mapped to expanded numbers, as shown here:

```
Router_E#show num-exp
Dest Digit Pattern = '5040'     Translation =
                                '7447'

Router_E#
```

POTS and VoIP Digit Manipulation Using Translation Profiles

Translation profiles work similarly to access control lists (ACL) on a router. With access lists, you create a unique ACL and provide permit and deny statements. You then apply the ACL to a router interface using the access-group command.

Translation profiles use the same approach as ACLs. Your first task is to create voice-translation rules with a unique tag for identification. Each voice-translation rule can contain up to 15 rules. The next step is to create a voice-translation profile and set the rules to be used for called or calling numbers. Lastly, the voice-translation profile is applied to the POTS or VoIP dial peer, using the translation-profile dial-peer command. It can also be set globally on the voice gateway if you desire. This profile can be applied to incoming or outgoing calls on the dial peer.

Translation profiles are extremely flexible and can be used to provide more granular control over modification scenarios than the other digit-manipulation tools previously described. The creation of a translation profile is a simple matter of entering into configuration mode and using the translation-profile *number* command, where you can tag the rule set by number. This example creates translation rule 1:

```
Router_F#configure terminal
Router_F(config)#voice translation-rule 1
Router_F(cfg-translation-rule)#
```

At this point, we are in cfg-translation-rule mode. Here we can create the individual rules that reside in translation rule 1. The proper syntax for this is

```
rule <1-15> /match-number-string/ /replacement-number-string/
```

Let's configure a few rules to match extensions 3111, 4111, and 5111 and set them all to 6000:

```
Router_F(cfg-translation-rule)#rule 1 /3111/ /6000/
Router_F(cfg-translation-rule)#rule 2 /4111/ /6000/
Router_F(cfg-translation-rule)#rule 3 /5111/ /6000/
Router_F(cfg-translation-rule)#exit
Router_F(config)#
```

> Keep in mind that it doesn't matter what digits precede the match numbers. The router is looking for this sequence anywhere it can. Therefore, if you were to dial 5553111 on an interface where this translation rule is applied, it would change the entire number to 6000.

Now that we have created our translation rules, we need to apply them to a voice-translation profile. We can select whether we want the profile to translate for called, calling, redirect-called, or redirect-target numbers. Here's an example of how to configure a voice-translation profile labeled to_6000 that includes all the rules from voice-translation rule 1:

```
Router_F(config)#voice translation-profile to_6000
Router_F(cfg-translation-profile)#translate ?
  called          Translation rule for the called-number
  calling         Translation rule for the calling-number
  redirect-called Translation rule for the redirect-number
  redirect-target Translation rule for the redirect-target

Router_F(cfg-translation-profile)#translate called 1
Router_F(cfg-translation-profile)#exit
Router_F(config)#
```

We have defined our voice-translation rules and have inserted those rules into a voice-translation profile, which specifies called or calling translations. We have yet to apply this voice-translation profile to anything, however. This is similar to creating a router ACL but not applying it to an interface. The final step is to use the translation-profile command to apply the voice-translation profile either to a POTS/VoIP dial peer or to an individual ephone-DN. The profile can be configured to translate for either incoming or outgoing call legs. In our example, we will configure a POTS dial peer to use the to_6000 voice-translation pattern on incoming calls. Here is the syntax:

```
Router_F(config)#dial-peer voice 100 pots
Router_F(config-dial-peer)#translation-profile ?
  incoming  Translation Profile for incoming call leg
  outgoing  Translation Profile for outgoing call leg

Router_F(config-dial-peer)#translation-profile incoming to_6000
Router_F(config-dial-peer)#end
Router_F#
```

> **NOTE** The rules can be applied to both incoming and outgoing call legs if you wish. You need to have both configurations set to do so.

We can verify that our voice-translation rules actually work as described by issuing the test voice translation-rule privileged exec command. Here you can see that all three of our numbers configured in rule 1 are converted to 6000:

```
Router_F#test voice translation-rule 1 3111
Matched with rule 1
Original number: 3111    Translated number: 6000
Original number type: none       Translated number type: none
Original number plan: none       Translated number plan: none

Router_F#test voice translation-rule 1 4111
Matched with rule 2
Original number: 4111    Translated number: 6000
Original number type: none       Translated number type: none
Original number plan: none       Translated number plan: none

Router_F#test voice translation-rule 1 5111
Matched with rule 3
Original number: 5111    Translated number: 6000
Original number type: none       Translated number type: none
Original number plan: none       Translated number plan: none
```

 Real World Scenario

VoIP to PSTN Failover Using Digit Manipulation and Preference Commands

Alexander is a lead IPT design consultant at a Cisco VAR. A customer based in Chicago recently approached him to discuss a problem that arose after an outage took down all PSTN lines at the company's Denver location. Both sites use the PSTN for all off-network calls. Because of the PSTN outage, employees in the Denver and Chicago locations could not communicate with each other over the phone. The company is looking for a way to provide redundancy using the established IP WAN that connects the two sites for data.

The solution that Alexander came up with was to utilize the WAN link for all calls between the two locations and to fall back to the PSTN lines only if there is an outage. Not only will this create a second path, which provides for high availability, it will also lower the PSTN costs because calls will be routed over the IP WAN and no long-distance charges will be incurred. The following diagram shows the new CUCM environment; you can see the redundancy that the new VoIP to PSTN failover design offers.

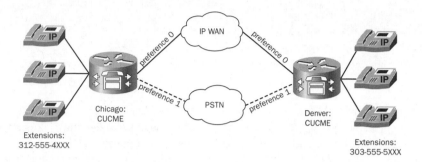

Using the preference command, Alexander can set the primary dial-peer path to be the IP WAN connection. If the WAN were to go down for some reason, the dial-peer would select the next-highest-preferred dial peer, which is the PSTN. Following are the configuration options that Alexander needed to add to each CUCM Express in Denver to configure redundant dial peers:

```
Denver-CUCME
Denver-CUCME#configure terminal
Denver-CUCME(config)#dial-peer voice 14000 voip
Denver-CUCME(config-dial-peer)#destination-pattern 4...
Denver-CUCME(config-dial-peer)#session target 172.16.1.1
Denver-CUCME(config-dial-peer)#preference 0
Denver-CUCME(config-dial-peer)#codec g729r8
Denver-CUCME(config-dial-peer)#exit
Denver-CUCME(config)#dial-peer voice 14001 pots
Denver-CUCME(config-dial-peer)#destination-pattern 4...
Denver-CUCME(config-dial-peer)#port 1/1:1
Denver-CUCME(config-dial-peer)#preference 1
Denver-CUCME(config-dial-peer)#prefix 1312555
```

Now on to the Chicago CUCM Express:

```
Chicago-CCME#configure terminal
Chicago-CCME(config)#dial-peer voice 15000 voip
Chicago-CCME(config-dial-peer)#destination-pattern 5...
Chicago-CCME(config-dial-peer)#session target 172.16.1.2
Chicago-CCME(config-dial-peer)#preference 0
Chicago-CCME(config-dial-peer)#codec g729r8
```

```
Chicago-CCME(config-dial-peer)#exit
Chicago-CCME(config)#dial-peer voice 15001 pots
Chicago-CCME(config-dial-peer)#destination-pattern 5...
Chicago-CCME(config-dial-peer)#port 1/1:1
Chicago-CCME(config-dial-peer)#preference 1
Chicago-CCME(config-dial-peer)#prefix 1303555
Chicago-CCME(config-dial-peer)#end
Chicago-CCME#
```

Now both CUCM Express routers will always prefer to send data over the IP WAN. Notice that Alexander is also requiring that any call destined for the IP WAN use the G.729 codec. This codec requires less bandwidth and allows for more simultaneous calls over a fixed-bandwidth link. The problem with H.323 and the G.729 protocol is that by default, H.323 sends the DTMF tones in band. This means that the tones will be compressed along with the voice. Because of the additional compression that G.729 performs, the DTMF tones are often unrecognizable when decompressed on the other side. To get around this problem, Alexander configured both voice gateways to send DTMF out of band using the H.245 standard format. He used the dtmf-relay h245-alphanumeric command to accomplish this. He added the commands to both voice gateways to complete the Denver configuration:

```
Denver-CUCME#configure terminal
Denver-CUCME(config)#dial-peer voice 14000 voip
Denver-CUCME(config-dial-peer)#dtmf-relay h245-alphanumeric
```

And on the Chicago CUCM Express:

```
Chicago-CCME#configure terminal
Chicago-CCME(config)#dial-peer voice 15000 voip
Chicago-CCME(config-dial-peer)#dtmf-relay h245-alphanumeric
```

If the WAN link were to have a failure, the session target IP address listed in the VoIP dial peer would no longer be in the routing table. When this happens, the dial peer is taken out of consideration from the call-routing process. Therefore, the next-highest preference that matches the destination pattern takes precedence. This happens to be the T1 POTS link that he configured at both sites. You'll notice that he used the prefix command to add a 1 and then the area code and office code numbers. These need to be provided to the PSTN so it knows the location of the offices.

Understanding the Digit-Manipulation Hierarchy

In a complex voice environment where dialed strings of numbers may go through multiple types of digit manipulation, you likely begin to question when one digit-manipulation method is run before another method is performed. With all the different digit manipulations occurring, it can get confusing to figure out what the final number will be. Figure 7.8 shows the *digit-manipulation hierarchy*.

FIGURE 7.8 The digit-manipulation hierarchy

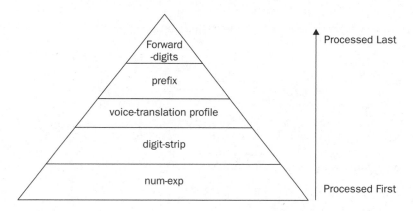

The method at the bottom (num-exp) is applied first. Then the next layer is applied, and so on until you reach the last manipulation process to be applied, which is the forward-digits option. This should help you figure out what happens when a dialed number is subject to two or more digit-manipulation processes.

Configuring a Trunk between Voice Gateways using H.323 and SIP Trunks

You may be surprised to hear this, but you've already seen an H.323 trunk configured between two voice gateways in the "Configuring VoIP Dial Peers over WAN Connections" section of this chapter. In case you missed this little fact, we'll go over how to configure a simple H.323 trunk between two voice gateways. Then you'll see how to configure those same two voice gateways for simple SIP trunking.

H.323 Trunking

Anytime you configure a VoIP dial peer between two voice gateways or CUCM Express systems, by default you are creating an H.323 trunk between the peer systems. Calls are then routed over the IP network when the destination pattern is matched. This type of H.323 trunk is the simplest to implement and it's all you will need to know how to configure within the limits of the CCNA Voice certification. Here is another quick example of how to configure H.323 trunking between voice gateways using the g.711 codec. We'll use Figure 7.9 as our example.

FIGURE 7.9   An example of H.323 gateway communication

Here is the configuration syntax for site A:

```
Site_A#configure terminal
Site_A(config)#dial-peer voice 500 voip
Site_A(config-dial-peer)#destination-pattern 5..
Site_A(config-dial-peer)#codec g711ulaw
Site_A(config-dial-peer)#session target ipv4:10.0.0.2
Site_A(config-dial-peer)#end
Site_A#
```
And here's the configuration for Site_B:

```
Site_B#configure terminal
Site_B(config)#dial-peer voice 400 voip
Site_B(config-dial-peer)#destination-pattern 4..

Site_B(config-dial-peer)#codec g711ulaw
Site_B(config-dial-peer)#session target ipv4:10.0.0.1
Site_B(config-dial-peer)#end
Site_B#
```

SIP Trunking

Configuration of a simple SIP trunk between two voice gateways involves using a command to change the signaling protocol from the default H.323 to SIP version 2. The session protocol sipv2 dial-peer command changes the trunk signaling to the proper format. As soon as the signaling is changed on both sides, your VoIP dial peer will use SIP signaling instead of H.323. Let's configure the same two-site setup as described in Figure 7.9, but this time we'll configure SIP trunking on our dial peers. Here is Site_A:

```
Site_A#configure terminal
Site_A(config)#dial-peer voice 400 voip
Site_A(config-dial-peer)#destination-pattern 4..
Site_A(config-dial-peer)#session protocol sipv2
Site_A(config-dial-peer)#codec g711ulaw
Site_A(config-dial-peer)#session target ipv4:10.0.0.1
Site_A(config-dial-peer)#end
Site_A#
```

And here's Site_B:

```
Site_B#configure terminal
Site_B(config)#dial-peer voice 500 voip
Site_B(config-dial-peer)#destination-pattern 5..
Site_B(config-dial-peer)#session protocol sipv2
Site_B(config-dial-peer)#codec g711ulaw
Site_B(config-dial-peer)#session target ipv4:10.0.0.2
Site_B(config-dial-peer)#end
Site_B#
```

That's really all there is to connecting two Cisco SIP voice gateway peers. Later on in this book, you'll learn how to connect to an ITSP with a SIP trunk and SIP user authentication using the UC500 series CUCM Express.

Summary

Chapter 7 began with a look at how to configure analog interfaces and then how to use POTS dial peers to route calls over the voice ports. We then moved on to discuss how to configure digital T1 CAS and PRI interfaces as well as how to use POTS dial peers to direct calls over the digital connections. Then you saw how to use VoIP dial peers to route calls to remote voice gateways across an IP WAN and learned some dial-plan strategies to help simplify the dial-peer setup and manipulation. We then discussed the voice-gateway decision-making process and various techniques to manipulate that process. Finally, we took a closer look at connecting voice gateways over an IP network using both H.323 and SIP signaling protocols.

While teleporting voice traffic across a voice gateway is not as spectacular as using the starship *Enterprise*'s teleporter, both function on the same principle of deconstructing something into a medium for transport so it can be reconstructed on the other end. Beam me up, Scotty!

Exam Essentials

Know how to configure FXS and FXO analog ports.   Understand how to apply caller-ID names/numbers, call progress tones, ring frequencies, and signaling information to analog interfaces.

Understand the purpose of PLAR. interfaces and how to configure them on FXS and FXO ports for both outbound and inbound calling.   PLAR interfaces create an automatic connection either when a phone goes off-hook (FXS) or when a call comes into the interface (FXO).

Know how to configure POTS dial peers for FXS and FXO analog ports.   With FXS ports, you use the extension number as the destination pattern and apply it to an FXS analog port. With FXO ports, you typically want to match many numbers for routing outbound calls either to the PSTN or another PBX. To match multiple numbers in the fewest destination patterns possible, you utilize dial-peer wildcards.

Know how to configure CAMA-signaled FXO ports for E.911 calling.   CAMA ports connect to a PSAP network rather than the PSTN. These connections use their own signaling protocol.

Know how to configure T1 CAS ports.   Understand the configuration options of framing type, linecode type, clock source, and ds0-group options of T1 CAS interfaces.

Know how to configure T1 PRI ports.   Understand the ISDN switch-type options available to you. Also understand the pri-group options, which set each voice timeslot for TDM. If you configure a fractional T1 PRI, remember that the D channel is always timeslot 23.

Know how to configure POTS dial peers for T1 CAS and PRI circuits.   Dial peers for T1 CAS and PRI circuits are very similar. The main difference is that the T1 PRI circuit always specifies the D channel in the port configuration.

Understand and know how to configure VoIP dial peers.   VoIP dial peers connect voice gateways over an IP network. The configuration process is similar to creating POTS dial peers except that instead of specifying a physical port to send data out of, you specify the IP address of the remote voice gateway.

Understand the necessity of creating a dial-plan strategy.   When designing a voice network, you want to limit the complexity of your dial-peer setups. Therefore, it is important to have a plan in place for phone number assignment in the environment that meets the needs for a business today and into the foreseeable future.

Understand the dial-peer decision-making process.   Know how voice gateways choose to route calls based on inbound and outbound dial peers. Understand how dial-peer 0 functions as the last resort.

Know how to manipulate numbers using digit-manipulation techniques.   Techniques such as digit-strip, prefix, destination-pattern, forward-digits, and translation-profiles can be used to help you forward the exact numbering scheme to the next voice gateway or endpoint.

Know how to configure H.323 and SIP trunks between voice gateways.   By default, creating a VoIP dial peer between two voice gateways results in the setup of an H.323 trunk. You can also easily change that trunk to use SIP signaling using the `session protocol sipv2` config-dial-peer command.

Written Lab 7.1

Write the answers to the following questions:

1. What is the config-voiceport command to set signaling for ground start?

2. What is the config-voiceport command to configure a PLAR to automatically ring extension 2111?

3. What config-dial-peer command tells the voice gateway to send *all* digits to the next call leg?

4. What is the config-controller command to set the framing type to Extended Super Frame?

5. When you want to set your full T1 CAS circuit timeslots to FXO Loop Start, what config-controller command do you enter?

6. You are configuring a T1 PRI circuit. What is the config command to set the ISDN switch to which your circuit connects to `primary-ni`?

7. How do you view a brief summary of the operational status of all of your POTS circuits on a voice gateway?

8. What VoIP config-dial-peer command sets the next call leg to 10.1.1.100?

9. You've just created a translation rule on your voice gateway to translate 401 to 501. How do you verify that the rule is working properly using the command line?

10. What config-dial-peer command sets the trunking signaling protocol to SIP version 2?

   (The answers to Written Lab 7.1 can be found following the answers to the review questions for this chapter.)

Hands-on Labs

To complete the labs in this section, you need a router with a voice-capable IOS, T1 PRI interface, Fast Ethernet interface, and two FXS ports for analog phones. The CUCM Express should be properly set up and ready for configuring IP phones. Each lab in this section builds on the last and follows the logical CUCM Express PBX model design as shown in Figure 7.10.

FIGURE 7.10   Diagram for the voice gateway labs

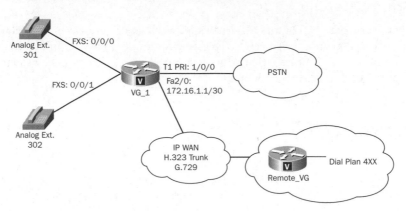

Here is a list of the labs in this chapter:

Lab 7.1: Configuring FXS Interfaces for Two Analog Phones

Lab 7.2: Configuring a T1 PRI Interface

Lab 7.3: Configuring an H.323 Trunk

Lab 7.4: Configuring Translation Profiles

Hands-on Lab 7.1: Configuring FXS Interfaces for Two Analog Phones

In this lab, we're going to configure a voice gateway that has two analog phones connected via FXS ports. The phones are located in the United States, so we can use the default cptone and ring frequencies. Table 7.6 lists the information needed to configure the ports:

TABLE 7.6   Information for port configuration

Extension	Caller-ID Number	Caller-ID Name
301	5558301	Marty Jones
302	5558302	Samantha Wilson

1. Log in to your CUCM Express router, and go into configuration mode by typing **enable** and then **configuration terminal**.

2. Enter config-voiceport mode by typing **voice-port 0/0/0**.

3. Configure FXS port 0/0/0 to have the seven-digit caller-id number by typing **station-id number 5558301**.

4. Enable caller ID by typing **caller-id enable**.

5. Configure FXS port 0/0/0 to have the correct caller-id name by typing **station-id name Marty Jones**.

6. Configure the next FXS port by typing **voice-port 0/0/1**.

7. Configure FXS port 0/0/1 to have the seven-digit caller-id number by typing **station-id number 5558302**.

8. Enter config-voiceport mode for the next FXS interface by typing **voice-port 0/0/0**.

9. Enable caller ID by typing **caller-id enable**.

10. Configure FXS port 0/0/1 to have the correct caller-id name by typing **station-id name Samantha Wilson**.

11. Exit config-voiceport mode by typing **Exit**.

12. Configure a POTS dial peer for FXS port 1 by typing **dial-peer voice 301 pots**. You will now be in config-dial-peer mode.

13. Configure the destination pattern to match the three-digit extension and have the dial peer point to FXS port 0/0/0 by typing **destination-pattern 301** and then **port 0/0/0**.

14. Configure a POTS dial peer for FXS port 2 by typing **dial-peer voice 302 pots**. You will now be in config-dial-peer mode.

15. Configure the destination pattern to match the three-digit extension and have the dial peer point to FXS port 0/0/1 by typing **destination-pattern 302** and then **port 0/0/1**.

16. Exit config-dial-peer mode by typing **end**.

Hands-on Lab 7.2: Configuring a T1 PRI Interface

1. Log in to your CUCM Express router and go into configuration mode by typing **enable** and then **configuration terminal**.

2. Configure the ISDN switch type to be primary-ni by typing **isdn switch-type primary-ni**.

3. Enter into config-controller mode by typing **controller t1 1/0/0**.

4. Set your pri-group to utilize all 23 POTs lines by typing **pri-group timeslots 1-24**.

5. Configure framing and linecoding types by typing **framing esf** and then **linecode b8zs**.

6. Set the T1 to receive clocking from the PSTN equipment by typing **clock source line**.

7. Exit config-controller mode by typing **Exit**.

8. Configure a POTS outbound dial peer for the T1 PRI by typing **dial-peer voice 10 pots**. You will now be in config-dial-peer mode.

9. Configure the destination pattern to match any 10-digit E.164 number and have the dial peer point to the T1 interface port 1/0/0 by typing **destination-pattern 91..........** and then **port 1/0/0:23**.

10. Exit config-dial-peer mode by typing **end**.

Hands-on Lab 7.3: Configuring an H.323 Trunk

This trunk connects to an already configured remote site that uses extensions in the 4XX range. We need to set up the physical Fast Ethernet. Assume that the remote site only has analog phones attached to FXS ports. Therefore, we don't have to worry about routing IP traffic to the remote site.

1. Log in to your CUCM Express router and go into configuration mode by typing **enable** and then **configuration terminal**.

2. Enter config-if mode by typing **interface fa2/0**.

3. Assign an IP address to match the diagram by typing **ip address 172.168.1.1 255.255.255.0**.

4. Exit config-if mode by typing **Exit**.

5. Configure a VoIP outbound dial peer for the WAN link by typing **dial-peer voice 10 pots**. You will now be in config-dial-peer mode.

6. Configure the destination pattern to match any 10-digit E.164 number and have the dial peer point to the T1 interface port 1/0/0 by typing **destination-pattern 91..........** and then **port 1/0/0:23**.

7. Configure a VoIP dial peer for the WAN interface by typing **dial-peer voice 400 voip**. You will now be in config-dial-peer mode.

8. Configure the destination pattern to match the four plus two additional wildcard digits and have the dial peer point to the remote-side WAN IP address of 172.16.1.2 by typing **destination-pattern 4..** and then **session-target ipv4:172.168.1.2**.

9. Make sure that the 4 is not stripped off when the number is sent to the remote voice gateway by typing **no digit-strip**.

10. Force the WAN to use a lower-bandwidth codec by typing **codec g729r8**.

11. Exit config-dial-peer mode by typing **end**.

Hands-on Lab 7.4: Configuring Translation Profiles

In this lab, we're going to configure translation profiles for our two analog phones attached to FXS voice-ports 0/0/0 and 0/0/1. Right now, the phones will ring when the three-digit extension is called. But callers from the PSTN will be dialing DIDs that don't correspond with our extensions. That means when PSTN calls come in, they will not go through, because we don't have a dial peer configured for the DID. To remedy this, we're going to create translation profiles for two PSTN DID numbers (555-4777 and 555-4952), mapping them to the three-digit FXS extensions, which will then be matched against the POTS dial peers we created in Lab 7.1.

1. Log in to your CUCM Express router and go into configuration mode by typing **enable** and then **configuration terminal**.

2. Enter cfg-translation-rule mode by typing **voice translation-rule 1**.

3. Add two rules to translate the seven-digit PSTN DIDs to the three-digit extensions assigned to the FXS interfaces by typing **rule 1 /5554777/ /301/** and then **rule 2 /5554952/ /302/**.

4. Exit cfg-translation-rule mode by typing **Exit**.

5. Enter cfg-translation-profile mode by typing **voice translation-profile from_pstn**.

6. Add our newly configured translation rule (rule 1) for called numbers to the translation profile by typing **translate called 1**.

7. Exit cfg-translation-profile mode by typing **Exit**.

8. Enter config-dial-peer mode for our already created T1 PRI dial peer by typing **dial-peer voice 10 pots**.

9. Add the translation profile (from_pstn) to search for and translate incoming DIDs from the PSTN by typing **translation-profile incoming from_pstn**.

10. Exit config-dial-peer mode by typing **end**.

Review Questions

1. What are the two types of dial peers?
   A. PSTN dial peer
   B. POTS dial peer
   C. VoIP dial peer
   D. IPT dial peer
   E. CUE dial peer

2. Which of the following outbound dial peers will finally be matched when a user at extension 4555 calls 5888?
   A. Destination pattern 4...
   B. Destination pattern 5...
   C. Destination pattern 5T
   D. Destination pattern 4T

3. You want to configure a VoIP target to point to 192.168.18.10. What is the proper syntax?
   A. `voip target ipv4:192.168.18.10`
   B. `session-target 192.168.18.10`
   C. `session target ipv4:192.168.18.10`
   D. `voip-target 192.168.18.10`

4. What type of signaling is commonly configured on FXS ports?
   A. SIPv2
   B. Loop start
   C. Line start
   D. B8zf
   E. Ground start

5. Which two dial-peer configurations will correctly route emergency service calls out CAMA port 1/0/1?

   A. Router(config)#dial-peer voice 911 pots

      Router(config-dial-peer)#destination-pattern .911

      Router(config-dial-peer)#port 1/0/1

   B. Router(config)#dial-peer voice 911pots

      Router(config-dial-peer)#destination-pattern 911

      Router(config-dial-peer)#port 1/0/1

   C. Router(config)#dial-peer voice 911pots

      Router(config-dial-peer)#destination-pattern 9911

      Router(config-dial-peer)#forward-digits all

      Router(config-dial-peer)#port 1/0/1

   D. Router(config)#dial-peer voice 911pots

      Router(config-dial-peer)#destination-pattern 911

      Router(config-dial-peer)#forward-digits all

      Router(config-dial-peer)#port 1/0/1

   E. Router(config)#dial-peer voice 911pots

      Router(config-dial-peer)#destination-pattern 9911

      Router(config-dial-peer)#prefix 911

      Router(config-dial-peer)#port 1/0/1

6. What term defines the need to modify the voltage of analog FXS endpoints to match the phones that require a different setting to properly ring?

   A. Ring frequency

   B. Cptone

   C. Dial plan

   D. DTMF

7. What describes the function when a user picks up a phone handset and the phone automatically dials a preconfigured extension?

   A. PLAR

   B. CAMA

   C. SRST

   D. Call leg

8. When configuring FXO dial-type, what two options do you have?

   A. POTS

   B. VoIP

   C. Pulse

   D. DTMF

9. What does the FXO interface command `ring number` do?

    A. Defines the outbound PSTN number to call

    B. Sets the ring frequency

    C. Sets the number of rings before the voice gateway answers the incoming call

    D. Sets the number of rings before the voice gateway forwards the call

10. What command can be used within a dial-peer statement to ensure that all digits are forwarded to the destination?

    A. `forward-digits all`

    B. `no digit-strip`

    C. `no prefix`

    D. `destination-pattern T`

11. What configuration setup is commonly configured on FXO ports to forward incoming calls to an operator or auto attendant?

    A. `digit-strip`

    B. PLAR

    C. `no digit-strip`

    D. CAMA

12. When you physically install T1 hardware on your voice gateway, what type of interfaces will your T1 interfaces be described as?

    A. Digital-port

    B. Session

    C. Controller

    D. Service-module

13. What term describes how an administrator determines where a T1 circuit will receive clocking information?

    A. NTP

    B. Time/date stamp

    C. Clock source

    D. Clock linecode

14. What global configuration option must be performed for T1 PRI circuits to communicate properly with the PSTN or connected PBX?

    A. Enable SIP signaling

    B. Enable SCCP signaling

    C. Set the E&M controller

    D. Set the ISDN switch type

15. What T1 PRI timeslot is always used as the destination port when configuring dial peers?

 A. Timeslot 1

 B. Timeslot 24

 C. Timeslot 30

 D. Timeslot 23

16. What is the VoIP equivalent to the POTS dial-peer `port` command?

 A. `destination-pattern`

 B. `session target`

 C. `ip route`

 D. `codec`

17. Why is it important to design a flexible dial-plan strategy for your network?

 A. To prevent routing loops.

 B. To comply with strictly enforced ITU-T E.164 guidelines.

 C. To efficiently route calls between sites with the fewest number of `destination-pattern` commands.

 D. Your PSTN or ITSP provider will give you your dial plan strategy. You simply need to follow their design.

18. Which POTS circuits carry DNIS information? Choose all that apply.

 A. FXO

 B. ISDN BRI

 C. ISDN PRI

 D. CAS T1

19. What is the default VoIP trunk-signaling protocol used on Cisco voice gateways?

 A. SIP

 B. MGCP

 C. H.323

 D. SCCP

20. Within the voice-gateway digit-manipulation hierarchy, which method is always applied last?

 A. Translation profile

 B. Digit-strip

 C. Destination-pattern

 D. Forward-digits

 E. Number expansion

Answers to Review Questions

1. B, C. The two types of dial peers are POTS and VoIP.

2. B. You can narrow the answer down to B and C based on the first digit matching the destination pattern. B is the more exact choice because it specifies that the extension is four digits in length.

3. C. The proper command syntax is `session target ipv4:192.168.18.10`.

4. B. FXS ports are most commonly configured with loop start signaling.

5. D, E. Don't forget that explicit matches are not forwarded to the destination. That means you must use the `forward-digits` command to send the three digits of 911 or use the `prefix` command to explicitly send 911 to the destination.

6. A. Changing the ring frequency informs the voice gateway what type of analog device is being used. Depending on where you are located, different phones use different ring frequencies, which are measured in Hertz.

7. A. A private line automatic ringdown (PLAR) acts as a hotline phone. When the phone goes off-hook, it will ring an extension without any user interaction.

8. C, D. The `dial-type` command deals with the type of digit signaling the port expects to hear from the PSTN. The two options are DTMF and pulse dialing.

9. C. The ring number signifies the maximum number of rings the voice gateway waits before answering the call.

10. B. The `no digit-strip` command ensures that all digits including those explicitly defined are forwarded to the destination.

11. B. PLAR is often used so the FXO interface answers the call directly on the port and immediately forwards it to the operator extension or AA pilot number.

12. C. The T1 hardware installed on a voice gateway will be seen as controller interfaces in the IOS configuration.

13. C. Clock source is the term to define where a T1 receives clocking information. The choices are free-running, internal, and line.

14. D. The ISDN switch type must be configured globally so Q.931 signaling can be sent to and received by our PRI peers.

15. D. PRI timeslot 23 (channel 24) is always used for out-of-band signaling. When configuring the destination port, you point it toward the D channel.

16. B. Both the `port` and `session target` commands tell the voice gateway where the next hop for calls should be routed.

17.   C. Proper planning should go into any new voice network to limit the number of `destination-pattern` commands. The fewer `destination-pattern` rules, the easier your voice gateway will be to troubleshoot and manage.

18. B, C, D. DNIS information is found only on digital circuits. FXO ports are analog and therefore cannot carry DNIS information.

19. C. By default, H.323 is used for signaling when you configure a VoIP trunk.

20. D. The forward-digits digit-manipulation method is performed after all other methods on Cisco voice gateways.

Answers to Written Lab 7.1

1. `signal loopStart`

2. `connection plar 2111`

3. `forward-digits all` or `no digit-strip`

4. `framing esf`

5. `ds0-group 0 timeslots 1-24 type fxo-loop-start`

6. `isdn switch-type primar-ni`

7. `show voice port summary`

8. `session target ipv4:10.1.1.100`

9. `test voice translation-rule 401`

10. `session protocol sipv2`

Chapter

8

Unity Express Overview and Installation

THE FOLLOWING CCNA VOICE EXAM OBJECTIVES ARE COVERED IN THIS CHAPTER:

✓ **Implement voice mail features using Cisco Unity Express.**

- ▪ Configure the foundational elements required for Cisco Unified Communications Manager Express to support Cisco Unity Express.

- ▪ Describe the features available in Cisco Unity Express.

✓ **Implement voice mail features using Cisco Unity Express.**

- ▪ Describe the Cisco Unity Express hardware platforms.

I have heard arguments that email has rendered voice mail obsolete. Despite what critics say, voice mail is far from dead. It's a vital part of business communication that is still widely used today. Think about it. Can you imagine calling a business and *not* being able to leave a voice mail? Sure, you can send an email, but voice mail messages add a personal touch that email cannot get across. It is also important to note that voice mail technology is continuing to evolve to provide users with advanced features and functionality that make it even more useful today than it was 5 to 10 years ago. In fact, I see email and voice mail continuing to merge to the point where it is difficult to separate the two.

In this chapter we will explore the various features available to users and groups in Cisco's voice mail tool, the Unity Express system. We'll then check out some of the more advanced functionality such as the ability to provide integrated messaging with IMAP email clients such as Microsoft Outlook. Then we'll move beyond the voice mail capabilities of Unity Express and explore other functions such as the auto attendant and optional automated voice response system. Cisco Unity Express (CUE) has a fairly complex licensing structure, and this chapter covers all the licensing for the various functions of Unity Express. I will show you how to install, initialize, and upgrade the CUE software. Finally, you'll learn a quick way to restore your Unity Express to factory default settings.

Understanding Unity Express Voice Mail Features

This section will describe voice mailbox users and groups that can be set up to use the system. Users are assigned individual subscriber mailboxes, while groups use a shared general-delivery mailbox. Once you've seen how users and groups are defined, I'll detail many of the features that mailbox owners can utilize. I'll then describe the different voice mail caller options available when people call in to Unity Express either to leave messages for other users/groups or to log in to their own mailbox remotely to check messages. Finally, I'll touch on some of the more advanced features that Unity Express offers.

Users/Subscribers

Unity Express users, known as *subscribers*, are individual accounts that are created to provide personal mailbox accounts for voice mail storage. The terms *user* and *subscriber* can be used interchangeably. These individual mailbox accounts are known as subscriber accounts. Owners of these accounts can customize their mailboxes to suit their needs. Each subscriber can be assigned a username, PIN, and password. These credentials allow a user to manage their account. The personal identification number (PIN) is used when the subscriber manages their mailbox using the *telephone user interface* (TUI). The username and password are used when the subscriber manages their account using the web GUI interface or other email access protocols.

Later in this chapter you'll see that users who have already been created as ephone-DN owners can be imported automatically into Unity Express. When this import occurs, a password and PIN can be any of the following:

- Randomly assigned
- Left blank
- Manually entered by the administrator

If you change a user's password from within the CUE operating system, the password for that user is updated on the CUCM Express automatically. However, if the change is made on the CUCM Express OS side, the password will not automatically be updated on Unity Express. You should use the Administration ➤ Synchronize Unity Express GUI option to make sure users and passwords are the same on both systems.

Voice mail subscribers configured on Unity Express use the following information to create individual mailboxes:

User Name   Full name: first, last.

Group   Name of the group of which the user is a member.

Password   Used for logging in to the Unity Express GUI.

PIN   Used to authenticate a user who is using the TUI. When a subscriber logs in to the TUI for the first time, they are required to change the default PIN.

Groups

Groups are collections of subscribers who have some sort of commonality. Typically, users within the same business function are bundled together to form a Unity Express group. For example, there may be a regional sales group and a customer service group. Members of a particular group can be either users or other groups. That is, entire groups can be contained within another group. For example, the regional sales group might be a member of the national sales group. A group is assigned a single telephone extension with a shared mailbox. A mailbox that is assigned to a group is called a *general delivery mailbox* (GDM). At any one time, only one member can access the GDM. There is no PIN assigned. The user first logs into their personal mail account and then can choose to access the GDM from the TUI interface. There are two types of group users:

Group member   Can access the general delivery mailbox to check messages and perform other mailbox functionality.

Group owner   Can add or delete group members and group owners. An owner is not considered a group member and therefore cannot access the GDM.

A group's owner is not automatically a member of the group. The owner account must also be set up as a member in order to access the GDM.

Mailbox Owner Features

There are literally dozens of mailbox features for both subscriber and group voice mailboxes. In this section, we're going to discuss the features that are most commonly deployed.

Spoken Name

When a user logs into their mailbox for the first time, they can record their spoken name to identify themselves as the owner of the mailbox. The spoken name is used when another user forwards a voice mail message, when the user does not record a personal greeting, or in the auto attendant when a caller chooses the user extension.

Personal Greeting

A user can set up a personal greeting for their voice mailbox. When a caller is transferred to a user's voice mailbox, the personal greeting is played, which typically asks the caller to leave a name, number, and reason for calling. If the mailbox user does not create a personal greeting, a CUE standard greeting is played in its place, which tells the caller to leave a message, either for extension XXXX or using the spoken name if one was recorded.

Alternate Greeting

An alternate greeting can be created for occasions when the user wants to switch quickly between a personal greeting and a different greeting. This is useful when the user needs to have two different greetings but does not wish to rerecord the personal greeting each time. When the alternate greeting is active, the personal greeting is in an inactive state but is still stored on the system.

Operator Assistance

The operator assistance feature is also called a "zero out" feature. It allows callers to press 0 to reach an operator. The actual extension that is called can be the default number defined by the Unity Express administrator, or it can be locally defined by the mailbox subscriber or group member. This feature lets callers opt out of leaving a message and attempt to speak with a live operator or assistant instead.

Tutorial

When a new subscriber or group mailbox is created, a user or group member can log in to their mailbox and use a TUI tutorial, which walks the user through basic setup of their mailbox. The voice prompts will step the user through setting up the following:

- Spoken name
- Greeting
- Change PIN
- Operator assistance

Message Waiting Indicator

Two different indicators inform users of new voice mails. The first, the *message waiting indicator* (MWI), is a red light found on all Cisco IP phones. This light is a prominent visual notification to the phone owner that they have a message waiting on the extension assigned to button 1 of a multiline phone. Only the extension assigned to button 1 uses the red light MWI. A second notification found on Cisco IP phones with LCD displays is the flashing envelope icon. This icon will flash next to the extension number on the button where the new voice mail was left. Figure 8.1 shows the flashing envelope icon next to extension 5004.

FIGURE 8.1   Flashing envelope MWI

This envelope icon indicates that a caller dialed extension 5004 and left a voice mail in the mailbox assigned to that extension. Also note that the red light on the phone is not lit. This is because extension 5004 is configured on button 2 of the phone, and the red light is used only when messages are waiting on button 1. A phone with multiple extensions may simultaneously have one extension tied to the MWI but have multiple lines with the envelope icons showing.

Message Notifications

The MWI described previously is a great way to notify users of a new voice mail when they are physically in front of their phone and can see the red light and flashing envelope icon. But as we know, many of our users are mobile and constantly away from their desks. They would have no idea that a new voice mail was waiting for them unless they periodically dialed in to check, a method that is not cost or time efficient. Fortunately, with the Unity Express version 3.1 and later versions, we can configure *message notifications* to alert users to a voice mail on any of the following:

- Another telephone (home, cellular, and so on)
- Numeric or text pager
- Email account

Message notification is globally enabled at the system level by the Unity Express administrator. The administrator then has the ability to control how message notifications are handled on a per-user or group basis. The administrator can also specify either that all new voice mail messages are sent to notification destinations or that only messages flagged as urgent are sent out.

Once the Unity Express administrator configures and enables the message-notification parameters, subscribers and group members can log in to their mailbox using either the TUI or GUI interface to specify the phone numbers and/or email addresses where the notifications are to be sent.

For email notifications to be sent, it is important that you remember to configure your Unity Express to point to an SMTP server. If you don't, emails will not be sent to users.

Users and/or group members can also configure cascading message notifications. This technique sets up a list of multiple notification destinations that have priorities assigned to them. The Unity Express will send an alert notification to the first destination and wait a defined period of time. If the timer expires and the new message has not been checked, the Unity Express system will move to the next destination and send a second notification, and so on.

Understanding Distribution Lists

Many times, you want to be able to send the same voice mail message to multiple people. You could call every extension associated with the person you wish the message to reach, but that would not be efficient. Instead, Unity Express offers the ability to create distribution lists, which allow users to create lists of subscribers so they can send a single voice mail message to multiple subscriber and/or GDM mailboxes. Think of it as forwarding an email to multiple email recipients. Unity Express supports two types of distribution lists:

- Public distribution lists
- Private distribution lists

Let's look at each of these so you can better understand the differences between the two.

Public Distribution Lists

A *public distribution list* is a list that is typically defined by the Unity Express system administrator. These lists are for any subscriber or group to use. It is common for public distribution lists to be created for the various departments that would need similar notifications. It is also common to see a public distribution list created grouping department managers together.

Private Distribution Lists

Private distribution lists are created by an individual subscriber or group. These lists can be used only by the owner of the private list. Users can customize a list that fits their specific job functions. These lists are commonly much more granular in nature than the public distribution lists available.

Mailbox Caller Features

When a caller dials an extension and is redirected because the user either is not available to answer the phone or is busy on another call, the call is most commonly redirected to a subscriber/group mailbox. At this point the calling party has several mailbox caller features available. This section will cover message recording options, operator assistance, and the ability to log in to the mailbox to check messages remotely.

Record Message Options

When a caller reaches a subscriber or group mailbox, they will be presented with a greeting of some sort informing the caller to leave a message. The caller then hears an audible beep on the phone handset as a signal that the Unity Express system has begun recording. When the caller has finished leaving a message, they can simply hang up the phone. As long as the message lasts two seconds or longer, the message is saved and is stored in the user's mailbox until they retrieve it.

Alternatively, after the caller leaves a message, they can press the # key on their handset to utilize the Record Message options available on the Unity Express system. These options are:

Review recorded message   Used if the caller would like to hear the message they just left.

Set the message priority as urgent   By default, mailbox messages are set with a normal priority. A caller can change this setting to urgent here. Depending on the mailbox configuration, flagging a message as urgent can trigger the CUE to kick off message notifications to quickly inform the mailbox owner of the urgent message.

Rerecord the message   Used to delete the previously recorded message and rerecord it.

Cancel the message   Used to delete the previously recorded message without rerecording it.

Operator Assistance

The operator assistance feature gives the caller a chance to talk to another person rather than leave a voice mail. For example, suppose a caller tries to reach extension 4172. The user for that extension is already on a call, so the incoming call is redirected to voice mail. The caller begins listening to the greeting, which tells them to leave their name and number. If the caller presses the 0 key on their phone before the message recording beep goes off, they are redirected to the extension configured as the operator for extension 4172. Individual extensions can have separate and different operators configured.

Mailbox Login

The mailbox login feature is for mailbox subscribers who are away from their desk and do not have access to their primary IP phone. The user can dial the phone number that is tied to the mailbox they wish to check. When the user begins hearing the voice mail greeting, they can press the * button. This action triggers the Unity Express system to ask for the extension and PIN associated with the mailbox they wish to access. Once the user is authenticated, they can access voice mail messages using the TUI as if they were using their primary phone at their desk.

Unity Express Advanced User Functionality

Besides using the standard TUI interface for checking voice mail messages on Unity Express, two additional methods offer alternatives to the TUI. The first method is called VoiceView Express. This allows the user to log in to their voice mail from any Cisco IP phone that supports XML. Using the LCD screen, the user can check their subscriber mailbox as well as any GDMs they are members of. The other advanced user voice mail functionality is called integrated messaging. This setup allows a user to check their voice mail and email from a single IMAP client. Let's take a closer look at each of these features.

VoiceView Express

The most common way to access and maintain voice mail features is through the TUI. An alternative method that Unity Express offers is called *VoiceView Express*. The CUCM Express and Unity Express software work together to let voice mail users listen to, send, and manage voice messages on a Cisco phone using the LCD display and softkeys. Figure 8.2 shows an IP Communicator logged into VoiceView Express.

FIGURE 8.2 VoiceView Express

The service uses XML to deliver information to the LCD display of the phone. To access VoiceView Express on a compatible Cisco phone, the user would press the Services button on the phone.

Integrated Messaging

For many, email has taken over the title for most-used communications method. If you are like me, you check your email far more frequently than your voice mail. To help streamline functions, Unity Express offers integrated messaging so your voice mail messages can be pulled off the CUE and placed in your Microsoft Outlook inbox or any compatible IMAP email client.

Integrated messaging merges your email and voice mail systems into a single point of communications reference. Unity Express uses IMAP to deliver messages to an email client capable of running IMAP version 4 rev 1. Note that integrated messaging is not unified messaging. With integrated messaging, you simply set up your email client to have two IMAP profiles, one for email and a second for voice mail. Figure 8.3 shows how your IMAP client software is then set up to pull from two different sources.

FIGURE 8.3   Integrated messaging

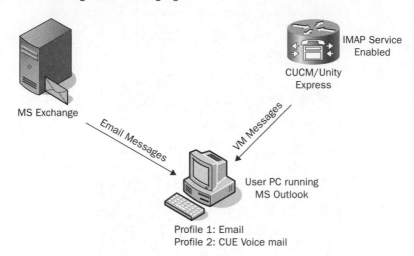

MS Exchange

Email Messages

VM Messages

IMAP Service
Enabled

CUCM/Unity
Express

User PC running
MS Outlook

Profile 1: Email
Profile 2: CUE Voice mail

Once this connection is set up, the user will receive voice mail messages as attached
.wav files.

Understanding Unity Express Auto Attendant Scripting Methods

The auto attendant (AA) feature of modern PBX systems has replaced a live operator as the
first point of contact for many businesses. The AA is a script that greets callers and either
asks them to enter a known extension for the person they are trying to reach or guides
the caller through various prompts on the script by asking them to press buttons on the
keypad. This script helps the caller navigate to the right person or department that will best
handle their needs. All Unity Express installations come standard with two default scripts.
The audio of the default files can be rerecorded to customize them to fit most businesses or
organizations. Some prompts have prerecorded audio on them, but you'll want to customize
them to personalize the AA experience. Let's take a closer look at the structure of the two
Unity Express preinstalled scripts.

Preinstalled Scripts

Two scripts have a basic mapping structure laid out to meet many AA needs for small to
medium-size businesses:

- Default Auto Attendant Script: `aa.aef`
- Auto Attendant Simple Script: `aasimple.aef`

These preinstalled custom scripts are similar in nature. Figure 8.4 displays the process flow for both of them.

The primary difference between the two preinstalled scripts is that the simple script utilizes a PlayExtensionsPrompt, which can be set up to say, for example, "To reach John, press 1. To reach Tammy, press 2." This type of script is generally useful only in smaller

FIGURE 8.4 The process flow for preinstalled scripts

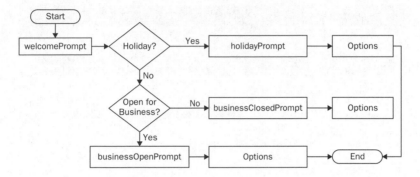

environments. The default script, on the other hand, allows callers to dial the extension if they know it already or to go through the dial-by-name feature.

There are two ways to change the audio contained within the various prompts. First, you can record your own audio using PC recording software. The files must be in the following format to function on the Unity Express system:

- G.711 u-law
- 8 kHz
- 8 bit
- Mono

A second and simpler method is to use the administration via telephone (AvT) functions by dialing into the TUI and recording prompts over the phone that are saved on the CUE in the proper format. This feature will be discussed in more depth later in this chapter.

Editor Express

The Cisco Unity *Editor Express* is a slimmed-down version of the Custom Script Editor that runs on Microsoft Windows. The Editor Express has the advantage of running directly on the Unity Express hardware. You simply log in to the web GUI, navigate to System ➢ Scripts, and click the New button. Figure 8.5 shows a screenshot of the Editor Express tool.

FIGURE 8.5 Editor Express

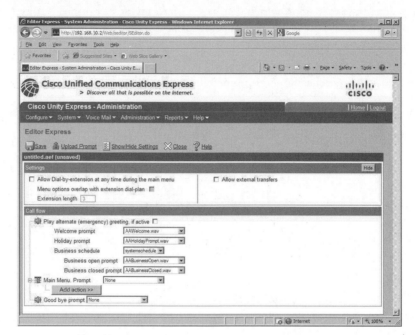

As you can see, the tool allows you to choose various options using drop-down menus. This editor does not have nearly as many configuration options as the full-blown Cisco script editor, but it may be enough to create the scripts that you need.

Unity Express Editor Application

If you require a fully customized AA script that the Editor Express tool cannot handle, you're in luck! Cisco also offers the *Unity Express Editor,* which is a far more robust application. This tool allows you to build and customize an AA script that is as complex as you desire.

The Cisco Unity Express Editor is an external Microsoft Windows application that is available for download on the cisco.com website. Figure 8.6 shows a screenshot of the CUE Editor application running on Windows XP.

FIGURE 8.6 The AA CUE Editor application

Once you create the script on your PC, you can save it as an `.aef` file and then upload the file to Unity Express. You can then set the script to be used as the primary AA script on the CUE.

Understanding Unity Express Interactive Voice Response

The *Interactive Voice Response* (IVR) functionality allows callers to interact with a voice menu much like an auto attendant, where the caller is prompted to press numbers on the telephone handset to work their way through the script. IVR provides additional capabilities, however, in the type of information a caller can receive. IVR has the ability to do the following:

- Query databases and present this information to the caller over the phone
- Send emails/faxes to customers based on caller responses on the IVR application

> To use the capabilities of IVR on your Unity Express system, you must purchase the proper IVR licensing from Cisco. Licensing of the Unity Express system is discussed in the next section.

Understanding CUCM Express Licensing

As with all Cisco hardware, you need proper licenses to run the CUE software. There are two separate Cisco license packages for legitimately running your Unity Express System with full functionality:

1. Unity Express Mailbox License package (required)

   - Mailbox license to run with the CUCM Express
   - Mailbox license to run with the CUCM or CUCMBE

2. Unity Express IVR License package (optional)

   Depending on which Cisco call-processing device you'll be connecting to, you will install either the cme license for interoperation with the CUCM Express or the ccm license for interoperation with the CUCM and CUCMBE. There are also differences in the number of mailboxes and sessions you can license depending on the type of hardware you plan to run Unity Express on. Table 8.1 lists all of the currently available Unity Express hardware devices and the maximum number of mailboxes, sessions, and storage hours for each.

TABLE 8.1   CUE hardware comparison

Hardware	AIM-CUE	NM-CUE	NM-CUE-EC	NME-CUE
Max mailboxes	50	100	250	250
Max sessions	6	8	16	24
Total VM storage	14	100	300	300

Let's now look at each of these in depth to see which software and licensing options are available from Cisco.

AIM-CUE

AIM-CUE offers the following licensing options:

cue-vm-license_XXmbx_cme_Y.Y.Y.pkg XX is the number of mailboxes the license supports. For the AIM module, the licenses can be for 12, 25, or 50 mailboxes. The cme within the filename tells us that this Unity Express software is designed to work with the CUCM Express system, and the notation Y.Y.Y represents the version of the Unity Express software.

cue-vm-license_XXmbx_ccm_Y.Y.Y.pkg XX is the number of mailboxes the license supports. For the AIM module, the licenses can be for 12, 25, or 50 mailboxes. The ccm within the filename tells us that this Unity Express software is designed to work with either the CUCMBE or CUCM call-processing system, and Y.Y.Y represents the version of the Unity Express software.

cue-vm-license_Xport_ivr_Y.Y.Y.pkg X is the number of simultaneous IVR sessions the license supports. For the AIM module, the licenses can be for 2, 4, 8, 16, or 20 sessions.

NM-CUE

NM-CUE offers the following licensing options:

cue-vm-license_XXmbx_cme_Y.Y.Y.pkg XX is the number of mailboxes the license supports. For the AIM module, the licenses can be for 12, 25, 50, or 100 mailboxes. The cme within the filename tells us that this Unity Express software is designed to work with the CUCM Express system, and Y.Y.Y represents the version of the Unity Express software.

cue-vm-license_XXmbx_ccm_Y.Y.Y.pkg XX is the number of mailboxes the license supports. For the AIM module, the licenses can be for 12, 25, 50, or 100 mailboxes. The ccm within the filename tells us that this Unity Express software is designed to work with either the CUCMBE or CUCM call processing system. Y.Y.Y represents the version of the Unity Express software.

cue-vm-license_Xport_ivr_Y.Y.Y.pkg X is the number of simultaneous IVR sessions the license supports. For the AIM module, the licenses can be for 2, 4, 8, 16, or 20 sessions.

NM-CUE-EC

NM-CUE-EC offers the following licensing options:

cue-vm-license_XXmbx_cme_Y.Y.Y.pkg XX is the number of mailboxes the license supports. For the AIM module, the licenses can be for 12, 25, 50, 100, or 250 mailboxes. The cme within the filename tells us that this Unity Express software is designed to work with the CUCM Express system. Y.Y.Y represents the version of the Unity Express software.

cue-vm-license_XXmbx_ccm_Y.Y.Y.pkg   XX is the number of mailboxes the license supports. For the AIM module, the licenses can be for 12, 25, 50, 100, or 250 mailboxes. The ccm within the filename tells us that this Unity Express software is designed to work with either the CUCMBE or CUCM call-processing system. Y.Y.Y represents the version of the Unity Express software.

cue-vm-license_Xport_ivr_Y.Y.Y.pkg   X is the number of simultaneous IVR sessions the license supports. For the AIM module, the licenses can be for 2, 4, 8, 16, and 20 sessions.

NME-CUE

NME-CUE offers the following licensing options:

cue-vm-license_XXmbx_cme_Y.Y.Y.pkg   XX is the number of mailboxes the license supports. For the AIM module, the licenses can be for 12, 25, 50, 100, or 250 mailboxes. The cme within the filename tells us that this Unity Express software is designed to work with the CUCM Express system, and Y.Y.Y represents the version of the Unity Express software.

cue-vm-license_XXmbx_ccm_Y.Y.Y.pkg   XX is the number of mailboxes the license supports. For the AIM module, the licenses can be for 12, 25, 50, 100, or 250 mailboxes. The ccm within the filename tells us that this Unity Express software is designed to work with either the CUCMBE or CUCM call-processing system, and Y.Y.Y represents the version of the Unity Express software.

cue-vm-license_Xport_ivr_Y.Y.Y.pkg   X is the number of simultaneous IVR sessions the license supports. For the AIM module, the licenses can be for 2, 4, 8, 16, or 20 sessions.

Installation and Initial Configuration of Unity Express on CUCM Express Routers

When either the AIM or NM Unity hardware module is properly inserted into a supported Cisco router, a new physical interface appears within the Cisco IOS. The interface will be labeled either Service-Engine or Integrated-Service-Engine, depending on the Unity Express hardware you are using. Running show version confirms that the service engine is installed:

```
Router#sh version
Cisco IOS Software, UC500 Software (UC500-ADVIPSERVICESK9-M), Version
12.4(11)XW7, RELEASE SOFTWARE (fc2)
```

```
Technical Support: http://www.cisco.com/techsupport
Copyright (c) 1986-2008 by Cisco Systems, Inc.
Compiled Wed 09-Apr-08 03:07 by prod_rel_team

ROM: System Bootstrap, Version 12.4(11r)XW3, RELEASE SOFTWARE (fc1)

Router uptime is 6 hours, 2 minutes
System returned to ROM by power-on
System image file is "flash:uc500-advipservicesk9-mz.124-11.XW7"

This product contains cryptographic features and is subject to United
States and local country laws governing import, export, transfer and
use. Delivery of Cisco cryptographic products does not imply
third-party authority to import, export, distribute or use encryption.
Importers, exporters, distributors and users are responsible for
compliance with U.S. and local country laws. By using this product you
agree to comply with applicable laws and regulations. If you are unable
to comply with U.S. and local laws, return this product immediately.

A summary of U.S. laws governing Cisco cryptographic products may be found at:
http://www.cisco.com/wwl/export/crypto/tool/stqrg.html

If you require further assistance please contact us by sending email to
export@cisco.com.

Cisco UC520-8U-4FXO-K9 (MPC8358) processor (revision 0x202) with 249856K/12288K
bytes of memory.
Processor board ID FTX130886A2
MPC8358 CPU Rev: Part Number 0x804A, Revision ID 0x20
14 User Licenses
10 FastEthernet interfaces
2 terminal lines
4 Voice FXO interfaces
4 Voice FXS interfaces
1 Voice MoH interface
1 cisco service engine(s)
128K bytes of non-volatile configuration memory.
125440K bytes of ATA CompactFlash (Read/Write)

Configuration register is 0x2102
```

Remember that the Unity Express should be thought of as a separate network device that just happens to be housed within the CUCM Express router. From a logical standpoint, the Service-Module is just like an Ethernet port that connects the router to the Unity Express hardware. The router side of the logical interface is the physical Integrated-Service-Engine interface. On the other side of this network connection is the Service-Module interface, which represents the IP endpoint of the Unity Express hardware. Figure 8.7 diagrams the logical network between the CUCM Express router and Unity Express hardware.

FIGURE 8.7 Logical network between CUCM and CUE

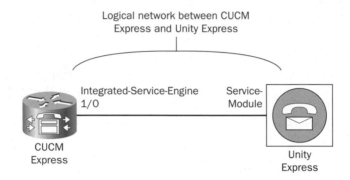

There are two methods for setting up this IP network so we can communicate with the Unity Express for operational and administration purposes. The first method is to use the `ip unnumbered` command on the Integrated-Service-Engine so we can use an already configured network on the CUCM Express rather than create a new one just for the purpose of connecting the Unity Express system. The second method is to create a separate point-to-point IP network between the Integrated-Service-Engine and the Service-Module. Let's look at how to configure each of these methods.

Configuring IP Unnumbered to Use Existing IP Network for Unity Express Connectivity

The *IP unnumbered* configuration method sets up the CUE so you don't have to waste a separate IP network for the sole purpose of Unity Express connectivity. By using the `ip unnumbered <interface>` config-interface command on the Integrated-Service-Engine, you can configure the Service-Module on an already configured IP subnet on the CUCM Express router. Figure 8.8 shows what this logical setup looks like:

FIGURE 8.8   Using ip unnumbered for CUE connectivity

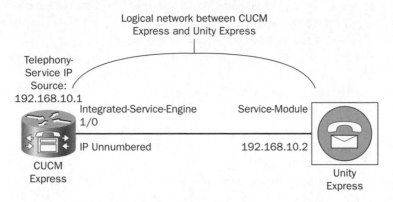

Notice that the Telephony-Service source IP address and the Service-Module IP address are on the same subnet. Both of these IP addresses use the /24 network that has been configured on interface loopback 0. A static route pointing to the Integrated-Service-Engine is then needed to tell the router how to reach the Unity Express system on the shared network. Here are the configuration commands to set up the logical network properly using IP unnumbered:

```
Router#configure terminal
Router(config)#interface loopback 0
Router(config-if)#ip address 192.168.10.1 255.255.255.0
Router(config)#interface integrated-Service-Engine 0/0
Router(config-if)#ip unnumbered loopback 0
Router(config-if)#service-module ip address 192.168.10.2 255.255.255.0
Router(config-if)#service-module ip default-gateway 192.168.10.1
Router(config-if)#exit
Router(config)#ip route 192.168.10.2 255.255.255.255 integrated-Service-Engine
0/0
Router(config)#
```

Now our Unity Express system is identified with the IP address 192.168.10.2/24, which resides on the same network as the source IP address for the CUCM Express system. This is the preferred method because we now have the CUCM Express and CUE sitting on the same network. This method is simpler and more easily understood by system administrators.

We can issue a show interfaces Integrated-Service-Engine 0/0 command to verify that our interface is up and sharing the loopback 0 IP address:

```
Router#show interfaces Integrated-Service-Engine 0/0
Integrated-Service-Engine0/0 is up, line protocol is up
```

```
Hardware is PQII_PRO_UEC, address is 0021.a02b.6081 (bia 0021.a02b.6081)
Interface is unnumbered. Using address of loopback 0 (192.168.10.1)
MTU 1500 bytes, BW 100000 Kbit, DLY 100 usec,
    reliability 255/255, txload 1/255, rxload 1/255
Encapsulation ARPA, loopback not set
ARP type: ARPA, ARP Timeout 04:00:00
Last input 00:00:03, output 00:00:03, output hang never
Last clearing of "show interface" counters never
Input queue: 0/75/0/0 (size/max/drops/flushes); Total output drops: 0
Queueing strategy: fifo
Output queue: 0/40 (size/max)
5 minute input rate 0 bits/sec, 0 packets/sec
5 minute output rate 0 bits/sec, 0 packets/sec
    21773 packets input, 9552774 bytes, 0 no buffer
    Received 826 broadcasts, 0 runts, 0 giants, 0 throttles
    0 input errors, 0 CRC, 0 frame, 0 overrun, 0 ignored
    0 input packets with dribble condition detected
    19172 packets output, 4603856 bytes, 0 underruns
    0 output errors, 0 collisions, 3 interface resets
    0 babbles, 0 late collision, 0 deferred
    0 lost carrier, 0 no carrier
    0 output buffer failures, 0 output buffers swapped out
Router#
```

We should also be able to ping our CUE Service-Module IP address of 192.168.10.2:

```
Router#ping 192.168.10.2

Type escape sequence to abort.
Sending 5, 100-byte ICMP Echos to 192.168.10.2, timeout is 2 seconds:
!!!!!
Success rate is 100 percent (5/5), round-trip min/avg/max = 1/3/4 ms
Router#
```

Configuring a Separate IP Network for Unity Express Connectivity

The second method for connecting the CUE to the CUCM is to configure a separate IP network between the Integrated-Service-Engine and the Service-Module. It is very similar to creating a router Ethernet interface with an IP address on the Integrated-Service-Engine physical interface. Then, within config-if mode, you configure an IP address and default-gateway within the same IP subnet space for the Unity Express hardware using the service-module command. Finally, for proper routing, a static route is needed so the router knows how to reach the Unity Express device on the other end of the network. Figure 8.9 shows our logical network with a 172.16.1.X/24 subnet created on the logical network segment.

FIGURE 8.9 Separate IP network for CUE connectivity

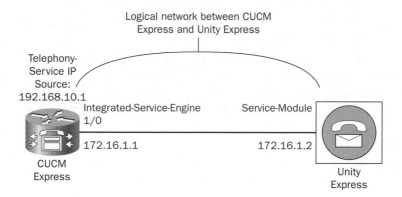

Here are the commands for configuring a separate IP network for Unity Express communication:

```
Router#configure terminal
Router(config)#interface integrated-Service-Engine 0/0
Router(config-if)#ip address 172.16.1.1 255.255.255.0
Router(config-if)#service-module ip address 172.16.1.2 255.255.255.0
Router(config-if)#service-module ip default-gateway 172.16.1.1
Router(config-if)#exit
Router(config)#ip route 172.16.1.2 255.255.255.255 integrated-Service-Engine 0/0
Router(config)#
```

We can once again issue a show interfaces Integrated-Service-Engine 0/0 command to verify that our interface is up using its own IP address:

```
Router#show interfaces Integrated-Service-Engine 0/0
Integrated-Service-Engine0/0 is up, line protocol is up
  Hardware is PQII_PRO_UEC, address is 0021.a02b.6081 (bia 0021.a02b.6081)
  Internet address is 172.16.1.1/24
  MTU 1500 bytes, BW 100000 Kbit, DLY 100 usec,
     reliability 255/255, txload 1/255, rxload 1/255
  Encapsulation ARPA, loopback not set
```

```
ARP type: ARPA, ARP Timeout 04:00:00
Last input 00:00:03, output 00:00:03, output hang never
Last clearing of "show interface" counters never
Input queue: 0/75/0/0 (size/max/drops/flushes); Total output drops: 0
Queueing strategy: fifo
Output queue: 0/40 (size/max)
5 minute input rate 0 bits/sec, 0 packets/sec
5 minute output rate 0 bits/sec, 0 packets/sec
   21773 packets input, 9552774 bytes, 0 no buffer
   Received 826 broadcasts, 0 runts, 0 giants, 0 throttles
   0 input errors, 0 CRC, 0 frame, 0 overrun, 0 ignored
   0 input packets with dribble condition detected
   19172 packets output, 4603856 bytes, 0 underruns
   0 output errors, 0 collisions, 3 interface resets
   0 babbles, 0 late collision, 0 deferred
   0 lost carrier, 0 no carrier
   0 output buffer failures, 0 output buffers swapped out
Router#
```

We should also be able to ping our CUE Service-Module IP address of 172.16.1.2:

```
Router#ping 172.16.1.2

Type escape sequence to abort.
Sending 5, 100-byte ICMP Echos to 172.16.1.2, timeout is 2 seconds:
!!!!!
Success rate is 100 percent (5/5), round-trip min/avg/max = 1/3/4 ms
Router#
```

We must configure two additional options on the CUCM Express prior to configuring the Unity Express system. First, we must create dial peers for our voice mail, auto attendant (AA), and administration via telephone (AvT) pilot numbers. Second, we need to create extensions for the message waiting indicator (MWI), which is the light on the phone that turns on when a phone receives a new voice mail message.

Configuring Dial Peers for Unity Express Functions

We need to configure three distinct dial peers on the CUCM Express to take advantage of voice mail, auto attendant (AA), and administration via telephone (AvT). We already know about the voice mail and auto attendant features, but *administration via telephone* is a new term for us. Administration via telephone is a way for telephone administrators to add/delete and modify audio prompts used by the Unity Express system. AvT offers a way for administrators to create these custom prompts without the need for a PC or sound-editing software. AvT also allows administrators to broadcast messages to all mailboxes on the Unity Express system.

When an ephone-DN is configured for voice mail, you need to specify an extension for the `call-forward busy` and `call-forward noan` commands to tell the CUCM Express to send the calls to the Unity Express system. This unique extension must be tied to a VoIP dial peer and forwarded over an SIP trunk to ultimately get to the Unity Express hardware located logically on the other side of the logical network we just configured. The auto attendant, AVT, and VoIP dial peers require their own unique extensions, but the setup for each is identical.

 Remember that the Unity Express system can use only SIP version 2 signaling between itself and the CUCM Express. No other signaling methods can be used.

Here is an example of how to configure dial peers for all three Unity Express functions:

```
Router#configure terminal
Router(config)#dial-peer voice 188 voip
Router(config-dial-peer)#description voice mail
Router(config-dial-peer)#destination-pattern 188
Router(config-dial-peer)#session protocol sipv2
Router(config-dial-peer)#session target ipv4:172.16.1.2
Router(config-dial-peer)#dtmf-relay sip-notify
Router(config-dial-peer)#codec g711ulaw
Router(config-dial-peer)#no vad
Router(config-dial-peer)#exit
Router(config)#dial-peer voice 189 voip
Router(config-dial-peer)#description aa
Router(config-dial-peer)#destination-pattern 189
Router(config-dial-peer)#session protocol sipv2
Router(config-dial-peer)#session target ipv4:172.16.1.2
Router(config-dial-peer)#dtmf-relay sip-notify
Router(config-dial-peer)#codec g711ulaw
Router(config-dial-peer)#no vad
Router(config-dial-peer)#exit
Router(config)#dial-peer voice 190 voip
Router(config-dial-peer)#description avt
Router(config-dial-peer)#destination-pattern 190
Router(config-dial-peer)#session protocol sipv2
Router(config-dial-peer)#session target ipv4:172.16.1.2
Router(config-dial-peer)#dtmf-relay sip-notify
Router(config-dial-peer)#codec g711ulaw
```

```
Router(config-dial-peer)#no vad
Router(config-dial-peer)#end
Router#
```

We've configured extensions 188, 189, and 190 as our destination patterns for each of these Unity Express features. We also specified that SIPv2 is the signaling protocol that is to be used, by including the `session protocol sipv2` config-dial-peer command.

The `dtmf-relay sip-notify` command is required because Unity Express uses the phone handset's tones to gather information needed to navigate through the voice mail, AA, and AvT menus. The command tells the CUCM Express to relay those tones over the SIP trunk to Unity Express.

We've statically assigned our codec to G.711. Remember that by default, dial peers are configured to use the G.729 codec. Unity Express can understand only the G.711 codec, so we must configure this or the dial peer will not work.

Finally, the `no vad` command tells the CUCM Express not to use Voice Activity Detection (VAD) across the SIP trunk. The Unity Express does not work properly with VAD enabled and must be turned off. VAD is enabled on all dial peers by default.

Configuring MWI Ephone-DNs

The message waiting indicator (MWI) feature informs phone users when one or more new voice mails are waiting in their voice mailbox. On almost every Cisco IP phone, a red light on the handset of the phone will light up in the event of a new message waiting in the phone owner's mailbox. When a new message arrives, the Unity Express system will call a configured ephone-DN that is specifically used for MWI. After all the new messages have been read, the Unity Express system will dial a second number to turn the light off. That means you set up MWI ephone-DNs similarly to any other standard ephone-DN; you must include an extension for MWI to function.

You must configure two MWI ephone-DNs: one to turn the MWI lamp on and the other to turn the lamp off. The numbers for these extensions have a static prefix and a wildcard ending where Unity Express appends the particular phone extension it wishes to reach. The following example shows two ephone-DNs being configured for MWI duty. Ephone-DN 11 turns the MWI light on and ephone-DN 12 turns it off. The prefix for the MWI DNs includes the letter a in this example. This is so a phone user cannot accidentally dial the MWI light extension to turn on/off a phone's light when there are no new messages in the user's mailbox. An administrator can use the letters a, b, c, and d for DTMF priority and override digits for the extension number. These are used in this situation to prevent users from inadvertently dialing the MWI extension to turn on and off the message lamp.

```
Router#configure terminal
Router(config)#ephone-dn 11
Router(config-ephone-dn)#number a11....
Router(config-ephone-dn)#mwi on
```

```
Router(config-ephone-dn)#exit
Router(config)#ephone-dn 12
Router(config-ephone-dn)#number a12....
Router(config-ephone-dn)#mwi off
Router(config-ephone-dn)#end
Router#
```

Now that we can reach our Unity Express system over IP and have our dial peers and MWI extensions set up, we will go through the process of upgrading the CUE software and then setting up the system using the GUI Initialization Wizard.

 Real World Scenario

AU: Verifying MWI Functionality without Leaving Your Chair

Marty has just completed configuring MWI on ephone-DN 20 for his boss. To test the MWI functionality, Marty calls his boss's phone and leaves a brief test message that should kick-start the MWI to turn on. When he walks over to his boss's office, Marty realizes that his boss is currently in a meeting. Not wanting to disturb his boss, Marty goes back to his desk to figure out a way to see if the MWI indicators were properly lit up. After trying out a few show commands on the CLI, Marty received the following output when issuing a show ephone 20 command:

Router#**show ephone 20**

```
ephone-20[1] Mac:0021.A02E.7D9A TCP socket:[5] activeLine:0 REGISTERED in SCCP
ver 12/9
mediaActive:0 offhook:0 ringing:0 ringRate: 0 reset:0 reset_sent:0 paging 0
debug:0 caps:9
IP:192.168.10.11 50271 7965  keepalive 6 max_line 6
button 1: dn 1  number 5000 CH1   IDLE  CH2    IDLE    mwi
Preferred Codec: g711ulaw
```

From this output, we can see that Marty's boss's phone is a 7965, which has one configured button with the extension 5000 assigned to it using ephone-DN 1. Also note that this line is a dual-line phone, thus the CH1 and CH2 IDLE status notifications. Finally, on the far right of the button 1 line, we see the mwi notification. This tells Marty that his test voice mail indeed triggered the MWI light to turn on. Now Marty can continue configuring other phones for MWI and be able to test the configurations without ever having to leave his desk.

Upgrading Unity Express Software

We've officially completed all the steps needed to get Unity Express networked with the CUCM Express. We can finally focus on getting Unity Express software up and running. To reach our Unity Express system via the command line, we log in to the CUCM Express and get into privileged-exec mode. We can then issue the following command:

```
Router#service-module integrated-Service-Engine 0/0 session
Trying 192.168.10.1, 2002 ... Open
UC500-CUE en
Password:
UC500-CUE#
```

By default, no enable password is set, so you can just hit Enter to get into the CUE privileged-exec mode.

One of the first steps you will likely want to take is to install the latest version of the Unity Express software, which can be downloaded from the cisco.com website. All of the necessary Unity Express files can be downloaded in a single zip file. You then extract that zip file and put it on an FTP server on your network in order to upload the new software to the Unity Express system. Figure 8.10 shows a screenshot of all the CUE software files needed to install the latest version of Unity Express on a UC500 series router.

FIGURE 8.10 CUE software files

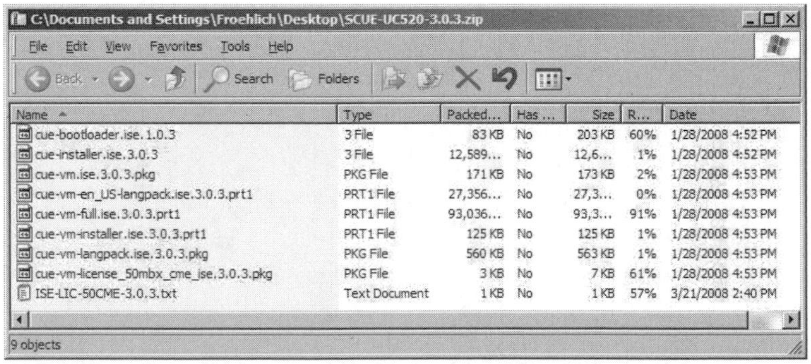

Table 8.2 lists the Unity Express software files and their functions. The x.x.x in the filename indicates the different version types available.

TABLE 8.2 Unity Express software files

Software Filename	Function
cue-bootloader.ise.x.x.x	Unity Express boot loader
cue-installer.ise.x.x.x	Unity Express install helper image
cue-vm.ise.x.x.x.pkg	Unity Express software package
cue-vm-en_US-langpack.ise.x.x.x.prt1	English (US) language package
cue-vm-full.ise.x.x.x.prt1	Voice mail application
cue-vm-installer.ise.x.x.x.prt1	Installer software
cue-vm-langpack.ise.x.x.x.pkg	Language package
cue-vm-license_50mbx_cme_ise.x.x.x.pkg	UC500 license package

To download and install a brand-new copy of the Unity Express software, we use the software install command. This offers several different options, as shown here:

```
UC500-CUE# software install ?
  abort      abort
  clean      clean download
  status     status
  upgrade    upgrade download

UC500-CUE#
```

The clean option specifies that this will be a brand-new install and not simply an upgrade. The difference between clean and upgrade is that an upgrade will keep any previously set configuration options and reapply them to the upgraded software. The status command lets us view the progress of a clean install or upgrade, and the abort command allows us to stop a currently running clean install or upgrade.

Once we choose a download option, we must specify the location of our FTP server and any username/password credentials needed.

There is also a `software download` command, which will download the necessary install files without running through the installation process. You can then go back at another time to run the install process. In our example the proper syntax to install software that has been locally downloaded onto Unity Express storage is `software install clean cue-vm.ise.3.0.3.pkg`. This command is very useful if you want to prepare for an install during the day and bring down the voice mail system at night to perform the upgrade.

Because this is a brand-new voice mail system, we'll use the `clean` option to ensure that our setup is configured with only the factory default settings. Here is the output of our software download and installation process:

```
UC500-CUE# software install clean url ftp://192.168.1.100/cue-vm.ise.3.0.3.pkg
username cisco
password for cisco :

WARNING:: This command will download the necessary software to
WARNING:: complete a clean install.  It is recommended that a backup be done
WARNING:: before installing software.

WARNING:: The system will briefly be brought to an offline state
WARNING:: This will terminate any active call and prevent new calls
WARNING:: from being processed.

Would you like to continue? [n] y

Downloading ftp cue-vm.ise.3.0.3.pkg
Bytes downloaded :  176977

Validating package signature ... done
 - Parsing package manifest files... complete.
Validating installed manifests ...........complete.
 - Checking Package dependencies... complete.

Downloading ftp cue-vm-langpack.ise.3.0.3.pkg
Bytes downloaded :  575607

Validating package signature ... done
Found Add-On Subsystem SID: e2e81cc6-39b5-47e1-9f83-b83c897fc50c Name: CUE
Voice Mail Language
```

Support Version: 3.0.0.0
Found Add-On Subsystem SID: c28339fa-f7ae-4732-85ab-fa6c68b5de0c Name: CUE
Voice Mail Italian Version: 3.0.0.0
Found Add-On Subsystem SID: 49f09114-e0b0-4721-8b85-04be2064920c
Name: CUE Voice Mail European Spanish Version: 3.0.0.0
Found Add-On Subsystem SID: 27e5e2ab-1622-4c02-8a0a-cfad0d932148
Name: CUE Voice Mail US English Version: 3.0.0.0
Found Add-On Subsystem SID: cf860289-67ac-4886-9295-a41e4c7a8487
Name: CUE Voice Mail European French Version: 3.0.0.0
Found Add-On Subsystem SID: f0a41398-3917-4d49-b5ab-c2b39a80c121
Name: CUE Voice Mail Latin American Spanish Version: 3.0.0.0
Found Add-On Subsystem SID: c4ca62e2-daff-40dc-b94e-bf20094bd700
Name: CUE Voice Mail Mexican Spanish Version: 3.0.0.0
Found Add-On Subsystem SID: 683674a5-e6ef-4c97-8e05-efbba1e6fe47
Name: CUE Voice Mail Canadian French Version: 3.0.0.0
Found Add-On Subsystem SID: fa803d25-9c89-4171-a14c-ec12d6ed6b8c
Name: CUE Voice Mail UK English Version: 3.0.0.0
Found Add-On Subsystem SID: 3f968fd0-6598-48e2-be1c-4af6c2e02e02
Name: CUE Voice Mail German Version: 3.0.0.0
Found Add-On Subsystem SID: 88f73a6c-884d-4838-b162-1b544dd6583f
Name: CUE Voice Mail Danish Version: 3.0.0.0
Found Add-On Subsystem SID: a2ba4f96-3452-40c3-83ad-c442cb6bf42f
Name: CUE Voice Mail Brazilian Portuguese Version: 3.0.0.0
 - Parsing package manifest files... complete.
 - Checking Package dependencies... complete.
 - Checking Manifest dependencies for subsystems in the install candidate list...
complete

Starting payload download
File : cue-vm-full.ise.3.0.3.prt1 Bytes : 95600813
Validating payloads match registered checksums...
 - cue-vm-full.ise.3.0.3.prt1
....verified
Extracting install scripts ...
starting_phase:
install-files.sh /dwnld/.script_work_order
add_file /dwnld/pkgdata/cue-vm-full.ise.3.0.3.prt1 13 /dwnld/scripts/e2e81cc6-
39b5-47e1-9f83-b83c897fc50c usr/bin/products/cue/lang_ui_script.py tgz
Scripts extraction complete.
Remove scripts work order /dwnld/.script_work_order
Running Script Processor for ui_install

At this point, the new software has been downloaded from the FTP server to storage on the Unity express system and the installation process begins. The install script that is run will ask you what language or languages you wish the Unity Express to run in. Depending on the hardware platform used, a different maximum number of language add-ons is allowed. This particular hardware allows for up to two languages to be installed. High-end ISR routers with Unity Express network modules can support up to five languages. The following shows that we ask that only US English be installed in the clean installation:

```
Maximum 2 language add-ons allowed for this platform.
Please select language(s) to install from the following list:

Language Installation Menu:

 # Selected   SKU     Language Name (version)
-------------------------------------------------------------------------
 1            ITA     CUE Voice Mail Italian (3.0.0.0)
 2            ESP     CUE Voice Mail European Spanish (3.0.0.0)
 3            ENU     CUE Voice Mail US English (3.0.0.0)
 4            FRA     CUE Voice Mail European French (3.0.0.0)
 5            ESO     CUE Voice Mail Latin American Spanish (3.0.0.0)
 6            ESM     CUE Voice Mail Mexican Spanish (3.0.0.0)
 7            FRC     CUE Voice Mail Canadian French (3.0.0.0)
 8            ENG     CUE Voice Mail UK English (3.0.0.0)
 9            DEU     CUE Voice Mail German (3.0.0.0)
10            DAN     CUE Voice Mail Danish (3.0.0.0)
11            PTB     CUE Voice Mail Brazilian Portuguese (3.0.0.0)
-------------------------------------------------------------------------

Available commands are:
# - enter the number for the language to select one
r # - remove the language for given #
i # - more information about the language for given #
x - Done with language selection

Enter Command:Enter Command:3

Language Installation Menu:

 # Selected   SKU     Language Name (version)
-------------------------------------------------------------------------
 1            ITA     CUE Voice Mail Italian (3.0.0.0)
 2            ESP     CUE Voice Mail European Spanish (3.0.0.0)
```

```
3        *     ENU    CUE Voice Mail US English (3.0.0.0)
4              FRA    CUE Voice Mail European French (3.0.0.0)
5              ESO    CUE Voice Mail Latin American Spanish (3.0.0.0)
6              ESM    CUE Voice Mail Mexican Spanish (3.0.0.0)
7              FRC    CUE Voice Mail Canadian French (3.0.0.0)
8              ENG    CUE Voice Mail UK English (3.0.0.0)
9              DEU    CUE Voice Mail German (3.0.0.0)
10             DAN    CUE Voice Mail Danish (3.0.0.0)
11             PTB    CUE Voice Mail Brazilian Portuguese (3.0.0.0)
--------------------------------------------------------------------

Available commands are:
# - enter the number for the language to select one
r # - remove the language for given #
i # - more information about the language for given #
x - Done with language selection

Enter Command:x
ui_install scripts executed successfully.
UC500-CUE#
```

Once you see the message that the ui_install scripts executed successfully, the software install process is complete. Unity Express will then reboot and come back online using the newly installed software.

We're not quite finished yet, however. Accompanying any new software install, we must also download and install the software licensing information. When we downloaded and extracted the zip file from cisco.com that contained the Unity Express software, a license file for the version of CUE for the UC500 hardware came with it. Different licenses are tied to the specific hardware platform Unity Express resides on. You must install the correct license that does not exceed hardware specifications. To accomplish this task, we again use the software install clean privileged exec command and specify the FTP location, filename, and any required authentication parameters. Here is an example of this process in action:

```
UC500-CUE# software install clean url ftp://192.168.1.100/cue-vm-license_50mbx_
cme_ise.3.0.3.pkg username cisco
password for cisco :

WARNING:: This command will download the necessary software to
WARNING:: complete a clean install.  It is recommended that a backup be done
WARNING:: before installing software.

WARNING:: The system will briefly be brought to an offline state
```

```
WARNING:: This will terminate any active call and prevent new calls
WARNING:: from being processed.

Would you like to continue? [n] y

Downloading ftp cue-vm-license_50mbx_cme_ise.3.0.3.pkg
Bytes downloaded :  6373

Validating package signature ... done
compatibility mode
 - Parsing package manifest files... complete.
Validating installed manifests ............complete.
 - Checking Package dependencies... complete.
 - Checking Manifest dependencies for subsystems in the install candidate
list...complete
```

We can now run a `show software license` privileged exec command to verify that our license is properly installed:

```
UC500-CUE# show software license
Installed license files:
 - voice mail_lic.sig : 50 MAILBOX LICENSE

Core:
 - Application mode: CCME
 - Total usable system ports: 6

Voice Mail/Auto Attendant:
 - Max system mailbox capacity time: 840
 - Default # of general delivery mailboxes: 15
 - Default # of personal mailboxes: 50

 - Max # of configurable mailboxes: 65

Interactive Voice Response:
 - Max # of IVR ports: Not Available

Languages:
 - Max installed languages: 2
 - Max enabled languages: 1
```

This command shows us our license maximums for the Unity Express system. We find the following licensing information within the output of this command:

- Maximum number of configurable mailboxes (65)
  - 50 personal mailboxes
  - 15 general delivery mailboxes
- Total number of simultaneous ports (lines) into Unity Express (6)
- Maximum number of mailbox minutes (840)
- Maximum number of IVR ports ("Not Available" because we need to purchase and install a separate IVR license to use this functionality)
- Maximum number of enabled (1) and installed (2) languages

Our Unity Express system is now installed and licensed. We can issue a show run privileged exec command to view the default configuration on the newly installed software. Remember that because this is a clean install, these settings are prebuilt configurations by the CUE software. We will run through the Installation Wizard to modify many of these configuration parameters:

```
UC500-CUE# show run
Generating configuration:

clock timezone America/Los_Angeles

hostname UC500-CUE

ip domain-name localdomain

system language preferred "en_US"

ntp server 10.1.10.2 prefer

software download server url "ftp://127.0.0.1/ftp" credentials hidden
"6u/dKTN/hsEuSoEfw4OXlF2eFHnZfyUTSd8ZZNgd+Y9J3x
lk2B35jOnfGWTYHfmPSd8ZZNgd+Y9J3x
lk2B35jOnfGWTYHfmPSd8ZZNgd+Y9J3xlk2B35jOnfGWTYHfgT"

groupname Administrators create
groupname Broadcasters create

username cisco create

groupname Administrators member cisco
groupname Administrators privilege ManagePrompts
```

```
groupname Administrators privilege broadcast
groupname Administrators privilege local-broadcast
groupname Administrators privilege ManagePublicList
groupname Administrators privilege ViewPrivateList
groupname Administrators privilege vm-imap
groupname Administrators privilege ViewHistoricalReports
groupname Administrators privilege ViewRealTimeReports
groupname Administrators privilege superuser
groupname Broadcasters privilege broadcast

restriction msg-notification create
restriction msg-notification min-digits 1
restriction msg-notification max-digits 30
restriction msg-notification dial-string preference 1 pattern * allowed

backup server url "ftp://127.0.0.1/ftp" credentials hidden
"EWlTygcMhYmj5tXhE/VNXHCkplVV4KjescbDaLa4fl4WLSPFvv1rWUnfGWTYHfmPSd8ZZNgd-
Y9J3xlk2B35jOnfGWTYHfmPSd8ZZNgd+Y9J3xlk2B35jOnfGWTYHfmP"

calendar biz-schedule systemschedule
 open day 1 from 00:00 to 24:00
 open day 2 from 00:00 to 24:00
 open day 3 from 00:00 to 24:00
 open day 4 from 00:00 to 24:00
 open day 5 from 00:00 to 24:00
 open day 6 from 00:00 to 24:00
 open day 7 from 00:00 to 24:00
 end schedule

ccn application autoattendant aa
 description "autoattendant"
 enabled
 maxsessions 6
 script "aa.aef"
 parameter "busClosedPrompt" "AABusinessClosed.wav"
 parameter "holidayPrompt" "AAHolidayPrompt.wav"
 parameter "welcomePrompt" "AAWelcome.wav"
 parameter "disconnectAfterMenu" "false"
 parameter "dialByFirstName" "false"
 parameter "allowExternalTransfers" "false"
 parameter "MaxRetry" "3"
 parameter "dialByExtnAnytime" "false"
```

```
 parameter "busOpenPrompt" "AABusinessOpen.wav"
 parameter "businessSchedule" "systemschedule"
 parameter "dialByExtnAnytimeInputLength" "4"
 parameter "operExtn" "0"
 end application

ccn application ciscomwiapplication aa
 description "ciscomwiapplication"
 enabled
 maxsessions 6
 script "setmwi.aef"
 parameter "CallControlGroupID" "0"
 parameter "strMWI_OFF_DN" "8001"
 parameter "strMWI_ON_DN" "8000"
 end application

ccn application msgnotification aa
 description "msgnotification"
 enabled
 maxsessions 6
 script "msgnotify.aef"
 parameter "logoutUri" "http://localhost/voice mail/vxmlscripts/mbxLogout.jsp"
 parameter "DelayBeforeSendDTMF" "1"
 end application

ccn application promptmgmt aa
 description "promptmgmt"
 enabled
 maxsessions 1
 script "promptmgmt.aef"
 end application

ccn application voice mail aa
 description "voice mail"
 enabled
 maxsessions 6
 script "voicebrowser.aef"
 parameter "logoutUri" "http://localhost/voice mail/vxmlscripts/mbxLogout.jsp"
 parameter "uri" "http://localhost/voice mail/vxmlscripts/login.vxml"
 end application

ccn engine
```

```
  end engine

ccn reporting historical
 database local
 description "UC500-CUE"
 end reporting

ccn subsystem sip
 end subsystem

ccn trigger http urlname msgnotifytrg
 application "msgnotification"
 enabled
 maxsessions 2
 end trigger

ccn trigger http urlname mwiapp
 application "ciscomwiapplication"
 enabled
 maxsessions 1
 end trigger

security password lockout policy temp-lock
security pin lockout policy temp-lock
service phone-authentication
 end phone-authentication

service voiceview
 enable
 end voiceview

voice mail default mailboxsize 775
voice mail broadcast recording time 300
voice mail notification restriction msg-notification

end
```

Some of these defaults will remain the same, and others will change to fit our environment. We could go ahead and configure the Unity Express system entirely through the command line. But the CCNA Voice exam tends to focus on the GUI for software initialization and configuration, so that's what this book will follow. Next, you'll learn to use the web GUI to run the Unity Express Initialization Wizard.

Unity Express Setup Using the Initialization Wizard

Using our example setup of configuring a separate IP network for CUE connectivity, we can open a web browser to http://172.16.1.2 and go through the GUI *Unity Express Initialization Wizard*.

In order to use either the CUCM Express or the Unity Express web GUI features, you must enable HTTP server functionality on the CUCM Express router. This configuration information can be found in Chapter 5 under the heading "Enabling the GUI Interface."

The first screen is the Authentication page, which asks you to log in with a User Name and Password, as shown in Figure 8.11.

FIGURE 8.11   The Unity Express authentication page

Notice that the page says "System is not initialized. Only Administrator logins are allowed" in bold red text. When we performed our upgrade, a general post-installation script was automatically run, which created a generic Administrator User Name and Password. The User Name is cisco and the Password is cisco. We enter the authentication information into the fields and click the Login button to proceed. The next screen presents four different options, as shown in Figure 8.12.

FIGURE 8.12   Initialization Wizard options

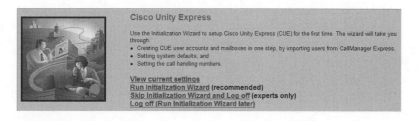

The first option is to view the current settings configured on the Unity Express system. These will be the factory default settings. The second option is to run the Initialization Wizard. The other two options let us skip the wizard or log off the system. We want to run through the Initialization Wizard, so we will click that link and begin the Initialization Wizard.

The Unity Express system wants to check the CUCM Express configuration for any information already configured on it that should be pulled into Unity Express. Items such as phone usernames/passwords and MWI configurations will automatically be read off the CUCM Express configuration and pulled into Unity Express. Figure 8.13 shows the CUCM Express login credentials page.

FIGURE 8.13 CUCM Express login credentials

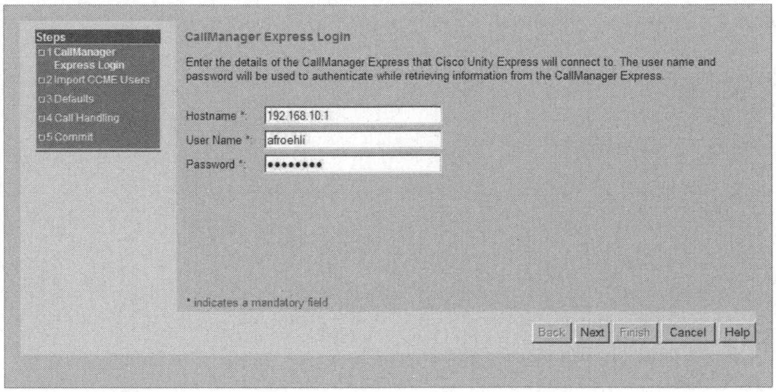

The Unity Express wants us to enter the Hostname of the CUCM Express system to which we will be connecting Unity Express. The IP address of the telephony-service source address should be already populated here. The User Name required is one of the local usernames created on the CUCM Express for managing the router. Enter the information and the password and click the Next button.

Using the supplied credentials, Unity Express automatically reads the CUCM Express configuration to see if any phone users have been previously configured on the system. If there are, the usernames, extensions, and privileges are imported into Unity Express. Figure 8.14 shows that our CUCM Express did not have any users configured at the time the Initialization Wizard was run.

FIGURE 8.14 Importing CUCM Express phone users

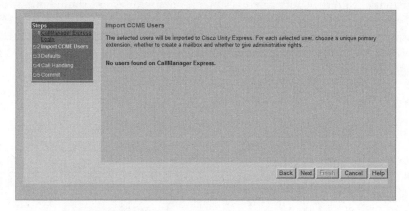

Click the Next button to continue the Initialization Wizard.

The next screen displays different default parameters for the Unity Express mailboxes. Figure 8.15 shows the page with the default settings.

FIGURE 8.15 Unity Express mailbox default settings

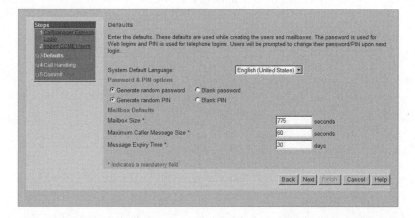

In this page, we can change the default mailbox language spoken in the automated voice mail prompts. We can also change the behavior for new mailbox password/PIN settings as well as mailbox size, message size, and message expiration time limits. You can either leave the default settings as is or change them to suit your preferences. Click the Next button to continue.

The Call Handling page lists the extension numbers for voice mail, auto attendant, and MWI functions within the Unity Express system. These extensions should match the dial-peer numbers we created on the CUCM Express earlier in the configuration process. Note that the MWI extensions were automatically pulled in by the CUCM Express. Figure 8.16 shows the screen with the proper extension numbers entered to match our CUCM Express dial-peer configurations.

FIGURE 8.16   CUCM Express call handling

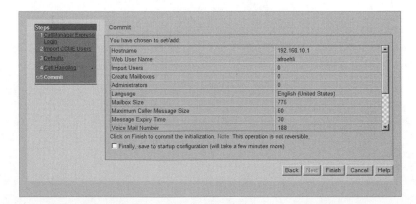

On this page, the only mandatory number to fill in is the voice mail pilot extension. All other fields can be left blank if you choose not to use the features. Click the Next button to continue the Initialization Wizard.

Finally, we are presented with a Commit page, which lists the settings that we just configured. If you want to make any changes to the configuration at this point, you can click the Back button to move backward through the wizard. If you are satisfied with the configuration settings, you can click the Finally, Save To Startup Configuration check box and click the Finish button shown in Figure 8.17.

FIGURE 8.17   Unity Express Initialization Wizard commit page

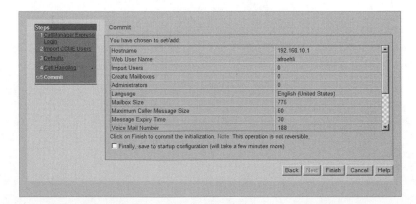

The wizard will then save the configurations on both the Unity Express and CUCM Express systems. Why does the process include saving the CUCM Express configuration? The Unity Express system added a `voice mail 188` command into the telephony-service section of its configuration using the supplied username and password you gave it during the wizard process. This command tells CUCM Express that to reach voice mail features, it should dial extension 188.

Restoring Unity Express to Factory Default Settings

Whether you're in a lab environment or in production, there will come a time when you will need to completely blow away your voice mail system and start from scratch. Cisco provides an easy way to use the command line to first suspend voice mail services and then set the configuration back to *factory default settings*. Keep in mind that once the process starts, there is no way to retrieve any voice mail, AA, or other configuration settings, so be very careful that you have backups of anything you might need! The following steps show how to restore Unity Express to factory default settings.

Step 1: Suspend Unity Express Services

The first step is to suspend voice mail service processes. To accomplish this, you must session in to the CUE device and get into privileged exec mode. You then can run the `offline` command. Unity Express will ask if you are sure you want to take voice mail offline. To proceed, type y and then press the Enter key, as shown in the following example:

```
Router#service-module integrated-Service-Engine 0/0 session
Trying 10.1.10.2, 2002 ... Open
UC500-CUE>
UC500-CUE> en
Password:
UC500-CUE# offline
!!!WARNING!!!: If you are going offline to do a backup, it is recommended
that you save the current running configuration using the 'write' command,
prior to going to the offline state.

Putting the system offline will terminate all end user sessions.

Are you sure you want to go offline[n]? : y
UC500-CUE(offline)#
```

Step 2: Restore Factory Defaults on Unity Express

Now that Unity Express is in an offline state, it will no longer process voice mail or auto attendant functions. You are now safe to reset the software to bring it back to a clean state, that is, before you made any configuration changes. To do that, run the `restore factory default` command, as shown here. Unity Express will again ask you if you are sure you want to perform this task; press y and the Enter key to continue.

```
UC500-CUE(offline)# restore factory default
!!!WARNING!!!: This operation will cause all configuration and data
on the system to be erased. This operation is not reversible.

Do you wish to continue[n]? : y
Restoring the system. Please wait .....done
System will be restored to factory default when it reloads.

Press any key to reload:

System reloading ....
<output removed>
```

The Cisco Unity Express system will erase everything saved on the system and reboot into factory default mode. It will then come up in an online state that is brand new and ready to be configured from scratch.

Summary

This chapter covered the typical and advanced voice mail features of Unity Express. We also looked at the additional CUE functionality of the auto attendant and Interactive Voice Response tools and then covered the proper licensing structure for your Unity Express. Finally, we got our hands on a Unity Express, and you learned how to upgrade, install, and initialize Unity Express to the point where you will be ready to begin configuring features on the system.

Now you have seen the types of voice mail features that Unity Express can provide. Voice mail technology has evolved to be much more than a method for people to leave messages while you are away from your desk. The capability to be notified of messages virtually anywhere in the world and the continuing integration with email make this technology a vital business communication tool that will continue to thrive for years to come.

Exam Essentials

Know the difference between subscriber and group mailboxes.   Subscriber mailboxes are for individual users. Group mailboxes are shared by a group of users.

Know the different types of message notifications.   Users can be informed of messages waiting within mailboxes through the flashing envelope icon on the LCD display or by the message waiting indicator light on the phone handset when using Cisco IP phones.

Understand the purpose and different types of distribution lists.   Distribution lists are used to send a single voice mail message to multiple recipients at the same time. Public distribution lists are globally set up by the voice administrator and can be used by anyone. Private distribution lists are created by individual users and can be used only by that individual.

Know the different types of mailbox caller features.   When a person leaves a message on a Unity Express voice mail system, they not only can leave a message but can also perform other functions such as reviewing, rerecording, canceling, and setting the message priority. They can also choose to use the operator assistance feature or even log in to their own mailbox if they have the proper security credentials in the form of a PIN.

Know the different types of Unity Express advanced user functionality.   Besides using the TUI for checking messages, administrators can configure VoiceView Express and/or integrated messaging to increase the flexibility for message retrieval.

Understand the components that make up the CUE auto attendant.   The auto attendant provides a flexible, automated, voice answering service for businesses. There are multiple ways of creating AA scripts, including using preinstalled scripts, the Editor Express, and the Custom Script Editor application.

Understand Interactive Voice Response.   IVR is an advanced automated voice system that lets users navigate through a menu system to receive up-to-date information that is pulled off a database and transformed into voice scripts. The Unity Express IVR also can be configured to send emails or faxes automatically based on caller responses to the IVR.

Understand CUE licensing.   There are two types of Unity Express mailbox licensing packages. Only one license is required based on the type of CUCM you are running. You purchase these licenses based on the number of mailboxes, ranging from 12 to 250. A separate IVR license is required if you plan to run the IVR application.

Know how to configure the CUE to communicate with CUCM Express.   The CUE is a completely separate device from a network and software point of view. You must be able to configure the CUE to properly communicate with CUCM Express over a logical IP connection. You then need to set up dial peers to forward voice calls to the CUE.

Know how to configure MWI ephone-DNs.   The message waiting indicator light requires specially configured ephone-DNs to turn on and off the MWI light and LCD indicator on Cisco IP phones.

Know how to upgrade Unity Express software.   Understand the different Unity Express software files and how to perform a software upgrade from scratch.

Know how to set up Unity Express using the Configuration Wizard.   Unity Express provides a web GUI wizard for the initial setup of the software. Understand what each step in the wizard is for.

Know how to restore Unity Express to factory defaults.   Understand the process required to suspend and reload the software to bring it back to its factory default settings.

Written Lab 8.1

Write the answers to the following questions:

1. What is the name of the mailbox that is shared by multiple users?

2. What term refers to a message notification that will continue to trigger alerts to different destinations until the notification is acknowledged?

3. Name the type of distribution list that is significant only to the user who created it.

4. What is a Unity Express voice mail retrieval method where users can use the Cisco IP phone LCD display and softkeys to check messages?

5. What is the name for the convergence of email and voice mail that is offered by Unity Express?

6. Name the AA script-editing software that runs on Microsoft Windows platforms.

7. What is the command used to set the Unity Express integrated service engine to share or borrow an IP address from the already configured loopback 0 interface?

8. Name the three dial peers commonly configured to point to a Unity Express system.

9. What command is used when setting up the SIP trunk between CUCM Express and Unity Express to tell the CUCM Express to not use voice audio detection?

10. What Unity Express software install command is used to upgrade the CUE software while maintaining and reusing the previous configuration on the system?

   (The answers to Written Lab 8.1 can be found following the answers to the review questions for this chapter.)

Hands-on Labs

To complete the labs in this section, you need a CUCM Express router with a Cisco Unity Express module. Each lab in this section builds on the last and will follow the CUCM Express to Unity Express integration according to the information found in Table 8.3.

TABLE 8.3 Lab parameters

Description	Parameter
Loopback 0 IP address	172.16.10.1/24
Service-Engine 0/1 IP address	IP unnumbered
Service-Module IP address	172.16.10.2/24
Voice mail pilot	297
AA extension	298
AvT extension	299
MWI light on	A11
MWI light off	A12

Here is a list of the labs in this chapter:

Lab 8.1: Configuring IP Network Connectivity Using the `ip unnumbered` Command

Lab 8.2: Configuring Unity Express Dial Peers

Lab 8.3: Configuring MWI Ephone-DNs

Hands-on Lab 8.1: Configuring IP Network Connectivity Using the *ip unnumbered* Command

In this lab, we're going to configure IP connectivity between the CUCM Express and Unity Express. We will be using the `ip unnumbered` technique for the virtual network connecting the two logically separated devices. Use Table 8.3 for the proper IP address and subnet mask information.

1.   Log in to your CUCM Express router and go into configuration mode by typing **enable** and then **configuration terminal**.

2.   Configure an IP address on the loopback interface by typing **interface loopback 0** and then **ip address 172.16.10.1 255.255.255.0**.

3.   Configure the Service-Engine to share an IP address with loopback 0 by typing **interface Service-Engine 0/1** and then **ip unnumbered loopback 0**.

4.   Configure networking on the service module by first adding the IP address and then adding a default gateway that points to the CUCM Express Service-Engine. To accomplish this, type **service-module ip address 172.16.10.2 255.255.255.0** and then **service-module ip default-gateway 172.16.10.1**.

5.   Exit config-interface mode by typing **exit**.

6.   Add a static route on the CUCM Express router that directs IP traffic destined to Unity Express. Type **ip route 172.16.10.2 255.255.255.255 Service-Engine 0/1**.

7.   Exit configuration mode by typing **end**.

Hands-on Lab 8.2: Configuring Unity Express Dial Peers

In the second lab, we will configure dial peers for the voice mail, AA, and AvT extensions that point to the IP address we assigned as the Unity Express. These SIP trunk dial peers will use the specific parameters required by Unity Express to function properly.

1.   Log in to your CUCM Express router and go into configuration mode by typing **enable** and then **configuration terminal**.

2.   We want to create a dial peer for our voice mail pilot extension according to the information in Table 8.3. To add a new dial peer, type **dial-peer voice 297 voip**.

3.   Add a description for our dial peer by typing **description VM Pilot**.

4.   Add our extension as the destination trigger by typing **destination-pattern 297**.

5.   Set the trunk protocol to SIP version 2 by typing **session protocol sipv2**.

6.   Point the dial-peer destination to the IP address of our Unity Express system by typing **session target ipv4:172.16.10.2**.

7.   Set the proper DTMF signaling by typing **dtmf-relay sip-notify**.

8.   Set the codec to G.711 by typing **codec g711ulaw**.

9.   Ensure that VAD is disabled by typing **no vad**.

10.   Repeat steps 2 through 9 for the AA and AvT extensions by replacing the descriptions and extensions to match those found in Table 8.3.

11.   Exit config-dial-peer mode by typing **end**.

Hands-on Lab 8.3: Configuring MWI Ephone-DNs

In the third and final lab, we will configure the message waiting indicator on and off ephone-DNs. These will then be triggered by Unity Express to give a visual alert to a user that they have a new voice message in their mailbox. Use the extensions given in Table 8.3. Also assume that Cisco IP phones configured on this system are three digits in length.

1. Log in to your CUCM Express router and go into configuration mode by typing **enable** and then **configuration terminal**.

2. Create a new ephone-DN for our MWI on signal. Use 111 as the label by typing **ephone-dn 111**.

3. Add the extension trigger and three-digit wildcard by typing **number a11...**.

4. Set this ephone-DN to be designated as our MWI on signal by typing **mwi on**.

5. Create a second ephone-DN for our MWI off signal. Use 112 as the label by typing **ephone-dn 112**.

6. Add the extension trigger and three-digit wildcard by typing **number a12...**.

7. Set this ephone-DN to be designated as our MWI off signal by typing **mwi off**.

8. Exit config-ephone-DN mode by typing **end**.

Review Questions

1. What name is used to describe a personal mailbox on Unity Express?

   A. General delivery

   B. VoiceView Express

   C. Caller ID

   D. Subscriber

   E. Integrated messaging

2. Where on the CUE GUI can you go to synchronize configurations that are shared between the CUCM Express and CUE Express?

   A. Administration ➤ Synchronize

   B. Administration ➤ Write Memory

   C. Synchronize ➤ CUCM Express

   D. Synchronize ➤ Write Memory

3. When a CUCM Express user is imported into Unity Express, which default PIN is *not* an option?

   A. Randomly generated

   B. Left blank

   C. Automatically set the same as the user extension

   D. Manually entered by the administrator

4. The red MWI light can be used on which Cisco phone button(s)?

   A. Button 1

   B. Button 1 or 2

   C. Any button with the feature ring configured

   D. Any phone button

5. When running the Unity Express Initialization Wizard, what information will *not* be imported from the CUCM Express configuration?

   A. MWI extensions

   B. MoH audio files

   C. Usernames

   D. User passwords

   E. Ephone-DN

6. Which of the following devices cannot be configured on Unity Express for message notification?

   A. PSTN telephone

   B. Cellular telephone

   C. Pager

   D. RFID

7. Which of the following is *not* an audio file requirement necessary to make your own audio prompts for the auto attendant?

   A. 8-bit

   B. 8 kHz

   C. G.711 a-law codec

   D. Mono

8. Auto attendant scripts are saved as what type of format?

   A. .wav

   B. .au

   C. G.711 u-law

   D. .aef

9. What Cisco feature allows callers to interact with a voice menu system to receive customized information or to trigger tasks such as sending faxes or email messages?

   A. AA

   B. IVR

   C. AvT

   D. TUI

10. When the Unity Express Initialization Wizard is complete and changes are being saved, why does the wizard also perform a configuration save on the CUCM Express?

    A. To ensure that the clocks are synchronized

    B. To update IP network changes that were made within the wizard

    C. To automatically update dial-peer rules on the CUCM Express

    D. To modify the MAC addresses of the ephones to match those found on Unity Express

11. Which of the following files is a CUE mailbox license for running up to 25 mailboxes on a CUCM Express system?

    A. cue-vm-license_25mbx_ccm_7.0.1.pkg

    B. cue-vm-license_25mbx_cme_7.0.1.pkg

    C. cue-vm-license_25mbx_ivr_7.0.1.pkg

    D. cue-vm-license_12mbx_ccm_7.0.1.pkg

12. What is the largest number of IVR licenses that can be purchased?

    A. 10

    B. 50

    C. 20

    D. 250

13. What is considered to be the logical interface of the Cisco Unity Express from an IP networking standpoint?

   A. Loopback 0

   B. Service-Module

   C. Integrated-Service-Engine 0/0

   D. FastEthernet 1/0/1

14. Which two statements about the Unity Express Initialization Wizard are *not* correct?

   A. Only administrators are able to log in and run the wizard for the first time.

   B. The wizard saves the configuration on Unity Express after each configuration section.

   C. Configuring an auto attendant extension is mandatory.

   D. Configuring a voice mail extension is mandatory.

15. A subscriber mailbox password serves what purpose?

   A. To allow a user to log in to their mailbox using the TUI

   B. To allow a user to log in to their mailbox using the web GUI

   C. To allow a user to log in to the AvT

   D. A one-time password used to set the PIN

16. Which of the following configurations is *not* required to configure IP networking properly for the Cisco Unity Express?

   A. IP address on the Integrated-Service-Engine

   B. IP address on the Service-Module

   C. Integrated-Service-Engine

   D. Dial peer for the voice mail pilot number

   E. Static route pointing the Service-Module IP address to the Integrated-Service-Engine interface

17. When configuring the SIP trunk between the CUCM Express and Unity Express systems, what does the `dtmf-relay sip-notify` config-dial-peer command do?

   A. Gathers and sends DTMF tones from Unity Express to the CUCM Express

   B. Gathers and sends DTMF tones from the CUCM Express to Unity Express

   C. Gathers and sends pulse tones from Unity Express to the CUCM Express

   D. Gathers and sends pulse tones from the CUCM Express to Unity Express

18. What type of dial peers are used to configure Unity Express pilot numbers for voice mail, AA, and AvT?

   A. PSTN dial peers

   B. POTS dial peers

   C. IPv4 dial peers

   D. VoIP dial peers

19. When performing a Unity Express software upgrade, what type of server can you use to transfer the software files to Unity Express storage?

    A. TFTP server

    B. CIFS server

    C. FTP server

    D. SMB server

20. The Call Handling page of the Unity Express Initialization Wizard lists all of the following extensions *except*:

    A. Voice mail number

    B. AvT number

    C. Voice mail operation extension

    D. MWI extensions

    E. Directory extension

Answers to Review Questions

1.   D. A subscriber mailbox is a personal mailbox assigned to a single user.

2.   A. To synchronize shared configurations between the CUCM Express and CUE, you navigate to Administration ➤ Synchronize within the Unity Express web GUI.

3.   C. The CUCM Express cannot automatically set the PIN to be the same as the user extension.

4.   A. The red MWI light can be used only for the primary extension, which is configured on button 1.

5.   B. Music on Hold (MoH) is solely handled by the CUCM Express, so there is no need for Unity Express to pull audio files over.

6.   D. All of the devices except RFID can be configured for message notification.

7.   C. The codec must be G.711 u-law.

8.   D. All scripts used by Unity Express are saved in the `.aef` format.

9.   B. The Interactive Voice Response (IVR) feature allows callers to interact by sending and receiving tailored information.

10. C. Changes such as those to voice mail dial peers need to be made on the CUCM Express for Unity Express to function properly. These changes are made to CUCM Express within the Initialization Wizard and then are automatically saved.

11. B. Option B is the correct CUE license for the CME for up to 25 mailbox licenses.

12. C. IVR licenses can be purchased in bundles of 2, 4, 8, 16, and 20.

13. B. The Service-Module is the logical representation of the Unity Express interface.

14. B, C. The wizard saves the configuration only at the end when the administrator commits to the changes. Also, the AA extension is not a mandatory field.

15. B. The subscriber password allows the user to log in to the web GUI to check messages or make changes to mailbox settings. The TUI uses a PIN for login purposes.

16. D. The dial-peer statements are required for proper functionality of the Unity Express system, but they are not necessary for IP networking.

17. B. The command is used to notify the CUCM Express that DTMF tones should be sent to Unity Express over the SIP trunk.

18. D. VoIP dial peers are configured for Unity Express pilot numbers and are directed over the SIP trunk.

19. C. An FTP server can be used to transfer the new software over to Unity Express storage for installation.

20. E. There is never a defined extension for either the local or corporate directory.

Answers to Written Lab 8.1

1. General delivery mailbox (GDM)

2. Cascading notification

3. Private distribution list

4. VoiceView Express

5. Integrated messaging

6. Custom Script Editor

7. `ip unnumbered loopback 0`

8. Voice mail, AvT, and AA pilot numbers

9. `no vad`

10. `software install upgrade`

Chapter

9

Unity Express Configuration

THE CCNA VOICE EXAM TOPICS COVERED IN THIS CHAPTER INCLUDE THE FOLLOWING:

✓ **Implement voice mail features using Cisco Unity Express.**

- Describe the features available in Cisco Unity Express.

- Configure basic voice mail features using Cisco Unity Express.

- Configure Auto Attendant services using Cisco Unity Express.

✓ **Communications Manager Express.**

- Explain basic troubleshooting methods for Cisco Unity Express.

A large part of any Unified Communications (UC) administrator's role is the implementation phase. This phase requires that the administrator have a solid understanding of how to configure a device to do what they intend it to do. Essentially the design creates a set of instructions, and the UC engineer must then carry out those instructions in the form of a configuration.

Chapter 9 is basically a set of instructions you can use to build various features that your business requires. Along the way you will learn what Unity Express is capable of by configuring it with the web GUI. To administrate CUE, you will also need to learn how to run file backups and restores as well as run and view trace files for troubleshooting.

Configuring Unity Express System Settings and Voice Mail Defaults

This section will guide you through the basics of setting up the Cisco Unity Express system settings and default voice mail capabilities. The system administrator will determine the settings required based on the geographic location of the system, Unity Express capabilities, and the needs of users and groups who utilize the mailboxes contained within the system. I'll first cover the general system settings for the CUE. After that, you'll learn how to set the systemwide default settings that will be used when creating new mailboxes for both subscribers and groups.

Configuring System Settings

System settings on the Unity Express are parameters that will likely be set only once throughout the life of the system. Functions such as time zones, DNS server settings, language settings, and call-in numbers fall within this category. Let's step through some of the most commonly used system settings. Keep in mind that you must be logged in with an administrator account to perform any of the systemwide configurations.

NTP and Time Zone

Just as in the CUCM Express, configuring a Network Time Protocol (NTP) server is vital for proper operation of Unity Express. Your mailbox subscribers need to have an accurate clock so they can determine the time a message was left for them. To point Unity Express at an NTP server, you first must log in with a user account that has administrative rights. Once you're logged in, go to System ➤ Network Time & Time Zone Settings. Figure 9.1 shows the configuration options available when configuring NTP and time zones.

FIGURE 9.1   Network time and time zone settings

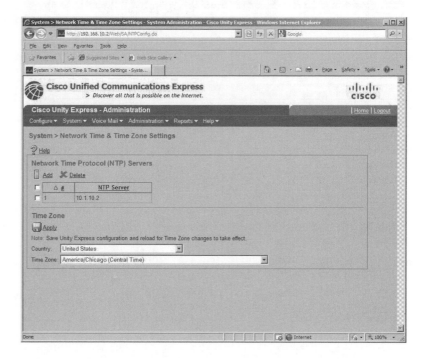

You can configure multiple NTP servers on the system by clicking the Add button and entering the IP address of the NTP server you wish to synchronize time with.

> After making any change on the Unity Express GUI, you must click the Apply button to activate the change and save it on the system.

Domain Name Settings

If you need your Unity Express to resolve hostnames to IP addresses within the system, then you will need to configure Domain Name System (DNS) settings. Features such as Integrated Messaging will often require the use of a DNS server in order to forward mail to an SMTP gateway that is configured with a domain name instead of an IP address. To configure these settings, navigate to System ➤ Domain Name Settings. Figure 9.2 shows the configuration options for setting the Unity Express local hostname and domain as well as the option to add a DNS server for domain name lookups.

FIGURE 9.2 Domain name settings

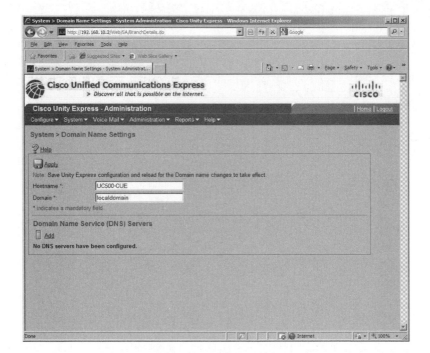

You will notice that the Hostname and Domain fields have already been populated. This is because the two settings are required and were given default names when the CUE was initialized.

If you wish to configure a DNS server, click the Add button and enter the IP address of the DNS server you want to resolve hostnames against.

Default Language

An administrator will want to set the System Default Language setting on the CUE to the primary language their voice mail users speak. This setting can also be changed at the user and group levels, but this is where the default is configured for all new users and groups set up on the system. To set the default language, go to System ➤ Language Settings. As shown in Figure 9.3, you select the default language from the drop-down list.

FIGURE 9.3   Setting the default language

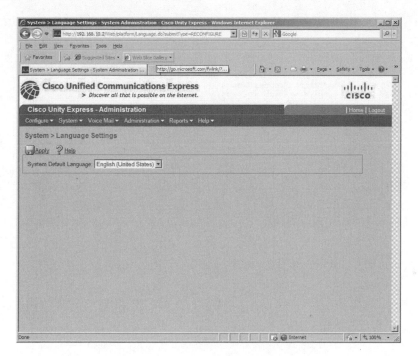

Depending on the capabilities of your Unity Express system and the language packages installed, you may have anywhere from one to five languages to choose from. The maximum number of language packages on a single CUE is five.

Call-in Numbers

Callers use three primary call-in numbers for Unity Express to reach CUE applications:

Voice mail   The access number used to access the Voice Mail application

Auto attendant   The access number used to access the Auto Attendant application

Promptmgmt   The access number used to access the Administration via Telephone (AvT) application

Figure 9.4 shows the currently configured call-in numbers for each of these applications.

FIGURE 9.4 Call-in numbers

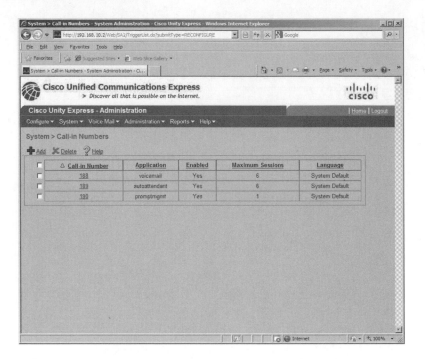

These numbers were previously configured in the Unity Express Initialization Wizard (Chapter 8). You can add additional numbers by clicking the Add button. You can also modify settings within the already configured numbers by clicking the number to pop up a screen where you can enter and save the changes. Figure 9.5 displays the settings that can be modified on call-in number profile 188.

FIGURE 9.5 Call-in number profile

The Application drop-down menu lists the three applications for which the number can be configured. Maximum Sessions is the maximum number of users who can dial in to the call-in number simultaneously. The voice prompt languages can also be modified here, and you can enable/disable a particular dial-in number if you need to.

Restriction Tables

You'll want to be able to control the telephone numbers that your users can modify when using Unity Express features such as message notification. Doing so protects the organization from users entering long-distance or international numbers. As you have learned, message notification allows users to set CUE to call remote telephone numbers for cellular phones or numeric pagers to notify them of new voice mails. *Restriction tables* can limit the types of numbers that can be entered. To add or modify a restriction table, navigate to System ➢ Restriction Tables. Figure 9.6 shows the configuration options available.

FIGURE 9.6   Restriction tables

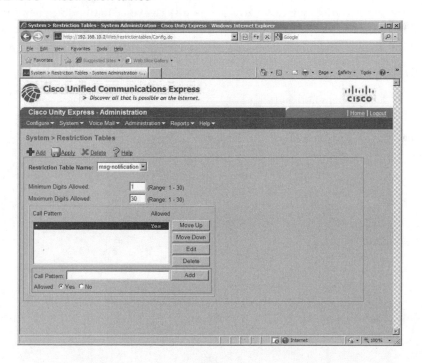

By default, a restriction table called msg-notification is already created for you. You can choose to add a new table by clicking the Add button, or you can modify the one already created. You have the ability to set the minimum and maximum number of digits allowed as well as to create allow/deny call patterns. These patterns use the * and dot (.) wildcards that we are already familiar with. Also keep in mind that the restriction table is read in top-down order; the entry at the top of the restriction table is read first, then the second, and so on. As soon as a match is made, the call is either allowed or denied based on the rule that is matched. Therefore, it is important to set your more-exact patterns at the top to match first, followed by more-general patterns that take advantage of wildcards. Next, we're going to look at configuring voice mail default settings.

Configuring Voice Mail Default Settings

When voice mailboxes are created, you can configure various parameters to customize them for each user or group who uses them. It is very likely, however, that most of your mailbox parameters will be identical. Because of this, you'll want to set the default settings within Unity Express to fit what the majority of your users will require. In this section you'll see how to configure default call handling, voice mail configuration defaults for the system, and voice mail defaults for individual mailboxes.

Voice Mail Call Handling

The default call-handling settings for voice mailbox users and groups are configured in the Voice Mail > Call Handling window. You can modify the voice mail pilot, operator, and AvT numbers. You can also specify the maximum number of sessions and languages used for voice mail and AvT prompts. To make changes to voice mail call handling, navigate to Voice Mail ➢ Call Handling. Figure 9.7 shows the available options.

FIGURE 9.7 Call-handling settings

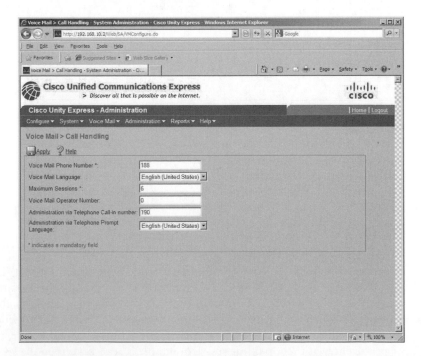

The fields have already been populated based on the responses we gave when running the Unity Express Initialization Wizard. If you need to modify these settings, you simply change and apply them here.

Voice Mail Configuration

In the voice mail configuration section, you can set all of the CUE systemwide settings for voice mail. To configure voice mail configuration default settings, go to Voice Mail ➢ VM Configuration. Figure 9.8 shows what the configuration screen options look like.

FIGURE 9.8 VM Configuration settings

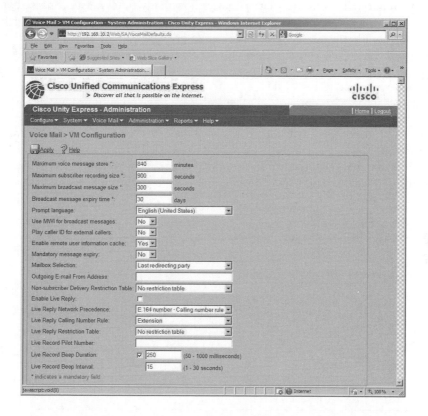

Looking at the figure, you can see that we can set the maximum time settings for overall voice mail, individual mailbox, broadcast message, and expiration limits here. There are also yes/no options for the following commonly used features:

Use MWI For Broadcast Messages   You can determine whether the message waiting indicator (MWI) light will be used when broadcast messages are sent to a mailbox.

Play Caller ID For External Callers   If off-network calls provide caller-ID information and the caller leaves a message, you can choose to be able to play that caller-ID information to the voice mail subscriber.

Mandatory Message Expiry   You can determine whether messages will be deleted after the absolute expiration time is up.

Another commonly used voice mail default setting we need to discuss is the Mailbox Selection drop-down menu. This option determines which voice mail a caller will be sent to when they are forwarded from one extension to another within Unity Express. By default, the setting is for the last redirecting party. This means the mailbox assigned to the last extension that redirected the call will get the voice mail. The other option is to use the original called party. That means that no matter how many times a user is passed around, if they end up going to voice mail, they will leave a message on the mailbox assigned to the original extension that was called. Let's look at an example.

Suppose a business has a single E.164 number that is used for customers to call. This number is answered by a receptionist. The receptionist's job is to figure out what the customer wants and to forward that call to the employee who can best assist. So a call comes into the receptionist at extension 3333. The receptionist answers the call and determines that the customer needs to talk to the billing department at extension 3444. The call is forwarded, but nobody picks up the call. Depending on the Mailbox Selection setting, the caller will then be directed to either the mailbox assigned to the receptionist or the mailbox assigned to the billing department. Figure 9.9 is a visual representation of what would happen in both the Last Redirecting Party and the Original Called Party scenarios.

FIGURE 9.9   Mailbox selection process flows

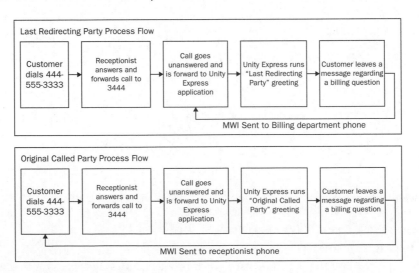

In our example, it is clear that we should configure our Mailbox Selection default setting to Last Redirecting Party, because we want the billing department rather than the receptionist to get the customer's voice message.

Voice Mail Defaults

Voice mail defaults set parameters for individual mailboxes. To make changes to these settings, navigate to Voice Mail ➤ VM Defaults. Figure 9.10 shows the settings that can be modified here.

FIGURE 9.10 Voice mail default settings

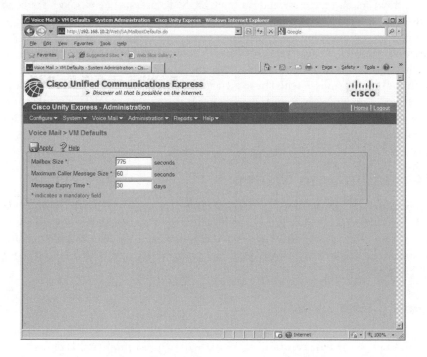

You can set the default individual mailbox size and message size in seconds. You can also set the message expiration time limit. If the system administrator has the Mandatory Message Expiry set to Yes in the VM Configuration settings, all saved messages will be deleted after the message is kept past the expiry time. If this setting is set to No, Unity Express will alert the user that the message will be deleted, but the user can choose to resave the message, which essentially resets the expiry timer back to 0.

Creating Users, Groups, and Mailboxes

We're now ready to begin adding new users and groups to the Unity Express system. You may already have users on the CUE from when you ran the Unity Express Initialization Wizard. If any users had been created on the CUCM Express, they would have been automatically imported into the CUE. At minimum, you should have the default cisco administrator account configured as a user.

To learn how to create users and groups, we'll use three different examples. First, we'll create a new user and assign a subscriber mailbox to them. Second, we'll create a group with multiple members who share a general delivery mailbox. Our last example will be to create a group within Unity Express that is strictly for CUE administration purposes using the AvT software feature. This administrator group will not have a mailbox assigned.

User Creation with Mailbox

Our first example will go through the process of creating a single Unity Express user with a subscriber mailbox. We'll configure user defaults that will be used as a template for all subsequent users. We'll then add a new user account, assign the user to an extension, and create a subscriber mailbox that links a CUCM phone extension with a CUE subscriber mailbox. Let's get started.

Configuring User Defaults

When creating a new user, Unity Express uses a default template to fill in much of the information required. As an administrator, you will want to modify this default user template to match the settings you wish to use for the majority of your CUE users. To modify user account default settings, navigate to Configure ➤ User Defaults. Figure 9.11 shows all of the default settings that can be modified.

FIGURE 9.11   User Defaults settings

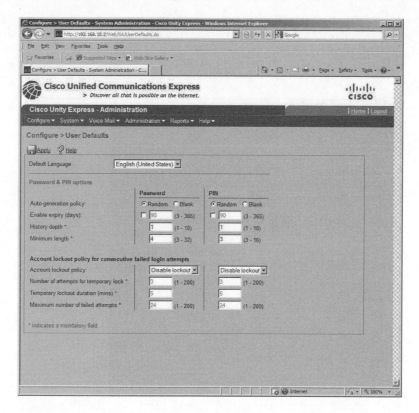

In this section, you can change the default auto-generation policy for assigning user PINs and passwords. You can also modify the minimum number of characters required for each. If security is of high importance to your organization, you have the option to set passwords to expire and force the user to use a password that has not been used previously. The History Depth setting dictates how many past passwords are kept, which means that the user cannot reuse them. For example, if History Depth is set to 2, when the user needs to change their password, they cannot set it to either of the previous two passwords that the account used.

You may also change the password/PIN lockout policy for all of your users. You can set the number of attempts, lockout time period, and whether the lockout policy is temporary, permanent, or disabled. If you choose to set the lockout policy to temporary or permanent, you can also set the number of attempts tried before an account is locked.

Creating a New User and Mailbox

We're now ready to create a new user account. To do so, go to Configure ➤ Users. The page will now display all of the currently configured users on Unity Express, as shown in Figure 9.12. At this point, there is only the default cisco user.

FIGURE 9.12   The Configure > Users window

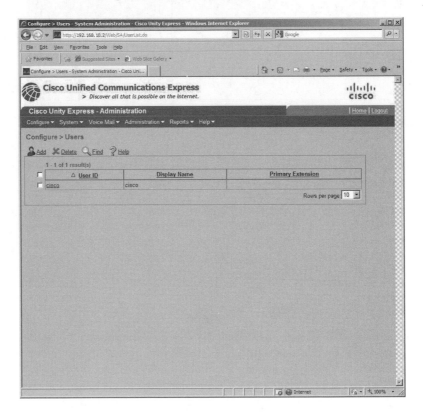

To create a new user, click the Add button. A new window will open that displays all of the configuration parameters we can set for our new Unity Express user. Figure 9.13 shows this window.

We can begin creating our new user (UserOne) by filling in the User ID, First Name, Last Name, Nick Name, and Display Name fields. Keep in mind that there cannot be any numbers, special characters, or spaces in the First or Last Name fields.

FIGURE 9.13 Adding a new user

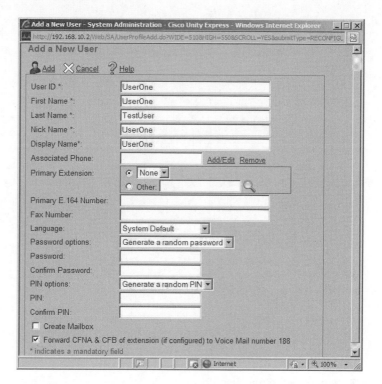

Next, we want to assign an extension (CUCM Express ephone-DN) to this user so that we can map the user to the extension and ultimately the extension to a voice mailbox. To get a list of all the already defined ephone-DNs, click the Other radio button and click the magnifying glass icon to the right of the blank field. A new window will open, titled Extension Option. Click the radio button of the ephone-DN you want to assign to the user. In this example, we chose extension 5001, as shown in Figure 9.14.

To save this extension assignment, click the Select Extension button in the upper left of the window. This will close the window and bring you back to the Add A New User window. We will finish the user configuration by choosing to specify a PIN and password as opposed to assigning them randomly or leaving them blank. Lastly, we'll check the Create Mailbox check box. We'll also leave the Forward CFNA & CFB Of Extension (If Configured) To Voice Mail Number 188 check box checked. This option tells us that our ephone-DN will be automatically set to forward calls that are not answered after 20 seconds or calls that cannot be answered because the user is already on the phone. The calls will be forwarded to extension 188, which is the voice mail call-in number. Figure 9.15 shows a completed user profile.

FIGURE 9.14 Selecting an extension for the new user

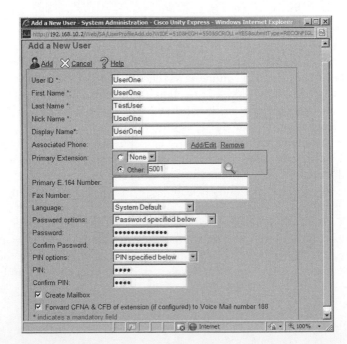

FIGURE 9.15 A completed new user form

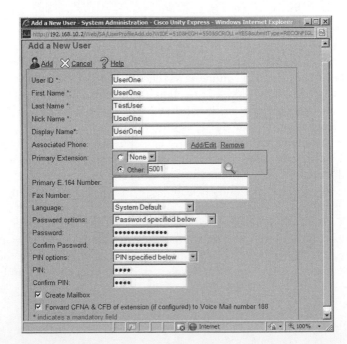

Because we checked the Create Mailbox check box when we created our new UserOne profile, Unity Express will automatically bring up the mailbox configuration options as soon as we click the Add button to actually create our new user.

A description of the mailbox will have been automatically created, containing the user ID of the user the mailbox belongs to.

You can also customize the operator-assistance number to whatever the mailbox owner wants. Maximum mailbox and message sizes can also be changed, although they must be less than or equal to the maximum sizes you configured globally in the voice mail default settings we configured previously in this chapter. Users can also modify the expiry time for messages and indicate whether they want to use the tutorial when first setting up the mailbox.

If you attempted to check the Enable Notification For This User/Group check box, you noticed that it didn't work. When you attempt to save the configuration by clicking the Add button, you will receive a warning message that states "Notification disabled system wide, cannot enable notification for owner." You'll learn how to enable Message Notification systemwide later in this chapter, so we can later check this box and successfully enable message-notification functionality.

Figure 9.16 shows the new mailbox configuration settings.

FIGURE 9.16   Adding a new mailbox

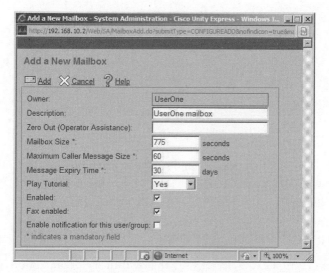

When you have finished setting the mailbox parameters, click the Add button so that Unity Express will build the mailbox for you.

Unity Express then takes you back to the original page of currently configured users. Figure 9.17 shows UserOne as a user on the Unity Express system.

FIGURE 9.17   A newly configured user

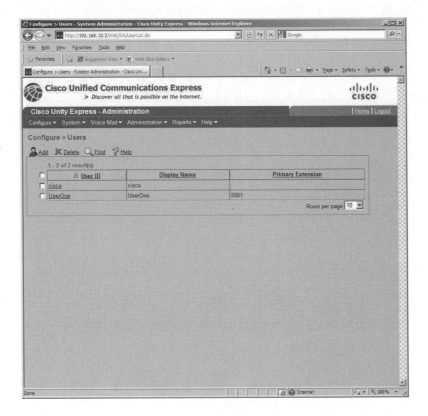

That is how you can configure a user and subscriber mailbox on the CUE. Next, you'll learn how to create a CUE group to share a general delivery mailbox (GDM) as well as a group used for administrative roles that do not require mailboxes.

Group Creation with Mailbox

In our first group-creation example, let's say that within the organization we have an IT support team of three members (UserOne, UserTwo, and UserThree). Employees who need technical support over the phone are told to call extension 5555. This extension is configured on button 2 of all three phones that make up the IT support group. If for some reason an employee dials 5555 and none of the three employees is able to answer the phone, after five rings the call will be forwarded to voice mail. The IT support team wants to use a GDM so that all three of them can be notified of a new voice mail as well as log in to check the GDM box. With these requirements in mind, let's create our IT support group with a GDM.

The first step in a new group creation is to navigate to Configure ➢ Groups. The next page displays all of the groups currently configured on Unity Express, as shown in Figure 9.18.

FIGURE 9.18   Configured groups

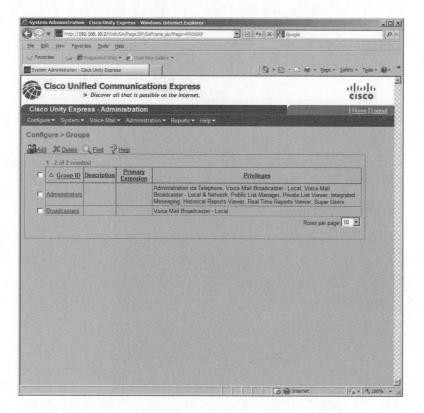

We want to build a new group from scratch, so click the Add button. A new window will pop up, asking you to enter details that identify the group and allow privileges as needed. Figure 9.19 shows the completed form for providing a new group for IT support. Notice that Create Mailbox is checked; this will create a single GDM that all members within the group will be able to access.

FIGURE 9.19 Adding a new group

 Don't forget that GDMs are accessed differently from standard subscriber voice mailboxes. With a GDM, a group member will log in to their personal subscriber account first and then access the GDM through the subscriber voice mail account. Only subscribers who are members of the GDM will have access to the group mailbox.

After you click the Add button to create the new group, a window will open that allows you to modify settings for our new general-deployment mailbox. Figure 9.20 shows this mailbox configuration screen.

FIGURE 9.20 The Add A New Mailbox window for groups

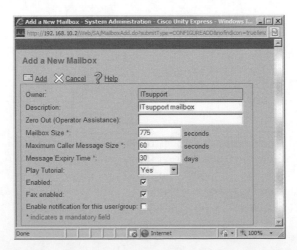

When you have finished configuring the GDM, click the Add button to have CUE build the new mailbox. You are then taken back to the main group page that lists all of the currently configured groups. Figure 9.21 shows this screen with our newly configured ITsupport group listed.

FIGURE 9.21   The newly configured group in the Configure > Groups window

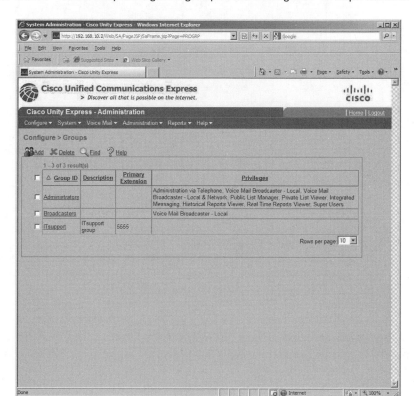

Now that our group is created, we need to add our three members to it so they can receive MWI and access the GDM to check messages. To accomplish this, click the ITsupport link. The ITsupport group profile will pop up as a new window. At the top of this window are tabs that contain various configuration settings within the new group. We want to add members to the group, so click the Owners/Members tab. The next screen shows us that we do not have any configured members; the table is blank. To add members, click the Subscribe Member button at the top. Now we are able to search for users we wish to include in the ITsupport group. If you click the magnifying glass without entering any additional information, the window will display all users configured within the CUE. Select the three users we want in the group, as shown in Figure 9.22.

FIGURE 9.22 Adding group subscribers

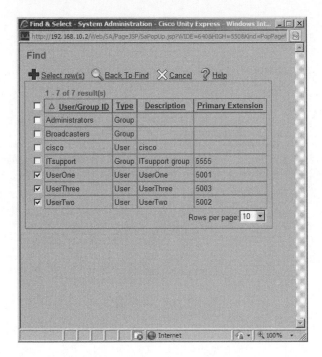

Once all three users are selected, click the Select Row(s) button. That's all there is to it. Now the three members have a shared mailbox for support calls that any of them can access.

Group Creation for Administrative Roles

Groups are used not only for shared GDM setups, as shown in the last example; we can also create administrator groups to give certain users access to various administrative roles on Unity Express. Listed here are the administrative privileges that can be assigned. A group can have one or many of the privileges assigned to a group:

Administration via Telephone (AvT)   AvT TUI access to change AA prompts.

Voice Mail Broadcaster—Local/Local and Network   AvT TUI access to send broadcast messages.

Private/Public List Manager   Web GUI access to view the existence and membership of configured private or public distribution lists. No changes can be made.

Integrated Messaging   Access to Integrated Messaging configurations using the web GUI.

Historical Reports Viewer   Access to view historical voice message using the web GUI.

Real Time Reports Viewer   Access to view real-time voice message reports using the web GUI.

Super Users   Full access to the CUE web GUI; can perform any configuration task.

By default, two administrator groups are preconfigured, Administrators and Broadcasters. Administrators have all the listed privileges assigned, while Broadcasters have only the Voice Mail Broadcaster—Local privileges. In this example, we are going to create an AvT group and assign a single member. This user will then be given the rights to utilize the Administration via Telephone (AvT) application within the CUE.

The first few steps of the group creation are identical to what we performed with the ITsupport group. Navigate to the Configure ➤ Groups section and click Add to bring up the group configuration settings. Fill out the Group ID, Full Name, and Description fields for our AvT group. Do not click the box to make a GDM, because this group does not need one. We will, however, give this group the right to access the AvT software contained within Unity Express for modifying auto attendant prompts and other voice-related recordings. Figure 9.23 shows the proper configuration settings for the AvT group.

FIGURE 9.23   Adding a new administrative group

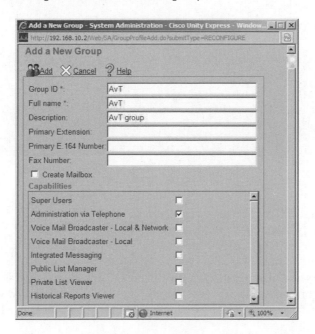

Click the Add button to create the new group. This action takes you back to the main screen, which shows all the groups in the CUE. This screen is shown in Figure 9.24.

FIGURE 9.24   The newly configured administrative group in the Configure > Groups window

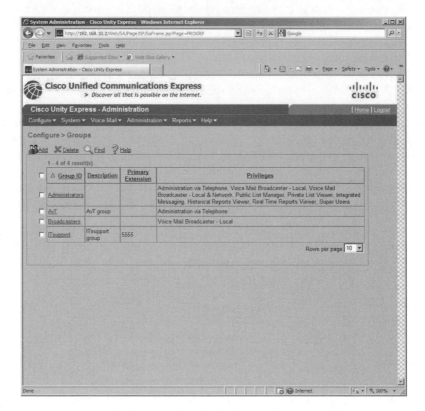

As we did with the ITsupport group, we need to add members to the AvT group. Select this group to modify it and then click the Owners/Members tab. The next screen shows us that we do not have any configured members, because the table is blank. To add members, click the Subscribe Member button at the top. Now we are able to search for users we wish to include in the AvT group. If you click the magnifying glass icon without entering any additional information, the window will display all users configured within the CUE. Figure 9.25 shows the search results listing all users configured on Unity Express.

FIGURE 9.25   Adding group subscribers

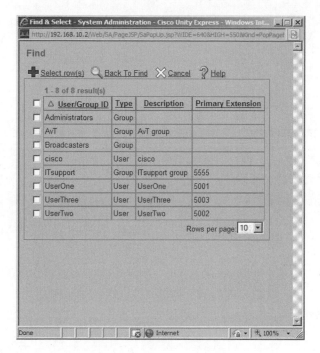

Check the box next to UserOne to make that user a member of this group, and click the Select Row(s) button. UserOne is now a member of the AvT group and can now access the AvT software features by dialing into the AvT pilot number configured on CUE. In the next section, we will go about configuring Auto Attendant. We will use UserOne in this section to record new AA prompts.

Configuring Auto Attendant

As you'll recall, when we ran through the Unity Express Initialization Wizard in the last chapter we were asked to assign an extension for the Auto Attendant application. Once an extension number is assigned, Unity Express will make the AA application available to anyone who dials this extension. This section will cover how to administrate the AA to change the AA scripts that users hear when they log in. Then we'll go over how to make changes to the system schedule to set your AA to function properly during both working and nonworking hours as well as holidays. Finally, we will use the AvT application to create the prompts to personalize the AA to our business.

Administrating the Auto Attendant Application

By default, AA will use the prebuilt `aa.aef` script. To make general changes to the AA setup, navigate to Voice Mail ➤ Auto Attendant ➤ Edit. Figure 9.26 shows the options available.

FIGURE 9.26   Modifying Auto Attendant settings

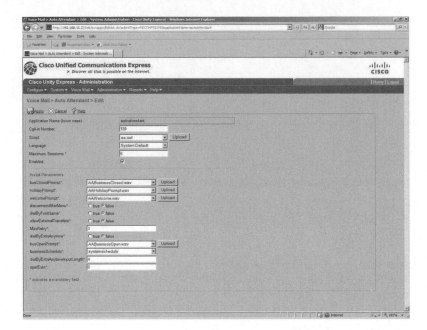

In this location you can make the following changes:

- Modify the AA call-in number.

- Select the script you wish to use.

- Upload custom-made scripts that were built with the Unity Express Editor PC software.

- Set the language used in the voice prompts.

- Set the Maximum Sessions

- Enable or disable AA.

- Modify or upload parameters within the AA script you have chosen to use.

- Change the prompts used by your AA script.

- Choose the business schedule that informs the AA software of office hours and holiday schedules. The AA uses this schedule to determine when to use various prompts such as BusOpenPrompt or BusClosedPrompt.

As soon as you have made all the necessary changes, click the Apply button to activate the modifications on the CUE.

Modifying the Business Hours Schedule

The *business hours schedule* is how the AA determines when to use the business open/ closed prompts that your AA script can utilize. Unity Express has a default schedule that you can modify, or you can choose to create your own schedule. To make changes to the business hours schedule, go to System ➤ Business Hours Settings. The default systemschedule business hours schedule comes up, as shown in Figure 9.27.

FIGURE 9.27   Business hours schedule

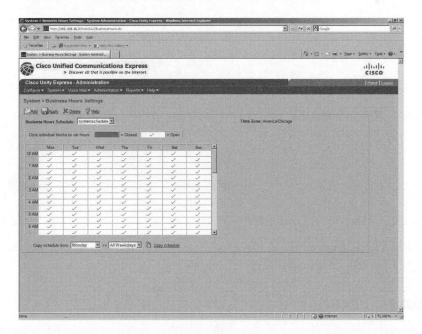

A table consisting of the days of the week and the time in 30-minute blocks is shown. You can click these blocks to set the open and closed hours for the business. As soon as you have made the necessary changes and clicked the Apply button, the office hour changes will be in effect and the AA script will change the prompts to use busOpenPrompt or busClosedPrompt based on these settings.

Configuring the Holiday Schedule

The AA also can use different prompts when the office is closed for a holiday. This is referred to as the *holiday schedule*. By default, no holidays are configured on the CUE. You must manually configure the holidays your office observes. To add holidays to the CUE, navigate to System ➤ Holiday Settings. Click the Add button to add a holiday. A new window will open that asks you to enter the year, date, and a description of the holiday. Figure 9.28 shows the Add A New Holiday screen.

FIGURE 9.28 Adding a new holiday to the holiday schedule

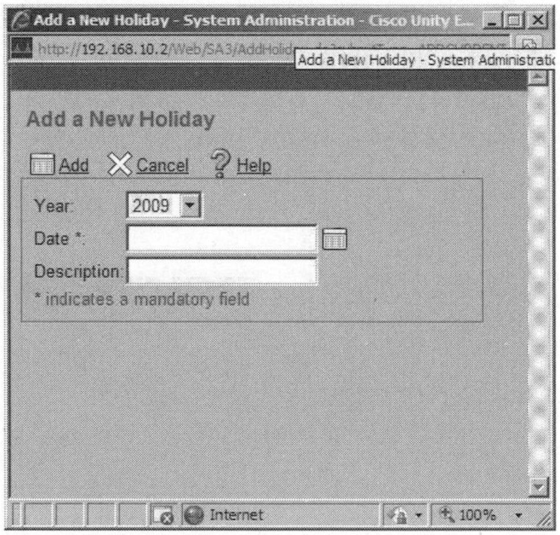

When you have entered all the proper information, click the Add button and the new holiday will be active on the Unity Express system.

Creating Custom Prompts Using the AvT

You can record your own custom prompts for the AA by utilizing the AvT feature. When you first initialized Unity Express, you created a call-in number that was specifically meant for AvT users to dial into. This application is referred to as promptmgmt on the CME web GUI. A user must have AvT privileges assigned in order to be properly authenticated and change the prompt messages. You learned how to assign those prompts in the "Group Creation for Administrative Roles" section of this chapter. When this user dials the call-in number and authenticates, they can enable alternate greetings on the fly in case of an emergency, such as bad weather that might keep employees from coming into the office. Users can also record their own prompts to use in the AA script for customization purposes. The default AA prompts that come on the CUE are very generic. Most businesses want a custom AA that at minimum says "Welcome to company XYZ" to inform callers of the name of the business they are calling. When the AvT user creates and saves a recorded prompt, this recording will be accessible on the CUE web GUI by going to System ➤ Prompts. Figure 9.29 shows the current saved custom prompts.

FIGURE 9.29   Custom prompts using AvT

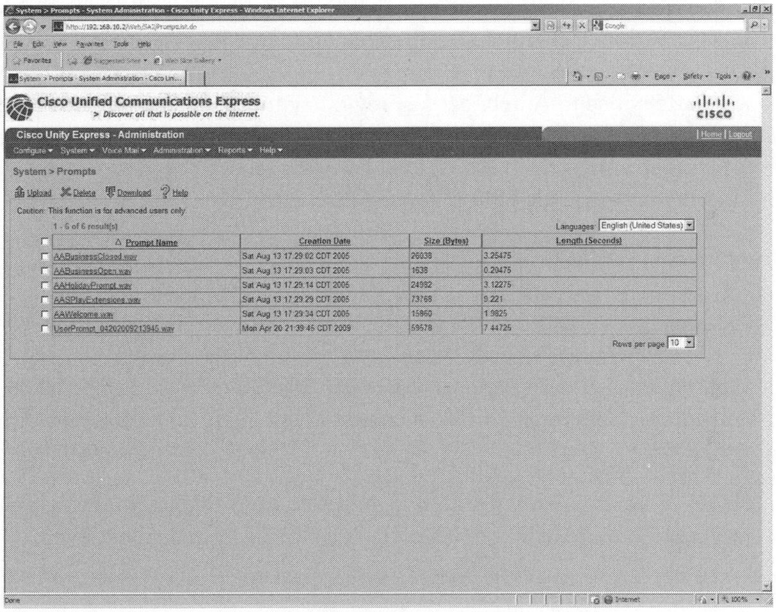

The prompt at the bottom that begins with "UserPrompt" is a custom voice file an AvT administrator has created and saved on the system. This new prompt can then be used within the active AA script to personalize the AA experience.

Configuring Message Notification

The *Message Notification* feature allows mailbox subscribers to be notified of a new voice mail message by calling a remote telephone such as a home or cellular phone. You can also configure Message Notification to send an email or alphanumeric page. The details here are subject to the restrictions discussed earlier.

SMTP Settings for Message Notification

Manhattan Optical is a distributor of glasses and contact lenses throughout the United States. The sales team is equipped with smartphones with email capabilities. A request has been sent to IT to see if it is possible to notify the sales team of new voice mail messages over email. Ann, the support engineer, has discovered with a little research that Unity Express has a feature called Message Notification that can remotely alert users of new voice messages via email.

Ann uses the web GUI and finds where Message Notification is configured for voice mail users. She enables Message Notification and clicks the Apply button to make the changes active on the configuration. But when she does, an error message appears, stating that an SMTP server must be configured for the proper sending of email notifications. This error makes complete sense to Ann because previously there was no need to configure SNMP within Unity Express. Now that Ann needs to send emails from Unity Express, she needs to identify a mail server from which to send messages. Logging in to the Unity Express command line, Ann issues the following command:

```
UC500-CUE#configure terminal
UC500-CUE(config)# smtp server address 10.68.20.10 authentication username
uc500 password VmP4ss
```

This command configures outgoing emails to use the SMTP server located at 10.68.20.10. This mail server requires authentication, so a username of uc500 and a password of VmP4ss were included.

Now that an SMTP server has been properly configured on Unity Express, the sales staff can be sent email notifications when new voice mails arrive in their mailboxes.

By default, Message Notification is disabled systemwide. Navigate to Voice Mail ➢ Message Notification ➢ Message Administration. Here you can check the box to enable Message Notification systemwide. Figure 9.30 shows this enable screen.

FIGURE 9.30 Message Notification systemwide settings

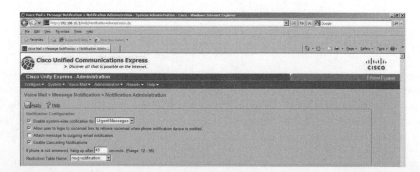

In addition to enabling Message Notification, the administrator can specify the following global settings, as listed in Table 9.1.

TABLE 9.1 Message Notification systemwide settings

Setting	Description	Options
Enable system-wide notification	Types of messages that will trigger message notification	All Messages will trigger message notification for any voice mail message. Urgent Messages will trigger message notification only when the calling party flags the message as urgent.
Allow user to login to voice mail box to retrieve voice mail when phone notification device is notified	With this box checked, when Unity Express calls a configured number on the message notification list, that user is allowed to automatically log in and check their messages. Otherwise, the user would have to terminate the call and dial back into Unity Express to retrieve messages.	Enabled or disabled.
Attach message to outgoing email notification	Will attach voice mail message to email notifications in a .wav format	Enabled or disabled.
Enable Cascading Notifications	Unity Express waits a period of time for the user to log in and check their messages. After a set time has expired, Unity Express will notify the next phone, email address, or pager on the list.	Enabled or disabled.
If phone is not answered, hang up after XX seconds	Amount of time Unity Express attempts to reach a notification number before the system considers the notification to have failed to reach the intended party.	Number of seconds between 12 and 96.
Restriction Table Name	A restriction table can be added to limit the phone numbers that can be used for message notification.	Any configured restriction table in the drop-down list.

In our example, we're going to enable Message Notification for urgent messages. The user will have the ability to log in to Unity Express automatically to retrieve messages. Also, we have enabled *Cascading Notifications* to cycle through any configured notification destination endpoints configured.

Now that we have Message Notification enabled globally, we can go into individual user accounts and enable Message Notification. To enable this feature on existing accounts, navigate to Configure ≻ Users and click the User ID of the user for whom you wish to set up message notification. Figure 9.31 shows that we have decided to enable Message Notification on UserOne's account.

FIGURE 9.31 Enabling Message Notification for a user or group

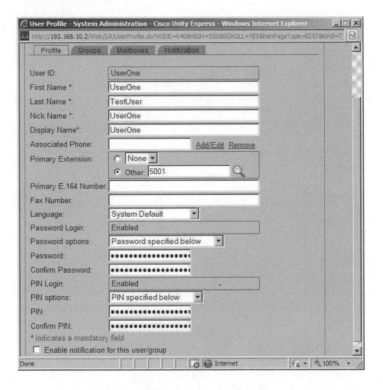

To enable notification, click the Enable Notification For This User/Group check box.

Next, click the Notification tab for UserOne. Here we can go ahead and set up the notification destination endpoints. There are several notification device types, for notification of telephones, pagers, and email addresses. To configure these options, choose the notification endpoint by clicking the link. The screen will then display options for you to enable notification for the device and to enter the information Unity Express needs to send alerts. For example, Figure 9.32 shows us enabling and configuring notification for a home telephone.

FIGURE 9.32 Configuring Message Notification: home phone

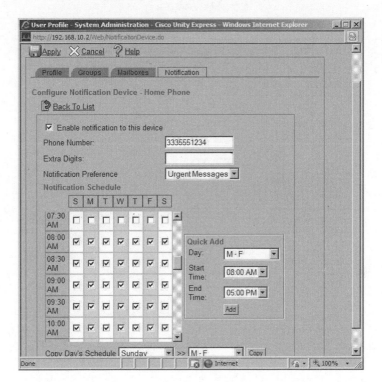

We've checked the Enable check box and added the telephone number we want Unity Express to call. We've also set the notification schedule to send alerts only when messages come in Monday through Friday from 8:00 a.m. to 5:00 p.m. Once you have finished setting up the notification endpoint, click the Apply button.

Unity Express will then bring us back to the main Message Notification screen for UserOne. Figure 9.33 now lists the Home Phone device type as enabled and the telephone number associated with this option.

Now that we have set up message notification for UserOne, when an urgent message is stored in the subscriber mailbox, Unity Express will call the home phone number of 333-555-1234 and inform UserOne that an urgent message is waiting for them. The user can then authenticate to their mailbox using their PIN and retrieve the message.

FIGURE 9.33   Configuring Message Notification: home phone enabled

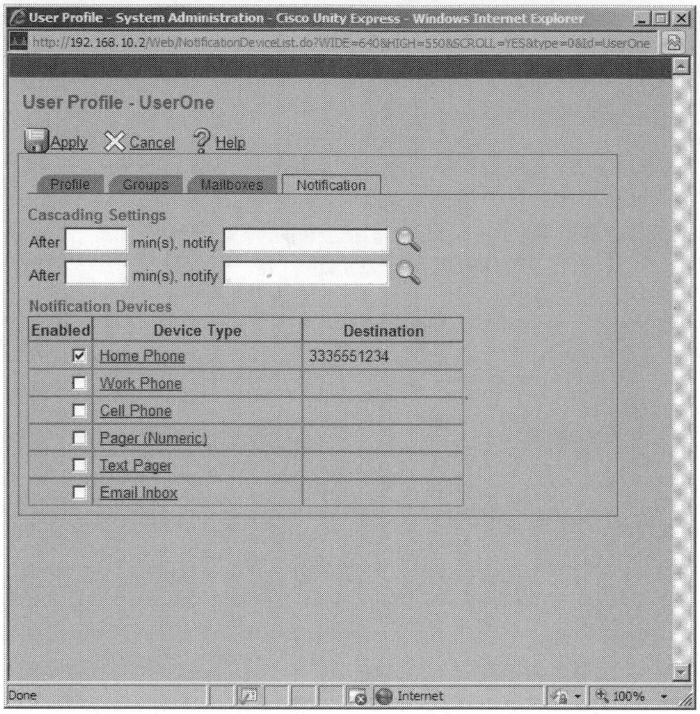

Administrating and Troubleshooting Unity Express

Unity Express administrators have multiple tools available to them to help keep the system running smoothly. This section will discuss how to synchronize configuration information contained within the CUCM Express and CUE databases. Then we'll talk about how to set up external backups of your CUE data in case of a failure. Finally, we'll talk about how to start and view trace files in real time to help troubleshoot any issues on the CUE.

Synchronizing Information

It is always important to keep in mind that the call-processing configuration of the CUCM Express is separate from the configuration of Unity Express. They are two completely separate devices that share a single hardware chassis. When you run the

Unity Express Initialization Wizard for the first time (as described in Chapter 8), this process pulls in information from the CUCM Express. This is the first *synchronization* performed between the two systems to ensure that all the data to be shared between the two systems is known by both devices. Any subsequent additions to either the CUCM Express or Unity Express may need to be synchronized; you can do this using the Synchronize feature in the CUE web GUI. For example, when the CUCM Express administrator creates a new ephone-DN, this information is not known to Unity Express. You must perform a synchronization between the two databases. To do this, navigate to Administration ➤ Synchronization Information. The synchronization will then be performed, and any changes will be displayed once the synch is complete.

Backing Up and Restoring Configurations

It is vital that you, as an administrator of a voice mail system, make regular backups of the configuration and user/group mailbox contents. Unity Express gives you the ability to back up data to an external server such as an FTP server and restore it from there.

To set up a server for external backups, go to Administration ➤ Backup/Restore ➤ Configuration. Figure 9.34 shows the configuration options.

FIGURE 9.34   The Backup/Restore > Configuration screen

The figure shows that our FTP server is located at 192.168.10.50. The FTP server username and password are set here for proper authentication. You can set the Maximum Revisions option to tell the system to keep a specific number of backups on the FTP server. Any backups above this number will be deleted, with the oldest backups deleted first.

Once your Backup/Restore server is set up, you can run a backup or restore by navigating to Administration ➤ Backup/Restore ➤ Start Backup or Administration ➤ Backup/Restore ➤ Start Restore.

Running a Unity Express Trace

A *trace* on Unity Express is the equivalent of the debug command on a Cisco router or switch. To run a trace, you must connect to Unity Express using the command line. Once you are connected, you run a trace for a particular *module* within the CUE. Modules are segments of Unity Express that handle different processes within the system. The following output shows us logging into the CUCM and displaying some of the trace modules available:

```
Router#service-module integrated-Service-Engine 0/0 session
Trying 192.168.10.1, 2002 ... Open
UC500-CUE> en
Password:
UC500-CUE# trace ?
  BackupRestore Module
  all           Every module, entity and activity
  caff-sip      Module
  capi          Module
  ccn           Module
  config-ccn    Module
  configapi     Module
  dbclient      Module
  dns           Module
  editorexpress Module
  entityManager Module
  imap          Module
  limitsManager Module

[output cut]
UC500-CUE#
```

To view the trace information in real time, we first must initiate a trace. For example, we'll initiate a full trace of the ccn module by running a trace ccn all privileged-exec command. The ccn trace is one example of many traces that can be run, as shown here:

```
UC500-CUE#trace ccn all
```

Now we can view the trace output in real time by doing a show trace buffer tail privileged EXEC command. The tail portion of the command tells Unity Express to print the last log message to the screen. Following is an example of this command:

```
UC500-CUE# show trace buffer tail
Press <CTRL-C> to exit...
```

```
1829 04/20 22:01:30.034 WFSP MISC 0 WFSysdbNdJCallStats::get exit
3313 04/20 22:07:34.670 DSSP LWRE 0 Received UDP packet on 192.168.10.2:5060 ,
source 192.168.10.1:60349
INVITE sip:188@192.168.10.2:5060 SIP/2.0
Via: SIP/2.0/UDP 192.168.10.1:5060;branch=z9hG4bK272504
Remote-Party-ID: <sip:5002@192.168.10.1>;party=calling;screen=no;privacy=off
From: <sip:5002@192.168.10.1>;tag=54322C-998
To: <sip:188@192.168.10.2>
Date: Fri, 03 Jul 2009 14:25:53 GMT
Call-ID: 4004C842-671411DE-80269C78-EC077092@192.168.10.1
Supported: 100rel,timer,resource-priority,replaces
Min-SE:   1800
Cisco-Guid: 1073935306-1729368542-2149686392-3959910546
User-Agent: Cisco-SIPGateway/IOS-12.x
Allow: INVITE, OPTIONS, BYE, CANCEL, ACK, PRACK, UPDATE, REFER, SUBSCRIBE,
NOTIFY, INFO, REGISTER
CSeq: 101 INVITE
Max-Forwards: 70
Timestamp: 1246631153
Contact: <sip:5002@192.168.10.1:5060>
Call-Info: <sip:192.168.10.1:5060>;method="NOTIFY;Event=telephone-event;
Duration=2000"
Expires: 180
Allow-Events: telephone-event
Content-Type: application/sdp
Content-Disposition: session;handling=required
Content-Length: 191

v=0
o=CiscoSystemsSIP-GW-UserAgent 5216 7538 IN IP4 192.168.10.1
s=SIP Call
c=IN IP4 192.168.10.1
t=0 0
m=audio 18456 RTP/AVP 0
c=IN IP4 192.168.10.1
a=rtpmap:0 PCMU/8000
a=ptime:20

--- end of packet ---
```

To end the trace, we exit out of the real-time monitoring and issue `no trace ccn all`. Trace files can come in handy when you are troubleshooting multiple CUE problems. Also, if you ever create a Cisco support case for a problem with Unity Express, one of the first pieces of information technical support requests is the output of a trace on the system.

Summary

In this chapter, we went over many of the different configuration, backup, and troubleshooting options for Unity Express. Using the web GUI, administrators can quickly and easily implement voice mail and Auto Attendant features that were laid out in the design phase of the project. You also learned how to back up and restore not only configurations but also any saved voice mail files. Finally, this chapter introduced you to the `trace` command, which is a powerful tool used for troubleshooting problems that might arise when implementing or supporting Unity Express.

In Chapter 10, you'll learn how to work with the SBCS platform and Cisco Configuration Assistant.

Exam Essentials

Know How to configure an NTP server for proper unity express timekeeping.   Mailbox subscribers require an accurate clock to ensure that they know when callers left messages. Using the CUE GUI, navigate to System ➤ Network Time & Time Zone Settings.

Understand when it is important to configure a DNS Server on unity express.   Whenever Unity Express needs to talk to an external server such as an SMTP server for sending voice mail as email attachments, you might configure the server using a domain name as opposed to an IP address. If you use a domain name, you need to configure Unity Express with a DNS server to resolve the domain name to an IP address.

Know how to modify the default language used on unity express.   To modify language settings, navigate to System ➤ Language Settings.

Understand the three common types of call-in numbers.   The three primary call-in numbers configured are the voice mail pilot, auto attendant, and AvT extensions.

Understand the purpose of restriction tables.   Restriction tables control the telephone numbers that Unity Express users can enter for message notification. These tables help to protect a company from expensive long-distance charges.

Know what default VM settings can be made on unity express.   Options such as mailbox/message size and expiration time limits can be set here; they are applied to all subscriber mailboxes by default.

Know how to create users, groups, and mailboxes using the unity express web GUI.   Users are individuals who usually are associated with their own personal subscriber mailbox. Groups consist of two or more people who share a GDM box as well as have individual mailboxes. All of these are set up using the Configure tab.

Understand that groups are created for both GDM and administrative purposes.   Besides their use for sharing GDMs, groups can also be created to serve administrative roles such as an Administration via Telephone (AvT) Administrators group.

Know how to configure auto attendant features using the Unity Express web GUI.   You can configure Auto Attendant by navigating to Voice Mail ➢ Auto Attendant. Here you can set up your scripts, set business/holiday hours, and manage custom prompts.

Understand the purpose of message notification.   Message Notification is a feature that alerts users of new voice messages by triggering automated calls or emails to a destination the user chooses.

Understand the process of synchronizing CUCM Express with Unity Express   The CUCM Express and Unity Express share information with each other, such as ephone-DNs and users. When you make an addition to shared information, you need to synchronize the two systems to ensure they both are aware of the change.

Know how to back up and restore the unity express configuration and Files.   You can back up and restore information to a remote location by navigating to Administration ➢ Backup/Restore and then choosing to configure the settings or run a backup or restore.

Know what a unity express `trace` command is used for.   A Unity Express trace is much like a debug on a Cisco router or switch. You can obtain information that is helpful for troubleshooting problems with your system.

Written Lab 9.1

Write the answers to the following questions:

1. Sam just checked his voice mail and found a new message waiting in his mailbox that said it was left at 2:00 p.m. today. This is impossible because it is only 1:15 p.m. What should the administrator check?

2. The mail administrator gave you the following SMTP gateway to use for Unity Express Integrated messaging: mail.fakecompany.com. What else do you need to do to ensure that SMTP is properly configured on the CUE?

3. What is the maximum number of language packages that can be used at once on a Unity Express system?

4. What can administrators use to limit the types of numbers they can enter for Message Notification?

5. What feature is used to control the reuse of passwords?

6. What two types of groups are used on Unity Express?

7. Using the Unity Express web GUI, where can you configure Auto Attendant features?

8. Where can you modify the operational hours of a business within the Unity Express web GUI?

9. Name the type of Message Notification in which Unity Express notifies one device, waits for the user to acknowledge the notification, and, if the message is not acknowledged after a period of time, alerts the next device (phone, pager, or email).

10. What tool does Unity Express use for troubleshooting purposes that is similar to the debug command used on Cisco routers and switches?

(The answers to Written Lab 9.1 can be found following the answers to the review questions for this chapter.)

Hands-on Labs

To complete the labs in this section, you need a UC500 with a Cisco Unity Express AIM module. Note that if you are using a different CUCM Express router and Unity Express network module, the commands used will be slightly different. Lab 9.2 also requires an FTP server to be connected to the network.

Here is a list of the labs in this chapter:

Lab 9.1: Viewing Real-Time Trace Logs

Lab 9.2: Saving and Retrieving Trace Log Files

Hands-on Lab 9.1: Viewing Real-Time Trace Logs

In this lab, we're going to run a trace on Unity Express and view the files in real time. We're going to focus on troubleshooting problems when leaving voice mail messages. The problem can be re-created, so our solution will be to turn on the trace, view the logs in real time, and then disable the trace.

1. Log in to your CUCM Express router and go into configuration mode by typing **enable**, entering your password, and then typing **configuration terminal**.

2. Session into the Unity Express AIM module by typing **service-module integrated-Service-Engine X/X session**. The X/X is the AIM module/slot where the hardware resides within the CUCM Express router.

3. Enter into privileged-exec mode by typing **enable** and entering your CUE password.

4. Turn on voice mail debugging by typing **trace voice mail debug all**.

5. Begin real-time viewing by typing **show trace buffer tail**.

6. Re-create the voice mail problem that is being experienced, and watch the trace debugs on the terminal screen.

7. Once the problem has been re-created and captured in real time, disable the trace by issuing **no trace voice mail debug all**.

Hands-on Lab 9.2: Saving and Retrieving Trace Log Files

Now let's say that by viewing the real-time trace debugs we ran in lab 9.1, we were unable to find the problem. We've decided to get some help from the Cisco Technical Assistance Center (TAC), and they have requested that we run the same trace and send it to them for viewing. This time, instead of viewing the real-time logs, we're going to have the logs written to the trace log file. To do this, first we will enable saving to a log file; then we will start our trace and re-create the problem. Finally, we'll disable the trace and FTP the log file to our desktop so we can forward it to TAC for review.

1. Log in to your CUCM Express router and go into configuration mode by typing **enable**, entering your password, and then typing **configuration terminal**.

2. Session into the Unity Express AIM module by typing **service-module integrated-Service-Engine X/X session**. The X/X is the AIM module/slot where the hardware resides within the CUCM Express router.

3. Enter into privileged-exec mode by typing **enable** and entering your CUE password.

4. Enable saving trace logs to a file stored on the compact flash by typing **log trace buffer save**.

5. Turn on voice mail debugging by typing **trace voice mail debug all**.

6. Re-create the voice mail problem that is being experienced, and watch the trace debugs on the terminal screen.

7. Once the problem has been re-created and captured in real time, disable the trace by issuing **no trace voice mail debug all**.

8. View the saved log files on the compact flash by typing **show logs**. The log file that Cisco TAC will want to see is called **atrace_save.log**.

9. Copy the **atrace_save.log** file from the compact flash to an external FTP server by typing **copy log atrace_save.log url ftp://user1:cisco@**$XX.XX.XX.XX$**/cue/atrace_save.log**, where $XX.XX.XX.XX$ is the IP address of your FTP server and there is a configured user named user1 with a password of cisco.

10. Once you have the log file on the FTP server, you can forward it to Cisco TAC for review.

Review Questions

1. For Integrated Messaging to work properly, what must be configured on Unity Express?

    A. DNS server

    B. DHCP server

    C. HTTP server

    D. SSH server

2. Languages within Unity Express can be set at all of the following levels except:

    A. Default level

    B. Admin level

    C. User level

    D. Group level

3. Where can you set the maximum number of voice mail sessions allowed within the Unity Express web GUI?

    A. Voice Mail ➤ VM Configuration

    B. Voice Mail ➤ Call Handling

    C. Configure ➤ User Defaults

    D. System ➤ User Defaults

4. By default, how is Unity Express configured to route a caller to the correct mailbox when calls are forwarded within the CUCM Express system and the call is not answered?

    A. Original called party

    B. General delivery mailbox

    C. Operator mailbox

    D. Last redirecting party

5. How can the administrator set a limit on how long any voice mail is saved on the Unity Express System?

    A. Ensure that Mandatory Message Expiry is set to No

    B. Ensure that Mandatory Message Expiry is set to Yes

    C. Ensure that Mandatory Message Expiry is set to Delete After 30 Days

    D. Ensure that Mandatory Message Expiry is set to Yes or Delete After 30 Days

6. What are the three types of user password/PIN lockout policies?

    A. Temporary

    B. Notify

    C. Permanent

    D. Disabled

    E. Static

7. When adding a new user mailbox, what is the result of creating a user mailbox by checking the Create Mailbox check box but unchecking the Forward CFNA & CFB Of Extension To Voice Mail Number option? Choose all that apply.

   A. The user will have a new mailbox created with the default mailbox parameters.

   B. The user will have a new mailbox, but it will be disabled.

   C. Calls going into the user extension will never go to voice mail when the user is either unable to answer or already on the phone.

   D. Calls going into the user extension will be redirected to the voice mailbox when the user is either unable to answer or already on the phone.

8. What does the Zero Out feature do?

   A. Resets the keypad to Unity Express default settings

   B. Resets the message expiry time to 30 days

   C. Provides an extension to forward calls within Unity Express voice mail to when the caller presses the 0 button

   D. Provides a way to reset the user PIN/password while using the Unity Express TUI

9. We want a group of users to be able to listen to group voice mail messages and be notified of new messages via the MWI. What type of GDM users are these?

   A. GDM operators

   B. GDM owners

   C. GDM members

   D. GDM super users

10. What are the two Unity Express groups available by default?

   A. Administrators

   B. Broadcasters

   C. AvT Administrators

   D. Super Users

   E. Historical Reports Viewers

11. What is the name of the Auto Attendant script used by default on Unity Express?

   A. `aa.aef`

   B. `aaDefault.wav`

   C. `aa.wav`

   D. `aaDefault.aef`

12. On the web GUI for Unity Express, which holidays are configured by default?

   A. Christmas Day

   B. New Year's Day

   C. Independence Day

   D. No holidays are configured

13. When an AvT administrator creates a new recording for the Auto Attendant, where can the newly recorded files be accessed using Unity Express GUI?

    A. Voice Mail ➢ Auto Attendant

    B. Voice Mail ➢ AvT

    C. System ➢ Prompts

    D. The files can be accessed only through the command line.

14. What step must be taken to properly configure Message Notification to work over email using Unity Express?

    A. Configure an SNMP server

    B. Enable network address translation (NAT) on Unity Express

    C. Configure an SMTP server

    D. Configure MWI on all ephones

15. What two types of messages can you choose for triggering message notification?

    A. Urgent messages

    B. Broadcast messages

    C. GDM messages

    D. All messages

16. When configuring Message Notification on the Unity Express web GUI, what does it mean when you check the "Allow user to login to voice mail box to retrieve voice mail when phone notification device is notified" check box?

    A. The user can call back in and access messages remotely.

    B. The user can have the voice mail automatically sent to an alphanumeric pager.

    C. The user can listen to their messages without terminating the call.

    D. The user can dial into their personal extension to retrieve messages.

17. Voice mail messages sent as email attachments on Unity Express are sent in what format?

    A. `.jpg`

    B. `.au`

    C. `.wav`

    D. `.mp3`

    E. `.mp4`

18. You've just finished configuring a backup FTP server to save configuration and mailbox contents onto a separate server. When configuring the backup server, you set the maximum number of revisions to five. What does this mean?

   A. Unity Express will monitor the number of backups on the FTP server and keep the five oldest revisions.

   B. Unity Express will monitor the number of backups on the FTP server and keep the five newest revisions.

   C. The FTP server will monitor the number of Unity Express backups and keep the five oldest revisions.

   D. The FTP server will monitor the number of Unity Express backups and keep the five newest revisions.

19. What is a trace in regard to Cisco Unity Express?

   A. A tool to trace analog phone calls on the PSTN

   B. A tool to trace voice messages back to the original calling party

   C. A tool similar to the debug command used for troubleshooting purposes

   D. A methodology used by voice engineers to route voice traffic to the proper subscriber or GDM

20. What two methods below will let you run a trace on Unity Express hardware?

   A. Web GUI

   B. CCA

   C. Console port

   D. SSH/Telnet

Answers to Review Questions

1. A. Your Unity Express system must be set up to properly resolve hostnames. Therefore, you must configure at least one DNS server.

2. B. Languages can be set at a global or default level as well as at user and group levels.

3. B. You can configure language settings and maximum sessions by using the Unity Express GUI and navigating to Voice Mail ➢ Call Handling.

4. D. The calls are sent to the extension mailbox that the user was last redirected to.

5. B. Mandatory Message Expiry can be set to either Yes or No. If you want all messages to be deleted after a specified period of time, you should set this to Yes.

6. A, C, D. The three types of lockout policies are temporary, permanent, and disabled.

7. A, C. Checking the Create Mailbox check box indeed makes a new mailbox for the user. However, if Forward CFNA & CFB Of Extension To Voice Mail Number is unchecked, calls to that extension that are either no-answer or busy will not be forwarded to the mailbox.

8. C. The Zero Out feature is a way the user/administrator can set an extension to forward operator-assistance calls to.

9. C. Standard GDM users can listen to messages and be notified of new messages using message waiting indicators.

10. A, B. By default, Administrators and Broadcasters groups are defined.

11. A. The script used by default on Unity Express AA setups is `aa.aef`.

12. D. By default, Unity Express does not have any holidays configured.

13. C. Prompts are found by navigating to System ➢ Prompts on the Unity Express GUI.

14. C. An SMTP server must be defined so that mail can be properly sent.

15. A, D. You can set Message Notification to trigger either on all messages or on those marked by the caller as urgent.

16. C. When a user receives a notification call on their home or mobile phone, they have the ability to listen to the message without having to dial back into Unity Express.

17. C. Messages attached to emails are sent as `.wav` files.

18. B. Unity Express is responsible for keeping track of the number of revisions saved on the FTP server. Once the number of revision files goes over five, Unity Express deletes the oldest revisions.

Backups are a manual process, and you can kick off the backup by using the web GUI to navigate to Administration ➢ Backup/Restore ➢ Start Backup.

19. C. A trace is similar to the debug command used for troubleshooting CUE.

20. C, D. The only way to run the trace tool is through the command line.

Answers to Written Lab 9.1

1. NTP and time zone settings

2. Configure a DNS server on Unity Express

3. Five

4. Restriction tables

5. History depth

6. GDM groups and Administrator groups

7. Voice Mail ➤ Auto Attendant

8. System ➤ Business Hours Settings

9. Cascading Notifications

10. Trace

Chapter

10

Introducing the SBCS Platform and Cisco Configuration Assistant

---

THE FOLLOWING CCNA VOICE EXAM OBJECTIVES ARE COVERED IN THIS CHAPTER:

✓ **Implement UC500 using Cisco Configuration Assistant.**

- Describe the function and operation of Cisco Configuration Assistant.

✓ **Describe the components of the Cisco Unified Communications Architecture.**

- Describe how the Unified Communications components work together to create the Cisco Unified Communications Architecture.

✓ **Perform basic maintenance and operations tasks to support the VoIP solution.**

- Explain basic maintenance and troubleshooting methods for UC500.

Auto-pilot...no assembly required...fly-by-wire...Plug and Play. All of these terms conjure up images of instant operability and simplicity that take the user out of the experience so that focus can be placed elsewhere. These same terms can be used to describe how Cisco envisioned the SBCS lineup of products.

In this chapter you'll get an overview of the Smart Business Communication System product lineup Cisco offers, targeted toward small businesses and branch offices. You'll learn how all these products are engineered to take as many of the difficult configuration and provisioning steps as possible out of the process. Last, the chapter will show you the Cisco Configuration Assistant application, an easy-to-use tool for the configuration of more advanced voice and data features that are not enabled by default.

The Smart Business Communications System

The Cisco *Smart Business Communications System (SBCS)* is a separate lineup that focuses on the needs of small- to medium-size businesses. Cisco's goal with the SBCS is not necessarily to be the cheapest solution. Instead, they're marketing the lineup to businesses that require feature-rich communications environments that are more commonly found in the larger enterprise-class hardware and software. In this sense, you really do get a bargain in terms of capabilities for your dollar. This section will briefly introduce the products that make up the SBCS lineup including the UC500 Series, the only platform that offers voice capabilities.

The SBCS Components

Cisco has spent a great deal of engineering time and effort to come up with the SBCS lineup for small businesses. There is a product within their offerings for virtually every need that a small business would require. Not only that, but they have designed all SBCS components to be extremely easy to deploy to remote offices. In fact, many basic capabilities are ready to go out of the box; essentially, the equipment can be almost Plug and Play if desired.

Let's take a closer look at each product currently available within the SBCS lineup.

Unified Communications 500 Series

There are two distinct chassis form-factor types for the UC500. The UC520-8U and UC520-16U models come in a "desktop" model chassis. The 8U and 16U in the model number stand for the number of IP phone users licensed on the system. The height of the units is 1.5 rack units. A *rack unit* (abbreviated U; don't confuse this with the model number) is a unit of measurement in the data/telecom world to describe the height of equipment. Each rack unit is 1.75~IN. It's possible to mount the desktop form-factor models in a 19~IN rack, but that requires the purchase of special mounting brackets.

The other form-factor model is for the UC520-24U, UC520-32U, and UC520-48U. This larger chassis is a full 19~IN wide, so it fits in a standard telecom rack, and no optional mounting extensions are needed. The height of the unit is 2U. It also has a built-in power supply; by contrast, the desktop version requires an external power brick. Table 10.1 breaks down the different hardware options available for the UC520 Series.

TABLE 10.1 UC500 Series Hardware Options

Hardware Options	Description	UC520-8U and 16U	UC520-24U, 32U, and 48U
Chassis form factor	Dimensions of the unit	Desktop	Standard 19~IN
Height	Height of the unit	1.5U	2U
Power supply	Type of power supply	External power brick	Built-in power supply
Console port	Used to connect directly to the UC500 via PC serial connection	1 port	1 port
Power over Ethernet (PoE)	10/100 BaseTX for 802.3af and up to 15.4W	8 ports	8 ports
Fixed FXS ports	Used to connect analog devices to the network	4 ports	4 ports
Fixed FXO ports	Used to connect to the PSTN for analog service	Optional, 4 ports	Optional, up to 8 ports

TABLE 10.1   UC500 Series Hardware Options (*Continued*)

Hardware Options	Description	UC520-8U and 16U	UC520-24U, 32U, and 48U
ISDN BRI ports	Used to connect to the PSTN for digital service	Optional, 2 ports	Optional, up to 6 ports
T1/E1 PRI ports	Used to connect to the PSTN for digital service	Not available	Optional 1 port
LAN expansion port	10/100 BASE-TX to uplink to SBCS switch for expansion	1 port	1 port
Voice expansion slot	VWIC slot to add additional analog/ digital ports	FXS, FXO, ISDN BRI, T1/E1	FXS, FXO, ISDN BRI, T1/E1
WAN Ethernet port	10/100 BASE-TX commonly used to connect to DSL or cable Internet services	1 port	1 port
MoH audio jack	3.5 mm port to connect to external audio source for MoH such as CD player or iPod	1 jack	1 jack
Compact flash (CF) slot	Used to store software and configuration files	1 slot	1 slot
Integrated wireless	Integrated WAP with a single antenna	1 WAP 802.11b/g	Not available

The first two illustrations present a visual representation of the majority of the hardware options available on the UC500 Series platform. The desktop and 19~IN rack form factors have the ports laid out in the same manner, so I'll show only the desktop form factor. Figure 10.1 illustrates the UC520 in the desktop form factor with the optional four FXO fixed ports included, and Figure 10.2 details the same desktop form factor UC520 with the optional two-port ISDN BRI included.

FIGURE 10.1   UC500 desktop chassis with fixed FXO ports

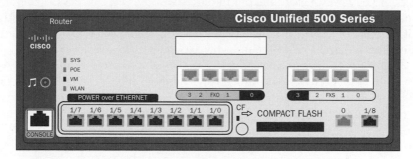

FIGURE 10.2   UC500 desktop chassis with fixed ISDN BRI ports

Note that you can have only the four FXO ports or the two ISDN BRI ports in a fixed setup. If you require additional FXO/BRI ports, you'll need to use the voice expansion slot.

The UC500 Series hardware is truly the heart of the SBCS lineup. With a single device, you get the following functionality:

- Cisco Unified Communications Manager Express

- Voice gateway functions using supported built-in FXS, FXO, ISDN-BRI, and other voice interfaces using the voice expansion port

- Unity Express for voice mail, auto attendant, and IVR capabilities

- Built-in Ethernet switch for voice and data connections

- Power over Ethernet (PoE) support

- VLAN configuration

- Quality of Service (QoS) capabilities

- IPSec VPN capabilities

- Firewall capabilities

- Static routing (no dynamic routing protocols are supported)

- Optional built-in wireless autonomous access point (desktop chassis only)

Keep in mind that the UC500 chassis devices are essentially fixed, with no expandability to add users. If you have 16 users and opt to purchase a UC520-16U desktop device, as soon as you require a 17th phone, you'll be required to upgrade to the larger chassis. Because of this lack of flexibility in field upgradability, you'll need to pay special attention to the future user requirements of the site where you are deploying the UC500.

Because this book focuses on voice, the UC500 Series is of utmost importance to us. We will cover the UC500 series out-of-the-box capabilities in more detail later in this chapter. The other non-voice features are not covered in this book, but it is important to know the other features that are available to you, so we will look briefly at the other SBCS series first.

 Real World Scenario

UC500 Power Failover Allows Good News to Reach Pet Owners

Heather is an employee at a veterinarian hospital in the Midwest. Her job is to keep owners up to date on the status of their pets after various surgical procedures the hospital performs there.

In the spring, the weather patterns can often lead to violent rainstorms with high winds. On this particular day, the storm managed to knock out the power to the hospital. The network equipment had proper UPS power, but after around 30 minutes, the batteries ran out and power was still not restored.

Heather still needed to contact a pet owner to update them on the successful surgery that was performed on a Labrador earlier that morning. Fortunately for Heather, the voice system that was installed in the hospital was a Cisco UC500. Cisco incorporated a high availability feature in the UC500 that allows users to make phone calls using analog phones connected to FXS ports for outbound calling on FXO ports even when there is no power to the system. The *power failover feature* allows the analog phone connected to an FXS port be switched directly to the FXO ports that are connected to the PSTN. This way, emergency calls can be made during occurrences when the UC500 loses power during an outage.

Secure Router 520 Series

At first glance, you might question why Cisco has included the Secure Router 520 (SR520) Series in the SBCS lineup. While it's true that the UC500 can provide router capabilities in the form of static routes, the Secure Router 520 Series supports many of the most popular dynamic routing protocols, which can greatly simplify larger and therefore more complex routing environments. The following features are supported on this platform:

- Dynamic routing protocol support

- Advanced firewalling and intrusion prevention system (IPS) capabilities

- Built-in Ethernet switch for voice and data connections

- Power over Ethernet (PoE) support

- VLAN configuration

- Quality of Service (QoS) capabilities

- IPSec and SSL VPN capabilities

- Optional built-in autonomous access point for wireless connectivity

Notice that voice gateway functions are not included. The 500 Series is a good option when you don't require the voice capabilities of the CUCM Express and Unity Express that are found in the UC500. It also includes more advanced security capabilities, including IPS functions that the UC500 does not support.

ESW 500 Series Switch

The Cisco ESW 500 Series switch lineup offers several hardware options for Fast or Gigabit Ethernet connectivity for your end devices and servers. It also offers the capability to connect to other switches using SFP uplink modules. Here is a list of features that the ESW 500 Series switch platforms offer:

- Fast Ethernet and Gigabit Ethernet switch ports in 24- or 48-port configurations

- Power over Ethernet (PoE) for up to 48 ports of Fast Ethernet and 24 ports of Gigabit Ethernet

- QoS capabilities for Layer 2 traffic identification and tagging

- Layer 2 security features such as IEEE 802.1X port security and access control lists (ACLs)

- VLAN configuration

- Optional redundant power supply

- Small Form-Factor Pluggable (SFP) expansion slots for uplinks to other network devices

Expansion is the name of the game for the ESW 500 Series switches. Typically, an office environment will include either the UC500 Series or the Secure Router 520 Series hardware. Both of these devices have an integrated switch. If an office requires additional switch ports, they'll typically buy one of the ESW 500 Series switches to expand the number of physical Ethernet ports available for use.

Cisco 500 Series Wireless Express

The SBCS lineup offers two different wireless options. One option is to purchase the wireless component that is built into either the UC500 or SR500 Series hardware. This provides a single autonomous access point. An *autonomous access point (AAP)* means that the wireless intelligence resides on the access point itself. A second way to implement wireless is to purchase and implement the Cisco 500 Series wireless express hardware, which consists of two pieces, the Cisco 521 and the optional 526 Wireless Express Mobility Controller. First, the Cisco 521 is a stand-alone wireless access point with the following capabilities:

- 802.11b/g functionality

- Integrated antennas

- Standards-based security

A Cisco 521 can run on its own in autonomous mode, and the Cisco Configuration Assistant can manage up to three 521s in a single location.

If your wireless implementation may expand beyond three wireless hotspots at a single location, you might want to consider the second piece of Cisco 500 Series wireless express hardware/software, the 526 Wireless Express Mobility Controller. When implemented, this device becomes the brain of your wireless network. The Cisco 521s are no longer considered autonomous. Instead, different software is used on the 521 hardware to make them "dumb" devices called *lightweight access points (LWAPs)*. All the configuration and maintenance are then performed at the 526 Wireless Express Mobility Controller, and only basic radio and Ethernet transport functionality is performed at the LWAP level. With this setup, you have the ability to control up to 12 LWAPs at a single location. The SBCS wireless controller also provides these additional benefits:

- A single point of wireless hardware and software management

- The ability to monitor wireless coverage automatically and make real-time changes to signal strength, gain, and wireless channel selection to optimize the wireless network

- Support for wireless mobility services to better support voice over wireless IP phones such as the Cisco 7921 and 7925

It is important to know the entire SBCS suite of products not only for the CCNA Voice exam but also to get an idea of the components available for designing and implementing networks for commercial environments. Now we're going to revisit the UC500 Series platform in more detail to show you all the various options available when ordering and setting up your voice network for small- to medium-size businesses.

Using the UC500 Series Platform out of the Box

As mentioned earlier, one clear benefit the SBCS platform has over its competition is the fact that straight out of the box, the devices are functional. No configuration is necessary to provide basic capabilities. This Plug and Play functionality is also true for the UC500

Series. As soon as you plug in the UC520, it powers up and loads a default configuration for voice and data usage. Also note that all of the licensing is already taken care of. Only when you need to upgrade software or add additional user licenses or other capabilities will you ever have to relicense the UC500.

The developers at Cisco made some assumptions about the default capabilities that users of the UC500 Series platform would want to have. Here is a list of the preconfigured features that you will find on bootup of the UC520:

- Separate voice and data VLANs.
- DHCP server for voice (10.1.1.0/24) and data (192.168.10.0/24) VLANs.
- Ethernet WAN port configured to receive IP address via DHCP for connection to standard DSL, cable modem, or any other consumer/small-business Internet service.
- Network Address Translation (NAT) on WAN port.
- Basic firewall access control list (ACL) protecting the inside network from the WAN port and between VLANs.
- HTTP and HTTPS GUI service setup.
- TFTP server configuration for IP phones using option 150.
- Basic FXS configuration of PLAR analog phones.
- Basic dial-peer setup for off-network calling using FXO interfaces.
- Telephony service set up to utilize CUCM Express in a key-system setup.
- Multicast MoH setup using the default `music-on-hold.au` file stored in flash.
- Auto-registration of phones enabled for Plug and Play setup of Cisco IP phones for a single extension. IP phones receive extensions beginning with 201, and analog phones receive assigned numbers beginning with 301.
- Basic voice mail configuration.

With all of these features preconfigured, some businesses may not need to configure the UC500 manually at all. It is highly recommend that you change at least the default administrator password, however.

NOTE If you've already made modifications to your UC500, you can restore the CUCM Express default configuration very easily. On the flash storage, you should find a file listed with a name similar to UC520-8U-4FXO-K9-factory-4.2.7.cfg. Depending on your hardware and factory-installed software, this filename will be slightly different. Once you find the factory default configuration, you can issue a copy flash: UC520-8U-4FXO-K9-factory-4.2.7.cfg startup-config privileged EXEC command. Then proceed to reboot your UC500 by issuing the reload command. Once the UC500 reboots, your CUCME comes up with the default configuration.

While the Plug and Play functionality is a nice option for quick or simple deployments, you've made a substantial investment in the UC500 Series hardware, so you may as well squeeze every useful feature you can out of it. In the next section, I'm going to introduce you to the Cisco Configuration Assistant, a tool that greatly simplifies the configuration and management of the SBCS platform. You will learn all about the software package and then learn how to install and discover your UC500 Series environment so you can begin the process of configuring the added features that aren't preconfigured out of the box.

Introducing the Cisco Configuration Assistant

Because the Smart Business Communications System is geared toward small- to medium-size commercial environments, Cisco has anticipated that there may not be a highly skilled network engineer on staff to configure and maintain complex networking equipment using the command line or even the web GUI configuration tools. The SBCS offers a third configuration and maintenance application called the *Cisco Configuration Assistant (CCA)* that further simplifies the process to the point where you can configure and manage the entire SBCS lineup using this single tool.

The Cisco Configuration Assistant application is simple to install and configure. This section discusses the CCA application in detail to provide you with the requirements and limitations of the tool.

CCA Requirements

This section details the system requirements for the CCA software to run on PC hardware. It also lists the requirements of the devices that are to be managed within CCA.

CCA Software Requirements

You can find the CCA software on the included CD when you purchase any SBCS product. If you no longer have the CD, you can download it for free from the cisco.com website, provided you have a valid CCO account. The application is a "fat" client, meaning it runs as an executable program on your Microsoft Windows PC. Here are the minimum system requirements needed to run CCA version 2.0, the latest version as of the writing of this book:

- Operating system: Windows XP Professional or Windows Vista Ultimate
- PC processor: 1-GHz Pentium IV
- Memory: 512 MB
- Screen resolution: 1024 × 768
- Disk space: 150 MB
- LAN connectivity: Fast Ethernet

The CCA software also relies heavily on both Adobe Flash and Java to execute the underlying CCA code. When you install the CCA application, both Flash and Java will be installed on the PC if they are not already set up.

CCA-Managed Device Requirements

In addition to the SBCS lineup detailed earlier, the CCA can manage a handful of other small-business Cisco devices. The CCA version 2.0 can currently manage the hardware shown in Table 10.2.

TABLE 10.2   CCA Version 2.0 Manageable Devices

Cisco Device	Model(s)
Routers	SBCS UC500Series
	SBCS SR520 Series
	Cisco 800 Series
Switches	SBCS ESW 500 Series
	Catalyst Express 500 Series
Wireless	SBCS 500 Series Access Point
	SBCS 500 Series Express Mobility Controller

CCA Limitations Per Site

There are limits to the number of devices that the CCA can manage per site. You can support a maximum of 25 devices on a network. The types of devices managed are limited as well. CCA can manage a maximum of the following devices:

- 5 Cisco UC500 Series or SR520 Series routers
- 15 ESW 500 Series switches
- 3 500 Series autonomous wireless access points
- 2 500 Series Wireless Express Mobility Controllers

Fortunately, these restrictions are a per-site limitation on the CCA. Within the CCA, you have the ability to manage an unlimited number of sites with the same tool. Each site then must abide by the maximum device limits.

 Previous to version 2.0 of the CCA application, a "site" was called a "community." These two terms can be used interchangeably.

Now that you have a better understanding of the capabilities and limitations of the CCA software, we can now cover how to install and set up the CCA to support a site using a UC500 Series router.

Setting Up CCA for Supporting the UC500 Series Platform

In this section, we'll go through the CCA software installation process and cover the main user interface buttons of the CCA GUI. Finally, we'll create a brand-new CCA site and take it to the point where the CCA automatically discovers our lab network. Let's get started.

Installing the CCA Software

Setting up the CCA software is very similar to installing any other Windows application. The installation file comes as a Windows executable. Following are the steps you'll go through to install the application on Windows XP:

1. Download the CCA version 2.x software, or insert the software CD that came with your SBCS hardware. The easiest way to find the CCA software on Cisco's website is to go to http://www.cisco.com/go/configassist. You then click the Download button on the right side of the screen. You will be required to log in to CCO to download the software.

2. Locate the file labeled Cisco-config-assistant-win-k9-2_0-en.exe. This is your installation file. It may look slightly different depending on the version you are about to install.

3. Double-click the executable and the installation process begins. The first thing the InstallShield Wizard checks is to make sure you are running a compatible version of Java and Flash.

4. You will be presented with an end-user license agreement (EULA). You must accept the EULA to continue the install process.

5. The installer will ask you what physical directory you would like the software to be installed in. By default, the location is C:\Program Files\Cisco Systems\CiscoSMB. Figure 10.3 shows this part of the install process.

   Either change the directory by clicking Browse and choosing an alternate location in which to install the CCA software files or accept the defaults. When finished, click the Next button. At this point the software will be installed on your PC. It may take several minutes for this process to complete.

6. When the installation is finished, you will be presented with the notification shown in Figure 10.4.

FIGURE 10.3 Specifying the install directory location

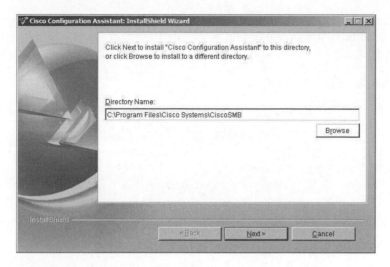

FIGURE 10.4 Successful CCA installation

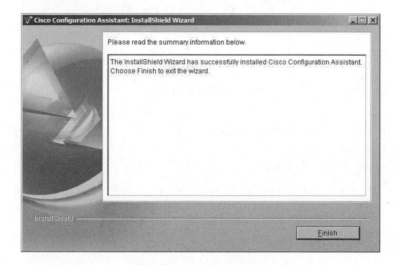

Click the Finish button to complete the installation process.

The installation will have created a shortcut on your desktop labeled "Cisco Configuration Assistant." The remainder of Chapter 10 will cover how to navigate the application as well as how to set the CCA to discover a UC500 and any connected Cisco IP phones. Chapter 11 will then cover the necessary steps to configure the UC500 system using the Configuration Assistant.

Navigating with the CCA User Interface

Before we start using CCA, let's cover the CCA navigation bars and the functions of each of the buttons. The two main navigation menus are the feature bar and the toolbar. Figure 10.5 highlights the two main menu interfaces.

FIGURE 10.5 CCA GUI navigation bars

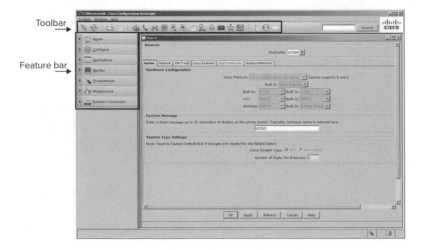

Let's go over what each of the icons mean on these two navigation bars.

Understanding the Feature Bar Interface

The *feature bar* is vertical and by default resides along the left side of the screen. Figure 10.6 shows the icons listed on the feature bar once a site has been discovered.

FIGURE 10.6 The feature bar

Each button of the feature bar serves a different purpose. The bar shows the features that can be configured for all of the devices you are managing at the site. Here's a breakdown of what can be done within each feature bar section:

Home   Here you can find access to the Dashboard, Topology, and Front Panel views. You can also run the various setup wizards.

Configure   Here you can manually configure routing, switching, security, telephony, and other features of the SBCS lineup that is on your network. This is where an administrator would commonly go to configure various options on the UC500 router.

Applications   Here you can modify general site settings and configure setup options for Smart Applications, which are optional applications on SBCS hardware. A Smart Application example on the UC500 is Unified Messaging.

Monitor   Here you can find various monitoring tools and voice status reports.

Troubleshoot   This button provides tools for troubleshooting network and voice problems.

Maintenance   Here you'll find tools for maintaining the software of your SBCS equipment, including software updates and license management.

Partners Connection   This provides access to Cisco's Small Business Support Community, where you can find product documentation, configuration information, and software downloads.

Understanding the Toolbar Interface

The *toolbar* has icons that deal with the configuration, management, and monitoring of your SBCS devices. Many of these buttons deal with the CCA application itself, whereas others are duplicates of what is included in the feature bar but with graphical icons for ease of understanding. Figure 10.7 displays the toolbar menu system with descriptions of each icon button.

FIGURE 10.7   THE TOOLBAR

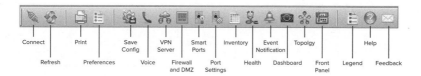

Let's briefly break down what each icon represents from a setup, configuration, and maintenance point of view.

Connect   Uses the CCA to connect to a different site or to an individual SBCS device.

Refresh   Updates the CCA views with the latest information.

Print   Prints the currently active CCA window or help window.

Preferences   Modifies the default CCA display preferences.

Save Configuration   Performs a `copy running-config startup-config` on the managed device.

Voice   Provides configuration options for voice communication.

VPN Server   Provides configuration options to set up a virtual private network (VPN).

Firewall and DMZ   Provides configuration options to set up firewall rules and to create a network demilitarized zone (DMZ).

Smart Ports   Allows you to configure various port security and management functions based on Cisco suggested roles.

Port Settings   Provides View and Modify Port settings.

Inventory   Displays the device hardware/software versions along with the management IP address and other information that identifies the device.

Health   Provides system measurements used to gauge the operational health of managed devices. These measurements include bandwidth utilization, CPU utilization, memory allocation, device temperature, and interface error statistics.

Event Notification   Displays any event-driven notifications for all discovered devices. This information can be useful when troubleshooting various problems. Events are considered to be a triggered condition that occurs on CCA monitored devices that Cisco has determined an administrator should know about. These events include:

- Temperature that exceeds the recommended threshold
- Fan malfunction
- Port that was placed into administratively shutdown mode
- FastEthernet port with a duplex mismatch
- A monitored device that went into an "unknown" state
- VLAN conflict

There are four different levels of event notification that correspond to syslog level types. The lower the level type is, the more severe the alert. Within the Event Notification CCA tool, Event Notification Types are defined as follows:

TABLE 10.3   Event Notification Types

Syslog Level	Event Notification Type
0-1	Critical Error
2-3	Error
4	Warning
5-7	Informational

Dashboard   Pulls up the Dashboard view, which is a great way to quickly display information about the health of your network and attached devices.

Topology   Pulls up the Network Topology view for all discovered devices at a site.

Front Panel   Displays a graphical representation of the physical front of your SBCS device. This is great for checking the status of various ports and LEDs.

Legend   Pulls up the Legend, which describes all icons, labels, and links available on the CCA.

Help   Pulls up the help utility for the active window, where you can search for CCA-related information for configuration, monitoring, and maintenance assistance.

Feedback   Pulls up a feedback page where you can leave feedback and suggestions regarding the CCA tool. This information is then reviewed by Cisco so they can make improvements to new versions of the CCA application.

Monitoring Your SBCS Equipment Using the CCA Dashboard

A monitoring tool within CCA that is new to version 2.0 and above is the Dashboard. This tool is designed to give the administrator quick and simple-to-understand monitoring tools that show SBCS device system health displays using various GUI graphs and charts. Figure 10.8 shows the Dashboard displaying health information for a UC500 Series device.

FIGURE 10.8   The CCA Dashboard

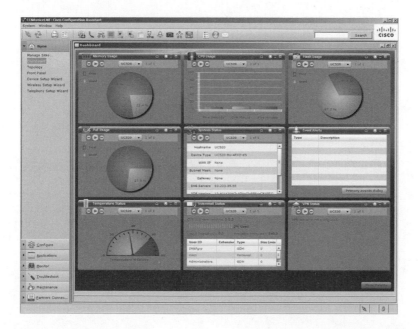

Now that you know the user interface a little better, we can go ahead and set up our first CCA-managed site.

Adding a New CCA Site

Figure 10.9 shows the initial screen you are presented with when you launch the CCA application.

FIGURE 10.9   The Customer Sites tab is initially empty

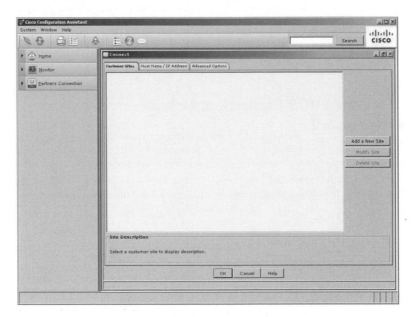

The first thing that we need to do to support an SBCS network is to add it by clicking the Add A New Site button. Remember that each site, or community, is managed separately. The CCA can manage multiple sites on the same application.

You should set your UC500 back to its default settings prior to adding it as a new customer site in the CCA. This way, you can start with a clean slate, using the default username/password for the administrator account (cisco/cisco). You also have the default VLANs and IP ranges for the various components.

A new window pops open, as shown in Figure 10.10.

FIGURE 10.10   Creating a new customer site

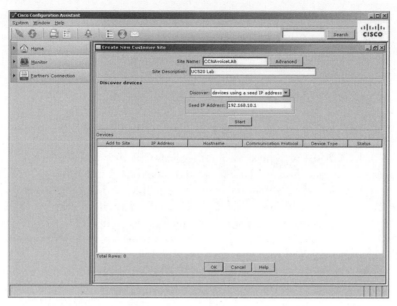

The next screen asks the administrator to fill out the following fields:

- Site Name
- Site Description
- Discover
  - Devices Using A Seed IP Address
  - Devices On A Subnet
  - Devices On An IP Address Range
  - A Single Device By IP

The default (and recommended) network-discovery method is to enter a seed IP address. The *seed address* is typically the heart or root of the network. In our example, the seed IP address of our network is the UC500. When we enter the IP address of the UC500 (192.168.10.1 by default) and click the Start button, the CCA will attempt to connect to the system using either HTTP or HTTPS. That means you must have one of these two services up and running to connect properly; otherwise, the discovery process will fail.

Once the CCA software connects using HTTP or HTTPS, you will be prompted to enter the proper administrator credentials for the UC500, as shown in Figure 10.11.

FIGURE 10.11 UC500 authentication

If you're connecting to a UC500 that has the default configuration, the default username and password are cisco/cisco.

As soon as the CCA software has been authenticated, a discovery process occurs. This *site discovery* process uses the UC500 seed device to look for other CCA-compatible devices such as ESW switches, IP phones, and other SCBS hardware. The term *seed* refers to using the central source of a single device to branch out and find other devices. But how does the CCA actually discover these other attached devices? It uses the Cisco Discovery Protocol (CDP). So another absolute requirement for proper CCA network visibility is that CDP is running on the devices that you wish to discover!

It can take several minutes for the discovery process to complete. When the CCA software is finished, it presents the user with a topology map of the seed device and any other devices it found using CDP during the discovery process. Figure 10.12 shows our small topology of a UC500 and two Cisco 7965 IP phones.

FIGURE 10.12 CCA topology

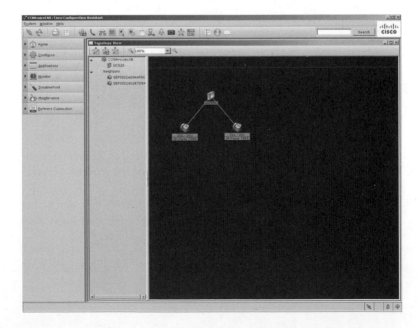

Make note of how the IP phones are considered "neighbors" of the seed UC500 device.

Summary

In Chapter 10 you learned the various hardware components that the SBCS lineup comprises. Each SBCS hardware device serves a different purpose within a small-business voice and data network. We then looked at the UC500 Series SBCS platform to examine both its hardware and software capabilities. From a configuration standpoint, the UC500 can be used literally right out of the box for many basic voice and data features. Last, the chapter introduced you to the Cisco Configuration Assistant and how it can configure and manage the different SBCS components from a simple-to-use GUI application that runs on Microsoft Windows computers. Now you have a better understanding of why the SBCS components that Cisco offers are an incredibly flexible hardware lineup both in their capabilities and in the way they are configured and maintained. In the next chapter you'll use the CCA to configure the UC500 platform's telephony functions in detail.

Exam Essentials

Know the different SBCS UC500 hardware options.   The UC500 system provides voice and data functionality for small businesses. Several different chassis and PSTN port configurations are available. In addition, a voice expansion slot is available for additional PSTN expandability.

Know the major SBCS hardware components.   In addition to the UC500, the SBCS lineup includes the Secure Router 500 Series, the ESW 500 Series Layer 2 switches, and the 500 Series wireless components.

Understand the UC500 Series preconfigured capabilities.   The UC500 is preconfigured to deliver voice and data services out of the box. This allows for extremely fast deployments for environments that require only a basic implementation.

Know what the CCA software is used for and how to install it.   The Cisco Configuration Assistant is a Windows-based application that is used to simplify the configuration and management of the SBCS lineup.

Know how to create and discover a new SBCS site using CCA.   A site is a network that utilizes SBCS hardware. You can use a seed address on the CCA to discover the SBCS network for configuration and monitoring purposes.

Written Lab 10.1

Write the answers to the following questions:

1. The UC520-16U comes in what chassis form factor?

2. Which SBCS hardware supports dynamic routing protocols?

3. What is the name of the feature that allows users to use analog phones connected to the PSTN over FXO interfaces when the UC500 has no power?

4. Which SBCS wireless component controls LWAPs?

5. Which operating systems are required in order to use the CCA?

6. Which two supplemental applications are required to be installed on the PC running CCA?

7. What is the maximum number of UC500 or SR500 Series SBCS devices that can be managed at a single site?

8. How many sites can be managed by CCA?

9. Within the feature bar of the CCA, what button would you click to update the software on your managed SBCS hardware?

10. On the toolbar of the CCA, what button would you click to display a graphical representation of the SBCS system you are managing?

(The answers to Written Lab 10.1 can be found following the answers to the review questions for this chapter.)

Review Questions

1. What two UC500 models use an external power supply?

   A. UC520-8U

   B. UC520-16U

   C. UC520-24U

   D. UC520-32U

   E. UC520-48U

2. How many rack units (U) does the UC500 desktop chassis consume?

   A. 1U

   B. 1.5U

   C. 2U

   D. 2.5U

3. What is the maximum number of fixed PRI interfaces that can be ordered on the desktop form factor UC500 system?

   A. 1

   B. 0

   C. 2

   D. 4

   E. 8

4. What is the name of the UC500 port that is used to uplink to an Ethernet switch such as the ESW 500 Series?

   A. WAN Ethernet port

   B. Compact flash slot

   C. Voice expansion slot

   D. FXO port

   E. LAN expansion port

5. What type of phone can be used when there is no power to a UC500 that is connected to the PSTN using FXO ports?

   A. Cisco 7900 Series IP phones

   B. Cisco 500 Series IP phones

   C. Cisco 7921 or 7925 wireless phones

   D. Analog phones

6. Which UC500 models support an integrated wireless access point? Choose all that apply.

   A. UC520-48U

   B. UC520-8U

   C. UC520-32U

   D. UC520-16U

   E. UC520-24U

7. What SBCS series hardware supports dynamic routing protocols?

   A. UC500 Series

   B. ESW 500 Series

   C. SR500 Series

   D. 500 Series Wireless Express Mobility Controller

8. If your site needs to manage more than three wireless access points, what additional device is recommended?

   A. 500 Series Express Wireless Mobility Controller

   B. SR500

   C. ESW 500

   D. LWAP

9. When the intelligence of a wireless access point is moved from the access point to a Wireless Express Mobility Controller, what term describes the access point?

   A. Hot spot

   B. Integrated antenna

   C. Autonomous

   D. Controlled

   E. Lightweight

10. Which of the following is *not* a benefit of using SBCS 500 Series Wireless Express Mobility Controllers?

   A. Single point of management.

   B. Ability to monitor wireless coverage of multiple access points at one time.

   C. Cisco IP 7921 and 7925 phones can be used only on wireless designs that use the Wireless Express Mobility Controller.

   D. Support for wireless mobility services.

11. What part of the out-of-the-box UC500 Series configuration is recommended to be changed?

   A. Auto-registration

   B. Default administrator password

   C. Network Address Translation

   D. Default access control list (ACL)

12. Which of the following is *not* a system requirement for installing the CCA on a Windows PC?

   A. Processor 1GHz Pentium IV

   B. 512 MB RAM

   C. 150 MB disk space

   D. LAN or WLAN connectivity

13. Which of the following hardware *cannot* be configured or supported using CCA?

   A. 800 Series router

   B. ESW 500 Series switch

   C. SR500 Series

   D. 500 Series Express Mobility Controller

   E. 1800 Series router

14. CCA requires which two additional applications to be installed on the Windows PC?

   A. Flash

   B. JavaScript

   C. Java

   D. Silverlight

   E. SBCS

15. What is the maximum number of ESW 500 Series devices that can be supported using CCA in a single site?

   A. 2

   B. 5

   C. 10

   D. 15

16. What are the names of the two main CCA navigation bars?

   A. Feature bar

   B. CCA bar

   C. Wizard bar

   D. Toolbar

17. Which of the following is not a feature bar button in CCA?

   A. Home

   B. Monitor

   C. Partners Connection

   D. Applications

   E. Wizard

18. Which of the following tasks can be achieved by using the Front Panel button on the CCA toolbar?

   A. Verify that the MoH lamp is lit on an IP phone

   B. View the network topology of the site

   C. Verify link up/down status of a Fast Ethernet port

   D. Reload the UC500 remotely.

19. What is the default method for a site discovery using CCA?

   A. Single device by IP

   B. IP address range

   C. Seed IP

   D. Subnet range

20. When using the seed IP address CCA site-discovery method, what does the seed device use to discover additional devices on the network to manage?

   A. ICMP

   B. HTTP or HTTPS

   C. SSH

   D. Telnet

   E. CDP

Answers to Review Questions

1. **A, B.** The two desktop chassis models of the UC520-8U and UC520-16U use an external power brick.

2. **B.** The desktop chassis form factor UC500 uses up 1.5U. Each rack unit is 1.75 inches.

3. **B.** The desktop model of the UC500 does not support any fixed PRI interfaces.

4. **E.** The LAN expansion port is used to uplink to a switch such as the ESW 500 Series for Ethernet port expandability.

5. **D.** Only analog phones connected to the FXS interfaces can utilize the power failover feature.

6. **B, D.** Only the desktop UC500 chassis supports the integrated wireless access point.

7. **C.** The Secure Router 500 Series hardware supports dynamic routing protocols. The UC500 supports only static routes.

8. **A.** The Wireless Express Mobility Controller is recommended for sites that have more than three Cisco wireless access points when using the CCA. The CCA can support only 3 autonomous APs at a single site. If the wireless APs are controlled by a Wireless Express Mobility Controller, then the CCA can support up to 12 LWAPs at a single site.

9. **E.** When the intelligence of an access point resides at the Wireless Express Mobility Controller, the access point is referred to as a lightweight access point (LWAP).

10. **C.** The Cisco 7921 and 7925 wireless IP phones can be used with wireless access points in both AAP and LWAP architectures. The Wireless Express Mobility Controller is not required.

11. **B.** The default administrator password should be changed at minimum.

12. **D.** A Fast Ethernet connection is required to connect the PC to the network. A WLAN connection is not supported when using the CCA.

13. **E.** All of the devices are supported except for the 1800 Series routers.

14. **A, C.** Java and Adobe Flash are required on the Windows desktop. If they are not installed on the system when CCA is installed, the CCA application installs them for you.

15. **D.** Up to 15 ESW switches are supported within a single site using CCA.

16. **A, D.** The feature bar is found vertically along the left side of the screen, and the toolbar is horizontal across the top of the application screen.

17. **E.** The Wizard is not a feature bar button within the CCA application.

18. C. The Front Panel button of the CCA toolbar displays a graphical representation of SBCS hardware such as the UC500. The only task that can be accomplished by using the Front Panel button is to verify the up/down link status on a Fast Ethernet port.

19. C. The default method for CCA site discovery is to enter a single seed IP address.

20. E. The seed device uses CDP to discover additional devices that the CCA can manage.

Answers to Written Lab 10.1

1. Desktop

2. Secure Router 500 Series

3. Power failover feature

4. Wireless Express Mobility Controller

5. Microsoft Windows XP or Vista Ultimate

6. Flash and Java

7. Five

8. Unlimited

9. Maintenance

10. Front Panel

Chapter

11

Configuring Telephony Functions Using the Cisco Configuration Assistant

THE FOLLOWING CCNA VOICE EXAM OBJECTIVES ARE COVERED IN THIS CHAPTER:

✓ **Implement UC500 using Cisco Configuration Assistant.**

- Describe the function and operation of Cisco Configuration Assistant.
- Configure UC500 device parameters.
- Configure UC500 network parameters.
- Configure UC500 dial plan and voice mail parameters.
- Configure UC500 SIP trunk parameters.
- Configure UC500 voice system features.
- Configure UC500 user parameters.

In Chapter 10 you learned that the Cisco Configuration Assistant (CCA) is a PC-based application that allows administrators of small networks to configure and administer various products within the Cisco SBCS lineup. In this chapter we're going to focus on configuration of the SBCS UC500 Series platform for voice functionality. The chapter will start by running through the Telephony Initialization tool settings to prepare the UC500 for proper configuration using the CCA. The remainder of the chapter details the different CCA voice-configuration options available to you. By the end of the chapter, you will have a thorough understanding of setting up a UC500 for various voice capabilities using the Cisco Configuration Assistant application.

Telephony Initialization

When you click any configuration option under Configure ➤ Telephony, a window pops open labeled Telephony Initialization, as shown in Figure 11.1.

FIGURE 11.1 The Telephony Initialization window

Because you're using the CCA for the first time, you are given the option to set up your CUCM to function as either a PBX or a key system. You can also choose the number of digits your phone extensions will have. This field is auto-filled with 3, indicating that your phone extensions will be three digits in length. Finally, you can optionally choose to add a voice mail access extension (pilot) number. In our example, we used 700 for our voice mail access extension. Click the OK button to continue.

At this point the CCA communicates with the CUCM and CUE to configure various default settings. This typically takes several minutes to complete. Once it is finished, you will receive a pop-up message that states "Voice system initialized." Click OK to continue. Now that our CCA has initialized our UC500, we can configure telephony functions starting within the Configure ➤ Telephony portion of the Feature bar.

Configuring the Telephony Region Using CCA

The first thing we're going to configure is the telephony region where our UC500 resides geographically, to match the telephone signaling and notification standards that users are accustomed to. To reach the Telephony Region configuration area, use the Feature toolbar and navigate to Configure ➤ Telephony ➤ Region. Figure 11.2 shows the Telephony Region options available to us.

FIGURE 11.2 The Telephony Region options

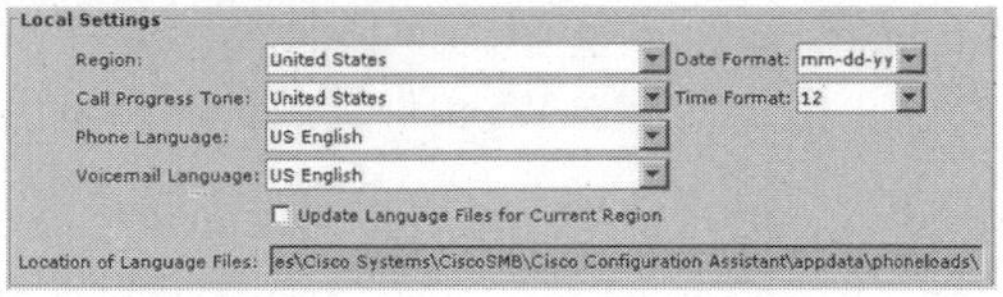

All of the configuration parameters displayed in the Region area should be familiar to you by now. You can modify the UC500 to fit the language, call-processing tones, and time/date formats of the local area of the user base.

Configuring Telephony Voice Features Using CCA

The next Telephony configuration area we're going to investigate comprises the voice features. To configure voice telephony options, navigate to Configure ➤ Telephony ➤ Voice in the Feature toolbar. When the voice configuration options open, you'll notice several tabs that segment the various voice features.

The next sections will cover the following tabs to show what you can configure within the CCA:

- System
- Network
- SIP Trunk
- Voice Features
- User Extensions

Configuring Voice System Options

The System tab is a great place to view the hardware setup of your UC500 system. During the CCA discovery process, the UC500 is analyzed and all hardware components are detected. Figure 11.3 shows the layout of the System tab. Within the Hardware Configuration section, you can see all of the built-in components and whether any module slots are filled or empty.

FIGURE 11.3   The Voice System options

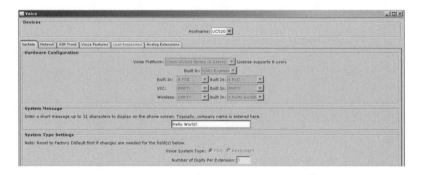

As you can see, from a configuration standpoint, the only portion that can be modified within the Setup tab is the System Message, which is the message displayed at the bottom of the Cisco IP phone just above the softkeys. In Figure 11.3, we've changed our System Message field to display "Hello World!"

Last, the System tab has a section labeled System Type Settings. This section shows the administrator whether the UC500 is set up to function in PBX or keysystem mode and how many digits per extension are used by default for the various phone and pilot extensions on the system. Recall that during the CCA Telephony Initialization stage, we were required to choose both the UC500 mode and the number of extension digits the CUCM Express should use for auto-assignment of analog and IP phones. These choices cannot be modified unless the administrator wants to reset the UC500 to factory defaults. That is why these choices are grayed out within the System tab. It is important to emphasize that, because of this lack of simple renumbering capability, you need to properly plan before installation.

The next tab we're going to look at is Network, which configures the IP networking capabilities for our voice VLAN on the UC500.

Configuring Voice Network Options

The Network tab within Voice Telephony configuration allows you to configure IP addressing for the call-processing unit and IP phones. Figure 11.4 displays the IP networking configuration options available.

FIGURE 11.4 The Voice Network options

The Voice VLAN section lets the administrator choose which configured VLAN to use for IP phones. Remember that by default on the UC500, two VLANs are defined. One VLAN is for data traffic and the other is for voice. CDP is used to automatically detect Cisco IP phones. If a Cisco phone is detected, that phone will be placed into the VLAN that is set here. If CDP is not enabled or not supported by the phone, the administrator will have to configure the phones manually later on.

The voice *DHCP scope* is also configured here. You define the IP network and subnet mask. You can also configure *excluded addresses* so the DHCP service does not accidentally hand out an IP address that is hard-coded, which would cause an IP address conflict. Last, you can set the Communications Manager Express IP address and subnet mask. If you choose to configure this IP address to be in the same subnet as your DHCP pool, as shown in the previous figure, make sure this IP address is one of the DHCP-excluded IP addresses.

Configuring SIP Trunk Options

The SIP Trunk tab is where you configure a trunk to another voice gateway or Internet Telephony Service Provider (ITSP) connection. For ITSP configurations, the CCA greatly simplifies the configuration process by providing SIP configuration templates for certified ITSP providers. As of the writing of this book, the list of certified ITSP providers includes the following:

- AT&T
- British Telecom (BT)
- Broadview
- Cbeyond
- Covad
- Fibernet
- Nuvox
- One Communications
- PAETEC (McLeod)
- XO Communications

Depending on the ITSP used, you will be required to fill out different information. For example, Figure 11.5 shows the options required if you set up an SIP trunk with AT&T's ITSP voice services.

FIGURE 11.5   AT&T ITSP SIP trunk configuration

 Real World Scenario

The Advantages of Using a Certified ITSP

A small Chicago-based business was tired of the expensive long-distance charges they were experiencing with their PSTN provider. Because the organization recently had a Cisco UC520 SBCS device installed, they wanted to pursue the option of setting up an SIP trunk with a Cisco-certified ITSP. After doing some research, the company's network administrator chose Covad as the ITSP for the business.

After calling Covad and signing an ITSP contract for an SIP trunk with eight DIDs, the network administrator was given detailed instructions on how to configure the UC520 to connect to the SIP gateway at the other end of the Covad SIP trunk using the Covad SIP Trunk template, as shown here:

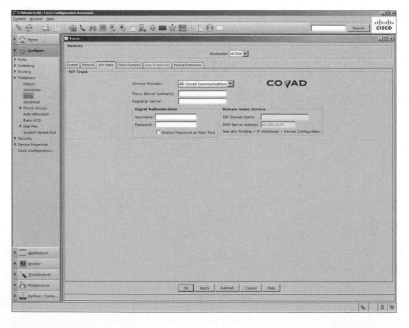

Setting up SIP trunks from Cisco-certified ITSPs is a snap because when you sign up for one of these services, the ITSP tells you the exact information to enter into the various SIP Trunk fields. It's just a matter of plugging the information into the fields and clicking the Apply button.

One additional SIP Trunk screen you should be aware of is the one used for all noncertified ITSPs. The Generic SIP Trunk Provider option provides many more fields that may be required by the non-certified ITSP. Figure 11.6 shows the SIP configuration fields available.

FIGURE 11.6   Generic SIP trunk configuration

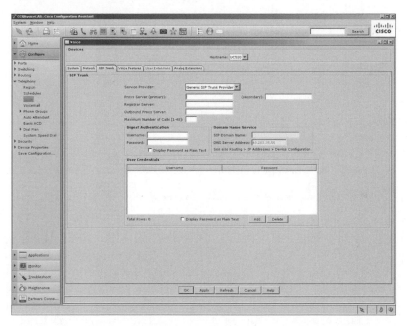

Even though the Generic SIP Trunk Provider option might take some trial and error by both you and the ITSP, it is still an available option so you are not solely locked into choosing a certified service provider.

Configuring Voice Features Options

The Voice Features tab is a bit of a mish-mash of configuration options. Cisco has determined that this grouping of features is commonly found in small to medium-size environments and therefore has made them easily configurable here using the CCA. Figure 11.7 displays the Voice Features tab layout.

FIGURE 11.7 Voice Features options

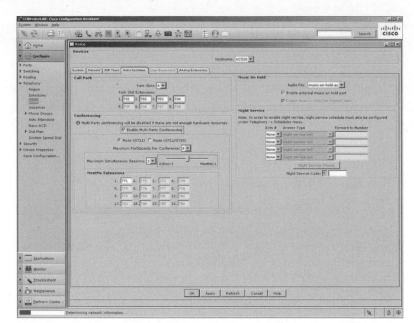

The tab is divided into four separate voice options. Let's briefly go over each feature and its configuration with CCA.

Call Park

Call parking is a very popular feature in small offices because it allows the user to quickly put a caller on hold and resume the call from another phone on the system. For example, let's say a clothing store clerk answers a call from a customer asking whether the store has a specific pair of shoes in a size 8. The clerk needs to check the inventory in the back of the store. Instead of placing the caller on hold, the clerk parks the caller. The clerk then goes to the back of the store to check the inventory. The clerk can then pick up a different phone located at the back of the store and dial the parking slot number to resume the call.

You can set call park slots for the temporary holding of calls onto special extensions. In Figure 11.7, we've enabled four call park slots with the extensions of 701 to 704.

Music on Hold

The Music On Hold section allows for a few modifications within the CCA application. The Audio File drop-down menu allows you to select music files that are stored on the UC500 flash in either a `.wav` or `.au` format.

The Enable External Music On Hold Port check box allows you to enable or disable the 3.5mm jack that allows an external audio source such as a CD or MP3 player to be used for MoH. When this box is checked, the music from the external jack takes precedence over the audio file stored on the UC500 flash.

The Enable Music On Hold For Internal Calls check box allows you to enable or disable MoH for calls that are on internal IP phones. When MoH is disabled for internal calls, any call placed on hold will hear the hold beep signal every few seconds instead of music. This saves UC500 resources such as memory and processor cycles that can be used for other tasks and features.

Conferencing

The Conferencing section allows for two types of multi-party conference calls. Recall that DSP resources are required for conferencing. Because of this, the CCA automatically calculates the amount of available resources and sets limits for the number of conferences that are allowed to be configured on the UC500. You can play around to balance the number of sessions with the maximum number of participants and the codec mode to set up conferencing as you see fit. Each of these three settings uses up a different amount of DSP resources.

 G.711-only mode is commonly used for deployments when conference call participants are mostly on-network. *Mixed mode* (G.711/G.729) is recommended for off-network participants that use an ITSP setup with SIP trunking. If the ITSP supports G.729, then your calls will use less bandwidth. Keep in mind that mixed mode uses more DSP resources than G.711 mode alone.

Once you have these settings configured to allocate the various DSP resources, you can choose between the two different types of conference-call sessions.

AdHoc conference calls let a user call one party and then call another so that all can talk to one another. This is often referred to as three-way calling, but this term can be a bit misleading, because often there are more than three parties in an AdHoc conference, depending on the Maximum Participants Per Conference setting. In our example, we allow up to eight parties per conference.

MeetMe conferences allow parties to dial an extension to "meet" others for a conference call. This is also called a conference bridge. In our example, we've enabled a single MeetMe conference bridge number of 771. Users who wish to establish a conference call on a Cisco IP phone can press the MeetMe softkey, which becomes available as soon as this feature is enabled. A confirmation tone is then generated back through the phone handset to the user. At this time, the user dials the 771 code to access the conference bridge.

Because we've set our codec to G711 and the maximum number of participants to 8, our DSP resources allow us to have two simultaneous conference sessions. Using the slider bar, we've decided to allow for one AdHoc and one MeetMe conference session in the example shown.

Night Service

The final section of the Voice Features tab is Night Service. We've already gone over the purpose of night service, when we discussed Call Forwarding options in Chapter 6. Just as a reminder, night service allows for simple forwarding to a different extension (such as the voice mail pilot number) based on the time of day. Because this feature is based on the time of day, there is a notification statement in the configuration section stating that you must tell the CCA what the office hours are. You will learn how to configure telephony schedules later in this chapter.

After you've made the configuration changes for the various voice features you've enabled, you can click the Apply button to save your changes. When you do this, you'll see an error message identifying errors that must be corrected before the CCA will make any configuration changes to the UC500 system. Figure 11.8 shows the configuration error message sent by the CCA.

FIGURE 11.8   CCA configuration error notification

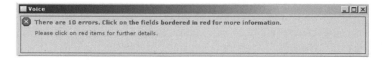

As you have seen throughout this book, many configuration features depend on the proper configuration of other features. Some configurations serve as building blocks to various features. The CCA has built-in intelligence to inform you of these dependencies. The 10 errors that CCA is complaining about were flagged because we must first fill out user extension fields prior to enabling conferencing on the system. Let's look at the User Extensions tab to correct the errors.

Configuring User Extensions Options

The User Extensions tab is where an administrator can add and delete analog and IP phones on the UC500. There also is an import feature for *bulk additions* of phones using standard .csv files.

During the initial seeding process, the CCA probed the UC500 and found that it had four FXS analog ports and two Cisco 7965 IP phones attached to Ethernet interfaces. Figure 11.9 shows that the CCA added the FXS ports and IP phones to the configuration.

In addition, it assigned the analog FXS port extensions between 301 and 304 and extensions 201 and 202 for the Cisco phones. Generic first/last names were also added to the analog phone ports. As stated in the error notification, CCA is alerting us that we must fill in the remaining first/last names as well as assign a user ID to all phone devices configured on the UC500.

FIGURE 11.9   User extension options

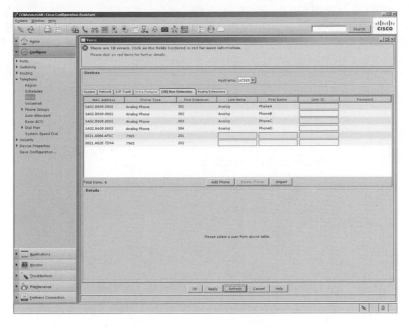

Let's go ahead and assign user IDs to the four analog phones. Figure 11.10 shows the CCA screen after adding these user IDs.

FIGURE 11.10   Adding analog phone user IDs

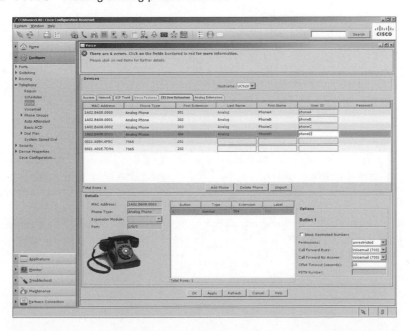

In the Details section for the PhoneD analog phone port, you can see that we can configure various call-blocking permissions as well as call-forward extensions. Also note that as we begin to correct our "errors," the error count in the alert drops. After we added the four user IDs to the analog phones, the number of errors detected by CCA went from 10 to 6.

To appease the CCA application, let's go ahead and configure usernames and IDs for the two IP phone users to correct the final six errors. Figure 11.11 shows the two users properly configured.

FIGURE 11.11 Adding IP phone user IDs

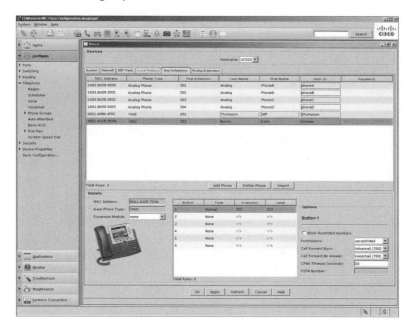

In the Details section of the Cisco 7965 IP phone, we have the ability to set up the phone button expansion module if we have one. We can also set up or modify any of the six phone buttons that are standard on the 7965 phone. Also note that there is a button to add any phones that the CCA did not detect initially when going through the discovery process.

When all configurations are finished, click the Apply button to apply the changes to the running configuration of the UC500. Next we'll modify, configure, and view voice mail features using the CCA.

Configuring Telephony Voice Mail Features Using CCA

The third Telephony configuration area we'll examine covers the voice mail options. To configure voice mail options, navigate to Configure ➢ Telephony ➢ Voice Mail in the Feature toolbar. You'll notice that there are two tabs within the voice mail configuration options: Setup and Mailboxes.

Obviously, since we're working with voice mail, we're dealing with Unity Express, which is integrated into the UC500 hardware. We're going to look at each of these tabs to see what voic email configuration options are possible using the Cisco Configuration Assistant.

Voice Mail Setup Options

The Unity Express setup options available on this tab deal with systemwide settings. Figure 11.12 displays the configuration options available to us.

FIGURE 11.12   Voice Mail Setup options

The Voice Mail Access Extension field is populated with extension 700. As you'll recall, when we initialized the telephony features within the UC500 using the CCA, we set the access extension at that time. If you want to, you can modify this number here.

There is also a place to add a PSTN number so users could dial in and check messages while they are off-network. This setting is optional. We added 5155557897 in our example.

Last, there are two check box options. The first is to enable or disable *VoiceView Express* so users can check their voice mail using softkeys on Cisco IP phones. The second check box is labeled *Live Reply*. This feature allows the user to return calls to parties who left voice mails directly from Unity Express. The alternative method of returning calls if Live Reply is disabled is that the user disconnects (hangs up the phone) from Unity Express and redials the number manually.

Voice Mail Mailbox Options

The second Voice Mail tab allows us to modify the preconfigured mailboxes for each of the extensions that were assigned in the User Extension tab of the Telephony Voice configuration options. Figure 11.13 shows the Mailboxes tab with extension 201 highlighted to illustrate the various configuration options available on the UC500 using CCA.

FIGURE 11.13 Voice Mail Mailboxes options

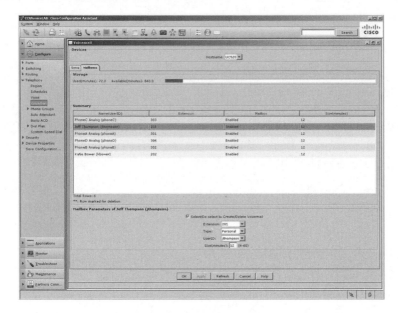

At the top of the screen is the Storage section. Here we can view the Unity Express storage capabilities. We can see how much storage has been allocated compared to the amount available. Capacity for Unity Express is expressed in minutes on a UC500.

Looking at user Jeff Thompson's individual mailbox, we see that by default, the mailbox is enabled. By unchecking the Select/De-select option, we can effectively disable the mailbox if we choose. Other parameters that can be modified include extension number, mailbox type, user ID assigned to the mailbox, and size of the mailbox itself. By default, each mailbox will hold 12 minutes of recorded messages.

Configuring Telephony Phone Groups Features Using CCA

The Phone Groups section is where we can configure various clusters of users to better handle communication based on the grouping of users/extensions that have similar roles in the organization. The following groups can be configured, modified, and deleted in this section:

- Hunt groups
- Paging groups
- Pickup groups

To locate this configuration area, use the Feature bar to navigate to Configure ➤ Telephony ➤ Phone Groups. Here's a look at how each of these sections is laid out in the CCA.

Hunt Groups

You set up hunt groups by using the Feature bar and navigating to Configure ➤ Telephony ➤ Phone Groups ➤ Hunt Groups. Up to 10 hunt groups can be defined using the CCA. As a reminder, hunt groups use a pilot number that people dial to reach a group of people who perform similar duties, such as a customer call center. Customer call centers can be ideal situations for hunt groups because the caller is looking to speak not to a specific person but rather to one of many people who are capable of servicing the caller's needs. The CCA then attempts to ring an extension that belongs to the hunt group based on various algorithms that can be set, including sequential or longest-idle time. If the first extension called does not answer after a defined period, CCA attempts to ring the next extension in the hunt group.

In the next example, the three-digit pilot numbers are already defined, but you can change them if you like. Figure 11.14 displays the Hunt Groups configuration screen.

FIGURE 11.14 Hunt Groups configuration

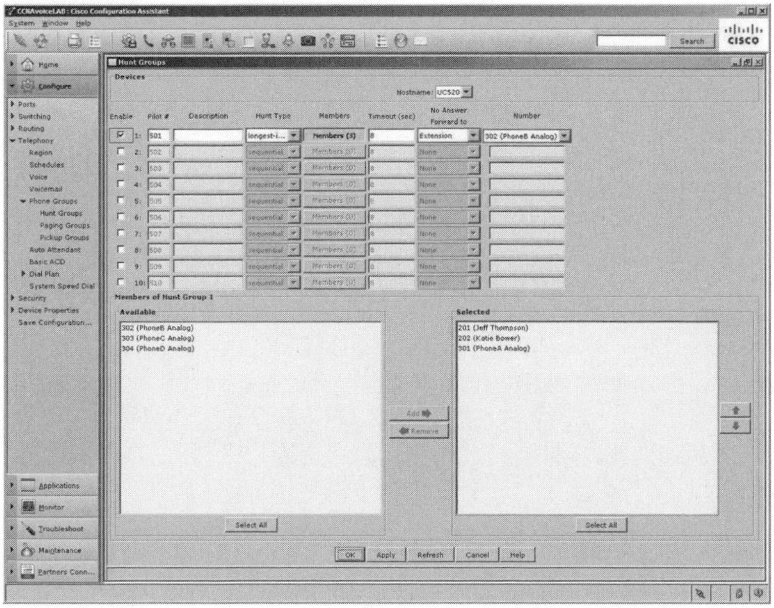

By default, all the hunt groups are disabled. To enable a hunt group, check the Enable check box located on the left. In this example, we've enabled hunt group pilot number 501. We've also changed the Hunt Type setting to Longest-Idle Time. You can select hunt group members from the Available section and click the right-arrow button to move them over to the Selected section. Extensions 201, 202, and 301 have been added as members of this group. Finally, we've set the No Answer Forward To drop-down list to ring extension 302 if none of the group members answers the call.

Paging Groups

To set up paging groups, use the Feature bar and navigate to Configure ➢ Telephony ➢ Phone Groups ➢ Paging Groups. The Paging Groups section is very similar in setup to the options for configuring hunt groups. And again, the purpose of these paging groups is to provide for a one-way broadcast of real-time voice to multiple group subscribers. Figure 11.15 shows the CCA layout for this section.

FIGURE 11.15 Paging Groups configuration

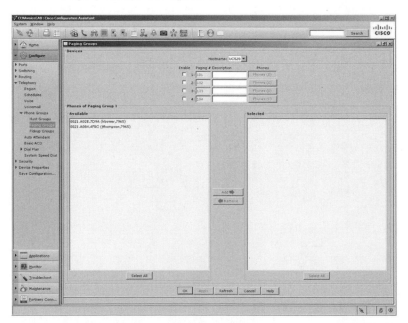

The Enable check box allows you to enable up to four paging groups on the UC500 with paging numbers that are predefined but can be modified. You can also describe each paging group so that administrators can better keep track of the purpose of the group. Finally, there is a listing of available phones and selected phones assigned to the paging group.

Notice that only IP phones can be part of a paging group. Therefore, the analog ports on our UC500 system are not included as Available choices.

Pickup Groups

Finally, you set up pickup groups in the Feature bar by navigating to Configure ➢ Telephony ➢ Phone Groups ➢ Pickup Groups. Users within a pickup group can use the GPickUp softkey to answer any ringing phone that belongs to the same pickup group. Again, this is a nice feature to have in call centers or places where multiple people perform the same functions. Figure 11.16 displays the CCA layout for configuring pickup groups.

FIGURE 11.16   Pickup Groups configuration

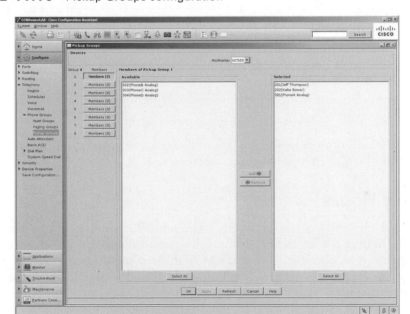

Up to eight pickup groups can be configured. In the screenshot, three group members have been added to pickup group 1. There is no enabling/disabling of the groups. To activate a pickup group, you simply move IP or analog phones from the Available list to the Selected list and click the Apply button.

That covers the different groups that can be set up within CCA version 2.0. Next, we'll explore how to set up business schedules including business hours, holidays, and night-service hours.

Configuring Telephony Schedules Using CCA

The SBCS UC500 system needs to be instructed about business and holiday working hours for two purposes. The first is to play the correct Auto Attendant prompts. One standard set of audio prompts can be played when the office is open, and another can be played to inform callers that the office is closed. The same goes for holiday hours when the business is closed.

The second reason for filling out a work schedule within the UC500 is to take advantage of the Night Service tool, which is a convenient feature to automatically forward incoming calls on an extension directly to voice mail when someone calls during non-working hours. You can set these schedules using the CCA by using the Feature toolbar and navigating to Configure ➤ Telephony ➤ Schedules. Three tabs set up scheduling, as shown here: Business Hours, Night Service, and Holiday.

Let's look at each of these tabs to see how to set up our office schedule for proper functionality of both the AA and Night Service features.

Business Hours

The Business Hours tab lets you set the hours when the office is open and people are able to take calls. Both of the standard AA scripts that come with the UC500 incorporate the business hours functionality. Times can be configured at half-hour intervals. A checked box means the office is open, while an unchecked box indicates closed times. So, for example, if your office has working hours from 7:30 A.M. to 5:30 P.M. Monday through Friday, then you would want to have the boxes checked between those hours on the schedule. By default, all boxes are checked, indicating your office is open seven days a week for all 24 hours of the day. You could manually go through and uncheck the hours that the office is closed, but you'll quickly see that it becomes time consuming and, honestly, quite boring. To make the setting of working hours a bit easier, the CCA has a widget to check or uncheck boxes based on time and day of the week. In Figure 11.17 I am using the widget to uncheck the boxes between the hours of 17:30 (5:30 P.M.) and 24:00 (12:00 A.M.).

When you click the Update Table button, all of the half-hour time boxes on Monday between those times become unchecked. To complete Monday's closed hours you should set the time from 00:00 to 08:30 using the time widget and click the Update Table button. Also note that you can have up to four different business-hour schedules. To enable a

FIGURE 11.17   The Business Hours tab

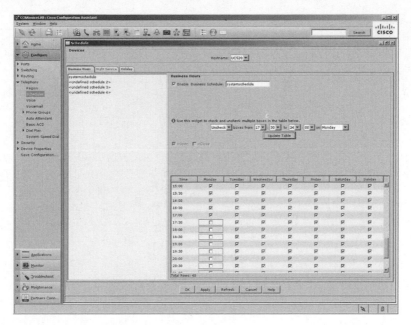

particular schedule, highlight it on the left and click the Enable Business Schedule check box. Only one schedule can be enabled at a time, however, so you must first uncheck the schedule that is currently enabled before enabling a new schedule.

Night Service

The night service schedule goes hand-in-hand with the Night Service option described in the "Configuring Voice Features Options" section of this chapter. Figure 11.18 displays the Night Service Schedule layout.

By default, all seven days of the week are set up for night service between the hours of 5:00 P.M. and 9:00 A.M. Since our office is open Monday through Friday from 8:30 to 5:30, we'll need to modify these settings. We can use the night service schedule to set the nonworking hours per day as 17:30 to 08:30 for Monday. We can then use the Copy Selected Row To drop-down list to select Tuesday and apply Monday's settings to Tuesday. We can continue to do this for Wednesday, Thursday, and Friday. Finally, our office is not open at all on Saturday and Sunday, so we can set our night service hours from 00:00 to 24:00 for Saturday and then highlight Saturday on the schedule and copy the hours over to Sunday. Once this setup is complete, any extensions that have the Night Service feature enabled will have calls immediately routed to voice mail (or any other configured extension chosen) when the office is closed.

FIGURE 11.18 The Night Service Schedule tab

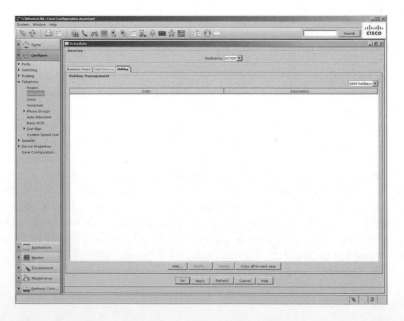

Holiday

The Holiday tab allows you to configure business holidays for use by the Auto Attendant. When these dates are set, the AA uses an alternate "holiday" greeting, informing callers that the office is closed for that holiday. Figure 11.19 displays the Holiday tab and its features.

FIGURE 11.19 The Holiday Schedule tab

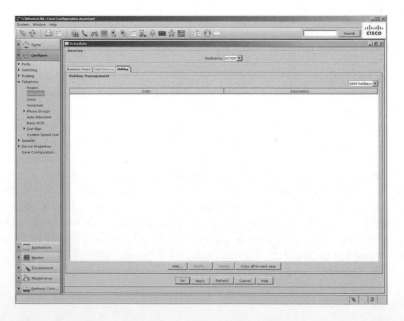

By default, no holidays are configured on the UC500 when using the CCA. If you want to add holidays, click the Add button, and the window shown in Figure 11.20 opens.

FIGURE 11.20   The Add A Holiday window

You can click on the calendar icon to select the holiday you wish to configure. You can then add a description to the holiday. In our example, we've configured July 4, 2009, and labeled it Independence Day. Keep in mind that because some holidays do not fall on the same calendar date every year, you'll have to manually configure holidays for each calendar year. The American holiday of Thanksgiving, for example, falls on the last Thursday in November of each year. Because the calendar date changes, you must configure holidays every year. The CCA allows you to configure holidays for the current year and one additional year out. The writing of this book occurred in 2009, so the CCA gave us the ability to configure holidays for 2009 and 2010.

Configuring Telephony Auto Attendant Features Using CCA

You can find the Auto Attendant configuration features within CCA by using the Feature toolbar to navigate to Configure ➢ Telephony ➢ Auto Attendant. When the window opens, you see three tabs for configuration of different AA options within CCA: Auto Attendant, Prompt Management, and Script Management.

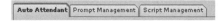

Let's go over these tabs to see what the configuration screens look like.

Auto Attendant

When you initially look at the Auto Attendant tab options, there are only three radio buttons to choose from, defining the mode you want for your auto attendant. The first mode is to turn Auto Attendant off, the second choice is to use the AA in standard mode, and the third is to use the AA in the more advanced multi-level mode. The difference between standard and multi-level mode is that standard has a single menu system whereas multi-level mode uses a more complex menu system for navigation. By default, the Auto Attendant mode is set to Off. Figure 11.21 shows the options available to you in standard AA mode:

FIGURE 11.21   Auto Attendant Standard mode settings

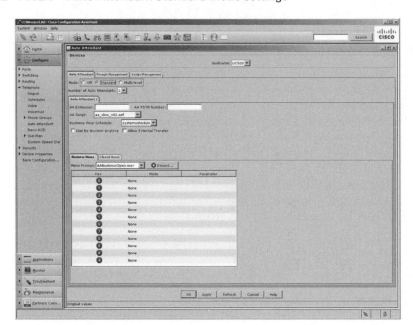

As you can see, the CCA allows you to configure all the standard AA options you've learned how to set using the Unity Express web GUI. Among the options to point out, the AA Extension number is the pilot extension to dial to use the AA. You also have a section to add the PSTN number for off-network calls to come into the AA. There also is an option to choose the business hour schedule you want to implement. Finally, you can configure dial pad key mappings so that when users press the digit on their handset, they move the AA script forward. For example, we can set the number 1 on the keypad to dial extension 201. The audio menu prompt will then have to be modified to tell the user to press 1 for Jeff Thompson, who resides at extension 201. So just how can we change the various prompts used by the AA? That question is answered in the next Auto Attendant tab, Prompt Management.

Prompt Management

The Prompt Management tab is where you can view, modify, add, or delete AA menu prompts. Figure 11.22 shows the Prompt Management tab configuration options.

FIGURE 11.22   The Prompt Management tab

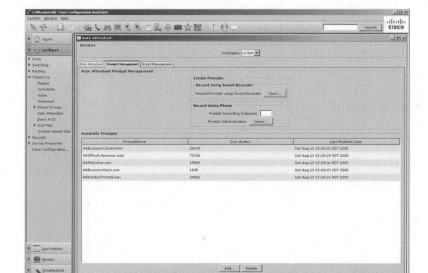

As you can see, five default AA prompts are available. You can choose to modify these default prompts or add new prompts if you desire. Either way, there are two different prompt-recording options using the CCA. The first method is to use the integrated *CCA Sound Recorder* option. This allows you to use your PC microphone to record the prompts and have them saved to the local drive of the PC where you have CCA running. Then, when you click the Apply button, CCA uses its built-in FTP service to transfer the new prompt file to the compact flash of the UC500. Figure 11.23 shows the recording window when you click the Open button next to Record Prompts Using Sound Recorder.

FIGURE 11.23   The CCA Auto Attendant Prompt Sound Recorder

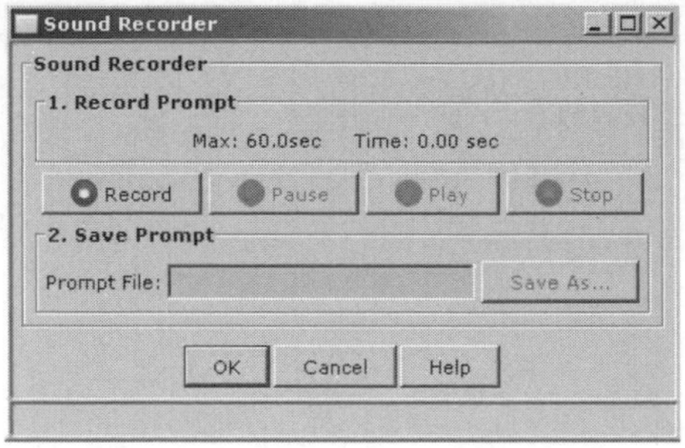

The recorder has all the standard Record, Pause, Play, and Stop buttons, as you would expect. Also note the limit of 60 seconds per prompt. When you save the prompt files for new recordings, make sure you are descriptive with the filenames so you can easily recall what the prompts are used for.

The second prompt-recording option is to enter a prompt-recording extension for users to dial in to record their own AA prompts using the same AvT functionality within Unity Express. We need to first assign at least one member to the AvT group. To do this within the CCA, we select the users we want to add as AvT users within the Prompt Administrators section. As soon as we've assigned our prompt administrator and applied the changes, we can use the prompt administrator's phone to dial the AA prompt-recording extension and use AvT to record, play back, and save our new AA prompts.

Script Management

Auto Attendant scripts were detailed in Chapter 8, so we won't go over their purpose here again in great detail. But as you will recall, we discussed three different methods to develop scripts. First, the administrator could use one of the two predefined scripts within Unity Express. The second and third methods are useful if an administrator needs to create their own customized scripts. The administrator can create scripts using the Editor Express tool that is built into Unity Express. Or, for even more scripting options, they can download and install the custom Script Editor application for Microsoft Windows. The Script Management tab within CCA allows users to upload, rename, or delete AA prompts. The CCA does not provide any way to create or modify the prompts, however. Figure 11.24 displays the Script Management tab with the predefined scripts available for use.

FIGURE 11.24   The AA Script Management tab

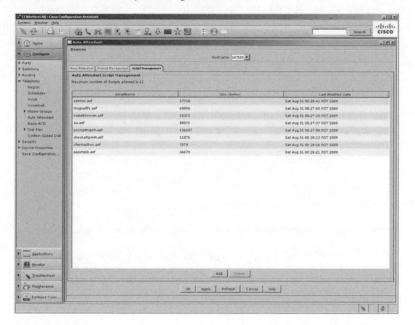

Please note that a maximum of 12 scripts can be stored on the UC500 at one time.

You now have a good understanding of the AA configuration options available within the Cisco Configuration Assistant. Next, you'll learn how to configure dial plans for both incoming and outgoing calls.

Configuring Telephony Dial Plans Using CCA

Incoming and outgoing dial peers can easily be configured using the CCA. To do so, use the Feature toolbar and go to Configure ➤ Telephony ➤ Dial Plans. You will see two sections, conveniently labeled Incoming and Outgoing.

Let's look at both of these configuration sections to see how we can create dial plans for inbound and outbound calls on our UC500 system.

Creating an Incoming Dial Plan

When we navigate to Configure ➤ Telephony ➤ Dial Plans ➤ Incoming, we see two configuration tabs: Incoming FXO Calls and Direct Dialing.

The Incoming FXO Calls tab is used to configure inbound rules for use by any idle FXO ports that are connected to the PSTN. The Direct Dialing tab is used for the creation of translation rules to map incoming DID numbers from digital PSTN trunks to internal extension numbers configured on the UC500 system. Let's take a closer look at the incoming dial-peer configuration options available to us using the CCA.

Incoming FXO Calls

If your UC500 comes equipped with FXO ports, the incoming dial peers are defined here. By default, each FXO port is assigned to extensions beginning with 201, as shown in Figure 11.25.

FIGURE 11.25 The Incoming FXO Calls tab

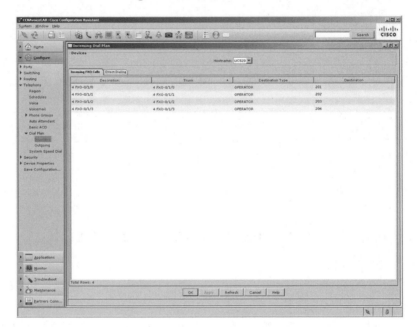

Why are the ports configured to forward to extensions beginning with 201? As you'll recall, the UC500 default auto-assign configuration sets IP phones with three-digit extensions beginning with extension 201. Because we have two 7965 phones configured, those phones use extensions 201 and 202. That means that if we have all four FXO ports configured, calls coming into 0/1/0 and 0/1/1 would be forwarded to the 7965 phones at extension 201 and 202, respectively. Calls that come into FXO ports 0/1/2 and 0/1/3 would receive a busy signal, because these extensions do not have an ephone-DN associated with them. To remedy this, we can change the ports to forward to 201 or 202. An even better idea would be to set all four FXO ports to dial the Auto Attendant extension of 700. That way, all external calls will first hit the AA to be directed to the intended person without any human interaction. To do this, you can manually enter the extension 700 into the Destination field or, better yet, use the Destination Type drop-down menu to choose AUTO_ATTENDANT. Once you do this, the destination extension is automatically set to the AA extension. Several Destination Type options are available for the administrator to choose from. Table 11.1 describes the most commonly used Destination Type options.

TABLE 11.1   FXO Destination Type options

Destination Type	Description
CO_LINE	Used for key system–configured UC500 systems
OPERATOR	Manually defines an extension to forward to using the Destination field
AUTO_ATTENDANT	Forwards to the configured AA extension
HUNT_GROUP	Forwards to a configured hunt group extension

Now that our FXO ports are configured, we can move on to discuss other inward direct-dialing configurations, using the Direct Dialing tab.

Direct Dialing

Chapters 3 and 7 made us well aware that for the PSTN, more options are available than just FXO ports. The Incoming FXO Calls tab helped us set up incoming dial peers for our four FXO ports, but what if we have a T1/E1, SIP, or ISDN BRI connection to our PSTN? The Direct Dialing tab is used to configure dial peers for these digital circuits. Figure 11.26 shows the CCA format for the Direct Dialing configuration tab.

Notice that the configuration options are grouped into two distinct sections. One section is called Direct Dial To Internal User Extensions. This essentially lets you create a one-to-one mapping of a digital line to an internal extension. For ease of configuration, the CCA allows you to group DID and extension ranges together in a single dial peer. Of course, this can work only if both your DIDs and internal extensions are contiguous.

FIGURE 11.26   The Direct Dialing tab

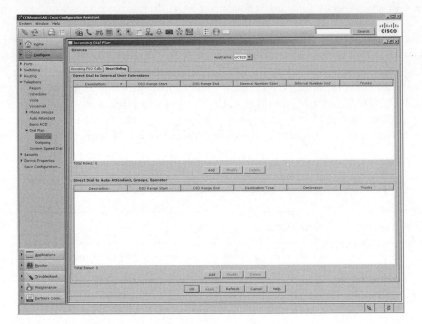

The second Direct Dialing tab section is Direct Dial To Auto-Attendant, Groups, Operator. This lets you direct digital circuits with DIDs to predefined AA, hunt group, or operator extensions. Again, if your DID ranges are contiguous, you can add multiple DIDs to a single dial-peer rule.

Creating an Outgoing Dial Plan

When we speak of off-network calling, we typically are referring to outbound calls to the PSTN using one or more PSTN interfaces such as FXO, ISDN, T1/E1, or even an IP WAN connection to an ITSP using SIP. In order to route calls out of these PSTN interfaces properly, we must create rules that trigger an off-network call when specific digit-entry conditions are matched. A very common method of implementing this trigger is to have all calls intended to reach someone off-network begin with the number 9. A prefix digit to trigger outgoing calls is called an access code. For example, if a user on our UC500 system wishes to make a local call to 555-8934, the person would dial 95558934. The prefix 9 would strictly be to let the UC500 know that the user wishes to make an off-network call.

This section shows how to use the CCA to set up outgoing dial plans on the UC500. To configure these dial plans, use the Feature toolbar on the left and navigate to Configure ➤ Telephony ➤ Dial Plans ➤ Outgoing. You'll find three outgoing dial plan configuration tabs: Outgoing Call Handling, PSTN Trunk Groups, and Caller Id.

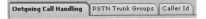

Let's review each of these outgoing dial plan tabs to understand what can be configured using the CCA.

Outgoing Call Handling

The CCA software includes prebuilt outgoing dial plan templates to greatly simplify standard dial plans for many countries or regions around the globe. The software predefines a dial plan that commonly suits the needs of most small businesses. Figure 11.27 displays the Outgoing Call Handling tab with the NANP template selected.

FIGURE 11.27   The Outgoing Call Handling tab showing the North American template

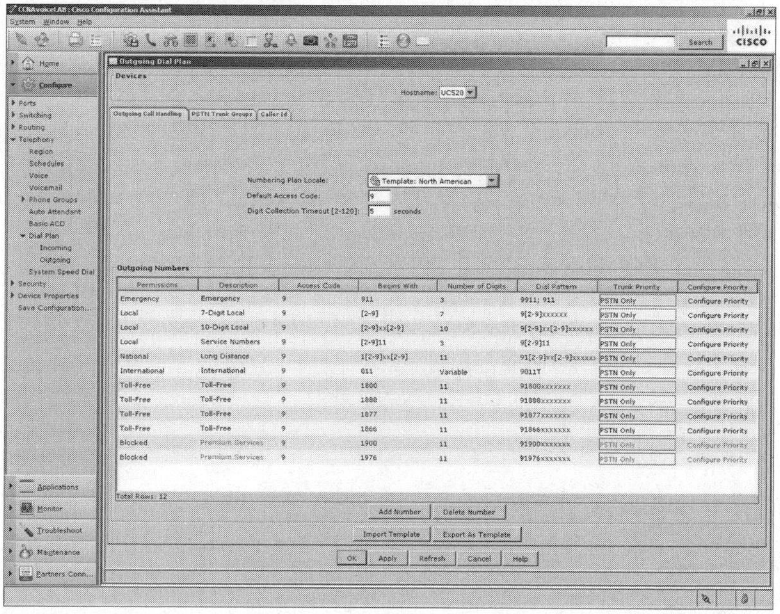

You can delete or modify any of the dial-plan rules in the template to meet your specific dial-plan requirements. You can also add rules using the Add Number template. You also have the ability to import .csv files or export the template for use on other systems if you choose. Also note that the default access code of 9 is chosen for this template by default, and the collection timeout for any dial patterns that use the T wildcard is 5 seconds.

The *Trunk Priority* column in the Outgoing Call Handling tab is where you can set a priority for the different PSTN trunk lines you have installed on the UC500. Here is a list of the Trunk Priority settings:

- PSTN Only
- SIP Only

- PSTN Then SIP
- SIP Then PSTN
- None

So, for example, if your company has both an SIP trunk and standard PSTN lines for off-network calling, it is likely that the SIP trunk calls will cost less. Therefore, you should choose the SIP Then PSTN trunk priority for all of your long-distance dial-plan rules. That way, the UC500 will route all calls over the lower-cost SIP trunk unless it is down. If the SIP trunk is unavailable, the UC500 will route calls over the PSTN instead. This also gives you site redundancy for off-network dialing.

PSTN Trunk Groups

When an on-network caller dials an off-network number, that call is matched by an outgoing dial plan. When a match is made, the voice gateway has the responsibility to choose one of the open PSTN lines for the outbound call. If the office has a single FXO line to the PSTN, the choice is obvious because there are no alternatives. But what if the site has two or more FXO lines and they both happen to be idle? Or what happens if you have a 23-channel T1 PRI and 19 of those channels are idle? How does the voice gateway choose which line to use next? The *PSTN Trunk Groups* tab allows you to create various trunk groups, and you can then choose from a list of hunt schemes how the UC500 will choose a phone line or channel to use. Figure 11.28 shows an example of a UC500 with a single group, labeled ALL_FXO, which includes four FXO lines.

FIGURE 11.28 The PSTN Trunk Groups tab

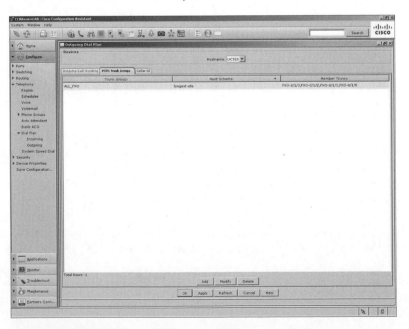

The hunt scheme that the ALL_FXO group is using is longest-idle. Here are all of the hunt schemes available for use:

- Longest-idle
- Round-robin
- Sequential
- Random
- Least-idle

Any PSTN connections that the UC500 supports (FXO, ISDN BRI, T1/E1, SIP) can be configured into trunk groups. Each group can utilize a different hunt scheme if you choose.

Caller Id

The Caller Id tab is used to assign a standard telephone number for all outbound calls to the PSTN when using digital circuits such as ISDN or T1/E1 lines. That means that a single main PSTN number will used for outgoing calls, which will show up on the called party's caller ID display.

 NOTE Remember that the Caller Id section is used only for digital circuits. Analog PSTN lines such as FXO ports can use only the assigned PSTN number defined by your provider for external caller ID.

Your choices for the main PSTN number are as follows:

- None
- Automated Attendant
- Other (Enter any PSTN number you choose)

There also is an option to set up a *Caller ID blocking code*. When it is activated, users can punch in this four-digit passcode (which must begin with an *) and then the PSTN number they wish to call. When the call is made, the caller ID information is still sent, but the sent caller ID number will be changed to say "Restricted" instead of an actual telephone number.

Last, the Caller Id tab has the ability to translate DIDs that were configured within the Direct Dialing tab in the Incoming Dial Plan section of the Feature toolbar. For each DID, you can choose whether to display the main PSTN number or the more unique DID of the extension that is making the call.

Summary

The UC500 is the sole SBCS device that provides voice functionality in the form of CUCM Express and Unity Express. It is very important for CCNA Voice students to familiarize themselves with the various UC500 configuration options available when using the CCA.

In this final chapter of the book, you have learned how to initialize the UC500 to prepare the device for setup using the CCA. Many of the most critical voice and voice mail features can be configured within the CCA Voice and Voice Mail sections. A section called Groups is where you can configure various hunt, paging, and pickup groups by placing voice users into different group categories. You then learned the two purposes for defining office-hour and holiday schedules and how these can be used by both the Auto Attendant and Night Service features. Last, the chapter showed how to define the different incoming and outgoing dial plans for off-network call routing on the UC500.

Exam Essentials

Know how to use the Telephony Initialization tool within CCA.   The CCA has a tool that is specifically designed to prepare the UC500 hardware to be configured using the CCA. Within this tool, you choose to set your UC500 up as either a PBX or a key system. You also determine the extension digit length and voice mail pilot extension if you want to enable Unity Express functions.

Know how to configure Telephony Region settings within CCA.   The CCA has a Telephony Region section, where you define the region the UC500 will be located in for signaling and telephone-notification options found in different parts of the world.

Know how to configure Voice features within CCA.   The Telephony Voice section is where you can configure system, IP network, SIP trunking, popular voice features, and user options.

Know how to configure Voice Mail features within CCA.   The CCA contains a Voice Mail section where you can configure global Unity Express settings such as pilot numbers and whether to enable features such as VoiceView Express and Live Reply. In this section, you can also modify mailboxes that were preconfigured based on the extensions that were configured in the Telephony Voice configuration section.

Know how to configure Phone Group features within CCA.   Hunt groups, paging groups, and pickup groups can be configured using CCA. In its Phone Groups section you can globally enable, add, delete, and modify groups as you see fit.

Understand why telephony schedules are important within the UC500 and how to configure them within CCA.   The UC500 needs to be aware of office hours to properly utilize the Auto Attendant office open/closed and holiday prompts. Another reason is to utilize the Night Service functionality. Three separate tabs within the CCA allow you to configure hours and dates for the office being open and night service hours as well as holidays when the office is closed.

Know the AA configuration capabilities that CCA offers.   CCA has several configurable options for Auto Attendant functionality. Within the Auto Attendant CCA section, you can enable AA for either standard script functionality or using a multi-level mode. In addition, you have several methods to create and manage AA voice prompts. Finally, you can manage custom scripts within CCA. Keep in mind, however, that the CCA does not offer any way to create custom scripts from scratch.

Know how to configure dial plans within CCA.   CCA provides separate Telephony configuration sections to configure incoming and outgoing dial plans. The Incoming dial plans section allows you to set up dial plans for analog and digital PSTN. Here you can determine how PSTN calls are handled when they arrive at the UC500. Outgoing dial plans deal with outgoing call handling, PSTN trunk groups, and caller ID information that can be controlled locally on the UC500 system.

Written Lab 11.1

Write the answers to the following questions:

1. When running through the CCA Telephony Initialization tool, what are the two CUCM model options available?

2. If you are going to configure a UC500 outside the United States, to what CCA Telephony section would you navigate to change the signaling and notification settings on the system?

3. What Telephony Voice configuration tab would you use to configure VLAN information on the UC500 within the CCA?

4. What Telephony Voice configuration tab would you navigate to if you wanted to set up a PSTN connection to an ITSP?

5. What SIP template drop-down choice would you select if you wanted to use a noncertified ITSP?

6. When configuring conferencing features on the CCA, which available codec mode uses the least amount of DSP resources?

7. When configuring the Night Service feature within CCA, what additional step are you notified to perform in order for Night Service to function properly?

8. What Unity Express feature that can be enabled using the CCA allows users who dial into their mailbox to automatically return calls from parties through the UC500?

9. What three groups can be configured on a UC500 using CCA?

10. When you use the CCA version 2.0 and navigate to Configure ➢ Telephony ➢ Schedules, what three tabs do you see?

(The answers to Written Lab 11.1 can be found following the answers to the review questions for this chapter.)

Review Questions

1. When configuring global Telephony Initialization settings using CCA, what two system mode options are available for you to choose between?

   A. Key system

   B. Hybrid

   C. Express

   D. Advanced

   E. PBX

2. Within the CCA, where can you modify region settings on the UC500?

   A. Configure ➤ Voice ➤ Region

   B. Setup ➤ Voice ➤ Region

   C. Configure ➤ Telephony ➤ Region

   D. Setup ➤ Telephony ➤ Region

3. When configuring Voice features by using CCA, what tab would you use to configure a connection to an ITSP on a UC500?

   A. User Extensions

   B. SIP Trunk

   C. Voice Features

   D. Network

   E. System

4. You wish to modify the voice VLAN ID used on your UC500. What Voice configuration tab would you use to modify this setting?

   A. Analog Extensions

   B. Setup

   C. Voice Features

   D. Network

   E. System

5. Using the CCA, you want to specify a DHCP pool of IP phones between 192.168.1.100 and 192.168.1.254. How would you accomplish this? Choose all that apply.

   A. Set the DHCP pool to 192.168.1.0 and the subnet mask to 255.255.255.0.

   B. Set the DHCP pool to 192.168.1.0 and the subnet mask to 255.255.255.128.

   C. Set the Excluded parameters to be from 192.168.1.100 to 192.168.1.254.

   D. Set the Excluded parameters to be from 192.168.1.1 to 192.168.1.99.

6. What determines the maximum number of simultaneous AdHoc and MeetMe sessions available on a UC500?

   A. Available CPU resources

   B. Available system memory

   C. Number of DSP resources

   D. Number of codec resources

7. What conference type requires users to dial a unique extension to join the call with other users?

   A. MeetMe

   B. Mixed Mode

   C. AdHoc

   D. DSP

8. What file type can be used to import multiple voice users at once using the Import button within CCA?

   A. `.doc`

   B. `.pdf`

   C. `.csv`

   D. `.exe`

   E. `.dat`

9. During the Telephony Initialization process, the CCA detects what type of ports and assigns generic first and last names to them?

   A. FXS

   B. FXO

   C. PRI

   D. BRI

   E. VoIP

   F. SIP

10. If you have made configuration errors, how does the CCA notify you?

   A. Any fields that have errors are bordered in green.

   B. Any fields that have errors are bordered in red.

   C. A pop-up window identifies any errors that need correcting.

   D. A new error tab is created that identifies any errors that need correcting.

11. What is the purpose of configuring a voice mail access PSTN number when configuring Unity Express Voice Mail features within the CCA?

   A. It enables on-network users to dial in to check their messages.

   B. It enables off-network users to dial in to check their messages.

   C. It enables on-network users to use Live Reply.

   D. It enables off-network users to use Live Reply.

12. What are the three CUCM Express phone groups that can be configured using CCA?

   A. Call group

   B. Conference group

   C. Paging group

   D. Hunt group

   E. Pickup group

13. How many years out can an administrator configure holidays for using the CCA?

   A. One

   B. Unlimited

   C. Zero

   D. Two

   E. Four

14. Which Telephony Schedule tabs within the CCA have configurations that are often used by Auto Attendant scripts? Choose all that apply.

   A. Business Hours

   B. Night Service

   C. Holiday

   D. Call Forward

15. When configuring Auto Attendant features using CCA, what tab would you navigate to in order to select the AA script you want to use?

   A. Holiday Schedule

   B. Auto Attendant

   C. Script Management

   D. Prompt Management

16. What are the three Auto Attendant modes within CCA that an administrator can choose from?

   A. Off

   B. On

   C. Standard

   D. Enable

   E. Multi-level

17. An administrator needs to record a new AA menu. What CCA Auto Attendant tab would they navigate to in order to accomplish this task?

    A. Auto Attendant

    B. Prompt Management

    C. Recording Management

    D. Script Management

18. Which of the following is *not* an FXO Destination Type option when configuring incoming FXO calls using the CCA?

    A. AUTO_ATTENDANT

    B. OPERATOR

    C. EMERGENCY_SERVICES

    D. HUNT_GROUP

    E. CO_LINE

19. What three options can be set up or modified on a UC500 using the CCA under the Telephony configuration section of the Feature bar?

    A. Voice VLAN

    B. Voice and Data VLANs

    C. Access Control Lists

    D. ITSP SIP Trunk

    E. Paging Groups

20. When configuring outgoing call handling on your UC500 using the CCA, what is the purpose of the default access code?

    A. An administrator password used to access the TUI

    B. Individual user codes for remote voice mail access

    C. A code to inform the UC500 that you wish to make an off-network call

    D. An administrator password used to modify the AA script

Answers to Review Questions

1. **A, E.** The two Telephony Initialization system mode options are PBX and key system.

2. **C.** All CCA configuration parameters specific to the UC500 are found within Configure ➤ Telephony on the Feature toolbar.

3. **B.** The UC500 has templates for certified Internet Telephony Service Providers (ITSP). There also is a configuration template for generic ITSPs. These templates can be found within the SIP Trunk tab when configuring Voice features using CCA.

4. **D.** When using the CCA to configure Voice features of the UC500, you would navigate to the Network tab to modify the voice VLAN.

5. **A, D.** The best option is to use a /24 subnet mask. You will then need to exclude the addresses from 1 to 99 so they are not handed out by the DHCP service.

6. **C.** DSP resources are hardware resources that ultimately determine the number of simultaneous conference sessions possible.

7. **A.** The MeetMe conference call type uses an extension that is dialed to meet other members who can join the call.

8. **C.** The CCA supports `.csv` files for bulk adds of voice users.

9. **A.** Generic first and last names are assigned to all FXS ports that are found during the Telephony Initialization process.

10. **B.** Errors are highlighted with a red border. These errors must be corrected before the CCA applies the changes.

11. **B.** This configuration setting lets you define a public PSTN number that users can dial when off-network so they can remotely check voice mail messages.

12. **C, D, E.** The three phone groups that can be configured within CCA are hunt, paging, and pickup.

13. **D.** You can configure holidays for the current year and one additional year out.

14. **A, C.** Both the Business Hours and Holiday schedule tabs contain configurations that can be used by AA scripts to play different voice messages depending on whether the office is open or closed. The Night Service tab configurations are not used by AA scripts because it is designed to immediately forward calls of individual user extensions to voice mail or an operator number without having that extension ring.

15. **B.** The Auto Attendant tab lets administrators choose the AA script they want to use by selecting one from a drop-down menu that lists all scripts on the UC500.

16. **B, C, E.** The three choices for AA script modes are Off, which disables AA on the system; Standard, which is a single-level AA script; and Multi-level, for a tiered AA script.

17. B. Administrators can view, modify, add, or delete AA menu prompts on the Prompt Management tab.

18. C. All of the Destination Type options are valid except for EMERGENCY_SERVICES.

19. A, D, E. Within the Telephony configuration section of the Feature bar, you can modify the voice VLAN, set up an ITSP SIP trunk, and configure paging groups. The other two options can also be configured using the CCA but not within the Telephony section.

20. C. The default access code is used to trigger an off-network call. By default, this number is set to 9.

Answers to Written Lab 11.1

1. PBX and key system

2. Region

3. Network

4. SIP Trunk

5. Generic SIP Trunk Provider

6. G.711

7. Configure the Night Service schedule

8. Live Reply

9. Hunt groups, paging groups, and pickup groups

10. Business Hours, Night Service, and Holiday

Appendix A

Design and Configuration Using the CCA Telephony Setup Wizard

According to the U.S. Small Business Administration, more than 600,000 new small businesses are started each year. Most of these businesses will require voice and data solutions, for which the SBCS lineup is perfectly tailored. One of the beauties of working on the design and build-out of a brand-new SBCS site is that you are free of having to deal with currently implemented voice and data systems. In engineering circles, a project that is brand new and lacks any constraints imposed by prior network equipment or designs is referred to as a "greenfield" project. New businesses that are just starting up and need a voice and data network give the design engineer the opportunity to design and configure a voice/data network as they see fit.

The Telephony Setup Wizard is an alternative configuration tool within CCA that strives to simplify basic voice and data provisioning of greenfield sites for small offices using the UC500 system. Cisco clearly is of the opinion that there is more than one way to skin a cat. An administrator can configure the UC500 using the command line, web GUI, CCA, or the Telephony Setup Wizard within CCA. Think of the Telephony Setup Wizard as training wheels for the CCA.

This appendix begins with an overview of the Telephony Setup Wizard and the requirements for its use. We'll then go over a mock greenfield case study, using a fictional business to help understand the types of questions you will need to ask the business owners when designing a voice and data network. Once we have compiled the information, you will learn how to use the Telephony Setup Wizard to rapidly implement a basic UC500 system. The wizard does not offer anything new from a configuration standpoint; rather, it gives you an additional method to configure your UC500 hardware.

CCA Telephony Setup Wizard Overview and Requirements

The CCA Telephony Setup Wizard (TSW) is a relatively new tool that became available in CCA version 2.0. This tool is intended for brand-new deployments with up to 24 users. It is used only for brand-new (greenfield) configurations. When you connect to a UC500 using the CCA for the first time, the TSW automatically loads. At this time, you can choose to configure your hardware using the wizard or the other CCA configuration methods you learned in Chapter 11. The following requirements must be met in order to use the TSW for your initial configuration:

- The UC500 must have a factory default configuration. If the UC500 was purchased new from Cisco, then the device will be ready to go. If the UC500 has been used at a different site or changes have been made to the factory default configuration, then the administrator will need to reset both the Unity Express and CUCM Express to factory default settings.

- The PC running the TSW software within the CCA application must have only a single network connection enabled. If the PC has both an Ethernet and a wireless connection enabled, one of them will have to be disabled; otherwise, the TSW will detect both network connections and you will be denied the opportunity to run the wizard.

- All of the IP phones that you wish to configure must be connected, fully booted, and their firmware upgraded before running the wizard. You should make sure that each phone is up and properly functioning with the factory default settings before beginning.

When the CCA detects that the UC500 has the default configuration, it will automatically run the wizard as soon as the CCA discovery process completes. Figure A.1 shows the TSW welcome screen.

FIGURE A.1   The Telephony Setup Wizard welcome screen

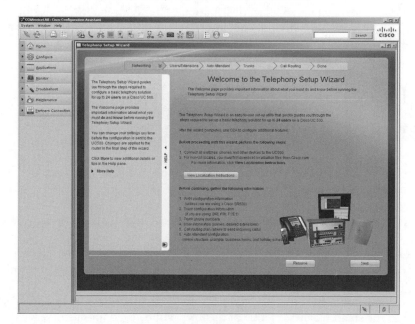

At the top of the TSW screen you can see the five steps of the configuration process:

1. Networking
2. Users/Extensions
3. Auto Attendant
4. Trunks
5. Call Routing

We'll cover these configuration steps in detail as we go through the information-gathering process from the owner of the fictional business we are setting up.

Running from top to bottom along the left side of the wizard screen within CCA is the Help section. Here you can find detailed descriptions of configuration parameters that the wizard is asking for on the screen. You can collapse the Help section to give yourself additional room on the screen.

Lastly, at the bottom of the screen are the wizard navigation buttons, used to progress forward and backward through the wizard. It is important to keep in mind that no changes to the UC500 are made until the administrator has run through the wizard in its entirety. If for some reason you close the CCA prior to applying the configuration, any configuration changes will not be saved and you can rerun the wizard without having to reset the UC500 to factory default settings.

Now that you understand the layout of the Telephony Setup Wizard, let's begin our fictional case study. In this case we will have a discussion with the owner of CC-NAV Inc., a company that is starting up a widget distribution center. Our goal with this discussion is to gather the information required to configure the UC500 for both voice and data needs. We will then walk through the configuration process using the CCA TSW.

The Information-Gathering Meeting for CC-NAV Inc.

Abe Jefferson, owner of CC-NAV Inc., set up a meeting to discuss the voice and data requirements for his new widget distribution center. The following is a review of how the meeting went:

CC-NAV is a brand-new business that sells and distributes widgets. It is located in Chicago, USA. The small company will have a single site with six employees. Each of these employees will need their own telephone for making/receiving calls as well as basic Internet access for email and web browsing. Abe has already contacted an ISP, and a standard DSL connection will be installed at the site using DHCP.

Abe also contacted his local phone company and is having four analog telephone lines run into the small business. Three of the lines will be used for customers calling for sales or shipping questions. The number that CC-NAV will advertise to potential customers is 312-555-8861. The fourth line will be dedicated for a fax machine. This number is 312-555-8863.

Abe has hired five employees to handle the daily operations of the new start-up. He provided us with an employee list that includes the name and job title of each employee. There will be two salespersons to handle customers wanting to order widgets. Mr. Jefferson also has two employees to handle warehouse and logistical duties to ensure that the widgets are shipped properly to customers once the orders are finalized. Overseeing both the sales and warehouse employees will be an operations manager, who will also be required to fill in as a member of the sales or warehouse staff when needed.

Abe foresees customers calling into a main CC-NAV telephone number that will be handled by an Auto Attendant system, where the customer can contact a salesperson for new sales or the warehouse for any shipping questions. A hunt group will be set up for both the sales and warehouse teams. If nobody in either hunt group is able to answer a call, the final extension tried will be that of the operations manager.

Unless there is a shipping problem, Abe believes that the shipping employees will not receive many calls. On the other hand, the sales department will (hopefully) receive many calls from customers wishing to order widgets. Because of this, Abe wants to provide high-end Cisco 7965 IP phones to his sales team and the operations manager. Abe also will receive a 7965 because, well, he's the boss! The two warehouse employees will be supplied with less-expensive analog phones that will be deployed in the warehouse section of the office.

All other parameters needed for the UC500 setup will be left up to the consultant (you) to determine. Now that we have had a thorough conversation with the business owner, let's use this information we've gathered to set up our voice and data network for CC-NAV using the Telephony Setup Wizard. In the next five sections of this case study, we will go through each TSW configuration step, lay out the configuration plan using what we learned during the information-gathering process, and configure our UC500 according to business specifications.

Configuring Networking Parameters Using the TSW

Now that we've gone through the information-gathering process to discover what we need to configure the UC500 for CC-NAV Inc, we can turn our attention to using the Telephony Setup Wizard to quickly configure the voice and data capabilities for the site. We'll start our configuration back at the TSW welcome screen you saw in Figure A.1. As stated earlier, it is important that the IP phones we wish to configure using the TSW are up and functioning. Once you have verified this, click the Next button to begin configuring the system and network parameters.

Configuring System Access

This screen requires that you name the UC500 and set up an administrator account. Abe never gave specific instructions on these steps, so we've taken the liberty of devising our own. As a consultant, it is very important that you document your configurations so you can provide them to the customer. You never know when you might have to come back and use this documentation for troubleshooting purposes! Table A.1 lists the required System Access fields and the information we will configure within them.

TABLE A.1   System Access parameters

Required Fields	Discovered Information
System Host Name	UC500_CC-NAV_Inc
Admin Username	Admin
Admin Password	cisco1

Figure A.2 shows the first configuration screen within the Networking parameters section.

FIGURE A.2   The System Access configuration screen

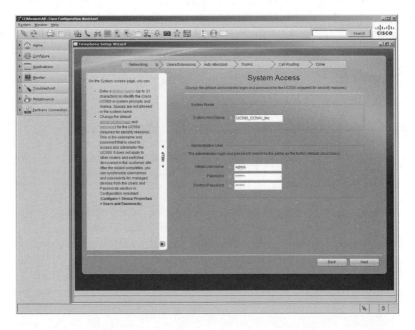

Enter the information into the fields as shown in the figure, and click the Next button to continue.

Configuring the System Locale

The next Networking configuration screen is Choose Locale. Here we set regional parameters that dictate the dial plan, time zone, and language used on the system. While we did not specifically ask Abe all of these questions, we did learn from our conversation that the business will be operated in Chicago, USA. Given this single piece of information, we can infer the configuration parameters shown in Table A.2.

TABLE A.2 System location parameters

Required Fields	Discovered Information
UC500 Location	Chicago, USA
Language	English
Dial Plan Locale	NANP
Time Zone	GMT -06:00
Daylight Savings Mode	Enabled

Figure A.3 shows the Choose Locale screen with the proper settings for a business located in Chicago.

FIGURE A.3 The Choose Locale configuration screen

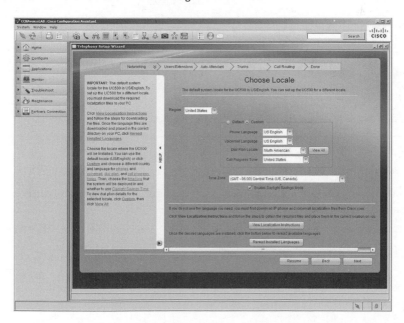

Enter the information into the fields as shown in the figure, and click Next to continue.

Configuring WAN/LAN Settings

The following two configuration screens deal with WAN and LAN settings. In our conversation with Abe, we learned that he has contacted an ISP and has ordered a DSL connection that requires our end device to be set to receive an IP address using DHCP. We also know that employees will use the network for both voice and data, so we should separate this traffic into separate VLANs, following Cisco best-practice methodology. There were no specific requirements for the addressing scheme used for the voice and data IP subnets, so we can configure them as we see fit. Table A.3 lists the IP network parameters we've decided to implement.

TABLE A.3 IP network parameters

Required Fields	Discovered Information
WAN/Internet	Standard DSL (using DHCP)
Data VLAN	1
Data IP Subnet	192.168.10.0/24
Data IP Gateway	192.168.10.1
Data Subnet DHCP Scope	192.168.10.10-240
Voice VLAN	100
Data IP Subnet	10.1.1.0/24
Data IP Gateway	10.1.1.1
Data Subnet DHCP Scope	10.1.1.10-240

The Configure WAN Connection screen is first. Figure A.4 shows the different WAN configuration options available to us, including these:

- DHCP
- Static IP

- PPPoE IP Negotiate
- PPPoE Static IP

FIGURE A.4   The WAN configuration screen

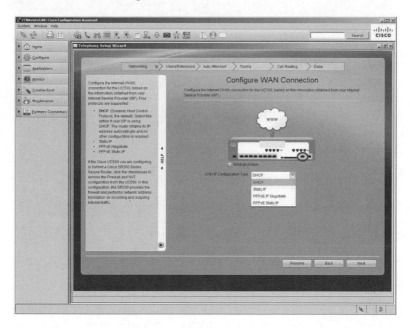

Because our site will be receiving an IP address from a DHCP server hosted by the ISP, we can simply choose the DHCP option and click Next to continue. If we were to choose one of the other options, we would have to add additional information including static IP addresses, subnet masks, or authentication information for Point-to-Point Protocol over Ethernet (PPPoE).

The next screen in the wizard allows us to configure the LAN portion of our IP network including IP subnet settings. Figure A.5 shows how we've set up our network to use the settings defined in Table A.3.

FIGURE A.5 The LAN configuration screen

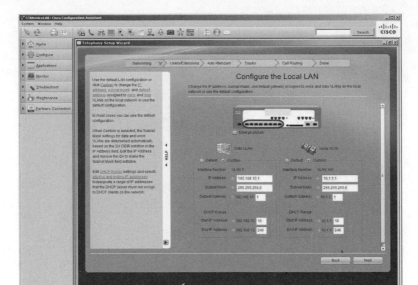

Notice how the VLAN information is listed but cannot be changed. This is one of the limitations to the TSW. To make configurations as simple as possible, Cisco removed the ability to change the VLAN ID because for most environments, the default VLANs of 1 and 100 will work just fine. In fact, we've decided not to modify any of the default LAN settings given. In our conversation with the owner, there was nothing that he said that would require us to stray away from the default settings provided by Cisco. Click the Next button to continue.

This final Networking configuration screen is a summary of all the decisions we've made thus far. Figure A.6 shows the Networking Summary screen.

FIGURE A.6 The Networking Summary screen

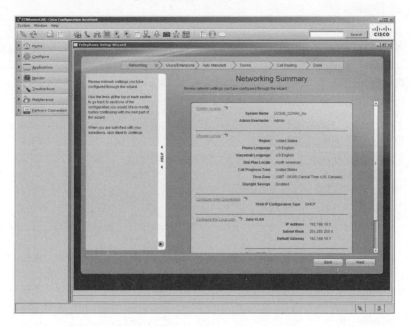

You can review your choices and click the Back button to make any modifications. Once you are satisfied, click the Next button to move on to the Users/Extensions configuration section.

Configuring User and Extension Parameters Using the TSW

The Users/Extensions configuration screens are used to set up all of the internal (non-PSTN) settings, including extensions, FXS ports, and telephone users for assigning phones and voice mail boxes to users. There are five configuration screens and one summary screen in the wizard. Let's plan out our configuration settings for each option and use the TSW to configure the UC500. First up on the list is defining the internal dialing structure.

Configuring Internal Dialing

Internal dialing refers to the extensions that will be configured on analog and IP telephones on the system. Internal extension lengths can be three, four, or five digits in length. By default, three digits are used. Because there are only a handful of phones on the system, the choice of three digits is logical for this environment. In addition, Table A.4 lists the other decisions we've made.

TABLE A.4 Internal dialing parameters

Required Fields	Discovered Information
Internal Extension Length	Three digits
Access Code	9
Prefix Digit for Voice Mail	6
Voice Mail Pilot Extension	299
AA Extension	298

The access code of 9 is for off-network calls, and the voice mail prefix digit is used for direct calls to the voice mail system for use by the AA (Automated Attendant). It will also be used by analog phones that do not have a default voice mail button, as Cisco IP phones do. Both the access code and prefix digit are restricted to a single number from 1 to 9, and the digit cannot be the first number of any configured extension or access code. Figure A.7 shows the internal dialing screen with the proper configurations for our case.

FIGURE A.7 The Define Internal Dialing screen

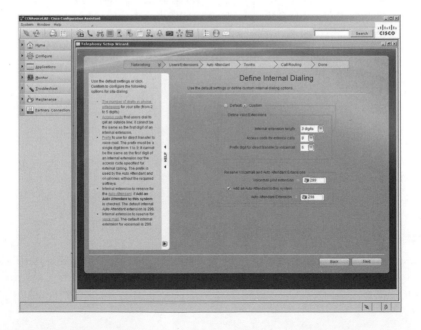

Enter the information into the fields as shown in the figure, and click the Next button to continue to the next screen in the wizard.

Configuring Analog Station (FXS) Ports

During our conversation with Abe Jefferson, it came to light that the business requires one shared fax machine and two analog phones for the warehouse workers. Given this information, we've come up with the necessary information to configure the FXS interfaces, as shown in Table A.5.

TABLE A.5   FXS port parameters

Required Fields	Discovered Information
Number of fax machines	1
Number of user analog phones	2

Our UC500 has four FXS ports, so we will disable 0/0/3 because we do not need it at this time. Port 0/0/0 will be set up as a common area phone/fax for our analog fax machine, and 0/0/1 and 0/0/2 will be configured as user ports. Figure A.8 shows the analog station ports configuration screen configured to match our business requirements.

FIGURE A.8   The Configure Analog Station Ports screen

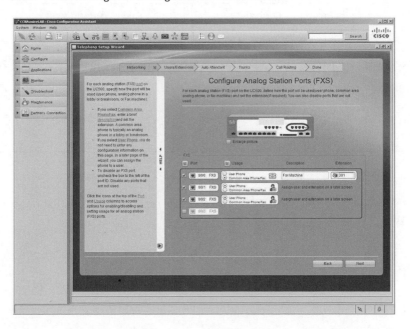

When we configure an FXS port as a common area phone or fax, you'll notice that a default extension of 301 appears. The Cisco default settings for three-digit extensions are that user extensions begin at extension 201 and common-area phones begin at 301. You can change these numbers to suit your needs as long as they don't interfere with other previously configured extensions or access codes such as voice mail pilot numbers or the access code.

Enter the information into the fields as shown in the figure, and click the Next button to continue through the wizard.

Configuring Phone Users and Extensions

Now it's time to define our users and user extensions on our PBX. The Define Users and Extensions screen allows us to enter the full first and last names of our phone users as well as assign an extension to them. Because we chose to use three-digit extensions on this system, the CCA auto-filled the user extension field with numbers beginning with 201. Using the information we gathered in our information-gathering conversation with the owner, we've come up with the user parameters in Table A.6 that we can use to configure the system.

TABLE A.6 User parameters

Name	User ID	Job Function	Phone Type	Extension
Abe Jefferson	ajefferson	Owner	Cisco 7965	201
David Miller	dmiller	Sales	Cisco 7965	202
Wendy Davis	wdavis	Sales	Cisco 7965	203
Sarah Foreman	sforeman	Operations manager	Cisco 7965	204
Chen Lee	clee	Warehouse/logistics	Analog	205
Michael Cross	mcross	Warehouse/logistics	Analog	206

Figure A.9 shows the Define Users and Extensions screen properly filled out for our six employees.

FIGURE A.9 The Define Users and Extensions screen

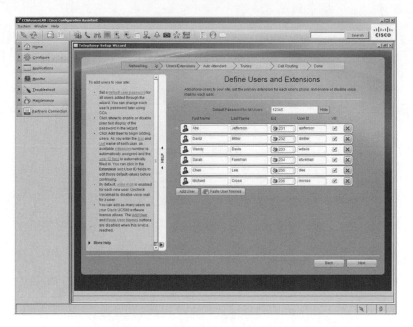

By default, each user password will initially be 12345. The user will be required to change this password the first time they log in. Also notice that we've decided to create individual subscriber voice mail boxes for each employee. These will be automatically created for us by the CCA. Click Next to move on to the next configuration screen.

Now we have users and extensions configured, but none of these users are assigned a phone. Figure A.10 shows us assigning a phone to each user. Each user configured is listed on the left of the screen, and a drop-down list shows all of the discovered IP phones as well as any enabled FXS ports available. Abe stated that he, the operations manager, and the sales team would be using Cisco 7965 phones. The two warehouse employees would use analog phones attached to the FXS ports on the UC500. Use Table A.6 to determine whether a user is assigned a Cisco 7965 or an analog phone.

FIGURE A.10   The Assign Phones screen

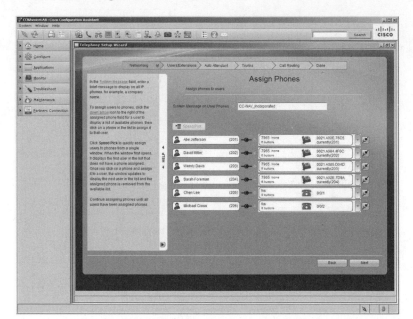

If we did not care which employee was assigned to a particular phone, we could have clicked the Speed Pick button, which randomly assigns a phone to a user. But because specific people are to receive a specific type of phone, we manually assigned them to our users. The system message that is displayed at the bottom of the LCD screen on the Cisco IP phones is also configured on this screen. Click the Next button to move on to the next configuration screen.

Configuring Hunt Groups

The last Users/Extensions configuration screen is used to create hunt and blast groups. A blast group is simply a hunt group that will ring multiple phones simultaneously. The first extension to answer the call gets the connection. Now that we have users assigned to phones, we can go ahead and create our hunt groups for the business. Abe would like to see two hunt groups created for business operations. One group would be for sales and the other for warehouse/logistics. We'll use the longest-idle-time method to determine which phone in the hunt group rings. Also keep in mind that Abe wants the "catch-all" extension to be the operations manager if nobody is able to field the call. Figure A.11 shows the hunt group setup screen with the proper configuration parameters entered in.

FIGURE A.11 The Define Hunt Groups and Blast Groups screen

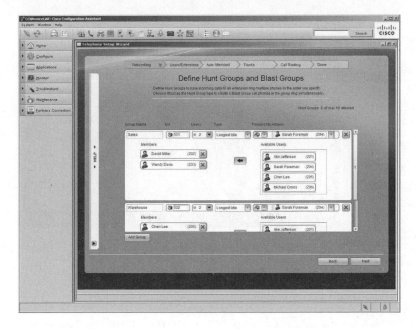

> **NOTE**
> This hunt group setup may not be ideal for some businesses. If the first two members fail to field the call, the forward will go directly to our operations manager (Sara Foreman). If she is not able to answer the call, it will be redirected to Sara's personal mailbox. Keep situations like this in mind when you are planning your hunt or blast groups.

The CCA configures hunt/blast groups to begin with extension 501 by default. You should also make sure to name your group so you can clearly understand what its purpose is. Once you have finished configuring your groups, click the Next button to continue.

The final Users/Extensions screen is a summary of all the settings made in this section. Figure A.12 shows the Users Summary screen.

FIGURE A.12   The Users Summary screen

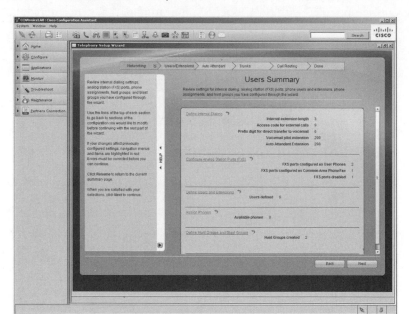

You can review your choices and click the Back button to make any modifications. Once you are satisfied, click the Next button to move on to the Auto-Attendant configuration section.

Configuring Auto Attendant Parameters Using the TSW

Our client has clearly stated that an automated attendant should be used to direct calls to either the sales or warehouse teams. Beyond that, it is up to us to determine the AA settings that a typical business such as CC-NAV would require. We'll first set up basic AA settings, such as the choice between a single and a dual schedule AA. We'll then move on to define the AA prompts and actions to the prompts. Finally, we'll define how to customize the AA prompts for CC-NAV Inc.

Defining the AA and Setting Working Hours

Figure A.13 shows the first of a series of AA choices that need to be made.

FIGURE A.13   The Define Auto Attendant screen

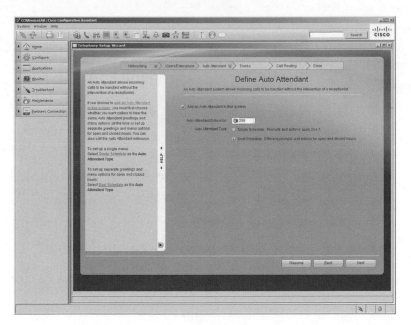

We must check the box to enable AA in the first place. We've already determined the AA pilot extension in previous TSW configuration steps, but we can modify it here if needed. The TSW allows for two AA types, which differ as follows:

Single Schedule   The single schedule presents the same AA script 24 hours a day regardless of the business being open or not.

Dual Schedule   The dual schedule provides two different AA scripts. One script is played during office hours, and the other is for after-hours and holiday calls. If this choice is selected, the administrator must define when the business is open as well as the holiday dates when the office is closed.

Since this is a small business that is unlikely to be run 24 hours a day, we've decided to configure a dual-schedule setup. Once you've configured our choices, click Next to continue.

Because of our choice to configure a dual schedule, we contacted Sarah Forman, the operations manager, who provided us with office hours and days when the office will be closed because of a holiday. This information will be used in the next two Auto Attendant configuration screens. Figure A.14 shows us setting the office working hours to be Monday through Friday from 8:00 A.M. to 5:00 P.M.

FIGURE A.14   The AA Business Hours definition screen

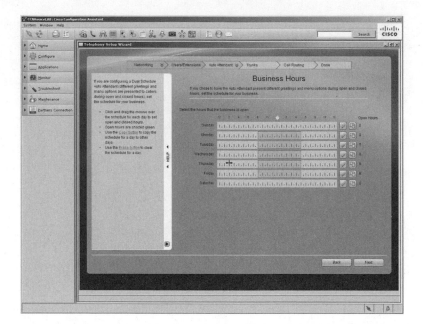

To modify the hours on the screen, you simply click and drag across the day you wish to modify. The working hours portion is then highlighted in green. Set the hours according to Sarah's input, and click the Next button to continue.

This next screen is to configure holiday hours for the business. The CCA offers a 12-month calendar where you can find the days you wish to define as a holiday. Click the holiday, name it, and that entire day will then use the after-hours AA script. By default, holiday hours are set for New Years and Christmas Day only. We've added additional holidays that are common in the United States. Figure A.15 shows our setup.

Make the necessary holiday additions, and click Next to continue to the next screen.

Defining AA Prompts and Actions

The Define Auto Attendant Prompts and Actions screen is where we define how the AA script progresses for each call. Because we decided to use a dual-schedule AA, both a Company Greeting and an After Hours Greeting are defined in Figure A.16.

FIGURE A.15   The AA Holiday Schedules definition screen

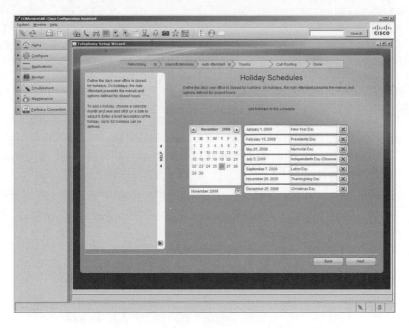

FIGURE A.16   Defining AA prompts and actions

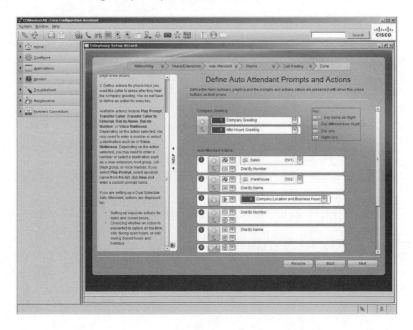

The Auto Attendant Actions section is where we can configure the prompts that will guide the user navigating through to reach the representative of CC-NAV they wish to contact. The numbers 1 through 8 to the left of the actions represents the keypad button a caller will press to initiate the action. In our example, we've mapped the Sales hunt group to button 1 and the Warehouse hunt group to button 2. Callers can also press 3 to hear a recording of office hours. Buttons 4 and 5 are used for the caller to either dial by number (if known) or to dial by name by using the keypad to spell out the last name of the employee.

Also very important to notice is the key in the upper-right corner of the screen. This key is used to define whether a button option is available for callers based on when they call. Defined office hours are considered to be "day" hours, and hours when the office is closed are "night" hours. Following are the different options you can apply to a particular button setup depending on when the user calls:

Day Same As Night   The AA button option is available regardless of when the user calls.

Day Different From Night   The AA button option is used for different purposes depending on the time of day the call is placed.

Day Only   The AA button option is available only during office hours.

Night Only   The AA button option is available only after office hours.

As you can see in Figure A.16, we've set our hunt groups to be available only when the office is open. During working hours the phone buttons used by the AA are set up as the following:

Button 1: Contact the Sales hunt group

Button 2: Contact the Warehouse hunt group

Button 3: Company location and business hours recording

Button 4: Dial user by extension

Button 5: Dial user by name

When the office is closed, the following button mappings are used on the AA system:

Button 1: Dial user by extension

Button 2: Dial user by name

Button 3: Company location and business hours recording

As you can see, buttons 1 and 2 are using the Day Different From Night option to create different actions for the button based on time of day. Button 3, which is a recording of the business location and hours, remains the same 24 hours a day and therefore uses the Day Same As Night option.

When you have made the proper configuration settings, click Next to continue.

Managing Auto Attendant Prompts

We have our AA scripts all defined, but we don't have any voice scripts to help the user navigate through them. Figure A.17 shows the different ways we can manage AA prompts using the TSW. As you can see, we will need to record three different AA prompts according to the settings we defined in the last step. The prompts we need to create are the Company Greeting, the After Hours Greeting, and the Company Location and Business Hours Recording.

FIGURE A.17 The Manage Auto Attendant Prompts screen

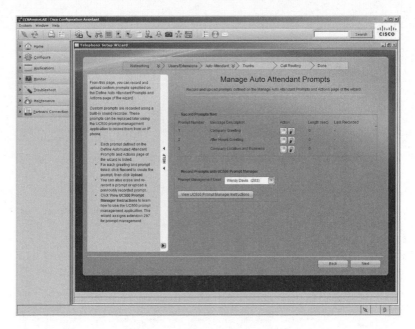

There are three ways we can add custom AA prompts to our UC500. One method is to create and save audio files using a separate voice-recording application. We can then upload the files as `.wav` or `.au` to the UC500 at this screen. To upload the files, click the folder icon in the Action column and locate the stored file to upload it. The files will then be stored onto the UC500 compact flash.

A second method is to use the TSW to record prompts directly to the UC500. This requires that the PC you are running the CCA on have a voice card and microphone. If it does, you can use this hardware to record the prompts and save them to the UC500 compact flash.

Finally, the last method is to use the UC500 Prompt Manager to record your custom prompts. This is the method we've chosen to create our recordings for our three prompts. Wendy Davis has agreed to record the AA prompts, so we have selected her phone extension to be the Prompt Management User. What this means is that Wendy can use her phone (and only her phone at extension 203) to dial into the prompt management pilot number and walk through the recording of the three custom prompts our AA needs. As you can see in the Help section, the TSW has assigned extension 297 for the prompt management pilot number. Wendy will dial this extension and use the built-in TUI to follow the directions to record and save our prompts to the UC500 compact flash.

When you have made the proper configuration settings, click Next to continue.

We are then presented with the Auto Attendant Summary screen, as shown in Figure A.18.

FIGURE A.18   The Auto Attendant Summary screen

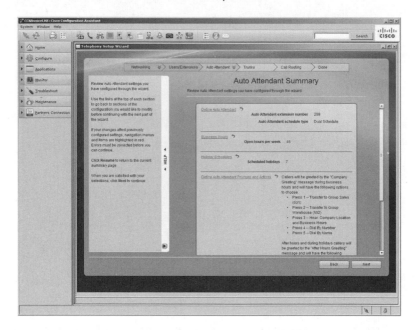

As in all other summary screens we've seen, we can review all our settings and go back to modify anything that we wish. Once you are satisfied, click the Next button to move on to configure the business PSTN trunk parameters.

Configuring Analog PSTN Trunk Parameters Using the TSW

The PSTN trunk parameters screen for our mock setup is fairly straightforward. We know that Abe has already contacted his local PSTN and ordered four PSTN lines. Three of those lines are to be used for incoming and outgoing calls, and the fourth line will be dedicated to a fax machine. All of the FXO interfaces will act as PBX-connected ports, meaning that incoming calls will be directed to one specific extension. And as we know, PBX extensions are unique to a single phone (unlike key system setups, where a number is defined on multiple phones and the first one to answer has control over that particular line).

Figure A.19 shows the PSTN configuration that we have defined for CC-NAV Inc.

FIGURE A.19   The analog trunk setup screen

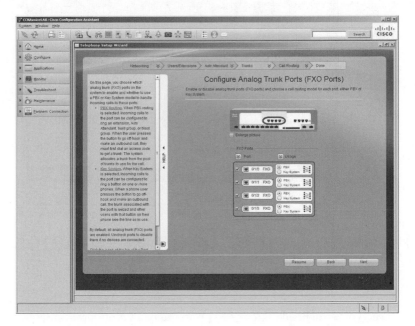

There are very few options to configure here, which limits our flexibility but also helps to simplify the TSW process, and that is what the tool is all about. We can enable or disable any of the four interfaces as well as define the action of the interface as being either a PBX or a key system port. In our case, we want to use all four FXO ports and we also want them to use the PBX model of functionality. Once you have made the necessary configuration changes, click Next to continue.

As you can see, we're already at the Trunking Summary page shown in Figure A.20.

This screen shows you how many ports will be disabled, set up as key system ports, or set up as PBX model ports. When you are satisfied, click Next to move to the last TSW section, Call Routing.

FIGURE A.20 The Trunking Summary screen

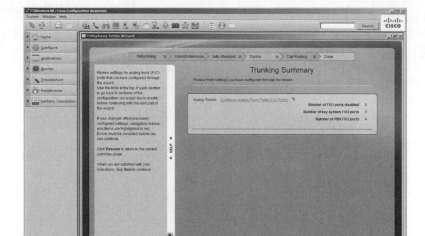

Configuring Call Routing Parameters Using the TSW

In the Trunks section we defined all four FXO ports to be PBX-modeled interfaces. In order to work when calls come inbound from the PSTN, the interfaces now must be assigned to an extension. In our initial conversation, we learned that CC-NAV would have two telephone numbers: the main number, which will be assigned to three PSTN lines, and a fourth line for a fax machine. We also know that all customers calling to place orders or inquire about shipping/logistics should go through an automated attendant to help them reach the right employee. We've created Table A.7 to assist us with defining which FXO port will be routed to the Auto Attendant or to the FXS port with the attached fax machine.

TABLE A.7 FXO port parameters

FXO Port	PSTN Number	Routed To
0/1/0	312-555-8861	Auto Attendant
0/1/1	312-555-8861	Auto Attendant
0/1/2	312-555-8861	Auto Attendant
0/1/3	312-555-8863	Fax machine

Now that we have the ports defined, we just need to configure them to be routed either to the AA pilot number or to the FXS fax port. Figure A.21 shows how we configure call handling for CC-NAV's FXO ports using the TSW.

FIGURE A.21   The incoming call-handling screen

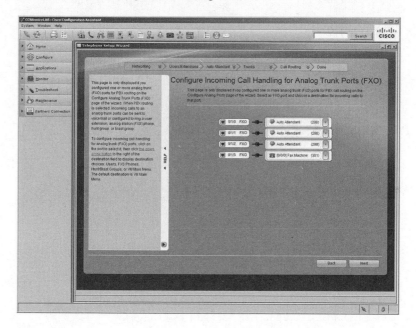

The configuration process is quite simple; all of the enabled FXO ports are listed on the left of the screen, and a drop-down list of all configured extensions is available to choose from. When inbound calls come into one of these four ports, the calls are promptly redirected to the extension without any manual intervention. The first three ports (FXO 0/1/0 to 0/1/2) are redirected to the AA so customers can use it to contact either the Sales or Warehouse group. Fax requests come in on the alternate PSTN number, which is then routed to the FXS interface with the attached analog fax machine on it. Once you have set the interfaces for proper routing, click Next to continue.

This again was another short configuration section. Figure A.22 shows the summary screen, which is little more than a confirmation of how the ports are defined as being routed either to the AA or to the FXS interface.

Once you are sure about your settings, click the Next button to move on to the final TSW configuration screen.

FIGURE A.22   The Call Routing Summary screen

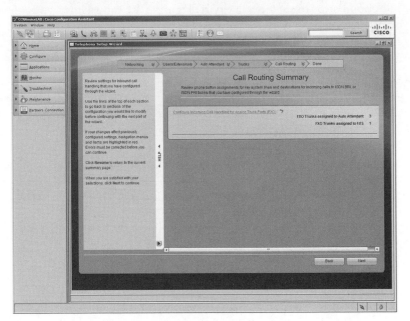

Final Review and Applying the Configuration Using the TSW

The Apply Configuration screen is the final opportunity to review all of the configuration settings we wish to make using the TSW. Up to this point, we've only defined what we want to configure, and no changes have actually been made on the UC500 system. Only when we click the Apply Configuration button, as shown in Figure A.23, will the wizard apply all the modifications onto the CUCM Express and Unity Express systems.

On this screen there are tabs for each of the five wizard configuration sections we went through. At any time, you can go back and modify any of these settings before you apply them to the system. Also note the red text stating that we have modified the VLAN information in the wizard, so we will lose IP connectivity to the UC500 system and will have to relaunch CCA using the new IP address on the VLAN.

Click the Apply Configuration button to put our new system configuration onto your UC500. The wizard then converts our settings to command-line form and applies and saves them to both the CUCM Express and Unity Express configurations. This process can take up to 28 minutes to complete, so please be patient.

As soon as the wizard finishes applying and saving the configuration, the employees at CC-NAV Inc. can test it out. Any modifications can then be made using the CCA telephony

FIGURE A.23   The Apply Configuration screen

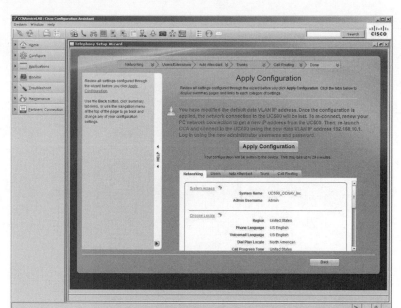

tools, web GUI tools, or even the command-line tools that have been taught throughout the course of this book. Any of these methods will get the job done and get our customers off and running on their new voice system.

Summary

The mock consulting example in this case study was used to show you what the Telephony Setup Wizard was designed to do. For brand-new and relatively straightforward setups for small businesses, the wizard is a great way to get a site up and running very quickly.

Appendix
B

About the Companion CD

IN THIS APPENDIX:

✓ What you'll find on the CD

✓ System requirements

✓ Using the CD

✓ Troubleshooting

What You'll Find on the CD

The following sections are arranged by category and summarize the software and other goodies you'll find on the CD. If you need help with installing the items provided on the CD, refer to the installation instructions in the "Using the CD" section of this appendix.

Some programs on the CD might fall into one of these categories:

Shareware programs are fully functional, free, trial versions of copyrighted programs. If you like particular programs, register with their authors for a nominal fee and receive licenses, enhanced versions, and technical support.

Freeware programs are free, copyrighted games, applications, and utilities. You can copy them to as many computers as you like — for free — but they offer no technical support.

GNU software is governed by its own license, which is included inside the folder of the GNU software. There are no restrictions on distribution of GNU software. See the GNU license at the root of the CD for more details.

Trial, *demo*, or *evaluation* versions of software are usually limited either by time or by functionality (such as not letting you save a project after you create it).

Sybex Test Engine

For Windows

The CD contains the Sybex test engine, which includes all of the assessment test and chapter review questions in electronic format, as well as two bonus exams located only on the CD.

PDF of the Book

For Windows

We have included an electronic version of the text in `.pdf` format. You can view the electronic version of the book with Adobe Reader.

Adobe Reader

For Windows

We've also included a copy of Adobe Reader so you can view PDF files that accompany the book's content. For more information on Adobe Reader or to check for a newer version, visit Adobe's website at www.adobe.com/products/reader/.

Electronic Flashcards

For Windows

These handy electronic flashcards are just what they sound like. One side contains a question or fill-in-the-blank question, and the other side shows the answer.

System Requirements

Make sure your computer meets the minimum system requirements shown in the following list. If your computer doesn't match up to most of these requirements, you may have problems using the software and files on the companion CD. For the latest and greatest information, please refer to the ReadMe file located at the root of the CD-ROM.

- A PC running Microsoft Windows 98, Windows 2000, Windows NT4 (with SP4 or later), Windows Me, Windows XP, or Windows Vista, and Windows 7.
- An Internet connection
- A CD-ROM drive

Using the CD

To install the items from the CD to your hard drive, follow these steps:

1. Insert the CD into your computer's CD-ROM drive. The license agreement appears.

Windows users: The interface won't launch if you have autorun disabled. In that case, click Start ➢ Run (for Windows Vista, Start ➢ All Programs ➢ Accessories Run). In the dialog box that appears, type D:\Start.exe. (Replace *D* with the proper letter if your CD drive uses a different letter. If you don't know the letter, see how your CD drive is listed under My Computer.) Click OK.

2. Read the license agreement, and then click the Accept button if you want to use the CD.

The CD interface appears. The interface allows you to access the content with just one or two clicks.

Troubleshooting

Wiley has attempted to provide programs that work on most computers with the minimum system requirements. Alas, your computer may differ, and some programs may not work properly for some reason.

The two likeliest problems are that you don't have enough memory (RAM) for the programs you want to use or you have other programs running that are affecting installation or running of a program. If you get an error message such as "Not enough memory" or "Setup cannot continue," try one or more of the following suggestions and then try using the software again:

Turn off any antivirus software running on your computer. Installation programs sometimes mimic virus activity and may make your computer incorrectly believe that it's being infected by a virus.

Close all running programs. The more programs you have running, the less memory is available to other programs. Installation programs typically update files and programs; so if you keep other programs running, installation may not work properly.

Have your local computer store add more RAM to your computer. This is, admittedly, a drastic and somewhat expensive step. However, adding more memory can really help the speed of your computer and allow more programs to run at the same time.

Customer Care

If you have trouble with the book's companion CD-ROM, please call the Wiley Product Technical Support phone number at (800) 762-2974. Outside the United States, call +1(317) 572-3994. You can also contact Wiley Product Technical Support at http://sybex.custhelp.com. John Wiley & Sons will provide technical support only for installation and other general quality-control items. For technical support on the applications themselves, consult the program's vendor or author.

To place additional orders or to request information about other Wiley products, please call (877) 762-2974.

Glossary

802.3af   An IETF standard PoE method for powering networked devices.

A

access control list (ACL)   A list of permission and/or deny statements that limit traffic flows on network devices.

Ad Hoc conference   A conference call feature within CUCM Express that lets a user call one party and then call another to enable all to talk to one another. The total number of parties called depends on the maximum participants setting.

address signaling   The transmission of digits to the remote party that the calling party wishes to dial. Address signaling can use either pulse dialing or DTMF.

Administration via telephone (AvT)   A method for telephone administrators to add/delete and modify audio prompts used by the Unity Express system using a telephone connected to the CUCM Express.

Analog Telephony Adapter (ATA)   A hardware device that allows standard analog telephones and fax machines to operate on an Ethernet LAN.

Automatic Number Identification (ANI)   A number or extension that represents the originating phone number. It is also referred to as caller ID.

Applications layer   The Cisco Unified Communications Model layer that adds additional value-added applications to supplement call-processing functions found in the Call Control layer.

auto attendant (AA)   An automated system with voice prompts to assist the caller to be routed to the proper contact using internal extensions.

autonomous access point (AAP)   A term used to define a wireless access point in which the wireless intelligence resides on the access point itself.

auto-QoS   A command on a Cisco network that automatically configures QoS techniques that are specifically designed for voice traffic. It helps to eliminate some of the complexity of configuring QoS manually.

B

Basic Rate Interface (BRI)   An ISDN circuit that gives you two 64Kbps channels for voice and one 16Kbps channel for out-of-band signaling.

bearer channel   An ISDN channel that is responsible for voice communication transport. Each channel provides 64Kbps of bandwidth.

binary   A numbering system that is used by electronic systems. It uses a series of 1s and 0s called bits to represent any numeric value.

bit   A binary digit used by computers to store information. A bit can have a value of either 1 or 0.

bulk additions   A CCA method of importing a list of phone extensions using a CSV-formatted spreadsheet.

Business Hours schedule   Used with the Unity Express Auto Attendant to determine when to use the business open/closed prompts.

C

Call Admission Control (CAC)   The function responsible for determining if the caller has the right to ring the requested number and for verifying that there is sufficient bandwidth available to complete a call.

Call Control layer   The Cisco Unified Communications Model layer that is responsible for call processing. This is where the CUCM hardware is found.

call detail record (CDR)   A CUCM Express feature that keeps track of all calls made on the CUCM Express system.

call history   A CUCM Express report that shows call origin and destination along with start and end dates/times.

call leg   A logical connection between dial-peer origination or termination points on IP networks.

call parking   A telephone feature that lets a user place a phone call in "parked" state using an unassigned ephone-DN and then resume the call from another phone.

call pickup   A telephone feature that allows a user to answer a remote extension on their local phone.

call progress tone (cptone)   A Cisco voice gateway command used to set the location tones for analog phones on FXS ports.

call transfer   A telephone feature that moves an active phone conversation from one phone extension to another.

call waiting   The ability for a phone to receive two or more simultaneous calls.

caller ID blocking code   A CCA option that, when activated, allows users to enter a code to block the caller ID information from reaching the called party.

Cascading Notifications   Unity Express message notification option that waits a period of time for the user to log in and check their messages. After a set time has expired, Unity Express will notify the next phone, email address, or pager on the list.

CCA sound recorder   A built-in tool that allows administrators to use a PC microphone to record AA prompts and have them saved to the local drive, where they can be uploaded to Unity Express.

central office (CO)   The last hop within the PSTN before it goes to the customer premise.

Centralized Automatic Message Accounting (CAMA)   A specialized circuit is that is used for Emergency 911 (E911) service in North America.

Channel Associated Signaling (CAS)   Digital circuit signaling that commonly uses in-band robbed-bit signaling to provide 24 56Kbps channels for voice.

Cisco Configuration Assistant (CCA)   A Windows-based application that greatly simplifies the configuration and management of devices within the Cisco SBCS platform.

Cisco phone user license   A license for each individual phone endpoint.

Cisco power injector   A midspan device that provides power to a single phone endpoint.

Cisco Unified Communications Manager (CUCM)   A server-based, call-processing platform for large enterprise organizations. Multiple servers can be clustered to support up to 30,000 endpoints.

Cisco Unified Communications Manager Business Edition (CUCMBE)   A server-based, call-processing and voice mail platform for medium-size businesses. It handles call processing and Unity Connection email on the same server for support for up to 500 endpoints.

Cisco Unified Communications Manager Express (CUCM Express)   A router-based, call-processing platform that runs on multiple Cisco ISR router platforms. It handles call processing for up to 240 users.

Cisco Unified Communications Publisher   A call-processing server that controls the read/write functions of the CUCM database.

Cisco Unified Communications Subscriber   A server that handles call-processing functions in CUCM clusters. These servers look to the publisher to access the CUCM database.

clock source   A Cisco voice gateway command that allows an administrator to determine where the T1 circuit synchronizes its timing clock.

cme-basic package   A CUCM Express bundled software TAR package that contains the more common Cisco phone load files and a limited amount of extras such as ringtones and desktop backgrounds.

cme-full package   A CUCM Express bundled software TAR package that contains all Cisco phone load files, ringtones, and desktop backgrounds available.

codec   Software that encodes and decodes digital streams. Codecs often compress the streams so they can be more efficiently transported.

common channel signaling (CCS)   Digital circuit signaling that uses an out-of-band channel for signaling.

compressed RTP (cRTP)   A compression method that eliminates header information prior to transport of RTP packets to conserve bandwidth.

compression   The process of encoding packets to use fewer bits. The packet is then sent across a link and decoded at the other end to be expanded to its original state. This helps to reduce bandwidth resources.

CUCM Express feature license   A license that determines how many phones you can run on the CUCM.

CUCM Express license bundles   A way to purchase IOS and CUCM Express licenses together with Cisco router hardware. These bundles simplify the licensing process.

D

default phone configuration   A file that informs a Cisco phone of all the general information it needs to communicate with the CUCM Express system.

DHCP scope   A range of IP addresses that the DHCP server uses to hand out to clients.

dial-peer 0   The last-resort method that POTS and/or VoIP inbound dial peers use when all other methods fail to match. Using this dial peer often results in suboptimal handling of voice traffic.

dial-plan strategy   A strategy developed to efficiently route calls between the remote sites with the fewest number of destination-pattern commands.

Dialed Number ID Service (DNIS)   A service offered by PSTNs on digital circuits that lets the CUCM Express determine which telephone number was dialed by a customer.

digit manipulation   Configuration methods used to modify or change one number into a different number to reach the intended destination.

digit prefix   A digit-manipulation method of adding additional digits and/or pauses to the beginning of the dialed number prior to passing it on to the next destination along the call path.

digit stripping   A digit-manipulation method used by Cisco voice gateways that removes the explicitly defined destination-pattern digits when configuring dial peers.

digital signal processor (DSP)   A specialized hardware chip that offloads voice processing from the main CPU. The chip can be used for analog-to-digital conversions, digital transcoding, and conference-call processing, among other functions.

direct inward dial (DID)   A PSTN service that allows for bundling of multiple analog circuits on a trunk. The PSTN will then assign full telephone numbers to this trunk and will strip off digits before sending them to the customer PBX. This process allows the numbers to use any of the analog lines on the trunk.

directory alias   A command used when identifying files to be serviced by the TFTP server when the files are organized in a directory structure. The alias helps the phones locate the directory where the files can be stored on the flash.

dual-line   The combining of two separate phone lines in one telephone button. This lets users of the phone place calls on hold or receive a second call when one line is in use.

dual-tone multi-frequency (DTMF)   A method that uses two audible tones to represent dialed digits. This in-band signaling method is then detected by the phone system and translated into dialed digits.

Dynamic Host Control Protocol (DHCP)   A service that dynamically assigns IP addresses and other network information to endpoint devices such as PCs and IP phones.

E

echo   A voice term used to describe the reflection of sound that arrives to the listener after the direct sound is heard.

Editor Express   A Unity Express web GUI editor that is used to create, delete, and edit automated attendant scripts. This is a slimmed-down version of the Unity Express Editor software that runs on Microsoft Windows.

encoding   The process of transforming information from one format into another.

Endpoints layer   The Cisco Unified Communications Model layer where voice endpoints are found, such as Cisco IP phones, soft phones, and video devices.

ephone   A configuration statement that represents physical phones on the CUCM Express. It is a number used to identify a particular device within the IOS.

ephone button separator   A CUCM Express command character that is used to set different rings, call waiting, overlay, and monitor options on an ephone.

ephone-DN   A configuration statement that represents the telephone extension configured on each phone.

ephone exempt   A CUCM Express command used to exempt an ephone completely from any call-blocking configurations.

ephone extension states   The six different operational states that an IP phone can be in.

ephone registration   The process an IP phone goes through to register to a CUCM.

excluded address   A specified IP address or range of addresses within the DHCP scope that the DHCP server does not hand out to DHCP clients.

expansion   An ephone button separator option used to expand line coverage for an overlay button.

Extended Super Frame (ESF)   A T1 framing type that bundles frames together more efficiently than its predecessor, SF.

F

factory default settings   The settings used when the hardware was direct from the factory.

Feature bar   A vertically positioned function bar that lists the various features that can be used to configure, monitor, and manage a particular SBCS device using the CCA.

firmware load file   A file on the CUCM Express used to tell the registering Cisco phones which firmware they are to download.

fixed delay   The time it takes to send an electrical or optical signal across a definable distance.

Foreign Exchange Office (FXO)   An interface that connects to a PBX or key system and assumes that all dial tones, ring indicators, and other call-progress signaling are provided locally by the PBX.

Foreign Exchange Station (FXS)   An interface that connects directly to an analog endpoint, such as an analog phone or fax machine.

forward digits   A digit-manipulation method of specifying the number of digits to be passed on to the next destination along the call path.

fractional T1   A service provided by many PSTNs that hands off a full T1 circuit but limits the number of usable channels.

frequency   The number of occurrences of a repeating event in a specific period of time.

G

G.711   The ITU standard audio codec that is uncompressed and requires 64 Kbps of bandwidth.

G.729   The ITU standard audio codec that is uncompressed and requires 8 Kbps of bandwidth. This codec uses a high-complexity compression algorithm.

G.729a   The ITU standard audio codec that is uncompressed and requires 8 Kbps of bandwidth. This codec uses a medium-complexity compression algorithm.

general delivery mailbox (GDM)   A mailbox that is assigned to a Unity Express group that is shared among subscribers.

glare   An anomaly that occurs when the local user and PSTN attempt to seize the analog circuit at the same time. Glare is often noticed on lines that use loopStart signaling.

graphical user interface (GUI)   A visual user interface that is more user friendly and intuitive than the command line.

ground start   The analog signaling method that grounds one side of the circuit before opening the circuit. Once the signal is grounded, the current on the analog line is allowed to flow and the user can make calls. This type of signaling prevents glare.

H

H.323   An ITU standards-based, peer-to-peer protocol. It is a bundle of multiple protocols defining signaling and control of voice and video data.

H.323 gatekeeper   A database that contains H.323 mappings (telephone numbers) to IP addresses.

Holiday schedule   Used with the Unity Express Auto Attendant to determine when to use holiday message greetings.

hunt group   A CUCM Express feature that assigns a pilot number that, when called, is answered by one of several extensions that take turns ringing first.

huntstop   A command that tells the CUCM Express to look for the next preferred ephone-DN if the most preferred phone is busy.

hybrid system   The combination of PBX and key-system functionalities.

I

in-band signaling   Signaling that is transported on the same wire as the voice traffic.

inbound dial peers   Information used to route calls that are inbound to the voice gateway.

informational signaling   Feedback generated from the phone switch to the user in the form of audible tones and/or voice messages to inform the user what stage a call is in.

Infrastructure layer   The Cisco Unified Communications Model layer responsible for moving IP packets from source to destination.

Inline Power (ILP)   A Cisco proprietary PoE option integrated into switches.

integrated voice gateway   The voice gateway architecture in which the voice gateway and CUCM Express system share the same hardware.

Intelligent Power Management (IPM)   A Cisco method using CDP to negotiate power allocation of 802.3af PoE devices.

Interactive Voice Response (IVR)   A Unity Express feature that allows callers to interact with a voice menu much like an automated attendant, where the caller is prompted to press numbers on the telephone handset to work their way through the script. IVR functionality requires a separate IVR license to run on Unity Express.

intercom   A CUCM Express feature that acts as a speed dial with automatic answer on the called party's speakerphone.

International Numbering Plan   An ITU E.164 standard numbering format that is globally used by PSTNs.

Internet Low Bandwidth Codec (iLBC)   A newer codec developed by VoIP industry leaders that uses between 13.3 and 15.2 Kbps of bandwidth and can tolerate moderate amounts of packet loss.

Internet Telephony Service Provider (ITSP)   A service provider that provides access to the PSTN using a VoIP trunk as opposed to standard switched circuits that legacy PSTN providers use.

inter-VLAN routing   The process of moving packets from devices between VLANs.

IOS compatibility matrix   A matrix found on the cisco.com website used to identify compatible IOS voice software and CUCM Express software.

IOS feature set   A license that determines the different features that can be run on an IOS-capable device.

IP Communicator   A Cisco softphone that runs on Microsoft Windows operating systems. The software emulates a 7900 series phone.

IP unnumbered   A Cisco IOS command that allows an interface to share the IP of another directly connected interface on the router.

ISDN switch type   A Cisco voice gateway command that specifies the ISDN switch a network's T1 provider uses.

J

jitter   The variations in time of arrival for time-sensitive packets.

K

keepalive   A message sent from one network device to another at predefined intervals to verify the operational status of a device or service.

key system   A phone switching system where phones are set up identically and share PSTN numbers.

L

latency   The time it takes a packet to be moved between two points.

Layer 3 switching   The creation of logical routed interfaces on switch hardware. Inter-VLAN routing is then transported over dedicated ASICs to provide wire-speed routing.

lightweight access point (LWAP)   A wireless access point in which the wireless intelligence is controlled by a separate device called a wireless controller. The access point is responsible only for acting as a bridge between the wireless interface and the Ethernet interface.

line seizure   A telephone line state when a phone transitions from an on-hook to an off-hook state.

Link Fragmentation and Interleaving (LFI)   A process that takes large data packets and fragments them into smaller, more manageable sizes. The interface then processes voice packets in between the newly fragmented data packets. This helps to eliminate variable delay and jitter.

Live Reply   A configuration option that allows the user to return calls to parties who left voice mails directly from Unity Express.

local directory   A shared directory system used to map names of telephone users with a telephone number.

local loop   The circuit between the customer site and the central office (CO).

loop start The analog signaling method that opens a circuit loop to the PSTN. The service request is signaled when the telephone handset is removed from the phone cradle, which enables loop current on the analog line to flow.

Low Latency Queuing (LLQ) A queuing technique that creates a strict-priority queue for voice traffic.

low-power mode The initial 802.3af boot phase that uses 6.3 W of power.

M

Mandatory Message Expiry An option that administrators can set on voice mail boxes where messages are deleted after an expiration timer has expired.

Mean Opinion Score (MOS) A quality measurement system that rates the quality of voice streams for a particular codec.

Media Gateway Control Protocol (MGCP) An IETF standard client-server communications signaling protocol used for signaling between voice gateways.

media termination point The use of DSP resources for tasks such as call parking, call transfers, and conference calling.

MeetMe conference A conference call feature within CUCM Express that allows parties to dial an extension to "meet" others for a conference call. Also referred to as a conference bridge.

Message Notification Unity Express feature that allows mailbox subscribers to be notified of a new voice mail message by calling a remote telephone/pager or the triggering of an email.

message waiting indicator (MWI) A visual indicator that notifies users of a new voice mail.

mixed mode Allows either G.711 or G.729 codecs to be used for voice conferencing.

monitor line An ephone button separator option used to monitor the status (on- or off-hook) of a single ephone-DN.

multilayer switch Another term for a Layer 3 switch.

multiplexing Combining multiple analog or digital signals over a single shared medium.

Music on Hold (MOH) Music supplied by a PBX or key-system device that plays music or any other kind of audio while the remote party is placed in a hold state.

N

network-locale   A CUCM Express command used to specify the tones and telephone cadence settings for a particular geographic region.

Network Time Protocol (NTP)   A service that synchronizes the internal clocks on networked equipment.

North American Numbering Plan (NANP)   A standard numbering format used by 24 countries in North America.

number expansion   A digit-manipulation method of translating extension numbers into full E.164 DIDs when sending calls out to the PSTN.

O

octo-line   The combining of eight separate phone lines in one telephone button. This lets users of the phone place calls on hold or receive a second call when the first line is in use.

off-premise exchange (OPX)   A Cisco voice gateway command option that, when used, forces the FXO port to wait until the FXS port goes off-hook before connecting the call.

outbound dial peers   Information used to route calls that are outbound from the voice gateway.

out-of-band signaling   The use of a separate transport medium such as a separate pair of wires to transport signaling.

overlay   An ephone button separator option used to associate multiple ephone-DNs with a single line button.

override code   A special passcode used by telephone users to override any call-blocking functions configured on the CUCM Express.

P

paging   A CUCM Express feature that acts as a one-way intercom.

peak amplitude   The variation in the frequency, either highest or lowest, over a 1-wavelength period, measured from a mean of 0.

peak-to-peak amplitude   The variation in the frequency over a 1-wavelength period. It measures the difference between the highest and lowest voltage of the waveform.

phantom power   Using the same wiring to power devices as Ethernet uses to transmit and receive data.

plain old telephone service (POTS)   Analog circuit from the PSTN that is commonly delivered to homes and businesses on two wires for full-duplex conversations.

POTS dial peer   A logical dial-string-to-port mapping used to configure traditional telephony devices.

power brick   Standard 110v AC unit that plugs directly into a single phone endpoint.

power failover feature   A UC500 feature that allows an analog phone connected to an FXS port to be switched directly to an FXO port during a loss of power to the unit.

powered patch panel   A device that sits in between an IP phone and a non-PoE-capable switch that provides power to multiple phone endpoints.

preference   A CUCM Express command often used to identify an ephone-DN that shares an extension number on multiple ephone-DNs. The lowest preference number will ring first.

Primary Rate Interface (PRI)   An ISDN circuit that provides 23 64Kbps channels for voice and one 64Kbps channel for out-of-band signaling.

Private Branch Exchange (PBX)   A phone switching system where phones are given unique features and extensions.

private distribution list   A private list of subscribers that can broadcast the same message simultaneously. These lists are created and maintained by the individual user and cannot be shared.

Private Line Automatic Ringdown (PLAR)   A specialized voice gateway port that will automatically ring any number configured on the port as soon as the phone goes off-hook.

PSTN Trunk Group   A CCA configuration section that allows an administrator to create various trunk groups and then choose from a list of hunt schemes how the UC500 will determine a phone line or channel to use.

public distribution list   A public list of subscribers that can be broadcast the same message simultaneously. These lists are commonly created and maintained by the Unity Express administrator.

public switched telephone network (PSTN)   A public network for switched telephony circuits. The network is governed by the ITU and uses E.164 numbering standards.

pulse code modulation (PCM)   The process of digitizing voice. The process used is to sample the audio, quantize the wave, and encode the digital stream.

pulse dialing   A method that uses on-/off-hook transitions at a specific rate to represent dialed digits. The changes in current flow on the line are sensed by the telephone system and translated into dialed digits.

Q

quality of service (QoS)   The identification and prioritizing of traffic flows to guarantee a level of performance.

quantization   The process or language used to encode sound waves into defined values.

R

rack unit (U)   A unit of measurement used to describe the height of data and telecommunications equipment that fits into standard 19~IN communication racks.

Real-time Transport Control Protocol (RTCP)   An IETF standard protocol that provides out-of-band monitoring of RTP streams for feedback and statistical purposes.

Real-time Transport Protocol (RTP)   An IETF standard protocol developed for the delivery of unicast and multicast voice/video streams.

reset   A CUCM Express command that performs a full reboot of a Cisco IP phone.

restart   A CUCM Express command that performs a quick reset of a Cisco IP phone.

Restriction Tables   A Unity Express feature that limits the types of phone numbers that can be dialed when using call-in message notification.

ring frequency   A Cisco voice gateway command used to adjust the strength of the ring in Hertz. The ring frequency sometimes needs to be modified to meet the standards of the phones that are attached to the FXS ports.

ring number   A Cisco voice gateway command used to specify the maximum number of rings detected by the router before answering the call.

robbed-bit signaling (RBS)   A specific type of T1 Channel Associated Signaling (CAS) that steals bits from the 24 channels and uses these bits for signaling purposes.

root web directory   The directory where the files are located for the web GUI.

S

sampling   The process of capturing and converting a sound signal into a numeric sequence.

seed address   A term used within the CCA application to describe the central point of an SBCS network. The application then uses the seed address and CDP to discover additional hardware the CCA can manage within the site.

separated voice gateway   The voice gateway architecture in which the voice gateway and CUCM Express system are on separate hardware devices.

Session Initiation Protocol (SIP)   An IETF standard peer-to-peer communications signaling method. Can be used between voice gateways or between call-processing units and endpoints.

session target   A Cisco command that specifies the VoIP dial-peer address to be used with matching telephone numbers for outgoing calls.

shared line   The term used to describe an ephone-DN that is applied to two or more IP phones.

SIP proxy   An SIP signaling architecture that is used for making requests on the behalf of endpoints. This helps to facilitate policy enforcement by the CUCM administrator.

site discovery   The CCA process of using a seed address and CDP to discover other SBCS devices on the network the CCA can manage.

Skinny Call Control Protocol (SCCP)   A Cisco proprietary client-server communications signaling protocol. Can be used between voice gateways or between call-processing units and endpoints.

Smart Business Communication System (SBCS)   A suite of Cisco hardware positioned for small to medium-size businesses.

source IP address   The IP address that defines the location of the CUCM Express call-processing unit.

Statistical Time-Division Multiplexing (STDM)   A multiplexing technique where a timeslot is reserved on the wire only when it is needed.

Super Frame (SF)   An older T1 framing type that has mostly been replaced by ESF.

supervisory signaling   Signaling used for setup and teardown of calls. A supervisory signal also indicates different states of a voice call.

survivable remote site telephony (SRST)   A cost-effective method to provide high-availability voice features to remote sites when a WAN failure occurs.

switch virtual interface (SVI)   A virtual interface created in software on Layer 3 switch hardware.

synchronization   The process of comparing shared information between the CUCM Express and Unity Express. Any additions or changes are then matched up on both devices based on the most recent updates.

syslog server   A server used to offload and store computer and network hardware log information for long periods of time.

T

telephone user interface (TUI)   An interactive voice interface used to manage Unity voice mail components using a telephone handset.

telephony service setup script   A basic command-line script that walks an administrator through a series of DHCP and voice questions to configure ephones and ephone-DN settings automatically.

Time-Division Multiplexing (TDM)   A multiplexing technique where each timeslot is given a specific order when the slot reoccurs. The timeslot is reserved whether it is used or not.

toll bar   A CUCM Express feature that lets administrators define when they wish to block calls from being made, on specific dates and/or during certain hours of the day.

toolbar   A horizontally positioned function bar that lists graphical icon buttons that are commonly used to configure, monitor, and support SBCS devices using the CCA.

trace   A Unity Express command used to view real-time informational messages for troubleshooting purposes. This command is similar to the "debug" command on Cisco IOS devices.

traffic classification   The process of identifying time-sensitive packets.

traffic marking   The process of flagging critical packets so the rest of the network can properly identify them and give them priority over all other traffic.

traffic queuing   The process of ordering certain types of traffic for transport based on markings used to identify the priority of the packet.

translation profile   A digit-manipulation method of creating translation rules, assigning them to a translation profile, and finally assigning the translation profile to a POTS or VoIP dial peer. This process allows administrators to be very flexible when manipulating digits on a voice gateway.

trunk   Phone lines coming into the PBX from the PSTN that can be used by any number of telephone extensions assigned to the trunk.

Trunk Priority   A CCA outgoing call-handling option where an administrator can set a priority for the different PSTN trunk lines installed on the UC500.

trust boundary   The point on an IP network where you begin enforcing queuing strategies.

U

Unity   A server-based appliance for voice mail that runs on the Microsoft Windows 2000 or 2003 operating system. A single server can support up to 15,000 mailboxes.

Unity Connection   Voice mail software that runs on a Linux-based server platform. It often accompanies CUCMBE implementations and can even reside on the same hardware. A single server can support up to 7,500 mailboxes.

Unity Express   A hardware device for voice mail that fits into specific Cisco router platforms. Comes in either an NM or an AIM form factor. Supports up to 250 mailboxes.

Unity Express Editor   A Microsoft Windows application that provides the most feature-rich and robust way to create and modify automated attendant scripts for Unity Express.

Unity Express group   A collection of subscribers who have some sort of commonality. Subscribers can be grouped together to either share a GDM or to share some sort of administrative right on the CUCM Express.

Unity Express Initialization Wizard   A web GUI-driven process that configures the global settings for Unity Express functionality.

Unity Express subscriber   An individual user account that is created to provide a personal mailbox account for voice mail storage.

UPC bar code   A common bar code symbol system that stores information, which can be read quickly using a bar code scanner.

user-locale   A CUCM Express command used to specify the language used on softkey and menu functions on Cisco phones.

V

variable delay   Variations in the time it takes to send an electrical or optical signal across a definable distance caused by queuing delays.

virtual LAN (VLAN)   A logical segmentation of the network that allows a group of devices to act as if it were on the same physical network.

VLAN trunk   A link between two Layer 2 switches that can transport traffic from multiple VLANs. It keeps the traffic between the VLANs separate by tagging each frame.

VLAN Trunking Protocol (VTP)   A messaging protocol that manages the addition, deletion, and changes of VLANs on a network.

Voice over IP (VoIP)   The delivery of voice communications over IP networks.

Voice VLAN   A dedicated VLAN specifically used for voice communications on an IP network.

VoiceView Express   A CUCM Express and Unity Express feature that lets voice mail users listen to, send, and manage messages on a Cisco phone using the LCD display and softkeys.

VoIP dial peer   A logical dial-string-to-IP-address mapping used to configure IPT telephony devices.

VTP Client   A VTP switch mode that listens to the VTP Server and copies the VLAN settings to its own VLAN database. It also forwards the VTP update messages from the server to other switches within the same VTP domain on its trunked links. This mode does not allow you to add, delete, or modify VLANs.

VTP Server   A VTP switch mode that allows an administrator to add, delete, and modify VLANs on the network over trunked links. All changes are propagated to other switches within the VTP domain.

VTP Transparent   A VTP switch mode that ignores updates locally but passes them on to connected neighbors.

W

watch phone   An ephone button separator option used to monitor the status (on- or off-hook) of all ephone-DNs assigned to a phone.

wavelength   The distance between each wave collected in an audio sample.

wildcard   A configuration method that lets an administrator use special characters to configure multiple off-network numbers without having to specify every allowable number.

write memory   A Cisco IOS command used to save the running configuration to the startup configuration.

Index

Note to the Reader: Throughout this index **boldfaced** page numbers indicate primary discussions of a topic. *Italicized* page numbers indicate illustrations.

V

Wiley Publishing, Inc.
End-User License Agreement

The Best CCNA Voice Book/CD Package on the Market!

Get ready for your CCNA Voice certification with the most comprehensive and challenging sample tests anywhere!

The Sybex Test Engine features:

- All the review questions, as covered in each chapter of the book.

- Challenging questions representative of those you'll find on the real exam.

- Two full-length bonus exams available only on the CD.

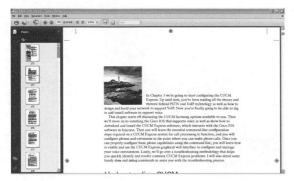

- An Assessment Test to narrow your focus to certain objective groups.

Search through the complete book in PDF!

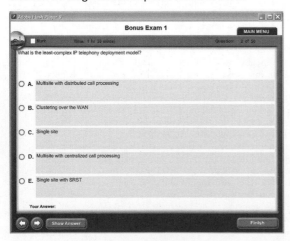

- Access the entire *CCNA Voice Study Guide* complete with figures and tables, in electronic format.

- Search the *CCNA Voice Study Guide* chapters to find information on any topic in seconds.

Use the Electronic Flashcards for PCs or Pocket PC devices to jog your memory and prep last minute for the exam!

- Reinforce your understanding of key concepts with these hardcore flashcard-style questions.

- Download the Flashcards to your Palm device and go on the road. Now you can study for the CCNA Voice exam (640-460) anytime, anywhere.

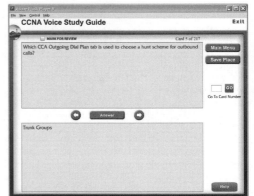

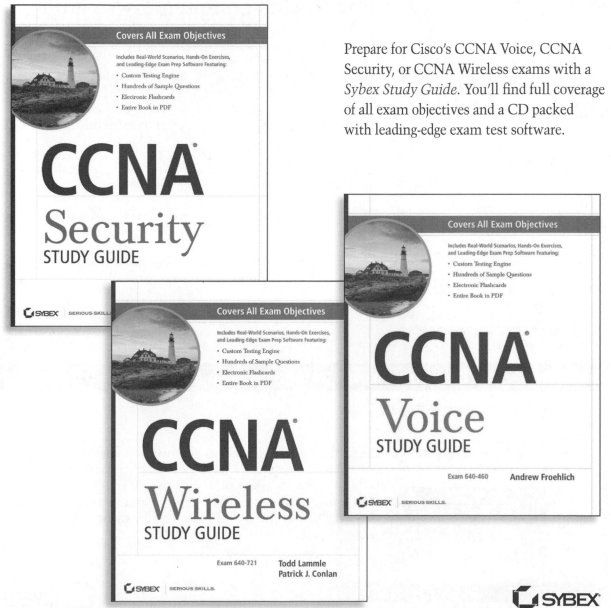

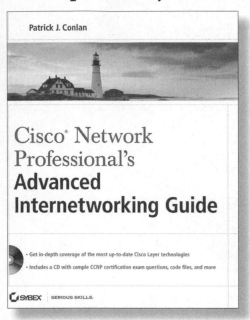